P. G. Wodehouse

P. G. Wodehouse

A CENTENARY CELEBRATION

1881–1981

James H. Heineman

Donald R. Bensen

EDITORS

THE PIERPONT MORGAN LIBRARY

OXFORD UNIVERSITY PRESS

NEW YORK · LONDON

Copyright © 1981 by The Pierpont Morgan Library
29 East 36 Street, New York, N.Y. 10016
Printed in the United States of America
Library of Congress catalogue card no. 81–83357
casebound edition ISBN 0–19–520357–7
paperbound edition ISBN 87598–073–2

JAMES H. HEINEMAN mustered his education in Belgium, England, and Switzerland where he gathered scant knowledge and no moss. His professional career, which has embraced investment banking, public utilities, and publishing, has provided him with some enjoyment, repeated anguish, and indifferent income. During World War II he served overseas in Military Intelligence, a term which an earlier edition of the Encyclopædia Britannica *listed several paragraphs beneath Animal Intelligence. His residence in several countries prompted a former friend to comment that Heineman was illiterate in four languages, and quite useless in three others. He was born on the fifth of May, a day he shares with Sören Kierkegaard, Sylvia Pankhurst, Karl Marx, and the first train robbery in the United States at North Bend, Ohio. He feels that the world would be an insane place were it not for Mozart, French cooking, his daughters, and Wodehouse.*

D. R. BENSEN, a Wodehouse reader from the age of eight, issued many Wodehouse reprints during his twenty-five years as an editor for several New York publishers, and has edited the forthcoming collection Wodehouse on Crime. *His ambition to become a serious Wodehouse collector was blighted by PGW's advice not to pick up a first edition of* The Gold Bat *for a dollar and a half, as it wasn't very good reading. He has had twenty-one books published, and is now at work on a limerick cycle dealing with the Old Testament.*

ADDENDUM
Page 97, column 2, line 21 should read: out on 8 August 1908 by A. E. Baerman who was Wodehouse's agent in

CORRIGENDUM
Page 105, column 1, lines 10–11 should read: Bertie Wooster and Jeeves first appeared in the story "Extricating Young Gussie,"

Table of Contents

ix	Key to the Endpaper Illustrations	
xi	Preface	Charles Ryskamp
xiii	Introduction	James H. Heineman
xviii	A Selective P. G. Wodehouse Chronology	

ESSAYS

3	How I Write My Books	P. G. Wodehouse
4	Dulwich Schooldays	Peter Southern
7	Writing a Biography of P. G. Wodehouse	Frances Donaldson
10	Lunching with Plum	Alec Waugh
13	Wodehouse's Editor: A Painless Job	Peter Schwed
15	The Wodehouses of Hollywood	Maureen O'Sullivan
18	Wodehouse the Writer of Lyrics	Benny Green
24	Wodehouse in Performance	Edward Duke
28	Letter from London, August 1939	John Hayward
31	Honoris Causa	Letty Grierson
34	Uncollected PGW	David A. Jasen
37	On Collecting P. G. Wodehouse	Charles E. Gould, Jr.
42	Holy or Unholy Writ	Richard Usborne
46	Wodehouse's *Punch* Verse	Peter Dickinson
49	Wodehouse and the Literary Scene	John Garrard
52	Wodehouse's American Illustrators	Walt Reed
56	Wodehouse's English Illustrators	Bevis Hillier
60	On Translating Wodehouse	Georg Svensson
63	Wodehouse on Crime	Isaac Asimov
67	Valley Fields	Richard Usborne

70	Wodehouse on Golf	John Garrard
73	Native Woodnotes Wild	Richard Usborne
77	Cats and Dogs	Margaret Garrard
81	New York	John Garrard
84	Where Is Blandings Castle?	Ann E. Wood

BIBLIOGRAPHY

91	A Bibliography of P. G. Wodehouse	Eileen McIlvaine
93	Novels and Semiautobiographical Works	
142	Omnibus Volumes	
152	Published Plays (Including Adaptations)	
157	Tauchnitz Editions	
158	Autograph Editions	
159	Anthologies with Wodehouse Contributions	
161	Introductions and Prefaces	
162	Translations	
184	The Dramatic Wodehouse: Stage and Screen	
193	Works about P. G. Wodehouse	
193	*Bibliographies*	
193	*Full-length studies*	
194	*Chapters devoted to Wodehouse*	
195	*Periodical articles*	
196	*References to Wodehouse in memoirs and biographies*	
196	*Related materials*	
197	*Imitations and parodies*	

Key to the Endpaper Illustrations

1   Lower left. In the water in New York harbor, Mr. Oscar Swenson, from Sweden, adds to his savings what he can catch from the folding money thrown from the dock—but not far enough—to the pretty American girl on the rail above, Wilhelmina ("Billie") Bennett. Flying through the air, in addition to the money-grabbing gull, is Englishman Sam Marlowe, pushed overboard by jostling passengers. *Three Men and a Maid*.

2   This is Hollywood in the days of Prohibition and the Depression. The ape carrying the baby is, in fact, Cyril Waddesley-Davenport, late of Balliol College, Oxford, who has done well in gorilla parts. This time, almost without thinking (because it happens so often in the movies), he has taken a baby from a pram and climbed aloft with it. Down below, right, is Montrose Mulliner kissing his Rosalie. Montrose will soon find himself on the level with the gorilla and able to seem to rescue the baby heroically, while thousands gasp and cheer. See "Monkey Business" in *Blandings Castle*.

3   The Oldest Member of the golf club, at ease (now that he has given up the game) on the terrace of the clubhouse, telling a tale to a captive audience. *Golf without Tears* and several subsequent collections of tee-side stories.

4   The Wrecking Crew, the fearsome foursome of old men, who have taken up golf too late in life and, with their herd of caddies, obstruct the fairways and roughs of any course. They are nicknamed, in exasperation, the First Grave-Digger, The Man with the Hoe, Old Father Time, and Consul, the Almost Human. Chester Meredith, playing for the course record in front of them, was just swinging down on his approach shot to the eighteenth, when he was hit in the plus-fours by a fluke shot from the First Grave-Digger. This loosened Chester's tongue, to the amazement and admiration—nay, love—of the beautiful Felicia Blakeney who was walking round with him. His love now returned, Chester holed out his next shot with a light flick of his mashie-niblick, and strode off with the record and the girl, while an unperturbed bird (lower right) brooded over a cache of golf balls.

5   Charlotte Mulliner, a poet, is overcome by the sporting atmosphere of Bludleigh Court and is firing little Wilfred Bassinger's airgun at that great white hunter, Colonel Sir Francis Pashley-Drake, sunbathing on top of the boathouse. He will escape into the reeds and Charlotte will then consider setting the reeds alight with a match to smoke him into the open for a second shot. "Unpleasantness at Bludleigh Court" in *Mr. Mulliner Speaking*.

6   From what he has in his pocket, that could be Freddie Widgeon dancing joyously with his Sally Foster, because his £1,000 of Silver River oil stock is going to make him rich. Little does he know that Thomas Molloy, who sold him the stock, is not in the business to make others rich. *Ice in the Bedroom*. Mellingham Hall, the house top left, is the white-elephant country mansion that Crispin Scrope has inherited and can't afford to keep in repair. *The Girl in Blue*. The lady with the cosh is probably Bertie Wooster's Aunt Dahlia putting Lord Sidcup to sleep before he can reveal that she has pawned the necklace her husband gave her. *Jeeves and the Feudal Spirit*. The couple enjoying their game of golf in the lake are William Bates and Jane Packard in "Rodney Fails to Qualify" in *Divots*.

7   The bar-parlour of the Angler's Rest, with Miss Postlethwaite drawing a pint for the local policeman and, at right, Mr. Mulliner.

8   A Hot-Scotch-and-a-Slice-of-Lemon telling a tall story to a Stout-and-Mild, a Gin-and-Ginger-Ale, and a Double-Whisky-and-Splash. The setting is the beginning of almost any story in the Mulliner saga.

9   We're at Blandings now. The Empress of Blandings, the great Black Berkshire sow, on whom a daily diet of 58,700 calories has been settled, pride of her owner, Clarence, ninth Earl of Emsworth of Blandings Castle, is standing aloof in her pen. Leaning on the fence admiringly is the ninth Earl himself, and standing with him is George Cyril Wellbeloved, pigman extraordinary. All three recur in a succession of novels. Wellbeloved appeared (or, rather, disappeared for a fortnight in the local slammer) first in "Pig-Hoo-o-o-o-ey!", a story in *Blandings Castle*.

10   Blandings Castle in the background, a loving couple in the middle distance, Beach the butler, "a dignified procession of one," and the Hon. Galahad Threepwood chatting up a pretty girl. Could she be Sue Brown, daughter of the only girl Gally ever loved? No, Sue was smaller than that. But Gally was helping girls and young men to pursue their loves in several Blandings Castle novels. Perhaps the lady in the foreground is Gally's disapproving

sister (all Gally's sisters disapprove of him, and we of them), Lady Constance Keeble. If so, from the look on Gally's face, he has scored off her yet again. *Summer Lightning, Heavy Weather, Full Moon, Pigs Have Wings, A Pelican at Blandings, Sunset at Blandings.*

11   Blandings Castle again. Lady Hermione Wedge (the one of Lord Emsworth's ten sisters who looks like a cook) in the background, and in the foreground her beautiful daughter, Veronica, frightened by Bill Lister, who is disguised as a gardener with an Assyrian beard. *Full Moon.*

12   More Blandings. Far left, secretary Rupert Baxter, the Efficient Baxter, in striped pajamas, locked out and throwing flower pots at (what turns out to be) his employer's, Lord Emsworth's, bedroom window. *Leave It to Psmith.* That's Psmith walking away east and wearing a monocle. The stout gentleman in the bushes must be Murchison, the Scotland Yard detective guarding croquet-playing Sir James Piper, Chancellor of the Exchequer. *Sunset at Blandings.* The boy with the camera has escaped from yet another Blandings novel. He is George, grandson of Lord Emsworth, who photographed his grandfather's clandestine cutting of the guy ropes in the tented field where the Church Lads Brigade are camping in the Castle grounds. *Service with a Smile.*

13   Edwin, the Boy Scout. (As the only son of an Earl, he must be Lord Something.) Behind is Bertie Wooster in the two-seater, talking to D'Arcy ("Stilton") Cheesewright, now a country copper pursuant of Lady Florence Craye up at the big house. Stilton is jealous of Bertie, whom he suspects of being pursuant of Florence too. Wee Nooke, the cottage that Lord Worplesdon has lent Bertie, is at the back, and it is soon to be burnt to ashes as a result of one of Boy Scout Edwin's Good Deeds of the Day. *Joy in the Morning.*

14   Jeeves fishing to pass the time before Wee Nooke goes up in flames. *Joy in the Morning.*

15   That is probably Skeldings Hall in the background, home of Roberta ("Bobbie") Wickham, and that could be Bobbie as she might have been, playing tennis with Algy Crufts, had not her mother, Lady Wickham, ordered her to drive Clifford Gandle (that bore!) to Hertford. "Mr. Potter Takes a Rest Cure" in *Blandings Castle and Elsewhere.* Lower down we are at Ditteridge, the Glossop place in Hampshire. Bingo Little is tutor and guardian to Oswald Glossop and in love with Oswald's sister, Honoria. Bingo arranges that Bertie shall push Oswald into the lake, Bingo shall rescue him, and Honoria, seeing the rescue, will fawn on Bingo. Well, it doesn't work out that way. Oswald goes into the lake from the bridge and a good sudden push from Bertie, but Bingo has disappeared and Bertie has to plunge to the rescue. Meanwhile, Oswald is swimming strongly to shore. The girl under the tree could be Daphne Braythwayt. It's Bertie, wet, in the foreground. "Scoring off Jeeves." The swan is part of another story, "Jeeves and the Impending Doom." The swan has chased the Rt. Hon. A. B. Filmer (that bore!), Cabinet Minister, onto the top of a sort of summer house on an island in the middle of the lake at Woollam Chersey—

16   —Bertie's Aunt Agatha's place. Then we change scenery to Totleigh Towers, Sir Watkyn Bassett's place. And here's Lord Sidcup (né Roderick Spode) getting knocked out, this time by the Rev. "Stinker" Pinker for assaulting the wretched Gussie Fink-Nottle (crouching on the ground in spectacles).

17   The admiring girl watching the fisticuffs is Stiffy Byng, the curate's fiancée. Indoors now, still at Totleigh Towers, that's Bertie Wooster crouched below the sofa. *Stiff Upper Lip, Jeeves.* The cow creamer on the round-topped table belongs to Uncle Tom Travers. It is coveted, pilfered, and traded by a disparate assortment of people all for the noblest of selfish motives.

18   And on the armchair, though not at Totleigh Towers, is Sir Roderick Glossop, famed loony-doctor. Behind him is any Wodehouse aunt with any captive niece. The black apparition at the window is Gussie Fink-Nottle again, again being chased by Roderick Spode/Sidcup, and frightening the daylights out of Anatole, the chef, whose bedroom is below. The half-seen young couple might be Tuppy Glossop and Angela Travers. (Sir Roderick Glossop is the only character who appears both in the Wooster/Jeeves saga and in the Blandings stories.)

19   The scene changes to the neighborhood of Bertie Wooster's bedroom in his Mayfair flat. His twin cousins, Claude and Eustace, have parked a dead salmon and a number of cats in his bedroom, trophies of an Oxford treasure hunt. This effectively wrecks any chance of Sir Roderick's allowing Bertie to marry his daughter, Honoria. Sir Roderick, who should know, thinks Bertie is a mental case, keeping fish and cats in the bedroom. "Sir Roderick Comes to Lunch" in *Jeeves.* Jeeves shimmers into the bedroom with the early morning restorative, while the Duke of Dunstable, moustache bristling, snorts his disapproval.

20   This particular morning is quite clearly the early morrow of the annual Oxford-Cambridge boatrace. Bertie glimpses daylight at home, having escaped dire punishment at the hands of the Beak at the Bosher Street police station for having abetted the pilfering of a helmet from a member of the constabulary. Bertie's banjo, on which he has been known to accompany himself in a heartfelt rendition of "Sonny Boy," has withstood the fray.

Preface

CHARLES RYSKAMP

It is fitting that this publication, celebrating the centenary of P. G. Wodehouse's birth, and the exhibition accompanying it should begin in the United States. Although Wodehouse's work is mainly set in England, his first considerable success was in this country, where he became at least as popular during his heyday as in his own and where he lived for about forty years.

Let us hope that Americans relish quite as much as do the English a playful mastery of their common language. And it is certain that Wodehouse was a master of words no less than wit. Nearly half a century ago, Hilaire Belloc created a minor storm by calling him "the best living writer of English," but the storm subsided when, on reflection, critics and questioners in the main had to acknowledge the justice of Belloc's judgment. Wodehouse did not address the burning questions of his time, nor any other, but what he chose to do, he did better than anyone else.

Wodehouse's success in the English-speaking world, then, may need little explanation. What is remarkable is how well his work has done in other countries—how truly universal his appeal is. A writer cannot be translated—and profitably published—in twenty and more languages if his only virtue is the ability to handle his own language adeptly. There are, for instance, sixty titles now in print in Italian translations, and it cannot be expected that more than a small part of Wodehouse's stylistic felicities survives the process.

Why, then, do Germans, Swedes, Turks, Italians, Japanese, Portuguese, Netherlanders, and all the others enjoy reading Wodehouse in the absence of one of his strongest suits? I would say that, in addition to his command of his native language, he had mastered the universal art of story-telling—of creating wholly fictional yet convincing characters and landscapes, and presenting them with a deftness and geniality that shines through in any language. *Jeeves* as a word has all but entered the English language and many others; and it is very cheering to imagine readers throughout the world lifting their eyes briefly from the printed page to glance over vast regions of steppe, expanses of jungle, terra-cotta towns clustered on sunburnt hills, dank polders, city skylines, or bee-haunted gardens, and then returning avidly to Market Blandings, Berkeley Mansions, the Drones Club, or the Anglers' Rest.

You may be surprised that Pelham Grenville Wodehouse appears in *Debrett's Peerage* (for so he does, identified as "Author and Dramatist," a collateral relation of the Wodehouses, Earls of Kimberley, and direct descendant of the fifth Baronet, Sir Armine Wodehouse, father of the first Baron Wodehouse), or that he lived for more than two decades in Remsenburg, Long Island; but those are not features of this book. The twenty-five essays in this volume and the extensive bibliography and checklists focus primarily on Wodehouse's work—on his genius as a writer.

Here you will be amazed by the extent and variety of his writings. This volume contains the record of the novelist, short story and feature writer, song lyricist, movie scriptwriter, versifier. P. G. Wodehouse was first paid for a piece of writing in 1900. He was completing a novel at the time of his death in hospital in 1975. The essays in this book attempt to recall the various achievements of the man; the bibliographical sections demonstrate the incredible output of more than seventy-five years of constant writing. You will find not only books and magazines, but also sheet music—among them the score and lyrics for the famous song "Bill" in *Showboat*—because Wodehouse helped to shape the modern American musical; there are scripts of plays and movies that he wrote or adapted; there are theatre posters and programs, as well as title pages, photographs, and illustrations for dust jackets or periodical publications.

This book is meant to please both the scholar and the fan. The same is true of the exhibition, which will open at The Pierpont Morgan Library on the evening of 15 October 1981, the one hundredth anniversary of P. G. Wodehouse's birth, continuing until 10 January 1982.

None of this would have been possible without the devotion—to P. G. Wodehouse and to the Morgan Library—of Mr. James H. Heineman. He is a Trustee of the Library and a publisher and collector. In his Introduction he tells his own story with a wit and skill which would have pleased his master: Mr. Heineman has been a fan since he was ten, a collector of Wodehouse's books since he first read one of these enchanting stories. Today his collection is unrivaled, and this publication and the exhibition would have been impossible without it, and without his enthusiasm, perseverance, and sheer hard work. Mr. Heineman, with his collaborators and with those who lent to the exhibition, has helped us to relive and cherish the worlds of Jeeves and Bertie Wooster, the denizens of Blandings Castle and the Drones Club, and the yarns of Mr. Mulliner and the Oldest Member. Once again we are traveling through that delightful country which none of us can live in but all can enjoy.

Introduction

JAMES H. HEINEMAN

A CELEBRATION of the birth of one of the masters of English comic writing requires no justification. However, the nature of this volume, so unlike the conventional exhibition catalogue—rather, an extended appreciation, with a bibliography and checklists—may call for a brief explanation.

The notion of the exhibition first came up in 1977, at a lunch with Charles Ryskamp, Director of The Pierpont Morgan Library, at the Century Association. The intellectual atmosphere of this institution is such that one's mind naturally turned to intellectual subjects and therefore in short order to P. G. Wodehouse. It may be that the Association's name reminded us of the fact of Wodehouse's centenary, then four years off; in any case, by the end of luncheon the Wodehouse celebration had been proposed. Mr. Ryskamp brought the proposal to the Library's Trustees, who approved, and the celebration was set in motion.

One circumstance that helped to carry the suggestion was that one of the Trustees—myself—had about the best collection of Wodehouse's books going, so that it seemed to be no great matter to get the exhibition together.

I must now rewind the tape to discuss the origins of this collection. As a youth of about ten, I fell under the spell of Wodehouse, and acquired his books as they came out. It is interesting that many Wodehouse fans became so at such an age; perhaps, having learned his craft producing boys' stories, he never lost the elements of fun and characterization which won his young first readers. For me, his intricate yet satisfyingly clear plots, the engaging *dramatis personae*, and the sunny Never-Never Land in which the books were set certainly appealed strongly. But I believe it was his use of language that most engaged me: not so much what are thought of as his unique idiosyncrasies, but the sheer music of his dialogue and narrative, its pristine quality. Winston Churchill has said, "Short words are best, and the old words, when short, best of all" (an almost ideal sentence, its own best example). A close reading of Wodehouse will show that much of his writing is good, plain discourse—which of course adds to the effect of his extravagances, such as his excellent and inventive use of slang (except American; there he had a regrettable fondness for discontinued items). Wodehouse almost always referred to his work as "my stuff"—a short word, an old word, a craftsman's word.

I was then living in my parents' house in Brussels, and would, with an embryonic collector's instinct, pick up the English editions and stow them on my bookshelves, unopened to maintain their unspoiled condition, relying when I could for reading on the paperbound Tauchnitz editions, then readily available on the Continent.

In 1944, as a soldier in the U.S. Army, I managed to make my way to my parents' home after an absence of some time, and found it, after four years of German occupation, surprisingly intact: the rugs, the fixtures, the furniture, even the flooring had not suffered. However, my Wodehouse books had vanished.

That was the end of what could be called collection A. In the years following the war, I kept on buying new Wodehouses as they came out, and, of course, reading them. After a while I had a fair number of books, which might be described as a clump on my shelves rather than a collection, though I did take care to keep them in fair condition.

Then, on an airplane journey, I took up and read with relish David Magee's fine book *Infinite Riches*, which describes his life as a book dealer. One thing that struck me with force was his discussion of Wodehouse as an author whose work could be collected at no great cost. Yes, first editions could be quite easily found for about four dollars, though the situation has changed a good deal since then! As I had quite a fair start, I set about turning what had been only an enthusiasm into an avocation and collection. By the time of that conversation at the Century Association, I had most of Wodehouse's books in their first English and American editions.

It was now agreed that there was to be a centenary exhibition, and that it would be in the main a display of my collection. And, as soon as that agreement had been reached, it became clear to me that it would be about as dull an exhibition as any cultural institution had ever mounted.

I mean, you can look at just so many title pages and dust jackets, mostly the same size and appearance, and then you are going to ask yourself what is to come next. When the answer is "nothing," there you are, collecting your umbrella from the cloakroom and shambling out onto Madison Avenue two hours earlier than you had expected.

At this point, the Library's needs and my own interests coincided. As a collector of Wodehouse's books, I had gone pretty well about as far as I could go. But there was a world of Wodehousiana remaining: manuscripts, phonograph records, letters, sheet music, film posters and stills, magazines, original artwork for illustrations, published translations—after all, a man who had so strongly affected not only literature but musical theatre and the films had to have left a number of traces along his way.

So I set about expanding my collection to include other Wodehouse material, emphasizing the sorts of thing that would enliven the exhibition and, by their diversity, have a graphic appeal which would please the museum-goer as well as gladden the collector. But, of course, this material had to be important and add to the understanding of Wodehouse.

I do have to say that the exhibition, and my collection, includes an item which is unique. You will, or should, recall the long-standing desire of Clarence, ninth Earl of Emsworth, to have an oil portrait of his Black Berkshire sow, Empress of Blandings, executed and hung in a position of honor in the Long Gallery of Blandings Castle among the paintings of his ancestors and notables. This wish was never realized in Wodehouse's books, though there is some suggestion that it might have been in the unfinished *Sunset at Blandings*. The visitor to the exhibition will see, indeed cannot avoid seeing, the amiable countenance of the Empress, handsomely framed, peering aristocratically at him. This excellent painting—might one term it *suidae generis?*—is very likely the only example extant of the fulfilling by actual persons of the ambitions of a fictional character.

I have now accounted for many of the items to be found in the exhibition. The bibliography and other allied material are the most complete yet published for Wodehouse. They are founded on the pioneer work of James Meriwether, David Magee, and David Jasen. The remainder of the book, some twenty-five articles by various hands—twenty-three of them never published before—dealing with some unexpected aspects of Wodehouse and his work, does, as I said at the beginning, call for some explanation.

It is certainly no surprise to find, in any publication dealing with Wodehouse, contributions from Richard Usborne, who has a long, honorable, and scholarly history of study and comment on this author. It is less expectable to encounter the names of Maureen O'Sullivan and Isaac Asimov, persons well known but not hitherto considered as Wodehouse experts. In their articles, as in the others, readers will look in vain for any shred of scholarly significance or profundity. Information and diversion will certainly be found in full measure: Wodehouse as a source of dramatic fare; Wodehouse's treatment of cats, crime, and golf; what the late and last Kaiser thought of Wodehouse; two instructively different approaches to collecting Wodehouse; what Blandings actually looks like; and a fund of reminiscence, comment, appreciation, and affection.

It seemed to us pointless to provide a detailed catalogue of what is in the exhibition. The items are there; at least half of them have never been exhibited before; and the exhibition cards will give all the information required for their contemplation by those attending. What would be appropriate for a publication for this centenary celebration, we felt, was to provide a measure of what Wodehouse himself for three-quarters of a century provided for all of us: cheerful, undemanding fun.

That is, of course, the keynote of the celebration. In preparing it, I have been struck by one thing about the people who concern themselves with Wodehouse's works—agents, publishers, and editors, as well as collectors and fans: how very happy they are to be so concerned. Nobody seems to collect Wodehouse out of a stern sense of duty or, except very seldom, greed. Pure enjoyment is the main thing.

I believe that this is partly because there is none of that tendency, as there is with so many authors, to delve deeply into Wodehouse's psyche or to try to achieve an admiring identification with someone superior to oneself. Wodehouse does not offer solutions to, or tragically trenchant comments on, the human condition, but instead does a good bit to ameliorate it by doling out large lashings of joy, warm laughter, and good cheer.

The geniality Wodehouse inspires is especially evident among collectors. The collector's temperament, alas, is not always large-minded and open-handed. He can be avid, petty, devious, given to dealing through agents in darkest secrecy and giving a miser's cackle at the prospect of scooping a treasure from under a rival's nose. Wodehouse does not draw out that kind of nastiness. Most Wodehouse collectors know each other and are friendly competitors, often tipping one another off to something good that has turned up (which the tipper-off doesn't happen to want). Until recently, money was not an important consideration, which of course goes a long way toward promoting good feeling.

One can see why this is so. One cannot be absorbed in Wodehouse without being influenced by his characters' examples of style, charm, decency, and pluck. When they act outrageously, they at least do so with an air, and almost never in meanness or spite. I don't say that an interest in Wodehouse amounts to a course in improving one's behavior, to be sure; but there is no denying that Wodehouse collectors are a milder lot than, say, those specializing in the messages of the gloomier Russians and the general decline of just about everything everywhere.

In his piece in this book Charles Gould quotes me as saying: "We don't collect Wodehouse; he collects us," and I stand by that. The many people, of such different backgrounds, whom Wodehouse has collected—for, make no mistake, it is more his doing than mine or the Morgan Library's—for this volume show in their writing that they wish only to share their enjoyment of Wodehouse. There is no one-upping, no attempt to impress with special knowledge or insight. This portion of the book should be considered as a remarkably varied appreciation of the works and character of a man who worked very hard so that we, his readers, might sit back and enjoy his stuff, as I hope you will do with these pieces.

If there is any fly at all in the perpetually efficacious Wodehouse ointment, it is the aggravating fact that for seventy-five years he made the very difficult seem so frightfully easy.

No introduction is complete, nor should it be, without the pleasure of expressing thanks to those people whose assistance, scholarship, time and patience were given to me so kindly and copiously. First on a long list of Wodehousians who have thus helped me in abundant measure is Richard Usborne, who quite possibly knows more about Wodehouse than did Wodehouse himself, and who has been unstinting in his guidance and understanding. Included in these thanks is Monica Usborne, whose cheerful hospitality and sumptuous repasts helped gather Wodehousians galore in her home and around her table at Hampstead for me to meet and from whom to learn. *Coprima inter pares* is Eileen McIlvaine, bibliographer, librarian, and scholar, and always as cheerful as a sunny Wodehouse day in June. Wodehouse people are usually a cheerful lot, but Eileen McIlvaine's cheerfulness extended beyond the call of patience when my questions would compete with a deadline she was trying to meet. There would be little of interest and usefulness in this book had not Richard Usborne and Eileen McIlvaine kept me pointed the right way.

I am also much indebted to Edward Cazalet, Q.C., Lady Wodehouse's grandson and P. G. Wodehouse's literary executor, for his encouragement, help, and the discreet opening of closed doors. To Lady Donaldson, who, with the blessing of the Wodehouse family, is writing the definitive Wodehouse biography, my thanks and gratitude are expressed for her judicious help in showing me what is important and what is more important. And to Lady Wodehouse go my warm thanks for her loving embrace of our cause.

I am most grateful for the encouragement and loyal help given to me by my friends at The Pierpont Morgan Library. Charles Ryskamp, the Library's Director, Herbert Cahoon, its Curator of Autograph Manuscripts, and Rigbie Turner, Assistant Curator of Autograph Manuscripts and Music Manuscripts, have not only made the preparation of this exhibition and this accompanying book easy, they have also made them thoroughly enjoyable. And Priscilla Barker and Ronnie Boriskin have made it all a delight. The exhibition is indebted to Francis Mason and Karen Powell for having brought it so effectively to the public attention.

And special thanks to Sara Feldman Guérin and Timothy Herstein for engineering so engagingly the exhibition itself.

To Kenneth Lohf, Librarian for Rare Books and Manuscripts, Columbia University Libraries, I express my special thanks for recommending the right person to undertake and complete a most important task—Eileen McIlvaine.

I am definitely indebted to Evelyne Ginestet d'Auzac de Lamartinie, whose thesis for the Doctorate in Letters at the Sorbonne, "Le Monde de P. G. Wodehouse," has provided me with information either unlearned or forgotten.

My gratitude and thanks go also to Donald Bensen, Wodehousian extraordinary, whose wide and deep knowledge of the canon was indispensable in editing this book. I also deeply thank the contributors of the articles appearing herein. When invited to write, each answered, "Yes, I'd love to" with a broad and happy smile.

I extend my appreciation also to Hilary Rubinstein and Scott Meredith, Wodehouse's British and American literary agents, for their permissions to quote from Wodehouse's many works, and for expressing their enthusiasm.

Had Polonius not met with a sticky end a few centuries ago, he would assuredly have enjoined me to be true to Wodehouse's own self. As a Wodehouse extremist responsible for this book and the exhibition, I have tried to live up to this directive. As a Trustee of the Library I thank every member of its staff, The Stinehour Press, and The Meriden Gravure Company for helping me to follow it.

But it is to P. G. Wodehouse himself that I am the most beholden. It is his works and the affection he engenders that have guaranteed the friendly collaboration of all those engaged in this centenary celebration.

A Selective P. G. Wodehouse Chronology

A CAREER spanning more than seven decades clearly contains so many significant dates that a full chronology would be unwieldy and tedious, and so inappropriate to Wodehouse. This listing is therefore in the main limited to unique occurrences—such as PGW's birth and marriage—and to "firsts"—first publication, first job, first appearances of his most famous characters. But, just to avoid a foolish consistency, some trivial and entertaining events have been included.

1881	15 Oct	Born, Guildford, Surrey, U.K.
1894	2 May	Entered Dulwich College
1900	Feb	Won 10/6 for prize contribution to *Public School Magazine*, "Some Aspects of Game-Captaincy"
	July	Completed Education at Dulwich
	Sept	Entered employ of Hong Kong and Shanghai Bank, London, at £80 per year
	Dec	Began writing column, "Under the Flail," for *Public School Magazine*
1901	June	Wrote nineteen short stories, all dreadful, during mumps attack
	16 Aug	First contributions to the newspaper *The Globe* published
1902	9 Sept	Quit Hong Kong and Shanghai Bank
	17 Sept	"An Unfinished Collection," first *Punch* article, published
	18 Sept	*The Pothunters*, first novel, published
1903	19 Mar	"The Peculiar Case of Flatherwick," first article for U.S. magazine *Vanity Fair*, published
	Aug	First full-time job writing: the "By the Way" column, *The Globe*
1904	Jan	Rents Threepwood, a house in the village of Emsworth—both names destined to ring down through the ages
	25 Apr	Arrives in New York on first visit to U.S.
	Aug	Becomes editor of "By the Way" at magnificent wage of 25 gns.
	10 Dec	First theatre lyric, "Put Me in My Little Cell," performed
1905	1 Jan	Resolves to learn banjo, later mercifully abandons this idea
	July	"The Wire Pullers," first *Strand Magazine* story, published
1906	19 Mar	Engaged to do comic lyrics for *The Beauty of Bath*, music provided by one Jerome Kern
	6 June	*Love among the Chickens*, first adult novel (and first to appear, two months on, in the U.S.), published—first appearance of Stanley Featherstonehaugh Ukridge
	17 Nov	Purchases a Darracq auto; after one lesson, crashes it into a hedge and never drives again
1907	1 Jan	Employed by Hicks Theatre as lyrist
	13 Oct	*Not George Washington*, novel with autobiographical elements, published
	6 Dec	Joins Gaiety Theatre as lyrist
1909	May	Arrives in New York on second U.S. trip; sells two stories in one day, wires resignation to *Globe*, settles in to enjoy success for indefinite period

	15 Sept	*Mike*—first appearance of Psmith—published, U.K.
1910	Feb	Success proving more indefinite than enjoyment, returns to England and the *Globe*
1911	21 June	Faints in Café Royal on being told funny story; not a critical response but result of a chill
	24 Aug	*A Gentleman of Leisure*, first play, opens, New York
1912	January	Becomes client of literary agent Ella King-Hall; remains so for twenty-two years
	14 Feb	*The Prince and Betty* published, U.S.
	1 May	Wildly different version of *The Prince and Betty* published, U.K.
1913	8 Apr	*Brother Alfred*, play in collaboration with Herbert Westbrook, opens, London; lasts two weeks
1914	4 Jan	*Nuts and Wine*, revue in collaboration with Charles Bovil, opens, London
	23 Jan	*The Man Upstairs*, first adult short-story collection, published, U.K.
	3 Aug	Meets Ethel Rowley in New York
	30 Sept	Marries Ethel Rowley
	1 Oct	Moves to Bellport, Long Island, at rental of $20 a month
1915	2 Mar	*A Gentleman of Leisure*, first film, released
	3 Sept	*Something New*, first Blandings Castle novel, published, U.S.
	15 Sept	"Extricating Young Gussie," first Jeeves story, published in *Saturday Evening Post*
	24 Dec	Introduced by Jerome Kern to Guy Bolton, New York
1916	25 Sept	*Miss Springtime*, first Bolton-Wodehouse-Kern musical, opens to rave reviews
1917	20 Feb	*Oh, Boy!*, first B-W-K "Princess" show, opens—biggest hit of New York season
	5 Nov	*Miss 1917*, B-W-K revue, opens and flops; also Guy Fawkes Day, which might explain disaster
1919	May	*My Man Jeeves*, first (partial) Jeeves collection, published, U.K.
1921	Mar	Returning to Prohibition-era U.S., pays Biltmore bellboy $17 for bottle of whisky
1922	3 Feb	*The Clicking of Cuthbert*, first golf collection, published, U.K.
1923	17 May	*The Inimitable Jeeves*, first all-Jeeves collection, published, U.K.
1925	25 Apr	Lunch with Sir Arthur Conan Doyle, a boyhood idol
1926	3 Nov	PGW's adaptation of Molnar's *The Play's the Thing* opens, New York
	8 Nov	*Oh, Kay!*, B-W-K show, gives Gertrude Lawrence her New York musical debut
1927	27 Sept	*Meet Mr. Mulliner*, first Mulliner collection, published, U.K.
	27 Dec	*Show Boat* opens, New York, featuring long-abandoned PGW lyric, "Bill"
1929	Aug	First visit to Hollywood
	Nov	Ethel Wodehouse negotiates six-month contract with MGM for PGW as screen writer
1930	8 May	To Hollywood to take up duties; assigned to work on script for musical *Rosalie*
	Oct	MGM renews contract for six months; *Rosalie* still unfinished
1931	7 June	In interview with *Los Angeles Times*, complains of too much pay for too little work, rocking Hollywood to its foundations, if any
	Nov	Returns to England, neither bloodied nor bowed; *Rosalie* remains unfinished and unfilmed
1932	Mar	Wodehouses settle in France
	10 Mar	*Louder and Funnier*, first essay collection, published, U.K.
	20 July	*Nothing but Wodehouse*, first omnibus, published, U.S.
1934	16 Mar	*Thank You, Jeeves*, first Jeeves novel, published, U.S.
	1 Sept	*A Century of Humour*, edited by PGW, published, U.K.
	21 Nov	*Anything Goes* opens, New York; of the original Bolton-Wodehouse script, jetti-

		soned because of Morro Castle disaster, two lines remain; these net PGW $500 a week for the run of the show
	23 Dec	Ethel Wodehouse acquires Wonder, longest-lived of all Wodehouse Pekes
1935	12 Apr	*Blandings Castle*, first (partial) Blandings collection, published, U.K.
	14 June	Original Bolton-Wodehouse version of *Anything Goes* opens, London; a success, and their last musical collaboration
	Dec	Sadly abandons his Monarch typewriter, with him since 1909, for a new machine
1936	3 Apr	*Young Men in Spats*, Drones Club collection, published, U.K.; first book appearance of Pongo Twistleton's alarming Uncle Fred
	26 June	Awarded medallion by Mark Twain Society
	10 Oct	Back in Hollywood under new contract with MGM; once more put to work on *Rosalie*
1937	May	Asked by RKO to adapt for the screen a novel by a promising writer; a congenial task, as the p.w. is P. G. Wodehouse
	4 Nov	Returns to France, to house at Le Touquet
1938	7 Oct	*The Code of the Woosters*—for many the ultimate Jeeves-Bertie novel—published, U.K./U.S.
1939	21 June	Granted honorary Litt.D. by Oxford
	18 Aug	*Uncle Fred in the Springtime*, first Uncle Fred novel, published, U.K.
1940	22 May	German Army occupies Le Touquet
	21 July	Interned by Germans, sent to Loos prison, where booked under the name of Widhorse; later confined with other internees in lunatic asylum in Tost, Silesia
1941	21 June	Released from Tost, allowed to live in Berlin
	26 June	Agrees to U.S. correspondent's request to broadcast to America on internment experiences; makes five broadcasts
	15 July	Attacked bitterly over BBC for broadcasts
1943	Sept	Wodehouses sent from Berlin to Paris
1944	20 Nov	Wodehouses arrested by French police for no clear cause; released, but PGW "detained" in hospital
	6 Dec	Foreign Minister Anthony Eden tells House of Commons no basis for any charges against PGW
1945	20 Jan	Released from hospital "detention"
1946	27 May	*Money in the Bank*, first of several novels written during detention, published, U.K.
1947	25 Apr	Wodehouses return to U.S.
1948	18 Apr	*The Play's the Thing* revived, New York, a hit again
	2 Sept	*Don't Listen, Ladies* opens, London; Bolton-Wodehouse adaptation of Sacha Guitry play; their last produced theatrical collaboration
1952	July	Wodehouses make final move, to house in Basket Neck Lane, Remsenburg, Long Island, New York
1953	5 Oct	*Bring on the Girls!*, collaborative memoir with Bolton, published, U.S.
	9 Oct	*Performing Flea*, letters to friend Bill Townend, published, U.K.
1955	16 Dec	Becomes U.S. citizen
1960	27 Jan	Notified of election to *Punch* Table, a signal honor
1962	20 June	*Author! Author!*, new version of *Performing Flea*, published, U.S.
1964	24 May	Long-playing record, *Jeeves*, issued, U.S.
1965	27 May	*The World of Wooster* series begins, BBC-TV
1967	16 Feb	*Blandings Castle* series begins, BBC-TV
	Nov	P. G. Wodehouse Animal Shelter opened, Remsenburg

1971	15 Oct	*Jeeves and the Tie That Binds* (U.S.) / *Much Obliged, Jeeves* (U.K.) published as part of ninetieth birthday celebration
1974	14 Apr	*Aunts Aren't Gentlemen*, last complete novel, published, U.K.
1975	1 Jan	Knighted by Queen Elizabeth II
	14 Feb	After a good morning's work on latest novel, dies
1977	24 Oct	*Sunset at Blandings*, incomplete novel with notes and scenarios, published, U.K.

Essays

How I Write My Books
P. G. WODEHOUSE

EDITOR'S NOTE: The reader is, of course, the final authority on what an author's works mean, how they are regarded by posterity, and what he was up to in his treatment of themes and situations; and ingenious and dedicated scholars routinely present interpretations and opinions which have been known to surprise their subjects quite as much as they have instructed the public, often more so. However, on the matter of just what it was he did, distinct from the underlying significance and symbolism, it is the author who has the first-hand knowledge; and it is appropriate here to let PGW say a word on this topic, in a piece which he contributed to *What I Think*, a writers' symposium published by George Newnes in London in 1926.

IN THE MATTER of plots, I find that I use, for short stories, a method exactly opposite to the one which gets me my best results in the case of novels—if in these earnest days I can apply such a dignified name to my longer yarns.

When I want to write a short story, I sit down on one chair, place the feet comfortably on another, put notebook, pencil, matches, pipe, and tobacco handily on my lap, select a character, and then keep on sitting till I have discovered what happened to him the time he forgot his wife's birthday or on the afternoon when he went to Wembley. In other words, the story grows out of the character. It may turn into an entirely different story half-way through, but the character remains the same.

A novel is another matter altogether, far less simple, and it is to the strain of getting plots for novels that I attribute the hideous, lined face and bald head which appear in my photographs.

A good novel ought to have a theme, so I start by trying to think of one. Failing in this, I dig up a scene—any scene, so long as it seems to have possibilities. I then take the actors in the scene and try to learn more about them. Then I think of other scenes, bung them down on a bit of paper, and pin this bit of paper to the first bit of paper. This goes on for about a week, by which time my drawer contains perhaps ten bits of paper, carefully pinned together and scrawled over with the sort of thing the fever-patient moans in his sleep.

Then, just as I am beginning to feel that nothing will emerge from this chaos, scene number fifteen suddenly clicks with scene number eight. I join them and write them down on another bit of paper. And then, when I am shaving or in my bath, it occurs to me that by turning the blackmailer into a dog-fancier and giving the girl an aunt who keeps rabbits, and eliminating the curate in favor of a pickle-manufacturer from Milwaukee, I have got a faint, shadowy suggestion of a plot.

At this point I really get going. I stand no nonsense from my characters. The pickle-manufacturer has to become a dowager duchess—and like it—in order to fit the scene where the dog-fancier (now a blackmailer once more) goes to the Hunt Ball so as to keep in with the girl's aunt, whose rabbits have been taken away from her and replaced by a racing-stable.

The final stage begins when one or two characters who can't be altered creep into the story. Then I know where I am.

As regards characters, some of those which have appeared in my stories have come from chance remarks from friends about men they have known. Years ago a cousin of mine told me that he was at Winchester with a long, thin, solemn, immaculately-dressed boy who used to wear an eyeglass and talk kindly, but not patronizingly, to the head master. The character, Psmith, who has appeared in several of my books, was based on my idea of that youth, whom I never met. Ukridge was a friend of W. Townend, the writer of sea-stories, who told me about him. Jeeves was an invention of my own. I was in the middle of a short story, when it suddenly struck me that a young man of my hero's mental calibre could not possibly have thought out the solution of the problem in which a friend of his was involved, and it seemed to me that a super-intelligent valet would just meet the case.

When it comes to the actual writing of a story, I always work on the typewriter. I have never tried dictation.

Reprinted with the kind permission of the estate of P. G. Wodehouse.

PELHAM GRENVILLE WODEHOUSE was born on 15 October 1881 in Guildford, Surrey, England, and died in Remsenburg, Long Island, U.S.A., on 14 February 1975. Between those dates, he wrote not far short of a hundred novels and collections of short stories, a series of brilliant theatrical lyrics, and whatever essays he found time for; he helped change the style of the musical theatre, created a number of immortal characters, and, though it was no part of his intention, inspired this book.

Dulwich Schooldays
PETER SOUTHERN

The most deadly error mortal man can make, with the exception of calling a school a college, is to call a college a school.
The Pothunters, 1902

EVERYBODY KNOWS that P. G. Wodehouse went to Dulwich College when he was a boy: the fact is proclaimed on the back of nearly every English paperback copy of his works. What is less generally appreciated is that he never left. Although the official records state that Wodehouse, having entered the school in May 1894, departed in July 1900, it becomes clear from his books and letters that Dulwich College occupied a place in his heart that schools can rarely achieve, and exerted a profound influence on his whole life, his enthusiasms, and his literary works. In return, the school remembers him with affection and pride, keeping personal mementos of him in the library.

Dulwich College is one of the major landmarks of South-East London. Founded in 1619 by the Shakespearean actor-manager Edward Alleyn, it was endowed with extensive lands which increased rapidly in value with the arrival of the railways and the absorption of the area into London's suburbs. By Wodehouse's day the school had built opulent new buildings in self-confident red brick a few hundred yards from the original site in Dulwich Village, and stood in sixty-five acres of remarkably rural scenery only seven miles from Piccadilly Circus (or for a crow, only five). The boarding houses preserve the pastoral atmosphere with names like Orchard, Elm Lawn, and Ivyholme. There were just over six hundred boys at the college in Wodehouse's time, mostly day boys and suburbanites, but including a steady proportion of boarders separated from their families out East.

Dulwich is a public school and preserves the image of such establishments much as it did at the turn of the century. The education is expensive, and the pupils are expected both by school and parents to get their money's worth. They work hard on a curriculum that changes only very slowly and well behind the times. They play games, chiefly team games like cricket and rugger, which are held to promote self-discipline and corporate loyalty. These games, so central to the formation of the British character, involve, in the case of cricket, at the highest level, five full days of play, broken only by the weather and meals, generally ending in a draw; and in the case of rugger, violent physical contact where progress is impeded by the rule that one may only pass the ball backwards. Over the years the pupils absorb the code of behavior, enforced by their peers, which is the least definable, yet held to be the most valuable, feature of such an education.

In the college today there are few visible records of distinguished former pupils (known as Old Alleynians, or O.A.s). The school elite, members of the cricket and rugger teams which represented the school, are soberly commemorated in the 1930s pavilion which dominates the sports field. There one can read the name of Wodehouse, P. G., as a member of the rugger XVs and cricket XIs of 1899 and 1900. For further details of his school career one must turn to the school magazine, *The Alleynian*, which he edited and which was mostly concerned with chronicling the deeds of individuals. The earliest reference, coming in his first term at the school, concerns an interform cricket match in 1894. The infant Wodehouse, batting number 11 (i.e., last) for Upper IIIb, made an inauspicious start to his cricketing career, being bowled by Green in both innings without scoring a run. However, his form won by three runs, and Wodehouse was considered to have done enough to earn promotion to number 10 in the next match, amassing two more scores of 0, one of them *not out*. In 1898 he had the further misfortune to be bowled by his elder brother, Armine, who had the infuriating habit in his schooldays of excelling at everything he put his hand to, whether in work or play. Nevertheless, by 1899 Wodehouse, P. G., was a regular member of the first team, but *The Alleynian* character sketch of him lacks nothing in frankness: "Bowled well against Tonbridge, but did nothing else. Does not use his head at all. A poor bat and very slack field." Rugger and boxing reports speak of his achievements with greater approval: "The ponderous Wodehous" showed "how boxing was really done in the best circles."

There was little in school magazines in those days that was not concerned with sport, but occasional drama critics noticed Wodehouse's early successes in the theatre. He was praised for his performances, in the two roles of a frog and a worshiper, in Aristophanes' *The Frogs*, although the reviewer was alarmed by the "muttered exclamations and throes of agony" which could be heard during his rapid costume change. His lighthearted acting style is also revealed in a review of W. S. Gilbert's *Rosencrantz and Guildenstern* which enthuses over his dance routine and some inventive byplay with a revolver. *The Alleynian* can also take the credit for publishing Wodehouse's earliest works: two poems, including "On the New Football Field":

> I raised my eye (which I had fixed
> Upon a book of Coptic),
> And close at hand a dauntless band
> Of diggers met my optic!

Another extraordinary publication, the Dulwich College *Form List*, allows one to trace the academic course followed by Wodehouse throughout his school career and his level of achievement in his main subjects. He seems never to have won a prize (not even, as Bertie Wooster had, for "Scripture Knowledge"), and he remained near the middle of any form he entered. The basic diet of the schoolboy of the 1890s was severely classical, which was just as well for Wodehouse, who had some talents in this direction and evidently had problems with subjects like mathematics and French. The ability to embark on long sentences and to emerge heading in the same direction that he had gone in was a skill that Wodehouse learned young and owed to his close acquaintance with classical authors like Thucydides. This should come as no surprise to those familiar with the Bertie-and-Jeeves relationship to find that their creator was raised on Plautus and in the sixth form would have been made to read the *Mostellaria*, in which a slave uses a series of subterfuges to protect his dissolute young master from the righteous indignation of his father who finds his house invaded by uninvited guests.

This classical bias is clearly visible also in the schools in which Wodehouse's earliest stories are set. When faced with the necessity to work, the boys are generally wrestling with Xenophon or puzzling over the Romans' extraordinary habit of throwing wings of horse across rivers. In *The White Feather*, the headmaster of Wrykyn faced changing educational patterns in much the same way as did Gilkes, the formidable Mast of Dulwich in Wodehouse's day. "To him the word 'Education' meant Classics. There was a Modern Side at Wrykyn, and an Engineering Side and also a Science Side; but in his heart he recognized but one Education—the Classics."

The schools about which Wodehouse wrote, Wrykyn, St. Austin's, Sedleigh, Beckford College, and Eckleton, are all Dulwich. It is certainly no accident that the old boys of St. Austin's are called O.A.s. The school building has three blocks, connected by cloisters, the masters' Common Room is in the middle block, the school caters for both boarders and day boys, and it was reached by a short train journey from Victoria Station. All this was and is true of Dulwich College too, though the train takes a minute longer than it did in the age of steam. A further coincidence, of a type that emerges frequently in studying the background to Wodehouse's works, is that *Tales of St. Austin's* was published only a year after an imposing house of the same name was built on a prime site in Dulwich Village. At all Wodehouse's schools, as at Dulwich, extra lesson on Saturday afternoon was considered the most fearful punishment. At Sedleigh the area outside the school block was known as the gravel; once a term there was Service Day, regarded as an effective whole holiday and an opportunity for informal sporting fixtures; and in the Great Hall there was an Honors Board bearing the names of those who, on leaving, distinguished themselves in those few activities the school chose to remember: Oxford, Cambridge, and the Indian Civil Service. This last feature has now gone from Dulwich College, submerged beneath a wallpaper reminiscent of a Chinese restaurant. That could never have happened at Sedleigh.

The most clear-cut reference to Dulwich occurs in *Psmith in the City*, when Mike, forced to seek employment in a bank (a gruesome fate which Wodehouse had shared), seeks lodgings near the college, which is described in some detail. Hundreds of Alleynian feet still tread each day the asphalt passage from the station to the fields. Perhaps the most obscure of all the reminders from Wodehouse's own schooldays is the lament of the missing pavilion hairbrush in *The Pothunters* (1902) which recalls a lengthy correspondence in *The Alleynian* on the same topic in 1898.

The code of the public schoolboy at the turn of the century comes across vividly in these early books. Arrogance ("sticking on side") is outlawed and punished by the boys themselves with an icy reserve. An easy insouciance is cultivated to conceal ambition and hard work. Fights among boys are extremely rare, "lower school scuffles" not counting. Smoking is "beastly bad" and confined to "rotters" and results in instant expulsion if discovered. Masters are to be ignored if possible and baited if not. Prep is generally cribbed, but "wholesale plagiarism should be kept for the school magazine."

The contacts with Dulwich were not broken when Wodehouse left in 1900. For some years he continued to write for *The Alleynian*, contributing reports on rugger matches and boxing tournaments. He maintained a deep emotional involvement in the fortunes of the school teams, which led him on one occasion to walk in a daze from Dulwich to central London, so moved was he by the stirring action on the field. The unbeaten cricket team of 1938 was rewarded by Wodehouse with a dinner and seats at the London Palladium, much to the delight of a future England player, Trevor Bailey, who was then fourteen; and more or less the last thing that Wodehouse did before leaving England for the last time in 1939 was to visit the college to watch a cricket match against St. Paul's. His later letters show a constant long-range interest in the results of the school teams and, shortly after the war, still recuperating from his experiences in German prison camps, he wrote, "Isn't it odd, when one ought to be worrying about the state of the world and one's troubles generally, that the only thing I can think of nowadays is that Dulwich looks like winning all its school matches." In his nearest approach to autobiography he remembered his schooldays as "six years of unbroken bliss."

The ill-timed broadcast talks he made from Germany to still-neutral America in 1941 clouded Wodehouse's subsequent relationships with his publics, English and American. Nowadays, when one reads the texts of them, the only object of wonder is that the Germans should have allowed themselves to be made the butt of some gentle humor; but in the rancorous climate of war-tired Europe the reaction was decidedly different and a venomous press campaign ensued in England. Although much about this incident remains uncertain, it seems clear that Dulwich College didn't turn vindictively upon its former hero. Malcolm Muggeridge has said that Wodehouse's name was "expunged from some roll or other" at the school, but there is no evidence of this. That some frostiness entered into the friendly relationship is clear from the fact that the president of the old boys' club is mildly pilloried under a feminized version of his name, Eustacia Pulbrook, in *The Mating Season*. The book was written while Wodehouse was still in France in 1946, and it may be supposed that some rumblings against him were still to be heard among the old boys. It is significant that the only place where anything approaching an apologia for the broadcasts appeared was *The Alleynian* of July 1945. The wild accusations of his other critics did not rate any reply, but Wodehouse was clearly anxious to straighten things out with his Dulwich friends. "Slacker" Christison, who devoted much of his life to the health of the Old Alleynian Club, kept an extensive collection of cuttings from many sources on the activities of his friend and schoolboy contemporary. Wodehouse wrote to his old school friend Bill Townend in 1950, "Last Thursday the OA New York dinner, ten of us, me in the chair. It really was a joy to get back into an atmosphere where one could discuss whether J. B. Smith was right in passing to his wing in the Haileybury match of 1907 . . . or was it 56 or 65 that R. J. Jones made v. St. Paul's in 1911." In 1951 he gave a complete set of his works to the college library.

The relationship with the college remained warm and constant, and the influence of the place never ceased to exert its force. Although the later books move away from the school setting, the southeastern suburbs of London remain prominent. Furthermore, many of the most popular set pieces in the works of Wodehouse retain an authentic school flavor. The Market Snodsbury Grammar School prize-giving in *Right-Ho, Jeeves!* (U.S.: *Brinkley Manor*) is the work of a man who knows his subject, who has squirmed through the embarrassments of visiting speakers and knows how boys react. The concerts and public occasions which are inflicted upon Wodehouse's characters have an awful truth about them and are reminiscent of *Alleynian* reports of similar gatherings. The time and the place have been captured perfectly—never has an author put to such productive use a case of arrested development.

Many of the landmarks that were firmly rooted in Wodehouse's memory and which surface in his works have sadly decayed or been obliterated in recent years. Brixton no longer has its Bon Marche (though eagle-eyed observers can still pick out the fading letters of the old shop's name); Sydenham lost its Crystal Palace in a blaze in 1936. Close to West Dulwich station (itself a recent victim of British Rail vandalism which turned it from the prototype Wild West station to a run-down bus shelter), on the site of the old Wodehouse home on the corner of the Croxted Road stands a dispiriting bungalow. But not all is lost. Hollyhocks and nasturtiums still bloom unconscious of the passage of time in Valley Fields, and over at the college the boys still remember P. G. Wodehouse with affection and, more important still, know where to find him on the bookshelf.

PETER SOUTHERN is a mediaeval historian who teaches at Westminster School in London. His previous job was at Dulwich College where he taught for five years, having been enticed there very largely by the Wodehouse connection. He was able to mount several exhibitions concerned with the life and works of Wodehouse during his stay at Dulwich and enjoyed the company of other Wodehouse enthusiasts who had gathered there. He still lives in Dulwich with his wife and two sons, only a moderate stone's throw from the former Wodehouse home.

Writing a Biography of P. G. Wodehouse

FRANCES DONALDSON

DINING TOGETHER a few years ago, an English literary agent, an American and an English publisher discussed who, among English contemporary writers, could reasonably be assured of a place in posterity. Unanimous agreement was reached on three names—Evelyn Waugh, Graham Greene, and P. G. Wodehouse. Asked the same question, ninety-nine out of a hundred educated Englishmen might name the first two, but the third would come as a surprise to many of them. Alone, surely, in the history of literature, Wodehouse, although primarily a popular novelist, writing for and read by millions of ordinary people in every country and every language in the world, was also a "writer's writer," an idol of intellectual society. And, although for nearly a century he has been praised by his most distinguished colleagues, the admiration of the second of these groups has still to be explained to the first.

The reasons for this are twofold. His talent for language was so great, so fresh, and so secure that the virtues which beguile the professional are exactly those which tend to disguise his qualities from the man who reads purely for pleasure. "In all the departments of his skill," Hilaire Belloc wrote, "Mr. Wodehouse is unique for simplicity and exactitude, which is as much as to say he is unique for the avoidance of frills. He gets the full effect, bang! One may say of him, as the traveler in the story, hearing Shakespeare for the first time, said of Hamlet: 'Doesn't he pull it off?' " The second reason is that Wodehouse adds to the confusion by putting his inspired prose, as well as a miraculous humor, at the service of plots which, although idiosyncratic, peopled by characters who have become household words, and told with enormous narrative skill, are, nevertheless, entirely of a popular kind.

The first task of a biographer therefore is by explanation and illustration to establish for the general reader the reasons why Wodehouse has achieved a lasting place in English literature; and he must do this conscious of the fact that, because of the tremendous interest in his subject, his words will also be read by many people who could do the job better themselves. I have put on the half title of my book some words written by Ogden Nash: "To inhabit the same world as Mr. Wodehouse is a high privilege; to inhabit the same volume, even as a doorkeeper, is perilous."

The second problem for a biographer of Wodehouse stems so immediately from the first that it might almost be considered part of it. There is very great difficulty in finding anything to say about his work which has not already been said in definitive form before. Over nearly ninety years and more than ninety books, so much space has been devoted to him by so many of our best writers that every thought which occurs to one turns out previously to have occurred to somebody else. At first one feels deprived of any originality one might have hoped to have, but further thought brings consolation. For, although so much has been written about Wodehouse, the best of it, apart from a distinguished analysis of his work by Richard Usborne, is not in books but in the files of old newspapers and literary magazines. Part of the duty of a biographer is to collect and present contemporary opinion in a more viable form, and I soon realized that, in return for the disadvantage of being bereft of my own ideas, I could by quotation call into collaboration most of the finest critical talents of the period.

Having thus with the help of others surmounted, I hope successfully, the initial problems, I was able to return to the sphere more properly my own—that of biography—and here I had the very distinct advantage of having known Wodehouse personally ever since I was about fourteen and, in addition, of having been very close to his stepdaughter, Leonora. Wodehouse adopted Leonora and he brought her up, and she was one of the very few people he loved and with whom he was at ease. I was at school with her and I always saw much of her until she died so tragically when she was barely forty. She was the best crib one could have to the character of this very peculiar, if not very complex, man, and she left a son and a daughter who have given me every help in writing my book.

First, I must say that I believe there is a very big difference between a political or historical biography and the kind of thing that I write. In all the books I have written, what has interested me is the person, rather than what he did or the period in which he lived. Of my book *Edward VIII*, people have often said how much they admired the enormous research I must have undertaken in order to be able to write it. This praise was undeserved. There was no research of the kind which would be needed for the life of, for instance, a politician, where a knowledge of the issues of fifty years can be merely background material. I had to grasp the political issues of the day only inasmuch as they touched the king, which is to say, often hardly at all. What was necessary was to understand a character, and then to present him in such a way that the reader will understand him too.

To do this needs a great deal of thought, deep and sustained consideration of moods and motives as well as of actions. One must live with the person one is writing about, sometimes for years at a time, and one must become very much engaged. A publisher once said to me that he preferred the second half of a book I had written to the first, because, he said, "it has more feeling." And he added that it is feeling which makes a book.

I think he was right and that the first rule for any biographer is that he must have some feeling for his subject, although I am not sure that it matters what that feeling is. David Cecil has said that he could never write a book about someone unless he was fond of him, but I have not found this necessary. In fact, I am inclined to think it makes the task more difficult. I came to dislike two of the subjects of my books, one of them rather intensely, and I found that in that case it is merely a matter of leaning over backwards to be fair; and, if you are right in your prejudices, the facts will speak for themselves and you will gain a reputation for great impartiality. When, on the other hand, one is fond of one's subject, although one must not succumb to the temptation to alter or suppress the facts, it is inevitable to try to present them in such a way that the reader does not find the subject unsympathetic. And this can take years off one's life.

I do not for a moment wish to suggest that there is a great deal about P. G. Wodehouse to give trouble to a biographer, because he was one of the kindest and most faultless men I have ever met. But he did get into trouble in 1941 for broadcasting on a German wavelength from Berlin to the United States of America, and this was a technical offense against his country which, although few people have believed that it was deliberately treacherous, many have been unable to understand or forgive. The test of whether the biographer is succeeding in his task must be that, when this episode is reached, he should so have contrived it that no direct confrontation with the reader is necessary. The latter should by now know Wodehouse so well that he does not need to be told that, given the circumstances in which Wodehouse found himself, it was inevitable that he should behave as he did; and inevitable, too, that he should then feel, as Lord Emsworth felt when, after swallowing his front stud, he came down to dinner having substituted for it a brass paper-fastener, that he simply could not understand what the fuss was about.

But I was assured, both by professional writers and those who knew Wodehouse well, that the final and insurmountable problem for anyone writing about him was the dullness of his personality and, with the exception of this one incident, of his life. While his tremendous output of novels and short stories, articles, musical comedies, lyrics, and verses ensured endless material for the critic, the biographer was faced with a large, silent recluse, who hardly ever made a joke, gave his considerable store of affection almost entirely to dogs, as a young man spent almost his entire day at his desk, and for the last twenty-five years of his life worked in the morning, walked in the afternoon, thought about work after tea, had a cocktail at six, an early dinner, and then went to bed.

At one time I was ready to give up in despair. However, just as I had called into service all those earlier writers who seemed to have stolen my thoughts, so I now turned for help to the Master himself. The pen is after all mightier than the sword, and, if I had no battles, no political crises, even no love affairs, I did have a vast store of published work to draw on for illustration of any point I wished to make, and, even more important, an unexpected quantity of unpublished papers. For what does a writer who is also a recluse do when he is not at work or walking the dogs, or when he finds himself in a prison camp? In the first case he writes letters, in the second he keeps a diary.

Wodehouse's output of letters can be compared to his output of fiction. He answered every fan letter personally and he wrote all his life to his friends, and, if the latter could be counted on the fingers of one hand, he nevertheless wrote to them regularly; while, because he succeeded as a writer early in life, they did their part by keeping the letters he wrote. When he was in the internment camp in Germany, he kept a diary or writer's notebook (not to be confused with something he called the Camp Book which was a full-length manuscript he wrote up from these notes and which has now disappeared).

I have been lucky enough to be allowed the full use of all this and much more besides, and, if, as I hope, I have to some extent succeeded in presenting Wodehouse to the world as he was, it is because of the immense help he gave me himself.

FRANCES DONALDSON was born in 1907, the daughter of Frederick Lonsdale, the playwright. She married John George Stuart Donaldson (now Lord Donaldson of Kingsbridge) in 1935. She has one son and two daughters. In 1940 she bought a farm and continued farming through the war and, with her husband, until 1968. Her first two books, Approach to Farming *and* Four Years' Harvest, *describe her experiences of wartime farming. Other books include* Freddy Lonsdale (Freddy *in USA*), The Marconi Scandal (*the history of a political scandal of 1912*), Evelyn Waugh: Portrait of a Country Neighbor, *and* Edward VIII, *winner of the 1975 Wolfson History Award and the book on which the television series* Edward and Mrs. Simpson *was based. Of herself she says: "I went to five schools but all for young ladies which taught me nothing, not even how to be a young lady—the education for girls of the middle to upper classes in those days being shocking. Nothing else to say, as all my hobbies being exercise ones have left me now."*

Lunching with Plum
ALEC WAUGH

I FIRST encountered Plum Wodehouse in August 1910 at Lord's, where he was playing cricket for the Authors against the Publishers. I remember the match well. Conan Doyle captained the Authors, S. S. Pawling the Publishers. Pawling, William Heinemann's partner, universally called "The Skipper," was one of the bulwarks of the Hampstead Cricket Club, which was known as the nursery of Middlesex cricket; he had played a few times for Middlesex.

That match at Lord's was a closely contested draw. (My score card, which I kept for many years, is now in the Haverford College Library.) Hugh de Selincourt was playing, author, later, of that classic *The Cricket Match*. Also Gunby Hadath, whose name, I discovered later, was as well known to readers of *The Captain* as Plum's. In the closing quarter of an hour of the match E. Temple Thurston took three quick wickets, the last clean bowled. But it was entered in the score card as "Stumped." Thurston was aggrieved. He felt that the impression would be given that the batsman had run out of his ground contemptuously and missed the ball—a complaint that suggests that Thurston didn't know much about the game.

I can remember nearly everything about the match except Plum's own innings. He went in first wicket down and made over sixty runs. I can only assume it was a sound, straightforward performance unmarked by brilliance or eccentricity of style; and the fact that I do not recall it proves that the name P. G. Wodehouse meant nothing to me. At my preparatory school popular magazines were not allowed. I consequently never saw *The Captain* in which Plum's school stories appeared. It was not till Christmas 1910 that a copy of *Mike* lay beside my Christmas stocking. Had I read *Mike* six months earlier, how eagerly I would have demanded to be introduced to its author!

Mike, for a schoolboy of twelve who was crazy about cricket had, in 1910, absolutely everything. It has some of the best descriptions of cricket that I have ever read. How cleverly the narrative is constructed so that the account of each match begins at a different point, so that sometimes it is told in retrospect. And then there is the introduction of Psmith—what wit, what *variety* of wit. He is as funny today as he was seventy years ago.

The creation of Psmith is one of the miracles of literature. There he suddenly was, in the middle of a serial written for schoolboys, a complete creation. Is there any parallel in literature? I cannot think of one. Suddenly, overnight, without warning, PGW discovered that he had this unique gift. What a surprise, what an excitement it must have been to him. How soon did he realize all the implications that were involved, or half the implications? He went on writing in *The Captain*. *Mike* was followed by *Psmith in the City* where, at the very start, Mike is still the hero; Psmith's entry is delayed. It is not till *Psmith, Journalist* that Mike is relegated to a very minor role. In *Leave It to Psmith* Mike fades away forever.

I came late, then, to my appreciation of PGW. My young brother Evelyn on the other hand had become an appreciator of the Master, as he always called him, at the age of seven. Wodehouse was Evelyn's nurse Lucy's favorite reading. Evelyn did not read of Psmith in *The Captain*. But the first clothbound editions of the Psmith saga contained reproductions from the original *Captain* illustrations so that for Evelyn from the very start the tall, elegant ex-Etonian with the monocle was a familiar sight.

My own high enthusiasm for PGW survived the 1914–18 War. I returned from eight months in a prisoner-of-war camp as the author of a story of public-school life that had become a *succès de scandale*. As such I was quite often interviewed, and I took every opportunity of paying tribute to Plum's work. When I was asked which books I would choose if I were shipwrecked on a desert island, I would always refer to "the ever-delightful *Mike*." It never occurred to me to wonder whether Plum was conscious of my hero-worship, but I presumed he was aware of my existence. As the author of so many school stories, he could hardly not have heard of *The Loom of Youth*. But I was very surprised—I was more than surprised—by an incident that took place in the spring of 1925. I returned from lunch to find on my office desk a message from "Mrs. Woodhouse" asking if I could dine with her that night. I

PLATE 1

Dulwich College, just south of London, which Wodehouse attended 1894–1900.

The Wodehouse corner in the Dulwich Library containing Wodehouse's pipe, desk, chair, typewriter, and other memorabilia.

The 1899 Dulwich cricket team.

PLATE 2

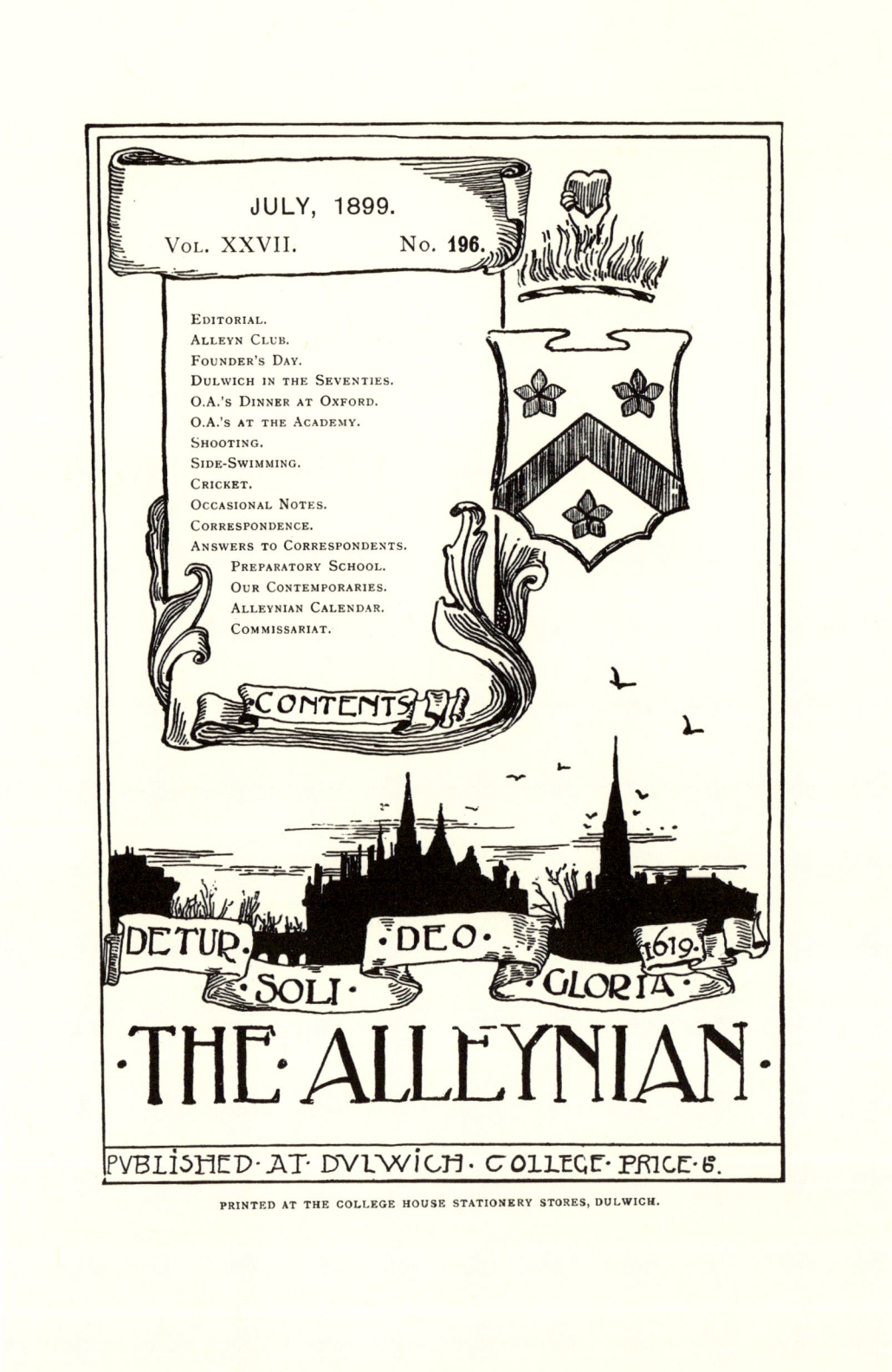

Wodehouse was editor of the *Alleynian*, the Dulwich College magazine, and contributed to it for most of his life.

PLATE 3

The *Captain*, a magazine for schoolboys published by George Newnes, carried stories by Wodehouse from February 1902 to 1913.

PLATE 4

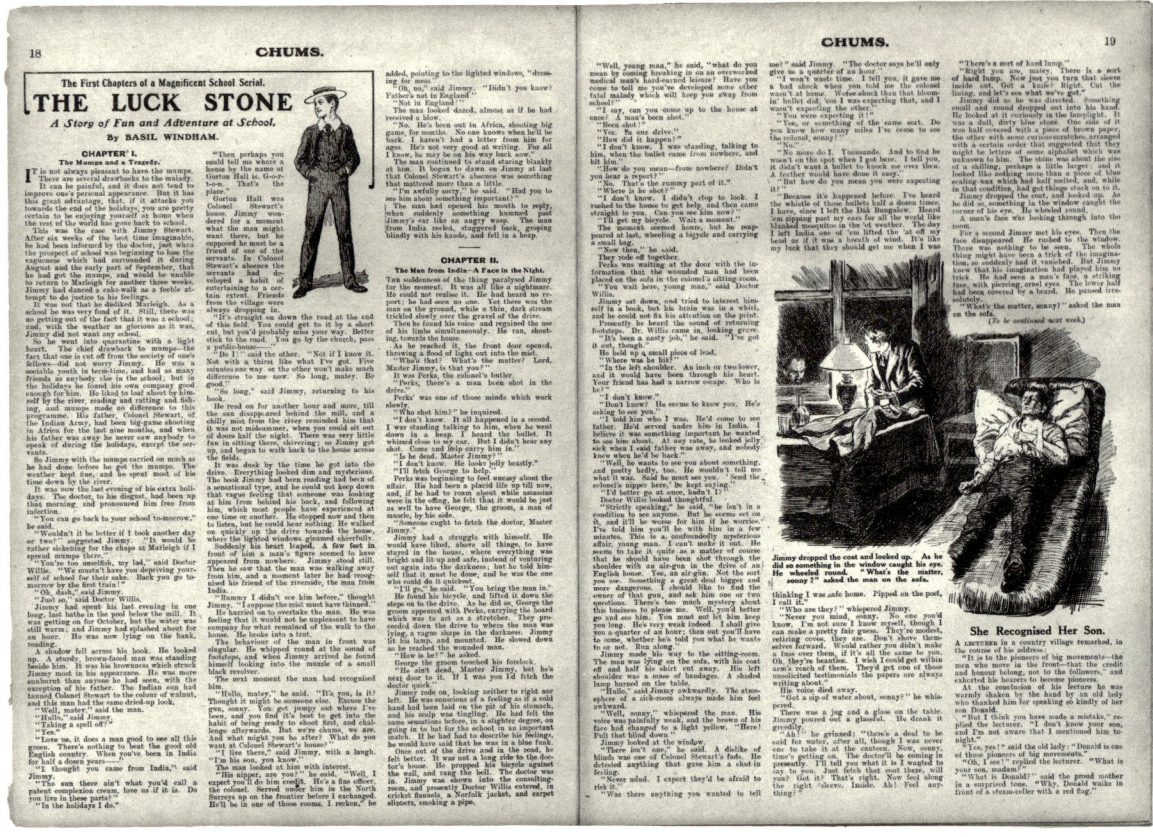

In *Chums* Wodehouse used the pseudonym Basil Wyndham.   *Courtesy of James B. Meriwether.*

A selection of a few early twentieth-century magazines which carried Wodehouse.

PLATE 5

The Pothunters: A School Story (1902) was Wodehouse's first book.

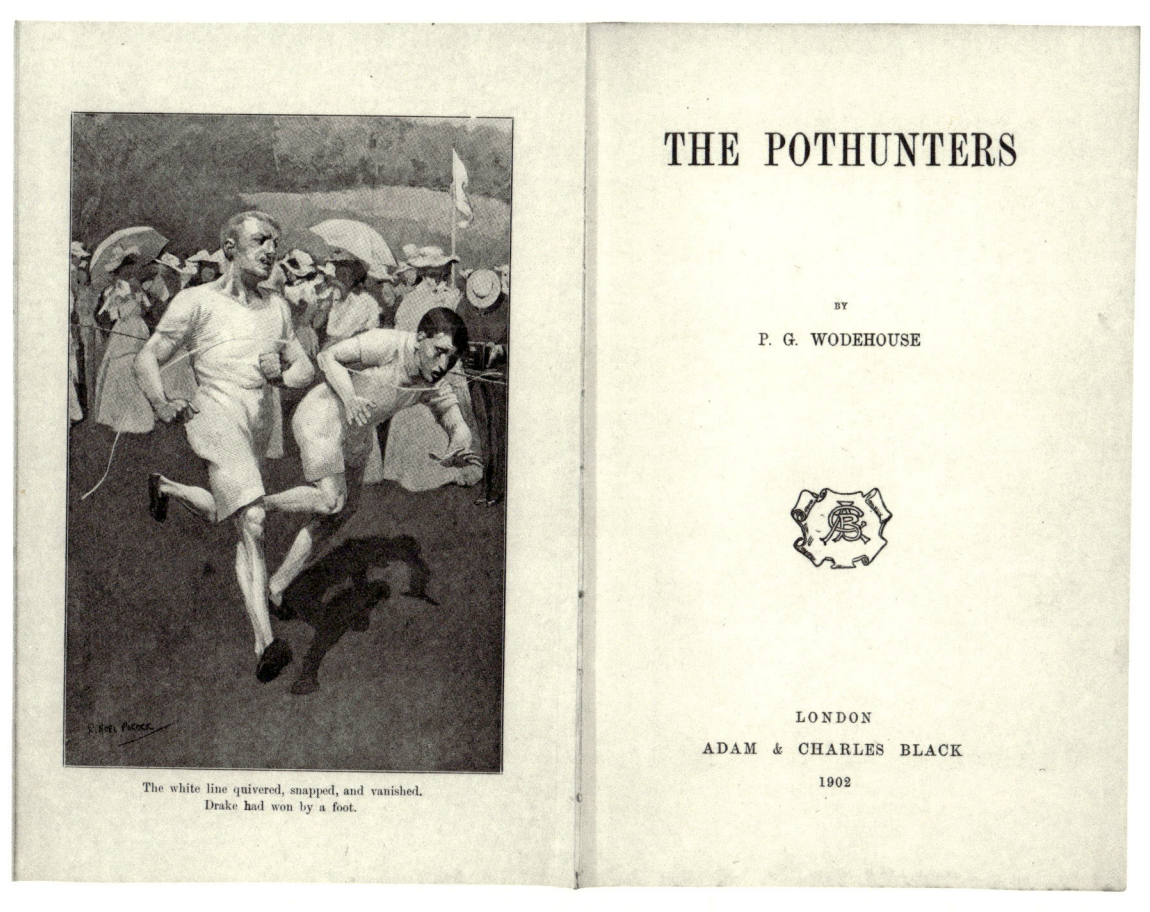

PLATE 6

Early books for youngsters.

1909

1904

1909

1903

PLATE 7

Love among the Chickens is Wodehouse's first adult novel and his first book published in the United States (1906).

The *By the Way Book* is a collection of humorous writings by Wodehouse which first appeared in the *Globe*, an evening London newspaper.

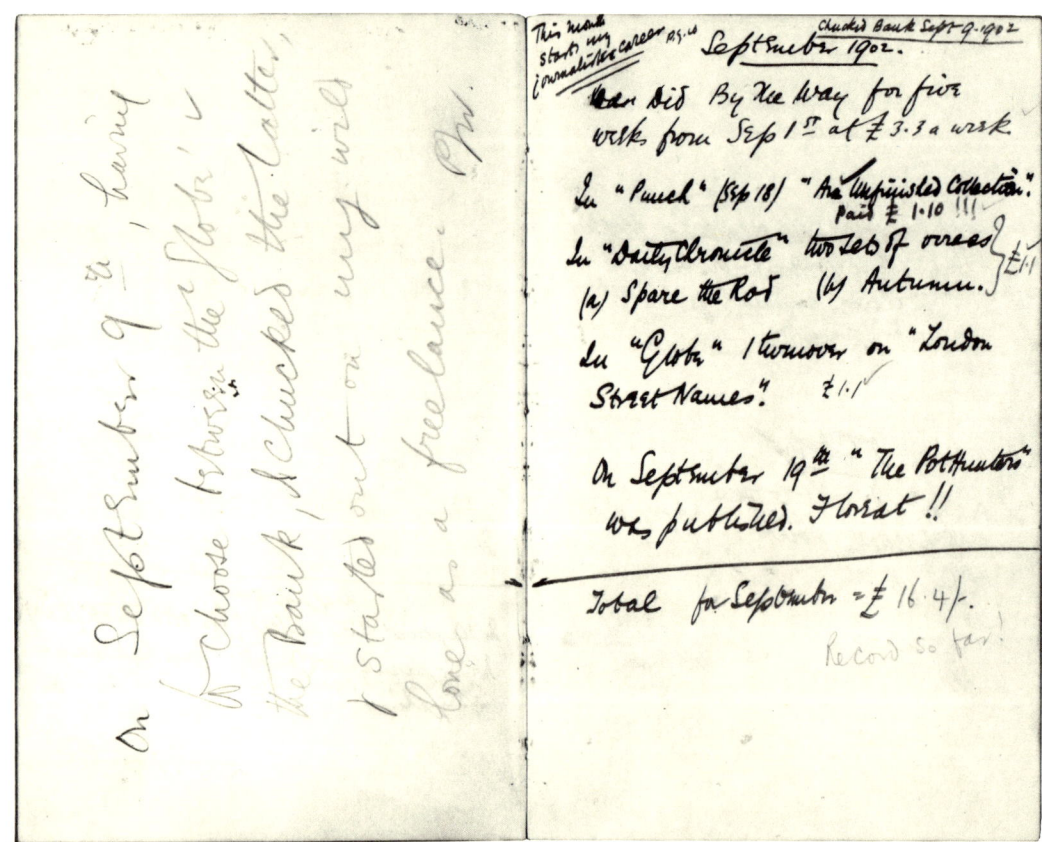

Selected pages from Wodehouse's account book, including the first payment he ever received for writing.
Courtesy of Derek Grimsdick.

Mem: I left
England for New York
on April 16, which
explains the poor
total of my
April receipts.

April 1904

Daily Chronicle
  A Warning (Ap 2) (10/6) ✓
  No Thin Blue Line (Ap 5) (10/6) ✓

In "Books of To-day"
  Moon Problems for Breakfast } (£4.4)
  Songs on the Situation }

In "Globe"   £4.14.6 | £2.12.6 ✓
  By the Way Ap 2–9 | 12–16 /

In "Punch"
  "Man's Inhumanity to Boy" (April 13) £1.16/

£13.18

378.0.10
22.15.10
405.15.10[?]

* Owen Hall, the author of "Sergeant Brue"
wrote & asked me to write this & said
it was excellent. Went & heard it
sung on Sat. Dec 10, & Monday Dec 12.
Encored both times. Audience laughed
several times during each verse
this time.

On this, the 13th December 1904, time 12 p.m. I set it
down that I have arrived. Letter from Cosmo
Hamilton congratulating me on my work &
promising commission to write lyrics for his next
piece. I have a lyric in "Sergeant Brue", another
probably in "The Cingalee", a serial in the
'Captain', 5 books published, I am editing
'By the Way', Pearson's have ten stories & two poems
of mine, I have finished the 'Kid Brady' stories,
I have a commission to do a weekly poem for
'Vanity Fair', and Pocock has [put?] 8/- permanently
onto Pearson's staff, so in future he will be the slot.   P.G.W.

December 1904

In 'Globe' £10/) £5✓ £5✓ £5 £5
By the Way: Dec 1–3: 5–10: 12–17: 19–24: 26–31.

In 'Vanity Fair'.
  Our Christmas Pantomimes (with B. Fletcher Robinson) (Dec 7)
  How to be a Journalist, though jugged ✗
  Prima facie Evidence (Dec 14)
  The Benefactor (Dec 21)   £5.9
  Tommy's Cap (Dec 28)

* In "Sergeant Brue" (at the Strand Theatre)
Lyric "Criminals' Trio" (£5.5) ✓

Total for December
  £33.4/-

Total for 1904
  £411.14.10

PLATE 10

A handful of theatre productions for which Wodehouse wrote the book or lyrics.

PLATE 11

PLATE 12

"Bill," possibly Wodehouse's most famous lyric, was originally written for Oh, Lady! Lady! for which Wodehouse wrote all the lyrics.

had a very close school friend called Woodhouse, but it was odd that his mother should be inviting me to dinner and at such short notice. I happened to be engaged that evening, so I rang back to say that I was sorry I could not come. The telephone number was unfamiliar. I presumed that his mother was calling from a house where she was playing bridge. My call got straight through. To my surprise a strange voice answered me, "What a pity—P.G. *will* be disappointed."

I stared bewildered at my inkpot. It was scarcely believable, but there was no other explanation. I had been invited, not by the mother of my friend *Woodhouse*, but by the wife of P. G. *Wodehouse*, whom I had never met. I could see what had happened. Plum and his wife were short a dinner guest and Plum had said, "I've always wanted to meet Alec Waugh. See if you can get him. He works with Chapman and Hall." And Chapman and Hall's telephone message-taker had rendered the name phonetically. If I had known who had invited me, I should certainly have excused myself from my engagement. "Damn!" I thought. "Shall I ever have another chance?"

I did. This time with a longer warning, three or four days. But again the invitation came over the telephone. "I'd love to," I said. I was invited to a block of furnished flats in Westminster.

Dining with PGW was for me a very great occasion. I am astonished that I can remember so little of it. I do not know whom I sat next to. I do not remember any of the conversation before the men were left with their port. There were ten or twelve at table. W. B. Maxwell was the chief guest. He was discussing the Beefsteak Club to which Plum had recently been elected. It was, I was to think many years later when I became a member myself, very much Plum's kind of club, though I do not think any of the Drones would have sought admission.

The Beefsteak is off Leicester Square in Irving Street. It is on the first floor and consists of a single long table that has room for twenty chairs. There are no small tables. There is no bar. There is a fireplace and a window seat where there is a writing desk and a table where newspapers and periodicals are laid out. No guests, only members, are allowed at lunch. A member on arrival signs his name downstairs. At the head of the stairs the porter, who is always known as "Charles," has a small office. The member orders his lunch and any beverages that he may require. Charles chooses his seat at the table. Two bedrooms are available for members.

Plum was, at dinner that night, telling Maxwell that he had felt shy when he presented himself unheralded at Charles's cubbyhole. No one was vouching for him. Maxwell reassured him: "The Beefsteak is the friendliest club in the world. There are no introductions. Charles shows you where you will sit. To be a member of the Beefsteak is all the introduction that you need. If you are inquisitive about whom you are sitting next to, you can ask Charles afterwards."

At the end of that first evening I told Plum how much enjoyment I had derived from *Mike*. He said, "I don't know how I managed it." Probably that was an exact estimate of the book. When he began to write it he had no idea that he was a humorist. He discovered himself in *Mike*. He asked me if I knew Denis Mackail's stories. I said that I did. "He's good, isn't he?" Plum said. I agreed. I wondered afterwards whether it was the answer Plum would have preferred. Mackail was at that time writing a series of short stories for *Nash's Magazine*, the *Strand*'s chief rival. Mackail's stories contained an Ukridge-type hero, and the illustrations were very much in the manner of the *Strand*'s. Is it possible that Plum slightly resented this? One does not associate Plum with jealousy, but Mackail was after all trespassing on Plum's territory. I wished my answer had been noncommittal.

I was not to meet Plum again till after the Second World War. It seems strange that we did not meet during the intervening years. We often moved in the same atmosphere, in London, in New York, in the South of France. We had many mutual friends, and those often brought me friendly messages. "You know my friend Alec Waugh," he'd say. "I hope that everything's going well with him." I was touched by that, so much so that, when we did meet again, in New York, I did not feel the apprehension that so often one does about remeeting a friend after a quarter of a century: Will we recognize each other? Will he be a completely different person? On that point I had been alerted. I had been put on my guard. The surprise was going to be how completely unchanged he was.

I had discussed him in New York with one of his American publishers. "We presumed," he had said, "that Plum would go on writing during the war. One cannot break the habit of a lifetime. He had, of course, published nothing, but he must have written something. He could not surely have gone on writing about Blandings, a world that had ceased to exist." But that is exactly what he had done: he had gone on writing exactly the same kind of book about a world that had never existed except in his own imagination.

In New York both Plum and I were members of the Coffee House Club. And it was through the Coffee House that we met, in, I think, 1950. During the next few years we were to lunch together several times, once or twice at the Century, my club, and once or twice at his club, the Lotos. In retrospect those five or six occasions blur together. He was so exactly the same person that each new meeting was another installment of the same conversation.

He looked exactly the same. He had not put on weight. He was always completely hairless. He was his familiar, massive, genial self. He had no peculiarities, of manner or expression. He was not funny. He never repeated jokes. There was no sparkle in his conversation. He did not indulge in reminiscences. There was a straightforward exchange of talk. The characters in his stories have characteristic turns of phrase. He never had. We would have two cocktails, then lunch. When he lunched with me we shared a bottle of wine. But he did not drink his share of the bottle.

He was quite unchanged. He was interested in exactly the same things that he had been a quarter of a century ago. He had kept astonishingly up to date with public-school athletics. "It is an extraordinary thing," he would say, "Marlborough beat Tonbridge and Tonbridge beat Uppingham, but Uppingham beat Marlborough. What do you make of that?" He talked eagerly about old school matches.

Our interest in school athletics was the closest of the links between us. "It's a curious thing," he said, "but you and I are almost the only English writers who really enjoyed our schooldays, all the way through. Most writers enjoyed their last two or three years when they had reached positions of authority. But nearly all of them hated their first years. You and I on the other hand liked it from the very start."

That, in fact, had been one of my chief problems as a public schoolboy. I had enjoyed it all too much. I had been to a very strict preparatory school. A spartan discipline had been maintained. I am the kind of person who usually manages to get a reasonable amount of enjoyment out of living, but it was not till I left my preparatory school that I realized what having a good time amounted to. My father had hated his first years at Sherborne; Evelyn hated his first years at Lancing; they both lived for their holidays. I on the other hand was always glad to get back to school. I had too good a time. I was always "above myself." I was constantly in conflict with authority, both masters and prefects. I was not very popular. In fact I was generally disapproved of. But the fact that I had liked school so much was a very special bond between Plum and myself. I have an idea in fact that Plum in his adult life never felt completely at home with Englishmen who had not enjoyed their schooldays from the start.

Evelyn and Plum did not meet until after the second war. And when they did they found it difficult to make contact. Evelyn had been a PGW fan from the very earliest days. Wodehouse was one of the few writers by whom Evelyn's own writing was influenced. He knew Plum's writing much better than I did. He was one of Plum's warmest champions after the war and he broadcast a warm critical tribute to Plum on his eightieth birthday. But from what I have been told, they did not find much in common when they met. They eventually discussed the inequities of income tax.

I myself always felt very much at ease with Plum. Our talk moved smoothly from one subject to another. Yet the ease was such that I find I cannot recall the matter of our conversations, only the pleasure of his company. Plum did not want to talk about himself; I might have been more imaginative, more pressing, and acted as, so to speak, an interviewer, learning much that might have interested and enlightened me. I did not, and am left with but the recollection that we met and lunched as friends.

I cannot say that I would want it any different.

ALEC WAUGH. In the last week of 1917 Alec Waugh was nineteen years old. He became engaged to be married to the daughter of author W. W. Jacobs. He sailed to join the British Expeditionary Force in France as a subaltern in the Machine Gun Corps, and he published a realistic story of English public school life that was soon in the best-seller lists: The Loom of Youth. *It was a succès de scandale. He has led a varied and dramatic life. He was taken prisoner in the big retreat in March 1918. He has been married three times, finally to the American writer Virginia Sorensen, Newbery Medallist, author of* Miracles on Maple Hill. *He wrote, in 1930, a travel book,* Hot Countries, *that was a Literary Guild Selection. He served in the Middle East in World War II. He has written a number of novels, his most successful being* Island in the Sun, *which was an international best-seller, with Harry Belafonte as its film star.*

Wodehouse's Editor: A Painless Job

PETER SCHWED

IN RECENT YEARS there have been several scholarly volumes devoted to the writings of P. G. Wodehouse and these naturally include in one way or another a complete list of his books. I tip my hat admiringly in the direction of anyone who actually has succeeded in scoring a perfect mark in that undertaking because I, admittedly no professional bibliographer, have tried to do it more than once over the past quarter of a century during which I have been his American editor. It's a little like trying to square the circle. Not only are the works of Wodehouse, like the flowering gardens of England (a paradise he is believed by some to have invented and populated almost entirely with bachelors, butlers, aunts, the peerage, clergymen, jolly girls some of whom have demoniacal ideas of fun, and golfers), numerically infinite, but, whether for good or bad reasons, English and American editions frequently bear different titles. Nor have I helped matters in this respect during the stretch of years since the glorious day in the early 1950s when Plum first came to Simon and Schuster and to me. Then and afterwards, he and his British publisher almost invariably had already agreed upon a title, but lots of the time I suggested a different one for the American publication. Three motives inspired my officiousness, to which, incidentally, Plum almost never showed anything except pleased acceptance. The first was that often the title seemed too British. The second was that the British titles often consisted of just two words that sounded very much like previous books (*Summer Moonshine*, *Full Moon*, *Spring Fever*, etc.), and my idea was that each title should be a very individual one in its own right (like *The Butler Did It*, *The Ice in the Bedroom*, etc.). The third reason was that I had the proud privilege of being Wodehouse's editor, but Plum's books needed virtually no editing. An editor is supposed to contribute *something*! So I became a gilder of the lily, and not too much else.

I don't intend here to venture very far into the domain of the academic analysts of the Wodehouse craft. I appreciate as much as anyone such things as his superb plot manipulation, his hilariously scholarly use of quotations from Shakespeare and the Bible to heighten narrative effect and all that sort of thing, but I'm content to let more serious types brood over such matters. Leave me alone simply to read Wodehouse and enjoy him.

Since so many people think of him only in connection with his glorious novels, because they are what one encounters in bookstores and reviews and advertising promotion, I can't forbear pointing out what enchanting reading you're missing if you know only the novels. For one thing, in my opinion nothing in the realm of Wodehousiana can top the best of his short stories, collections of which are harder to find today than years ago when the genre was more popular. But *The Most of P. G. Wodehouse* is still very much in print and that is the book I'd give to someone who had never read the Master, and wanted to start. In that volume he or she will encounter positive gems of short stories, each as good as the one preceding or following it, about Jeeves and Bertie Wooster, or Mulliner, or Ukridge, or the Drones Club, or the Oldest Member, and then, as a final gorgeous prize, the complete hilarious novel *The Luck of the Bodkins*. Anybody who doesn't treasure this volume after reading it is someone you don't want to know.

Still, short stories after all are also fiction and so, perhaps, not that different from novels; but vintage Wodehouse comes in many bottles. His riotously funny nonfiction enchanted readers of *Punch* for decades and many of the best examples have appeared in book form—*Over Seventy* in England and *America, I Like You* in the United States are different collections but share a number of the same pieces. A really ardent Wodehouse admirer might find most interesting of all the letters that he wrote to his lifelong friend, William Townend (an author himself), over a lengthy period of time. The letters appeared in England in the book entitled *Performing Flea*; I always felt that it was one of the best textbooks about writing that I had ever read. Twenty years after its publication I urged Plum to revise and update it and give American readers a chance to read this unique Wodehouse production. He did so and we published it in the United States under the title *Author! Author!* Of course it's funny—what did

Plum ever write that wasn't?—but it's more than that. It's a valuable tool for an embryonic writer and, if you're a Wodehouse fan, no biographer could tell you nearly as much about how he wrote as he does himself in these pages.

Some of my favorite Wodehouse inspirations are found in his light verse, but others are writing specifically about that in this book so I will not intrude upon their territory—at least not much. However, since all we Wodehouse fanatics are more welcome dinner guests than we might otherwise be by dint of quoting superb lines from the Master, and since many of my particular pets come from his poetry, allow me to spring at least one of them briefly on you here even though you will meet it again as part of a complete poem elsewhere. It's from "Printer's Error," a poem which in my opinion would surely have made Keats throw in the towel had he come across it at the time he was writing "Ode on a Grecian Urn," particularly the stage in it when "I" (Wodehouse) point a gun at "the printer who had printed 'not' when I had written 'now' ":

> "Prepare," I said, "to meet your God,
> Or, as you'd say, your Goo or Bod,
> Or possibly your Gow!"

Enough. The theory behind my being asked to write this article wasn't to let me get by, using the easy tactic of quoting Wodehouse, even though that would be a lot better than anything I might say. The idea was that, over the course of so long an author-editor relationship, I'd have a few personal recollections that others wouldn't know about.

Well, when I first met Plum he was a promising lad of seventy and he had just about that many books under his belt already. One might have felt that the well and the man might run dry pretty soon. But Plum went on for more than twenty more years, delivering a new and invariably wonderful book to me virtually every year. He was like the regular striking of a 365-day clock if there were such a thing. During the first few years Plum and Ethel lived in the city in the penthouse of 1000 Park Avenue together with the inevitable complement of X dogs and Y cats. So Plum used to toddle into the Simon and Schuster office himself each year and deliver his new manuscript by hand. I rather wondered why his first experience didn't discourage him. That year we had a not-very-literate receptionist who not only didn't recognize his name but had an intriguing habit of wiping her memory and slate clean of anything that took place before she went off on a coffee break. When Plum arrived that day she seated him in a dark corner and dashed off to get hers before the Danish pastry ran out. Plum, ever a courteous and philosophical man as well as a shy one, sat in his corner and puffed his pipe. And sat. And sat.

I had been in a meeting out of which I expected to be called immediately upon the Great One's arrival, but when the meeting ended and there had been no word, I went out to the receptionist's desk to see if there had been a message about Mr. Wodehouse's being delayed. The receptionist was still mulling this difficult query over in her mind when an elderly gentleman emerged from his dark corner beaming, and came towards me with one hand outstretched and a manuscript held in the other. He had been waiting patiently without ever inquiring about the delay for almost an hour, but he shook off all my apologies. "I've had plenty of practice," he said, "in doctors' waiting rooms."

That quiet, good-humored acceptance of the chips as they happened to fall was typical of Plum. He was not only a gentleman, he was a gentle man who never used his sharp wit as a weapon in personal relationships. He saved that for his writing, and among friends in a living room or around a dinner table he invariably was the appreciative listener, laughing approvingly at others' feeble *bons mots*.

When he came to the office we always had a festive luncheon to celebrate the completion of the new book and, as he was leaving, I would start to rummage around in my office closet. That was because two situations seemed ordained on those days: it rained heavily at noon and Plum never came equipped for rain. I learned to keep a supply of cheap, plastic raincoats and old, discarded hats and caps in that closet for such occasions. (No umbrellas; despite his British upbringing, Plum was not an umbrella type.) He would don my humble, quite hideous raingear, look at himself admiringly in a mirror, tilt the hat or cap at a rakish angle and observe how smart his outfit now was, and then wander off back to Ethel and the dogs and cats, humming softly. We did also meet on other dates throughout the year at his New York apartment or mine, but then Ethel was overseeing his comfort. My primary role was to be at the office on those wonderful days when a new manuscript was ready, with a table booked at a good restaurant and a moderately functional plastic raincoat and beat-up head covering ready in the closet.

In later years, when the Wodehouses moved to Remsenburg and Plum was getting close to being eighty, he virtually never came to the city. So I would make at least an annual pilgrimage out to the far eastern stretches of Long Island to be nuzzled by even more dogs and cats, sip a huge, delicious, beautifully chilled martini with Plum as we watched his favorite soap opera of the moment on television at noon, enjoy a splendid luncheon with him and Ethel afterward, and then receive that year's Holy Grail—the latest book manuscript to emerge from that perpetual-motion machine, the Wodehouse typewriter. Incidentally, Plum typed his stuff himself and no touch-system nonsense about it either!

Throughout the year I regularly sent him a flow of the mystery novels he so dearly loved to read, but when I visited him at Remsenburg I also brought a gift. We were both pipe smokers, of the breed that can never have too many pipes, so a new one with a big bowl from his favorite shop, Wilkie's, was most likely to be my offering; but in one early year, as a change, I made a grave mistake. I brought him a couple of pounds of Dunhill's best and most expensive tobacco. The exquisite courtesy upon which I've commented earlier prompted Plum to beam at me and make a big fuss over the gift, but later I learned better, and I suspect he gave it to the deserving poor. For Plum never really liked any good tobacco in his beautiful pipes. What did he like? The cheapest and dryest cigar he could find, crumbled to shreds in his fingers and then rammed into his pipe bowl! Ah well . . . even the greatest of idols may have the toe of one foot made of clay.

The last time I ever visited Plum at Remsenburg was in January 1975. He had just been made a Knight of the British Empire on the Queen's New Year's list, but since he was then ninety-three years old and not in good health he had been unable to make the trip to Buckingham Palace to receive his honors. So I scoured the Army-Navy stores on West 42nd Street until I managed to find one that had an elaborate ceremonial sword—the fact that it was Japanese could be overlooked. Armed with it, Scott Meredith, his long-time agent and friend, and I drove the hundred miles to Remsenburg and there, in the Wodehouse living room with Ethel as witness, carried out the rite of dubbing Plum a KBE. A cooperative photographer recorded the ceremony for posterity and, it now turns out, this book.

The one manuscript of Plum's I did not receive from him personally was the last. After his death, ninety pages of typescript and a sheaf of notes and outlines were delivered to me—the first draft of about two-thirds of a Blandings Castle novel. This, edited by Richard Usborne, was published in 1977 as *Sunset at Blandings*, and provides a fascinating picture of Wodehouse at work, showing for once the way in which this meticulous craftsman labored to produce the final effect of effortless ease.

It is worth noting that he was working on it the day he died. What could be more typical of Plum than working straight through to the end?

PETER SCHWED, P. G. Wodehouse's American editor for a quarter of a century, only had one point of contention with his favorite author. Wodehouse claimed that he had read more books not worth reading than any other man, and Schwed insisted that, if it were true, it was merely because Plum was older. While continuing to be the active Chairman of the Editorial Board of Simon and Schuster, Schwed has done a good deal of writing himself in recent years, both articles and books. He is a considerably better tennis player than Wodehouse was ever a golfer and has always had a considerable local reputation if, in his own words, "the local scene was no larger than one square mile."

The Wodehouses of Hollywood

MAUREEN O'SULLIVAN

MILLIONS OF PEOPLE have been gladdened by P. G. Wodehouse's works. Some hundreds were friends, acquaintances, or co-workers. Fewer than a hundred were honored by having one of his books dedicated to them. And a very few had the distinction of serving as a model for one of his characters. I don't know if I am the only person who fits into all four categories, but there can't be too many of us, and I count the distinction as a rare privilege and delight.

When I met Plummie and Ethel Wodehouse, I was not yet twenty, a budding screen actress, and he was one of the many writers under contract to M.G.M. in Hollywood. But in Ireland and at school in England I had read many of his books, so I was aware of his fame and standing. Ethel soon invited me to their house and gave me some blunt and sensible advice on a stormy romance I was going through. She was irresistible, and it was impossible to feel shy with Plummie. He was large and affable, very English and rather vague, quietly amusing rather than frighteningly witty—he was, in fact, lovable.

In their Spanish-style house on Benedict Canyon Drive, complete with pool and tennis court, Ethel had managed to create an English garden, in which, in the shade of a rose-covered trellis, she served a full English tea, including watercress sandwiches on the thinnest imaginable bread, while Plummie worked away in a small house behind the pool.

After Ethel had given me a few home truths about my problems, Plummie came out from his little house, blinking vaguely in the sunlight. His day's work was finished—time for a walk. The Wodehouses loved to walk. A turn or so to the left and then to the right brought us—in those days, not by any means now—into the country. Miss Winks, their adored Pekingese, ran happily beside us.

So began a great and lasting friendship with the Wodehouses. In a way I became closer to Plummie than to Ethel. There were times when she did not want to take walks with us, and then we rambled over the hills with Miss Winks, or perhaps walked all over Beverly Hills gossiping and telling each other our thoughts and feelings, as if we were the oldest of friends.

Soon their daughter Leonora arrived from England. She was actually Ethel's daughter from a previous marriage, but was in fact more like Plummie. They adored each other. There was something magical about Leonora—whenever I pick up a book of reminiscences of that period, I am apt to find accounts of her captivating the author with her gentle wit and strange beauty.

Ethel loved to dance—"for the exercise," she said. So the house was always filled with suitable dancing partners. They had to be young to keep up with Ethel's extraordinary energy, and tall, because Ethel was fairly tall herself. There were some shorter ones—usually English and pimply—who always fell in love with me. Somehow the attractive ones didn't.

I don't know if that was because of my habit of turning up at her dinner parties wearing the clearly fake jewelry which was all I had. (This was before costume jewelry made its debut.) Ethel solved this problem, as she was to solve many others; she took me aside and said, "Darling, never wear jewelry unless it is real. It is better to wear nothing." And she took me upstairs and gave me one of her lovely bracelets. All the same, it was still the short, spotty guests who hung after me.

Given Ethel, Leonora, and Miss Winks, Plummie would have been happy anywhere. I can still picture him, floating motionless and happy in the pool, looking at his toes or at the clear blue of the California sky, while presumably working out the next bit of writing complexity. Ethel knew how to protect him from all intrusion, and we knew better than to speak to him unless he started the conversation.

"Nothing I hate like a good view!" he once said to me as he sat at his typewriter, facing the wall. It was a good thing he felt that way; contract writers at M.G.M. worked in small, often windowless cells on what was called Writers' Row, and were expected to be there from nine or nine-thirty until clocking-out time at five-thirty, with an hour out for lunch. Plummie's picture of studio life and the writer's plight in his Hollywood stories was exaggerated, but a good deal less so than outside readers might think.

I used to walk down Writers' Row, looking with awe at the nameplates on the office doors: Aldous Huxley, F. Scott Fitzgerald, Lillian Hellman, George S. Kaufman, Robert Benchley, Donald Ogden Stewart. It was typical of the studio system of the time that these brilliant writers seldom got their completed works on the screen. (I recently saw a film Scott Fitzgerald once told me he was working on, and he did not have even the tiniest screen credit.) Their assignments were turned over to the producers, and more practiced—and less talented—screen writers were given their scripts to mold into what was supposedly more suitable form for filming.

Under this system many a writer went to pieces, and complaints echoed constantly around the pool at the Garden of Allah. Paid large sums of money, the embittered writers sunned themselves in enforced idleness and consoled themselves with alcohol. I asked Plummie if he didn't hate the whole thing. "Not at all," he replied. "I just pretend that I'm in jail. And it's a very nice jail, where they pay you well, and let you out for lunch and on Sundays"—Saturdays were working days then.

From someone else that might have been taken as bitterness, but it was no more and no less than what Plummie felt. He was too—*innocent* is perhaps the word—to speak other than what he felt. After he had been in Hollywood a year, a reporter interviewed him, and got more than she—and Plummie's bosses—had bargained for. He cheerfully recounted his film writing career so far, and said, "It dazes me." Asked where the dazing came in, he answered, "They paid me two thousand dollars a week—a hundred and four thousand dollars—and I cannot see what they engaged me for." M.G.M. had been, he said,

> extremely nice to me. But I feel as if I had cheated them.
>
> You see, I understood I was engaged to write stories for the screen. After all, I have twenty novels, a score of successful plays and countless magazine stories to my credit. Yet, apparently, they had the greatest difficulty in finding anything for me to do.
>
> Twice during the year they brought completed scenarios of other people's stories to me and asked me to do some dialogue. Fifteen or sixteen people had tinkered with those stories. The dialogue was really quite adequate. All I did was to touch it up here and there.
>
> Then they set me to work on a story called "Rosalie," which was to have some musical numbers. It was a pleasant little thing and I put three months on it. When it was finished they thanked me politely and remarked that as musicals didn't seem to be going so well they guessed they would not use it.
>
> That about sums up what I was called upon to do for my hundred four thousand dollars. Isn't it amazing?

It particularly amazed the Eastern financiers who were bankrolling the studios; and in a surprisingly short time the free-spending movie magnates found that the purse strings were being drawn uncomfortably tight. There was a lot of resentment against Plummie in Hollywood, and *Variety* a week or so later carried a rather spiteful report claiming that he was habitually arrogant about refusing to attend story conferences! Plummie would no more have "gone Hollywood" in that way than he would have partnered Joan Crawford in an Apache dance.

He let the storm pass over him, and set to work on his new novel, *Hot Water*. To my pleased astonishment, he dedicated it to me—"with love from Ethel, Leonora, Miss Winks, John-John and the Author." He told me that he had modeled the heroine after me. As she is described as having "a nice little figure and nice little legs, and a way about her that made you feel that something wonderful was about to happen," I didn't feel like arguing with him.

Plummie called the girl Jane. Neither of us had any notion that within a few years I would be known around the world by that name—not as a Wodehouse heroine but as Tarzan's mate.

Plummie and Ethel left Hollywood soon after, but whatever hurt feelings there were in the film community didn't last, and he was invited back for another stint of screenwriting a few years later; I was married by now, and my husband and I renewed our friendship with the Wodehouses as though no time at all had passed. Then Plummie and Ethel left for Europe. When the war came and France fell, I was appalled to hear that they had been interned by the Germans. There was little news until June of 1941, when I received, with some surprise, a telegram from Berlin—not a usual occurrence in Hollywood in those days!—reading:

> LOVE TO YOU BOTH LISTEN IN TONIGHT FRIDAY JUNE 27TH OVER STATION DJD 25.49 MTS DJB 19.74 MTS DZD 28.43 MTS 6.00 PM PACIFIC TIME. PLUM

My husband managed to work out how to tune the short-wave radio to bring in the broadcast. Over the squeaks and crackles of the short wave came Plummie's unmistakable tones: "If anyone listening to me seems to detect in my remarks a slight goofiness. . . ." And then, characteristic and—given the locale from which he was broadcasting—astonishing, his comments on German occupation:

> One's reactions on finding oneself suddenly surrounded by the armed strength of a hostile power are rather interesting. The first time you see a German soldier in your garden, your impulse is to jump ten feet straight up into the air, and you do so. But

this feeling of embarrassment soon passes. A week later you find you are only jumping five feet. And in the end familiarity so breeds indifference that you are able to sustain without a tremor the spectacle of men in steel helmets riding round your lawn on bicycles and even the discovery that two or three of them have dropped in and are taking a bath in your bathroom. The motto of the German army in occupied territory is "What's yours is mine," and any nonsense about an Englishman's home being his castle is soon dispelled.

It was marvelous to hear Plummie's voice again, and to know that he was alive, well, and undaunted —though it seemed remarkable that he could get away with saying what he was about his internment experiences; it seemed pretty dumb of the Nazis to let him blandly mock them and their methods, as he was clearly doing.

All the same, there was a tremendous storm about the broadcasts from Berlin, which, after the war, bewildered and saddened Plummie, though good sense eventually prevailed. Asked about it a long time later, he said shortly, "I was a damned fool"— but it seems to me that, just as with the Hollywood interview, ten years before, he had been asked to say what he thought and had done so, without taking what most people would consider normal account of where and to whom he was saying it. And, as then, the upshot had come as a surprise to him. I don't quite know how it is that a man who could concoct the most ingenious plots in his novels could be as guileless in his nonwriting life as Plummie was; it may be that he used up all his craftiness in his work and had none left over for the everyday world.

I had many letters from Plummie during the more than forty years of our friendship—but only one from Sir Pelham Wodehouse, written not long after the bestowal of his knighthood in 1975, and only a few weeks before he died. He did not mean it as a farewell, but it can stand as one, and I treasure it for that.

January 24th 1975

How lovely getting such a nice long letter from you. I am such an old wreck that I seldom go to the theatre but am proud of you when you did 1000 performances.

Those days in Hollywood seem like yesterday. I am in good form mentally and writing all the time. My legs have gone back on me and I have a stick all the time but I suppose one is bound to get something when one is 93!

Since the news of my knighthood broke, life has been very hectic, with hundreds of interviews and photographs. Getting a bit calmer now. Ethel sends oceans of love and the same from me. Ever, Plummie.

MAUREEN O'SULLIVAN was brought from her native Ireland to Hollywood in the early 1930s by a perceptive talent scout, and gained almost immediate fame from her portrayal of Tarzan's mate, Jane, in a long-lasting series also starring Johnny Weissmuller. In addition to the creations of Edgar Rice Burroughs, she brought to screen life the characters of Charles Dickens (in David Copperfield*) and Jane Austen (in* Pride and Prejudice*). In recent years, her career has been mainly on the stage, with several memorable productions to her credit, recently and notably in the current* Morning's at Seven*, for her work in which she shared a Best Ensemble Acting Tony award with her colleagues. She is the widow of the late director John Farrow, and the mother of the actress Mia Farrow.*

Wodehouse the Writer of Lyrics

BENNY GREEN

BETWEEN 1904 and 1928 P. G. Wodehouse contributed either some or all of the lyrics to twenty-nine musical comedies, collaborated on twenty libretti and published more than three hundred songs. It was honorable work executed with stunning technical command and an originality which influenced profoundly the course of the American theatre lyric, and it must be accounted one of those curious quirks of literary history that the British, who are inclined to regard Wodehouse the novelist as one of their more priceless national possessions, should have remained in almost total ignorance of this important aspect of his career. Never in all the years he labored in the vineyards of musical comedy was Wodehouse under any illusions regarding the lowly status of the work in the hierarchy of the theatre, either in Hollywood or on Broadway. In a short story called "The Castaways," when the script writer Bulstrode Mulliner is interviewed by that maniacal embodiment of the spirit of the Perfecto-Zizzbaum Motion Picture Corporation, Jacob Z. Schnellenhamer, the great man ponders aloud the problem of where to house the new hack:

> "Miss Stern," he said, addressing his secretary, "what vacant offices have we on the lot?"
> "There is Room 40 in the Leper Colony."
> "I thought there was a song-writer there."
> "He passed away Tuesday."
> "Has the body been removed?"[1]

As for Schnellenhamer's Broadway counterparts, in a chapter of reminiscence Wodehouse observed of that excessively felonious entrepreneur Colonel Henry Savage: "He walked with a slight limp, having probably in the course of his career been bitten in the leg by some indignant author."[2]

The picture of the gentle, trusting English public schoolboy wandering into this thieves' kitchen calls to mind that Wodehouse hero who was like "a well-dressed Daniel introduced into a den of singularly irritable lions." In contrast, Wodehouse appears to have been perfectly aware from the very beginning of the nature of the people he was dealing with. In fact, for a man whose fate it would always have been to be dubbed by Central Casting as a bumbling innocent, his perceptions were razor-sharp. For not only did he know by a kind of commonsensical instinct that the professional lyricist could expect no deference from paymasters incapable of rhyming "moon" with "June" or indeed with anything, he grasped also the thorny proposition that the artifact itself was very often so idiotic as actually to render itself quaint. When, in the story "Bill the Bloodhound" the detective Henry Pifield Rice falls in love with a chorus girl and follows her into the cast of a touring show, he is hardly likely to gain much cerebral nourishment from the libretto:

> The plot of "The Girl from Brighton" had by then reached a critical stage. The situation was as follows: The hero, having been disinherited by his wealthy and titled father for falling in love with the heroine, a poor shop girl, has disguised himself (by wearing a different colored necktie) and has come in pursuit of her to a well-known seaside resort, where, having disguised herself by changing her dress, she is serving as a waitress in the Rotunda, on the Esplanade. The family butler, disguised as a Bath-chair man, has followed the hero, and the wealthy and titled father, disguised as an Italian opera singer, has come to the place for a reason which, though extremely sound, for the moment eludes the memory. Anyhow, he is there, and they all meet on the Esplanade. Each recognizes the other, but thinks he himself is unrecognized. *Exeunt* all, hurriedly, leaving the heroine alone on stage. It is a crisis in her life. She meets it bravely. She sings a song entitled "My Honolulu Queen," with chorus of Japanese girls and Bulgarian officers.[3]

What years of exasperated amusement those few lines represent can only be imagined, but it occurred neither to Wodehouse nor to any of the other great lyricists of the period that the imbecility of plot and characterization might be an impediment to the composition of literate songs. This was the very essence of their art, to secrete within a lunatic body a tiny residue of wit and technical finesse. Wodehouse knew all about these working conditions and accepted their limitations cheerfully, perhaps even exultantly, realizing that to a comic novelist it was all grist to the mill, and that the enormities of temperament displayed by the real-life counterparts of Schnellenhamer and company were nothing less than brilliantly absurd character sketches acted out free of charge most obligingly for the convenience of the most gifted literary farceur of the century.

In the story "Mother's Knee," Wodehouse brings out two salient points about the songwriting world of his day, its administrative cynicism and its frankly piratical foundations. When the aspiring songwriter Wilson Hymack first composes his song "It's a Long Way Back to Mother's Knee" and is advised by the narrator to play it to a publisher, Hymack's disgusted response is an interesting pointer to Wodehouse's own experience of the profession: "No thanks. Much obliged, but I'm not going to play that melody in any publisher's office with his hired gang of Tin-Pan Alley composers listening at the keyhole and taking

---

1. "The Castaways" in *Blandings Castle*.
2. *Bring on the Girls!* P. G. Wodehouse and Guy Bolton.
3. *The Man with Two Left Feet*.

notes." What is this rare pearl about which Hymack is so obsessively protective? Wodehouse knows that there is only one way to convey its essence, and that is to create it—which he does:

One night a young man wandered through the glitter of Broadway:
His money he had squandered. For a meal he couldn't pay.
He thought about the village where his boyhood he had spent,
And yearned for all the simple joys with which he'd been content.
He looked upon the city, so frivolous and gay,
And, as he heaved a weary sigh, these words he then did say:
It's a long way back to mother's knee, mother's knee, mother's knee:
It's a long way back to mother's knee,
Where I used to stand and prattle
With my teddy bear and rattle:
Oh, those childhood days in Tennessee,
They sure look good to me!
It's a long way back, but I'm gonna start today.
I'm going back, believe me, oh! I'm going back (I want to go!)
I'm going back—back—on the seven-three
To the dear old shack where I used to be!
I'm going back to my mother's knee![4]

It might seem at first sight that in perpetrating the bathetic lunacy of his parody, Wodehouse has gone much too far, except that when measured against the straight-faced solemnity of successes like "Back Home in Tennessee" and "Mammy," to say nothing of the comically execrable "Sonny Boy," a piece like "Mother's Knee" emerges as a really rather mild-mannered example of the genre. When the song is eventually performed in public, a music publisher called Blumenthal bestows upon it the loftiest accolade of his grubby profession:

It was sure-fire, he said. The words, stated Mr. Blumenthal, were gooey enough to hurt, and the tune reminded him of every other song-hit he had ever heard. There was, in Mr. Blumenthal's opinion, nothing to stop the thing selling a million copies.[5]

4. *Indiscretions of Archie.*
5. Ibid.

Wodehouse's depiction of the songwriting profession as a conspiracy in which all its generals are striving to win the war before the last is more or less accurate, and the egregious Blumenthal may be taken as a composite portrait of Tin Pan Alley rather than any one of its captains of industry. That in other cases Wodehouse was being more specific as a portraitist there can be no shadow of doubt. In *The Inimitable Jeeves* (*Jeeves* in the U.S.), Cyril Bassington-Bassington gets a small part in a Broadway revue called *Ask Dad*. At the dress rehearsals, the producer, a Napoleonic screwball called Blumenfeld, intimidates the performers by exposing them to the merciless decisions of a small and distastefully precocious schoolboy, who has only to say, "Pop, that number's no good" for people to be fired and scenes rewritten. One of the characters explains:

It may be pure fatherly love, or he may regard him as a mascot. My own idea is that he thinks the kid has exactly the amount of intelligence of the average member of the audience, and that what makes a hit with him will please the general public. While, conversely, what he doesn't like will be too rotten for anyone.

Where has Wodehouse dredged up his mad idea? One of the first Broadway impresarios he had encountered was a man called Abraham Erlanger, whose barber was paid to read aloud to him, in French, extracts from the collected letters of Napoleon, and who was rumored to keep a loaded revolver in his desk, in case, Wodehouse somewhere speculates, he should ever find himself confronted by the Duke of Wellington. When Wodehouse had his first interview with Erlanger, he found the great man seated behind the desk:

Lounging in a chair beside him was a small boy in knickerbockers, who gave the collaborators a cold look as they entered, as if he did not think too highly of book writers and lyrists. . . . It turned out later that the stripling was some sort of relation, a nephew or the son of a cousin or something, and he was a very valued and esteemed cog in the Erlanger organization. Aged twelve years, he had been selected by Erlanger as possessing exactly the intelligence of the average New York theatre audience. If he liked something, Erlanger reasoned, the public would like it too. If he didn't, they wouldn't.[6]

6. *Bring on the Girls!* P. G. Wodehouse and Guy Bolton.

Not that the aspiring lyricist necessarily disapproved of such dreadful men. After Erlanger has granted Wodehouse his first commission, the happy apprentice rationalizes his master's excesses by asking, "Why shouldn't a fellow shoot a chap from time to time if the situation seemed to call for it? What's the sense of having a loaded revolver if you never use it?"

It must be said that from the sepulchral quietude of Dulwich College, where as a schoolboy Wodehouse's versifying tendencies first began to emerge, to the shot and shell of Abraham Erlanger's Broadway campaigns may well be defined as the longest journey in the world. However, as there has never been, nor ever will be, any conventional path to professionalism as a songwriter, Wodehouse's progression may be taken as typical enough. His first journalistic post was with a periodical called *The Globe*, for whose "By the Way" column he was required to write a daily squib in rhyme concerning some topical event. From here to the composition of light verses to music for the Edwardian musical theatre was a natural enough transition, although Wodehouse was extremely lucky in his first collaborator, an unknown American symphonist manqué called Jerome Kern. Between them the two men concocted for the Adelphi Theatre a song about a prominent politician entitled "Mr. Chamberlain." Years later, when Kern, now a successful lion of the younger school of indigenous American popular composers, resumed his partnership with Wodehouse, by this time freelancing as a critic and short story writer in New York, the upshot was a series of unambitious musicals which revolutionized the entire concept of how America's songs should sound, and how its musical comedy settings should look.

The Princess Theatre on 39th Street, administered by the resourceful Elizabeth Marbury, had only 299 seats, a numerical curiosity explained by the fact that the theatre had been built by the Shubert brothers, compared to whose entrepreneurial shenanigans the excesses of an Erlanger are seen to be the harmless gambols of a spring lamb; the fire regulations of the time applied only to theatres with 300 or more seats, so the Shuberts, not particularly anguished by the thought that circumstances might conceivably set fire to audience and performers, had thoughtfully installed 299 seats. The aesthetic consequences were profound. Miss Marbury's triumvirate of Kern, librettist Guy Bolton, and lyricist Wodehouse began writing musical comedies tailored to the lilliputian dimensions of the building in which they were to be presented: not more than two sets, not more than twelve girls, not more than eleven musicians. The chorus disappeared, and with it conventional Hapsburgian hothouse passion. No more crown princes masquerading as butlers, no more milkmaids who turn out in the end to be dowager duchesses, no more cast lists reading like extracts from the *Alamanach de Gotha*. Most interesting of all, no more lyrics which strove through blowsy euphemism to elevate mutual attraction between the sexes to some kind of mystical experience.

What Wodehouse started to do the moment he began working at the Princess was to exchange the inanities of Ruritania for those of Main Street. In terms of technique, of vocabulary, of production values, the effect was so extraordinary that the great lyricists to come in the American musical theatre, men like Ira Gershwin, Oscar Hammerstein, Howard Dietz, Lorenz Hart, all of them a few years younger than Wodehouse, were to be lavish in their acknowledgment of the stylistic debt they owed him. Just as Berlin, Kern, and George Gershwin were creating colloquial American theatre music, so Wodehouse was creating its lyric counterpart.

He brought to this task a range of comic effects and innocent romantic tendernesses which continue to illuminate musical trifles written two generations ago. One has only to glance at his verses to see that they dealt in the currency of everyday life:

> I was often kissed 'neath the mistletoe
> By small boys excited with tea.
> If I'd known that you existed,
> I'd have scratched them and resisted, dear,
> But I never knew about you, oh, the pain of it,
> And you never knew about me.

The thought of the Merry Widow singing those lines at the Prince of Pilsen is enough to demonstrate the extent to which Wodehouse was changing the face of the American song. "You Never Knew about Me," written in 1917, is an item especially pertinent to the neglected question of how far his Broadway career affected his style as a novelist, as we shall see; for the moment he seemed to casual observers to be running two intensely demanding but disconnected careers concurrently. In 1917 he was involved in the freakish number of six New York first nights, having completed all the lyrics of *Kitty Darlin'* and *The*

Riviera Girl, written all the lyrics and part of the book of *Have a Heart, Oh, Boy!* and *Leave It to Jane*, and contributed sketches to *Miss 1917*. Apart from the notorious Harry B. Smith, no Broadway writer had ever committed himself to so many assignments in one season, and yet in that same year Wodehouse the novelist published *Piccadilly Jim* and *Uneasy Money*, besides contributing stories to the *Strand* and *The Saturday Evening Post*. He was, in effect, a part-time lyricist, a status which did not inhibit his more renowned successors from naming themselves as his disciples, of whose numerous testimonies that of Ira Gershwin can stand for all the rest:

> Wodehouse's talent in this field has never been fully recognized. So far as I'm concerned, no one wrote more charming lyrics than he in the period from just before World War I to the Twenties. Certainly I admired him greatly, and in a letter to me (November 10, 1961) he wrote that Richard Rodgers had sent him a telegram, not only congratulating him on his eightieth birthday but telling him how much Larry Hart, Oscar Hammerstein and Dick himself had been taught by Plum through the years.[7]

Because of circumstances more to do with the leisurely pace of Kern's evolving maturity than of Wodehouse's, none of the Princess Theatre songs has won fame as a standard item, the exception being "Bill," which, although it was eventually incorporated into *Show Boat* years after the Kern-Wodehouse partnership had dissolved, originally appeared in *Oh, Lady! Lady!* in 1919; the fact that five years before the first Gershwin brothers' musical, six before the debut of Rodgers and Hart, and ten before Porter's, Wodehouse should have been exploiting the anticlimactic of "I love him because he's . . . I don't know . . ." is a useful demonstration of his lyric flair and an explanation for the delight and reverence with which the rising wits of the American musical theatre greeted his casual democratization of the genre; as Alan Lerner later wrote of the Princess Theatre days, "Although Wodehouse was English, those smallish musicals inaugurated the American musical."[8] If the Bill of Kern's song sounds indubitably English, Wodehouse swiftly mastered the same trick on Broadway that he was bringing to a fine art as a novelist in *Psmith, Journalist* and *Piccadilly Jim*, the development of the perfect mid-Atlantic style. In the song "Cleopatterer," the flavor of the vocabulary and the willful facetiousness with which it is deployed is quite Runyonesque:

> She gave those poor Egyptian ginks
> Something else to watch besides the sphinx.

There is a fine Leacockian frenzy about the lines to Napoleon inspired by the minatory breadbasket of the great Erlanger:

> Napoleon was a little guy,
> They used to call him Shorty.
> He only stood about so high,
> His chest was under forty. . . .
> But though his waist was large, he faced
> And overcame all foemen.
> He knew quite well it's brains that tell
> And not a guy's abdomen.

As in his novels, Wodehouse was a dazzling eclectic, having assimilated everything from the old music-hall nuances which pervade the very being of his "A Packet of Seeds" to the jolly coarsenesses of vaudeville echoing through "When It's Tulip Time in Sing-Sing":

> For the little birds each spring sing
> "Aren't you coming back to Sing-Sing?"

Wodehouse's boyhood hero, W. S. Gilbert, peeps from behind the arras of "The Schnitza Kommisski," while the sentiments of "Till the Clouds Roll By" return us to that lap of romantic innocence usually associated with the early Ira Gershwin and Lorenz Hart. By the time he wrote his last stage lyrics, with Rudolf Friml in 1928 for *The Three Musketeers*, even Edmund Wilson, who hardly took Wodehouse's artistic pretensions seriously, could grudgingly concede that "there exists a kind of blended Anglo-American jargon in the insouciant British tradition, which I believe to be mainly the creation of the Englishman P. G. Wodehouse, who lived for years in the United States and whose American musical comedies, written with Jerome Kern, have been as popular as his English novels."[9]

Regarding those novels, it is revealing that Wodehouse's long experience as a musical comedy lyricist endowed him with an ability unique in the modern novel, *to hear what his characters were singing*. Several contemporary novelists, particularly F. Scott

---

7. Letter to Benny Green from Ira Gershwin.
8. "The Street Where I Live." Alan Jay Lerner, 1978.
9. "Talking American" in *The Shores of Light*. Edmund Wilson.

Fitzgerald and John O'Hara, have perceived the journalistic value of popular songs for locating the precise year of the action, but Wodehouse remains the only novelist to quote chapter and verse, and even, on one remarkable occasion, to use contrasting songwriting styles for the delineation of character. It is fascinating enough that Freddie Threepwood should indulge a weakness for the words of "April Showers" while Miss Peavey in *Leave it to Psmith* prefers "The Beale Street Blues," that Samuel Bulpitt in *Summer Moonshine* is a mine of information regarding the texts of "Pennies from Heaven," "Alice Blue Gown," "What'll I Do?" and "Happy Days Are Here Again," that Orlo Vosper in *Pigs Have Wings* is partial to "My Sweetie Went Away," that Mr. Pickering in *Uneasy Money* betrays a regrettable tendency to break into "I'll Sing Thee Songs of Araby," that Galahad Threepwood is sufficiently acquainted with the works of Noel Coward to quote "Mad Dogs and Englishmen" to the Duke of Dunstable, himself a figment of W. S. Gilbert's imagination, that Wilfred Alsop in *Galahad at Blandings* (U.S.: *A Pelican at Blandings*) is thoroughly conversant with Irving Berlin's "Another Cup of Coffee, Another Piece of Pie," that Mr. Cobbold in *Spring Fever* keeps bursting into "My Son Josh-uay," and that Bertie Wooster is actually willing to render "Sonny Boy" in public. But it is in *Quick Service* that Wodehouse actually extends the machinery of characterization by defining the contrast between the wet fish Lord Holbeton and the dashing hero Joss Weatherby as the antipathy between those two archetypal compositions "Trees" and "Old Man River." At the climax of the battle between the two men for the hand of the heroine, Holbeton, rendering "Trees" while sauntering towards the denouement, has just "got as far as the line about nests of robins in the hair and was rendering it with even more than his customary brio," when he is confronted by the hero, who also happens to be singing—at which point Wodehouse defines his credo regarding popular song of the modern epoch: "When a man singing 'Trees' meets a man singing 'Old Man River,' something has to give. They cannot both continue to function. Lord Holbeton generously decides to be the one to yield."[10] Or to put it another way, the school of indigenous American composers led by Wodehouse's old comrade from the Princess Theatre days, Jerome Kern, has finally ousted the Victorian aspidistra school of balladry. And as "Old Man River" comes from the same stage work which features Wodehouse's own most famous lyric, "Bill," the passage, and indeed the entire novel, may be taken as the author's modest reassertion of his own theories regarding the sensibilities of the modern song.

In fact, Wodehouse's work in the theatre, so far from being a whimsical aberration on the part of a dedicated novelist, cannot be separated from the fiction. For apart from the fact that on numerous occasions Wodehouse explained how his system of constructing a novel and apportioning segments of action to this or that character was governed by his experience of casting performers in musical comedies, it appears that the innocuous rhyming couplets of his days on Broadway lingered in the brain of the aging novelist, there to influence the cadences of his prose dreams. When in his ninety-second year Wodehouse embarked on the odyssey of Mr. Ephraim Trout, Hollywood lawyer, in *Bachelors Anonymous*, he defined his hero's regrettable neglect of silken dalliance by observing that "Mr. Trout had once kissed a girl of six under the mistletoe at a Christmas party, but there his sex life had come to an abrupt halt." And so the lines in a 1917 lyric emerge more than half a century later in a context far removed from the arena of Elizabeth Marbury. The songwriter in Wodehouse never died; it slumbered sometimes for long periods, but was likely to wake up with a melodious snort at any moment and reassert the engaging banalities of its methods and beliefs.

BENNY GREEN is a professional jazz saxophonist who has played with a range of orchestras embracing the Stan Kenton Band and the Galteymore Irish Dance Group. He began writing on musical subjects as a musician, and joined the London Observer *as jazz critic in 1958, staying for nineteen years. Since 1959 he has been a regular broadcaster on a variety of subjects for the BBC, including series on the history of the Hollywood musical and a history of popular music in the twentieth century. His published works include three volumes of music criticism and a biography of Fred Astaire. In the theatre he wrote book and lyrics of a musical life of Bernard Shaw, rewrote the libretto for the 1971 London revival of* Show Boat *and wrote two Cole Porter compilations for London's Mermaid Theatre,* Cole *(1974) and* Oh, Mr. Porter *(1977). To coincide with the Wodehouse centenary he is publishing a literary biography of Wodehouse and an annotated edition of Wodehouse's stage lyrics.*

---

10. *Quick Service.*

Wodehouse in Performance
EDWARD DUKE

THERE ARE moments in the life of an actor when he is what is euphemistically described as "resting." It was during one of these moments a few years ago that I decided to fill in the time by writing a play. This would have a spectacular part for myself, would run forever, and would lead inevitably to stardom and Hollywood. A modest and straightforward project, except for one practical problem: what would the play be about?

I had always been an ardent fan of P. G. Wodehouse, and considered that he was badly served on the English stage. I had seen a friend play Bertie Wooster at a provincial repertory theatre in a disastrous adaptation of *Ring for Jeeves*. The musical *Jeeves*, presented in the West End with the most distinguished backing, had closed after three weeks. These and similar failures decided my course. I would write the definitive Wooster/Jeeves play. I am always inspired by failure, feeling that I could do whatever it is better. The flaws become self-evident and I usually think I know how to rectify them. It is an arrogant conceit on my part, but not such a bad starting point. Having seen Wodehouse fail, I would now make him succeed.

I decided to work with my brother, James, also a Wodehouse enthusiast, on a two-act farce loosely drawn from *The Code of the Woosters* and *Stiff Upper Lip, Jeeves*. We worked out our own convoluted plot, machining it in such a way as to fit in as many of our favorite bits as possible. That is where we made our first and biggest error. You cannot have the action of a farce held up every five minutes while your leading character explains the recuperative properties of red peppers and raw eggs beaten up in Worcester sauce, even if this has made you laugh since infancy. We also found that Wodehouse on the page, while always funny, did not flow easily off the tongue. A great line like "Aunt Agatha had the air of one who, while picking flowers on the railway, is caught by the down-express in the small of the back" is wonderful to read but would never get a laugh in the theatre; there is simply too much information to take in. Also the proper timing of the line is impossible to attain. One of the ways you get laughs from an audience is by signaling a rhythm to them, and when they hear it they know that what you are saying is supposed to be funny.

Oscar Wilde was the master of rhythm of the spoken word. Lady Bracknell in *The Importance of Being Earnest* says: "Come along, Gwendolen; we have already missed one train, if not two. If we miss any more we shall be exposed to comment on the platform." The actress hardly has to do any work; the lines will do it for her: "Come along, Gwendolen [*beat*] we have already missed one train [*beat*] if not two [*beat*] if we miss any more we shall be exposed to comment on the platform." The words themselves are unimportant, but the rhythm is irresistible. Now Wodehouse is designed to be read, not spoken, and the words mean a great deal; but too many words baffle an audience and—dare I say it?—eventually bore them. Plot and situation are vital to hold them, and this was our difficulty with *What-Ho, Wooster*, as we called the play. In going more for Wodehouse the humorist as opposed to Wodehouse the storyteller, the play just became too long and there was not enough variety in it. Wodehouse himself says in his introduction to *The Jeeves Omnibus* that you should never sit down and read his work in one long stint, but should take him in small doses. I now see his point: he is a soufflé, as opposed to a *timbale de ris de veau Toulousienne*. Our mistakes in *What-Ho, Wooster* were the mistakes of our predecessors. We thought, "Here is a great and prolific writer; let us just filch all his finest passages and hang them on a plot tailored to include them." The whole *What-Ho, Wooster* experience was vital when I came to work on *Jeeves Takes Charge*. Without having been through it, I would never have understood the most important point about Wodehouse—one that I shall come to in a moment.

Soon after this I ceased to "rest" and for two years put aside thoughts of Hollywood and stardom in favor of playing small parts in the West End. But there was a nagging feeling in the back of my mind that I was getting nowhere fast and that, unless I created something of my own soon, my so-called career would never get off the ground—but what to do? *What-Ho, Wooster* obviously wasn't going to catapult me to fame, but had I exhausted Wodehouse? I went on holiday to Greece and took all the Jeeves books I could lay my hands on, mainly because they make excellent holiday reading but also because I wanted to see if I could get any more ideas out of them. Sitting on a beach in Spetsai ploughing through *Carry on, Jeeves*, it suddenly dawned on me that what was really funny about Wodehouse was not so much the dialogue but the *narrative*. The great chunks of dialogue in *What-Ho, Wooster* had left no room, I suddenly realized, for Bertie's vital comments on the action. So, having discovered this, what was I going to do about it? Was I going to have Bertie step outside the action and make remarks on what was going on? No, because that would only hold things up. The only way, it seemed to me, of making it work was having Bertie come on stage and tell the *whole* story, playing *all* the parts himself. I would make it into a one-man show, and, having recently discovered that Bertie was supposed to be twenty-four, the actor to play him was me.

My course was set, and on my return to England I started to work very seriously on a fifty-minute one-man show. I decided to tell two stories as different from each other as possible. It seemed to me that many people would not know anything about Wooster or Jeeves and I would have to educate them. It therefore followed that I must start with what was ostensibly the first story about Jeeves coming to take up his position at Bertie's flat. This story required no previous knowledge on the part of the audience. It involves, you will remember, the matter of Bertie's engagement to Lady Florence Craye, the dubious autobiography of her Uncle Willoughby, and the poisonous Boy Scout Edwin. The next problem was what should come after this. "The Great Sermon Handicap," a great personal favorite, would have been impossible to stage; there were too many characters in it, and I made it my rule that there should never be more than three people on stage, so to speak, at the same time. There is just so much an actor can do on his own without confusing his audience. I then had a foolhardy idea of following it with the one story Jeeves narrates, "Bertie Changes His Mind," which I had always found very funny. It is the one about the girls' school and the speech which Bertie made to the assembled young ladies. My instincts told me it could be made to work. I decided that my program was to be "Jeeves Takes Charge" and "Bertie Changes His Mind."

In my zeal I read them both into a tape recorder, but when I listened to the playback it was boring, monotonous, and literary. Also it was much too long. There was a moment of panic when I realized what a task I had undertaken. However, gritting my teeth, I cut both stories to shreds leaving only the facts and Bertie's funnier moments of narrative. The Jeeves story was shorter anyway, but he narrates in a heavy ponderous way, so that a lot of his narrative had to be cut. Whereas on the page we smile at his long-windedness, on stage he would merely have seemed pompous.

I hired a fringe theatre for a month around Christmas, and used various friends to design a set and costumes. Though Wodehouse was primarily an author and not a playwright, I felt that we had to steer very clear of the literary atmosphere that surrounds one-man shows. You know, somebody comes on in a bow-tie and reads from a lectern, and succeeds in sending a polite audience into a deep untroubled sleep. I would be performing in a theatre, so therefore the show must be theatrical. I made certain decisions about the lighting and the set. The scenery and furniture would be black and white, in the style of the period, as would my costumes. Between the two stories there would be a very quick change from Bertie to Jeeves so that I would remain dressed in each story as the narrator. The characters in the stories would be suggested by movement and voice only. The whole feeling would be informal from the start with Bertie mixing a cocktail and chatting to the audience in his flat in Berkeley Mansions. Bertie's flat would be the basis for all the scenes, suggested by subtle changes of lighting. For example, when Bertie goes into Uncle Willoughby's garden and "hears a snail clear its throat a mile away," the stage becomes dappled and the indoor plants on the set are picked out by spotlights to give the illusion of being out of doors.

I started to learn it at a rate of two pages a day. This is the hard slog of the actor's life, but for me it is the most important. It is when I am learning a part that I get most of my ideas on how to play it. Bertie Wooster was the most problematic of the characters, with Jeeves in second place. These are both very complex people and there is a big danger of playing them as just another upper-class featherbrained young man about town and his valet. Bertie is a nice young man, intelligent within limits, endowed with a nice sense of humor and a gift for the *mot juste*. Wodehouse uses enormous literary skill to give Bertie ingeniously witty things to say while setting him up as a clown. No ordinary clown could think up lines like "He was a tall, drooping, cove who looked as if he had been stuffed in a hurry by an incompetent taxidermist." Also, Jeeves is not just a valet; he is a gentleman's personal gentleman with a brain that makes his head bulge out at the back. He is extremely fond of the opposite sex and is often known to shift a nifty shoe on the dance floor. I had to suggest all of these things in my performance if it was to succeed.

What would Bertie look like? At first I pictured him with slightly receding sandy-colored hair and a monocle, with a suggestion of buck teeth. I am very dark and extremely tall, so I got myself a wig. Should he have a stammer? There was nothing in the books to suggest he had; also, there was no evidence that he sported a monocle. I decided against the wig and the stammer but stuck to the monocle. It would be a good signal to the audience: if the monocle was in, I was Bertie; out, I was one of the others. The voice was the hardest part of the whole exercise. The upper-class folk of that era—approximately 1925—placed their voices right at the back of their throats and hardly moved their lips. Obviously this wouldn't be feasible, as I wouldn't be heard past the first row and would thereby irritate the audience; worse still, I would be hoarse after five minutes. I had the idea of placing some sounds at the back and the rest forward in the mask of the face but with a very pronounced accent. This seemed to work, although I still found it a strain on the vocal cords. Then I found that by pushing my teeth forward, which I had to do to get the buck-teeth effect, the voice followed suit and soon I had a voice that went with the face. I also gave Bertie a nervous baying laugh whenever the situation got tricky. Soon I found this wonderfully rounded character taking over to such an extent that it used to take some time after rehearsal to get rid of Bertie Wooster.

Jeeves was, of course, very difficult for me as I am half his age—I place him at about forty-five—and many of my actor friends tried to dissuade me from tackling the second story in which Jeeves is the narrator. I was adamant, however, and started studying him in detail. I knew that he was dark with a large head and piercing eyes, that he moved from "spot A to spot B like some sort of gas," and that he was tall. Also he never showed emotion other than to raise his right eyebrow. I could find out nothing about his voice, but thought that it was probably a rich and even baritone. This part of the show would require a great deal of discipline, and I decided to work out his every movement down to the last footfall. Whereas Bertie's movements would be lanky and fairly disorganized, Jeeves would know exactly what he was going to do next, and this would help to give the feeling of a well-ordered mind. It would also help me with portraying his age and sagacity. As an adolescent in Japan, I had spent some time studying and observing the Kabuki theatre, and the actors there had taught me a walk which gave the impression of gliding. I used this walk for Jeeves, and bent my right arm as if I were permanently holding a tray. This was another useful signal to the audience, like Bertie's monocle. I also never moved my face, and concentrated my eyes on a spot in the audience—the green Exit signs were helpful. I was more surprised than anyone at the success of the second story, and realized that I needed to have no fears about playing Jeeves, because the audience had already seen me do it in the first story which I narrated as Bertie.

Having sorted the two protagonists out, I started on the smaller parts. These I felt could verge on the side of caricature as long as they had a firm basis in reality. Lady Florence Craye, for instance, "a girl with a wonderful profile," would always be seen nose-up and sideways on. Edwin, the Boy Scout, "as foul a pestilence that ever wore khaki shorts," would have a penchant for picking his nose. Uncle Willoughby, "who'd been a bit on the Tabasco side in his youth," would have been played by Sir Ralph Richardson if they had done a film, I felt sure, so I played him as Sir Ralph. Peggy Mainwaring, the little schoolgirl in "Bertie Changes His Mind," I had enormous fun with. She is described as "a red-haired young person with a snub nose and an extremely large grin," and I gave her a lisp and a "W" instead of an "R." She also had trouble, I felt, with keeping her knickers up. The headmistress was so obviously Dame Edith Evans that that was how I played her.

In rehearsal, it became evident how to stage the piece. As long as I had a clear idea in my mind of the geography of the various rooms, roads and gardens, then the audience would too. The characters' heights were important; if Edwin, the Boy Scout, was talking to Uncle Willoughby, he would be looking up to him, and vice versa. We worked out a few simple tricks to push the story along. With Bertie in the smoking-room, Uncle Willoughby would be reading a newspaper. Looking to the left, I would be Uncle Willoughby talking to Bertie; looking to the right, I would be Bertie, concealed by the newspaper, shaking with terror. In the second story, we used the armchair as a car with three people in it: Jeeves in a bowler hat driving, Peggy Mainwaring in the middle, and Bertie on the left. By tilting the hat to three different angles I was able to suggest a cramped car with this appalling schoolgirl "devouring some sticky species of sweetmeat" in the middle.

The show opened at the Young Vic Studio to a small amount of press coverage, and, owing to snowstorms and a rail strike, small houses as well. But this was a crucial period in the birth of the piece as I could gauge what was working and what wasn't without being under too much important scrutiny. In other words, I could make my mistakes. Two technical points were made clear in performance: first, owing to the extreme energy and pace of the writing, there could not be one moment of flagging on my part if I was going to keep the interest of the audience. This was fairly tiring but vital. Second, one needs as much breath to play Wodehouse as Shakespeare. If I took a breath in the middle of the line before a laugh, the laugh would be diminished. When you read a sentence, you read it in one, getting the full impact immediately. I had to do the same when speaking. This was especially true of Jeeves; try saying, in one breath: "I was at one time in her father Lord Worplesdon's employment, but I tendered my resignation because I could not see eye to eye with his Lordship in his desire to dine in dress trousers, a shooting-coat and a flannel shirt," and you will get some idea of the strenuousness of the exercise.

One other thing was made clear to me, and this was that the show was basically a success. People laughed where they were supposed to and left having enjoyed themselves. It became obvious to me that I would have to come up with a second act if the piece was to have real commercial possibilities. After my season at the Young Vic, I was invited to perform a longer show at the Kings Lynn Festival. What would I do about my second part?

I was wary of trying just another short story—I felt it would be too much of a good thing and would lose the impact of the first act. In the end I had no choice, so I read "Without the Option" from a lectern. It was not a success; my feelings about doing another short story were right. The audience was bored.

I had two more invitations to perform a longer version of the show around England, so I set about working on a second act in detail. One of the things that always slightly bothered me about the first act was that, because of the nature of the stories, I couldn't get in all the pieces of classic Wodehouse that the public knows. Things like Bertie's aunts, Anatole the chef, and Gussie Fink-Nottle's drunken prize-giving scene. Surely having set up the ins and outs of the Wooster/Jeeves relationship in the first act, I could now just come on and do a Wooster stand-up routine with perhaps a song and a dance: Bertie Wooster Live at Carnegie Hall! That is basically what I did. I made a framework of two scenes and gave myself a slight plot to work on. Bertie is in his bedroom chatting to the audience about his aunts; he keeps being interrupted by Aunt Dahlia on the telephone—if he doesn't speak at her village concert on "the life and times of a debonair boulevardier," he won't get any more of Anatole's cooking. Bertie refuses, and when she suggests he sing "Sonny Boy" and tap-dance as well, he gets furious and shouts, "*Never!*" There is a quick scene-change into a large tent with Aunt Dahlia's voice over the P.A. system announcing: "The next item will be my nephew, Bertram Wooster, lecturing on the life and times of a debonair boulevardier." Bertie then enters, slightly inebriated, and tells the audience that it reminds him of the time Gussie Fink-Nottle had to "dish the prizes out at the local grammar school and broke the habit of a lifetime." After this twenty-minute sequence—in my view the strongest comic scene Wodehouse ever wrote and probably the high point of my show—he pays a tribute to the golden days at the Drones Club, sings "Sonny Boy," badly, and does a riotous tap-dance bringing the play to a rousing finish.

The second act was never a problem to rehearse or perform, as I could be much freer, not so constricted by the discipline of the first act. Quite by accident, and to my amazement, the show now built, scene after scene, into an enormous climax and a great success. I was even more amazed when I was invited to play a three-week season at the Lyric Studio, Hammersmith, and we played to capacity business and rave notices. Again, all the old problems of stamina and vocal strain came up, but I was fit enough to cope with them, and eventually the show became easier to do. The Wodehouse magic carried it forward.

In my view the greatest humorist of the twentieth century has enabled me to see my shortcomings as an actor and helped me to overcome them. He has also handed me a great script to play with. I hope I have served him as well.

EDWARD DUKE is an expert on P. G. Wodehouse (having been introduced to his stories at the age of seven by his father) and has written a play, What Ho Wooster. *He felt Wodehouse had been ill-served on the English stage, and believed that the only way to present this raconteur was in a narrative style—hence* Jeeves Takes Charge, *a solid West End success. Duke started his career at the age of fourteen at the Kabuki theatre in Tokyo, Japan, studying various techniques of Oriental theatre. In England he has appeared in repertory in such plays as* Rosencrantz and Guildenstern Are Dead, Arms and the Man, Conduct Unbecoming, Jane Eyre, Hamlet, *and* French without Tears. *He has appeared on the West End stage in* Why Not Stay for Breakfast *and* Filumena. *He has also appeared on the screen and on television.*

Letter from London, August 1939
JOHN HAYWARD

EDITOR'S NOTE: All but two of the pieces in this book—this one and PGW's "How I Write My Books" —were written for it, and so deal with Wodehouse in complete retrospect. John Hayward, a well-known literary critic, for some time provided Bonniers of Stockholm, publishers in Swedish translation of many English authors, including Wodehouse, with comments on the British publishing scene, of which this is one; and we have included it because it gives a view of the place Wodehouse held halfway through his writing career, which ran from 1901 to 1975. What is clear—whether it is surprising must rest with each reader—is that Wodehouse had by this time achieved everything that he was going to and yet for another three and a half decades cheerfully turned out work which kept him at that summit.

Maureen O'Sullivan touches briefly on the matter of PGW's captivity by the Germans in 1940 in another contribution; for those who are still troubled by this matter, it might be instructive to note Mr. Hayward's statement, made some months before that event, that "he has always refused to listen to unpleasant news or to read the newspapers when trouble is brewing."

IF I WERE asked to name the outstanding literary event of the year in this country, I should be very much inclined to say that it was the decision this summer of Oxford University to confer upon the famous humorist Mr. P. G. Wodehouse its honorary degree of Doctor of Letters. Oxford does not bestow such favors lightly—least of all on those without claim to academic distinction. Mr. T. S. Eliot, for example, who was given an honorary degree at Cambridge this summer, has yet to be honored in this way by his old university. I was present at the ceremony in the Sheldonian Theatre, when the Public Orator greeted Mr. Wodehouse in neat Horatian hexameters, and later at the lunch, given by the Vice-Chancellor, in the historic Codrington Library in All Souls College, and I do not think there was anyone at either of those distinguished gatherings who could have doubted for a moment who was the hero of the day. It was not the Spanish Grandee, the British admiral, the famous American jurist, the great Shakespearean scholar, but plain PGW, as he is called by his English readers, the creator of Jeeves, Bertie Wooster, Lord Emsworth, and other surely immortal eccentrics.

I happen to know that the initiative on this unprecedented occasion was taken by Dr. Gordon, the Vice-Chancellor of the university, himself a distinguished man of letters, and that he had no difficulty in persuading his learned colleagues of Mr. Wodehouse's fitness to receive the highest honor Oxford can bestow for literary merit. In conferring it, Dr.

Gordon addressed him as *Vir lepidissime, facetissime, venustissime, jocosissime, ridibundissime*. It was a striking tribute to his popularity with readers of every age and class, from the venerable savant to the schoolboy, from the eminent public servant to the merest "gentleman of leisure"; and with, one might add, at least one British prime minister—the late Earl of Oxford and Asquith, who was a passionate addict of the Master's works and never traveled without a copy of one of them. It seems, moreover, that his extraordinary vogue is by no means confined to English-speaking people. Almost all his recent novels have been translated into the most unexpected languages. He is, for instance, something of a best-seller in Soviet Russia of all places, and he has always been a favorite with the Czechs and the Italians.

I cannot conceive, though, how his novels read in translation. Admittedly their masterly plots would lose nothing by translation into any language under the sun, notwithstanding their essentially English and, to a lesser degree, American setting, for Mr. Wodehouse has a genius for creating dramatic surprise and inventing absurd situations. But I am puzzled to know how any translation could possibly convey the inimitable verbal wit, the grotesquely distorted literary echoes and the pure fantasy of simile and metaphor that are Mr. Wodehouse's chief claim to literary distinction. I suspect that very few even of his English readers are aware of the wide range of his reading and of how aptly, like the Devil in the old saying, he can "quote Scripture to his purpose." It is surprising that none of those pertinacious American students for the Ph.D. degree, at a loss for a subject for research, has yet thought of writing a dissertation on the influence of, say, Shakespeare on the work of P. G. Wodehouse! If this ever happens, it would be easy to show how almost every single novel of his contains passages that prove, explicitly or implicitly, his familiarity with the work not only of Shakespeare but of a large number of the best English writers from Chaucer onwards. The "common reader," as Dr. Johnson defined him, has probably never paid much attention to these literary influences and allusions in his work; he is only concerned that Mr. Wodehouse should continue to be amusing. For the same reason he has probably never bothered himself about Mr. Wodehouse's literary style, which is in a high degree polished and correct. While it is something of an exaggeration to say, as Hilaire Belloc does in his preface to the recently published *Week-End Wodehouse*, that "Mr. Wodehouse is the best writer of English now living," he is beyond question a writer who knows exactly what he wants to say and the best way of saying it.

He is, I suppose, what is called a born writer. He was certainly never educated to be one. Of aristocratic birth—he is a kinsman of the Earl of Kimberley and a collateral descendant, therefore, of no less a person than Anne Boleyn, the wife of Henry VIII—he went, according to the custom of his class, to an English "public school." For financial reasons, though, he did not follow the usual practice of continuing his education at Oxford or Cambridge but went, like his hero Psmith, straight from school into a bank in the City. This was at the turn of the century. It was while working at the bank and living in modest rooms in Chelsea that he began to write short stories in his spare time. These, as well as his early novels, were school stories and were first published serially in boys' magazines like *The Captain*. I have met very few people, even among Mr. Wodehouse's most passionate admirers, who have read them or, indeed, know their titles—*The Pothunters* (his first book), *A Prefect's Uncle*, *Tales of St. Austin's*, and so on. But I have met people, unacquainted with his later work and the tales of Jeeves and of Blandings Castle, who recall, with sentimental regret for their own boyhood, the stirring accounts of cricket matches and midnight escapades that used to appear regularly in *The Captain* in the early 1900s.

Although there is not a great deal of money in this sort of work, Mr. Wodehouse was soon earning enough, after working hours, to justify the risk of throwing up his job at the bank and settling down seriously to live by his pen. It was an important decision for a young man to take. When he made it he was by no means an established writer, and, in fact, he recalls an occasion when no less than eight rejected manuscripts arrived by one post. But he was encouraged by the offer of a temporary job, which later became permanent, on the staff of the old *Globe* newspaper, to which he contributed a daily column entitled "By the Way," extracts from which were subsequently published, in book form, by him and a collaborator in a little-known volume called *The Globe By the Way Book*. He contributed regularly also a good deal of anonymous work to *Punch*, including light verse for which, his friend Herbert

Westbrook tells me, he had a remarkable facility.

His first novel, as distinct from a school story, *Love Among the Chickens*, appeared as long ago as 1906, but it was not until five years later that he gave up writing for boys and produced *A Gentleman of Leisure*, the first of many typical and inimitable studies devoted to the fanciful and absurd adventures of rich and witless young men. And it was not for another ten years, until 1919, that the immortal Jeeves, the greatest of his creations, appeared on the scene. Jeeves's first entry into the world was made in a very humble fashion, in a small, poorly printed volume, bound in cheap red cloth and priced at ninepence. This is now a rare first edition, almost impossible to find in good condition, and is eagerly sought for by collectors. It is not generally known, however, that there is an earlier volume than this in which Jeeves makes a single, tantalizing appearance. It is a collection of nondescript short stories, entitled *The Man with Two Left Feet* and published in 1917. Mr. Wodehouse has confessed that he did not at first consider the possibility of exploiting the character of the "gentleman's personal gentleman." In this forgotten story, in which a manservant named Jeeves merely announces a visitor and then retires, there is certainly no hint of a suave, ubiquitous valet who was later to become the guide, philosopher, and friend of Bertie Wooster. As a matter of fact and accuracy, it is possible to trace the evolution of Jeeves a stage further back still. This interesting biographical or historical fact has not hitherto been disclosed, and I am grateful to Mr. Westbrook for supplying me with the information on which it is based. He informs me that the character of Jeeves was in part founded upon a hint in a short dramatic sketch—"After the Show"—in which he and Wodehouse collaborated. I have read the manuscript of this piece and it seems to me clear that Barlow, the valet who appears in it, is, if not exactly the prototype, at least an adumbration of Jeeves; and, moreover, that his young master, the Hon. Aubrey Forde-Rasche, is a precursor of Bertie Wooster and all the other young-men-about-town of Mr. Wodehouse's subsequent novels and stories.

It was Jeeves who clinched PGW's reputation as the outstanding English humorist of his time. His popularity, it is true, had been growing steadily during the war years 1914–18, while he was in the United States, and it was noticeably enhanced in 1918 by the publication of *Piccadilly Jim*, which is still one of his most popular books. But it was not until after the war that he became firmly established in the best-seller class, not only in England but also, though on a smaller scale, in foreign countries as well. His market value had increased commensurably with his popularity. For his early stories he had been accustomed to receive about ten pounds; by the beginning of the 1920s he was in a position to command anything up to four or five hundred pounds. By this time he was also beginning to earn considerable sums in serial and film rights.

Mr. Wodehouse has always been a fluent writer, and for the last thirty years and more he has produced at least one book a year. Ranged together on the shelves, they make an impressive showing—fifty-eight volumes in all, as many, incidentally, as there are years to his age. Yet, with the approach of his sixtieth year, he is still at the height of his powers and, in appearance, much younger than his age. Tall, heavily built, with a bland, genial face and eyes that twinkle humorously through horn-rimmed spectacles, he looks for all the world like the ideal uncle of fiction. Looking at him, one would say that he has never known what trouble is. In a sense, one would not be far wrong, for a friend who has known him intimately for the last thirty years tells me that he has always refused to listen to unpleasant news or to read the newspapers when trouble is brewing. Thus, he cannot bear being told about misfortune or ill-health. It is somehow in keeping with his character and temperament that he should have made his home in a pleasure resort—Le Touquet—where his only domestic concern is the welfare of his dogs and his only serious interest, his work. His detachment from the world around him is reflected in his novels, which offer the reader an easy escape from life, as, in a different way, detective stories do. His fantasy world is one in which perpetual summer reigns and virtue always finds its reward; where the course of true love is never denied a happy ending and sex never rears its ugly head or poverty endures for more than a season. I have always felt that his heroes and heroines are blissfully unaware of the "facts of life." Historically, the Wodehousian world bears a superficial and glamorous resemblance, I suppose, to the palmy days of Edwardian England—an age to which, in these troubled times, one looks back with nostalgic, not to say sentimental, regret. It is one that has been described brilliantly, in the form of a novel, by Miss Sackville-West in *The Edwardians*, and by the Duke of Portland in his almost fabulous autobiography, *Men, Women and Things*. It is an age that will never return, a golden age that never existed outside the imagination, but which has a kind of reality in the dreams of those who, by a willing suspension of disbelief, stretch out their hands to grasp, as Proust did, the eternal illusion of *le temps perdu*. The Wodehousian Arcadia is infinitely remote from the world of the present—as remote as Cytherea of the "Land of Heart's Desire."

Reproduced with kind permission of the copyright owner.

JOHN DAVY HAYWARD, 1905–65, scholar, bibliographer, and collector. Although he suffered from muscular dystrophy from the age of ten, he had a brilliant academic career. While still an undergraduate at Cambridge where he won a scholarship, he produced the first twentieth-century edition of Rochester. At the age of twenty-four he did an edition of John Donne. Since he was condemned to a wheelchair, his flat became a literary center. After the war he shared a flat with T. S. Eliot until the latter remarried. He is "the gentleman in white spats" in Eliot's dedication of Old Possum's Book of Practical Cats. Hayward produced anthologies on St. Evremonde, Swift, Donne, Dr. Johnson, and Eliot. He collected Wodehouse first editions.

Honoris Causa
LETTY GRIERSON

IN THE SUMMER of 1939, I accompanied my father, H. J. C. Grierson, to Oxford, where he was to receive an honorary degree. Another of the three candidates for the D.Litt. was P. G. Wodehouse; and they walked side by side in the procession from the Vice-Chancellor's college (where the traditional feast is champagne and peaches) to the Sheldonian Theatre in which the *Encaenia* always takes place. Graduation processions often bring together strange partners. Elisabeth Murray, taken as a child to see her grandfather, Sir James Murray, editor of the *Oxford English Dictionary* and founder of the art of historical lexicography, in a similar parade through the streets of Cambridge, did not think of asking who was the quiet little man who walked beside Grandfather Dictionary's bearded figure. She was to learn much later that it was Thomas Hardy.[1]

My father had reached the stage in an academic career (he was seventy-three) when honorary degrees tend to accrue. It had become something of a joke—in fact he *had* a little joke about it: "I have an honorary degree for every letter in the alphabet," and with a deprecating giggle he'd reel out: "Amsterdam, Bordeaux, Cambridge, Dublin, Edinburgh . . . ," his voice trailing off as though he'd run out of breath, not place names. He also said the best part of the whole business was the people you met standing in line (referring of course to the graduation procession)—Cordell Hull at Princeton, André Maurois at Columbia, and now Wodehouse. And how he enjoyed the Commencement cartoons that appeared every June in *The New Yorker*! ("I see no mention of an honorary degree for you, Sir," says the usher running his finger down his list and addressing the next-in-line candidate who has stepped forward expecting to be capped.)

It was on the way to the Sheldonian that my father first felt the impact of the Wodehouse cult in the English universities (he spoke of it later with a faint chagrin). The pageantry of the occasion and the settled, late-June weather ("twelve noon on the third Wednesday in the ninth week of the Trinity—summer—Full Term" has been the time and date of the *Encaenia*[2] since the Middle Ages) draw out everyone to watch what Sir John Betjeman has called "the ribbon of learning" winding its way through Radcliffe Square. Undergraduates especially crowded close and cheered Wodehouse with respectful hilar-

---

1. K. M. Elisabeth Murray, *Caught in a Web of Words* (Yale University Press, 1977).

2. For a full description of the *Encaenia*, see John Betjeman, *An Oxford University Chest* (Oxford University Press, 1979). I am indebted to Joellyn Ausanka of the press for putting this invaluable book into my hands when my memory of times and places was flagging.

ity. I myself was familiar with the cult, having met it in full force as an undergraduate at Cambridge twelve years earlier. I believe it was less strong, perhaps hardly existed, in the Scottish universities. We were a dour lot. Nor was it at that time as prevalent at Girton and Newnham as at the men's colleges.[3] Women were still in such a minority at the two great universities that we worked harder, carried our scholarship less lightly—in other words had less time for outside reading.

I had my own reasons for being a little shy of Wodehouse in my college days. I loved the jargon, the sheer Wodehouse-ese that all the men I knew at Cambridge used, and I imitated it shamelessly—but I never went back to first sources. Why was this? I suspected him of being a male chauvinist. In those far-off days I'd have had no word for male chauvinism (and what a comfort it is to have one), but I was well acquainted with the phenomenon, in life and in literature. I knew that Wodehouse dealt in maiden aunts and flappers and I reckoned that British humorists usually were humorous at the expense of women. It was not until much later, in America and working for Donald Bensen who was bringing him out in paperback, that I found how wrong I was about Wodehouse. Few of his men are as plucky and sensible as the best of his women, and none of his women plumb the depths of silliness as deeply as many of his men.

But now back to June of 1939, that last Midsummer Day before the war. It is, I recall, the sort of day that brightens most Wodehouse stories—and is so rare in the England of stern reality—bright, warm, and clear.

The public has been advised to take its reserved seats early in the gallery of the Sheldonian. An organ recital, largely Bach and Handel, helps to pass the time—but it stops abruptly and yields to some brave Purcell trumpet airs as the procession begins to file in and take its places on the dais and in the amphitheatre. We are all on our feet now and will not sit again until after the national anthem. It is then that I see Wodehouse for the first time. Benign and beaming, he surveys the scene. There is too a kind of freshness in his presence, a lack of blaséness, which the austerity of his simple academic dress

---

[3]. I am unable to break the habit of a lifetime of referring to students at Oxford and Cambridge as "men" and "women." The shock is still with me of the general reaction when, newly arrived from Scotland, I referred to a scruffy-looking freshman at Sidney Sussex College as a "boy."

(black gown and mortarboard) brings out. He was, I believe, receiving his first degree, honorary or otherwise. My filial eye passes to my own special candidate and I am distressed to see that he is looking a wee bit grumpy, swathed though he is in the scarlet gown of his alma mater, a sort of John-Knoxy black velvet academic hat scrunched down on his head. For sheer flattery there is nothing like your mortarboard, with its long swinging tassle, its stiff yet flexible brim, which can be tipped to a rakish angle without endangering the equilibrium of the whole.

The candidates are certainly a distinguished lot. I have of course my own opinion of which is the most noteworthy, but Lord Lothian, Charles Massey (the High Commissioner for Canada), and America's Justice Felix Frankfurter, along with an admiral, a chief justice of India, an eminent scientist, and an equally eminent scholar—and Wodehouse—do form an impressive group.

The ceremony begins, and the Public Orator, Dr. Cyril Bailey, takes each candidate in turn by the hand and presents him to the Vice-Chancellor of the university with a little citation in Latin. These citations are traditionally "full of puns and quips for the initiated"—in-jokes, in other words. That dealing with my father is in fact fairly sober, praising him for being the first to recognize the importance of the poems of John Donne and to edit them—though I am not sure whether he takes the introductory description of him, as one "Scotch by birth and nature, who *nevertheless* [italics mine] learned the gentle character of the English language in Christ Church," as a sly dig or a piece of bland Sassenach effrontery.

There is no question about the eulogy for Wodehouse. It is delivered in rolling hexameters, and ingeniously brings in Bertie Wooster, Jeeves, Mr. Mulliner, the Earl of Emsworth, and Psmith—a glorious, respectful, and affectionate burlesque. It is during this that I observe my father, his face alight with enjoyment, and relished extraordinarily verbal ingenuity in that language and in English.

Dr. Bailey descends into prose for his conclusion, presenting to the assembly their *festivum caput*—which can be roughly translated as "great guy"—and "our Petronius, or should I say Terence?"

And then it is done with, and I finally catch up with the new D.Litt.s on the steps of the Sheldonian, chatting happily, with my father explaining to his new colleague with what ingenuity the activities of his creations had been translated to the antique world. "Fidus Achates" for Jeeves was, he thought, particularly felicitous.

It was perhaps a curious confrontation, the scholar and the popular writer; but people who are dedicated to what they do and are beyond question excellent at it do have a great deal in common.

I cannot in good conscience refer to the Public Orator's citation of Wodehouse so favorably without reproducing it so that the reader may form his own opinion. The English translation which follows the Latin text was very kindly prepared by Vlasta Podzemmy of the Brearly School. The editor of this portion of this book has, perhaps wisely and perhaps not, chosen to alter Miss Podzemmy's translation of the versified portion of the citation and render it in an approximation of the original meter.

> Ecce auctor magicus, quo non expertior alter
> delectare animos hominum risumque movere.
> Namque novas scaenae personas intulit et res
> ridiculas cuique adiunxit. Cui non bene notus
> dives opum iuvenis, comisque animique benigni,
> nec quod vult fecisse capax, nisi fidus Achates
> ipse doli fabricator adest vestisque decentis
> arbiter? Aut comes ille loquax et ventre rotundo
> cui patruusque neposque agnatorum et domus omnis
> miranda in vita—sic narrat—fata obierunt?
> Nobilis est etiam Clarens, fundique paterni
> et suis eximiae dominus, Psmitheusque "relicta
> cui fac cuncta," Augustus item qui novit amores
> ranicularum, aliusque alio sub sidere natus.
> Non vitia autem hominum naso suspendit adunco
> sed tenera pietate notat, peccataque ridet.
> Hoc quoque, lingua etsi repleat plebeia chartas,
> non incomposito patitur pede currere verba,
> concinnus, lepidus, puri sermonis amator.

> Quid multa? Quem novere omnes, testimonio non eget. Praesento vobis festivum caput—Petroniumne dicam an Terentium nostrum?—Pelham Grenville Wodehouse, Societatis Regiae Litterarum sodalem, ut admittatur honoris causa ad gradum Doctoris in litteris.

Behold the magic author, more skilled than any other
In pleasing minds of men and moving them to laughter.
A host of characters he has created, then
Endowed each one with traits incomparably absurd.
Who knows not well that youth, rich, friendly,
    open-handed,
Who may not move or act without his staunch Achates,
Himself a subtle plotter, and stern sartorial mentor?
Can any fail to know that talkative and rotund
Chap whose uncles, nephews, cousins—the
    whole household—
Lead lives awash in marvels (so at least he tells us)?
Far-famed is Clarence, master of ancestral lands
And of his own prized pig—and Psmith ("Leave
    everything
To him")—Augustus too, who pores upon the newts'
Amours—and all those others, born to stranger stars.
And yet he turns not up his nose at human follies
But, rather, kindly notes them and finds them cause
    for mirth.
And though he fills his books with lively, common
    language,
His prose runs not about on awkward feet, for he
Is polished, witty, and most ardent lover of
    unblemished writing.

> What more? The man we all know does not need my praise to introduce him. I present to you that great guy—should I say our Petronius or Terence? —Pelham Grenville Wodehouse, member of the Royal Society of Literature, so that he may be admitted, for honor, to the degree of Doctor of Letters.

LETTY GRIERSON was born and grew up in Scotland. After graduating from Edinburgh and Cambridge Universities, she came to the United States as a graduate student at Bryn Mawr. At that time her father, H. J. C. Grierson, was working on his edition of the letters of Sir Walter Scott, and asked her to look up and make copies of those letters of Scott that were in the Morgan Library. It was while Ms. Grierson was working at the Morgan that she met her future husband, Dr. Hellmut Lehmann-Haupt, who was also doing some work there. They were married in 1933 and have three sons. Ms. Grierson now lives in New York and is a freelance editor and writer.

Uncollected PGW

DAVID A. JASEN

I FIRST got interested in P. G. Wodehouse's life after I had read about four of his books while in high school. He quickly became my favorite author, and I wanted to know all about the man. This led me, before the start of my senior year at college, to meet him. I was living on the south shore of Long Island at Long Beach; so was he, but about seventy-five miles away, in Remsenburg. I got out the map and located this minuscule hamlet, then went off one sunny day to seek him out. Arriving in the afternoon, I introduced myself. I had a humor column for our weekly college newspaper and gave as my excuse for meeting him that I wanted to interview him. He readily and graciously consented, adding that he walked the dogs at this time of day and I could accompany them. His two dogs were Jed, a dachshund, and Bill, a large mongrel. At the end of the three-quarters of an hour's interview/walk, he took me into his study where he showed me his collection of his own books, took down a reprint of *Blandings Castle*, which he had mentioned during the interview as containing his favorite short stories, and autographed it to me.

After my column was published—and I had received a splendid handwritten note of thanks from him—I discovered that many fellow students, teachers, and administrators were fans of his and that Wodehouse wasn't my private preserve after all. All this response encouraged me to find out as much as possible about his life (he was seventy-seven at the time, and had just had published *Cocktail Time*). I was attending American University, in Washington, D.C., and so had access to the Library of Congress, where I went through their card files and got out everything they had on him. When I returned home for the Easter vacation, I called him up and asked if I could see him. He remembered me and cordially invited me to lunch. Because I had expressed interest in his theatrical career (about which he had written nothing except *Bring on the Girls!*), he also invited his longtime theatrical collaborator and friend, Guy Bolton, to the luncheon. This meeting whetted my appetite, and I tracked down their theatrical agent, John Rumsey, of The American Play Company, who lent me several scripts of their old musical comedies. Louis Aborn, of Tams-Witmark, furnished the musical scores, and I began to get a good picture of how great the Bolton-Wodehouse contribution was to the American musical comedy. Further study at the New York Public Library—in their Reference Room, Theatre Collection, Music Collection, and Genealogy Room—prompted an idea which was beginning to grow: to do a really thorough job of research to find out *all* about his life, private and professional, and write a biography of him. Planning to write the first biography of the greatest and most prolific humorist of the twentieth century required two major efforts: researching the facts of his life including tracking down friends, family, and business associates; and trying to locate and read all of his published writings. When I broached the subject, he was clearly taken aback, but good-naturedly said I could be his official biographer. He warned me that some fellow had tried to do it several years before but that nothing had come of it as the man had got sidetracked with research on Peveril, Plum's older brother. I promised him I would keep to the main line.

I made plans to go to England during my next annual vacation. Plum was extremely helpful, writing to family, friends, and business associates, asking them to give me whatever help I needed. They all responded warmly, and my biography, *P. G. Wodehouse: A Portrait of a Master*, is a result. In London, I spent a good deal of time at both the British Museum in Bloomsbury and at their Newspaper Library at Colindale, digging up every reference they had and reading large amounts of his work from obscure publications.

On my return to the United States, I met Peter Schwed of Simon and Schuster, his current publisher, and Henry Morrison, who handled his work at the Scott Meredith Literary Agency. With their kind permission, I went through their files, and was later lucky enough to do the same with Plum's previous literary agents, both here and in England.

During my next visit to England, J. D. Grimsdick of Herbert Jenkins Ltd., Plum's publisher since 1919, lent me the diary that Plum had kept from his initial sale in February 1900 to February 1908. This was the major source of information for those years, and helped to jog Plum's memory as he recalled interesting associations from each work.

During this period, I became a supercollector: I collected facts and anecdotes about his life, as well as getting involved with first editions, English and American, of his work, magazine appearances, sheet music, playbills, scripts, clippings, articles on him, reviews of his work, recordings, piano rolls, letters, and photographs. While I was working on the biography, it became apparent that another tool for the collector was needed, and I set about meeting that need. *A Bibliography and Reader's Guide to the First Editions of P. G. Wodehouse* was my answer. In it I set down the specific details needed for collectors readily to identify Plum's first editions. Occasionally it was easy, but all too often it was impossible without the aid of publishers' files and copyright copies on deposit at the Library of Congress and at the British Museum.

In the course of all this, I gathered various items which I had especially enjoyed reading but which had never been collected in book form. This lack was somewhat surprising, as Plum's thriftiness with his writings was a byword. He was usually very careful to see that a short story was published in magazines in England and the United States before being put into a book which was then published in both countries. But during my years of research I was constantly coming across material not to be found in his published volumes. When I got what I thought was a generous representative sampling of the variety of materials—school, sporting, romantic, and humorous short stories, humorous articles, articles on sports, and poems—I brought my selection to Plum, asking if he would agree that these should be preserved between hard covers. He not only enthusiastically approved, but volunteered to write the foreword. Unfortunately, he died before he could write it, and the foreword was written by his good friend and onetime editor Malcolm Muggeridge.

The first of these posthumous publications of his early writings, never before published in book form in the United States (and some never before published in book form in England), was entitled *The Uncollected Wodehouse*. Continuum, which had issued the biography, was the publisher; and a couple of years later, I was asked by them to gather more of this little-known material. The book was issued as *The Swoop! and Other Stories*, including several stories from the early years of *The Captain* and *Pearson's Magazine*. His very rare novel, *Not George Washington*, has finally made its debut in the United States, after seventy-three years. The latest offering in the Continuum Wodehouse collection is *The Eighteen-Carat Kid and Other Stories*, which includes his only story written for children, *William Tell Told Again*, and his first published short stories in *The Public School Magazine* and in the *Strand*, where he was published continuously for an amazing thirty-five years. There is enough suitable material for another volume or two, which I hope will be issued in due course.

The present and possible future collections of this type employ material dating from the first decade and a half of the century. Plum's writings after the First World War narrowed to two major types: serials for the magazines which were later published in book form, and humorous short stories for the magazines, which were also published in hard-cover collections. During the 1950s he started writing humorous articles again. Many of these were published in his "autobiographical" works *America, I Like You, Over Seventy,* and *Author! Author!*

It was during his formative years that he wrote voluminously and in a variety of literary forms: columns about contemporary public schools, articles, short stories, lyrics, verse, plays, libretti, and serials. Here is where the treasures of uncollected Wodehousiana lay, in the many forgotten newspapers and magazines which proliferated in prewar London and New York.

The first writing for which Wodehouse was paid, "Some Aspects of Game-Captaincy," appeared in A. and C. Black's *Public School Magazine* for February 1900. He received 10/6 for it as first prize in their sponsored contest. A year later he began to appear regularly in its pages with articles about schools, sports, and adolescent literature, and with humorous short stories about young public school boys. Many of his contributions were not signed, adding to the difficulties of research. There is a similar problem with his writing for the American *Vanity Fair* magazine from 1914 to 1918, where he appeared under several pseudonyms as well as his own name. Plum's diary provides us with the key to his anonymous contributions and prices paid for them, and the publishers' files allow us to sort out the pseudonymous ones.

1902 was a banner year for Wodehouse, beginning with the publication of many stories and the first of his serials in Newnes's *The Captain: A Magazine for Boys and Old Boys*. It had been created to rival *The Public School Magazine*, which proceeded to go out of business in March 1902. *The Captain* reigned supreme, and Plum became one of its major contributors. It was also the year in which his first serial was published as a book, *The Pothunters*, the year he started a remarkable sixty-three-year association with *Punch*, the venerable British humor magazine, and the year he began his professional writing career with the century-old newspaper *The Globe*.

There is much in the way of unrepublished He-and-She jokes and turnovers which Plum ground out over the next seven years at *The Globe*. What is undoubtedly his rarest volume, *The Globe By the Way Book*, a shilling paperback co-authored with Herbert Westbrook, is a collection of his "By the Way" columns and vividly demonstrates that most topical humor loses its meaning very quickly. I can't imagine anyone in 1981 on either side of the Atlantic thinking anything in that book funny. To be sure, the advertisements have a lovely period charm to them, but that wasn't the purpose of the book.

After his newspaper stint, Plum wrote very little in the way of topical articles for the magazines, but rather concentrated on general themes—the theatre, Hollywood, butlers. Although he used a number of them in *Louder and Funnier*, many others as good and as funny exist but have not been reprinted; *The Uncollected Wodehouse* contains some more.

Since his school days at Dulwich College (1894–1900) provided Plum with many happy memories and an opportunity to develop his various talents and abilities, it is only reasonable that the major portion of his writings for the newspapers and magazines reflected that interest. Just as the theatre, detective fiction, and media interviewers would pervade his nonfiction in later years, so did the activities of the public school and its sports figure largely in his early writings.

It was not until he came to the United States in 1909 and had two short stories sold in the same day that he began to shift ground and write what magazine editors wanted from him: romances with a humorous touch. Sometimes the humor is barely in evidence, but from 1915 onward it gradually takes over, until in the late 1920s the romance is incidental to the Wodehouse story. Most of the uncollected stories date from the early short story period (1909–16).

The first Bertie Wooster–Jeeves short story was collected in *The Man with Two Left Feet*, but it has never been placed in any of the Jeeves anthologies. And, as far as American collectors are concerned, it might as well never have been published in the United States at all, as the book was issued in the heart of the depression by a publisher of reprints. However, from the literary agent's file card we learn that Doubleday, Doran and Company, Plum's regular publisher at the time, rejected the collection and allowed the A. L. Burt Company to publish it. Thus, thinking it a reprint, as the title page included the line "By arrangement with Doubleday, Doran & Company, Inc.," many collectors passed it by. It is an extremely scarce item today.

With such cavalier treatment of the first Bertie-Jeeves story, we shouldn't be surprised at what befell Plum's first series character, Reggie Pepper. He initially appeared in the story "Disentangling Young Duggie" in the 30 March 1912 issue of *Collier's*, which ran in the August 1912 issue of the *Strand* as "Disentangling Old Percy." This story has still to be collected in a Wodehouse volume. The last of the seven Reggie Pepper stories, however, has finally reappeared in *The Uncollected Wodehouse* under the title "The Test Case."

One type of literary form Wodehouse worked in which has not as yet been collected is the short-short story told in verse. Plum did these during the middle of the first decade of the century. They dealt with animals, sports, card games, and the cockney. This last category held a strong fascination for Plum, though he gained his reputation from writing about the upper classes. Often in these early years he would write a poem, short story, or article in cockney dialect, providing a curious contrast to the rest of the Wodehouse oeuvre.

Collecting the uncollected PGW has long been a hobby of mine, and I take great pleasure in being able to offer fellow collectors and enthusiasts choice selections from time to time. I recently had a chance to publish another kind of uncollected Wodehouse, when Sam Carr of the English firm of B. T. Batsford Ltd. asked if I would put together a pictorial book of Plum's theatrical life. *The Theatre of P. G. Wodehouse* contains many rare photographs of Plum and his theatrical associates never before seen, in the context of all of his productions—musicals and straight plays—with opening-night cast credits and the titles of those published songs to which he wrote the lyrics.

And there is another project that needs doing: a collected book of his lyrics. Not only was he the first lyricist working on the American stage whose lyrics either advanced the plot or added substance to the characterization, but he was recognized by peers as being among the very best. When Ira Gershwin, Lorenz Hart, Oscar Hammerstein II, Howard Dietz, and Richard Rodgers go out of their way to praise Plum's lyrics, I feel these lyrics need to be rescued from the vagaries of their present existence in the form of single, unprotected pieces of sheet music. Since most songs from Broadway shows were not best sellers, the print runs were not very large; and they have become increasingly scarce, so that it is virtually impossible to gather a complete set today. I think Plum was at his wittiest when he produced his humorous historical lyrics, such as "Napoleon" and "Cleopatterer." His most famous lyric, of course, was "Bill," later incorporated into *Show Boat*, but originally written for *Oh, Lady! Lady!*

And what about the libretti for the musicals which Plum worked on with Guy Bolton? Shouldn't they, too, be collected? And why not a collected volume of two of his straight plays? They illustrate yet another facet of his career.

Plum's "golden years" in musical comedy were from 1917 to 1924. In those days the recording industry was still in comparative infancy, with recording being acoustic instead of electric, as we now have it. The acoustic process limited both the upper and lower registers, with the result that the sounds were rather boxy. Singers of popular songs were hired for their clarity of diction and the range of their voices. There were no original-cast recordings of musical plays, and one was lucky to find a singer who would record any selection from a Broadway show. It is therefore gratifying that Folkways Records has issued a long-playing disc, "The Theatre Lyrics of P. G. Wodehouse" which features rare contemporary recordings of some of his outstanding lyrics, mostly to the music of Jerome Kern.

For the collector of visual graphics, there are the magazine and book illustrations—not quite Plum, but supplementing Plum. However, that is beyond the scope of this article.

While much has already been accomplished, there is still work to be done. It is still possible to discover uncollected Wodehouse in several areas, and these considerable joys remain to the collector.

DAVID A. JASEN is widely known for his writings on, and bibliographies of, P. G. Wodehouse. More recently he has edited some of Wodehouse's uncollected works. He also plays ragtime piano.

On Collecting P. G. Wodehouse

CHARLES E. GOULD, JR.

To BEGIN on the stuffiest, most pedantic note possible, you *can't* collect P. G. Wodehouse, except by metonymy. And a very good thing, too. When Wodehouse died in 1975, I was a child of some thirty-one summers; and I confess now that it has been to me a secret source of pleasure and self-congratulation that I never, on a summer's day, from noon to dewy eve, drove the easy drive to Remsenburg to drape myself, like Lord Emsworth over the Empress's sty, over Wodehouse's front fence and say, "Here I am, having read and enjoyed all your books; do you work regular hours or wait for inspiration?" If reports of his sublime modesty are to be believed, he'd at least have affected to think I thought he was Edgar Wallace; at best he'd have asked me in for a drink, or maybe a cup of tea; and I could have "collected" him. I'm glad I didn't; but I do wish I'd met him.

In that contradiction reposes what seems to me to be the Collector's Dilemma: destined to have everything, he must guard diligently against the old curse of wanting merely to possess. I tell myself that the aging Wodehouse would have been delighted to see me, to add me to his own collection of fanatic fans, decent devotees, and learned letter-writers; but he would not have been. His life was writing those books, not accumulating enthusiasts for them—though as a collector I have come to discover that he answered all his fan mail, sometimes twice, and that far from holding himself as an icon among twentieth-century writers, he must have held himself something of an iconoclast. One hears chilling tales of famous (however reputable they may have been) authors who merely for the sake of doing down the collectors would have secretaries sign their letters "in his absence," and all the weary work of getting the great man's signature to be done over again.

But not Wodehouse. Not only did he reply to letters; unlike the Thomas Hardy whose gloomy work he strove so unceasingly to emulate, Wodehouse would inscribe and return to the bare-faced collector a novel which the b.-f.c. had sent him with that very goal in mind. That's how some of us managed to get Wodehouse books inscribed to us, and I say that more as a testimony to his generosity than to our grasping cleverness. It is clear that Wodehouse understood Lord Emsworth's Scarab Syndrome, however little he himself shared it. As a matter of fact, I have been told that Wodehouse shared few if any of our collectors' acquisitive instincts, being content, as his daughter Leonora wrote in *The American Magazine* for October 1931, with "an occasional dollar to buy tobacco with and an account at a bookshop." "He would sell a check for five hundred dollars to anyone at any time for a dollar-fifty net cash," she wrote; and I not only believe that, but regard his attitude as being worthy of emulation by the collector.

I have a friend in England who lies awake nights worrying that my Collector's Impulse will overcome my Reader's, and that I will spoil the fun of reading Wodehouse, for myself at least, by engaging wholly in sordid commercial traffic merely to acquire things. His fears are groundless, of course; but only because my soul is so pure. That is surely a danger which *other* collectors must face, and guard diligently against. *Guard diligently against*: that is my recurrent theme—as against the troops of Midian, who prowl and prowl around; for, after all, it is not the mere possession of these things that makes the collector what he is, nor is it the acquiring, nor the discovering, nor the delight of acquiring or discovering, that makes the collector's life worth living. It is, rather, that he is collecting what Wodehouse *did*, what he *made*, what indeed—if the authorities are to be believed—made *his* life worth living.

There is, as Vergil and Wordsworth knew, a life in things, and it is possible to see into it. The collector's impulse to acquire, at best, allies itself with that possibility. It may, of course, permit itself off-moments, as Lord Emsworth's characteristically does: it is a noble achievement to come up with something no other collector has got, especially if he was trying particularly hard to get it; but while Wodehouse would understand that, and doubtless applaud it with a chuckle, we do not serve his memory or his work as best we might if that is our governing precept. It is my wish here to dismiss the charge that collectors are mere acquisitors, that their impassioned quest to *have* everything stops with that. It doesn't. It must be true that a first edition is closer to the spirit that produced it than is a uniform-edition reprint; a first edition in dust wrapper is a stage closer, a typescript closer still, a manuscript or holograph letter as close as we can go. It is not ignoble so to seek; but it is not exactly natural, either. Not everybody cares about such proximity to the originating spirit; and that, above all, is what I think the collector does do.

II

Just what he cares about as material for collecting, however, is worth a certain amount of consideration. R. B. D. French, whose book about Wodehouse is to my mind the most spirited yet to appear, has been content for decades to have only a reading copy of each title. His contentment with the text alone has been such that from time to time he would swap first editions for reading copies, the only proviso being that the reading copy be readable. Such contentment argues a purity of soul greater than mine, and perhaps a spiritual proximity to the original greater than mine as well. But such collectors do exist, and they are not to be despised. Indeed, I was once one myself, in the dear dead days beyond recall, when my object was merely to have a reading copy of every *book*—not even of every title, but simply of every book—that Wodehouse wrote. I blush to remember a letter I wrote to Herbert Jenkins some years ago, begging them to sort out the duplicity of variant titles (this was, of course, before Mr. Jasen's invaluable bibliography appeared), and being gratified to learn that I already had *Company for Henry*, though on this side it called itself *The Purloined Paperweight*. I remember with a chill that runs up and down the spine my unreadiness to pay two dollars for a first edition of *Big Money*, simply because I already had *Big Money* in a second edition. (I sprung the two dollars anyway, and was rewarded for my extravagance: I found that the illustrated endpapers in the second edition were reversed from those in the first: not everybody knows this; now you do, no extra charge.) Even more to my shame, I remember walking halfway across the West End of London and then, having decided that I was not too proud to add a mere anthology edited by Wodehouse to my collection, back again to shell out the astronomical sum of fifty pence for *A Century of Humour*. But far worse than that, I recall the impecunious ignorance with which I once turned down the unsolicited offer of a copy of Lady Cynthia Asquith's *The Treasure Ship*, containing the first book publication of "Pillingshot, Detective."

If a sorrow's crown of sorrow is remembering happier things, it must also be that part of the secret pleasure experienced by any collector emerges from his memory not only of the treasure he has quietly wrested from the possession of the unalert or uninitiated, but also of the treasure he has somehow let slip through his grasp. For one's satisfaction in the purity of his soul, there's nothing like the one that got away. Somebody is kicking himself for letting go a first English edition of *Leave It to Psmith*, published in 1923 but dated 1924, thinking it was a later edition; somebody somewhere has passed up or passed on the A. L. Burt publication of *The Man with Two Left Feet*, thinking it was a reprint; and perhaps there is even someone who has let pass through his hands a copy of the chimerical *White Hope*, which somehow crept into Simon and Schuster's list of books by P. G. Wodehouse about 1962 and has been there ever since.

What every collector wants, presumably, for starters, is a complete run of all the Wodehouse books, in both English and American first editions, in dust wrappers, all in mint or at least very fine condition. Such a perfect collection may exist. It is, I think, true that Wodehouse himself did not have one; or that, if he did, he did not spend the happy hours telling it over that a collector would have done. In short, it must be true that to some degree the collector is indeed motivated, or even governed, by the material, by the wish to acquire, by the desire to have his hands on the objective correlative of what finally is a spiritual reality.

And what a wealth of objective correlatives there is, thanks to the prolific genius of that presiding spirit! Not only are there the books; there is the sheet music; there are the magazines, the covers of the magazines, the illustrations for the magazines; the dust wrappers, the illustrations for the dust wrappers, the illustrations for the books and endpapers; the theatre programs, the posters; the articles, reviews, and advertisements; the letters, the manuscripts, and the sort of memorabilia which Wodehouse himself made fun of people for collecting. Remember the lengths, in "High Stakes," to which Bradbury Fisher is prepared to go in order to acquire from Gladstone Botts "the authentic baffy used by Bobby Jones in his first important contest," and that at the end of the story he cables his London agents "to instruct them to buy J. H. Taylor's shirt stud for my collection."

That sort of thing is hardly a step beyond the graceful plea made by Mr. Richard Usborne in a letter to the London *Times* in June 1980, for somebody to come forth with the striped umbrella which Wodehouse won as a trophy in a golf tournament in North Carolina. I hope that, or a cricket cap or shirt stud (or brass paper fastener, which would have served the nonsartorial Wodehouse as well as it served Lord Emsworth) turns up; but the man who once remarked to an interviewer, "Ah, yes, what memories I would have if only I could remember them," was hardly likely to look after his own memorabilia or, I suspect, to look upon our manic desire to do so with anything but wry amusement. After all (in the company of Fielding and Dickens), he even lost track of his own characters: in *Jeeves and the Tie That Binds*, Bertie's headmaster Aubrey Upjohn emerges inexplicably as Arnold Abney, a pedagogue who had appeared only once, nearly sixty years earlier, in *The Little Nugget*. "I can't think how I came to make such a bloomer," Wodehouse wrote to me in 1972 (in what is now a *collectible* letter). "Comes of writing so much."

And, of course, that's just what it comes of. Part of the fascination and delight which keep the Wodehouse collector going is that there *is* so much, though much of what there is becomes scarcer and scarcer. As James Heineman, whose Wodehouse collection is the Empress of Wodehouse collections, remarked recently, "We don't collect Wodehouse; he collects us." Always beyond our own luck or skill or pocketbook; always beyond the cooperation or connivance of the dealers with whom we trade; always beyond the bulk or purity of our collection and collecting, are the brain and spirit of the creative genius who wrote so much.

III

It was a rather auntlike creature (actually an elderly cousin once removed) who got me started, with *Blandings Castle*. In those days of banished youth I was spending my summers reading the sort of thing (I say this with all due respect) that Jeeves likes: Spinoza, with an occasional dash of Marcus Aurelius or St. Augustine just to keep things light. Otway could wait: no harm, I said to myself in phrases which Wodehouse himself was uttering at about the same time, in seeing what this frivolous youngster had to say. (I had no idea that he was a spavined septuagenarian, let alone that he was still writing.) What he had to say was, of course, captivating; and I began to "collect" him for the best possible reason: simply to have more of his books to read. The auntlike creature's supply ran to about eleven, one of which had been spoiled when she threw it at me in astonished rage that I had grown roughly to man's estate without ever hearing of P. G. Wodehouse and one of which, I discovered a few years later, was the first printing of *Biffen's Millions* which says "P. J. Wodehouse" on the spine. A somewhat overwritten letter to Simon and Schuster about that brought a most cordial and subtle reply from Peter Schwed; but even it did not suggest to me except in a vague way that I was handling "collector's items." Would that it had done, for in those days one could with some regularity find Wodehouse on secondhand shelves for fifty cents or a dollar (if one still can, please tell me where); and I often did, but what I was "collecting" then was simply one copy of each book, without much regard for condition, and that one edition might be more pleasant to have than another had simply never occurred to me.

It was my wife, to her yet undiminished pecuniary regret, who really started the trouble. Seeing my glassy stare as in the dusty recesses of some church basement sale I fondled a Wodehouse book trying to remember whether I had a copy or not, she began to say, "Oh, go ahead and buy it." From there it was but a step to noticing editions, cataloguing what I had, keeping with me a list, producing a wants list ... and the rest can be imagined readily enough by any collector. You tell yourself you can take it or leave it alone, but one day you find you're hooked, and that's that.

If, as I have already suggested it is, it is mildly though perversely pleasant to recall or imagine the gems one has missed out on, it is of course not the least of the collector's pleasures to reflect upon the associations that his collecting has generated. These for me have been mainly dealers: most of my best friends think I'm crazy; but they, and even passing acquaintances, have sent me things which they assumed, rightly, that in my lunacy I would like to have. And though over the years I have known dealers both patronizing and impatient about a name they have often mispronounced, more often than not they have been helpful and even indulgent in their dealings with a collector. With increasing frequency, of course, they are now saying, "Wodehouse? Can't keep him on the shelves." But it is still possible, every now and then, to find something on the shelves, because Wodehouse is an author whose books people want to read, and that is a pleasant truth, a safeguard against his becoming a mere collectible.

Any collector, I suppose, takes pleasure in showing off his collection, especially to other collectors who will pay him the high compliment of furious envy. Wodehouse novels abound with such people, including Lord Emsworth in the Scarab Phase and Uncle Tom and his old silver. There is, however, always the risk, perhaps less grave in life than in literature, that a prize piece will be pinched, and the mortal fear that one's secret sources will be found out. But perhaps the dark doings at Blandings Castle and Brinkley Court need not trouble us here. Nobody has ever pinched anything from me (though by the letter of Wodehouse's own law in *Stiff Upper Lip, Jeeves*, if you are a collector it is not in the strictest sense of the word pinching if you pinch from another collector); and I have never pinched anything myself. I am, however, as politely cagey as I can be, and I urge upon others the same reticence about where things can be found. There is no doubt, as Joseph Connolly and others have pointed out, that the Wodehouse market is growing or, as you may prefer, inflating itself; and I am ready to acknowledge my share of the responsibility. As a chaste sign in a nameless bookstore in an unknown town in an unidentified state (where I still find Wodehouse appearing on the shelves) says, "The more you pay for it, the more it's worth."

Beyond a certain point, or beyond a certain level of casual satisfaction, collecting by its nature does imply competitiveness as well as acquisitiveness; and though I have said that at its best collecting is not governed by these, clearly the best *collections* have been; for there is, after all, a limited supply of the raw material of which a fine collection can be made. The impulse to upgrade and refine can become a quite legitimate *need* to the serious collector; and the desire for completeness can become a scholarly or aesthetic obligation. In such lofty mode have I from time to time justified spending the household food budget on a copy with a dust wrapper I had never before seen, or on a copy of *Jeeves* on whose flyleaf no loving idiot had inscribed in purple crayon, "To Old Popsie, from MacKintosh, with the hope that this gift may lead to feelings warmer and deeper than those of ordinary friendship."

IV

Nobody needs from me advice on how to go about it; but I do have a few rules of the collector's thumb which may be presented very briefly: (1) Never correct a bookseller's pronunciation of the name Wodehouse, nor explain that he, though immortal, is dead. If you can suggest that you share the prejudice that he wrote foolish stories for the simple-minded, that's all to the good, especially if you have managed the appearance of one who is "only shopping for a friend." (2) In the same vein, try not to appear too knowledgeable: the dullest dealer may be put on guard by your feverish quest for the inverted watermark on page 55, or by your remarking aloud that you have never before seen *that* title in a *yellow* binding. (3) The quest for magazines containing Wodehouse stories or serials may frequently be disguised as the much more believable (if far less sensible) quest for F. Scott Fitzgerald, Ernest Hemingway, W. Somerset Maugham, Agatha Christie, or Kenneth L. Roberts; these names, among many dealers in ephemera, are known quantities, and may well be commanding a respectable price already; letting on that you are looking for, indeed buying, something else altogether can only cause alarm and confusion. Many dealers fear their own prices as much as we do. (4) Do not allow your brow to sickly o'er with the pale cast of helpless misery if a dealer tells you (as sooner or later one will) that oh, yes, he sold a *Pothunters*, mind in dust wrapper, only last week for about ten, too bad you missed it; just smile coyly and remark, "Oh, yes, there are some about."

Those who know me best will recognize in this seemingly cynical advice the eye of chilled steel and gimlet voice which have made me the force I am in the collector's world; armed therewith, you too are ready to go bravely into its marts and thoroughfares. It is a world as fascinating for its uncertainty as for its certainty, as stimulating for its frustrations as for its satisfactions. Just as no two books, unless perhaps absolutely mint, are identical, so are no two collections identical. Each acquisition will have both a character and a history of its own; and however individually minor or unimportant these may seem, they combine to give the collection a character of its own too. One man's thingummy may well be another man's major general, and there is blessedly no reason for any collector to be embarrassed about what he has or does not have. If a book captures the spirit of its creator for the imagination of its owner, it's worth collecting: we can hardly find fault with that, and the book with the missing spine may well be the soul of the collection. In the final analysis, I think, Mr. Heineman is predictably right: we are not so much the collectors as the collected, and time cannot wither nor custom stale the infinite variety of what we are up to, so spacious was the achievement of the man who put us up to it.

CHARLES E. GOULD, JR., took his B.A. in Latin at Bowdoin College. Rem acu tetigisti, *one of Jeeves's things, is about as far as he got; and at the University of Connecticut he took his M.A. in English, concentrating on that famous quatrain by James Graham, first Marquess of Montrose. For ten years he has taught English at Kent School. He would like to describe himself as "a bald-headed, spectacled plug-ugly," and may eventually deserve to do so, but for the moment must settle for far less:* opisthognathous *about sums it up.*

Holy or Unholy Writ

RICHARD USBORNE

"Clarence, what year was that terrible argument between young Gregory Parsloe and Lord Burper? When Parsloe stole the old chap's glasses and sold them at a shop in the Edgware Road? '96? I should have said later than that. Perhaps you're right, though."

Lady Constance cried out.

"Galahad! You're not going to print stories like that about our nearest neighbor?"

"Certainly I am. It's the best story in my book...."

WAIT A MINUTE. There's something wrong there, surely. I thought Parsloe had pinched Lord Burper's *false teeth*, and had *pawned* them in the Edgware Road. But the book here says "glasses" and "sold." And later on Galahad refers to the great story of Parsloe and the snowballs. *Snowballs?* No, no. It was the story of Parsloe and the *prawns* which broke butler Beach into a most unbutlerine roar of laughter when he read it in his deck chair near the laurel bush outside the back door of the castle. It was in Gally's Reminiscences, that dreaded *succès de scandale* that was never published. The autograph manuscript was eaten up in her sty by the Empress of Blandings. The horrible Percy Pilbeam had hidden it under the straw there, not knowing that the building was to be the new bijou residence of Lord Emsworth's prize-winning pig. "False teeth," "pawned," and "prawns" are certainly the readings in Wodehouse's *Summer Lightning* (published 1929 by Herbert Jenkins, later Barrie and Jenkins, later Hutchinsons, London, and as *Fish Preferred* by Doubleday, Doran, New York).

The book in front of me at the moment is P. G. Wodehouse's *Summer Lightning*, adapted by Tony Augarde for the Oxford University Press in its Alpha General Fiction series, good books simplified, for foreign students learning English, into a basic vocabulary of fifteen hundred words. And in those fifteen hundred was no room, obviously, for "false teeth," "pawn," or "prawn."

Some years ago a competitor on the BBC-TV "Mastermind" program had offered "P. G. Wodehouse's books" as his special subject. The BBC asked me to give them twenty or more questions to ask him, with the answers. Now, what if one of my questions had been "Give one of the stories about Sir Gregory Parsloe that Galahad Threepwood was going to put into his Reminiscences," and what if the expert had answered, "Lord Burper's glasses that Parsloe had sold in the Edgware Road" or "The story of the snowballs"? Magnus Magnussen would have looked at his card and said, "I can't give you that. It says here 'prawns,' not 'snowballs,' and it was Lord Burper's false teeth, not glasses, and Parsloe didn't sell them, he pawned them, in the Edgware Road." Wouldn't the competitor have had a genuine grievance against the BBC, and the BBC a genuine grievance against me, and I against the Oxford University Press?

The very pricey market these days for first editions and original manuscripts and typescripts of Wodehouse's works may be partially explained by the fact that there are so many known variants of them now legitimately in print that the *ipsissima verba* are that much the more precious. Some bookworm must soon establish a canon, agreed on by all Wodehouse publishers, and then make a variorum volume.

Wodehouse himself reran certain stories. For instance, in the hard-to-find original *My Man Jeeves* there are tales told by and about Reggie Pepper which in *Carry on, Jeeves*, *The Jeeves Omnibus*, and *The World of Jeeves* are told, with minor changes, by and about Bertie Wooster. Then that early novel, *The Prince and Betty* (the British Library has this, incidentally, in Esperanto as well as English), appeared first in America, published in February 1912 by W. J. Watt and Company. The main character in this is Rupert Smith, an American from Harvard. He animates a sleepy New York magazine, *Peaceful Moments*, and turns it into a crusading, anti-slum-landlord force for good. In the English version, published in May 1912 by Mills and Boon, there is no New York sequence, no *Peaceful Moments*. There is still a Prince, of Mervo (a Mediterranean island), and still a Betty Silver, whom he eventually wins, but in England, not America. Then, three years later, *Psmith, Journalist* was published, by Adam

PLATE 13

As a regular contributor to England's most popular magazine, the *Strand*, Wodehouse was often a headliner.

PLATE 14

A sampling of magazines in which Wodehouse's stories and articles regularly appeared.

PLATE 15

PLATE 16

A Jeeves provenance.

P. G. WODEHOUSE
REMSENBURG, N. Y.

October 20.1960

Dear Mr Simmons.

Thank you for your letter. That's very interesting about Jeeves and the J.S.Fletcher book. If it was published in 1931, he did the pinching, not me, for my Jeeves dates back to 1916.

But, my gosh, you'd think a writer like Fletcher would have known of the existence of Jeeves by 1931, for I had had four Jeeves books out by then.

I was watching a county match on the Cheltenham ground before the first war, and one of the Gloucestershire bowlers was called Jeeves. I suppose the name stuck in my mind, and I named my Jeeves after him.

I will certainly do some Ukridge stories if I can get the requisite ideas! At the moment I am half way through a Blandings Castle novel.

Yours sincerely

P.G. Wodehouse

Found—the looks of Goole's own Jeeves

A photograph has come to light in the Goole Times files of Percy Jeeves, the Goole-bred professional cricketer on whom P. G. Wodehouse based the famous immaculate gentleman's gentleman of the Bertie Wooster stories.

Jeeves, who lived with his parents initially in a house in Parliament Street, was renowned during his tragically short career with Warwickshire for impeccable grooming, spotless flannels and smartly ironed shirts. It was this appearance which inspired Wodehouse, a cricket fan often to be found at Edgbaston during the summers of 1913 and 1914.

Our picture shows the gentlemanly hairstyle and the perfectly-placed cap, but time has dimmed the impression of how neat were the other items of his dress. Nonetheless his stance has poise and the grace of the halcyon days of English cricket in which he lived.

Along with this photograph, published in the Goole Times of August 4, 1916, there is a profoundly sad report which reads: "It is with deep regret that we have to announce the death in action of Pte Percy Jeeves, son of a Mr and Mrs E. Jeeves, of Manuel Street, Goole."

With a similar sense of honour to that of his smooth but quick-thinking fictional descendant, Jeeves had enlisted at the commencement of the first world war and was drafted to France in October, 1915.

During the brutal assault on human life and dignity which became known as the battle of the Somme, a portion of a German shell put an end to the life and career of what Wisden described as "one of the great bowlers of the future."

Percy Jeeves' parents were still living in Goole when their 28-year-old son died. His father, Edwin Jeeves, was well-known as one of the longest-serving guards with the Lancashire and Yorkshire railway company, and worked on the Haxey route for many years.

The biography of Percy Jeeves has been written in this newspaper before. He made his cricketing name in Goole as the star of the Alexandra Street Board School side, made his debut with the Goole Town second eleven at the age of 17, was transferred to the first eleven in the same season, and in 1909 took up a professional engagement with Hawes Cricket Club.

These, of course, were the days when some of the game's best-known characters played professionally in the minor leagues. The great Syd Barnes, still considered by many England's greatest ever bowler, would play wherever an offer was made. Jeeves made his county debut for Warwickshire against the Australians in 1912, while qualifying for that county, but only had two seasons before the war in which he showed his great promise.

Frank R. Foster, the great Warwicks and England fast bowler, described him as "the greatest all-rounder in the game in 1914." Expected to develop as a bowler, he was not terrifically fast but got a lot of life off the pitch.

He also played football for Swinefleet United FC in the Goole and District League, and the only photograph previously known to exist of him dates from this period, though it is too faded to reproduce.

Percy Jeeves once played for Players against Gentlemen at the Oval. Immaculate as Wodehoue's well-known and well-loved character, he was one of the most gentlemanly Players ever to have turned in a match-winning performance.

Private Jeeves

7.6.78.   Back 98 Boothferry Road,
                       Goole,
                       North Humberside.

Dear Lord Donaldson,

I remember reading some time ago that your wife was planning to write a book on P.G.Wodehouse. Perhaps she will find this article of mine from the Goole Times of some help. There are, in fact, more pictures in the possession of a member of the Jeeves family, and there was an earlier article with more details which I could look up if it was useful.

Yours sincerely,

Brian Groom

Jeeves as seen by various illustrators.

PLATE 18

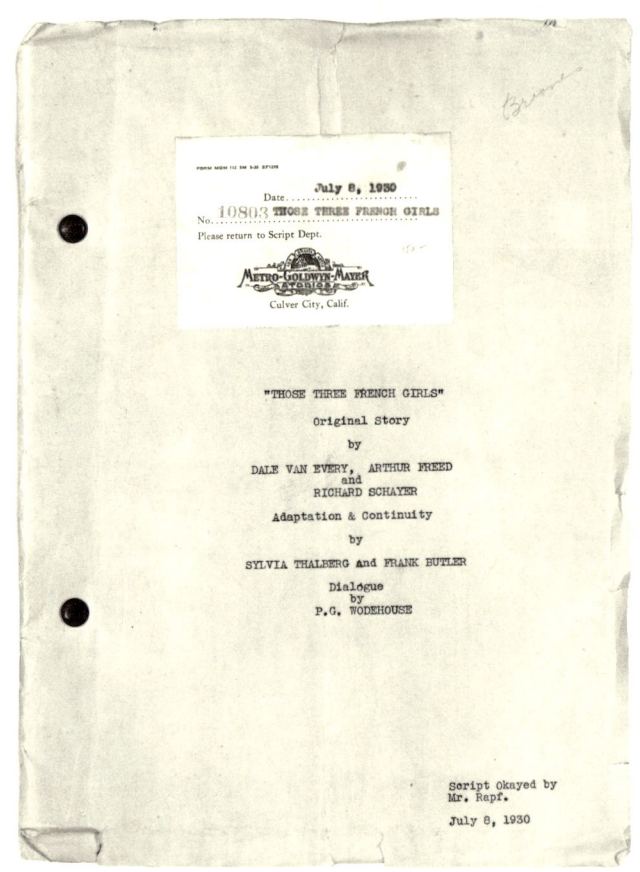

The script, a poster, and a still of the movie *Those Three French Girls* (1930) for which Wodehouse wrote the dialogue.

PLATE 19

The sheet music of the play (1934) and the 1956 movie poster of Cole Porter's *Anything Goes* with book by P. G. Wodehouse.

A film adaptation (1936) starring Robert Montgomery of Wodehouse's novel *Piccadilly Jim* (1924).

PLATE 21

A Damsel in Distress (1937) featured Fred Astaire, Joan Fontaine, Gracie Allen, George Burns; Wodehouse wrote the novel and the script.

PLATE 22

Jeeves achieves movie stardom.
His name all but enters
the English language.

PLATE 23

A few of the plays Wodehouse made possible.

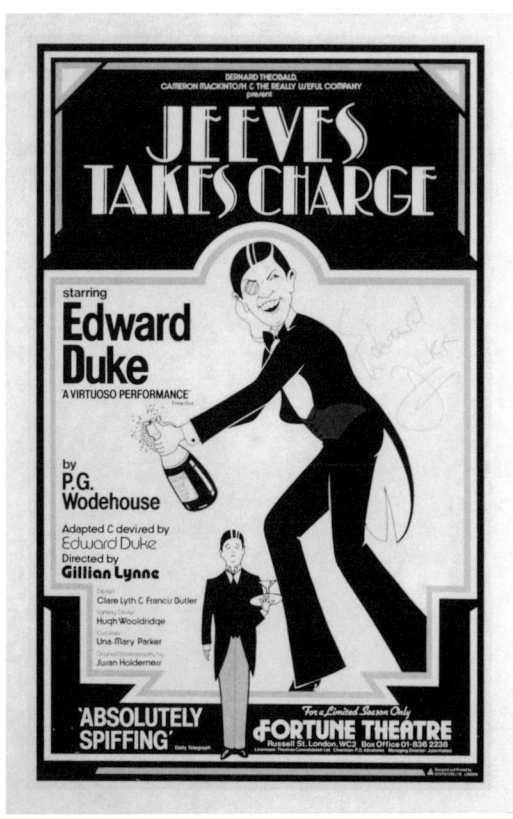
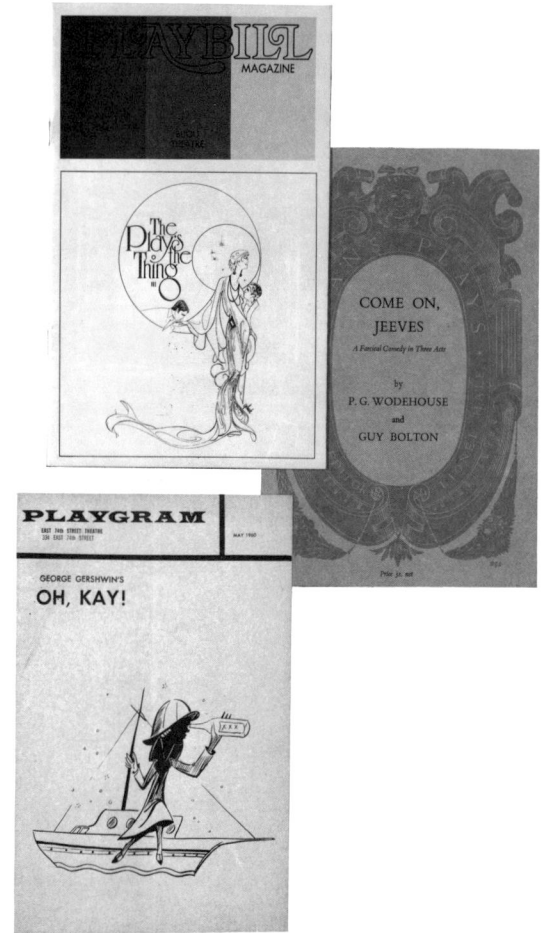
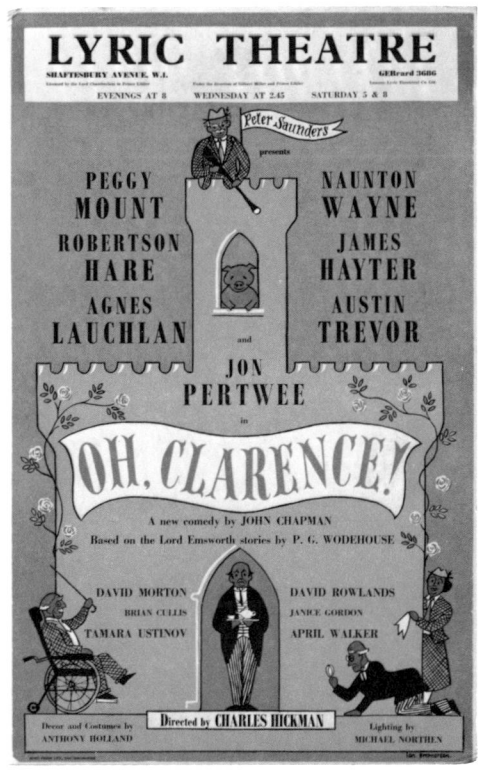

PLATE 24

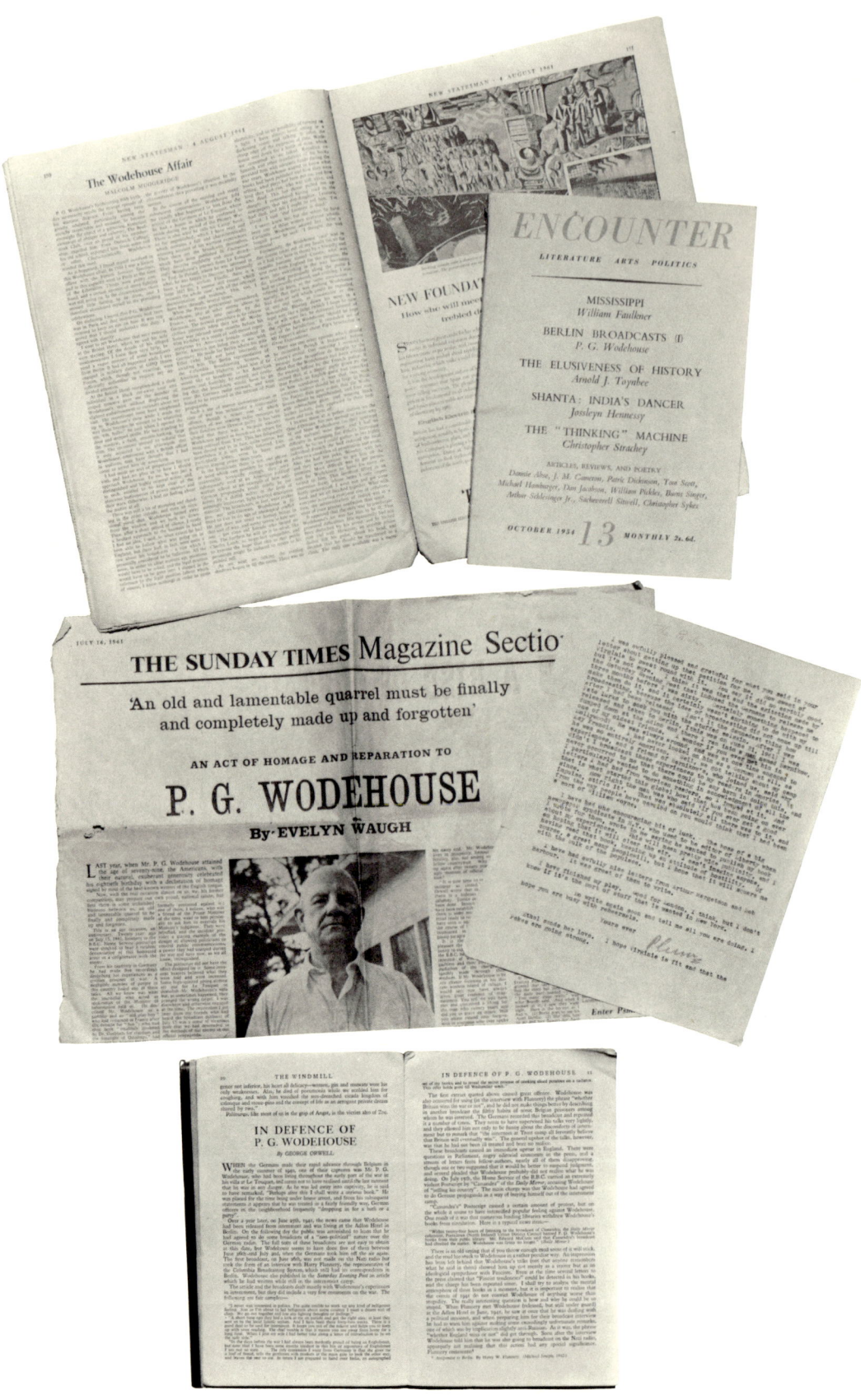

The Berlin broadcasts explained by (clockwise from top left) Malcolm Muggeridge, *New Statesman*, 1961; P. G. Wodehouse, *Encounter*, 1954; P. G. Wodehouse, letter to Guy Bolton, 1945; George Orwell, *The Windmill*, 1945; Evelyn Waugh, *The Sunday Times*, 1961.

and Charles Black, in London (but never in America). In *Psmith, Journalist* Englishman Rupert Smith, who calls himself Psmith, of Eton, Sedleigh, and Cambridge University, comes to New York and takes over, and animates, the magazine *Cosy Moments* and turns it into a crusading etc., etc., as in the American version of *The Prince and Betty*. Autophagous cannibalism? Abuse of copyright? Author's bounty? Bookworms and bibliographers, fettle your footnotes!

Wodehouse allowed his own ending of *Much Obliged, Jeeves* (1971) to be changed (by Peter Schwed of Simon and Schuster, I believe) in the American edition, renamed *Jeeves and the Tie That Binds*. We have recently seen Jeeves's life story run completely off the Wodehouse rails in C. Northcote Parkinson's *Jeeves*. In that merry molehill of myth Jeeves ends up as landlord of, and sole storyteller in, The Angler's Rest public house on the Shropshire estate of the Earl of Yaxley (né Bertram Wooster) and his Countess (née Roberta Wickham). You mustn't believe a word of it. I have myself, in adapting two Wooster/Jeeves novels for BBC radio, changed the Rev. "Stinker" Pinker from an all-England rugby footballer into a Pegasus association footballer. And, more heinous, I have given dear Aunt Dahlia oaths and repartee that are not in the sacred texts. But those were words, winged and never in print. I could plead for mitigation of punishment, if any, on that score, I think.

We bookworms (for, adaptation jobs apart, I count myself a Wodehouse bookworm) must keep the lifelines clear back to the original sources. A small point. When the single-volume *Mike* (1912) was, in 1953, split into two books, *Mike at Wrykyn* and *Mike and Psmith*, Wodehouse's English publisher updated the names of the real-life star all-England cricketers in it. C. B. Fry had been a great maker of centuries in Test Matches before 1912, for instance. In the 1953 reprint he became David Sheppard, who, at that date, was the cricketer every schoolboy would have wished to be; playing for Cambridge, Sussex, and England (twenty-two Test Matches), and he was to be England's captain the next year, 1954. At the time I am writing this Sheppard is the Anglican Bishop of Liverpool and, if I read the ecclesiastical gossip column aright, he may be an archbishop by the time of the Wodehouse centenary. What English schoolboy of today sees the cricket cap under the mitre?

I give you an even smaller point—a point pointed out to me by Wodehouse's, and my, friend Alec Waugh. In *The Inimitable Jeeves* (1923) there is a story "The Delayed Exit of Claude and Eustace." Bertie's twin cousins Claude and Eustace, in London when they should have been heading for jobs that were waiting for them in South Africa, were thrusting their unwelcome young attentions on Bertie's beautiful actress friend, Marion Wardour. At Jeeves's suggestion, Miss Wardour told the boys she was heading for South Africa herself, to take up a theatrical engagement, but would be traveling overland to Madeira to join the ship there. So Claude and Eustace both, but separately, asked Jeeves to book them passages (at Bertie's expense) for South Africa on the boat sailing tomorrow from Southampton. Little did either know that the other would be on board. Little did either know that Jeeves had booked them into the same double cabin. Little did either know that Miss Wardour had no intention of joining them, or the ship, at Madeira. The slip, that persists in the autograph edition of *The Inimitable Jeeves*, but which Wodehouse corrected for *The Jeeves Omnibus* (1931) and *The World of Jeeves* (1967), is that you couldn't travel overland to Madeira, since it is an island. "Overland" becomes "by another boat" in the two volumes of the collected Bertie/Jeeves stories.

Then we must reckon for the one-shotter shortened versions of novels that Wodehouse often sold for prebook publication in magazines. The story, told in 18,000 words in one issue of, say, *The Ladies' Home Journal*, appeared next week at 65,000-word length in hardback on the bookstalls. Wodehouse did his own cutting. I haven't closely compared texts, an 18,000-word one-shotter against the full novel. But if he meant false teeth, pawned and prawns, he would have said so. The length was constricted to 18,000, but the Wodehouse vocabulary wasn't filleted down to 1500 words.

I have just received my May/June issue of the current (1980) *Saturday Evening Post*. In it there is a rerun of the "Jeeves Takes Charge" story that they first ran sixty-four years earlier, in 1916. I am more than a little disturbed. I find, first, an illustration of Bertie with a monocle and an ear-to-ear red moustache. Did Wodehouse ever specify a monocle for Bertie? I do not think the "Spot of Art" story is conclusive. About moustaches I am on surer ground. Twice Bertie grew moustaches, in defiance of

Jeeves's disapproval, and both times they were small, like David Niven's. In one case Jeeves said it looked like a stain of mulligatawny soup on the upper lip. In both cases the moustaches were forfeit at the end of the story or novel. Well, illustrations to Wodehouse stories and decorations for dust jackets of Wodehouse books can claim—or anyway they enjoy—a license. The Empress of Blandings is still frequently—indeed, on the cover of the Oxford University Press 1500-word-vocabulary *Summer Lightning*—pictured as a pink-and-white porker. She is, and was, specified twice in the texts as a Black Berkshire.

But Bertie's moustache and monocle are not my chief complaint against the 1980 rerun of "Jeeves Takes Charge." In its second paragraph Bertie is telling us how he came to be spending a week at Easeby, his Uncle Willoughby's place in Shropshire. He says: "I generally did this in the summer, *for the old boy liked to have me round and, being down in his will for a substantial chunk of the right stuff,* I always obliged him. . . ."

"Jeeves Takes Charge," which relates Jeeves's arrival from the agency, is the first story in terms of fictional chronology. In the happy half century and more of real time and of multiplication of Bertie/Jeeves books, no explanation is ever given for Bertie's never-failing pecuniosity, solvency, easy circumstances. Call it anything but "oofiness." "Oofy" Prosser is the rich man of the Drones: certainly Bertie is not in the Oofy class. Bertie once refers to himself as "stagnant with the stuff" and never has to borrow a fiver "till the end of the month" as so many of his friends at the Drones do. He is never poverty-stricken. He is never employed. His income is undoubtedly unearned. Where then did the money come from?

According to the extra twenty-seven words (my italics, above) now injected in that part of "Jeeves Takes Charge" Mark 2, a sizable chunk of his capital would have come from his Uncle Willoughby . . . his late Uncle Willoughby. We never hear of him, or Easeby, again in the last sixty-plus years of Wodehouse's prolific output.

Later in the rerun story in the *Post* the financial point is again touched on. It reads: ". . . as I was more or less dependent on Uncle Willoughby I couldn't very well marry without his approval. . . ." This amplifies the suggestion that Bertie relied on Uncle Willoughby at death to set him up for life.

But in all the texts of the collected stories the sentence reads: ". . . as *at that time* I was more or less dependent on Uncle Willoughby," etc., etc. . . . The May/June 1980 *Post* does not have that important "at that time." Why? We had known that at that time Bertie was getting an allowance from his uncle. We assumed that he became self-financing somehow later and we had amused ourselves theorizing about the "how" of somehow. The *Post* today clearly doesn't like loose ends and has solved the problem for us. Is it our duty to accept this post-mortem solution? I think not. We bookworms must surely keep our noses clean . . . keep them stuck into the primary sources. And now—only now—I find that the *Post* version *is* the primary source. Wodehouse himself altered it in republication.

It is difficult enough in a corpus of seventy or more books of Wodehouse fiction, and in a succession of new editions of Wodehouse in English in England and America, to spot variants from the originals. We wallow in a blissful world of formidable aunts, prize pigs, fizzy girls with masculine-seeming Christian names (Bobbie, Stiffy, Corky, etc.), endless house parties, goof golfers, hammock weather all summer long in England(!), dyspeptic American millionaires, jobless younger sons, portly and porty butlers, delightfully fiendish children, small dogs that nip ankles, Scotch gardeners, bossy fiancées (how many did Bertie have? I make it at least a dozen, one at a time), bishops buoyant with Buck-U-Uppo, and crusty magistrates, on the bench or retired, rich with the fines of decades in their bank balances. But the price of our contentment must be constant vigilance—to enjoy, if we will, the thought of your Parsloe selling Lord Burper's glasses in the Edgware Road. But we must take it with a knowing pinch of salt, knowing the true, the original, the vintage P. G. Wodehouse text. It was Lord Burper's *false teeth*—Lord Emsworth vouched for that: he had seen them in a small cigar box—and Parsloe had *pawned* them.

There is one further source of unholy writ which bookworms should study, the misprint due to faulty typesetting and faulty proofreading. In my copy (first edition, 1971, Barrie and Jenkins) of *Much Obliged, Jeeves* I find Boko Littleworth for Boko Fittleworth, Worpledon for Worplesdon, county for country, Steeple Bumpleigh for Woollam Chersey, and Arnold Abney for Aubrey Upjohn (as Bertie's headmaster at preparatory school). And why Bertie's old Communist "man" Brinkley has changed his name to Bingley is never explained. *We* can see why: it's because to have Brinkley the ex-valet now living near Aunt Dahlia's place, Brinkley Court, would jar. But old (aged ninety) Wodehouse should have been helped over that hurdle by an alert editor somewhere if not by his own ingenuity.

Then, last horror, Jeeves, on page 191, quotes a line and a half of "Lucretius, sir, 99–55 BC," and misses out an essential *"quod."* (These errors also appear in the American edition, entitled *Jeeves and the Tie That Binds*.)

Well, let Wodehouse himself have the last words, in felicitous verse:

PRINTER'S ERROR

As o'er my latest book I pored,
   Enjoying it immensely,
I suddenly exclaimed "Good Lord!"
   And gripped the volume tensely.
"Golly!" I cried. I writhed in pain.
"They've done it on me once again!"
   And furrows creased my brow.
I'd written (which I thought quite good)
"Ruth, ripening into womanhood,
Was now a girl who knocked men flat
And frequently got whistled at,"
And some vile, careless, casual gook
Had spoiled the best thing in the book
   By printing "not"
     (Yes, "not," great Scott!)
       When I had written "now."

On murder in the first degree
   The Law, I knew, is rigid:
Its attitude, if A kills B,
   To A is always frigid.
It counts it not a trivial slip
If on behalf of authorship
   You liquidate compositors.
This kind of conduct it abhors
   And seldom will allow.
Nevertheless, I deemed it best
And in the public interest
To buy a gun, to oil it well,
Inserting what is called a shell,
   And go and pot
    With sudden shot
      This printer who had printed "not"
        When I had written "now."

I tracked the bounder to his den
   Through private information:
I said, "Good afternoon," and then
   Explained the situation:
"I'm not a fussy man," I said.
"I smile when you put 'rid' for 'red'
And 'bad' for 'bed' and 'hoad' for 'head'
   And 'bolge' instead of 'bough.'
When 'wone' appears in lieu of 'wine'
Or if you alter 'Cohn' to 'Schine,'
   I never make a row.
I know how easy errors are.
But this time you have gone too far
By printing 'not' when you knew what
   I really wrote was 'now.'
Prepare," I said, "to meet your God
Or, as you'd say, your Goo or Bod,
   Or possibly your Gow."

A few weeks later into court
   I came to stand my trial.
The Judge was quite a decent sort,
   He said, "Well, cocky, I'll
Be passing sentence in a jiff
And so, my poor unhappy stiff,
If you have anything to say,
Now is the moment. Fire away.
   You have?"
     I said, "And how!
Me lud, the facts I don't dispute.
I did, I own it freely, shoot
This printer through the collar stud.
What else could I have done, me lud?
   He's printed 'not' . . ."
    The Judge said, "*What!*
      When you had written 'now'?
God bless my soul! Gadzooks!" said he.
"The blighters did that once to me.
   A dirty trick, I trow.
I hereby quash and override
The jury's verdict. Gosh!" he cried.
"Give me your hand. Yes, I insist,
You splendid fellow! Case dismissed."
   (Cheers, and a Voice "Wow-wow!")

A statue stands against the sky,
   Lifelike and rather pretty.
'Twas recently erected by
   The P.E.N. committee.
And many a passer-by is stirred,
For on the plinth, if that's the word,

In golden letters you may read
"This is the man who did the deed.
  His hand set to the plough,
He did not sheathe the sword, but got
A gun at great expense and shot
The human blot who'd printed 'not'
  When he had written 'now.'
He acted with no thought of self,
Not for advancement, not for pelf,
But just because it made him hot
To think the man had printed 'not'
  When he had written 'now.' "

RICHARD USBORNE is the author of Clubland Heroes, Wodehouse at Work to the End, *and* A Wodehouse Companion; *editor of* Vintage Wodehouse *and* Sunset at Blandings. *He was educated at Charterhouse and Balliol College, Oxford. He sometimes reviews books for the BBC,* Times Literary Supplement, *and other media. His hobby is writing light verse. His American wife is from Albuquerque, New Mexico. Together they look after a beautiful 1693 house in North West London for the National Trust.*

Wodehouse's *Punch* Verse

PETER DICKINSON

In 1966 I was reading *Pigs Have Wings* aloud to my daughters, and the elder one, then aged eleven, had a sudden compulsion to write to the author and tell him his work was to her taste. As far as I know this is the only time she has ever experienced such an urge. Because I was then on the editorial staff of *Punch*, the London humorous magazine, and because Wodehouse had become (or rather, as I shall explain in a minute, rebecome) an occasional contributor, I sent him Philippa's letter, with a covering note on *Punch* writing-paper.

Wodehouse responded as I'd rather hoped, with a charming handwritten letter to Philippa; much more surprisingly, he typed another to me, specifically to say that he admired the quality of verse then being written in *Punch*. I took this to be mere politeness, because my own contributions to the magazine were mostly verse—and mostly, it must be said, pretty run-of-the-mill. I didn't then know that more than sixty years earlier Wodehouse had been writing almost weekly for *Punch*, very often in verse. In fact this long-ago outpouring had provided an important part of his young bachelor income. He had given up his safe, snug job in a City bank and was determined to make a living as a writer. I now suspect that in his mid-eighties and out of a mixture of loyalty and nostalgia, he would at least have *tried* to like anything that appeared in *Punch* and was printed in the form of verse.

There was another attraction. Light verse, for some reason, demands to be written in a rather old-fashioned way. The language can, and should, be as modern as you like, but it should still not merely scan and rhyme, but should do so with felicitous ingenuity. It should pour itself, without any contortions, into apparently complex molds. There is an enormous satisfaction in reading what could be, say, an extract from a legal document, full of whereases and notwithstandings, which the poet has contrived to arrange into triple-rhyming decasyllabic quatrains, with the odd internal rhyme for the hell of it.

This was the sort of thing that Wodehouse liked, together with the typical frills of English light verse, such as the sudden letdown from mock-romance to slang. He liked the idea of an established form being made to learn new tricks. He liked the unbuttoned, conversational style, moving within strict measures. (His novels, *mutatis mutandis*, could be described in very similar terms.) He liked the established but not yet ossified tradition—this one goes back beyond Byron, and includes Barham of *The Ingoldsby Legends*, C. S. Calverley, and of course the Gilbert of both the Savoy Operas and *The Bab Ballads*. Some of Wodehouse's own early verse is very Gilbertian, both in theme and style; and one of his very last pieces in *Punch* is in triple-rhyming dactylic heptameters with internal rhymes, the exact (and immensely difficult) meter of several Gilbert patter songs.

Wodehouse's first contribution to the paper was

in prose, and therefore outside my brief—but I won't let that stop me, as it was an article that, as assistant editor of *Punch*, I was still rejecting, in one form or another, at least twice a year some sixty years later; it was the one about the man who is building up a unique collection of rejection slips which will be ruined by the acceptance of this very article. Wodehouse's was a variant on the main theme, but a not particularly variant variant. That first Wodehouse contribution was in September 1902, and by the end of the year he had three pieces of verse accepted, two of which, incidentally, are included in Kingsley Amis's recent *Oxford Book of Light Verse*. (Did Mr. Amis look at any other year of *Punch* volumes, I wonder? Or at the verse of any other contributors in that particular year?)

What are they like? Could one honestly say that one detected a marked difference from other verses appearing around that time? I think not. The then editor, Owen Seaman, was himself a writer of verse, with a thoroughly schoolmasterly attitude to the trade (he had been a schoolmaster). He liked verse smooth and correct; he didn't care for strong feelings or blunt attacks; he preferred superficial little poems about courtship and love (one of Wodehouse's is a "Gourmet's Love Song," about a man regretting all the things he can't eat because he has lost his appetite over a girl). Seaman also liked verses with a topical peg, a quote from a newspaper, or a current event. Wodehouse welcomed the return of Buffalo Bill Cody to London with a set of triple-rhymed verses, rhyming "tomahawk" with "from a hawk," and "fortuitous" with "displease, when we view it, us," and ending:

Still, when your ochred and plume-covered savages
   Make preparations for raising the hair,
And when your cowboys are stemming their ravages,
   I, may it please you to know, shall be there.
One, if no more, of the thousands who pen you in
   Looks on your feats with a pleasure that's genuine.[1]

The year 1903 was much fatter, with forty-seven contributions—almost one a week—eighteen of them verse. It's hard not to wonder whether *Punch* was short of material. I don't mean that Wodehouse's contributions were below par, far from it; but it's the way the editors slopped them in, often two in the same short issue, and once two on the same page. Of course this was possible both because Wodehouse's themes and styles were very varied and because none of the articles was signed. In those days only very senior contributors were allowed to append as much as their initials to their stuff—even the editor signed his verses "O.S." This tradition lasted a very long time, initials and pseudonyms becoming rather more frequent in the thirties, and real names later still, though newcomers were still expected to see their work unsigned as late as 1952. Wodehouse did not get his own initials on any contribution to *Punch* until 1930. Even then I bet there was a good deal of argument about it, as he had contributed only half-a-dozen pieces since 1907. Of course he was famous by 1930, but what is fame compared to a really good old stuffy English tradition?

Back to 1903. The chief thing that strikes one is the variety. One does not normally think of Wodehouse as a particularly versatile writer, rather as a man who early found two or three things he could do well, and then proceeded to perfect those performances until they were immaculate. But these early verses disclose other potential Wodehouses. There are, for instance, a couple of parodies of Kipling, a writer for whose verse one would have thought he had very little sympathy. There is an attack—quite sharp—on the self-promoting novelist Hall Caine, who had announced that he was going to Iceland to gather material for his next novel; after listing suitable bits of local color Wodehouse ends:

   Though other things he will not miss,
      Those mentioned are enough
   To suit the purposes of this
      Preliminary puff;
   Others will follow, for we know
      A chance will not be lost
   To save this Saga of the Snow
      From turning out a "frost."[2]

There is an antimilitaristic poem about a proposal to train boys at an early age in the arts of war. This must refer to the beginnings of Baden-Powell's Boy Scout movement, apparently not even christened as yet. If so it is the first appearance of Wodehouse's lifelong irreverence about Boy Scouts, which recurs in the decks, from *The Swoop!* (1909) to the last appearance of "young blighted Edwin," Boy Scout son of Lord Worplesdon, in *Joy in the Morning* (1947). But in that early poem the open note of scorn and

---

1. "To William (Whom We Have Missed)," *Punch* 123 (31 Dec. 1902): 460.

2. "The Coming Saga," *Punch* 125 (29 July 1903): 63.

even (within the limitations of the genre) of sorrow rings strangely now.

There are poems which are almost music-hall songs; one can imagine the ode celebrating the return of Sherlock Holmes being brayed out by a chorus line. And then, enchantingly, there are pieces, or casual phrases, which foreshadow the mature Wodehouse. The saga of the young man who one night, as if by accident, tied the absolutely perfect bow tie and ruined his life trying to do it again might easily have occurred in the Drones; and what about this? In the poem a theatre manager is hiring thugs to assassinate his juvenile lead, who has grown old and fat and won't retire:

> And the black-souled ruffians muttered "Done!
> Prompt despatch is our aim and boast:
> We'll send him poison by every post;
> We'll speedily fill him with well-aimed lead
> And daily with sandbags we'll ply his head . . ."[3]

One can almost envisage the episode in the novel when, for classically Wodehousian reasons, the asinine hero is trying to persuade the Chicago gang-leader that he is capable of dark and dreadful mayhem, and uses exactly those words, done into prose.

In the following few years the spate lessens to around one contribution a month. I can't imagine that *Punch* paid particularly well—the honor would have been thought sufficient, even when blurred by anonymity. By this time Wodehouse had discovered he could make more money in the theatre, writing or updating lyrics. His short stories were being accepted in England and America. He always had a novel on the stocks. The incentive, both financial and psychological, to write verse must have dwindled, and he can't have had all that spare energy for it, either. Still he contributed to *Punch*, verse and prose, fairly regularly. The style remains much the same, and so do the subjects, but they haven't the gusto of the earlier pieces. Between the wars there is almost nothing from Wodehouse in *Punch* (in 1919 a neat poem about two civil servants who know each other only by memos; a mock-rustic ballad about warble-flies in 1930). Then Malcolm Muggeridge persuaded him back into the paper when he took over as editor in 1953.

He wrote partly out of friendship for Malcolm, for whom he had a great regard, and partly (I believe) out of affection for *Punch*. Mostly his contributions were "Our Man in America" pieces—cock-eyed reporting on the loopier aspects of the American scene—but once or twice a year he would send us a bit of verse. I find these late poems oddly moving, considering that was the last thing Wodehouse intended them to be. They are so obviously written for fun. They are leisurely and relaxed, very confident, largely nonsense and difficult to quote; but here's a verse from "Song about Whiskers," whose argument, if you can call it an argument, was that America hadn't been the same since beards went out (this was 1955, remember).

> What this country needs is men with whiskers
> Like the men of an earlier date.
> They were never heels and loafers
> And they looked like busted sofas
> Or Excelsior in a crate.
> Whitman's verse, there is none to match it,
> And you couldn't see his face unless you used a hatchet.
> What this country needs is men with whiskers
> Like the men who made her great.[4]

What I get from these last few poems is a sense of immense geniality, of pleasure in writing something he didn't have to write, and what's more in writing it for *Punch*, because that was the proper place for such things to appear in, just as it had been fifty years ago, when a clever young man had left his job as a bank clerk in London to see if he could earn his living by writing.

PETER DICKINSON is nowadays an author of prize-winning detective novels and children's books, but for nearly twenty years in the fifties and sixties he was Assistant Editor at Punch *magazine. As such he was responsible, among other things, for the selection of verse, and also wrote a great deal himself, ranging from nonsense verses through political satire to near-poetry. He belongs to the last generation to have enjoyed (if that's the word) the same kind of education as PGW, with almost total emphasis on Greek and Latin, including the composition of verses in the strict and difficult meters of those languages. He is married and has four children. He speaks in an accent Lord Emsworth would have been familiar with (e.g., pronouncing "golf" with a mute "l"). In* Who's Who *he lists his recreation as "manual labor."*

---

3. "Actor James," *Punch* 125 (29 July 1903): 60.

4. "Song about Whiskers," *Punch* 229 (28 Sept. 1955): 352.

Wodehouse and the Literary Scene

JOHN GARRARD

ALTHOUGH in the course of his works Wodehouse comments favorably on a number of authors—Evelyn Waugh, William Shakespeare, Marcus Aurelius, and Robert Benchley spring to mind—he does not seem to have had much esteem for his colleagues in general, and there are in his letters some pretty unflattering references to various established literary reputations.

> In our country authors as a class are no oil paintings. You have only to go to one of those literary dinners to test the truth of this. At such a binge you will see tall authors, short authors, stout authors, thin authors and authors of medium height and girth, but all of these authors, without exception, look like something that would be passed over with a disdainful jerk of the beak by the least fastidious buzzard in the Gobi desert.[1]

That, alas, was fact, but the theme recurs in his fiction, and the literary gathering seems to have been a regular nightmare of his. He has some harsh words for the meetings of the Wood Hills Literary Society in which that fine young golfer Cuthbert Banks gets involved.

> It is all very well to excite pity and terror as Aristotle recommends, but there are limits. In the ancient Greek tragedies it was an ironclad rule that all the real rough stuff should take place off stage, and I shall follow this admirable principle. It will suffice if I merely say that J. Cuthbert Banks had a thin time.

What, in fact, happened to him was that he was subjected to:

> eleven debates and fourteen lectures on *vers libre* Poetry, the Seventeenth-Century Essayists, the Neo-Scandinavian Movement in Portuguese Literature, and other subjects of a similar nature. . . .[2]

Then there was the annual dance of the Pen and Ink Club (president: Miss Julia Ukridge). It was here that the narrator Corky (but I am sure it was really Wodehouse himself speaking) mentions "that curious gray hopelessness which always afflicts me when I am confronted with literary people in bulk." Typical of the creatures discovered under this particular flat stone was Charlton Prout, the club secretary:

> It was a refined tenor voice that had addressed me, and it was a refined tenor-looking man whom I saw. He was young and fattish, with a Jovian coiffure and pince-nez attached to a black cord. . . . He was much too sleek and had no right to do his hair like that.

Accused of writing "A Shriek in the Night" and "Who Killed Jasper Bossom?" he says:

> You must be confusing me with some other—ah—writer. My work is on somewhat different lines. The reviewers usually describe the sort of thing I do as Pastels in Prose.[3]

Poor Prout's present-day counterpart would be wearing ragged jeans and dirty tennis shoes and, with his steel-rimmed spectacles, would look like a car coming through a hedgerow. It is questionable whether this sort of thing constitutes an improvement on the original model.

If Wodehouse really disliked anybody it was probably, as Usborne says in *Wodehouse at Work*, the phony and pretentious literary man.

It was said of him that "he had read more books not worth reading than any man in England": of course, he knew the classics as well, but the lower strata of literature—most notably the "woman's romance" (no longer termed the "shopgirl's novel") and the thriller obviously fascinated him, and they and their producers make glorious appearances in many of his books.

Pride of place must go to Mrs. Richard M. (Bingo) Little, a.k.a. Rosie M. Banks, "author of some of the most pronounced and widely read tripe ever put on the market." Published works include *A Red, Red Summer Rose*, *Madcap Myrtle*, *Only a Factory Girl*, *The Woman Who Braved All*, and *Mervyn Keene, Clubman*. Rosie pursues her craft out of conviction, not cynicism, and thinks Bingo must

---

1. *Over Seventy*.
2. *Golf without Tears*: "The Clicking of Cuthbert."
3. *Ukridge*: VI, "Ukridge Sees Her Through."

have been a king in Babylon when she was a Christian slave.[4]

It was these women's habit of using their most sacred and intimate affairs as raw material for their works that horrified Wodehouse. In an ill-advised descent into non-fiction, a piece entitled "How I Keep the Love of My Husband-Baby," Rosie refers to Bingo as "half god, half prattling, mischievous child."[5] Egbert Mulliner, intrepid assistant editor of a literary weekly, which ranks high among the Dangerous Trades, becomes engaged to Evangeline Pembury, having first carefully ascertained that she has never written any novels or short stories. But inevitably, two months later, Evangeline has written a novel called *Parted Ways*.

> Evangeline's novel was a horrible, an indecent production. Not in the sense that it would be likely to bring a blush to any cheek but his, but because she had put on paper in bald words every detail of the only romance that had ever come under her notice —her own.

There was the entire courtship including the first kiss and the proposal—given verbatim. "Egbert shuddered to think that he could have polluted the air with such frightful horseradish."[6]

Sparing only a passing glance for Cora McGuffy Spotsworth who looked like a snake with hips and whose love scenes had to be printed on asbestos,[7] and for Leila Yorke, whose titles included *For True Love Only*, *Heather o' the Hills*, *Sweet Jennie Dean*, and *Cupid the Archer*,[8] we must tear ourselves away from these lush pastures and go on to consider the detective or thriller story.

The thriller-writer James Rodman may be taken as expressing Wodehouse's approach to this genre:

> He held rigid views on the art of the novel and always maintained that an artist with a true reverence for his craft should not descend to gooey love stories, but should stick austerely to revolvers, cries in the night, missing papers, mysterious Chinamen and dead bodies—with or without a gash in the throat.

He goes to live at Honeysuckle Cottage, once the residence of the late Leila J. Pinckney, in her time a formidable rival of Rosie M. Banks and the rest in the production of sentimental tripe, and is busy finishing *The Secret Nine* (hero, Lester Gage). As the story takes shape in James's typewriter, Gage hears a faint noise, tiptoes to the door and flings it open, his revolver poised.

> On the mat stood the most beautiful girl he had ever beheld. A veritable child of Faerie. She eyed him for a moment with a saucy smile; then with a pretty roguish look of reproof shook a dainty forefinger at him.
> "I believe you've forgotten me, Mr. Gage!" she fluted with a mock severity which her eyes belied.

Rodman is horrified; what he had intended to happen was that a dying man should fall in and, after gasping, "The beetle! Tell Scotland Yard that the blue beetle is...," expire on the hearthrug. But the spirit of Leila J. Pinckney is overpowering, affecting all who come to her cottage, and only the most miraculous of circumstances preserves James from the clutches of a child of Faerie of his own and leaves him to produce thrillers of the proper austerity.[9]

The revolutionary effect that the environment can have on a literary artist is also the theme of Mr. Mulliner's story of "The Unpleasantness at Bludleigh Court." His niece Charlotte "was one of those gentle, dreamy, wistful girls who take what I have sometimes felt to be a mean advantage of having an ample private income to write Vignettes in Verse," and she found a soul-mate in a godlike young man called Aubrey Trefusis who wrote Pastels in Prose (like another littérateur we met earlier), with whom she discovered that she had many opinions in common including an intense loathing for all blood sports. Yet on a visit to Aubrey's ancestral home, Bludleigh Court, Lesser Bludleigh, near Goresby-on-the-Ouse, Bedfordshire, inhabited by his rapidly hunting family and "decorated throughout with groves of glass cases containing the goggle-eyed remnants of birds and beasts ... selected portions of ... gnus, moose, elks, zebus, antelopes, giraffes, mountain goats and wapiti," so potent is the influence of this stately abattoir, that Charlotte, having quarreled with Aubrey who had interrupted his wooing to chivvy a rat, is surprised when the *Animal Lovers' Gazette* refuses to accept her Vignette in Verse entitled "Good Gnus":

---

4. *The Inimitable Jeeves*: I, "Jeeves Exerts the Old Cerebellum"; II, "No Wedding Bells for Bingo."
5. *Carry on, Jeeves*: IX, "Clustering round Young Bingo."
6. *Mulliner Nights*: VII, "Best Seller."
7. *Nothing Serious*: "Feet of Clay."
8. *Meet Mr. Mulliner*: IX, "Honeysuckle Cottage."

9. Ibid.

> When Afric's sun is sinking low,
> And shadows wander to and fro,
>   And everywhere there's in the air
>   A hush that's deep and solemn;
> Then is the time good men and true
> With View Halloo pursue the gnu:
>   (The safest spot to put your shot
>   Is through the spinal column).[10]

Poets usually get fairly harsh treatment throughout the works, probably because most are obscure or pretentious or both. They are bearable only when inept or, as was Psmith on his visit to Blandings Castle, in the guise of Ralston McTodd, the powerful young singer of Saskatoon, conscious frauds:

> "I sometimes think, Miss Peavey, that flowers must be the souls of little children who have died in their innocence."
>
> "What a beautiful thought, Mr. McTodd!" exclaimed Miss Peavey rapturously.
>
> "Yes," agreed Psmith. "Don't pinch it. It's copyright."

It is indicative of Wodehouse's attitude toward the craft that the reader thinks more of the poetess Peavey when she turns out to be a jewel thief.[11]

Poets might be born, not made, but the unmaking of them was a consummation devoutly to be wished. Before his purification by golf and marriage, Rodney Spelvin "had once been a poet, and a very virulent one too: the sort of man who would produce a slim volume of verse bound in squashy mauve leather at the drop of a hat." "Virulent" was perhaps too mild a term: " 'Only last week a man, a coarse editor, asked me what my sonnet "Wine of Desire" *meant*.' He laughed indulgently. 'I gave him answer 'twas a sonnet, not a mining prospectus.' "[12]

But the poetry virus does not die; it only sleeps. Fatherhood revived it at its deadliest in Rodney, who celebrated his son in such lines as:

> Timothy Bobbin has ten little toes.
> He takes them out walking wherever he goes.
> And if Timothy gets a cold in the head,
> His ten little toes stay with him in bed.

There was a good deal more nauseating stuff of this kind, but salvation was at hand. As Rodney shaped up for a vital shot in an important golf match, a clear, childish voice broke the silence: "Dadee! Are daisies little bits of the stars that have been chipped off by the angels?"

The shot was missed disastrously, retribution followed, and it is implied that little Timothy was most unlikely to have piped up with any more sentiments of that kind.[13]

Wodehouse was a great admirer of A.A. Milne's plays, but he couldn't stomach Christopher Robin, and this story is one of the very rare instances where he allows himself a little ferocity on paper.

To this gallery of professional scribes must be added some unlikely amateurs in the shape of Monty Bodkin, acting editor of *Tiny Tots*, and Bingo Little, editor of *Wee Tots* (P. P. Purkiss, proprietor). Poor Monty didn't last long for, in the absence of the editor, he had to provide the editorial "Uncle Woggly to His Chicks," and, for some reason, the paper's owner, Lord Tilbury, took exception to the tone he adopted.

> Well, chickabiddies, how are you all? Minding what Nursie says and eating your spinach like good little men? That's right. I know the stuff tastes like a motorman's glove, but they say there's iron in it, and that's what puts hair on the chest.[14]

Bingo, on the other hand, proved to be more durable, possibly because Fate put him in the position of being able to blackmail P. P. Purkiss, and because he was able to compose a thoughtful editorial on "What Tiny Hands Can Do for Nannie."[15] I should like to have been able to read that, but Wodehouse, unfortunately, does not give us a sample.

Finally we have Bertie Wooster himself who was prevailed upon to write a few authoritative words on "What the Well-Dressed Man Is Wearing" for his Aunt Dahlia's magazine *Milady's Boudoir*. "A deuce of a job it had been, taxing the physique to the utmost. I don't wonder now that all these author blokes have bald heads and faces like birds who have suffered." Jeeves approved of some of the contents —"The sock passage is quite in the proper vein, sir"—but not of others.

> "Come to the bit about soft silk shirts for evening wear?" I asked carelessly.
>
> "Yes, sir," said Jeeves, in a low cold voice, as if he had been bitten in the leg by a personal friend. "And if I may be pardoned for saying so . . ."

---

10. *Mr. Mulliner Speaking*: V, "The Unpleasantness at Bludleigh Court."
11. *Leave It to Psmith*: VI, "Lord Emsworth Meets a Poet."
12. *The Heart of a Goof*: VII, "Rodney Fails to Qualify."
13. *Nothing Serious*: "Rodney Has a Relapse."
14. *Heavy Weather*.
15. *Nothing Serious*: "The Shadow Passes."

Bertie spoke of his article with pride ever after—but, of course, his soft silk shirts were sent back to the makers before he had a chance even to try them on.[16]

This has been a lighthearted piece because it is impossible to write pompously about Wodehouse, that least pompous of men. But he did, in fact, take his own craft of writing very seriously indeed, writing and rewriting endlessly until he achieved the exact effect he wanted. Carlyle said that genius meant the transcendent capacity of taking trouble. Wodehouse certainly had that kind of genius; but I should have said that a truer definition would be the achievement of something that could never be accomplished merely by taking infinite trouble.

JOHN GARRARD is sixty-four years of age. He had the good luck to be introduced by a small friend to the works of P. G. Wodehouse in 1926. Since then, as schoolboy (miserable), student (apprehensive), soldier (terrified), and toy manufacturer (over-taxed), he has needed a lot of cheering up. The Wodehouse treatment was prescribed fifty-five years ago, and it still works. He and his wife, Margaret, live in London. They have been married for thirty years and have two married daughters, one of whom lives in New York. His hobbies are literature and golf—he is better at golf.

16. *Carry on, Jeeves*: IX, "Clustering round Young Bingo."

Wodehouse's American Illustrators
WALT REED

THE ASSOCIATION of writers with artists has a long history, going back almost to the invention of printing. However, that association has usually been a *ménage à trois*, involving the printer or publisher as well.

Like most such triangles, relationships among the three are vastly complicated. First, it is not an equilateral triangle. The publisher is the entrepreneur who initiates the printing of a book, so the status of author and illustrator are almost invariably subordinate. The publisher has the prerogative of purchasing a manuscript or not, and with him also resides the decision about which—if any—artist shall be hired to illustrate the text. Although they may have personal preferences, rarely do the authors have a voice in the selection of the illustrators of their stories. Nor does the artist choose his author.

Since the contribution of the illustrator to the reader's reception of the story can be highly significant, publishers of most magazines or books rely on an art editor to select the most appropriate artist for a given manuscript. The qualities that make a good illustrator are quite specialized. An ability to dramatize a given situation is essential. The illustrator must cast the characters in keeping with the author's descriptions and choose those descriptive passages of text which will intrigue the casual viewer into reading the text, while not giving away the plot. Added to this is the artist's own personality which affects his point of view and creates that recognizable style that distinguishes one artist from another. This artistic charisma is somewhat akin to the movie actor's "star quality."

A good art editor is aware of readers' tastes as well as the capabilities of the illustrators available to him, and attempts to create a successful marriage of artist and writer. However, no marriage was ever more platonic. It is not even necessary for the two ever to meet. Occasionally, an artist may contact the author for some technical information or clarification about the story setting, or sometimes a grateful writer may pen a "thank you" note to an illustrator who does an especially sympathetic pictorial interpretation of the story; but generally each goes his own way.

Despite this lack of personal contact, the almost chance combination of illustrator and author has often resulted in long, successful associations in print, the work of each enhancing that of the other. The illustrator Frederick Dorr Steele, for instance, was best known for his illustrations of the Sherlock Holmes stories in America; Reginald Birch for *Little Lord Fauntleroy* and other stories by Frances Hodgson Burnett; and Arthur William Brown illustrated the Lawyer Ephraim Tutt series of stories by Arthur Train in *The Saturday Evening Post* for more than twenty years.

P. G. Wodehouse is notable (among other reasons) for the large number and variety of artists who illustrated his work. Part of this is due to his longevity; he simply outlived many of his early interpreters. The principal reason for this variety, however, was his appearance in so many different publications. Over the years, since his first novel was published in 1902, Wodehouse wrote more than seventy books and more than three hundred short stories; the substantial number of his essays and articles, plays, musical comedy lyrics, and motion picture scenarios is impressive, but did not significantly involve the chief concern of this article, illustration.

The universality of his stories has made them equally popular in England and America, and his books have been translated into many other languages, as diverse as Czech, Japanese, and Portuguese. In America Wodehouse was published in nearly every major magazine, each of which tended to have its own stable of illustrators. The rivalry between competing publications was such that, even though the illustrators worked on a freelance basis, it was clearly understood that one could not, for instance, work for both *The Saturday Evening Post* and *Collier's* simultaneously. Not that there weren't occasional defections from one camp to the other—or reconciliations after a proper interval—but usually such loyalties were maintained for the artist's working lifetime.

These limitations did not apply as much to authors, and Wodehouse appears to have avoided any such constraints. He sold his work to the *Post* and *Collier's* as well as to *Liberty* magazine when it was competing to move up from its position as number three of the weeklies. In short order his work had been published in most magazines of any stature, including *Munsey's, Popular, McClure's,* and *Vanity Fair*, in the last of which his work appeared under several pseudonyms, among them J. Plum, Pelham Grenville, and C. P. West (for Central Park West).

Publication in different magazines of course meant illustration by different artists—in Wodehouse's case, a veritable illustrators' *Who's Who*. A comprehensive but probably not complete list is given at the end of this article.

Wodehouse's stories presented an interesting challenge to those assigned to embellish them. The cast of characters tended to be much the same, despite changes of name or locale—idle and not-too-bright upper-class young men pursuing or being pursued by beautiful but strong-willed young heroines, resourceful valets or other servants, eccentric uncles, aunts, brothers-in-law, prize-winning pigs, and members of the Drones Club—stock types, perhaps, but providing colorful material for an illustrator.

It is fascinating to compare the interpretations of these similar characters by such a dissimilar group of illustrators. Nowhere is there more diversity shown than in the artistic interpretations of Wodehouse's most famous creation, Jeeves. Since the author does not oblige with any description more detailed than "a tallish man, with one of those dark, shrewd faces," Jeeves has been variously depicted as thin, fat, young, and old. Wallace Morgan (1873–1948) follows a middle course by making him slim and middle-aged.

Tony Sarg (1882–1942), who illustrated "The Aunt and the Sluggard" in *The Saturday Evening Post* in 1916, presents Jeeves as youthful and handsome while Bertie Wooster is pictured as plump and middle-aged. Generally, Bertie or his equivalent is illustrated as young and even somewhat good-looking. James Montgomery Flagg (1877–1960), however, does not hesitate to satirize his lack of intelligence and gives him an undershot lower jaw. His Jeeves, while proper, was more bemused and solicitous than pompous. We don't know which illustrator's visualizations pleased Wodehouse most. However, we do know from a letter written to his friend and collaborator Guy Bolton that the movie interpretation of Jeeves by Arthur Treacher was not in keeping with his idea of the character.

The artist who was perhaps most successful in interpreting the Wodehouse characters was Flagg, who did a large number of the stories for *Cosmopolitan* magazine during the thirties. He was a somewhat raffish personality who always delighted in lampooning the mighty, and he entered into the spirit of the stories with gusto. His emphasis on characterization made the individuals very real people. Flagg, who liked to affect a monocle himself, also gave one to Bertie Wooster. Flagg's pen-and-ink technique, which he employed for most of the stories, had great dash and style about it; this he had borrowed from his great predecessor, Charles Dana Gibson, often combining it with a watercolor wash, but adding his own wit and spontaneity, which suited the plots admirably.

Wallace Morgan, however, came closest to being the "official" Wodehouse illustrator, doing more stories for more different magazines than even Flagg. His association began with "Brother Alfred" in *Collier's* in 1913, and he did many other short stories for the magazine as well as the serials, "The Little Warrior" in 1920 and "The Medicine Girl" in 1931. Morgan was also sought out by the art editor of *Liberty* in 1926 and 1927 to illustrate another long series of short stories. He further surmounted the crossover taboo by doing illustrations for the serials "The Code of the Woosters" and "Summer Moonshine" for *The Saturday Evening Post* in 1938 and 1937 and "Laughing Gas" for *This Week* magazine in 1935.

Morgan's approach could not have been more different in style and technique from Flagg's. His emphasis was on the gesture and action of the whole figure rather than on facial expression or character type. Morgan worked with charcoal, which did not suit a detailed rendering but which allowed him to focus on the broader, more distant view in which the whole situation could be presented as a tableau.

One of the earlier and more dignified interpreters of Wodehouse was Frederic Rodrigo Gruger (1871–1953). His contribution was done for *The Saturday Evening Post* in 1915 for the story "Something New." Gruger was valued by the *Post*'s editor, George Horace Lorimer, who wanted to be sure that Gruger constantly had a *Post* manuscript to keep him busy. This rare—for illustrators—kind of security permitted Gruger to take extended trips abroad where he could continue to work on his illustrations. For several months, in fact, he leased a large English country manor, Darent Hulme, at Seven Oaks, Kent, complete with six servants, two gardeners, and a chauffeur. Lord Dunsany had the neighboring estate. With his first-hand knowledge of the milieu, Gruger also tended to give more emphasis to the setting than the actors.

Henry Raleigh (1880–1944) was a natural for Wodehouse. He did the upper-crust social scene with great style, but other than a few short stories and the serialized "Right-Ho, Jeeves" for *The Saturday Evening Post* in 1934, which were very successful, his associations were with other authors.

The only woman illustrator—there weren't many in the field—to interpret Wodehouse was May Wilson Preston (1873–1949). Her forte was humor and she did the serial "Heavy Weather," for the *Post* in 1933. One may enjoy the light, impressionistic drawings (she had studied under Whistler in Paris) but not look for much fact in them. For instance, the Empress of Blandings, Lord Emsworth's prize black pig, is pretty clearly shown as being white—an error made by many artists who have depicted her.

Robert Fawcett (1903–67), a Canadian by birth and trained at the Slade School in England, appears to have read his Wodehouse manuscripts more carefully. In his interpretation for "Pigs Have Wings" in *Collier's* in 1952, his Empress is properly black. And in order not to offend anyone, Fawcett himself posed for the villainous Sir Gregory Parsloe, owner of the rival pig Queen of Matchingham. Fawcett also illustrated "Big Business" for *Collier's* and had a superb ability to delineate both character and setting.

It appears that one of the early illustrators, Lucius W. Hitchcock (1868–1942), did not have much sense of humor. In his interpretation of "Creatures of Impulse" for *McClure's* magazine in 1914, he plays the story straight with little suggestion that he thought it was funny.

In contrast, Floyd Davis (1896–1966), who alternated at *Collier's* with Wallace Morgan in illustrating Wodehouse, created a memorably zany cast of characters for "Hot Water" in 1932. Each actor was outlandishly but carefully visualized for the reader, a great help, since Wodehouse plots are so convoluted and the cast of characters so numerous that it is often necessary to go back to the synopsis to find out who is trying to outmaneuver whom. Davis leaves no doubt about who the heroes or villians are, but they are so ludicrous that we love them all.

Similarly, Harry Beckhoff (1901–79) relied on broad humor in his *Collier's* illustrations for "Big Money" (1930) and "Phipps to the Rescue" (1950). But where Floyd Davis was almost savage in his satire, Beckhoff's characters are shown more kindly. They also look reasonably normal, if occasionally eccentric, in action. His butler Phipps, the hero of the story, is rather clearly modeled on Arthur Treacher.

James W. Williamson (1899–) draws with an understated sense of humor that nicely complemented the Wodehouse stories "Uncle Fred in the Springtime," "The Editor Regrets," "Bramley Is So Bracing," and "Tee for Two" in *The Saturday Evening Post*. Whether his pigs would pass muster must be left for a more expert appraisal.

A subsequent *Post* serial, "Money in the Bank" in 1941 was illustrated by Rudolph Pott, who was chosen perhaps because of the marked similarity of his style to that of Williamson.

Generally, the action in Wodehouse stories tends to be limited to conversation, and delicious it is, but occasionally a violent episode does flare up. This, of course, is what the illustrator looks for. Wallace Morgan's depiction of a dowager being chased around a swimming pool and Flagg's portrayal of a vengeful kick about to be applied to the seat of the pants of an obnoxious small boy are notable examples of Wodehouse in action.

There also seems to be a tendency for Wodehouse characters to climb up on the furniture or to crawl out from under beds.

The Wodehouse males occasionally resort to fisticuffs but usually tend to glower and threaten. It is the women who are the more forceful, driving the men to action or throwing things, if necessary.

The world of Bertie Wooster and company was almost extinct even when Wodehouse began writing about it; certainly World War I finished it. Yet the characters were timeless, and illustrators tended to keep them in a more or less contemporary setting. Even so, there is a great interpretative difference in the outlook of Lucius Hitchcock or F. R. Gruger in the teens and that of Gilbert Bundy (1911–55). Bundy was one of the most popular of the illustrators of the forties, and he couldn't resist making his characters up to the minute in "Quick Service," serialized in *The Saturday Evening Post*. In one picture, he indicates how much the old order has changed when a young man in the position of valet cheekily sits down with the hostess!

Some of the most recent appearances of Wodehouse in print indicate this modernizing process even more strongly. In the post-television years, the family weekly and monthly magazines have become almost extinct; those that still exist print very little fiction. The profession of illustration has gone through a similar alteration. The concept of a picture made to interpret the characters and setting of a story for the readers has greatly changed. Now the requirement is for a picture to decorate a page arrestingly. The artist is given an allowed amount of space but with almost complete latitude about how to fill it.

Bill Charmatz (1925–) is a popular contemporary book and magazine illustrator who has provided a new look for Wodehouse in the pages of *Playboy*. He reduces the elements in his pictures almost to poster shapes and colors. They look bright and lively on the page and invite the viewer to interpret what they mean and in the process to read the story.

If traditional illustration has seemed to disappear, however, old periodicals have been replaced by new ones and a new generation of artists has given a fresh look to books and magazines. Certainly Wodehouse reads as well as ever, and the present and past illustrations of his stories will serve as a guide for understanding his times and a springboard for future pictorial interpretations of his humor. Certainly we owe it to the pleasure given us to preserve all the Wodehouse memorabilia possible and to pass it along for the future. A world dominated by computer technology and printouts needs it more than ever.

WODEHOUSE'S LEADING AMERICAN BOOK AND MAGAZINE ILLUSTRATORS

H. R. Ballinger, Harry Beckhoff, Lonnie Bee, Earl Blossom, Austin Briggs, Arthur William Brown, Gilbert Bundy, Frederick Chapman, Bill Charmatz, Mario Cooper, John Crosman, Floyd Davis, Roy Doty, Robert Fawcett, James Montgomery Flagg, Alan Foster, Edward Gorey, Will Grefé, F. R. Gruger, John Huehnergarth, Joseph Isom, Martin Justice, Wyncie King, Charles LaSalle, Joseph Low, Charles D. Mitchell, Wallace Morgan, Harold J. Mowat, Alexander Popini, Rudolph Pott, May Wilson Preston, Henry Raleigh, Robert O. Reid, Herbert F. Roese, Rosenblum, Hy Roth, Tony Sarg, Charles Saxon, James Schucker, Silverstein, Joseph Simont, Haddon Sundblom, C. A. Voight, Jerry Warshaw, Gustavus C. Widney, James W. Williamson, George Wright.

Some illustrations were also commissioned by Wodehouse's book publishers, but these were in the main undistinguished, though the cartoonist Rea Irvin's work for *Hot Water* is crisp and decorative.

WALT REED. It was as an art student that Walt Reed was attracted by Wallace Morgan illustrations to his first P. G. Wodehouse story. He has been a lifelong fan of both ever since. Reed studied art at the New York–Phoenix Art Institute under Franklin Booth. He has been immersed in the history of illustration, and has written several books on the subject, including The Illustrator in America, 1900–1960s.

Wodehouse's English Illustrators

BEVIS HILLIER

LEWIS CARROLL and P. G. Wodehouse have more in common than their assured place among the greatest English humorists. Both had associations with Guildford, the county town (or "capital") of Surrey. In a quite Wodehousian way, Guildford has withstood the encroachments of the twentieth century which have reduced so much of Surrey to a sprawling suburb of London; even the High Street is still set with cobblestones. Carroll died there, in his sisters' house, in 1898. Wodehouse was born in Guildford seventeen years earlier, so the infant Pelham Grenville might have been dandled at the knee of the Reverend C. L. Dodgson, his local alias, if the author of *Alice* had not been notoriously less susceptible to small boys than to small girls. Both wrote verse as funny as their prose. Politically, both were romantic but dogged reactionaries. And both, on occasion, could be critical of the artists who illustrated their works; but there was a world of difference between their attitudes.

The Victorian artist Harry Furniss has left a droll description of the tribulations he endured as illustrator of Carroll's *Sylvie and Bruno*. He accepted the commission in 1885 after Sir John Tenniel, the illustrator of *Alice's Adventures in Wonderland* and *Through the Looking-Glass*, had refused to illustrate another story for Carroll, who in turn told Furniss that he disliked all Tenniel's drawings for the *Alice* books, except for Humpty Dumpty. As Furniss observes, it was as if Gilbert had said he did not admire Sullivan's music. Tenniel told Furniss that he could not tolerate "that conceited old don" any more, and added, "I'll give you a week, old chap; you will never put up with that fellow a day longer."

For Carroll, it was a case of out of the frying-pan, into the Furniss. Against all the odds, the two men managed to get on with each other most of the time; but Furniss found Carroll "captious":

> He subjected every illustration, when finished, to a minute examination under a magnifying glass. His practice was to take a square inch of the drawing, count the lines I had made in that space, and compare their number with those on a square inch of illustration made for *Alice* by Tenniel! And in due course I would receive a long essay on the subject from Dodgson the mathematician. Naturally this led to disagreements, particularly when it came to foreshortening a figure, such as "Sylvie and the Dead Hare," which is a question for the eye, not for the foot-rule and compass. In fact, over the criticism of one drawing I pretended that I could stand Dodgson the Don no longer, and wrote to Carroll the author declining to complete the work. He replied pathetically: "It is a severe disappointment to me to find that, on account of a single inch of picture as to which we disagree, you decline to carry out your engagement."[1]

Wodehouse was too genial and generous-spirited to adopt Carroll's pettifogging attitude to his illustrators (though the contention between Furniss and Carroll would evidently have worked very well in a Wodehouse story). He was capable of making a sharpish remark about one of them in a letter to a third party, as when he wrote to Bill Townend, himself an early Wodehouse illustrator: "God may have forgiven Herbert Jenkins for their cover picture of Mr. Mulliner, but I never shall." Again, some of the artists who appear in his stories might give the (wrong) impression that Wodehouse's opinion of artists in general was jaundiced. Though in "The Spot of Art" we have the soupy Gwladys Pendelbury and the even worse Lucius Pim (whose hair waved—a sure sign of untrustworthiness to baldpate Wodehouse's jaundiced eye) both painting, they are more than balanced by a succession of cheerfully bad painters such as George Finch in *The Small Bachelor*, Bill Lister in *Full Moon*, and Jeff Bennison in the unfinished *Sunset at Blandings*.

T. M. R. Whitwell, one of Wodehouse's earliest illustrators in *The Captain* magazine, was not a bit like the wavy-haired, bounderish Lucius Pim type of artist. He was a clean-cut Edwardian "blade" with acceptably straight hair and a bushy moustache. A line drawing of Whitwell appears in W. F. Thomas's illustration of *The Captain*'s New Year's party of 1911. Wodehouse himself, a rather prim, trim,

---

1. Harry Furniss, *Some Victorian Men* (London: John Lane, The Bodley Head, 1924), p. 76.

clerkish young fellow, appears in the same drawing. So does the illustrator H. M. Brock, whose work conjured up that period for John Betjeman when recalling his first interview in the awesome headmaster's study of Highgate Junior School:

> The gold clock ticked; the waiting furniture
> Shone like a color-plate by H. M. Brock. . . .

Brock was the adept illustrator, in pen-and-ink drawings, of Wodehouse's *Love among the Chickens* (1906). Mention of this book inevitably requires mention of the illustrator with whom Wodehouse was most friendly, William Townend. The two had been schoolfellows and shared a study at Dulwich College. Townend did the twelve illustrations which were used in the first edition of Wodehouse's *The White Feather* (1907). If Lewis Carroll was a writer who suggested illustrations to his illustrator, Townend was an illustrator who suggested plots to his author. The first edition of *Love among the Chickens* was informally dedicated to him in a preface:

> William Townend, Artist,
> if this should ever meet the eye of.
>
> Dear Bill, In the case of a book of this kind it is only right that the responsibility should be fixed. I take this opportunity of exposing you. But for the help I derived from your almost insolent familiarity with the habits of chickens, I should probably have been compelled to give up writing this book and go back to work again. Yours ever, P.G.W.

It seems rather unfair that Brock should have been chosen to illustrate *Love among the Chickens* rather than Townend, who inspired it. He eventually abandoned the artist's life for that of writing; that selection of letters from Wodehouse to him that made up *Performing Flea* (1953) (U.S. version: *Author! Author!* [1962]) packs a lot of wonderfully sage advice for fiction writers.

The majority of Wodehouse's novels were published with no illustrations: the main scope for the illustrators was in their serializations and the short stories in magazines, and wrappers for the novels and collections. The short-lived *Public School Magazine* was among the first to print his work under a byline. He began by writing its "Notes," for example, an attack on "the master who forces the human boy to take down notes for dictation" (1901). They illustrated this with crosshatched vignettes by R. Noel Pocock, who also supplied the single headpiece illustration (of a rugby football player) to Wodehouse's "Football, My Dear Sir, Why—," which begins with a passage already recognizable as in the classic Wodehousian manner:

> I think I may claim the distinction of being the only male adult in the United Kingdom (exclusive of those who are unable to write) who has never written a song about football, rhyming "leather" with "weather" and placing the adjectives "glorious" and "wintry" before the latter word. At one time there were three of us, myself, a Mr. Williams of Upper Tooting, and a Mr. Smythe of South Penge. That was early in the '80s. Since then Mr. Smythe has died, while Mr. Williams took to drink in the summer of 1890, and now writes odes to prominent players for the football edition of the *Upper Tooting Sporting Lynx*.

In *The Public School Magazine* in 1902 Pocock illustrated the story which was to reappear later that year as Wodehouse's first novel, *The Pothunters*, and the next year provided the frontispiece for Wodehouse's second novel, *A Prefect's Uncle*. He is always competent, never inspired. For the twelve full-page illustrations for *Tales of St. Austin's* (1903), Pocock was joined by Whitwell, and by E. F. Skinner, who has a more precise style than the other two. Whitwell then went on to do eight illustrations for *The Gold Bat*, published in 1904.

In the same year, with *William Tell Told Again* (printed, as it happens, in Guildford) a new illustrator appears, Philip Dadd. Dadd's drawings are dated 1900, which makes them the earliest drawings to appear in a Wodehouse book; indeed, predating Wodehouse's first book. The publisher had commissioned an illustrated book, then taken a dislike to the text supplied and, after a few years, asked the up-and-coming Wodehouse to provide something better. The drawings are unmistakably in the style of John Hassall, a famous poster artist of the time. Hassall is depicted with Wodehouse and the others at *The Captain*'s 1911 New Year's party.

When Wodehouse first broke into it in 1905, publication in *The Strand Magazine* was the supreme accolade for an artist or a writer. Wodehouse's first contribution, "The Wire-Pullers," a cricket story, was illustrated by W. G. Stacey, who also illustrated his later cricket epic, "The Lost Bowlers." By the time of the First World War, Wodehouse was contributing a prodigal amount to the *Strand*.

By then the illustrators included W. Heath Robinson, the designer of preposterous machinery (who was also to draw a jacket for a Wodehouse novel), Will Owen, who designed the "Bisto Kids" poster, Lewis Baumer, who lived almost as far into the twentieth century as Wodehouse, George Morrow, Frank Reynolds, Harry Rountree, and G. E. Studdy, well known for his cheeky mongrel dogs. But the majority of Wodehouse's stories were illustrated by the most successful poster artist of his day, Alfred Leete, who designed the recruiting poster which showed Lord Kitchener pointing an accusing finger, with the slogan "Your Country Needs YOU!" Leete's strong, swashbuckling pen-and-ink drawings illustrate "Bill the Bloodhound" (1915) and many other Wodehouse tales. But other *Strand* artists were also let loose on his stories, including Treyer Evans whose drawings for "The Love-r-ly Silver Cup" (1915) are very dashing and anticipate Art Déco drawings of the "Fish" type (Miss Fish was perhaps the most successful pupil of the Hassall Drawing School); E. H. Shepard, of later "Pooh" fame, who illustrated a number of the Wodehouse golf stories; and J. A. Shepherd, a *Strand* old stager who specialized in animals with human expressions —he illustrated Wodehouse's "The Mixer," a story told largely by a dog. Baumer executed a particularly effective illustration for "Wilton's Holiday" (1915) above the caption "He had developed a sort of wistful expression—I am convinced that he practised it before the mirror after his bath."

Just over twenty years before, Sidney Paget's illustrations to Conan Doyle's Sherlock Holmes stories in the *Strand* had established the canonical image of the ascetic detective with his deerstalker hat and curved meerschaum. The actors who played Holmes in the movies, notably Basil Rathbone, were obliged to adopt this appearance: any other would have been unacceptable to the public. But no *Strand* illustrator achieved a similar feat for Wodehouse; and the reason was that Wodehouse had not yet found his authentic voice. So long as he wrote about public schoolboys and pompous bank managers, the likes of Whitwell, Pocock, and Leete could interpret him appropriately. They were manly, stiff-upper-lip artists, quite unlike the effete or scatty daubers of Wodehouse's fiction.

By 1922 and 1923, when Wodehouse was well into what might be called his Art Déco period, he was still being illustrated by artists of an 1890s stamp, "black-and-white men" of the Phil May type, such as A. Wallis Mills, who illustrated "Comrade Bingo," a Jeeves story in the *Strand* of May 1922, or Reginald Cleaver who did the drawings for "The Long Arm of Looney Coote" in December 1923. By this time the *Strand* had A. K. Macdonald in its stable. He was strong on fairies and nubile princesses *en déshabillé* in stores for Christmas numbers of glossy magazines. He might have adapted well to the Madelines, Florences, and henpecked earls of Wodehouse's later prime. But Wodehouse was then still being seen as a writer of "rattling good yarns," not as the immortalizer of the goofy dream world which particularly appealed in the 1920s as an antidote to the horrors of the Great War.

The illustrator who, for the *Strand*, best hit off the Wodehouse manner was Gilbert Wilkinson. He was a versatile and very prolific artist who drew cartoons for the *Daily Herald* and covers and illustrations for *Woman*, *John Bull*, and *Passing Show*. He gave us the Drones Club exquisite as cleverly as Battling Billson, the Bobbie Wickham–type girl as characteristically as Billson's own barmaid fiancée, Flossie. He made Lord Emsworth short and stubby, which he wasn't, and he made the Empress of Blandings white, which *she* wasn't. But he did the *Strand* and Wodehouse proud.

For dust wrappers one gets the feeling that Herbert Jenkins didn't pay top prices. But Heath Robinson must have charged a considerable fee when he did the jacket for *If I Were You* in 1931. The picture is of Anthony, fifth Earl of Droitwich, pursuing his trade of barber. One of the greatest rarities sought after by Wodehouse collectors is the cover that Rex Whistler did for Faber and Faber for the book of essays *Louder and Funnier*, which shows a bust of the Master wreathed in smiles and laurel.

Abbey drew most of the covers for Herbert Jenkins in the 1930s, but for *Summer Moonshine* a new artist, Ian Fenwick, took over. Frank Ford came later, with a similar, but cleaner, line. He did *Money in the Bank* and *Joy in the Morning* post–World War II, followed by *Spring Fever*, *Uncle Dynamite*, *The Mating Season*, *Nothing Serious*, *The Old Reliable*, and *Barmy in Wonderland*.

Sir Osbert Lancaster, the distinguished illustrator who depicted that other tour-de-force of idyllic nostalgia, Max Beerbohm's *Zuleika Dobson*, both in book form and in murals for the Randolph Hotel,

Oxford, made his debut as a Wodehouse jacket designer in 1967 with *Company for Henry*. The Ashby Hall of the story is rendered as a superb Strawberry-Hill-Gothic mansion. Its squire, seated in a deck chair in the grounds, oddly resembles the novelist Anthony Powell. Equally, the left-hand figure on the wrapper of *Do Butlers Burgle Banks?* looks like Tom Driberg, the raffish Labor Member of Parliament. *Much Obliged, Jeeves* (1971) gives us Lancaster's vision of Jeeves, to my mind too vacantly benign and butlerine a figure. The supreme butler (Jeeves is, after all, a valet) is in the act of lighting the candles on a cake of which the surrounding frill reads "1881–1971" in celebration of the Master's ninetieth birthday.

Leslie Illingworth, whose main work was in *Punch* and the *Daily Mail*, was one of the illustrators Penguin used for Wodehouse when their covers went pictorial. But recent Penguins have covers by Ionicus (J. C. Armitage). He is a most accomplished artist. His figures almost all have a kind of baby-faced innocence, and perhaps they lack the dash of devil-may-care insouciance which enlivens the Wodehouse text. But all Wodehouse lovers must be grateful to him for the delightful aerial-view plan of Blandings which appears as endpapers for *Sunset at Blandings* (Chatto and Windus, 1977), and for its dust jacket. This shows the castle in architectural detail, full frontal, that follows most of the guidelines established in the whole canon of Blandings novels and stories.

At their best, the various illustrators of Wodehouse's stories have contributed a sense of style, of setting, of action which decorates the text and diverts the reader. But no depiction of Jeeves, of Bertie, of Gally, Lord Emsworth, of the Rogues' Gallery of Aunts, of Mr. Mulliner and his far-flung relatives is or can be as vivid as the portraits each reader draws for himself as he reads and rereads.

WODEHOUSE'S LEADING BRITISH BOOK AND MAGAZINE ILLUSTRATORS

A numeral following a name indicates the number of magazine stories illustrated by that illustrator. The letters D/W indicate that the illustrator designed the dust wrapper for a book. In certain important cases the name of the book or its character is mentioned.

Abbey (D/W), Lewis Auner (2), Armand Bath (*Love among the Chickens*), H. M. Brock (2), Gordon Browne (2), René Bull (2), Reginald Cleaver (first published picture of Ukridge), Charles Crombie (27), Philip Dadd (*William Tell Told Again*), Treyer Evans (8), Fenwick (D/W), Frank Ford (D/W), Victor Hall (1), Dudley Hardy (D/W), C. Harrison (*The Swoop!*), Harvey (D/W), Alfred Leete (22, including the first published picture of Bertie Wooster and Jeeves), Wilmot Lunt (1), Frank Marston (D/W), Wallis Mills (33), George Morrow (1), C. Morse (D/W), R. Noel Pocock (*The Pothunters, A Prefect's Uncle*), Alexander Popini (2), Harry Rountree (1), Sax (D/W), Ernest H. Shepard (5), J. A. Shepherd (1), Joseph Simpson (8), A. T. Smith (1), W. R. Stott (1), J. H. Thorpe (2), William Townend (*The White Feather*), Clarence Underworld (1), T. M. R. Whitwell (*Mike, The Head of Kay's, Psmith in the City*), Gilbert Wilkinson (28).

BEVIS HILLIER, formerly Editor of The Connoisseur *magazine, is the author of several books on art and antiques, including* Art Deco of the 1920s and 30s *(1968) which began the revival of interwar styles in the late 1960s and early 1970s. As Guest Curator of the Minneapolis Institute of Arts, Minnesota, he coorganized the huge Art Déco exhibition held there in 1971. He is Chairman of the Thirties Society of Great Britain. In 1975 he was created Commendatore of the Italian Order of Merit for "services to art." He is currently writing the authorized biography of Sir John Betjeman, the British Poet Laureate.*

On Translating Wodehouse

GEORG SVENSSON
Translated from the Swedish by Paul Britten Austin

IN THE ART of inventing an ingenious story, supremely farcical, with a series of unexpected, dramatic climaxes, and a sting in the tail, P. G. Wodehouse has few peers among British writers. Whether working in the novel or short-story form, he is a brilliant storyteller. Yet it wasn't this faculty that gave him his unique position as an entertainer and made him so boundlessly popular.

His comical situations, his capacity of creating funny but not excessively caricatured individuals, and of rendering their appearances, their whole way of being and their mental life—insofar as they may be said to evince any—are all immensely diverting. What a joy it is to travel in Wodehouse's company through the English landscape, with its castles and parks, its little villages and railway halts, or to stroll through the London streets and then pop in at some club or office! How amusing is his sharp eye for the differences between British and American life-styles and personalities. To open a Wodehouse book and enter its enchanted world is to shut the door behind one, firmly and finally, on a world that is showing a distressing tendency to become steadily more unpleasant. In Wodehouse's world the cat purrs and the fire crackles in the grate, and all you have to do is take off your slippers, sink back into your armchair, and tell the rest of the world to go to the devil.

And this, surely, is enough for anyone to feel blissfully at home? Not quite so blissful, even so, as one can feel in Wodehouse's company at its best. The real secret, the magic wand of his power, is the virtuoso use of language, in his special mode of self-expression. Actually his style is deceivingly simple, and flows pleasantly on with an appearance of limpid naturalness, yet at the same time it is, paradoxically, saturated with idiosyncrasies.

Wodehouse can express himself simply and straight to the point; indeed, if he didn't, he would soon become wearisome to read. Yet every now and then he permits himself turns of speech and complex periphrases, comprising literary or historical allusions, allegorical tropes and (more or less shockingly distorted) quotations, all of which add up to an imagistic style that is madly comic. Wodehouse's books are packed with these verbal acrobatics; yet as a man of the theatre he knows they must never be allowed to tread more closely on each other's heels than will allow the audience's laughter to settle before the next one.

Thus Wodehouse's success can be said to be due about fifty percent to his comic situations and portrait gallery of characters, fifty percent to his imaginative and humorous use of language. Strictly speaking, such an author ought to be untranslatable. Yet Wodehouse is one of the most frequently translated of all modern authors. Not necessarily, however, one of the *best* translated; his style, I imagine, must be harder to render in some languages than in others. I would suspect that the Wodehouse you get in French or Icelandic is not the Wodehouse you would expect; but here I may be quite wrong. In the last resort I believe it to be a question of whether, in any given tongue, he has had the luck to encounter as translator a kindred spirit, with a wide knowledge of English and an unusual virtuosity in handling his own language.

In Denmark, a Scandinavian country considered to swarm with wits and humorists, Wodehouse has hardly been translated at all. In another Scandinavian country, Sweden, whose life-style is often accused of being wooden to the point of tedium, virtually his entire output has been translated, and is also boundlessly popular. Sweden and Denmark are separated only by a narrow stretch of water. But when it comes to P. G. Wodehouse, the Öresund Strait widens out until it is as broad as the Atlantic.

At the same time Sweden is a country containing any number of Anglophiles, and English is widely read. Many Swedes, not merely Wodehouse addicts either, therefore prefer to read him in English. I should guess that at the peak of his popularity a good many thousand copies of the English editions of his books were sold in Swedish bookshops. And yet most of his works are also available in Swedish translation, and have enjoyed considerable success. When they first appeared, these must have sold in average editions of upwards of ten thousand copies (a lot for a population of between seven and eight million); and they have afterwards been reprinted sometimes several times over in pocket editions.

PGW was himself amazed and delighted that his books should go so well in Sweden. In a letter to me which was included in a collection presented to me on the occasion of my sixtieth birthday he wrote:

> I am glad of this opportunity to tell you how grateful I am to you for all the trouble you have taken to put me over with the Swedish public. I am so intensely spiritual that money means nothing to me, but I must confess that the cheques that Mr. Watt sends me for my Swedish sales do give me a gentle thrill. Whenever a book of mine is going what my publisher calls "slowly" in the USA, I cheer up because I know that everything is going to be all right in Sweden, thanks to you. [It was I who acted as his publisher and editor at Bonniers.]

The first Wodehouse book to be translated into Swedish was *Piccadilly Jim*. It came out in 1920, only two years after the original, and after that a new Wodehouse book appeared in Swedish translation almost annually, until at his death there were seventy of them. Two major anthologies, edited by myself, have also been published.

At first these Wodehouse translations did not sell too well, as can be seen from the frequency with which he changed his Swedish publishers. But from 1934 onwards he stuck with Bonniers. And the reason why he then established himself with the publisher, his critics, and his public is obvious. He had found a translator with a congenial sense of humor who was amazingly clever at rendering his verbal acrobatics into Swedish.

Vilgot Hammarling, a journalist, was the London correspondent of the big daily paper *Dagens Nyheter*. Hammarling had every qualification to be an ideal Wodehouse translator. He spoke English like a native. He was a brilliant stylist. Profoundly saturated in British culture, he was familiar with life in every class of British society. Even if Hammarling might not have been accepted as a member of the Drones Club, he had seen the inside of many other clubs and pubs, observing at close quarters all the types who populate Wodehouse's novels and short stories. Above all he loved Wodehouse's books and had an ear finely attuned to his special brand of humor.

Between 1934 and 1940 Hammarling translated *Leave It to Psmith*, *Heavy Weather*, *Summer Lightning*, *Thank You, Jeeves*, and *Carry on, Jeeves*. That is to say, it was with the Blandings books and Jeeves that Bonniers first seriously got going and turned Wodehouse into a Swedish best-seller.

Today, taking out one of these old Hammarling translations, one notices in every sentence how lovingly he has gone to work at it, obviously chuckling to himself and purring with delight as he turns and twists it this way and that to find its definitive Swedish form and then stands back to admire the resultant turn of phrase. I have had immense enjoyment from comparing, sentence by sentence, word for word, Wodehouse's original with Hammarling's version; and I must confess that, as far as I can judge, these two versions are so close to each other that one would need the kind of camera they use at finishing posts to see who has won.

But not even the cleverest Wodehouse translator can transpose his work word for word into another language. A few random samples of Hammarling's translation of *Heavy Weather* reveal certain liberties taken when he has felt some expression, or even name, could benefit from being exchanged for another. Lord Tilbury's newspaper empire is no longer the Mammoth Publishing Company but Elephant Publishers Ltd. *Tiny Tots*, that journal for the very young, is called in Swedish *The Littlest Ones' Own*, and its hard-hitting columnist Uncle Woggly becomes Farbror Svante, which sounds more in character for Swedish ears. When Ronnie Fish, warning Sue Brown against the attentions of P. Frobisher Pilbeam, refers to him as "the Pilbeam perisher," this, of course, is a verbal subtlety that utterly defies our Swedish tongue; so Hammarling simply has to be content with Ronnie calling Pilbeam "loathsome." Only on one minuscule point am I not prepared to go along with Hammarling's deviations from the sacred original English text. Wodehouse opens his third chapter with a—literal—bird's-eye view of Blandings Castle. Unleashing a bird, which flies over that stately home, he allows it—for safety's sake holding up one claw against the sun—to observe the goings-on on the castle terrace. Hammarling, not content with this bird's being merely an anonymous feathered friend, turns it specifically into an eagle, a fowl famed, as we all know, for its eagle eye. But is this quite right? Surely eagles are quite out of place in the Blandings idyll, are creatures altogether too menacing to be allowed to flutter about in those sacred precincts. Nor are eagles so numerous in Shropshire that they cannot be swiftly counted.

Yet no matter with what intensity of close-up one scrutinizes Hammarling, such petty torts are the most one can accuse him of. Otherwise his translations come perfectly up to the mark. Above all, their *tone* is exactly that of the original. Hammarling and Wodehouse, as humorists, are perfectly in tune.

By and by Hammarling found he had too much else to do. Attached to the Swedish Legation in London as press attaché, he stayed there for the rest of his life, and left the task of translating Wodehouse behind him.

So Wodehouse's Swedish publishers had to find him another translator. Once again they, and Wodehouse, had a stroke of luck. Birgitta Hammar had been introduced to Wodehouse's enchanted garden by her husband, a fanatical Wodehousian. Already well known as a translator from German and English, she had a particularly good hand with humorous books (she also translated Damon Runyon and James Thurber). But Wodehouse was to be her great love. Thanks to her, no fewer than forty-four Wodehouse books became available in Swedish. Instantly it was obvious she had the same qualifications for the job as Vilgot Hammarling. Her translations, too, are labors of love; sparing no pains to get as close as possible to the original, they analyze every sentence for allegorical nuances or for possible hidden allusions to personages or quotations from world literature. And whenever she really got stuck she made no bones about consulting authorities, among them the Master himself.

Birgitta Hammar has told us what translating Wodehouse was like. One of the big difficulties, she says, is the Swedish language's lack of synonyms, at least compared with English. On the same page Wodehouse can call policemen *cops, coppers, peelers, flatfeet, rozzers,* and *fuzz*. We Swedes, too, have sobriquets for our police, many of them not at all flattering. But nothing like so many! The upper- and lower-class slang Wodehouse loves to employ just will not translate into Swedish; and in having recourse to equivalents one is always in danger of awakening the wrong connotations and associations. The same applies, of course, to dialects. How, for instance, to bring out the differences between British and American English?

Another of her difficulties, Birgitta Hammar says, were the quotations. English possesses an inexhaustible treasure-house of old sayings; and Wodehouse draws on it, endlessly. In his book *Wodehouse at Work* Richard Usborne writes that on Jeeves's lips alone he has found quotations from Pliny the younger, Whittier, Fitzgerald, Shelley, Kipling, Keats, Scott, Wordsworth, Emerson, Marcus Aurelius, Shakespeare, Browning, Rosie M. Banks, Moore, Vergil, Gray, Burns, Byron, etc., as well—to make an end—as "whoever it was wrote 'The Wreck of the Hesperus.'" (It was Longfellow, Birgitta Hammar remarks.)

Sometimes Wodehouse gives the sources of his quotations, sometimes he just slips them insidiously into his text. Sometimes they are classical quotations, renderable in recognized Swedish translations, sometimes not; and then the poor translator suddenly has to translate not merely Wodehouse but also Tennyson or Wordsworth.

Worst of all for a Wodehouse translator, Birgitta Hammar laments, are the puns. In ninety-nine cases out of a hundred they are wholly untranslatable. At the same time the action often demands that they *shall* be translated even so, or at least replaced by some Swedish equivalent. And the translator finds he has one more gray hair on his or her already graying head. Not without a trace of bitterness Mrs. Hammar, in the ordinary way of things a good-natured woman, accuses Wodehouse of showing no sympathy at all for his translators, as she in fact herself once told him in a letter.

Notwithstanding these difficulties, Birgitta Hammar must be regarded as having been remarkably successful in transferring Wodehouse's jargon into Swedish. Personally I admire her rendering of the inane chat at the Drones Club, or the gossip at the Anglers' Rest, not to mention the priceless interchanges between Jeeves and Bertie Wooster. Here I do hesitate to use the word *achievement*. It is thanks to these translations, I'm sure, that Wodehouse's books will remain among our immortal classics—even in Swedish.

GEORG SVENSSON (b. 1904) has blended an avocation and a vocation. In 1925 he came across P. G. Wodehouse, and he has been a true believer ever since—reading, enjoying, and publishing the works of the Master in Swedish. Georg Svensson is Vice-President and Vice-Chairman of the Albert Bonnier Publishing Company. In 1932 he founded Bonnier's Literary Magazine (BLM) *and remained its editor for seventeen years, publishing articles on and about Wodehouse. Other than being a Wodehouse man, Mr. Svensson has been an author of books, chairman of the Society for Book Crafts, an active art historian, and the recipient of an honorary doctorate bestowed by Stockholm University. He has also compiled, edited, and published* Alla Tiders Wodehouse.

Wodehouse on Crime

ISAAC ASIMOV

ODD THAT I should have been asked to write on this subject, for it is something I have brooded on quietly during the nearly fifty years that I have been studying P. G. Wodehouse's books with careful attention.

I doubt that there is any facet of Wodehouse's writing that I have not thoroughly considered. I have even noted an occasional lightheartedness in his prose, a trifle of humor (probably unintentional) that brought a slight smile to my face.

Yet it is not the traces of humor that are characteristic of Wodehouse, not that which marks his writing indelibly. It is rather his attitude toward crime, the manner in which wickedness and evil drench very nearly every page and sentence of his tales.

Let me be frank! The level of morality in the Wodehouse canon would have been looked at askance in the foc's'l of a pirate ship. Hard-boiled Wall Street financiers would have pursed their lips in dismay. The average inmate of Sing Sing would have reacted with a sharp intake of breath and a startled "What ho!"

Consider the characters in which the canon abounds, the characters who serve as protagonists. (I was about to say "heroes," but no Wodehouse protagonist can be considered a hero in even the most liberal and diluted sense of the word.)

They are, almost invariably, gentlemen of leisure —with their leisure seriously interfered with by the fact that they usually have no money. Leisure is what they nevertheless cling to with an ardor worthy of a better cause: finding support through loans, at gaining which they are not proficient; wagers, at winning which they are less proficient; and crime, at which their inproficiency is more than made up for by their blackhearted ardor.

Fortunately for Britain, this ardor is largely canceled by the fact that these wastrels are definite guffins, with considerably more than a touch of the gaby to them. Were that not so, one would tremble for the land in which so many members of its upper classes have all the impulses of that master criminal, the late Professor Moriarty, and lack only the brainpower that should go with them—any brainpower at all, actually.

Consider Bertram Wilberforce Wooster. Bertie is considered by many to be the most lovable of Wodehouse's guffins, though I have always considered it significant that Bertie's very own Aunt Agatha, a woman of the most rigid standards and of unsurpassable probity, has the lowest opinion of him and expresses herself on the subject in the strongest terms. Bertie testifies to this himself, which is a very important point, for he is the one principal Wodehousian individual whose story is told in the first person, so that the manifestations of evil he reveals are particularly striking.

What do we know of this Wooster by his own account? To begin with, it is clear that there is not a policeman's helmet that is safe when he is within 3.2 kilometers of it (two miles of it, before Great Britain went metric).

It is needless to expand upon the importance of the London bobby—or the village constable, for that matter—and the manner in which they, unarmed and ill-paid, maintain, with unobtrusive gentleness, England's reputation as the most orderly and law-abiding nation in the world. It is these men, these heroes of order, who are humiliated and left helmetless by the Woosters of the world.

It would not be so bad if Wodehouse were to see to it that this dreadful crime was duly punished; and, indeed, there are occasions when this Wooster and others of his loathsome breed are brought before the beak (or, as he is popularly known among the British criminal classes, the "magistrate"). Unfortunately, the punishment is never appropriately heavy.

A particularly eagle-eyed guardian of the law is Sir Watkyn Bassett of the Bosher Street Station. On one occasion, expressing himself with generous warmth, he fined this odious assaulter of policemen the ridiculously small sum of five pounds, without even a prison sentence to go with it. Yet Bertie had the gall to complain, and to pretend that a simple reprimand would have met the requirements of the case.

It was this same Sir Watkyn who witnessed Bertie's casual attempt to steal another man's umbrella (a crime worse than car theft in rain-drenched Britain). It was also Sir Watkyn who came to realize that there wasn't a cow creamer in England that could expect to remain unpinched until such time as Bertie was incarcerated in the lowest dungeon beneath the castle moat, and well loaded with gyves, to boot. Even then, a wise bookie would be wary of offering odds that Bertie would not make it somehow.

It must be remembered that Wooster, in all his crimes, is aided and abetted by one Reginald Jeeves. Secure in his "cover" as a "gentleman's gentleman," he applies a coolly vicious brain to Bertie's service. It is clear that he does this for money alone since he can scarcely be motivated by admiration for one he contemptuously dismisses as "mentally negligible."

In tale after tale, the monster Jeeves manages to help Bertie escape from the punishment he so richly deserves. Jeeves's least reprehensible tools are lies and misdirection, though he does not hesitate to sink to further depths, as when he impersonates a Scotland Yard detective and pretends that his employer is one Alpine Joe, a common criminal—though there only the name and not the character is misrepresented!

It is not enough, however, that Wodehouse treats the dregs of society such as Bertie and Jeeves as though they were admirable creatures. No, not content with this, he holds up the truly virtuous members of the human species to ridicule and scorn and very often to outright slander. And surely the denigration of the good is even more to be deplored than the exaltation of the wicked.

Consider Sir Watkyn Bassett, whose devotion to truth and justice is undeniable, else he would scarcely undertake the arduous responsibility of the magistracy. Still, despite his heavy labors, he is a man of sunny disposition who keeps the courtroom a place of rollicking laughter with his gibes and sallies.

Yet Sir Watkyn is vilified constantly. Bertie never mentions him without remarks of concentrated slanderous intent. On several occasions, he openly maintains that Sir Watkyn's considerable fortune was obtained by keeping for his own use those five-pound fines he levies on malefactors, a ridiculous contention in view of the fact that a simple calculation will demonstrate that a fortune cannot be amassed in this manner. A handsome bit of pocket money, yes; a respectable fortune, no.

Worse yet, think of Roderick Spode, later Lord Sidcup. Roderick Spode is a person who—though admittedly leader for a while of a fascist group—is a person who is so thoroughly British as to be incapable of a criminal or even unethical act.

Whereas Bertie uses his sexual allure mercilessly, entrapping flighty and helpless maidens unused to the way of city roués—Florence Craye and Honoria Glossop spring to mind—and then callously leaving them in the lurch, Spode is never seen to address any woman in terms of anything but the deepest respect.

Indeed, such is Spode's eagerness to be of service to women that he designs women's underclothing—something which the villainous Jeeves betrays, with no flutter of his nonexistent conscience, although by the standards of his club, the Junior Ganymede, it ought to have remained in sanctified secrecy forever.

Spode has, in fact, been in love with the poetic Madeline Bassett since she was so high (however high that might have been) and has never by word or deed pressed his suit when he thought she loved another, a state of affairs that is almost continuous.

Yet Spode, too, is treated with contempt throughout the canon.

Nor is it only discrete, though indiscreet, acts of crime in which men such as Bertie are involved. There are the more continuous vices which can be observed.

Every person in the tales for whom Wodehouse attempts to elicit any sympathy at all is lost without a continuing and generous supply of alcoholic beverages. No crisis is so small, no turn of events so trivial, as to obviate the necessity for alcoholic stimulants. It should induce no surprise in us that the only individuals in the canon who are described as soberly subsisting on nonalcoholic beverages are uniformly presented as undesirables of the lowest sort. Those teetotalers, moreover, are occasionally induced to drink, through the machinations of the Woosters and the Jeeveses of the Wodehouse world. I need only adduce in proof of this the sad case of Augustus Fink-Nottle who, under the influence of such induced intoxication, made a mess of the prize-awarding ceremonies at the Market Snodsbury Grammar School.

Let us leave Wooster and Jeeves and turn to one Mulliner, whose first name goes unrecorded, probably in order to save him from the obloquy a right-thinking world would otherwise visit upon him.

Mr. Mulliner, clearly a dedicated sot, does not merely drink—he is never seen *anywhere* but in a "public house," as the British pub is familiarly known to the proletariat. There he chronicles the sordid careers of his assorted relatives, any one of whom could step into the ranks of the Dillinger gang with no questions asked.

Mr. Mulliner's nephew, Cyril, is, for instance, in love with the beauteous Amelia Bassett. Were the tale not Wodehouse's, Cyril would win his fair damsel by his loving ways and many virtues, even as you and I have done on innumerable occasions with uniform success (at least in *my* case).

This is not how Cyril operates, you may be sure. He does not hesitate for a moment to employ extortion and blackmail, stealing a murder mystery from Amelia's aging mother—whose large heart makes her a good friend of African tribal chiefs and man-eating pumas—and using his possession of this vital commodity to extort from her permission to marry her daughter. In the process, he also vilely slanders the innocent Lester Mapledurham, a wholly virtuous big-game hunter.

Another nephew, Adrian Mulliner, is a detective, member of a profession wholly devoted to the cause of goodness and the triumph of innocence. Yet, although this Adrian encounters a gaggle of British noblemen of Wodehousian persuasion—that is, noblemen who are, uniformly, petty crooks and cardsharps—our detective arrests none of them. Indeed, he marries the daughter of one of them, recognizing, perhaps, the impossibility of marrying into any well-born family in Great Britain without becoming intimately related to a den of thieves.

Still another nephew, Osbert Mulliner, is a liar and a hypocrite. On the scene at a time when two massive burglars, in an argument over the etiquette of the drawing room, lay each other low with massive blows such as lesser men achieve by swinging battleaxes, Osbert does not hesitate (despite his weedy physique) to claim to have committed the carnage himself. Do others turn away, sickened, at this disrespect for the sanctity of truth? Not in Wodehouse, they don't. Osbert gets the girl.

A fourth nephew, Mordred Mulliner, is drawn into a plot for arson by one of Britain's inevitably criminal nobility and does not shrink in horror at all. He is perfectly willing to collaborate.

But we must turn from the Mulliners, since no one can long gaze into so appalling a sink of iniquity without sinkening—I mean, sickening.

Let us, for a change of pace, though scarcely a change of sickishness—I mean sinkishness—contemplate Stanley Featherstonehaugh Ukridge, who is perhaps the most blatantly disgraceful of all Wodehouse's characters.

I say this in full knowledge that Bingo Little is capable of stealing ten pounds belonging to his infant son in order to bet it on the races, though he is well aware that he has never backed a winner in the history of the sport.

I say this despite the fact that Lord Ickenham thinks nothing of impersonating a variety of people in rapid succession and inducing his nephew Pongo to wreak havoc on the claws of an innocent parrot, while he himself slanders individuals who are absent and cannot defend themselves.

I say this remembering the way in which Dahlia Travers (forgetting her careful upbringing on the foxhunting fields of Great Britain) stands ready at a moment's notice to engage in burglary or grand theft, all accompanied by fruity epithets even Wodehouse dares not place on the printed page, in order to retain the services of her cook, the divine Anatole, or restore the finances of her periodical *Milady's Boudoir*.

Ukridge is a consummate ne'er-do-well who lives on what he can obtain by fraud from tradesmen or borrow from his luckless acquaintances. The most regular victim is George Tupper, a member of the Foreign Office who is forever interrupted in his difficult task of withstanding the cajoleries of sensuous female spies who are after the secret naval plans, in order to fail to withstand the far less desirable cajolery of Ukridge who is usually after at least five pounds.

This is far from the full extent of Ukridge's villainy. He does not hesitate on occasion to organize a group of like-minded cronies (and all the cronies in Wodehouse are like-minded when it comes to criminal conspiracy) for the purpose of defrauding an innocent insurance company by deliberately arranging an accident.

There is no sympathy at all for the sufferings of the directors of the company at being defrauded; there is no concern for the way in which their caviar will turn to ashes in their mouths, for the decay of their stately mansions, for the suffering of their wives, who must hesitate over their next minks, and their daughters, who must wonder fearfully where their next dozen cocktail dresses are to come from.

There is no slightest hint of any remorse at any of this. However, when one of the syndicate, *not* Ukridge, collects and refuses to share with his partners in crime, *then* the tears flow! Nowhere else can you find the naked face of the Wodehousian inversion of ethics so clearly shown.

And yet I doubt that a single library has ever banned a Wodehouse book because of the clear and present danger it presents to public morality! It is useless to try to find any group of Wodehouse's characters that is free of the taint of evil and crime.

Heroines, as a class, are a purer and sweeter kind of being than are the men they love—but not in Wodehouse. What of Roberta Wickham, a woman of outstanding *espièglerie*? (This French word is always left untranslated for reasons we can well imagine; for what about a beautiful girl is likely to be outstanding, eh?) Yet Roberta, despite her physical charms, finds her main delight in luring people to attempt the piercing of a man's hot-water bottle while he lies asleep. To understand the devilishness of this, remember Britain's foul climate and its lack of central heating.

There is also Stephanie Byng, a small heroine, who cannot rest until she maneuvers her fiancé (a man in holy orders, mark you) into attempting the foul crime of stealing the helmet of country constable Eustace Oates.

Women older than our heroines are no better. One would suppose that of all human beings, mothers, as a class, are most worthy of veneration. Yet when Cyril Fotheringay-Phipps agrees to be in charge of the Village Mothers on their annual outing, for the sake of his great love for Angelica Briscoe, it quickly turns out that the Mothers live for pleasure alone and that they are, one and all, friends in semihuman shape.

Nor are innocent little children in any way innocent. Thomas Gregson (the son of Bertie's Aunt Agatha) is widely held to be the scourge of the Midland counties. Nor is Bertie's other cousin, Bonzo Travers, much of an improvement. Even girl-children participate in the universal evil. One need only mention the kid Clementina, absent without leave from her school and, at the tender age of thirteen, indifferent to any sense of decency. For those who know their Wodehouse muppets, the lurid excuses of such films as *The Exorcist* and *The Omen* inspire merely a politely stifled yawn.

Babies? Ha! With utter lack of feeling Wodehousian babies demonstrate their innate blackness of heart on their very faces, for all are incredibly ugly.

There is, for instance, Algernon Aubrey Little, Bingo's infant son. Bingo, having failed to raise a small sum by conscienceless groveling to the Drones Club millionaire, Oofy Prosser (who is constantly vilified for his reluctance to contribute to the further decay of the moral fiber of wastrels by subsidizing them), is reduced to trading on the outstanding ugliness of his infant—and Algernon Aubrey, worthy son of such a father, maliciously allows a competing infant to look uglier, when a timely grimace might have saved the wretched Bingo.

The goings-on at Blandings Castle need not detain us. To be sure, Galahad Threepwood is engaged in writing an autobiography that will totally ruin the reputation of every friend and associate he ever had. To be equally sure, the Empress of Blandings, Lord Emsworth's prize pig, is kidnapped so frequently and so relentlessly that she can scarcely have time to eat. To be finally sure, the efficient, intelligent and virtuous Rupert Baxter is relentlessly pilloried simply because he does not fit into the vice and evil that surround him. Despite all this, Blandings is saved by the fact that Lord Emsworth himself is too far gone in senility to be truly evil.

Yet if this is a spark of the good, how quenched it is by the appalling thought that even the Wodehouse animals are evil! It suffices to refer to Stephanie Byng's Aberdeen terrier, the dog Bartholomew, which not only has teeth that bite like the serpent and sting like the adder, but is afflicted with doggie odor as well.

Cats are, perhaps, better, but even the saintly Webster is seduced by the demon rum into behavior which, for squalor and impropriety can scarcely be exceeded—and, mark you, like all Wodehouse's characters, once debauched he never recovers.

It is a relief to turn from this pervasive miasma of villainy to the occasional professional crook who appears. There is, preeminently, Soapy Molloy and his wife, Dolly. How different they are from this vast legion of amateurs of evil!

The Molloys are businesspeople, that is all. It is their peculiar task to relieve others of the burden of unnecessary wealth, taking all its cares and concerns on their own shoulders.

The point is that *they do not succeed*. They never succeed. Not once do they succeed. In fact, none of the professional crooks succeeds.

The moral is plain. In the world of Wodehousian crime, the merely talented professional is as putty in the hands of the heartless fiends who pass as "respectable" people by the degraded standards of the canon.

And yet there are those who feign to find Wodehouse amusing!

ISAAC ASIMOV was born in 1920 in the U.S.S.R.: a fortunate emigration by his parents during his infancy made him culturally and spiritually a native of Brooklyn, New York. Asimov has pursued his youthful interest in science and science fiction to such an extent that he has at the time of going to press had published more than 230 books in those fields (and in others, such as his guides to the Bible and Shakespeare, and collections of limericks), and will certainly by the time this is in readers' hands have published half-a-dozen more at least. Asimov admits (or claims) that his character Henry the waiter, in his "Black Widowers" detective stories, is modeled on Jeeves. He lives in New York City with his wife, the psychologist and writer Janet Jeppson.

Valley Fields
RICHARD USBORNE

I HAVE ALWAYS wondered why Wodehouse called it Mitching Hill in the 1936 short story "Uncle Fred Flits By." He had, eleven years before, established Valley Fields in *Sam the Sudden* (*Sam in the Suburbs* in the U.S.) and *Big Money* (1931); and when, in the novel *Uncle Fred in the Springtime* (1939), Uncle Fred harks back nostalgically to the events of "Uncle Fred Flits By," he three times refers to the scene of his misbehavior as Valley Fields. Mitching Hill, forsooth! "Uncle Fred Flits By" is, and must be taken as, set in Valley Fields, which, in its turn is, of course—and I quote Wodehouse's preface, written when he was ninety-plus, to a new edition of *Sam the Sudden*—"a thin disguise for the Dulwich where so many of my happiest hours have been spent. . . . I hope that in the thirty-three years since I have seen it Valley Fields has not ceased to be a 'fragrant backwater' (so described by Major Flood-Smith of Castlewood). Though I did read somewhere about a firm of builders wanting to put up a block of flats in Broxted Road, where I once lived in the first house on the left as you come up from the station. Gad, sir, if anyone had tried to do that in my time, I'd have horsewhipped them on the steps of their club, if they had a club."

And in 1948 he wrote, in a letter from New York, "Awful, the bomb damage in Dulwich. But what pains me most—oddly—is to hear that The Alleyn's Head has been destroyed. I used to have bread and cheese and beer in the taproom there whenever I went to see a match."

Two years in the wake of a distinguished elder brother, Pelham Wodehouse was at Dulwich College for six years and a term, 1894–1900. In his first term, as a dayboy (there were, and still are, more dayboys than boarders at Dulwich), he lodged at the house of an assistant master at the school, in East Dulwich; in his second, he became a boarder, in the house where now the Master lives. Then his parents came back from Hong Kong and took a house in Dulwich; so young Pelham lived with them there and was once more a dayboy. When his family moved to Shropshire, he became a boarder again. After he had left school and was a junior trainee in the Hong Kong and Shanghai Bank in the City of London, there was a period when he (like Mike Jackson, a slightly autobiographical character in *Psmith in the City*) had digs near his old school. And, as a more and more eminent Old Boy, he often came down to watch school football and cricket matches. He had been in the school XI and XV in his day, and now he sometimes wrote accounts of the school matches in *The Alleynian*, of which he had himself been a joint editor.

He had loved his school, his schooldays, and Dulwich itself. Say what you like about Wodehouse the chronicler of dukes, earls, and occasionally mere baronets, of Mayfair idlers at the Drones Club, of huge country castles and mansions, Wodehouse the man, as Wodehouse the boy, had his heart in the right place, and that place was Valley Fields.

"In the course of a long life I have flitted about a

bit," he wrote in the *Sam* preface; "I have had homes in Mayfair, in Park Avenue, New York, in Beverly Hills, California, and other posh localities, but I have always been a suburbanite at heart, and it is when I get a plot calling for a suburban setting that I really roll up my sleeves and give of my best." George Bernard Shaw (I think) said of Jane Austen (I know) that he knew her writing (not writings) so well that he could tell the places where she had put down her pen and gone to make herself a cup of tea. I shall never again, alas, read a Wodehouse novel for the first time. But in the late 1950s and through the 1960s, at first readings I had accurate presentiments, when a Mayfairish plot became too rich with butlers, earls, debs, and cocktails, that we would find ourselves, "like swimmers into cleanness leaping" (to pinch a poetic bit from Rupert Brooke), in Valley Fields.

"I fancy one gets there by omnibuses and things," says Pongo's Uncle Fred after lunch in Pongo's flat in the Albany, when the old goat proposes to take his nephew to visit the home of his ancestors. And they did. Lord Ickenham loved it, "stopping at intervals like a pointing dog and saying that it must have been just about here that he plugged the gardener in the trousers seat with his bow and arrow and that over there he had been sick after his first cigar, and he now paused in front of a villa which for some unknown reason called itself The Cedars." It is difficult to stop quoting from that gorgeous story. Suffice it to say that a nasty young spring breeze and downpour of rain drove these two interlopers to shelter in the windy porch of The Cedars, and soon Uncle Fred was introducing himself to the lone maidservant as the vet came, with his deaf-and-dumb assistant (Pongo), to clip the claws of the parrot he had seen through the front parlor windows. "Tap your teeth with a pencil," said his uncle to Pongo when instructing him on how to behave as a deaf-and-dumb assistant veterinary surgeon, "and try to smell of iodoform."

Perhaps Wodehouse felt at the time that Uncle Fred and Pongo had gone too far in fooling the (pleasant but peasant) lower-middle-class citizens of the suburb, and had therefore dubbed it Mitching Hill lest beloved Valley Fields feel the slight. Certainly the venue was Valley Fields for Uncle Fred in memory, and for Wodehouse from the start. And, yes, one does still get there by omnibuses and things. The Number 3 from Piccadilly Circus, free to us old-age pensioners on Saturdays and Sundays and between 0930 and 1600 hours on weekdays, but costing the thick end of £1 sterling to striplings, goes all the way to the corner of Croxleigh Road. The train from Victoria (to West Dulwich station), which cost the Earl of Hoddesdon (*Big Money*) a shilling and a penny first-class, now has no class distinctions and, at the time of writing, costs you rather, but not much, less than the bus. It is also quicker than the bus, if less interesting. Berry Conway in the same book could sprint from The Nook in Mulberry Grove to the station in about eighty-three seconds. I am sure young Wodehouse, whose £80-a-year salary at the bank would have been docked for repeated late arrival in the mornings, timed the sprint from "the first house on the left in Broxted Road" (or would it have been "last house on the right" as he hurtled down *to* the station?).

Berry Conway, otherwise a West End clubman, lived in Valley Fields, with Mrs. Hannah Wisdom, his housekeeper and old nannie, because that was all he could afford. His friend Lord Biskerton (The Biscuit), son of the Earl of Hoddesdon, above, came down there to live because he wanted to disappear from his creditors and his fiancée for a spell. And The Biscuit's father, the indigent sixth Earl, came down to find his son.

"How is the guv'nor? Pretty fit and insolvent? Still stealing the cat's milk and nosing about in the streets for cigar ends?"

"His health and finances are in much the same state as usual."

"Poor old chap!" said The Biscuit sympathetically . . .

The sixth Earl was foolish enough to come to Valley Fields wearing a gray top hat. What Valley Fields thought of toffs in gray toppers you must read for yourself.

Mulberry Grove, Ogilvy Street, Burberry Road, Roxborough Road, Mafeking Road, and their detached and semi-d. villas—The Cedars, San Rafael, Mon Repos, Peacehaven, Castlewood, The Nook—these and many more housed many nice people in peace. Well, comparative peace. Claire Lippett in *Sam the Sudden* had a revolver; and *The Ice in the Bedroom*, which, after *Sam the Sudden* and *Big Money*, dwells most lovingly on Valley Fields, brings Leila Yorke, best-selling romantic novelist, to that Elysian suburb, equipped for obscure reasons with a shotgun and ammunition, which stand her in good stead in a confrontation with those ageless crooks, the Molloys and Chimp Twist, and disturb the peace like anything.

The presiding spirit of the place is Mr. Cornelius of The Nook, house-agent and historian of Valley Fields, with long white druidical beard, pet rabbits, and vast wealth that he keeps secret from his wife (he doesn't want her to move him away from the suburb that he loves and, probably, make him go to the opera and play polo). Mr. Cornelius in *The Ice in the Bedroom* (1961) is not a day older than he was in *Sam the Sudden*; and to support his love for his "native land," Valley Fields, he is still quoting those twelve lines from Walter Scott ("Breathes there a man with soul so dead" and so on). Though not their own, their native land—so far as is known—Valley Fields had a magnetic attraction for many other Wodehouse characters. Ex-butler Keggs—if it's the same Keggs every time, he has buttled for many masters, in England and America—owns a number of Valley Fields villas, and Mr. Cornelius rents them for him. Maudie Stubbs, niece of Sebastian Beach, butler of Blandings Castle (Maudie Montrose, barmaid of the Criterion that was, Lady Parsloe-Parsloe of Matchingham Hall that's to be), had a "neat little house" in Valley Fields. Gertrude Butterwick's father lives in West Dulwich (same thing). An old nanny in *Bachelors Anonymous* lives in Valley Fields. Lord Tilbury was twice debagged in Valley Fields. The secretary, later wife, of Cedric Mulliner, dapper Mayfair snob, lived there. The Rev. Aubrey Jerningham, author of "Is There a Hell?" lives there, the new vicar. And that's not all. I hope I've made my point.

Wodehouse never did come back to his beloved suburb. He had probably had bread and cheese and beer in the old Alleyn's Head that winter day in 1933 when he came to watch the Dulwich-Sherborne match on the school grounds. Dulwich was leading five to three at the end of the first half and, against odds, they held their lead through to the end. But Old Boy Wodehouse wasn't able to endure the strain of watching to the end. He walked round the roads outside the grounds until the great cheering told him that the match was over and the home team, his old school, had won. He then *walked* the seven miles from Dulwich to the Dorchester Hotel in Mayfair, where he was staying, in a state of great happiness, and, he said, he could not remember anything about those seven miles through the streets of London: Herne Hill, Brixton, Clapham (cross the river), Sloane Square, Hyde Park, Park Lane. He was playing the game over in his mind—what he had had the courage to see, and the rest in his prescient imagination.

Wodehouse was at Dulwich, with his old school friend Bill Townend, watching a cricket match in July 1939. But that was the last time he walked in Valley Fields. It stayed plentifully and lovingly in his memory and his books for another thirty-odd years. I would gladly subscribe something of the cost if someone put up a notice somewhere in acknowledgment, such as

YOU ARE NOW ENTERING
[OR LEAVING]
THE AREA OF DULWICH, LONDON SE 19,
WHICH SIR PELHAM WODEHOUSE,
ONCE A SCHOOLBOY HERE,
GLORIFIED AS "VALLEY FIELDS"
IN MANY NOVELS AND STORIES.

Wodehouse on Golf
JOHN GARRARD

"YOU HIT A BALL with a stick until it falls into a hole."[1] This stark definition of the royal and ancient game comes, rather surprisingly, from the lips of the Oldest Member who, elsewhere in the course of a considerable oeuvre, never fails to treat it with all proper reverence.

The Oldest Member appears on the terraces or in the bars of what seem to be a number of different golf clubs on either side of the Atlantic, always ready to listen sympathetically to the predicaments of his juniors and to ensure—if necessary by attaching himself to their lapels or coattails—that they hear from his apparently inexhaustible repertoire some tale of golf or golfers from which a moral can be drawn to comfort them in their distress. He is the narrator of almost all the Wodehouse golfing stories, and he ranks with the other supreme spellbinders, Mulliner and Wooster. His art, indeed, is such that he can be read with pleasure and profit even by the lower forms of life, players of tennis, croquet, bowls, and the like. In the hands of the Master, the microcosm of golf assumes a universal significance.

Wodehouse himself had been a useful and enthusiastic cricketer and footballer in his schooldays and a more than useful boxer as well, and he followed the fortunes of his old school, Dulwich, in these sports to the end of his life. It was golf, which he did not take up until middle age, which seems to have moved his deeper emotions and to have inspired some of his profoundest and most moving passages. Writing at the age of ninety-two, he says:

> Whenever you see me with a furrowed brow you can be sure that what is on my mind is the thought that if only I had taken up golf earlier and devoted my whole time to it instead of fooling about writing stories and things, I might have got my handicap down to eighteen. . . . It is this reflection that has always made my writing so somber, its whole aroma like that of muddy shoes in a Russian locker room.[2]

Indeed, his very first golf story, "The Clicking of Cuthbert,"[3] has a strong Russian flavor with Vladimir Brusiloff, the novelist who specializes in gray studies of hopeless misery, trapped in the inferno of a meeting of the suburban Wood Hills Literary Society. This tale has a happy ending, for Vladimir is also an enthusiastic golfer and finds a kindred spirit in these unlikely surroundings in the young Cuthbert Banks, winner of the French Open. Cuthbert is there not so much in pursuit of culture as of Adeline Smethurst, his hostess's daughter. She has, so far, spurned him in favor of Raymond Parsloe Devine who, as the most Russian of the younger English novelists, occupies a seemingly unassailable standing both in the literary society and in Adeline's affections. But everything changes when Cuthbert is introduced to the effervescent Muscovite:

> "Banks!" cried Vladimir Brusiloff. "Not Cootaboot Banks. . . . My dear young man, I saw you win ze French Open. . . . Will you permit one who is but eighteen at Nijni-Novgorod to salute you."

The famous Russian novelist's open admiration of Cuthbert inspires similar feelings in Adeline, obliterating those she had held for Parsloe Devine. And as Vladimir and Cuthbert go off to shoot a few holes together, Adeline says tenderly:

> "May I come, too, and walk round with you?"
> Cuthbert's bosom heaved.
> "Oh," he said, with a tremor in his voice, "that you would walk round with me for life!"

It may have saddened Wodehouse's life that he never rose from the ranks of the golfing rabbits; but it is to this we owe the marvelous series of portraits of creatures who inhabit the golfing underworld, whose dark doings would otherwise have gone unrecorded.

First, the Wrecking Crew, a quartet of retired businessmen who had taken up the noble game late in life because their doctors had ordered them air and exercise. They were the Man with the Ace, Old Father Time, Consul the Almost Human, and—if there can be said to be grades in such a subspecies—their star performer, the First Grave-Digger.

---

1. *Golf without Tears*: VIII, "The Heel of Achilles."
2. *The Golfing Omnibus*: Introduction.
3. *Golf without Tears*: I, "The Clicking of Cuthbert."

He differed from his colleagues in that, while they were content to peck cautiously at the ball, he never spared himself in his efforts to do it a violent injury.[4]

To impatient golfers playing behind them, the Wrecking Crew, "moving with their caddies in mass formation, looked like one of those great race migrations of the Middle Ages."

Then there was the loquacious George Mackintosh who, to cure himself of shyness, had taken a correspondence course—all too effective—on "how to become a convincing talker." In the end, the only partner he could find was old Major Moseby whose hearing had petered out as long ago as the year '98. George's fianceé, Celia Tennant, was forced to take decisive action, with her mashie, as she explained to the Oldest Member.

> "I have no fiancé," she said in a dull, hard voice.
> "You have broken off the engagement?"
> "Not exactly. And yet—well, I suppose it amounts to that."
> "I don't quite understand."
> "Well the fact is," said Celia in a burst of girlish frankness, "I rather think I've killed George."[5]

George Mackintosh was undoubtedly better dead, but it had taken a woman's intuition to see it.

Continuing our tour of the golfing Rogues' Gallery or Chamber of Horrors, we come to Alexander Paterson, the slow player whose antics and contortions before performing the simple act of hitting a stationary ball are far too lengthy to be recounted here. Bearing in mind that statisticians estimate that the average of crime amongst good golfers is lower than in any other class of the community, except possibly bishops, Paterson determined to play golf with two young men in his employ before deciding which of them to appoint as treasurer of his company. It seemed a foregone conclusion, for Rupert Dixon was exceptionally self-controlled, whereas Mitchell Holmes was both nervy—he missed putts because of the uproar of the butterflies in the adjoining meadows—and impatient. He would be driven frantic by the Paterson style of play; moreover, he had a great gift of language and used it unsparingly. Mitchell managed to get as far as the fourteenth hole without quite reaching boiling point, but then the worst happened: his caddy crunched an apple as Mitchell drove, and the ball disappeared into the ravine.

Mitchell dropped his club and turned. His face was working horribly. "Mitchell!" I cried. "My boy! Reflect! Be calm."

"Calm! What's the use of being calm when people are chewing apples in thousands all round you? What *is* this, anyway—a golf match or a pleasant day's outing for the children of the poor? Apples! Go on, my boy, take another bite. Take several. Enjoy yourself! Never mind if it seems to cause me a fleeting annoyance. Go on with your lunch! You probably had a light breakfast, eh, and are feeling a little peckish, yes? If you wait here, I will run to the clubhouse and get you a sandwich and a bottle of ginger-ale. Make yourself at home, you lovable little fellow! Sit down and have a good time."

Then he conceded the match to Paterson, who at once offered him the post of treasurer. As Paterson later explained to the Oldest Member:

> "I have come to the conclusion that what the Paterson Dyeing and Refining Company really needs is a treasurer whom I can beat at golf. And I have discovered the ideal man.
>
> "Why," he went on, a look of holy enthusiasm on his fine old face, "do you realize that I can always lick the stuffing out of that boy, good player as he is, simply by taking a little trouble? I can make him get the wind up every time, simply by taking one or two extra practice swings! That is the sort of man I need for a responsible post in my office."[6]

There is a quick glance at the golfing wife:

> "It has always seemed to me a strange and unaccountable thing that nowadays, when gloom is at such a premium in the world's literature and all around us stern young pessimists are bringing home the bacon with their studies in the grayly grim, no writer has thought of turning his pen to a realistic portrayal of the golfing wife. No subject could be more poignant, and yet it has been completely neglected. One can only suppose that even modern novelists feel that the line should be drawn somewhere."[7]

These harsh words do not apply to the queenly

---

4. *The Heart of a Goof*: IV, "Chester Forgets Himself."
5. *Golf without Tears*: V, "The Salvation of George Mackintosh."
6. Ibid.: VI, "Ordeal by Golf."
7. *The Heart of a Goof*: III, "Keeping in with Vosper."

Clarice Plinlimmon, née Fitch, big-game hunter and explorer. In the early days of his courtship, Ernest Plinlimmon, the average adjuster, groveled before her and was duly spurned, her ideal being more on the lines of Sir Jasper Medallion-Carteret—who, in the novel she was reading, caught the heroine a juicy one with his hunting crop just on the spot where it would make her think a bit.

> "It is killing me, this great love of mine," he said. "I cannot eat, cannot sleep. It has begun to affect my work. Sometimes in my office, as I start to adjust an average her face rises between me and it, so that I adjust it all crooked and have to start over again."

Fortunately, for "average adjusters are like Chartered Accountants—when they love they give their hearts forever," Ernest accidentally hits Clarice with a golf ball, cracks her on the shin with his putter, and, flinging his arms out in a passionate gesture of remorse, blacks her eye. All this adds up to a passable imitation of Sir Jasper. Clarice throws her arms round him and they live happily ever after.[8]

Of course, even golf does not always provide the happy ending. Even the Oldest Member once advised a man to give it up—Jenkinson, the goof.

> A goof.... One of those unfortunate beings who have allowed this noblest of sports to get too great a grip upon them ... his goofery unfits him for the battles of life. Jenkinson, for example, was once a man with a glowing future in the hay, corn and feed business, but a constant stream of hooks, tops and slices gradually made him so diffident and mistrustful of himself, that he let opportunity after opportunity slip, with the result that other, sterner, hay, corn and feed merchants passed him in the race. Every time he had the chance to carry through some big deal in hay, or to execute some flashing *coup* in corn and feed, the fatal diffidence generated by a hundred rotten rounds would undo him. I understand his bankruptcy may be expected at any moment.[9]

But *nil desperandum*. Think of Rollo Podmarsh, whose love for the charming Mary Kent proved to be his means of salvation:

> Titanic emotions were surging in Rollo's bosom as he addressed his ball.... "Oh, Mary! Mary!" he breathed to himself as he swung.... If you were a golfer, you would realize that in selecting just that invocation to breathe to himself, Rollo Podmarsh had hit, by sheer accident, on the ideal method of achieving a fine drive. The first two words, tensely breathed, are just sufficient to take a man with the proper slowness to the top of his swing; the first syllable of the second "Mary" exactly coincides with the striking of the ball; and the final "ry!" takes care of the follow-through. The consequence was that Rollo's ball, instead of hopping down the hill like an embarrassed duck, as was its usual practice, sang off the tee with a scream like a shell and ... came to rest within easy distance of the green.

At the short second hole, as he took his mashie from the bag,

> ... he *knew* that his first shot would soar successfully on to the green. "Ah, Mary!" he breathed as he swung.... In altering and shortening his soliloquy at this juncture Rollo had done the very thing any good pro would have recommended. If he had murmured, "Oh, Mary! Mary!" as before, he would have over-swung. "Ah, Mary!" was exactly right for a half-swing with the mashie. His ball shot up in a beautiful arc, and trickled to within six inches of the hole.[10]

No doubt Mr. Nicklaus, as he comes to the eighteenth tee in Augusta, needing a four to win the Masters' championship, mutters some such formula to himself, assuming, of course, that Mrs. Nicklaus's name does not happen to be Berengaria or Jane. Many of the girls in the golfing stories do have polysyllabic names which are of no special help to their admirers. The partner whom Wilmot Byng had "selected for life's medal round was a charming girl named Gwendoline Poskitt." Rodney Spelvin, although feeling unworthy even "to polish the blade of her niblick," marries Anastasia Bates. Angus McTavish is engaged to Evangeline Brackett, a devoted and serious golfer who on the short fourteenth got "one of those lucky twos which, as James Braid once said to J. H. Taylor, seem like a dome of many-colored glass to stain the white radiance of Eternity."

In the preface to *The Heart of a Goof* Wodehouse "noticed with regret, a disposition on the part of certain writers to speak of Golf as a trivial theme, unworthy of the pen of a thinker." He was certainly not guilty of such a fault himself.

---

8. *Lord Emsworth and Others*: V, "There's Always Golf."
9. *The Heart of a Goof*: I, "The Heart of a Goof."
10. Ibid.: VI, "The Awakening of Rollo Podmarsh."

Perhaps the most outstanding virtue of this noble pursuit is the fact that it is a medicine for the soul. Its great service to humanity is that it teaches human beings that, whatever petty triumphs they have achieved in other walks of life, they are after all merely human. It acts as a corrective against sinful pride. I attribute the insane arrogance of the later Roman emperors almost entirely to the fact that, never having played golf, they never knew that strange chastening humility which is engendered by a topped chip-shot. If Cleopatra had been outed in the first round of the Ladies' Singles, we should have heard a lot less of her proud imperiousness.

This piece of historical insight Wodehouse used to good effect in his account of Merolchazzar, long-ago king of (presumably Mideastern) Oom, in which the monarch is intrigued by the uncouth posturings of a Scots captive equipped with a hoe and a stone. Once the barbarian has invoked his alien deity, Gowf, with the magic words, "Dinna press or sway the heid and keep yer e'e on the ba'," the infection seizes hold of Merolchazzar, and, shortly, all of Oom. It is, naturally enough, a benign disease, softening Merolchazzar's autocratic rule, defanging a priestly rebellion, and eventually cementing by marriage an alliance between Oom and the Outer Isles, whose Princess (possessed of—or by—her own Caledonian slave), has recently won the Ladies' Open.[11]

Statecraft and politics are not so handled nowadays, more's the pity.

Wodehouse may have been a twenty-four-handicap man on the golf course, but when it came to writing about the game he was plus two, and, indeed, the handicap committee would have had difficulty in finding anyone to make any sort of a match with him, even on those terms. With his typewriter he could give anyone else a stroke a hole and beat them out of sight. Writing about games has been the business of many authors in the English language over the last two hundred years or so. Those who have transformed this business into an art are a select and exalted company—William Hazlitt, Charles Dickens, Bernard Darwin, and P. G. Wodehouse.

11. *Golf without Tears*: X, "The Coming of Gowf."

Native Woodnotes Wild

RICHARD USBORNE

ONE WAY of writing successful novels is mine—making the thing practically a fairy story and ignoring real life altogether." So wrote Wodehouse in a letter to his friend Bill Townend in 1934.

I have heard it said, and seen it in print, that on a moonless night in 1942, during the Second World War, the German Secret Service dropped a spy onto Dartmoor in Devonshire; he was wearing spats and was soon marched off with gyves on his wrists. The theory is that the decision-makers at German Secret Service headquarters were, to a man, overcredulous readers of P. G. Wodehouse and thought that spats were still the proper wear for a young Englishman, not only in Mayfair but anywhere south of Scotland.

If so, they were at least a quarter of a century out in their reckoning. In the First World War a German spy in spats might have passed unnoticed in England, or, say, might not instantly have been nabbed as an impostor. But Wodehouse was not being translated into German then, and, anyway, it was not till spats had virtually disappeared off the feet of the young men in England that Wodehouse wrote about them. He gave the title *Young Men in Spats* to a collection of Drones Club short stories as late as 1936. I was a very clothes-conscious young man in London then, and I don't think I would have known where to buy spats if I had wanted them for a fancy dress party.

The German ex-Kaiser—the All-Highest until the defeat of Germany in 1918—in postwar exile in Holland had discovered the works of Wodehouse, could read them in English, loved them and used to read them aloud, in English, to the officers of his loyal but reduced staff. They were not as good at English, or at Wodehouse, as their master, who not only kept them to (seated) attention for the length of a Wodehouse short story o' nights, but, when he had read a passage which he judged specially funny, he read it again for his own pleasure and, he thought, theirs.

There is no evidence that Hitler, Germany's All-Highest in the Second World War, knew his Wodehouse scriptures. But his official interpreter, Dr. Paul Schmidt, was a devotee, and the word may have seeped round the Chancellery that the young upper-class Englishman wore spats and a monocle, had a valet, butter-colored hair, no chin, and no job, and threw crusty bread rolls and sugar lumps from table to table in his club dining room.

To me, an Englishman, one of the great charms and great unrealities of the Wodehouse books is his depiction of English weather. His own preferred season in England was autumn—a walk in the park with his Pekes on a still, gray November afternoon was what he liked best of all. But in his books England seems to enjoy perpetual high summer: sunshine by day, velvety warmth at night.

I am looking particularly at the Blandings Castle books, partly because I am just surfacing from my *n*th rereading of the whole Blandings canon, partly because it spans as near as (dammit) sixty publishing years—*Something Fresh* (1915) to *Sunset at Blandings* (1977). In fact there is a nip in the air at the beginning of *Something Fresh*. As Ashe Marson and Joan Valentine (he as a valet to an American millionaire, she as lady's maid to the millionaire's daughter) are trundled up to the castle from Market Blandings station in the uncovered horse-drawn cart reserved for servants and luggage, the cold east evening wind turns Ashe into "a mere chunk of frozen misery." And when he arrives and is taken to meet "Mr. Beach," the butler, in his pantry, he is given a welcoming whisky toddy. There is a fire in the grate and a kettle simmering on the hob.

In all the subsequent books, did Beach ever dispense hot drinks to his callers? Never, surely. It is port that Galahad came for, port that American Penny Donaldson demanded, port that Beach himself drank as a rule after he had served the postprandial tea in the drawing room and had locked all the outer doors for the night. Never again a fire in the grate, or a hob, or a kettle. In that first Blandings book it is early spring. Wodehouse refers to the house party, in honor of Freddie Threepwood's engagement to the millionaire's daughter, as occurring between the shooting and hunting seasons—which only shows that the young (well, in his early thirties) Wodehouse was not a shooting or hunting man. But in all the books to come the season is hay-harvest summer. Lord Emsworth goes down to the lake every morning to swim before breakfast, and at night to the Empress's sty just to listen to her breathing in her surfeited sleep. Lord Emsworth's resident younger brother Galahad and Lord Ickenham on visits assume that there will be a hammock under the big cedar for their morning cerebrations. In one book Galahad races his disliked sister Julia to the hammock after breakfast. It sounds as though the hammock is there all day and all night in summer. Tea is served on the lawn (a procession of two footmen carrying the essentials, followed by Beach to add authority) and after-dinner coffee on the terrace or in an arbor. And, further afield, three miles from the castle, the Emsworth Arms public house is serving teas and drinks on the lawn that runs down to the river. The snakeless meadows between are basking in summer, real summer: hammock weather, barring a few thunderstorms to drive quarreling young couples into woodland shelters and each other's arms.

I can think of only three Wodehouse short stories set in winter, and I am sure that research would prove that all three had been written to magazine editors' requests for seasonal stuff for their Christmas numbers. In "The Knightly Quest of Mervyn," Mr. Mulliner's cousin's son Mervyn is challenged by his adored object to prove his adoration by getting her some strawberries. The season, winter, is required for the story, but the weather gets no mention until, while he was going for a meditative walk through the messuages and pleasances of his uncle's place, Blotsam Castle, "the east wind went through his plus fours like a javelin." The cold wind drove Mervyn into his uncle's hothouses, where he found ripe strawberries growing in abundance. And so.... Then there was the "Jeeves and the Yuletide Spirit" story. Bertie, in love with the adorable and deplorable Bobbie Wickham at the time, had been invited by Lady Wickham to Skeldings for Christmas. Without Christmas and the (unmentioned) cold, not everybody would have had hot-water bottles in their beds, and it would not have been quite so indu-

PLATE 25

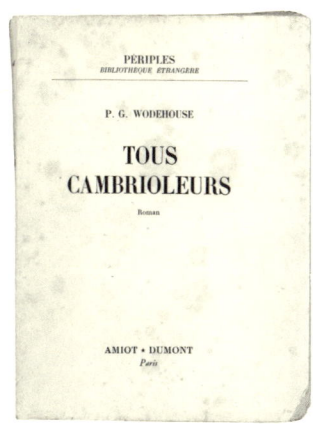
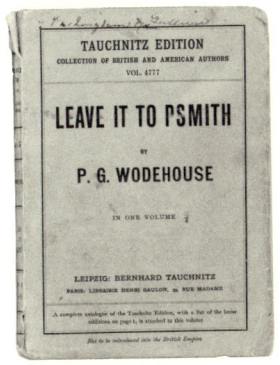

Leave It to Psmith in any other language.

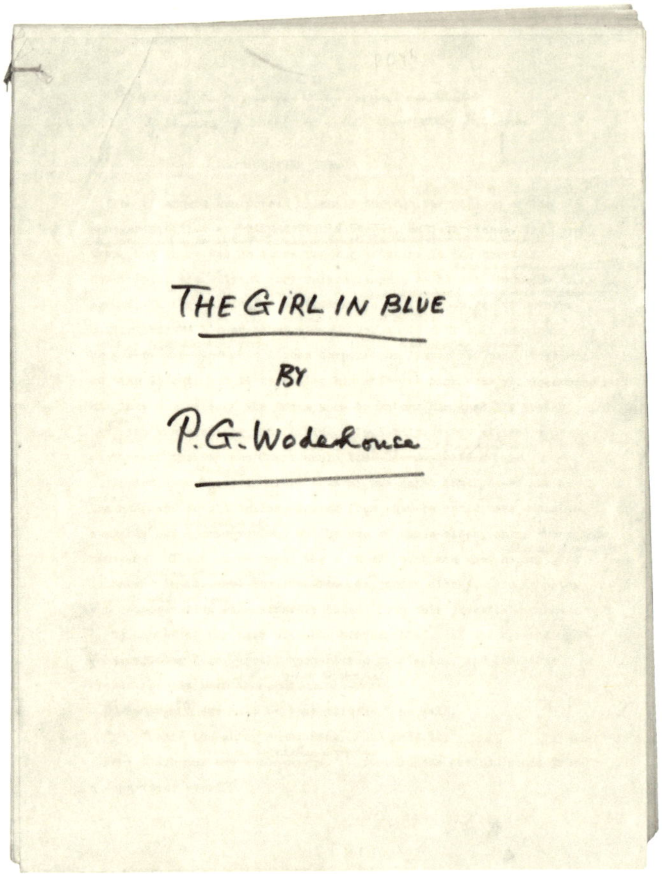

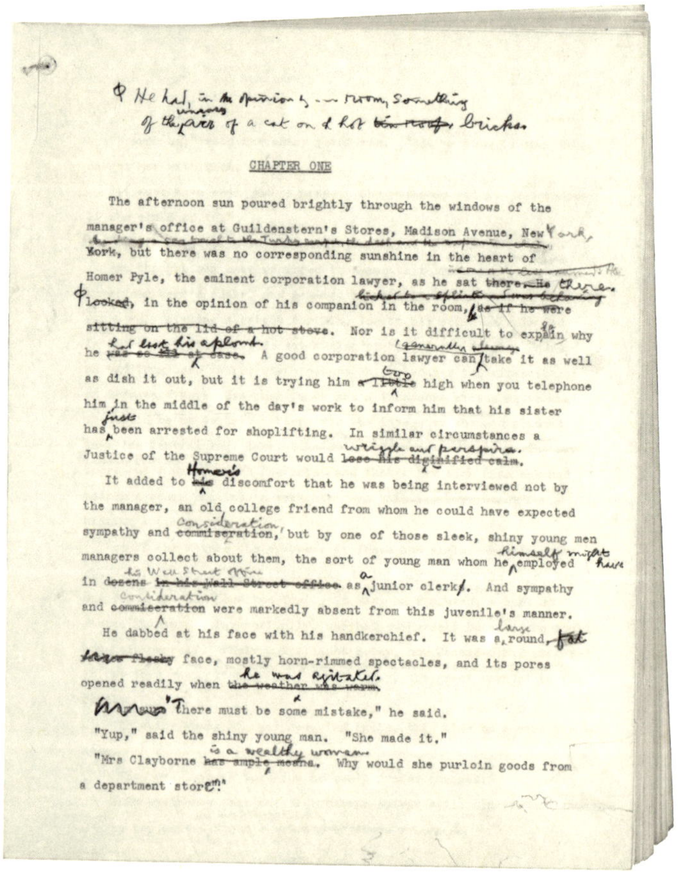

CHAPTER ONE

The afternoon sun poured brightly through the windows of the manager's office at Guildenstern's Stores, Madison Avenue, New York, but there was no corresponding sunshine in the heart of Homer Pyle, the eminent corporation lawyer, as he sat there. He looked, in the opinion of his companion in the room, as if he were sitting on the lid of a hot stove. Nor is it difficult to explain why he was so ill at ease. A good corporation lawyer can take it as well as dish it out, but it is trying him a little high when you telephone him in the middle of the day's work to inform him that his sister has been arrested for shoplifting. In similar circumstances a Justice of the Supreme Court would lose his dignified calm.

It added to his discomfort that he was being interviewed not by the manager, an old college friend from whom he could have expected sympathy and commiseration, but by one of those sleek, shiny young men managers collect about them, the sort of young man whom he employed in dozens in his Wall Street office as junior clerks. And sympathy and commiseration were markedly absent from this juvenile's manner.

He dabbed at his face with his handkerchief. It was a round, large fleshy face, mostly horn-rimmed spectacles, and its pores opened readily when the weather was warm.

"There must be some mistake," he said.

"Yup," said the shiny young man. "She made it."

"Mrs Clayborne has ample means. Why would she purloin goods from a department store?"

The original typescript with Wodehouse's revision in his own hand of *The Girl in Blue* (1971).

PLATE 27

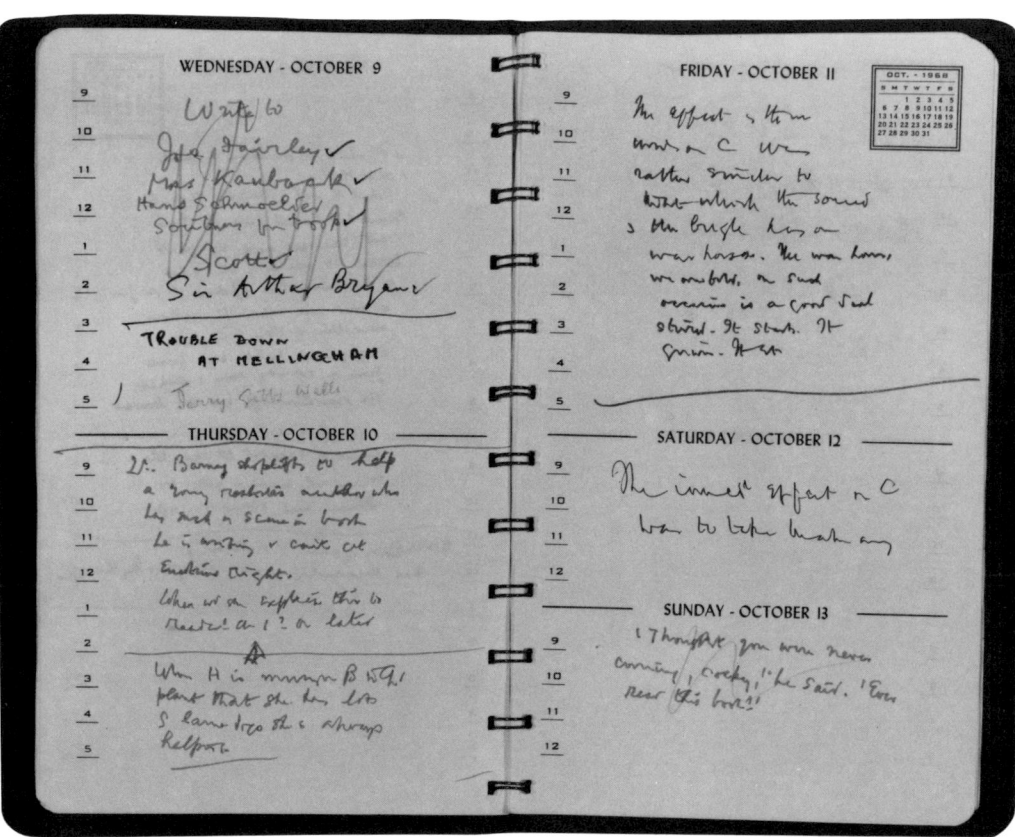

Preliminary notes in a desk diary from the local insurance agent for *The Girl in Blue*.

PLATE 28

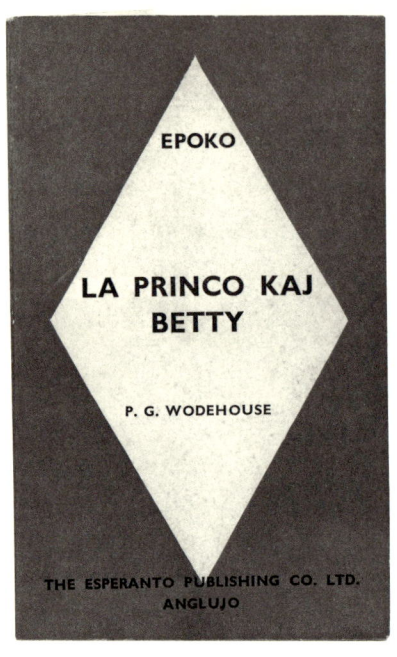

The Prince and Betty in Esperanto; *The Small Bachelor* in Czech; *Summer Moonshine* in Finnish; *The Mating Season* in Swedish.

PLATE 29

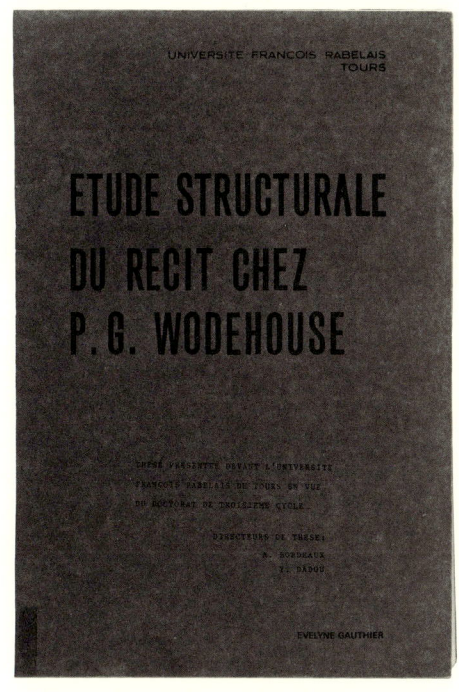
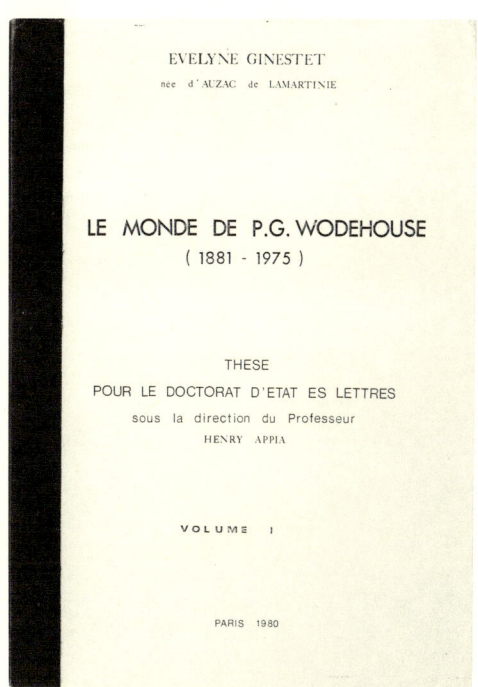
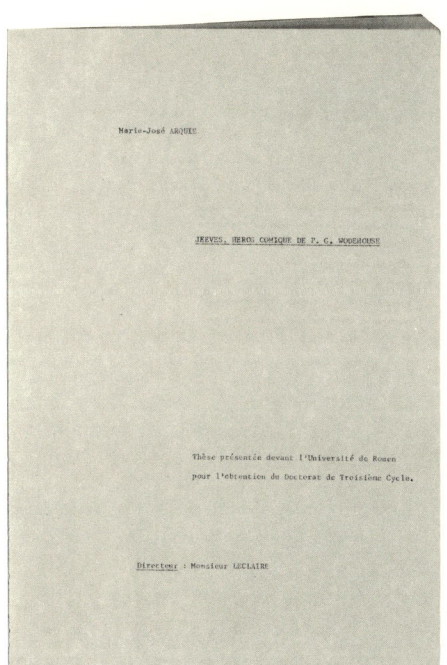

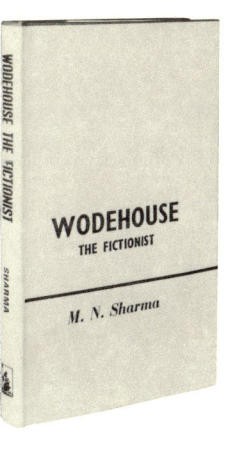

Five doctoral dissertations on Wodehouse: three from France, one from India, and one from the United States. (Clockwise from upper left, courtesy of: Université François Rabelais de Tours, Université de la Sorbonne Nouvelle, Meerut University, Michigan State University, Université de Rouen.)

PLATE 30

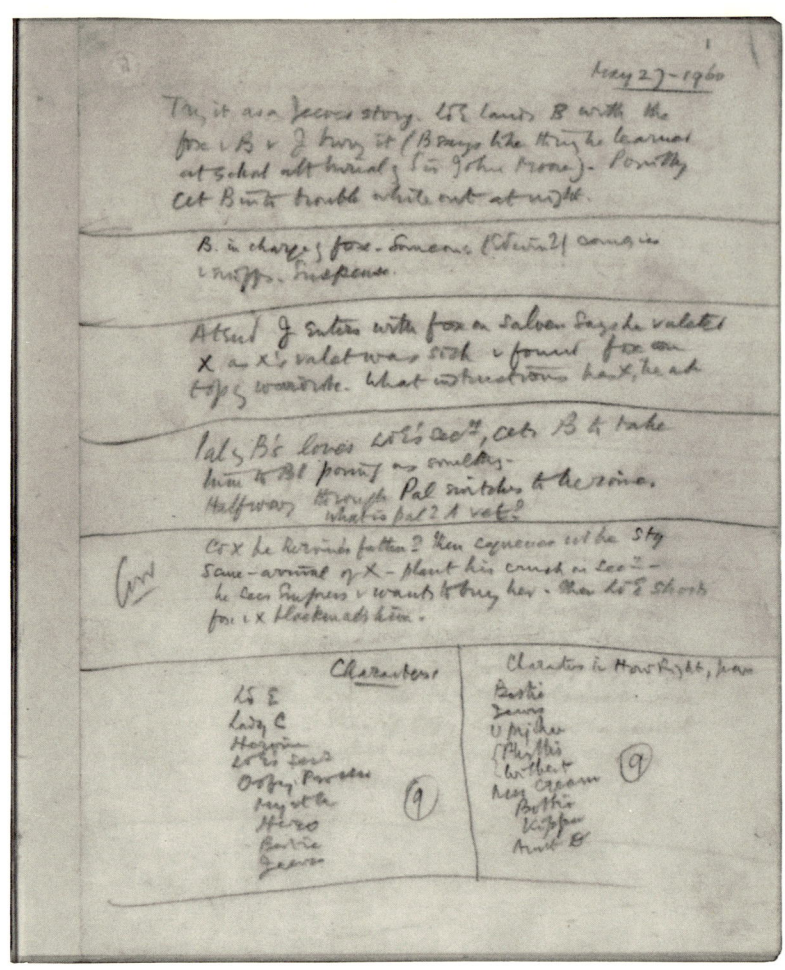

Original manuscript notes of *Service with a Smile* (1961) with dust wrappers of the English (left) and American (right) editions.

1000 Park Avenue
New York

Sept 27. 1951

Dear Mr Simmons.

Thank you so much for your letter. I am afraid I have been a long time answering it. I was finishing up a new novel, and as always when I am doing that I neglect my correspondence.

I am so glad you like Ukridge. He has always been one of my favourite characters. I will certainly try to do some more stories about him.

Ukridge is a real character. He was drawn from a friend of mine with whom I used to run about London from 1903 onwards. I have not seen him for years, and I suppose he is old and respectable now!

As regards Blandings, I am in a spot of difficulty. Do houses like Blandings exist in England today? I,m afraid not. What I shall do, if I can get a good plot, is to ignore modern conditions and just dish the old place up again making it full of butlers, footmen etc.

Best wishes
Yours sincerely

P. G. Wodehouse

Apley Hall, Bridgnorth. "I have always pictured Blandings Castle as somewhere near Bridgnorth in Shropshire, where I lived as a boy" (Wodehouse letter to Bengt Appelkvist, 12 April 1963).

PLATE 32

GUESTS AT THE CASTLE
(A Blandings Castle novel)
BY
P. G. Wodehouse

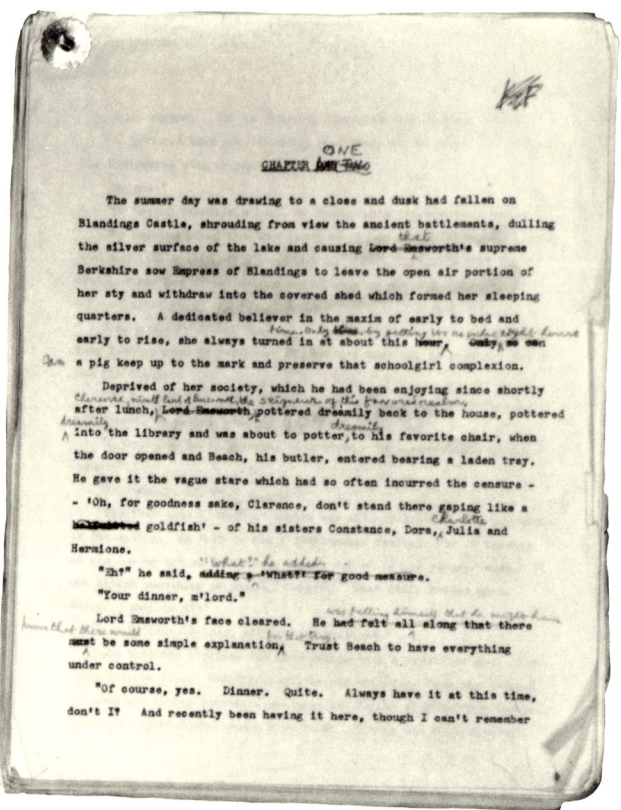

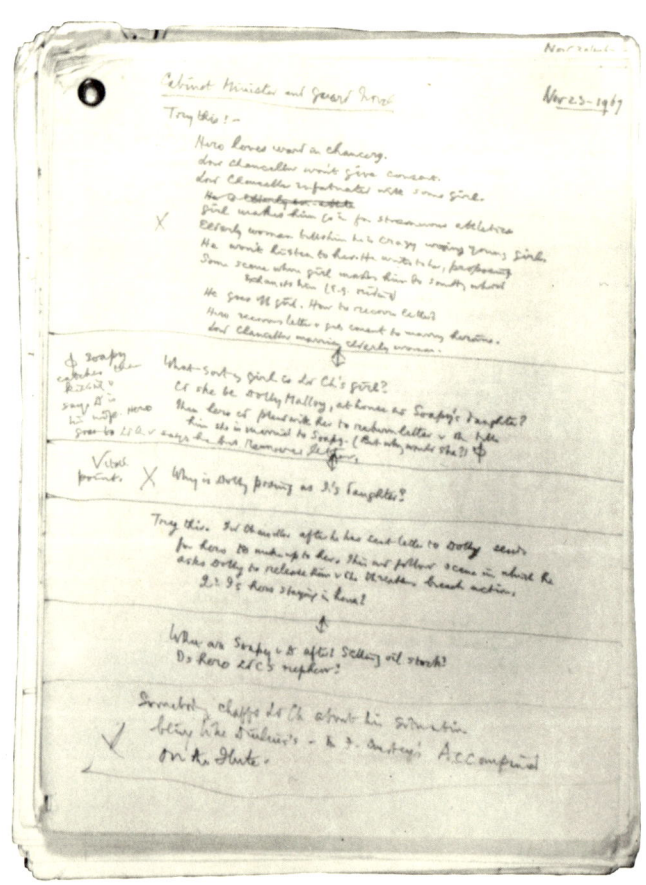

PLATE 33

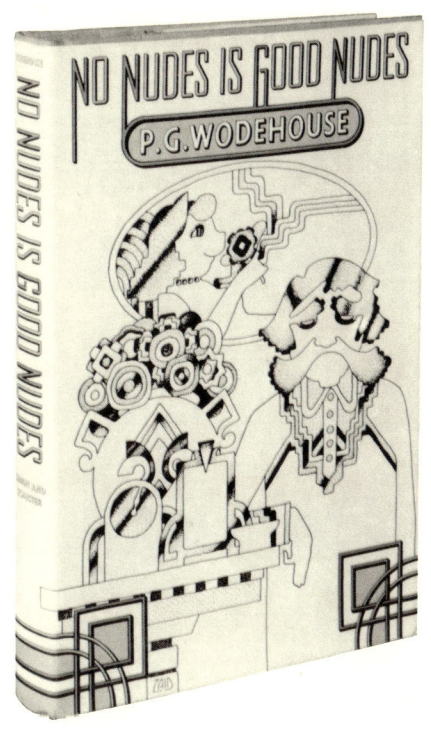

Typescript and handwritten notes of "Guests at the Castle" which was published in England as *A Pelican at Blandings* (1969) and in the United States as *No Nudes Is Good Nudes* (1970).

PLATE 34

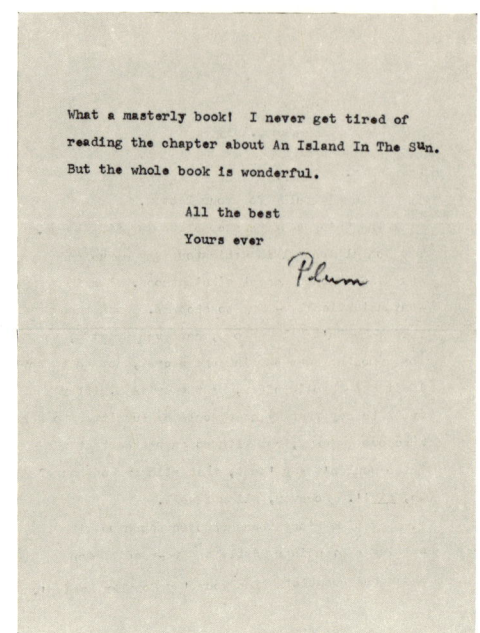

Letter from Wodehouse acknowledging Alec Waugh's congratulations on the knighthood.

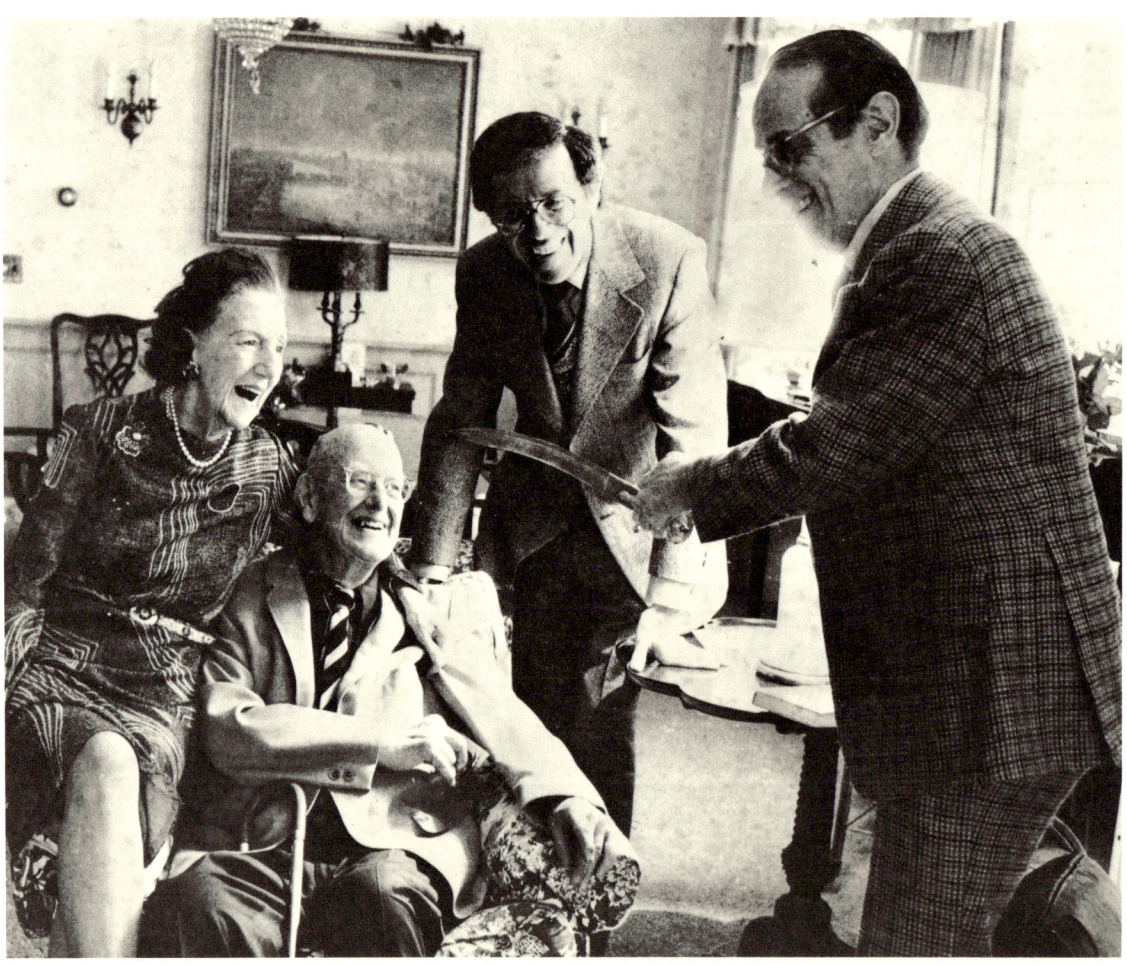

Peter Schwed (extreme right), Wodehouse's American editor and publisher, and Scott Meredith, Wodehouse's American agent, dub Wodehouse Sir Pelham, as Lady Wodehouse cheers.

PLATE 35

Ionicus maps his view of Blandings Castle, which are the endpapers for *Sunset at Blandings*.

P. G. Wodehouse's last novel (1977), for which sixteen of twenty-two chapters had been completed.

PLATE 36

All roads lead to Wodehouse characters. Supporting the signpost is Kimberley, the Wodehouse family name mentioned in Debrett's as early as 1536.
Photograph by Ian Yeomans.

cive of cold feet to have your personal h.w.b. punctured by a long darning needle on the end of a stick in the small hours at the hand of a practical joker. Then "The Ordeal of Young Tuppy"—that needed a match of village rugby football, essentially a winter game.

So . . . real summer? Not the way it happens in England. Wodehouse has got it all romantic and all wrong. England has rotten weather in summer. Winter is worse, but we expect that. For some reason we expect, year after year, that the summer will live up to its name, will produce even a quarter of the hot days that Wodehouse's stories postulate. We talk, these days, in wonder about the long, hot summer of (was it?) 1975, when we got a bushel or two of sour little black grapes off the vine on the south-facing wall (good for adding to the apples for jams, jellies, and tarts); when there was no rain for the whole of the Wimbledon fortnight; when there were five days of cricket in one or two of the five-day cricket Test Matches. And I remember—and tell of it too often—fireflies in the garden in Surrey in 1947. I had never seen fireflies in England before, and have never since. Yes, in those two egregious summers there were mornings (eleven-thirty to one o'clock) when you could read your P. G. Wodehouse in a hammock under a tree without catching a chill, afternoons when you knew you ought to have watered the dahlias that morning before the sun got at them, when the dog sought shade and slept upside down, evenings when loving couples could be heard warmly embracing beyond the fence on the heath. But never months-long summers such as Wodehouse gives us. I wonder how many foreigners have, from reading Wodehouse, come to England in summer without the necessary overcoats, warm underwear, and umbrellas. You?

Jobless young men with valets? I have never moved around in the best English social circles. I suppose there are still occasional young men in England who are totally unemployed, want to remain so, and, like Bertie Wooster, are happy to spend the afternoon at the club flipping playing cards into a top hat. Bertie and his Drones Club friends, from Oofy Prosser to Freddie Widgeon, did nothing, on inherited money or allowances doled out by uncles, and did it very well. It suited Wodehouse for his books to have them footloose.

Jeeves is Bertie's valet, cook, chauffeur, friend, and adviser. And he is a joy. But you note that very few of Bertie's friends at the Drones have "men." Oofy, yes. Harold Pendlebury-Davenport, yes. And Archibald Mulliner—the one who lived in the Albany, Mayfair, and imitated so well a hen laying an egg—yes, he had Meadowes, who was a long-standing member of The League for The Dawn of Freedom and who helped his master to turn socialist and go and try getting bread into the martyred proletariat in Bottleton East, far from Mayfair. It was Archibald himself who got martyred that evening—also a fortnight's imprisonment. Happily there was no indication that Meadowes discontinued his service just because his master, temporary Comrade Mulliner, was a jailbird. Nor did it stop Aurelia Cammarleigh from loving her wayward swain and eventually, we suppose, marrying him. (One of Meadowes's jobs for his young master had been to go into the park and carve AM/AC in a heart on the trunk of a tree.) I wonder how many members of the Drones had spent nights, or weeks, in prison cells. Bertie Wooster was in jug more than once. On the nights of the Oxford and Cambridge boat race and rugger match, you might think, reading Wodehouse, that London's West End seethed every year with young gentlemen in top hats, tail coats, and white ties, either trying to find a policeman so as to steal his helmet (the forward push is essential before the upward lift) or, having so tried and failed, being marched off to chokey, to face the magistrate next morning. I may say that for my first two years at Oxford I looked for trouble and excitement round Piccadilly Circus on boat race night and the rugger match, and nothing stirred, nobody seethed, the Criterion bar was only sparsely populated, Romano's and the Empire Grill silent and sedate and no policemen walked helmetless or anxious. Had they ever, even in Wodehouse's young days?

Bertie and Jeeves were, when at full strength, creatures of the 1920s and after. *Something Fresh*, published during the First World War, was of an earlier era. In that book practically all the members of the house party at Blandings had brought valet or maid. Freddie Threepwood had a valet. So did Lord Emsworth. (Lord E. for the last time. If ever a man needed a valet, it was Lord E., much more than he needed a secretary.) In postwar books Uncle Fred, Lord Ickenham, had no valet, Pongo no valet, Galahad no valet—even rich, self-indulgent old bachelor Sir Gregory Parsloe-Parsloe, Bart., no valet. But Bertie continues with his faithful Jeeves (except for occasional breaks) to the end of the road. Hands up, anybody, in England or America, who has had a gentleman's personal gentleman, or a friend who has had one, since World War I—a man to cook and valet and drive the car and read to you when you're sleepless (as did Ashe Marson, valet to dyspeptic Mr. Peters in *Something Fresh*), a man who comes with you when you go to visit family or friends, in hotels, on yachts, indeed on round-the-world cruises. I see no hands, and rest my case.

Show me a clergyman now who has a butler—in Wodehouse almost every man of the cloth above rank of curate has one. Where today (I ask you) do house parties drift into weeks and fortnights? How many homes have knife-and-boots boys or page boys in blue and buttony uniforms? Where can, or could, justices of the peace in England repose on a settee in their own homes and sentence a suspected miscreant to a fortnight's imprisonment without trial, without lawyers, and without argument? Lord Emsworth thinks he can, and clearly he has been a J.P. for many years and should know the ropes. Sir Watkyn Bassett, in his retirement from London magistracy, is almost as peremptory as Lord Emsworth as a J.P. in his Worcestershire home. Where in England since World War I did a country public house, or *any* public house, have its doors open to casual drinkers all day and most of the night? The Emsworth Arms (G. Ovens, proprietor) in Market Blandings knows no rules or opening and closing times. Many a weary traveler to the castle from London steps, in mid-afternoon, across from the railway station to the Emsworth Arms for a strengthening pint or courage-giving second pint of the home brew before facing the walk to the castle or the drive there in Jno. Robinson's station taxi.

Home brew? Yes, there are still public houses, owned by their landlords, not by breweries, where you can get home-brewed beer. Few now, and far between. But find me a village concert. Find me a steam train. Wodehouse has trains puffing and whistling in the slips at Paddington or Waterloo station long after England's railways have gone electric.

Wodehouse at his best was blissfully out-of-date. I don't say his books present a never-never land. He just ignores time and dates when he wants to.

I mentioned, in the butlerian context, curates and vicars. To an Englishman (myself), Wodehouse's treatment of office-holders of the Anglican Church, from curate to archbishop, is knowledgeable, frequent, and, without ever being irreverent to the Church, very funny. I do not remember a single instance of an American clergyman in such of his books as are set in America. Is there one? Now Wodehouse, from the age of twenty to ninety-three, spent much more of his time in America than he did in England. After World War II, when the Wodehouses lived in America (he took American citizenship in addition to his British), editors of American magazines begged him to write his funny stories for them with American characters and settings. He tried hard, but it was against the grain of his brain and typewriter. After finishing one novel, he wrote triumphantly to his friend Bill Townend that he had achieved a positively all-American novel with only the butler English (*The Old Reliable*, a revision of *Spring Fever* and now set in America; there is, in addition to Phipps the butler, an English Lord Topham). But no American clergy anywhere. And I know why. The Anglican Church was, perhaps still is, very strongly involved in the education of young middle-class England. Between the age of seven and eighteen Wodehouse had divinity, as it was called, as quite a substantial part of the curricula of his schools. Chapel, sermons on Sundays, examinations in Old and New Testament texts and history, and the classics, Latin and Greek, still given many more hours of class than mathematics, French, or engineering (the despised "modern" side). Many of the colleges of Oxford and Cambridge, and many of the so-called public schools (meaning private and fee-paying) in England were church foundations and, since Latin and Greek were obligatory to candidates for holy orders, Latin and Greek, along with church and chapel, "divinity" and Bible readings were things that the middle-class English boy got at any school that prepared for the two major universities. What I am saying is that Wodehouse, as a middle-class English boy, got "divinity" in full measure in his formative years, many of his schoolmasters, and certainly his headmasters, being in holy orders. And in his school holidays, his parents being half a world away in Hong Kong, he went to stay with uncles and aunts, several of the uncles being vicars of country parishes. So young Pelham got the Anglican Church (twice on Sundays in the holidays and chapel twice on Sundays at school) into his metronomically burgeoning mind as strongly as he did cricket and football. When he began to write fiction, set in England, churches and churchmen came into his typewriter and onto his pages with pleasant frequency and absolute confidence. The prose rhythms of Holy Writ, and parsonical phraseology from the pulpit, came back to him easily, having been tamped down in his mind in impressionable boyhood. Some of his very best stories are on church subjects—"The Bishop's Move," "Mulliner's Buck-U-Uppo," "The Story of Webster," "Cats Will Be Cats," "The Voice from the Past," "Gala Night," "Anselm Gets His Chance" from the Mulliner corpus alone; "Company for Gertrude" from the Blandings short stories; "The Great Sermon Handicap" and many more from the Bertie/Jeeves books, plus the Rev. "Stinker" Pinker, the Rev. Cuthbert Bailey, and several other splendid men of God.

But in the books and stories he wrote about America, not a clergyman in sight anywhere, is there?[1]

[1]. Well, yes, there is—the Rev. Gideon Voules, of Flushing, N.Y., in *The Small Bachelor*. But there's not an American trait in the Rev. Gideon, who might as plausibly have been imported into the narrative from Fulham as from Flushing.—DRB

If Wodehouse knew anything about the Christian Church in America, he didn't know enough to play with it in his stories. He said somewhere in a letter, and at a time when American editors of magazines were begging him for short stories with American characters throughout, "The fact is, I don't find Americans funny." The fact was, he had been educated as a boy in England and he knew England deeply enough to find it funny, to play with it. He kept his English accent till his death: in his voice because he was a very private person and not much of a talker; in his fiction because only there did he feel secure. He could, even in a German internment camp, write about England without reference books, spinning the stuff out of his guts. An England that had gone, perhaps never existed—but, real or fabulous, it was what he knew down to its bedrock. His stories about Hollywood are very funny (as near as he ever came to satire). But there or elsewhere in America, not a Man of God in sight. Significant, I think.

Cats and Dogs
MARGARET GARRARD

THERE IS a wide variety of livestock to be found in the works of Wodehouse—some wild, such as gnus, armadillos, snails, and snakes spring to mind; some domesticated, such as Lord Emsworth's supreme Black Berkshire sow the Empress of Blandings, the schoolboy's white mouse and sundry parrots; some human, including the gorilla who, rather unexpectedly, addressed Montrose Mulliner in the accents of Balliol College, Oxford;[1] and some partially human, such as The Wrecking Crew, a foursome of elderly golfers who infested the Oldest Member's club:

> They are the direct lineal descendants of the Gadarene swine. Every time they come out, I expect to see them rush down the hill from the first tee and hurl themselves into the lake at the second.[2]

[1]. *Blandings Castle*: "Monkey Business" (p. 215 of H.J. 2nd printing).
[2]. *Heart of a Goof*: "Chester Forgets Himself."

All these are worthy of full consideration, but it was dogs and cats that were the really important animals in Wodehouse's own life. He had several dogs in the early days at his house Threepwood in the village of Emsworth in Hampshire. Later on, his lifelong friend Bill Townend said that it was almost impossible to think of Plum without a Peke as a companion. In his letters to Townend, Wodehouse talks much of his Pekes, first of all Susan, and later Winky and Boo. They will not let him go for walks, they fight and they give each other Dirty Looks. In one of these letters he told a touching story of the alley cat that he adopted when, years before, he had a penthouse on the twenty-second floor of an office building on East 41st Street:

> I took him in, and for a few days he was a docile and appreciative guest seeming to be contented with regular meals and a spacious roof for purposes of exercise.

But all the while, it appeared, the old wild life had been calling to him, and one morning he nipped out of the door and headed for the open spaces. And not having the intelligence to ring for the lift, he started to walk downstairs.

I stood above and watched him with a heavy heart, for I knew that he was asking for it and that remorse must inevitably creep in. And so it proved. For the first few floors he was jauntiness itself. He walked with an air, carrying his tail like a banner. And then suddenly—it must have been on floor twelve—I could see the thought strike him like a bullet that this was going on forever and that he had got to Hell and was being heavily penalized for not having been a better cat. He sat down and stared bleakly into an eternity of going on and on and arriving nowhere. If ever a cat regretted that he had not stayed put, this cat was that cat.[3]

Nearer the end of his life, we see Wodehouse on the dust cover of *Over Seventy* holding a large cat. Finally, near their home on Long Island, he and his wife, Ethel, had financed a sort of hotel for stray dogs and cats with a full staff including three vets.

Since Wodehouse preferred to write from a basis of direct personal experience, it is not surprising that cats and dogs come into his writings more than any other animals. It is some of their principal appearances in his works that are to be evoked here.

He must have known many different breeds of dogs. Alsatians, Pekes, Scotties, Yorkshire terriers, Airedales, Sealyhams, bulldogs, bull-terriers, spaniels, poodles, Kerry Blues, wolfhounds, pugs, a Tanganyikan lion-dog, and miscellaneous mongrels are all mentioned. More often than not the dogs act aggressively at some moment, but, in spite of this, there is always a feeling of affectionate understanding of dogs' behavior. The aggression is to enable the dog to play an important part in the plot. One or two examples will illustrate how the dog characters put the humans at a disadvantage.

When Bertie and Jeeves were staying in New York, one of the trials of having Motty Pershore as an unbidden guest was the bull-terrier Rollo that Motty had won in a raffle while he was out on a binge. Jeeves, after quelling the animal by his personal magnetism, assured Bertie that, in time, he too would be on friendly terms with the dog as "Rollo will learn to distinguish your peculiar scent."

3. *Performing Flea* (London, 1953), p. 90.

"What do you mean my peculiar scent? Correct the impression that I intend to hang about in the hall while life slips by, in the hope that one of these days the dashed animal will decide that I smell all right."[4]

Then there was that "mobile flea storage depot," the poodle Alphonse, who was so important to Horace Bewstridge. Trying to consolidate himself with the connections of his loved one, Vera Witherby, Horace had made some brief notes for his own guidance. These concluded with the phrase: "A. Concil. If poss. p., but w.o. for s.d.a."

Horace explained that this was to remind him to conciliate Alphonse: "He is a dog of wide influence and cannot be ignored." The remainder of the cryptic phrase he translated as "If possible, pat, but watch out for sudden dash at ankles. He is extraordinarily quick on his feet."[5]

It was an Aberdeen terrier, Stiffy Byng's Bartholomew, that was chosen to play a dynamic role in one of the central episodes of that masterwork *The Code of the Woosters*. Bertie was staying at Totleigh Towers and had just set off down the drive in the hope of meeting Stiffy Byng and asking her to return a compromising notebook dropped by Gussie Fink-Nottle. Bertie had been told to look out for Stiffy's dog Bartholomew.

As the shades of evening are drawing in on Totleigh Towers, Bertie observes a policeman bicycling up the drive, and also observes that

> it was patent that his attention had not yet been drawn to the fact that he was being chivvied—in the strong, silent, earnest manner characteristic of this breed of animal—by a fine Aberdeen terrier. There he was, riding comfortably along, sniffing the fragrant evening breeze; and there was the Scottie, all whiskers and eyebrows, hareing after him hell-for-leather.

The inevitable disaster occurred, and the officer of the law came a smeller.

> One moment he was with us, all merry and bright; the next he was in the ditch, a sort of macédoine of arms and legs and wheels, with the terrier standing on the edge, looking down at him with that rather offensive expression of virtuous smugness which I have often noticed on the faces of Aberdeen terriers in their clashes with humanity.

4. *Carry on, Jeeves*: III, "Jeeves and the Unbidden Guest."
5. *Nothing Serious*: "Excelsior."

A few chapters further on, for excellent plot reasons, Bertie and Jeeves together and in silence enter Stiffy's bedroom in her absence.

> I was standing there, hoping for the best, when my meditations were broken in upon by an odd, gargling sort of noise, something like static and something like distant thunder, and to cut a long story short, this proved to proceed from the larynx of the dog Bartholomew.
>
> He was standing on the bed, stropping his front paws on the coverlet, and so easy was it to read the message in his eyes that we acted like two minds with but a single thought. At the exact moment when I soared like an eagle on to the chest of drawers, Jeeves was skimming like a swallow on to the top of the cupboard. The animal hopped from the bed, and advancing into the middle of the room, took a seat, breathing through the nose with a curious whistling sound, and looking at us from under his eyebrows like a Scottish elder rebuking sin from the pulpit.[6]

As was to be expected, there are plenty of Pekingese scattered through the stories. Sometimes they are peaceful and amiable. More often they are given to biting, screaming, or going off like bombs when offended. In the smoking room of the Drones Club, a Bean is described as displaying to some Eggs and Piefaces a nasty flesh wound received from "a blasted man-eating Peke with teeth like needles and a disposition that led it to take offense at the merest trifle."[7]

There is, in addition, a recurring theme of Pekes attacking and putting to flight much larger dogs. In *Nothing Serious* Celia Todd's Pekingese Pirbright had a thwarted confrontation with the wolfhound of Agnes Flack, the female champion of the Oldest Member's golf club; then later on, after he has drunk, and enjoyed, some of Smallwood Bessemer's tonic port, cleaned up the wolfhound in under one minute; thereafter, they were the best of friends.

Usually it is Alsatians who get cleaned up by Pekes. A hint of some hidden background to this theme is to be found in the dedication of *Louder and Funnier* published in 1932: "To George Blake, A Splendid Fellow and Very Sound on Pekes. But he should guard against the tendency to claim that his Peke fights Alsatians. Mine is the only one that does this."

The most notable development of the Alsatian-Peke motif occurred during Freddie Widgeon's harrowing weekend at Matcham Scratchings, the cat-infested ancestral seat of Sir Mortimer Prenderby in Oxfordshire. On retiring for the night, relieved to get away from the cats downstairs, Freddie perceived on his bed a fine Alsatian dog, named Wilhelm.

> Its manner was plainly resentful. It fixed Freddie with a cold yellow eye and curled its upper lip slightly, the better to display a long, white tooth. It also twitched its nose and gave a *sotto-voce* imitation of distant thunder.

Later, after Freddie had been forced to retreat to the top of a wardrobe, there came through the door an object which, in the dim light, he was at first not able to identify: "It looked something like a pen-wiper and something like a piece of a hearth-rug." When the Alsatian tried to investigate, it turned out to be a Peke puppy which, of course, exploded and chased the Alsatian right out of the bedroom.[8]

There are other dogs whose intervention help the hero or heroine to a happy ending. Such a past is often given to mongrels. It was William, "a mixture of Airedale, setter, bull-terrier and mastiff," who saved James Rodman from the malign influences at work at Honeysuckle Cottage.[9] But even more influential was the mongrel Bottles:

> a fine dog, though of uncertain breed. His mother had been a popular local belle with a good deal of sex appeal, and the question of his paternity was one that would have set a Genealogical College pursing its lips perplexedly.

At Blandings Castle, Freddie Threepwood was trying to impress Lady Alcester (the owner of four Pekingese, two Poms, a Yorkshire terrier, five Sealyhams, a Borzoi, and an Airedale) with the qualities of Donaldson's Dog Joy, the product of his father-in-law's firm. After the failure of his attempt to demonstrate the wholesomeness of the biscuits by eating one himself, Freddie produced Bottles as a fine example of a dog fed from his earliest youth on Donaldson's Dog Joy. But Bottles spoilt the effect by allowing himself to be routed by one of Lady Alcester's Pekes which, in the manner we have come

---

6. *The Code of the Woosters.*
7. *Eggs, Beans and Crumpets*: "Bingo and the Peke Crisis."
8. *Young Men in Spats*: V, "Good-bye to All Cats."
9. *Meet Mr. Mulliner*: IX, "Honeysuckle Cottage."

to expect, went off like a bomb. In the end, Bottles redeemed this failure by a performance in the after-dinner dog fight with the Airedale that so impressed Lady Alcester that she gave Freddie an order for two tons of Donaldson's Dog Joy.[10]

Most of the cats that Wodehouse used in his stories were mere pawns in the action. At Matcham Scratchings the cats get sat upon or thrown, alive or dead, out of the window.[11] When Sir Roderick Glossop came to lunch with Bertie, it was the disclosure by Jeeves of the presence in the bedroom of three cats—"the black one, the tabby one and the small lemon-colored animal, sir"—that first caused the eminent nerve specialist to have his doubts about Bertie.[12]

But, when we come to the story of the immortal Webster—"one of the best things I have ever done," Wodehouse said—we have to deal with a cat who is *different*.

> He was the property of the Dean of Bolsover, who, on being raised to a bishopric and sailing from England to take up his episcopal duties at his See of Bongo-Bongo in West Africa, left the animal in the care of his nephew Lancelot Mulliner who was an artist living in Chelsea. . . . Webster for a time completely revolutionized Lancelot's life. His early upbringing at the Deanery had made him austere and censorious, and he exerted on Lancelot the full force of a powerful and bigoted personality. It was as if Savonarola or some minor prophet had suddenly been introduced into the carefree, Bohemian atmosphere of the studio. . . . But one day, Lancelot discovered that the animal, for all its apparently rigid principles, had feet of clay and was no better than the rest of us. He happened to drop a bottle of alcoholic liquor and the cat drank deeply of its contents.[13]

To Lancelot's enormous relief, it now turned out that Webster, that seeming pillar of virtue, was one of the boys after all.

> Webster, like the stag at eve, had now drunk his fill. He had left the pool of alcohol and was walking round in slow, meditative circles. From time to time he mewed tentatively, as if he were trying to say "British Constitution." His failure to articulate the syllables appeared to tickle him, for at the end of each attempt he would utter a slow amused chuckle. It was at about this moment that he suddenly broke into a rhythmic dance, not unlike the old Saraband.[14]

From that moment this once saintly cat became a Bohemian of Bohemians. His days were a welter of brawlings and loose gallantry. His personal appearance suffered badly until he came to look "like the late Legs Diamond after a social evening with a few old friends." At this point the unexpected news of the immediate return of the Bishop threw Lancelot into despair at the thought of what his uncle would say on beholding this wreck. Before such a distressing encounter could occur, the Bishop had to send for Lancelot to come and rescue him from Widdrington Manor, Bottleby-in-the-Vale, Hants, where he was in imminent danger of being trapped into marriage with the chatelaine, Lady Widdrington, "one of those agate-eyed, purposeful, tweed-clad women of whom rural England seems to have a monopoly."

It was a common interest in cats that had originally thrown the Bishop together with Lady Widdrington, who owned an orange-colored animal called Percy.

> He was pure poison. Orange of body and inky-black of soul . . . there was about this animal none of Webster's jolly, whole-hearted, swashbuckling rowdiness. Webster was the sort of cat who would charge, roaring and ranting, to dispute with some rival the possession of a decaying sardine, but there was no more vice in him than in the late John L. Sullivan. Percy, on the other hand, for all his sleek exterior, was mean and bitter. He had no music in his soul, and was fit for treasons, stratagems and spoils. One could picture him stealing milk from a sick tabby.

In the end it was not Lancelot, but Webster who saved the Bishop. In the study at Widdrington Manor, the Bishop sat with his head in his hands, refusing all Lancelot's attempts at consolation. Here Webster arrived, having been sent down from London by train in a hamper, and almost at once engaged in a major battle with the evil Percy. This encounter, in which Percy realized he had gone out of his class and was put to flight, inspired the Bishop to face up to Lady Widdrington and break the bonds that held him. Overcome with admiration and grati-

---

10. *Blandings Castle*: V, "The Go-Getter."
11. *Young Men in Spats*: V, "Good-bye to All Cats."
12. *The Inimitable Jeeves*: VIII, "Sir Roderick Comes to Lunch."
13. *Mulliner Nights*: II, "The Story of Webster"; III, "Cats Will Be Cats."
14. Ibid.

tude, the Bishop found that he had never esteemed his cat so highly as that moment.

He stooped and gathered Webster into his arms, and Lancelot, after one quick look at them, stole silently out. This sacred moment was not for his eyes.[15]

15. Ibid.

MARGARET GARRARD. For the last sixteen years she has been teaching in London working with young children and, therefore, concerned mostly with reading, writing, and arithmetic. Her original subject was history, which she read at Newnham College, Cambridge, from which she graduated in 1945. A variety of jobs since then has included several years in the Civil Service, first with the United Kingdom Official War Histories and later with the Government Information Services. Her first contact with P. G. Wodehouse was reading the school stories in old bound volumes of The Captain *magazine. Since then reading Wodehouse has never stopped. A small piece of research on the actual site of Blandings Castle was her contribution to a Wodehouse seminar in 1975, led by Richard Usborne.*

New York
JOHN GARRARD

New York is a large city conveniently situated on the edge of America, so that you step off the liner right on to it without an effort. You can't lose your way. You go out of a barn and down some stairs, and there you are, right in among it. The only possible objection any reasonable chappie could find to the place is that they loose you into it from the boat at such an ungodly hour.

. . . I was surprised to find the streets quite full. People were bustling along as if it was some reasonable hour and not the gray dawn. . . . Going to business or something, I take it. Wonderful Johnnies!

The odd part of it was that after the first shock of seeing all this frightful energy the thing didn't seem so strange. I've spoken to fellows since who've been to New York, and they tell me they found it just the same. Apparently there's something in the air, either the ozone or the phosphates or something, which makes you sit up and take notice. A kind of zip, as it were. A sort of bally freedom, if you know what I mean, that gets into your blood and bucks you up and makes you feel that—

God's in his heaven,
All's right with the world

and you don't care if you've got odd socks on.

THIS IS Bertie Wooster speaking after his arrival in New York on the first and most disastrous of his missions, "Extricating Young Gussie."[1] Jeeves, whom Bertie had only recently acquired, wasn't called in to help that time. Things were very different thereafter.

Wodehouse wrote a lot about New York and, indeed, became practically a New Yorker himself. In this he differed from many of his compatriots who tried to describe the place, notably, the formidable Lady Malvern, who

fitted into my biggest armchair as if it had been built round her by someone who knew they were wearing armchairs tight about the hips that season. She had bright bulging eyes and a lot of yellow hair and when she spoke showed about fifty-seven front teeth. . . .

"You see, Mr. Wooster, I am in America principally on business. No doubt you read my book *India and the Indians*? My publishers are anxious for me to write a companion volume on the United States. I shall not be able to spend more than a month in the country, but a month should be ample. I was less than a month in India, and my dear friend Sir Roger Cremorne wrote his *America from Within* after a stay of only two weeks."[2]

Fortunately, England has been able to supply some more acceptable imports than Lady Malvern.

1. *The Man with Two Left Feet*: "Extricating Young Gussie."
2. *Carry on, Jeeves*: II, "Jeeves and the Unbidden Guest."

In their attitude towards America, visiting Englishmen invariably incline to extremes, either detesting all that therein is, or becoming enthusiasts on the subject of the country, its climate and institutions. Archie belonged to the second class. He liked America, and got on splendidly with Americans from the start. He was a friendly soul, a mixer; and in New York, that city of mixers, he found himself at home. . . .

There were moments when it seemed to him as though New York had simply been waiting for him to arrive before giving the word to let the revels commence.[3]

Archie, of course, was Archie Moffam (pronounced Moom to rhyme with Bluffinghame), who struck it lucky, and rich, when he married Lucille, daughter of Daniel Brewster, proprietor of the Cosmopolis Hotel.

To a visitor to New York who has the ability to make himself liked, it almost appears as though the leading industry of that city was the issuing of two weeks'-invitation cards to clubs. Archie had been showered with these evidences of his popularity. There were the fashionable clubs along Fifth Avenue, to which his friend Reggie van Tuyl introduced him. There were the businessmen's clubs of which he was made free by more solid citizens. And best of all, there were the Lambs, the Players, the Friars, the Coffee House, and Pen and Ink and other resorts of the artist, the author, the actor and the Bohemian.[4]

Wodehouse first visited New York in 1904, and established himself there soon afterwards as a provider of wholesome fiction for pulp magazines. Writing in 1957, he says:

The greatest change in the fifty-three years 1904–1957 is the improvement in American manners. In 1904, I found residents in the home of the brave and the land of the free, though probably delightful chaps if you get to know them, rather on the brusque side. They shoved you in the street and then asked you who you were shoving, and used, when spoken to, only one side of the mouth when replying.

Things are different nowadays:

. . . from New Jersey comes the news that an unidentified assailant plunged a knife into the shoulder of a Mr. James Dobson the other day, spun him round, and then, seeing his face, clicked his tongue remorsefully. "Oh, I beg your pardon," he said, "I got the wrong guy."

Frank and manly. You find yourself in the wrong, admit it and apologize.[5]

In fact New York gives a friendly welcome to most of the characters inflicted on it by Wodehouse, although the erratic lives of some of them periodically lead to slight brushes with the representatives of law and order.

Here is Cyril Bassington-Bassington, speaking in prison:

"I mean to say, why don't they wear helmets like they do in London? Why do they look like postmen? It isn't fair on a fellow. I was simply standing on the pavement looking at things when a fellow who looked like a postman prodded me in the ribs with a club. I didn't see why I should have a postman prodding me. Why the dickens should a fellow come three thousand miles to be prodded by postmen?"

"The point is well taken," said George. "What did you do?"

"I gave him a shove, you know, I've got a frightfully nasty temper, you know. All the Bassington-Bassingtons have frightfully nasty tempers, don't you know? And then he biffed me in the eye and carried me off to this frightful place."[6]

Although they have a regrettable habit of going about disguised as postmen, many distinguished and conscientious New York City police officers appear in the Works. The star is the aspiring vers libre poet Garroway in *The Small Bachelor*. He first appears on the roof outside the small bachelor's apartment, with his literary mentor, the formidable Hamilton Beamish, to be told by the latter, somewhat to his surprise, how stark and grim is the life of the Great City. He later reads the resulting verses to Hamilton Beamish; they are poorly received, Beamish having fallen in love in the meanwhile.

"Streets!
Grim, relentless, sordid streets!
Miles of poignant streets,

---

3. *Indiscretions of Archie.*
4. Ibid.

5. *Over Seventy.*
6. *Jeeves*: "A Letter of Introduction."

> East, West, North,
> And stretching starkly South;
> Sad, hopeless, dismal, cheerless, chilling
> Streets!"

Hamilton Beamish raised his eyebrows.

> "I pace the mournful streets
> With aching heart."

"Why?" asked Hamilton Beamish.

"It is part of my duties, sir. Each patrolman is assigned a certain portion of the city as a beat."[7]

Later, Officer Garroway is earnestly sought by one Sigsbee Horatio Waddington; Sigsbee H. has unfortunately forgotten Garroway's name—could it be Garrity? Or Mulcahy?

Now, a man who goes about New York looking for a policeman named Mulcahy has quite an afternoon's work in hand. So has the man who seeks a Garrity. For one who pursues both there is not a dull moment. Flitting hither and thither about the city and questioning the various officers he encountered, Sigsbee H. Waddington soon began to cover the ground. The policeman on point duty in Times Square said that there was a Mulcahy up near Grant's Tomb and a choice of Garritys at Columbus Circle and Irving Place. The Grant's Tomb Mulcahy, expressing regret that he could not himself supply the happy ending, recommended the Hundred-and-Twenty-Fifth Street Mulcahy or—alternatively—the one down on Third Avenue and Sixteenth. The Garrity at Columbus Circle spoke highly of a Garrity near the Battery, and the Garrity at Irving Place seemed to think that his cousin up in the Bronx might fill the long-felt want. By the time the clocks were striking five, Mr. Waddington had come definitely to the decision that what the world wanted to make it a place fit for heroes to live in was fewer and better Mulcahys. At five-thirty, returning from the Bronx, he would have supported any amendment to the Constitution which Congress might have cared to introduce, totally prohibiting Garritys. At six sharp, he became suddenly convinced that the name of the man he sought was Murphy.[8]

Although Wodehouse was generally well disposed to the force and wrote of it sympathetically, he gave another side of the picture in the sinister police captain MacEachern in *A Gentleman of Leisure*. MacEachern had achieved his successive promotions by purchase, and his rank of captain enabled him to become wealthy by the opportunities that it gave for graft. He is not funny at all, and it is difficult for the reader not to feel that there was some basis in fact for Wodehouse's portrait of this very unpleasant figure. Harsh reality of this sort does not often appear in his writing, but there is more than a glimpse of it in *Psmith, Journalist*, published in 1915.

Wodehouse was very much at home in the lordly mansions of Riverside Drive, and the millionaires' apartments on Park Avenue, as well as the artists' hideouts around Washington Square; but after Psmith becomes deputy editor of *Cosy Moments* ("Moments in the Nursery" by Louella Granville Waterman, "Moments of Mirth" by B. Henderson Asher, "Moments of Budding Girlhood" by Julia Burdett Parslow, etc.), a very different aspect of the city appears. He accidentally wanders into a noisome alley called Pleasant Street somewhere on the Lower East Side and, having inspected some of the tenements there, decides to transform *Cosy Moments* into a hard-hitting crusader against the slum landlords.

This leads to involvement in gang warfare and violent conflict with a landlord who happens to be commissioner of buildings for the city and is running for alderman. In his preface, Wodehouse says the incidents in the novel are based on fact, and it all seems very far from the world of Bertie Wooster and Archie Moffam, though the grim landscape is lightened by Psmith, who is in excellent form, and by a cat-loving gang leader.

Cosy Moments cannot have been the daily reading of Freddie Widgeon, that notable Drone, on his arrival after a voyage during which his quiet and saintly manner had persuaded the misguided Mavis Peasemarch to accept his proposal of marriage.

> The only thing in the nature of a flaw in life in New York was that the populace, to judge from the daily papers, didn't seem to be so ideally happy in its love life as he was.... It looked as if everybody in the place was cutting up their wives and hiding them in sacks in the Jersey marshes.... It saddened him when he opened his illustrated tabloid of a morning to have to try to eat eggs and bacon while gazing at a photograph of Mae Belle McGinnis taken when she was not looking her best because

---

7. *The Small Bachelor.*
8. Ibid.

Mr. McGinnis had just settled some domestic dispute with the meat axe.

Also, there seemed to him far too much of all that stuff about Sugar Daddy being Discovered in Love Nest as Blizzard Grips City.[9]

But, although meat axes and sugar daddies played —and no doubt still play—their parts in New York life, they never got more than a passing glance in the works of Wodehouse. For him New York was a place of happiness and success, and this is reflected in his writing. So many of his books are concerned with it that it has not been possible to do more than flit and sip, like the butterflies so much disapproved of by his graver characters, amongst the material available. It is not the least of the distinctions of this great city that it was here, thanks to George Horace Lorimer of *The Saturday Evening Post*, and to the New York theatre, that P. G. Wodehouse, the most English of writers, knew the first real successes of his life.

The attentive reader will have observed that the foregoing pages consist largely of quotations from the works of P. G. Wodehouse. It seems very unlikely that anyone will object to this; but, if they do, we quote—once again!—the words of the Master, this time on *Bartlett's Familiar Quotations.*

I wonder if Bartlett has been as good a friend to other authors as he has been to me. . . . It so happens I am not very bright, and find it hard to think up anything very clever off my own bat, but give me my Bartlett and I will slay you.

It has always been a puzzle to me how Bartlett did it. . . . One can see, of course, how he started. I picture him at a loose end one morning, going about shuffling his feet and whistling and kicking stones, and his mother looked out of the window and said:

"John, dear, I wish you wouldn't fidget like that. Why don't you find something to *do*?"

"Such as . . . ?" said John Bartlett (born at Plymouth, Mass., in 1820).

"Dig in the garden."

"Don't want to dig in the garden."

"Or spin your top."

"Don't *want* to spin my top."

"Then why not compile a book of familiar quotations, a collection of passages, phrases and proverbs, traced to their sources in ancient and modern literature?"

John Bartlett's face lit up. . . .[10]

9. *Young Men in Spats.*

10. *Over Seventy.*

Where Is Blandings Castle?

ANN E. WOOD

I FOUND Blandings Castle by accident. At least, I never meant to go looking for it. I was spending some time in Cheltenham, a pleasant place to work, and the panorama of the Cotswolds was a restful sight above the typewriter. So the days went well, but there wasn't much to do in the evenings, and I began to read the Blandings novels. Written over a period of fifty years, they conveyed an impression, stronger with each book, of having been set in a place the author knew and loved. A nagging thought began to beset me that there must be an actual "Blandings" somewhere in Shropshire—and that clues to where it was could be found in the books.

True, others had tried to find it, but most got bogged down inside Wodehouse's imaginary castle where the rooms had a kaleidoscopic quality. They moved about from book to book, and anyone who worries about details such as whether Lord Emsworth's favorite authority on pigs was named Augustus Whipple or Whiffle should lay off Blandings novels entirely for a while. The castle was a mixture of stately homes Wodehouse knew all during his life. The site and countryside had to be a misty boyhood memory of Victorian England.

So I went looking for a castle in the air somewhere along the Severn River. It was a pleasant pastime for balmy summer days, looking at castles and pubs with gardens that border the river. It seemed to me that the answer to the puzzle should be near Bridgnorth, where Wodehouse said he spent some of his happiest boyhood days. Sure enough, a few miles outside that picturesque town a driveway leaves the traffic on the A442 behind and rambles through woods and over fields to a great house that sits framed by terraces on the Severn—just as it says in the books.

There is no shortage of castles in Shropshire, but many clearly were never the kind to visit for a gentle summer vacation. They were dank, windowless piles of stones with only enough slits in the walls to enable the occupants to hurl something, preferably fatal, on the heads of anyone arriving uninvited. I was looking for something more hospitable, and I found it, in the end, by following the directions in *Uncle Fred in the Springtime* (1939):

> To reach Blandings Castle from Market Blandings you leave the latter, if you can bear to tear yourself away from one of the most picturesque little towns in England, by way of the High Street. This, ending in a flurry of old-world cottages, takes you to a broad highway, running between leafy hedges that border pasture land and barley fields, and you come eventually to the great stone gates by the main lodge and through these to a drive which winds uphill for some three-quarters of a mile.

But I didn't find it by myself. So much has changed —though much remains the same—since the Wodehouse family rented a house in Stableford, just beyond Bridgnorth, eighty-five years ago, that one needs help to see a bygone era.

Ask around Bridgnorth about the past, and you will soon be led to Ernest H. Pee, a merry, eighty-two-year-old man whose love of local history keeps him young, and whose passion for accuracy keeps local writers on their toes. He had an extensive library of old books on the subject. Margaret Rutter, the mayor's wife, helps him with his research, acting as an extra pair of eyes, as his own eyesight is failing. With their help I found the world of Blandings, one that began back before the turn of the century, when a quiet boy, reunited with his long-absent parents, apparently spent a lot of time during his summer holidays from prep school storing up memories of village England and pub life while his father played croquet.

The first afternoon, as we settled down in Mr. Pee's littered study among the dusty old books, I read descriptions that I had culled from the Blandings novels of the castle, Market Blandings, and how to get from one to the other and on to London. Time after time Mr. Pee's face lit up with the joy of rediscovery, and he and Mrs. Rutter expressed their amazement as the landscape that they knew emerged. Sometimes the haze of time or Wodehouse fancy would blur the picture, but it was there and made clearer by Mr. Pee as he gazed at the ceiling and saw the past in his mind's eye. Sometimes he had to mull something over for a while. He listened one day to a list of pubs in Market Blandings and the next morning handed me a list of pubs in Bridgnorth when he was a boy.

"You see what he did?" he said happily. "He just changed things a bit. The Stitch in Time is the Bird in Hand."

Wodehouse's view of the place he called Market Blandings grew kinder as time passed, softening into the perennially sunny, amiable landscape he is known for. There is a bite in *Something Fresh*, published in 1915, which may be one reason the folks back there have shown no eagerness to claim him.

> The village of Market Blandings is one of those sleepy hamlets which modern progress has failed to touch, except by the addition of a railroad station and a room over the grocer's shop where moving-pictures are on view on Tuesdays and Fridays. The church is Norman, and the intelligence of the majority of the natives is palaeozoic.

Mr. Pee smiled and said, "He got it, all right. Shrewsbury woke up for the flower show once a year and then went back to sleep. Bridgnorth was on the edge of the industrial boom around Coalport in the middle of the 1800s, but by the end of the century Bridgnorth had gone to sleep and didn't wake up again until the Second World War."

> It was market day and the normal stagnation of the place was temporarily relieved and brightened by pigs that eluded their keepers and a bull calf which caught a stout farmer at the psychological moment when he was tying his shoe-lace and lifted him six feet.

Mr. Pee listened to that description from *Something Fresh,* nodding his head and exclaiming, "That's it. That's it."

In the old days farmers drove all the livestock they wanted to sell into the center of town on market day to the square. The animals had to pass through the narrow streets and sometimes ended up in a shop if the door was carelessly latched, causing havoc inside.

"I remember one day," he recalled, "a whole flock of sheep crowded into a cobbler's shop, nearly scaring a girl to death. She couldn't budge for the animals all around her, but, you know, when they were driven out, not one thing was damaged. Someone said that the shop had never had so many feet inside it without doing any business, but the cobbler was too shaken up to laugh."

Piece by piece we put together a picture of the real world of Bridgnorth next to the fictional world of Blandings, and they blended into one. Bridgnorth, sitting on its rock above the Severn is so picturesque that its streets in summertime are filled with tourists admiring its charms, and by 1933 the *Heavy Weather* Wodehouse's view of Market Blandings had mellowed:

> There it stands dreaming the centuries away, a jewel in the green heart of Shropshire. Artists who come to paint its old gray houses and fishermen who angle for bream in the lazy river are united on this point. The idea that the place could possibly be rendered more pleasing to the eye is one at which they would scoff—and have scoffed many a night over their pipes and tankards at the Emsworth Arms.

It wasn't hard to find the establishment made famous as the Emsworth Arms. There has long been a pub bearing the name of the owner of the estate that touches the edges of Bridgnorth and dominates the town. When the estate changed hands a century ago, the name of the pub also changed, and the Whitmore Arms became Foster's Arms. At the height of the tourist season disco music fills the rooms, but we could take our pints into the garden and watch the anglers along the Severn.

Sitting in the sunshine, Mr. Pee solved a mystery that Oxford students have argued about in common rooms for decades. How did Psmith, the Efficient Baxter, or anyone else get so easily to and from London without changing trains when there was no through service on old railway schedules?

"There used to be certain cars on several trains, I think it was four a day each way, that were switched at Hartlebury. All you had to do was get in the right car, and you could ride straight through," he said.

As the pictures of Bridgnorth and Market Blandings merged, my curiosity about the estate on the edge of town, Apley, grew stronger. My companions showed a strange reluctance to go there. True, Mr. Pee sent me to the estate office in Bridgnorth for a pass to the property. Just mentioning his name got it issued right away. But getting them to consider going within Apley's borders was a problem, and it was a problem of class.

I was a foreigner and could be expected to do unconventional things. Mr. Pee is a retired florist. He had been at the Apley Hall long ago, but around at the back door. Mrs. Rutter's husband is a car dealer, as well as mayor, and she had seen the estate from the public footpath on the river bank opposite. I could venture, so to speak, into the master's domain, but they felt uncomfortable at pushing past the green baize door that divides his world from theirs.

"You don't understand how it was in the old days," Mr. Pee said. "We boys tugged our caps when the squire came to town, and the girls curtseyed. There was always the feeling that if anyone misbehaved something would happen. We felt it hanging over us."

A feudal aura lingered. The Whitmores owned the estate for three hundred and fifty years until they sold it to the Fosters in 1868. A descendant of that family still owns it. For centuries the local parliamentary candidates were chosen and supplied by those families. They were the Law and sometimes the Church, too.

I wanted to roam about the estate. Mrs. Rutter's curiosity finally prompted her to accompany me. She had been to London to be entertained by the Lord Mayor, and, as mayoress, she had entertained this grand personage in Bridgnorth, but she had never been up the driveway to the Hall, until one day I waved the estate pass, and said, "Why not? It's legal." In a burst of daring she turned in at the gates, drove by the No Trespassing signs, and entered the forbidden lands.

After a mile or so, an iron fence blocked the road. The gate was locked, but the footpath was open. Mrs. Rutter, now caught by the adventure, smiled wickedly, and said, "We can walk from here." She parked in a clearing, and we set off like guilty schoolchildren to explore. We left the mayor of Bridgnorth's car neatly parked next to a No Trespassing sign. As we walked along past green fields, we entered an English Shangri-la. The Blandings lands were there, little changed, before our eyes.

> The air was fragrant with indescribable English scents. Somewhere in the distance sheepbells tinkled; rabbits, waggling white tails bolted across the path; and once a herd of agitated deer made a brief appearance among the trees.—*Leave It to Psmith* (1923).

Nearby some pigs rooted happily in a field, freer and thinner than the Empress of Blandings in her splendid isolation. All in all, the differences between reality and fiction were agreeable, but Mrs. Rutter's black patent leather pumps were dusty, and I was thirsty when Apley Hall came into view before us.

We stood looking at the great, gray house with its castellated roof, and the Wodehouse vision of Blandings and the pictures from the Shropshire history books merged. There was no doubt that Lord Emsworth was somewhere near, rumpled and absent-minded as ever. We saw the Hall, as a fifteen-year-old boy first saw it in 1896—if we squinted a bit and imagined it cared for by an army of workers. It was built on a gentle rise in a secluded valley by the Severn in 1811, incorporating part of an older house. It was so fine that Queen Adelaide considered moving in after the death of William IV. Rumors of unhealthy river fogs scared her off. These fogs have apparently never bothered the owners.

> Huge and gray and majestic, adorned with turrets and battlements in great profusion, it unquestionably takes the eye. Even Tipton Plumsoll, though not as a rule given to poetic rhapsodies, had become lyrical on first beholding it, making a noise with his tongue like the popping of a cork and saying "Some joint!"—*Galahad at Blandings* (1965).

The exterior of the Hall is weathered, and the clock on the stable tower has stopped. The present owner lives on one of the estate farms. The Hall is leased to a boys' school, housing its classrooms, dormitories, and offices, and the stables have been made into additional classrooms, but little else is changed. In the past century a railroad appeared and then vanished from the opposite bank of the Severn, and now Apley Hall sits untouched by outside eyes, hidden by the forested ridges that encircle its valley.

Our tales of exploring this frontier three miles from his doorstep made Mr. Pee wistful. We had peered in every window, walked through any open door and followed footpaths until we were hot and tired, but there was still more to be seen, and he meant to see it with us.

Our expedition had to be timed to accommodate everyone's stomach. Mr. Pee preferred to stay at home in the morning after breakfast. Mrs. Rutter had to be home to cook lunch for the mayor at noon, and also to provide tea for her youngest child, Alec, ten, on his return from school.

On the day of our great tour of the whole estate we scooped Alec up after school, and we all missed tea so that we could complete our adventure before the mayor got home for dinner. In the early afternoon we looked for the house in Stableford—which, like Bridgnorth, abuts the Apley grounds—where the Wodehouse family had lived. Mr. Pee knew every road and turning on the way. Mrs. Rutter knew all the people we encountered. She hailed a man walking along a lane, and he in turn introduced us to his mother, who owns Stableford Hall, and some old ladies drinking tea in a cottage kitchen nearby. In an hour or so we met very nearly the entire population of Stableford.

There was some debate over teacups about which was the right house. There are only four or five to choose from, and we had by then been in two. A few telephone calls settled the matter, and we were on our way again, this time to Hays Bank, the house the Wodehouse family rented in 1896 for six years. The present occupant took time out from packing for a summer holiday to show us around. It is not a grand house, but is solid and two-storied. The driveway goes through a farmyard and over a cattle grid to the front door. Opposite that is the croquet lawn, an unmarked memento of the Wodehouses. A development company from Bilston was building new houses on a hillside in Bridgnorth and calling the area Upper Blandings, but there was still no noticeable local eagerness to claim Wodehouse.

As a grand finale to our tour of the estate, we returned to the Hall and the parkland around it, taking Mr. Pee through the main gates and up the driveway. And luck was with us. At the picket fence one of the teachers from the school was unlocking the gate. The way was open for us. We drove slowly along the mile or so up to the Hall and stopped by the front door. "I've never been *here* before," Mr. Pee said. He was beyond the green baize door at last. To Alec the great house by the river was a fairy-tale place. Mrs. Rutter and I felt quite pleased with ourselves as they admired the view. It was a sight right out of the *Shropshire Gazetteer* of 1824, and from *Leave It to Psmith*, published in 1923:

> The castle, which is one of the oldest inhabited houses in England, stands upon a knoll of rising ground at the southern end of the celebrated vale of Blandings in the county of Shropshire. Away in the blue distance wooded hills ran down to where the Severn gleamed like an unsheathed sword; while up from the river rolling park-land, mounting and dipping, surged in a green wave almost to the castle walls.

ANN E. WOOD, born in Illinois, comes from a newspaper family. She has spent fifteen years as a journalist in Washington, twelve of which as a White House correspondent for the New York Daily News. *More recently as a freelancer based in England she has written for* United Features Syndicate, *the London* Evening Standard, *and the* Smithsonian *magazine. While in Shropshire writing a story on private railroads for the* Smithsonian, *she realized that the immediate world around her was familiar through her reading of P. G. Wodehouse.*

Bibliography

A Bibliography of P. G. Wodehouse

EILEEN McILVAINE

THIS BIBLIOGRAPHY has several begats. John Hayward, the editor, critic, and bibliophile, reviewed many of Wodehouse's books in *The Spectator* in the 1930s and developed a collection of Wodehouse's novels around the review copies he received from the London publisher Herbert Jenkins (later Barrie and Jenkins, now part of the Hutchinson Publishing Group). With this start Hayward began a bibliography of first editions—especially English ones. Some of the earliest publication dates in the bibliography come from Hayward's correspondence with the publishers Adam & Charles Black and Methuen in London, and Macmillan in New York.

Hayward's collection passed on to David Magee, an English rare book dealer living in San Francisco. Magee had already begun collecting Wodehouse and maintained an extensive bibliographic correspondence which he described thus: "Swapping bibliographical information is to me as reading detective fiction might be to others."[1] Much of this information regarding the fine points of first issue, e.g., details of binding, number of advertisements, etc., was incorporated into the descriptive bibliography of Wodehouse firsts which he began to compile. Among these correspondents were David Jasen, Professor of Fine Arts, C. W. Post College, James B. Meriwether, Professor of English and American Literature, University of South Carolina, and Brian W. Hennem, a bookseller in London. From all this work Magee provided Peter Schwed, chief editor at Simon and Schuster and Wodehouse's editor, with one of the earliest complete checklists of titles, which Simon and Schuster included on the dust wrapper of *The Most of P. G. Wodehouse* (1960).

The Hayward-Magee collection, the correspondence, and the beginnings of the descriptive bibliography came to James H. Heineman and form the basis of this bibliography. Mr. Heineman has more than doubled the Magee collection and added much in areas previously not well covered. The enlarged collection, of course, offers great advantages to the bibliographer; to give an example, by being able to compare editions one is able to resolve many questions in describing first issue.

Besides the Magee checklists three other bibliographies of Wodehouse works have appeared. David Jasen issued *A Bibliography and Reader's Guide to First Editions of P. G. Wodehouse* in which he identifies first editions published in the United States and England as well as some magazine stories, plays on which Wodehouse collaborated, and movies made from Wodehouse novels. Richard Usborne in *Wodehouse at Work to the End* concluded his study with a Wodehouse checklist of first editions and movies and plays. And Joseph Connolly ended *P. G. Wodehouse: An Illustrated Biography* with a bibliography of Wodehouse first editions including a description of dust wrappers.[2]

Among the most interesting and amusing sources of Wodehouse bibliographical information are the sales catalogues issued by the journalist Barrie Phelps in London and Instructor of English Charles Gould of Kent School in Connecticut.

As the collection of essays in this catalog so

---

1. David Magee, *Infinite Riches* (New York: Paul S. Eriksson, 1973), p. 244.

2. David Jasen, *A Bibliography and Reader's Guide to First Editions of P. G. Wodehouse* (Hamden, Conn.: Archon Books, 1970). Richard Usborne, *Wodehouse at Work to the End* (London: Herbert Jenkins, 1976). Joseph Connolly, *P. G. Wodehouse: An Illustrated Biography* (London: Orbis, 1979).

clearly indicates, Wodehouse had a long and prolific career. His stories, serials, and articles on English football first appeared in boys' magazines in the early part of the century. Two of the publishers of these journals, Adam & Charles Black and George Newnes, were the earliest publishers of Wodehouse's novels. Between 1903 and 1909 Wodehouse branched out, contributing a humor column to a daily London newspaper, *The Globe*, and into writing lyrics for musical revues. From there it was but a step to collaborating on plays, with Sir Seymour Hicks, Ian Hay, and Guy Bolton. By this time he was writing adult novels (usually serialized) and short stories and humorous articles in magazines such as the *Strand*, *Saturday Evening Post*, *Collier's*, *Cosmopolitan*, and *Punch*. There were also omnibus volumes which are still being issued.

So besides novels, semiautobiographical works, collected short stories, omnibus volumes, plays, and song lyrics, the bibliographer must contend with the innumerable reprints, contributions to anthologies, introductions and prefaces written for books of friends and acquaintances, and translations. Thus a Wodehouse bibliography may never be complete, as more works are reprinted or more magazine articles and anthologies come to light. But the range of the works and the elusiveness of some of the publications are part of the pleasure, challenge, and frustration for the bibliographer.

For the early years of Wodehouse's career, February 1900 – February 1908, much information can be gleaned from an account book he kept, "Money Received for Literary Work." It is rather touching to note his glee upon September 9, 1902, the day he gave up his job at the Hong Kong and Shanghai Bank in London to become a full-time writer. Later, when Wodehouse became more recognized, he was cited in many of the standard bibliographical tools, and collected in libraries such as the New York Public Library, the Lilly Library of Indiana University, and the British Library.

The present bibliography aims to be as complete as possible for first editions of both English and American publications of novels, collected works, semiautobiographical works, and published plays. Included in each entry are descriptions and notes to distinguish the various editions. The format is adapted from that used by many of the "Soho Bibliographies" published by Rupert Hart Davis. And thus we come full circle, for John Hayward was the encouraging hand behind that series.

Not complete are the sections listing Wodehouse's single contributions to volumes: the introductions and prefaces and the single stories in anthologies. Since Wodehouse was glad to help promote another writer's book, there are many such introductions (note the help Wodehouse gave Denis Mackail by writing a note of praise used as a telegram on the dust wrapper of *Romance to the Rescue*[3]).

Magazine contributions are cited only incidentally, for a complete listing would require an additional volume. Where known, the original publication in a magazine is given, which should indicate the wide range of journals for which Wodehouse wrote.

EILEEN McILVAINE was born in a small North Carolina town and educated at High Point College and the University of North Carolina at Chapel Hill. She was a reference librarian at the University of North Carolina Library and since then has been at Columbia University Library, except for a short time as acting librarian at the American School of Classical Studies at Athens. In private life she is Mrs. Edgar R. Koerner. Ms. McIlvaine carried a sign in Chapel Hill during the civil rights movement, was in Athens to observe the arrival of the military junta, and came to Columbia just in time for the troubles. For the last three years she has worked in the tranquility of Wodehouseland.

---

3. Denis Mackail, *Romance to the Rescue* (Boston: Houghton Mifflin, 1921).

Novels and Semiautobiographical Works

A CHRONOLOGICAL LIST

1902	*The Pothunters*	1927	*Meet Mr. Mulliner*
1903	*A Prefect's Uncle*	1928	*Money for Nothing*
1903	*Tales of St. Austin's*	1929	*Mr. Mulliner Speaking*
1904	*The Gold Bat*	1929	*Fish Preferred / Summer Lightning*
1904	*William Tell Told Again*	1930	*Very Good, Jeeves*
1905	*The Head of Kay's*	1931	*Big Money*
1906	*Love among the Chickens*	1931	*If I Were You*
1907	*The White Feather*	1932	*Louder and Funnier*
1907	*Not George Washington*	1932	*Doctor Sally*
1908	*The Globe By the Way Book*	1932	*Hot Water*
1909	*The Swoop*	1933	*Mulliner Nights*
1909	*Mike / Enter Psmith / Mike at Wrykyn / Mike and Psmith*	1933	*The Great Sermon Handicap*
		1933	*Heavy Weather*
1910	*The Intrusion of Jimmy / A Gentleman of Leisure*	1934	*Thank You, Jeeves*
1910	*Psmith in the City*	1934	*Right Ho, Jeeves / Brinkley Manor*
1912	*The Prince and Betty / Psmith, Journalist*	1935	*Blandings Castle and Elsewhere*
1913	*The Little Nugget*	1935	*The Luck of the Bodkins*
1914	*The Man Upstairs*	1936	*Young Men in Spats*
1915	*Something New / Something Fresh*	1936	*Laughing Gas*
1916	*Uneasy Money*	1937	*Lord Emsworth and Others*
1917	*Piccadilly Jim*	1937	*Crime Wave at Blandings*
1917	*The Man with Two Left Feet*	1937	*Summer Moonshine*
1919	*My Man Jeeves*	1938	*The Code of the Woosters*
1919	*Their Mutual Child / The Coming of Bill*	1939	*Uncle Fred in the Springtime*
1919	*A Damsel in Distress*	1940	*Eggs, Beans and Crumpets*
1920	*The Little Warrior / Jill the Reckless*	1940	*Quick Service*
1921	*Indiscretions of Archie*	1942	*Money in the Bank*
1922	*The Clicking of Cuthbert / Golf without Tears*	1946	*Joy in the Morning*
1922	*Three Men and a Maid / The Girl on the Boat*	1947	*Full Moon*
1922	*The Adventures of Sally / Mostly Sally*	1948	*Spring Fever*
1923	*The Inimitable Jeeves / Jeeves*	1948	*Uncle Dynamite*
1923	*Leave It to Psmith*	1949	*The Mating Season*
1924	*Ukridge / He Rather Enjoyed It*	1950	*Nothing Serious*
1924	*Bill the Conqueror*	1951	*The Old Reliable*
1925	*Carry On, Jeeves!*	1952	*Barmy in Wonderland / Angel Cake*
1925	*Sam the Sudden / Sam in the Suburbs*	1952	*Pigs Have Wings*
1926	*The Heart of a Goof / Divots*	1953	*Ring for Jeeves / The Return of Jeeves*
1927	*The Small Bachelor*	1953	*Bring on the Girls!*

1953	*Performing Flea / Author! Author!*	1966	*Plum Pie*
1954	*Jeeves and the Feudal Spirit / Bertie Wooster Sees It Through*	1967	*The Purloined Paperweight / Company for Henry*
1956	*French Leave*	1968	*Do Butlers Burgle Banks?*
1956	*America, I Like You / Over Seventy*	1969	*A Pelican at Blandings / No Nudes Is Good Nudes*
1957	*Something Fishy / The Butler Did It*	1970	*The Girl in Blue*
1958	*Cocktail Time*	1971	*Much Obliged, Jeeves / Jeeves and the Tie That Binds*
1959	*A Few Quick Ones*		
1960	*How Right You Are, Jeeves / Jeeves in the Offing*	1972	*Pearls, Girls and Monty Bodkin / The Plot That Thickened*
1961	*The Ice in the Bedroom*		
1961	*Service with a Smile*	1973	*Bachelors Anonymous*
1963	*Stiff Upper Lip, Jeeves*	1974	*Aunts Aren't Gentlemen / The Cat-Nappers*
1964	*Biffen's Millions / Frozen Assets*	1977	*Sunset at Blandings*
1965	*The Brinkmanship of Galahad Threepwood / Galahad at Blandings*		

A1A The Pothunters

THE POTHUNTERS | BY | P. G. WODEHOUSE | [publisher's device] | LONDON | ADAM & CHARLES BLACK | 1902

COLLATION: [1–2] *blank*; [3] *half title*; [4] *blank; frontispiece* [inserted]; [5] *title page*; [6] *blank*; [7] *dedication:* To Joan, Effie, and Ernestine Bowes-Lyon.; [8] *blank*; [9] Contents; [10] *blank*; [11] List of Illustrations; [12] *blank*; 13–272, *text* (*bottom of page 272, printer's note:* Printed by M'Farlane & Erskine, Edinburgh)

PUBLISHED: 18 September 1902 (price 3s6d); British Library reception date 19 September 1902

COVER: Royal blue cloth, silver lettering on spine; silver loving cup on front cover and spine

SIZE: 12.5 × 19 cm. (5 × 7 ½")

A1B American edition

The American edition was issued by Macmillan, New York, 1902, from imported sheets ($1.50).

NOTES: Adam and Charles Black subsequently bound sheets of the first edition in gray-blue pictorial cloth, gold and light blue lettering; the cover illustration is from the frontispiece and the illustration on the spine is from half of the illustration opposite page 30. The title page is dated 1902. This second binding has also been issued with an eight-page advertising supplement, "Beautiful Books for Young People"; the latest Wodehouse title is *Mike*, published 1909.

Black reprinted in 1924 (British Library reception date 1 September 1924), 272 pages (2s6d), in series Black's Boys Library; this edition was reissued 1925. Macmillan issued from imported sheets, 1924 ($1.00).

This boy's story, the first Wodehouse in book form, originally appeared in *Public School Magazine*, January, February, March 1902, with illustrations by R. Noel Pocock. For the book the frontispiece and nine full-page illustrations were taken from the magazine serial.

Adam and Charles Black paid ten percent royalty on all copies of the book which were sold.

A2A A Prefect's Uncle

A PREFECT'S UNCLE | BY | P. G. WODEHOUSE | AUTHOR OF "THE POTHUNTERS" | *CONTAINING EIGHT PAGE ILLUSTRATIONS BY R. NOEL POCOCK* | [publisher's device] | LONDON | ADAM & CHARLES BLACK | 1903

COLLATION: [i] *half title*; [ii] By the Same Author [*advertisement for* The Pothunters 3s6d]; *frontispiece* [inserted]; [iii] *title page*; [iv] *blank*; [v] *dedication:* To W. Townend; [vi] Contents; [vii] List of Illustrations; [viii] *blank*; [1]–264, *text*

PUBLISHED: 11 September 1903 (price 3s6d); British Library reception date 12 September 1903

COVER: Red pictorial cloth; pink, gold, gray lettering; gray, red, pink, black drawing on front cover (same as frontispiece) and on spine (half of illustration opposite page 114)

SIZE: 12.5 × 19 cm. (5 × 7½")

A2B American edition

The American edition was issued by Macmillan, New York, October 1903, from imported sheets ($1.25).

NOTES: Black reprinted in 1924 (British Library reception date 1 September 1924) in the series Black's Boys Library (2s6d), 264 pages; this edition was reissued in 1925. Both of these printings are not illustrated except for a colored frontispiece. Macmillan, New York, issued the 1924 edition from imported plates ($1.25).

Wodehouse received an advance on May 1903 of £7.14.

A3A Tales of St. Austin's

TALES OF | ST AUSTIN'S | BY | P. G. WODEHOUSE | AUTHOR OF "THE POTHUNTERS, "A PREFECT'S UNCLE, ETC. | *CONTAINING TWELVE FULL-PAGE ILLUSTRATIONS BY* | *T. M. R. WHITWELL, R. NOEL POCOCK, AND* | *E. F. SKINNER* | LONDON | ADAM & CHARLES BLACK | 1903

COLLATION: [i] *half title*; [ii] By the Same Author; *frontispiece by Whitwell [inserted]*; [iii] *title page*; [iv] *blank*; [v] *dedication:* ad matrem; [vi] *blank*; [vii] Preface; [viii] *blank*; [ix] Contents; [x] *blank*; [xi] Illustrations; [xii] *blank*; 1–282, *text* (*bottom of page 282, printer's note:* Printed by M'Farlane & Erskine, Edinburgh); [283–84] *advertisements*

PUBLISHED: 10 November 1903 (price 3s6d); British Library reception date 12 November 1903

COVER: Light red pictorial cloth; gold and black lettering; gray, gold, and black drawing on front cover (from the frontispiece) and on spine (from illustrations opposite page 8); lettering on spine in gold

SIZE: 12.5 × 19.25 cm. (5 × 7⅝")

CONTENTS: How Pillingshot Scored, pp. 1–13; The Odd Trick, pp. 15–26; L'Affaire Uncle John, pp. 27–40; Harrison's Slight Error, pp. 41–54; Bradshaw's Little Story, pp. 55–66; A Shocking Affair, pp. 67–85; The Babe and the Dragon, pp. 87–98; The Manoeuvres of Charteris, pp. 99–180; How Payne Bucked Up, pp. 181–92; Author! pp. 193–206; "The Tabby Terror," pp. 207–18; The Prize Poem, pp. 219–32; Work, pp. 233–48; Notes, pp. 249–60; Now, Talking about Cricket–, pp. 261–72; The Tom Brown Question, pp. 273–82.

NOTES: Black reissued in 1903 in light red cloth with gold and black lettering on the spine. This printing was also issued in olive-green pictorial cloth, with gold lettering on the spine and with blue, black, and yellow drawing. Black printed a new edition September 1923 (British Library reception date 11 September 1923) in red cloth with black lettering; the frontispiece by J. H. Hartley is the only illustration (2s6d).

"Most of these stories originally appeared in the *Captain*. . . . The rest are from the *Public School Magazine*. The story entitled 'A Shocking Affair' appears in print for the first time. 'This was one of our failures.'" —Preface.

The illustrations in the book are the same as those used in the magazines.

A4A The Gold Bat

THE GOLD BAT | BY | P. G. WODEHOUSE | AUTHOR OF "A PREFECT'S UNCLE," "THE POTHUNTERS," ETC. | *CONTAINING EIGHT FULL-PAGE ILLUSTRATIONS* | *BY T. M. R. WHITWELL* | [publisher's device] | LONDON | ADAM & CHARLES BLACK | 1904

COLLATION: [i] *half title*; [ii] By the Same Author [*three titles ending* Tales of St. Austin's]; *frontispiece [inserted]*; [iii] *title page*; [iv] *blank*; [v] *dedication:* To That Prince of Slackers, Herbert Westbrook; [vi] Contents; [vii] Illustrations; [viii] *blank*; [1]–277, *text*; [278] *blank*; [279–80] *advertisements for three Wodehouse books*

PUBLISHED: 13 September 1904 (price 3s6d); British Library reception date 14 September 1904

COVER: Dark red pictorial cloth; gray, gold, yellow, black lettering and drawings; drawing on front cover from illustration opposite page 254; drawing on spine from page 202

SIZE: 31.8 × 20 cm. (5½ × 7⅞")

A4B American edition

The American edition was issued by Macmillan, New York, 1923, from imported sheets ($1.00).

NOTES: The first edition was reprinted in 1923 by Black (British Library reception date 11 September 1932), 277 pages, in the series Black's Boys and Girls

Library (2s6d); this printing is illustrated only by a colored frontispiece.

Later printings by Adam and Charles Black have an eight-page insert of advertisements identical to the later edition of *The Pothunters* (latest Wodehouse book advertised is *Mike*, published 1909).

The 1933 printing gives this publishing history: First published September 1904, reprinted 1911, this edition published September 1923, reprinted 1926 and 1932.

The story was serialized in the *Captain* October 1903 – March 1904 with illustrations by T. M. R. Whitwell.

A5A William Tell Told Again

WILLIAM TELL | TOLD AGAIN | P. G. WODEHOUSE | AUTHOR OF "THE POT-HUNTERS," "A PREFECT'S UNCLE," "THE GOLD BAT," | "TALES OF ST. AUSTIN'S" | WITH | *ILLUSTRATIONS IN COLOUR BY PHILIP DADD* | *DESCRIBED IN VERSE BY JOHN W. HOUGHTON* | [publisher's device in red] | LONDON | ADAM & CHARLES BLACK | 1904

COLLATION: [i] *half title*; [ii] *blank; colored frontispiece signed* Philip Dadd 1900; [iii] *title page*; [iv] *blank*; [v] *dedication:* To Biddy O'Sullivan for a Christmas Present; [vi] *blank*; vii, List of Illustrations; [viii] *poem (untitled)*; 1–[106] *text (bottom of page 106, printer's note:* Billing and Sons, Ltd., Printers, Guildford); [107–8] *advertisements for all four Wodehouse books*

PUBLISHED: 11 November 1904 (price 6s); British Library reception date 16 November 1904

COVER: Stone-colored pictorial cloth, gold lettering; green, black, brown drawing same as frontispiece; gilt top pages

SIZE: 16 × 22.6 cm. (6 3/8 × 8 1/2")

DUST WRAPPER: Illustration on dust wrapper signed P.D., same as plate x opposite page 60

NOTE: Fifteen verses by John W. Houghton; sixteen illustrations by Philip Dadd

A5B American edition

The American edition was issued by Macmillan, New York, December 1904, from imported sheets ($2.00).

NOTES: This title was issued by Black in many variant bindings: (1) same as first edition with twelve-page advertising supplement inserted. The latest Wodehouse book is *The White Feather* (1907);
(2) tan pictorial cloth, gold lettering; brown, green, and black drawings; gilt top pages; title page dated 1904; two pages of advertisements for Wodehouse books (same advertisements as first printing);
(3) red pictorial cloth, black lettering; brown, green, and black drawing; no date on title page but publisher's address; thicker, cheaper paper; no advertisements;
(4) green pictorial cloth, black lettering; tan, pea-green and black drawing; no date on title page but publisher's address; thicker, cheaper paper; no advertisements.

Philip Dadd was commissioned by Adam and Charles Black to submit drawings for "King Hildebrand's Ring"; these were used for *William Tell Told Again*. Wodehouse was paid fifteen guineas on publication for writing 15,000 words. (From Adam & Charles Black correspondence.)

A6A The Head of Kay's

THE | HEAD OF KAY'S | BY | P. G. WODEHOUSE | AUTHOR OF "A PREFECT'S UNCLE," "THE GOLD BAT," ETC. | *CONTAINING EIGHT FULL-PAGE ILLUSTRATIONS* | *BY T. M. R. WHITWELL.* | LONDON | ADAM & CHARLES BLACK | 1905

COLLATION: [i] *half title*; [ii] By the Same Author [*four titles*]; *frontispiece* [*inserted*]; [iii] *title page*; [iv] *blank*; [v] *dedication:* To my father; [vi] Preface; [vii] Contents; [viii] Illustrations; [1]–280, *text (bottom of page 280, printer's note:* Printed by M'Farlane and Erskine, Edinburgh)

PUBLISHED: 5 October 1905 (price 3s6d); British Library reception date 7 October 1905

COVER: Dark red pictorial cloth, gold lettering on spine, yellow lettering on front cover; red, black, gray, and yellow drawing on cover and also on spine

SIZE: 13.5 × 19.75 cm. (5 3/8 × 7 3/4")

NOTE: Frontispiece and seven illustrations by Whitwell inserted

A6B First American edition

The American edition was issued by Macmillan, New York, 1922, from imported sheets ($1.00).

NOTES: Adam and Charles Black reissued 1905(?) with an eight-page supplement, "List of Books for Boys and Girls"; the latest Wodehouse book advertised is *The Head of Kay's*. Reissued 1909(?) with an eight-page advertising insert, "Beautiful Books for Young People"; *Mike* (1909) is the latest Wodehouse book advertised. A new edition was issued October 1922 (British Library reception date 20 September 1922), 280 pages with a colored frontispiece; this edition was reissued 1923, 1924, 1928 in the series Black's Boys Library.

"When this story was appearing serially in the *Captain* [October 1904 – March 1905], some anonymous idiot wrote to the editors pointing out certain errors in the camp chapters. I am obliged. . . ."—Preface. Wodehouse received £60 for the serial, and by October 1905 £17.10 in royalties on the book.

A7A Love among the Chickens

LOVE AMONG | THE CHICKENS | BY P. G. WODEHOUSE | [publisher's device] | LONDON: GEORGE NEWNES, LIMITED | SOUTHAMPTON STREET, STRAND, W.C.

COLLATION: [i] *half title*; [ii] By the Same Author [*five titles ending with* The Head of Kay's]; *frontispiece* [*inserted*] *by* H. M. Brock; [iii] *title page*; [iv] *blank*; [v] *dedication:* To Sir Bargrave and Lady Deane; [vi] *blank*; [vii] Preface; [viii] *blank*; ix–x, Contents; [1]–312, *text* (*bottom of page 312, printer's note:* Printed by Ballantyne, Hanson and Co. Edinburgh and London)

PUBLISHED: June 1906 (price 6s); British Library reception date 29 April 1907 for second printing

SIZE: 12.5 × 19 cm. (5 × 7½")

COVER: Tan pictorial cloth, with green, orange, black drawing

NOTE: Three illustrations by H. M. Brock and frontispiece (inserted).

NOTES: There is some confusion about the publication date of Wodehouse's first adult novel: the copyright page of the second printing states it was first published July 1906; the publishing company, George Newnes, in a letter reported June 1906; while Wodehouse's own records and the *English Catalogue* give August. The British Library did not receive a copy of the printing but registered the second printing (British Library reception date 29 April 1907). Newnes also reissued August 1910 (6d).

From the Preface: "William Townend, artist. . . . Dear Bill—In the case of a book of this kind it is only right that the responsibility should be fixed. I take this opportunity of exposing you. But for the help I derived from your almost insolent familiarity with the habits of chickens, I should probably have been compelled to give up writing this book and go back to work again."

A7B First American edition

LOVE AMONG | THE CHICKENS | A STORY | OF THE HAPS AND MISHAPS ON | AN ENGLISH CHICKEN FARM | BY P. G. WODEHOUSE | ILLUSTRATED BY | ARMAND BOTH | NEW YORK | THE CIRCLE PUBLISHING COMPANY | 1909 [in decorative frame]

COLLATION: [i] *half title*; [ii] *blank*; *frontispiece* [*inserted*]; [iii] *title page*; [iv] *copyright page:* Copyright, 1908 by A. E. Baerman [publisher's device]; v–vi, Contents; List of Illustrations [*inserted*]; 1–[350] *text*

PUBLISHED: 11 May 1909 (price $1.50)

COVER: Tan pictorial cloth, blue lettering; pictorial design in red and blue

SIZE: 13.5 × 19.33 cm. (5⅜ × 7⅝")

NOTE: Frontispiece and five illustrations by Armand (both inserted).

NOTES: This was Wodehouse's first novel to be published in the United States. The copyright was taken out by A. E. Baerman who was Wodehouse's agent in New York for a short time.

"But I remember ages ago a crook agent pinched all the serial money for my Love among the Chickens, had it published as a book—copyright by him, and when the movies wanted it, I had to pay him $250 to release the rights." (Letter to Guy Bolton, 9 February 1951.)

A7C Second English edition

LOVE AMONG | THE CHICKENS | BY | P. G. WODEHOUSE | *ENTIRELY REWRITTEN* | *FOR THIS EDITION* | HERBERT JENKINS LIMITED | 3 YORK STREET, ST. JAMES'S | LONDON S.W.I MCMXXI [double-rule frame]

COLLATION: [i] *half title*; [ii] What This Story Is About, Other Books by the Same Author [*six titles ending* Indiscretions of Archie]; [iii] *title page*; [iv] *copyright page:* [publisher's device] Popular edition entirely rewritten by the author Printed in Great Britain by Purnell and Sons Paulton, Somerset, England; [v]–vi, *dedication:* Dedication to W. Townend; [vii]–viii, Contents; [1]–256, *text*

PUBLISHED: June(?) 1921

COVER: Blue cloth, darker blue lettering

SIZE: 19.5 × 13 cm. (5 × 7¾")

NOTES: There is no copy of this, the revised edition, in the British Library. The earliest copy of the Herbert Jenkins edition I have seen has *Jill the Reckless* ending the titles on the list of Wodehouse books. Both David Jasen and Joseph Connolly state that *Indiscretions of Archie* is the last title. This editon went through at least thirteen printings completing 104,208 copies.

From the dedication: "You will notice that I have practically re-written the book. There was some pretty bad work in it, and it had 'dated.' As an instance of the way in which the march of modern civilisation has left the 1906 edition behind, I may mention that on page twenty-one I was able to make Ukridge speak of selling eggs at six for five-pence!"

A8A The White Feather

THE | WHITE FEATHER | BY | P. G. WODEHOUSE | AUTHOR OF "THE GOLD BAT," "THE POTHUNTERS," "A PREFECT'S UNCLE," ETC. | *CONTAINING TWELVE FULL-PAGE* | *ILLUSTRATIONS BY W. TOWNEND* | LONDON | ADAM & CHARLES BLACK | 1907

COLLATION: [i] half title; [ii] By the Same Author Large crown 8vo . . . Price 3s.6d. each [*five titles*]; *frontispiece* [*inserted*]; [iii] *title page*; [iv] *blank*; [v] *dedication:* To my brother Dick; [vi] Preface; [vii] Contents; [viii] Illustrations by W. Townend; [1]–284, *text*

PUBLISHED: 9 October 1907 (price 3s6d); British Library reception date 11 October 1907

COVER: Tan pictorial cloth; black and tan lettering; black, white, tan drawing (from illustration opposite page 72)

SIZE: 14×20.25 cm. (5½×8")

A8B American edition

The American edition was issued by Macmillan, New York, 1922, from imported sheets ($1.00).

NOTES: Adam and Charles Black reissued in 1907 with an eight-page advertising supplement, "Beautiful Books for Young People," and again in 1913. The story was reprinted in October 1922 (British Library reception date 20 September 1922), 284 pages (2s6d). The verso of the title page of the 1922 reissue states: "First published in 1907; reprinted in 1913; this edition published in 1922, reprinted in 1922."

Macmillan reissued in 1928 ($1.00).

"The time of this story is a year and a term later than that of 'The Gold Bat.' The history of Wrykyn in between those two books is dealt with in a number of short stories, some of them brainy in the extreme, which have appeared in various magazines. I wanted Messrs. Black to publish these, but they were light on their feet and kept away—a painful exhibition of the White Feather."—Preface.

The tale first appeared as a serial in the *Captain* October 1905 – March 1906 with the same illustrations by T. M. R. Whitwell.

A9A Not George Washington

NOT | GEORGE | WASHINGTON | BY | HERBERT WESTBROOK | AND | P. G. WODEHOUSE | *Author of "Love Among the Chickens"* | CASSELL AND COMPANY, LIMITED | LONDON, PARIS, NEW YORK, TORONTO AND MELBOURNE | MCMVII ALL RIGHTS RESERVED

COLLATION: [i] *half title*; [ii] *blank; frontispiece* [*inserted*] *in color by* John E. Sutcliffe; [iii] *title page*; [iv] *blank*; [v] *dedication:* To Ella King-Hall; [vi] *blank*; [vii]–viii, Contents; [1]–279, *text*; [280] *printer's note:* Printed by Cassell & Company, Limited, La Belle Sauvage, London, E.C.

PUBLISHED: 18 October 1907 (price 6s; $1.50); British Library reception date 25 October 1907

COVER: Orange-brown cloth, gold lettering

SIZE: 13×20 cm. (5¼×7⅞")

NOTES: The first edition has eight small circles under the title on the front cover and "Cassell & Cassell" in gold on the bottom of the backstrip. At the stitching between pages 96 and 97 is "9–1907."

There are at least two variants, both 13×19.75 cm. (5¼×7¾"): (1) eight gold circles under the title on the front cover but "Cassell" in gold on the bottom of the backstrip of the spine and lacking "9–1907"; (2) seven gold circles under the title on the front cover, "Cassell" in gold on the bottom of the spine and "9–1907" on the inside of the stitching on page 96.

Ella King-Hall was Wodehouse's agent and Westbrook's wife. Wodehouse received an advance of £13.10.

A10A The Globe By the Way Book

THE | GLOBE | BY THE WAY | BOOK | A LITERARY QUICK-LUNCH | FOR PEOPLE WHO HAVE ONLY GOT | FIVE MINUTES TO SPARE | Illustrated by | W. K. HASELDEN | *Of the DAILY MIRROR* | Written by | P. G. WODEHOUSE | AND | HERBERT WESTBROOK | "THE GLOBE" PUBLISHING CO. | 367 STRAND

COLLATION: i–iv, *advertisements*; [1] *title page*; 2, "They're-off!"—Extract from the National Anthem; 3–[4], Preface; 5–144, *text*; *between pages 32 and 33 of text a ten-page insert:* A Chat about the Globe, *signed* C.P.

PUBLISHED: June 1908 (price 1s); British Library reception date 18 July 1908

COVER: Red paper cover with white lettering and drawing

COVER TITLE: By the Way 1/- Book 1/- Profusely Illustrated

SIZE: 16.75×21 cm. (6⅝×8¼")

NOTE: Compilation of Wodehouse-Westbrook columns, "By the Way," in the *Globe*.

A11A The Swoop

THE SWOOP! | OR | HOW CLARENCE SAVED ENGLAND | *A Tale of the Great Invasion* | BY | P. G. WODEHOUSE | Author of "The Gold Bat," "The Head of Kay's," etc. | [publisher's monogram] | LONDON: ALSTON RIVERS, LIMITED | BROOKE STREET, HOLBORN BARS | 1909

COLLATION: [1] *half title*; [2] *full-page illustration by C. Harrison* [line drawing]; [3] *title page*; [4] *copyright page:* London: Printed by William Clowes and Sons, Limited, Duke Street, Stamford Street, S.E., and Great Windmill Street, W.; [5] Preface [*signed* P. G. Wodehouse, The Bomb-Proof Shelter, London, W.]; [6] *blank*; [7]–122, *text*; 123–26, *advertisements*; [127–28] *blank*

PUBLISHED: 16 April 1909 (price 1s); British Library reception date 16 April 1909

COVER: Orange wrappers, black-and-white drawings and letters

SIZE: 12.25×18.25 cm. (4¾×7⅛")

NOTES: Line drawings throughout by C. Harrison. Designed to be sold for a shilling in railroad stalls, etc. *The Swoop* and *The Globe By the Way Book* are among the rarest Wodehousiana.

Wodehouse adapted the plot for publication in *Vanity Fair*, July–August 1915, "The Military Invasion of America, a Tale of the German-Japanese Invasion in 1916."

A12A Mike

MIKE | A PUBLIC SCHOOL STORY | BY | P. G. WODEHOUSE | AUTHOR OF "THE GOLD BAT," "A PREFECT'S | UNCLE," ETC. | CONTAINING TWELVE FULL-PAGE | ILLUSTRATIONS BY | T. M. R. WHITWELL | [publisher's device] | LONDON | ADAM AND CHARLES BLACK | 1909

COLLATION: [1] *half title*; [ii] By the Same Author [*six titles*]; *frontispiece* [*inserted*]; [iii] *title page*; [iv] *blank*; [v] *dedication:* To Alan Durand; [vi] *blank*; [vii]–ix, Contents; [x] *blank*; [xi] List of Illustrations; [xii] *blank*; 1–339, *text*; [340] *printer's note:* Printed by Ballantyne & Co. Limited, Tavistock Street, Covent Garden, London

PUBLISHED: 15 September 1909 (price 3s6d); British Library reception date 15 September 1909

COVER: Olive-green cloth; gold, black, green lettering; white, red, black drawing

SIZE: 13.50×20.25 cm. (5½×8")

NOTE: Of the original fifty-nine chapters, chapters 30–59 were published with a few changes in 1935 as *Enter Psmith*. In 1953, chapters 1–29 were issued entitled *Mike at Wrykyn* with a few changes, and the last thirty chapters were reissued as *Mike and Psmith* following the 1935 *Enter Psmith*.

A12B First American edition

The American edition was issued by Macmillan, New York, February 1910, from imported sheets ($1.50).

NOTES: Black reprinted "with four full-page illustrations in colour by J. H. Hartley" (frontispiece, pages 84, 200, 266) in 1924, 339 pages (British Library reception date 1 September 1924) (3s6d). The copyright page of the 1928 printing reads: "First published, with 12 page illustrations, September 1909; reprinted in 1910, 1916 and 1919; this edition published 1924; reprinted 1925 and 1928."

Macmillan reissued in 1924 from imported sheets ($1.75).

Originally written as two serials in the *Captain*: "Jackson Junior" and "The Lost Lambs," April 1907 – September 1908, illustrated by T. M. R. Whitwell.

A12C Mike / Enter Psmith

ENTER | PSMITH | BY | P. G. WODEHOUSE | AUTHOR OF "PSMITH IN THE CITY," "PSMITH, JOURNALIST," ETC. | A. & C. BLACK, LTD. | 4, 5 & 6 SOHO SQUARE, LONDON, W.1

COLLATION: [1] *half title and series note:* Black's Novel Library; [ii] *advertisements*; [iii] *title page*; [iv] *copyright page:* Published Spring, 1935 . . . Printed by Billing and Sons, Ltd., Guildford and Esher; v, Publisher's Note;

[vi] *blank*; vii, Contents; [viii] *blank*; 1–247, *text*; [248] *blank*

PUBLISHED: 14 February 1935 (price 2s6d); British Library reception date 14 February 1935

COVER: Jade-blue (blue-green) cloth, bright red letters

SIZE: 12.75×19 cm. (5×7½″)

DUST WRAPPER: Drawing by J. H. Hartley

NOTE: Chapters 30–59 of *Mike* were published with a few changes as *Enter Psmith*. This was reissued by Herbert Jenkins in 1953 entitled *Mike and Psmith*.

A12D American edition

The American edition of *Enter Psmith* was issued by Macmillan, New York, 17 September 1935, offset from the English edition (price $.75).

A12E Mike / Mike at Wrykyn

MIKE AT WRYKYN | *By* | P. G. WODEHOUSE | Author of "Mike and Psmith" | LONDON: HERBERT JENKINS

COLLATION: [1] *half title*; [2] *synopsis*; [3] *title page*; [4] *copyright page*: First published by Herbert Jenkins Ltd. 1953 . . . Printed in Great Britain by Wyman & Sons Ltd., London, Fakenham and Reading; [5–6] Contents; 7–[189] *text*; [190] *blank*; [191] *synopsis of* Mike and Psmith; [192] Books by P. G. Wodehouse

PUBLISHED: February 1953 (price 6s); British Library reception date 31 January 1953

COVER: Bright red cloth, black lettering

SIZE: 12.75×19 cm. (5×7½″)

DUST WRAPPER: Drawing by W. Spence

NOTE: Chapters 1–29 of *Mike* were published with a few changes as *Mike at Wrykyn*.

A13A The Intrusion of Jimmy

The | INTRUSION | OF JIMMY | by | P. G. WODEHOUSE | NEW YORK | [publisher's monogram] | W. J. WATT | & COMPANY | PUBLISHERS | [publisher's device] [single-rule frame]

COLLATION: [i] *half title*; [ii] *blank*; *colored frontispiece* [*inserted*]; [iii] *title page*; [iv] *copyright page*: Copyright, 1910, by W. J. Watt & Co. Published May. Press of Braunworth & Co. Bookbinders and Printers, Brooklyn, N.Y.; [v–vi] Contents; 1–314, *text*

PUBLISHED: 11 May 1910 (price $1.50)

COVER: Olive-green and black cloth, black drawing, gold lettering, round portrait pasted on cover; green lettering on spine

SIZE: 13×19.25 cm. (5⅛×7⅝″)

NOTE: One colored and four black-and-white illustrations by Will Grefé.

NOTES: The American edition was reprinted by Grosset & Dunlap, New York, in 1911, 314 pages ($.50), and by G. Howard Watt, 1929, 314 pages.

A13B First English edition

A GENTLEMAN OF | LEISURE | BY | P. G. WODEHOUSE | [publisher's device] | LONDON: ALSTON RIVERS LTD. | BROOKE ST., HOLBORN BARS | 1910

COLLATION: [i] *half title*; [ii] *advertisements* [*twelve titles ending* The Globe By the Way Book]; [iii] *title page*; [iv] *copyright page*: copyright in the U.S.A.; [v] *dedication*: To Herbert Westbrook . . . ; [vi] *blank*; vii–viii, Contents; [1]–347, *text*; [348] *printer's note*: Printed by Hazell, Watson & Viney Ld., London and Aylesbury.; 349–51, *advertisements*; [352] *blank*

PUBLISHED: 15 November 1910 (price 7s6d); British Library reception date 15 November 1910

COVER: Royal blue cloth, gold letters

SIZE: 12.5×19 cm. (4⅞×7½″)

DUST WRAPPER: Dark red, black letters; 7/6 on spine

NOTES: Reprinted by Herbert Jenkins February 1911 with a dedication: "To Douglas Fairbanks who many years ago played 'Jimmy' in the dramatized version of this novel." Jenkins issued at least fifteen reprints completing 120,078 copies.

George Newnes also reprinted this title, August 1911 (British Library reception date 5 February 1912), in Newnes Sixpenny Copyright Novels (126 pages). Newnes reprinted again December 1920, January 1929, and October 1931.

Wodehouse and John Stapleton adapted as a play, *A Gentleman of Leisure*, 1911.

A14A Psmith in the City

PSMITH | IN THE CITY | A SEQUEL TO "MIKE" | BY | P. G. WODEHOUSE | AUTHOR OF "THE GOLD BAT" "A PREFECT'S UNCLE" "THE | WHITE FEATHER" "TALES OF ST. AUSTIN'S" ETC. | WITH TWELVE FULL PAGE ILLUSTRATIONS | BY | T. M. R. WHITWELL | LONDON | ADAM AND CHARLES BLACK | 1910

COLLATION: [i] *half title*; [ii] By the Same Author [*seven titles ending with* Mike]; *frontispiece* [*inserted*]; [iii] *title page*; [iv] *blank*; [v] *dedication:* To Leslie Havergal Bradshaw; [vi] *blank*; [vii] Preface; [viii] *blank*; ix–x, Contents; [xi] List of Illustrations by T. M. R. Whitwell; [xii] *blank*; 1–266, *text* (*bottom of page 266, printer's note:* Printed by Ballantine & Co. Limited . . .); [267] Books by P. G. Wodehouse; [268] Books for Boys

PUBLISHED: 23 September 1910 (price 3s6d); British Library reception date 23 September 1910

BINDING: Blue pictorial cloth, gold, tan, black, and gray letters and drawing

SIZE: 13.8 × 20.25 cm. (5½ × 8″)

NOTE: Frontispiece and eleven illustrations by T. M. R. Whitwell are inserted.

A14B American edition

The American edition was issued by Macmillan, New York, November 1910, from imported sheets ($1.50).

NOTES: Black reprinted in 1923 (British Library reception date 15 March 1923), 266 pages (2s6d), without any illustration. The copyright page of the 1930 edition gives this publishing history: "Published September 1910, Reprinted 1919; This edition published March 1923, Reprinted twice 1923, twice 1924, twice 1925, 1926, 1928, 1930." The thirteenth reprint appeared in 1941, the fourteenth reprint in 1950.

"Mike and Psmith first appeared in a book called 'Mike.' This story opens about a month after they have left school."—Preface.

A15A The Prince and Betty

The PRINCE | and BETTY | [illustrated with two oval portraits] | by | P. G. WODEHOVSE | Author of | "The INTRVSION of JIMMY" | Illustrations by | WILL GREFÉ | NEW YORK | W. J. WATT & COMPANY | PVBLISHERS

COLLATION: [i–iv] *blank*; [v] *half title*; [vi] *blank*; *frontispiece* [*inserted*]; *title page* and *copyright page* [*inserted*]: Copyright, 1912, by W. J. Watt & Company Published January; [vii–viii] Contents; [ix] *half title*; [x] *blank*; 1–300, *text*; [301–302] *blank*

PUBLISHED: 14 February 1912 (price $1.25)

COVER: Black cloth with two oval portraits pasted on front cover; gold lettering on spine and front cover

SIZE: 12.75 × 19.25 cm. (5 × 7½″)

DUST WRAPPER: Drawing by Grefé

NOTES: The Watt edition was reissued with "Popular Edition" stamped on the bottom of the spine. The front cover of the reissue is dark blue cloth with a pasted-on illustration in color of the same illustration facing page 64 and is 1/16″ thinner.

Serialized in the *Strand*, February–April 1912, illustrated by Dudley Hardy.

A15B First English edition

THE | PRINCE AND BETTY | BY | P. G. WODEHOUSE | MILLS & BOON, LIMITED | 49 RUPERT STREET | LONDON W.

COLLATION: [i] *half title*; [ii] *advertisement*; [iii] *title page*; [iv] *copyright page:* By the Same Author [*four titles*] Published 1912; [v] *dedication:* To Ellaline Terriss from The Hermit; [vi] *blank*; [1]–282, *text* (*bottom of page 282, printer's note:* Turnbull and Spears, Printers, Edinburgh)

PUBLISHED: 1 May 1912 (price 6s); British Library reception date 1 May 1912

COVER: Light red cloth, black lettering on front cover; gold lettering on spine.

SIZE: 13 × 19.5 cm. (5¼ × 7¾″)

NOTE: Totally revised plot with scene shifted to London, Psmith dropped.

A15C Second English edition

PSMITH | JOURNALIST | BY | P. G. WODEHOUSE | AUTHOR OF "THE WHITE FEATHER" "MIKE" | "PSMITH IN THE CITY" ETC. | CONTAINING TWELVE FULL-PAGE ILLUSTRATIONS | FROM DRAWINGS BY T. M. R. WHITWELL | A. & C. BLACK, LTD. | 4, 5 & 6 SOHO SQUARE, LONDON, W. | 1915

COLLATION: [i] *half title*; [ii] By the Same Author [*eight titles*]; *frontispiece* [*inserted*]; [iii] *title page*; [iv] *blank*; v, Preface (*signed* P. G. Wodehouse, N.Y., 1915); [vi] *blank*; vii, Contents; viii, List of Illustrations; 1–247, *text* (*bottom of page 247, printer's note:* Printed at the Complete Press, West Norwood, London); [248] *blank*

PUBLISHED: 29 September 1915 (price 3s6d); British Library reception date 29 September 1915

COVER: Blue pictorial cloth; black, gold, cream, yellow, and blue lettering and drawing

SIZE: 13.5 × 20 cm. (5½ × 7⅞″)

DUST WRAPPER: Brown paper jacket with identical drawing to front cover.

A15D Second American edition

The American edition of *Psmith, Journalist* was issued by Macmillan, New York, 1915, from English sheets ($1.25).

NOTES: The plot was lifted from the American edition of *The Prince and Betty* with the love interest dropped. Eleven illustrations and frontispiece (inserted).

The Adam and Charles Black 1924 reprint gives the publishing history: "First published, with 8 illustrations, in 1915. This edition published in March, 1923; Reprinted July and October, 1923; February, 1924." Also reissued 1928.

The Macmillan printing was given a Library of Congress card number: 16–17497 and was reviewed in the *New York Times*, 26 December 1915.

The *Captain* ran the serial entitled "Psmith Journalist" illustrated by T. M. R. Whitwell, October 1909 – February 1910.

A16A The Little Nugget

THE LITTLE NUGGET | BY | P. G. WODEHOUSE | METHUEN & CO. LTD. | 36 ESSEX STREET W.C. | LONDON

COLLATION: [i] *half title*; [ii] *blank*; [iii] *title page*; [iv] *copyright page:* First published in 1913; [1]–303, *text*; [304] *printer's note:* Printed by Morrison & Gibb Limited Edinburgh; [1]–8, Methuen's Popular Novels [*dated*] Autumn 1913; [1–31] A Selection of Books Published by Methuen . . . May 1913; [32] *blank* [*advertising supplement inserted*]

PUBLISHED: 28 August 1913 (price 6s); British Library reception date 1 September 1913

COVER: Red cloth, gold letters and decorations on spine, lettered in blind on front cover

SIZE: 13×19.5 cm. (5¼×7¾″)

NOTES: Methuen reissued at least nineteen times through 1955, beginning with the second and third editions, January 1914; fourth edition (cheap edition), 13 October 1921.

Munsey's Magazine commissioned and published the story in their August 1913 issue, illustrated by William B. King. The *Captain* published it in its earliest form as a serial entitled "The Eighteen Carat Kid," January–March 1913, illustrated by H. M. Brock.

A16B First American edition

THE | LITTLE NUGGET | BY | P. G. WODEHOUSE | *Author of "The Intrusion of Jimmy," Etc.* | ILLUSTRATIONS BY | WILL GREFÉ | [*publisher's monogram*] | New York | W. J. WATT & COMPANY | PUBLISHERS

COLLATION: *frontispiece* [*inserted*]; [i] *title page*; [ii] *copyright page:* Copyright, 1914, by W. J. Watt & Company Published January; [iii] *half title*; [iv] *blank*; [1]–300, *text*

PUBLISHED: 10 January 1914 (price $1.25)

COVER: Black cloth, gold letters, black outline against gold background.

SIZE: 12.75×19.25 cm. (5×7⅛″)

NOTE: Frontispiece and two inserted illustrations by Will Grefé.

NOTES: The American edition was reprinted by Grosset & Dunlap, New York [1915?], 300 pages ($.75), and by The Curtiss Press [1929], 300 pages ($2.00).

A17A The Man Upstairs and Other Stories

THE | MAN UPSTAIRS | AND OTHER STORIES | BY | P. G. WODEHOUSE | AUTHOR OF "THE LITTLE NUGGET" | METHUEN & CO. LTD. | 36 ESSEX STREET W.C. | LONDON

COLLATION: [i–ii] *blank*; [iii] *half title*; [iv] *blank*; [v] *title page*; [vi] *copyright page:* First Published in 1914 [*in italics*]; vii, Contents; [viii] *blank*; 1–316, *text* (*bottom of page 316, printer's note:* William Brendon and Son, Ltd. Printers, Plymouth); 1–31, A Selection of Books Published by Methuen and Co. Ltd. . . . [*dated*] 25/10/13; 32, *blank* [*advertising supplement inserted*]

PUBLISHED: 23 January 1914 (price 6s); British Library reception date 27 January 1914

COVER: Dark brown cloth; gold lettering and decoration on spine, brown letters blind-stamped on cover

SIZE: 13.75×19.5 cm. (5×7⅝″)

CONTENTS: The Man Upstairs, pp. 1–17; Something to Worry About, pp. 18–34; Deep Waters, pp. 35–53; When Doctors Disagree, pp. 54–71; By Advice of Counsel, pp. 72–83; Rough-Hew Them How We Will, pp. 84–97; The Man Who Disliked Cats, pp. 98–113; Ruth in Exile, pp. 114–30; Archibald's Benefit, pp. 131–48; The Man, the Maid, and the Miasma, pp. 149–63; The Good Angel, pp. 164–80; Pots o' Money, pp. 181–98; Out of School, pp. 199–211; Three from Dunsterville, pp. 212–28; The Tuppenny Millionaire, pp. 229–44; Ahead of Schedule, pp. 245–60; Sir Agravaine, a Tale of King Alfred's Round Table, pp. 261–77; The Goal-

Keeper and the Plutocrat, pp. 278–91; In Alcala, pp. 292–316

NOTES: Methuen reissued the title through at least nineteen editions: twice in November 1922, four times in 1923, twice in 1924, through 1954.

Stories first appeared in *Ainslee's* (1909), *Strand* (1910–13), *Cosmopolitan* (1910), *Collier's* (1910–12), *London Magazine* (1911), *Pearson's Magazine* (1912).

A18A Something New

SOMETHING NEW | BY | PELHAM GRENVILLE WODEHOUSE | [publisher's device] | ILLUSTRATED BY | F. R. GRUGER | D. APPLETON AND COMPANY | NEW YORK 1915

COLLATION: [i] *half title*; [ii] *blank*; *frontispiece* [*inserted*]; [iii] *title page*; [iv] *copyright page*: Copyright, 1915, by D. Appleton and Company, Copyright 1915, by The Curtis Publishing Company . . . ; [v] List of Illustrations; [vi] *blank*; 1–[347] *text*; [348–50] *blank*

PUBLISHED: 3 September 1915 (price $1.35)

COVER: Red cloth, gold lettering, gray and gold scarabs on front cover, gold scarabs on spine

SIZE: 13×19.25 cm. (5×7⅝″)

NOTE: Frontispiece and three illustrations by F. R. Gruger inserted.

A18B First English edition

SOMETHING | FRESH | BY | P. G. WODEHOUSE | METHUEN & CO. LTD. | 36 ESSEX STREET W.C. | LONDON

COLLATION: [i] *half title*; [ii] By the Same Author: The Little Nugget, The Man Upstairs; [iii] *title page*; [iv] *copyright page*: First published in 1915; 1–315, *text*; [316] *printer's note*: Printed in Great Britain by Butler & Tanner . . . ; [317–20] *advertisements*; [1–31] A Selection of Books published by Methuen . . . [*bottom of page 31, printer's note*: Printed by Morrison & Gibb . . . 8/5/15]; [32] *blank* [*advertising supplement inserted*]

PUBLISHED: 16 September 1915 (price 6s); British Library reception date 13 September 1915

BINDING: Blue-green cloth, black letters

SIZE: 13×19.5 cm. (5¼×7¾″)

NOTE: Some revision from American edition.

NOTES: *Something New* was reprinted by A. L. Burt, Chicago, in 1931, 346 pages ($.75); and reprinted by Dodd, Mead, and Company, New York, 1930, 346 pages.

Methuen published *Something Fresh* in at least twenty editions (through 1951); the edition number is clearly indicated on the copyright page.

Something New is the beginning of the Blandings Castle saga about which Wodehouse later recalled: "In my first Blandings novel—circa 1915—I said that Lord Emsworth joined the Senior Conservative Club in the year 1885 (I think) and was at Eton in the sixties. So that when I write about him today, I am writing of a man well over a hundred." (Letter to Bennett Cerf, 12 August 1957.)

Wodehouse published twenty-one serials in the *Saturday Evening Post* and was paid $3,500 for this first one (appearing 26 June – 14 August 1915). The *Saturday Evening Post* became his preferred magazine in the United States. "Fancy I deliver my serial in the last half of March—they pay the entire cheque at the beginning of April—they start the story in May—and they are through with it in six or seven weeks." (Letter to Paul Reynolds, 18 April 1933.)

A19A Uneasy Money

UNEASY MONEY | BY | PELHAM GRENVILLE WODEHOUSE | AUTHOR OF "SOMETHING NEW" | [publisher's device] | ILLUSTRATED BY | CLARENCE F. UNDERWOOD | D. APPLETON AND COMPANY | NEW YORK 1916

COLLATION: [i] *half title*; [ii] *blank*; *frontispiece* [*inserted*]; [iii] *title page*; [iv] *copyright page*: Copyright, 1916, by D. Appleton . . . Copyright, 1915, 1916, by The Curtis Publishing Company . . . ; [v] *dedication*: To My Wife, Bless Her; [vi] *blank*; [vii] List of Illustrations; [viii] *blank*; 1–[326] *text*; [327–28] *blank*

PUBLISHED: 17 March 1916 (price $1.35)

COVER: Light red cloth, gold letters and decorations

SIZE: 13×19.25 cm. (5⅛×7⅝″)

NOTE: Frontispiece and seven illustrations by Clarence F. Underwood.

A19B First English edition

UNEASY MONEY | BY | P. G. WODEHOUSE | METHUEN & CO. LTD. | 36 ESSEX STREET W.C. | LONDON

COLLATION: [i] *half title*; [ii] By the Same Author [*five titles beginning* Love among the Chickens, *ending* Something Fresh]; [iii] *title page*; [iv] *copyright page*:

First published in 1917; [1]–279, *text*; [280] *printer's note:* Printed in Great Britain by Butler & Tanner, Frome and London; [1]–31, A Selection of Books Published by Methuen . . . [*dated*] 6/7/17; [32] *blank* [*advertising supplement inserted*]

PUBLISHED: 4 October 1917 (price 5s); British Library reception date 5 October 1917

COVER: Light red cloth, black lettering

SIZE: 13 × 19.5 cm. (5⅛ × 7¾")

NOTES: The English edition is considerably cut from the American and *Strand* publications. Methuen reprinted at least twenty-one editions, beginning second edition, April 1918, four editions 1922, three editions 1923, twice 1924, through 1950.

The American edition was reprinted by Macaulay Company, New York, [1920], [326] pages ($1.00).

The novel was serialized in the *Saturday Evening Post*, 4 December 1916 – 15 January 1916, and the *Strand*, December 1916 – June 1917, both illustrated by Clarence F. Underwood.

A20A Piccadilly Jim

PICCADILLY JIM | BY | PELHAM GRENVILLE WODEHOUSE | Author of "Uneasy Money," etc. | *ILLUSTRATIONS BY* | *MAY WILSON PRESTON* | [publisher's device] | NEW YORK | DODD, MEAD AND COMPANY | 1917

COLLATION: [i] *half title*; [ii] Novels by Pelham Grenville Wodehouse [*seven titles*]; *frontispiece* [*inserted*]; [iii] *title page*; [iv] *copyright page:* Copyright, 1916 By Pelham Grenville Wodehouse; [v] *dedication:* To my step-daughter Lenora . . . ; [vi] *blank*; [vii] Contents; [viii] *blank*; [ix] Illustrations; [x] *blank*; [xi] *half title*; [xii] *blank*; 1–363, *text*; [364] *blank*

PUBLISHED: 24 February 1917 (price $1.40)

SIZE: 13 × 19.33 cm. (5⅛ × 7⅝")

COVER: Yellow cloth, black lettering

NOTE: Frontispiece and seven illustrations (all inserted) by May Wilson Preston.

A20B First English edition

PICCADILLY | JIM | BY | P. G. WODEHOUSE | [publisher's device] | HERBERT JENKINS LIMITED | YORK STREET, ST JAMES'S | LONDON, S.W. 1 [three ornaments] [double-rule frame]

COLLATION: [i] *half title*; [ii] *blank*; [iii] *title page*; [iv] *copyright page:* Printed by Wm. Brendon and Son, Ltd., Plymouth, England; [1]–316, *text*

PUBLISHED: May 1918 (price 6s); British Library reception date 7 September 1918

COVER: Mustard cloth, black letters

SIZE: 13 × 19.25 cm. (5 × 7⅝")

NOTES: The Dodd, Mead edition was published at least three times: first and second editions printed before publication; third edition printed 26 February 1917 (from copyright page of the third edition). It was also reprinted in New York by Grosset, 1920, 363 pages ($1.00), and by A. L. Burt [1931?] 363 pages ($.75). This was the first novel published by Herbert Jenkins who as Barrie & Jenkins and now The Hutchinson Publishing Group still reissue the novels. "I didn't sell over two thousand till I went to Jenkins with Piccadilly Jim. . . ." (*Performing Flea*, p. 35.)

Herbert Jenkins reissued their twenty-fourth printing completing 261,000 copies about 1935.

Guy Bolton dramatized the novel in 1918; it was made into a silent film, 1919, and in 1934 the motion picture rights were sold to M.G.M. for $5,000. M.G.M. produced *Piccadilly Jim* in 1936 with Robert Montgomery and Madge Evans.

A21A The Man with Two Left Feet

THE MAN WITH TWO | LEFT FEET | AND OTHER STORIES | BY | P. G. WODEHOUSE | METHUEN & CO. LTD. | 36 ESSEX STREET W.C. | LONDON

COLLATION: [i] *half title*; [ii] By the Same Author The Little Nugget, The Man Upstairs, Something Fresh; [iii] *title page*; [iv] *copyright page:* First Published in 1917; v, Contents; [vi] *blank*; 1–297, *text*; [298] *printer's note:* Printed by Jarrold & Sons, Ltd., Norwich, England; [1]–31, A Selection of Books Published by Methuen . . . [*dated*] 4/10/16; [32] *blank* [*advertising supplement inserted*]

PUBLISHED: 8 March 1917 (price 5s); British Library reception date 8 March 1917

COVER:: Red cloth, black letters

SIZE: 13 × 19.5 cm. (5 × 7¾")

CONTENTS: Bill the Bloodhound, pp. 1–24; Extricating Young Gussie, pp. 25–54; *Wilton's Holiday, pp. 55–74; *The Mixer – I, He Meets a Shy Gentleman, pp. 75–96; II, He Moves in Society, pp. 97–117; *Crowned

Heads, pp. 119–41; At Geisenheimer's, pp. 143–66; The Making of Mac's, pp. 167–89; One Touch of Nature, pp. 191–207; Black for Luck, pp. 209–32; The Romance of an Ugly Policeman, pp. 233–52; A Sea of Troubles, pp. 253–70; The Man with Two Left Feet, pp. 271–97. (*Asterisks indicate stories not in the American edition.)

NOTES: Methuen reissued twice in 1922, three times in 1923, etc., through 1952.

The Bertie Wooster character first appeared as Reggie Pepper in the story "Extricating Young Gussie," in the *Strand*, January 1916, and the *Saturday Evening Post*, 18 September 1915.

The stories were first published in various issues of the *Strand*, March 1911 – May 1916, and in the United States in a number of popular magazines: *Red Book*, June 1915 – July 1915; *Saturday Evening Post*, 21 August 1915 – 18 March 1916; *Pearson's Magazine*, April 1915; *McClure's Magazine*, September 1914; *Collier's*, 26 August 1911.

A21B First American edition

THE MAN [raised above line] WITH | 2 [a shoe on either side] | LEFT FEET | BY | P. G. WODEHOUSE | A. L. BURT COMPANY | PUBLISHERS | New York Chicago | By Arrangement with Doubleday, Doran & Company, Inc.

COLLATION: [i] *title page*; [ii] *copyright page*: Copyright, 1911, 1914, 1915, 1916, 1933 by P. G. Wodehouse . . . Printed . . . at The Country Life Press, Garden City, N.Y., First edition; [iii] Contents; [iv] *blank*; 1–283, *text*; [284] *blank*

PUBLISHED: 1 February 1933 (price $.75)

COVER: Orange cloth, black letters, on front cover black 2 with drawing of shoe on either side

SIZE: 13.2×19.4 cm. (5⅛×7⅝")

CONTENTS: The Man with Two Left Feet, pp. 1–28; Bill the Bloodhound, pp. 29–52; Extricating Young Gussie, pp. 53–82; At Geisenheimer's, pp. 83–107; The Making of Mac's, pp. 108–30; One Touch of Nature, pp. 131–48; Black for Luck, pp. 149–73; Romance of an Ugly Policeman, pp. 174–94; A Sea of Trouble, pp. 195–213; *Absent Treatment, pp. 214–34; *Rallying Round Old George, pp. 235–60; *Doing Clarence a Bit of Good, pp. 261–83. (*Asterisks indicate stories not in the English edition but which appeared in *My Man Jeeves* [London, 1919].)

NOTE: Permission to print granted by Doubleday, Doran who never published themselves although holding the rights.

A22A My Man Jeeves

MY MAN JEEVES | BY | P. G. WODEHOUSE | LONDON | GEORGE NEWNES, LIMITED

COLLATION: [1-2] *blanks pasted down as front endpapers*; [3-4] *blank flyleaf*; [5] *half title*; [6] *blank*; [7] *title page*; [8] *blank*; [9] Contents; [10] *blank*; 11–251, *text (bottom of page 251, printer's note:* Printed in Great Britain by Butler & Tanner, Frome and London); [252] *blank*; [253-54] *list of Newnes 1/9 novels*; [255-56] *pasted-down pages*

PUBLISHED: May 1919 (price 1s9d); British Library reception date 10 June 1919

COVER: Light red cloth, black lettering and decoration on spine; blind-stamped design in front cover; paper very brittle due to poor quality

SIZE: 11×17.5 cm. (4⅜×7")

CONTENTS: Leave it to Jeeves, pp. 11–40; Jeeves and the Unbidden Guest, pp. 41–73; Jeeves and the Hard-boiled Egg, pp. 75–106; Absent Treatment, pp. 107–29; Helping Freddie, pp. 131–53; Rallying Round Old George, pp. 155–82; Doing Clarence a Bit of Good, pp. 183–208; The Aunt and the Sluggard, pp. 209–51.

NOTES: The month of publication is given as May in a letter from Newnes giving publication dates; that is the month used here although Richard Usborne gives June (*Wodehouse at Work to the End*) and the British Library reception date is June.

Newnes reissued July 1920 (British Library reception date 6 August 1920) on thicker but equally poor quality paper, a quarter inch taller, price 2s; the printer's note reads: "Printed by Hazell, Watson & Viney Ld."

There were later reprints by Newnes: February 1926 (cheap edition), November 1928 (Newnes new-size edition), May 1931 (cheap edition).

All of the stories first appeared in the *Strand* between March 1911 and August 1917. Four of the stories were first published in the United States in *Saturday Evening Post*, 5 February 1916 – 3 March 1917; *Collier's* published one 26 August 1911.

A23A Their Mutual Child

THEIR | MUTUAL CHILD | BY | PELHAM GRENVILLE WODEHOUSE | AUTHOR OF | "PICCADILLY JIM," "A GENTLEMAN OF LEISURE," | ETC. | [publisher's monogram] | BONI AND LIVERIGHT | NEW YORK 1919

COLLATION: [1] *half title*; [2] *blank*; [3] *title page*; [4]

copyright page: Copyright, 1919, by P. G. Wodehouse; [5] Contents; [6] *blank*; [7] *half title*; [8] *blank*; 9–284, *text*

PUBLISHED: 5 August 1919 (price $1.60)

COVER: Gray-blue cloth, white letters

SIZE: 13 × 19 cm. (5 × 7½″)

A23B First English edition

THE COMING | OF BILL | BY | P. G. WODEHOUSE | HERBERT JENKINS LIMITED | 3 YORK STREET, SAINT JAMES'S | LONDON, S.W.1 [two ornaments] MCMXX [double-rule frame]

COLLATION: [1] *half title*; [2] By the Same Author Damsel in Distress, Piccadilly Jim, etc. [3] *title page*; [4] *copyright page:* Printed by William Clowes and Sons Limited London and Beccles; 5–6, Contents; 7–251, *text*; [252] *blank*; [253–256] *advertisements*

PUBLISHED: 1 July 1920 (price 3s6d); British Library reception date 8 June 1920

COVER: Red cloth, black letters

SIZE: 13 × 19.5 cm. (5 × 7⅝″)

NOTES: Herbert Jenkins gave the publication date of 1 July 1920, though the *English Catalogue* reports June 1920, and the British Library received it 8 June 1920.

Herbert Jenkins reissued *The Coming of Bill* in at least eighteen printings, completing 103,511 copies [1939?], and reissued it again in the Autograph Edition 1966.

The story first appeared in *Munsey's Magazine*, May 1914, entitled "The White Hope" illustrated by E. M. Ashe. ". . . The White Hope is the book which was The Coming of Bill in England and Their Mutual Child over here. . . . It was written in 1910 in the days when Bob Davis edited the Munsey pulps and we young authors used to go to him for plots. He would take a turn around the room and come up with a complete plot for a serial, usually horrible but of course saleable to Munsey's! He gave me the plot of this one and I wrote it, but I have never thought highly of it. . . ." (Letter to David Magee, 14 July 1964.)

A24A A Damsel in Distress

A DAMSEL | IN | DISTRESS | BY | PELHAM GRENVILLE WODEHOUSE | AUTHOR OF "UNEASY MONEY," "PICCADILLY JIM," | "SOMETHING NEW," ETC., ETC. | NEW [publisher's device] YORK | GEORGE H. DORAN COMPANY [double-rule frame]

COLLATION: [1] *half title*; [2] *blank*; [3] *title page*; [4] *copyright page:* Copyright, 1919, by George H. Doran Company . . . ; [5] *dedication:* To Maud and Ivan Caryll; [6] *blank*; [7] *half title*; [8] *blank*; 9–302, *text*; [303–4] *blank*

PUBLISHED: 4 October 1919 (price $1.00)

COVER: Brown cloth, black letters and decorations against orange-red background

SIZE: 13 × 19.33 cm. (5⅛ × 7⅝″)

DUST WRAPPER: $1.00

A24B First English edition

A DAMSEL | IN DISTRESS | BY | P. G. WODEHOUSE | HERBERT JENKINS LIMITED | 3 YORK STREET, ST. JAMES'S | LONDON S.W.1 MCMXX [double-rule frame]

COLLATION: [1] *half title*; [2] By the Same Author Piccadilly Jim a book of laughter now in its Seventh Thousand. Cr. 8vo.; [3] *title page*; [4] *copyright page:* [publisher's device] Printed . . . by Chance and Bland, Gloucester; [5] *half title*; [6] *blank*; [7]–319, *text*; [320] *blank*

PUBLISHED: 15 October 1919 (price 6s); British Library reception date 16 October 1919

COVER: Deep red cloth with black letters

SIZE: 12.5 × 19.25 cm. (5 × 7⅝″)

DUST WRAPPER: Illustrated by Ealring (?); 6/ green label

NOTES: The American edition was reprinted by A. L. Burt, New York, 1922, 302 pages, ($.75). Herbert Jenkins reissued many times through 1975; by the twentieth printing, about 1939(?), they had issued 207,036 copies.

With Ian Hay adapted as a play produced in London, 1928; issued as a silent film, 1928; and again in 1937 with music by George Gershwin, lyrics by Ira Gershwin, starring Fred Astaire and Joan Fontaine.

A25A The Little Warrior

THE | LITTLE WARRIOR | BY | PELHAM GRENVILLE WODEHOUSE | AUTHOR OF "A DAMSEL IN DISTRESS," "PICCADILLY JIM" | "UNEASY MONEY," "SOMETHING NEW," ETC. | NEW [publisher's device] YORK | GEORGE H. DORAN COMPANY [double-rule frame]

COLLATION: [1] *half title*; [2] *blank*; [3] *title page*; [4]

copyright page: Copyright, 1920, by George H. Doran Company copyright, 1920, by P. F. Collier & Son Co. . . . ; [5] *half title*; [6] *blank*; 7–384, *text*

PUBLISHED: 8 October 1920 (price $2.00)

COVER: Tan cloth, green and tan lettering and decorations

SIZE: 13.25×19.5 cm. (5¼×7¾″)

A25B First English edition

JILL THE | RECKLESS | BY | P. G. WODEHOUSE | HERBERT JENKINS LIMITED | 3 YORK STREET ST. JAMES'S | LONDON S.W.1 [two ornaments] MCMXXI [double-rule frame]

COLLATION: [1] *half title*; [2] What This Story Is About, Other Books by the Same Author [*six titles beginning* Piccadilly Jim, *ending* Indiscretions of Archie]; [3] *title page*; [4] *copyright page:* [publisher's device] The Mayflower Press, Plymouth England. William Brendon & Son, Ltd.; [5] Contents; [6] *blank*; [7] *dedication:* To my wife, bless her; [8] *blank*; 9–313, *text*; [314] *blank*; [315–20] *advertisements*

PUBLISHED: 4 July 1921 (price 7s6d); British Library reception date 2 July 1921

COVER: Blue cloth, black letters and decoration

SIZE: 12.5×19.25 cm. (4⅞×7½″)

NOTES: A. L. Burt, New York, reprinted the American edition [1923], 384 pages ($.75). Herbert Jenkins reprinted through 1958; 1922 printed by Athenaeum Printing Works; the thirteenth printing, about 1935, completed 110,638 copies; the Autograph Edition, 1958.

Serial in *Collier's*, titled "Little Warrior," 12 June 1920 – 28 August 1920, illustrated by Wallace Morgan.

A26A Indiscretions of Archie

INDISCRETIONS | OF ARCHIE | BY | P. G. WODEHOUSE | HERBERT JENKINS LIMITED | 3 YORK STREET SAINT JAMES'S | LONDON S.W.1 MCMXXI

COLLATION: [1] *half title*; [2] What This Story Is About, Other Books by the Same Author [*six titles ending* A Gentleman of Leisure]; [3] *title page*; [4] *copyright page:* [publisher's device] Printed in Great Britain by Butler & Tanner Frome and London; [5] *dedication:* Dedication to B. W. King-Hall; [6] *blank*; 7–8, Contents; 9–320, *text*

PUBLISHED: 14 February 1921 (price 7s6d); British Library reception date 12 February 1921

COVER: Light blue cloth, dark blue lettering and designs

SIZE: 12.75×19 cm. (5×7½″)

DUST WRAPPER: Illustrated by C. Morse; 7/6 green label

A26B First American edition

INDISCRETIONS | OF ARCHIE | BY | P. G. WODEHOUSE | AUTHOR OF "THE LITTLE WARRIOR," "A | DAMSEL IN DISTRESS," "UNEASY | MONEY," ETC. | NEW [publisher's device] YORK | GEORGE H. DORAN COMPANY [double-rule frame]

COLLATION: [1] *synopsis*; [2] *blank*; [3] *title page*; [4] *copyright page:* Copyright, 1921, by George H. Doran Company, copyright, 1920, by International Magazine Company (Cosmopolitan Magazine) . . . ; [5] *dedication:* Dedication to B. W. King-Hall . . . ; [6] *blank*; vii–viii, Contents; [9] *half title*; [10] *blank*; 11–303, *text*, [304–8] *blank*

PUBLISHED: 15 July 1921 (price $1.75)

COVER: Tan cloth, green lettering

SIZE: 13.3×19.7 cm. (5¼×7¾″)

NOTES: Herbert Jenkins reissued the novel through 1978, the thirteenth printing, about 1935, completing 120,288 copies.

A reissue by George H. Doran is identical to the first edition except for the dust wrapper which states: "Second large printing." A. L. Burt, New York, reprinted [1923], 303 pages ($.75).

A27A The Clicking of Cuthbert

THE | CLICKING | OF | CUTHBERT | BY | P. G. WODEHOUSE | HERBERT JENKINS LIMITED | 3 YORK STREET ST. JAMES'S | LONDON S.W.1 [two ornaments] MCMXXII [double-rule frame]

COLLATION: [1] *half title*; [2] What This Story Is About [*eight titles beginning* Piccadilly Jim *and ending* The Girl on the Boat]; [3] *title page*; [4] *copyright page:* [publisher's device] Printed in Great Britain by Love & Malcomson, Ltd. London and Redhill.; [5] *dedication*; [6] *blank*; [7]–viii, Fore! [*signed* P. G. Wodehouse]; [9] Contents; [10] *blank*; 11–256, *text*

PRINTED: 3 February 1922 (price 7s6d?); British Library reception date 3 February 1922

COVER: Sage green pictorial cloth, dark green letters and drawing, publisher's device on back cover

SIZE: 12.5×19 cm. (5×7½″)

CONTENTS: The Clicking of Cuthbert, pp. 11–31; A Woman Is Only a Woman, pp. 32–57; A Mixed Threesome, pp. 58–81; Sundered Hearts, pp. 82–105; The Salvation of George Mackintosh, pp. 106–27; Ordeal by Golf, pp. 128–54; The Long Hole, pp. 155–79; The Heel of Achilles, pp. 180–201; The Rough Stuff, pp. 202–30; The Coming of Gowf, pp. 231–56.

A27B First American edition

GOLF WITHOUT | TEARS | BY | P. G. WODEHOUSE | NEW [publisher's device] YORK | GEORGE H. DORAN COMPANY [double-rule frame]

COLLATION: [i–ii] blank; [1] synopsis; [2] By P. G. Wodehouse [eight titles ending A Damsel in Distress]; [3] title page; [4] copyright page: Copyright, 1919, 1920, 1921, 1922, 1924, by P. G. Wodehouse [publisher's monogram] Golf without Tears–A–Printed in the United States of America; [5] dedication: Dedication to the immortal memory of John Henrie and Pat Rogie . . . ; [6] blank; vii–ix, Fore!; [10] blank; [11] Contents; [12] blank; [13] half title; [14] blank; 15–330, text; [331–34] blank

PUBLISHED: 28 May 1924 (price $2.50)

COVER: Green cloth, darker green lettering (decorated endpapers)

SIZE: 14×21 cm. (5⅝×8¼″)

NOTE: Rewritten to convert English scenes to American ones.

CONTENTS: The Clicking of Cuthbert, pp. 15–42; A Woman Is Only a Woman, pp. 43–77; A Mixed Threesome, pp. 78–108; Sundered Hearts, pp. 109–40; The Salvation of George Mackintosh, pp. 141–69; Ordeal by Golf, pp. 170–204; The Long Hole, pp. 205–34; The Heel of Achilles, pp. 235–62; The Rough Stuff, pp. 263–98; The Coming of Gowf, pp. 299–330.

NOTES: Herbert Jenkins also issued the first edition in sage-green-colored pebble cloth, 1922; their fourteenth printing, about 1935, completed 100,435 copies.

In New York, A. L. Burt reprinted the American edition [1926?], 330 pages ($.75).

Six of the short stories were made into silent films in 1924.

The stories first appeared in the *Strand* October 1919 – November 1921, and in *McClure's Magazine*, June 1920 – March 1922, and *Saturday Evening Post*, 7 June 1919.

A28A Three Men and a Maid

THREE MEN AND | A MAID | BY | P. G. WODEHOUSE | AUTHOR OF "INDISCRETIONS OF ARCHIE," "THE | LITTLE WARRIOR," "PICCADILLY JIM," | "UNEASY MONEY," ETC. | NEW [publisher's device] YORK | GEORGE H. DORAN COMPANY [double-rule frame]

COLLATION: [1] half title; [2] By P. G. Wodehouse Three Men and a Maid, Indiscretions of Archie, The Little Warrior, A Damsel in Distress; [3] title page; [4] copyright page: Copyright 1922, by George H. Doran. [publisher's monogram] copyright 1921 by the Crowell Publishing Company . . . ; [5] half title; [6] blank; 7–304, text

PUBLISHED: 26 April 1922 (price $1.75)

COVER: Dark brown cloth, darker brown lettering and design.

SIZE: 13.25×19.5 cm. (5¼×7¾″)

A28B First English edition

THE GIRL | ON THE BOAT | BY | P. G. WODEHOUSE | HERBERT JENKINS LIMITED | 3 YORK STREET, ST. JAMES'S | LONDON, S.W.1 [two ornaments] MCMXXII [double-rule frame]

COLLATION: [i] half title; [ii] What This Story Is About, By the Same Author [eight titles beginning Piccadilly Jim and ending with The Clicking of Cuthbert]; [iii] title page; [iv] copyright page: [publisher's device] Printed in Great Britain by Love and Malcomson, Ltd. London and Redhill; [v]–vi, Preface: One Moment! [signed P. G. Wodehouse, Constitutional Club, Northumberland Avenue]; [vii] Contents; [viii] blank; [ix] half title; [x] blank; 11–312, text; [313–20] advertisements

PUBLISHED: 15 June 1922 (price 7s6d); British Library reception date 16 June 1922

COVER: Orange pictorial cloth, red-brown lettering and picture

SIZE: 12.5×19.25 cm. (4¾×7⅝″)

DUST WRAPPER: Book jacket by Heath Robinson; 7/6

NOTES: Herbert Jenkins is still reprinting this title; the thireenth printing, about 1935, completed 103,781 copies; the latest reprint is dated 1978.

A. L. Burt, New York, reissued [1923] and [1928], 304 pages ($.75).

Under the title "Three Men and a Maid," serialized in *Pan*, February 1921 – September 1921, and in *Woman's*

Home Companion, October – December 1921, illustrated by J. Simont.

A29A The Adventures of Sally / Mostly Sally

THE | ADVENTURES | OF SALLY | BY | P. G. WODEHOUSE | HERBERT JENKINS LIMITED | 3 YORK STREET ST. JAMES'S | LONDON, S.W. 1 [two ornaments] MCMXXIII [double-rule frame]

COLLATION: [i] *half title*; [ii] What This Story Is About, By the Same Author [*nine titles beginning* Piccadilly Jim *ending with* The Girl on the Boat]; [iii] *title page*; [iv] *copyright page:* [publisher's device] Printed in Great Britain by Garden City Press, Letchworth; v, *dedication:* Dedication to George Grossmith; [vi] *blank*; vii, Contents; [viii] *blank*; 9–312, *text*; [313–21] *advertisements*

PUBLISHED: 17 October 1922 (publisher postdated to 1923) (price 7s6d); British Library reception date 18 October 1922

COVER: Orange cloth, brown letters and drawing

SIZE: 12.5×19.25 cm. (5×7⅝″)

NOTES: Herbert Jenkins reprinted many times: March 1925 (twelve titles on page ii); the twelfth printing making 92,484 copies; the latest reprint, 1979.

Wodehouse was working with Grossmith on *The Cabaret Girl*.

A29B First American edition

MOSTLY SALLY | BY | P. G. WODEHOUSE | NEW [publisher's device] YORK | GEORGE H. DORAN COMPANY [double-rule frame]

COLLATION: [1] *half title*; [2] By P. G. Wodehouse [*five titles ending* A Damsel in Distress]; [3] *title page*; [4] *copyright page:* Copyright, 1923, by George H. Doran Company [publisher's monogram] Mostly Sally. II . . . ; [5] *half title*; [6] *blank*; 7–317, *text*; [318–20] *blank*

PUBLISHED: 23 March 1923 (price $2.00)

COVER: Light green (pea) cloth, dark red lettering and decoration

SIZE: 13.25×19.25 cm. (5⅛×7¾″)

DUST WRAPPER

NOTES: George H. Doran reissued the first edition without the publisher's monogram on the copyright page. A. L. Burt reprinted, 1924 ($.75).

Serialized in *Collier's*, 8 October 1921 – 31 December 1921.

A30A The Inimitable Jeeves

THE | INIMITABLE | JEEVES | BY | P. G. WODEHOUSE | HERBERT JENKINS LIMITED | 3 YORK STREET. ST. JAMES'S | LONDON S.W.1 [two ornaments] MCMXXIII

COLLATION: [1] *half title*; [2] *synopsis of story*, [*ten titles beginning* Piccadilly Jim *and ending* Clicking of Cuthbert] [3] *title page*; [4] *copyright page:* [publisher's device] Printed in Great Britain by Wyman & Sons, Ltd., London, Reading and Fakenham; 5, Contents; [6] *blank*; 7–255, *text*; [256] *blank*

PUBLISHED: 17 May 1923 (price 3s6d); British Library reception date 17 May 1923

COVER: Light green pictorial cloth, dark green letters and drawings, publisher's device on spine

SIZE: 12.5×19 cm. (5×7½″)

DUST WRAPPER: Illustrations by Gates(?); green label 3/6

A30B First American edition

JEEVES | BY | P. G. WODEHOUSE | NEW [publisher's device] YORK | GEORGE H. DORAN COMPANY [double-rule frame]

COLLATION: [1] *synopsis*; [2] By P. G. Wodehouse [*six titles*]; [3] *title page*; [4] *copyright page:* Copyright, 1923, by George H. Doran Company [publisher's monogram] Jeeves I . . . ; [5] Contents; [6] *blank*; [7] *half title*; [8] *blank*; 9–288, *text*

PUBLISHED: 28 September 1923 (price $2.00)

COVER: Light brown (mustard) cloth, black letters

SIZE: 13.5×19.5 cm. (5⅜×7¾″)

CONTENTS: Jeeves Exerts the Old Cerebellum – No Wedding Bells for Bingo (magazine title: Jeeves in the Springtime); Aunt Agatha Speaks Her Mind – Pearls Mean Tears (magazine title: Aunt Agatha Takes the Count); The Pride of the Woosters Is Wounded – The Hero's Reward (magazine title: Scoring off Jeeves); Introducing Claude and Eustace – Sir Roderick Comes to Lunch (magazine title: Sir Roderick Comes to Lunch); A Letter of Introduction – Startling Dressiness of a Lift Attendant (magazine title: Jeeves and the Chump Cyril); Comrade Bingo – Bingo Has a Bad Goodwood (magazine title: Comrade Bingo); The Great Sermon Handicap; The Purity of the Turf; The Metropolitan Touch; The Delayed Exit of Claude and Eustace; Bingo and the Little Woman – All's Well (magazine title: Bingo and the Little Woman).

NOTES: Herbert Jenkins reissued 1924 (eleven titles on page ii ending *Leave It to Psmith*); twenty-fourth reprint about 1949; the Autograph Edition 1956, reprinted 1973 and 1978.

The American edition was revised to make a collection of short stories. About 7,000 copies of the original Doran edition were sold, of the Burt reprint (1925) about 16,000 copies. (From copyright page of the Pocket Books edition, 1932.)

Serialized in the *Strand*, August 1918 – December 1922 and in *Cosmopolitan*, December 1921 – December 1922.

First appearance of Bingo Little.

"The Great Sermon Handicap" was reprinted separately (*see* A49A).

A31A Leave It to Psmith

LEAVE IT | TO PSMITH | BY | P. G. WODEHOUSE | HERBERT JENKINS LIMITED | 3 YORK STREET ST. JAMES'S | LONDON S.W.1 [two ornaments] MCMXXIV [double-rule frame]

COLLATION: [1] *half title*; [2] What This Story Is About, Other Books by the Same Author [*eleven titles beginning* Adventures of Sally, *ending* Love among the Chickens]; [3] *title page*; [4] *copyright page*: [publisher's device] Printed in Great Britain by Wyman & Sons Ltd., London, Reading and Fakenham; v, Contents; [6] *dedication*: To my daughter, Leonora, Queen of her species; 7–327, *text*; [328] *blank*

PUBLISHED: 30 November, 1923 (price 7s6d); British Library reception date 30 November 1923

COVER: Green cloth, dark green lettering and decorations

SIZE: 13×19 cm. (5¼×7½″)

A31B First American edition

LEAVE IT TO | PSMITH | BY | P. G. WODEHOUSE | NEW [publisher's device] YORK | GEORGE H. DORAN COMPANY [double-rule frame]

COLLATION: [i–ii] *blank*; [1] *synopsis*; [2] Books by P. G. Wodehouse [*eight titles*]; [3] *title page*; [4] *copyright page*: Copyright 1923, 1924, By P. G. Wodehouse [publisher's monogram] Leave It to Psmith –B– . . . ; [5] *dedication*: To my daughter, Leonora . . . ; [6] *blank*; [7] Contents; [8] *blank*; [9] *half title*; [10] *blank*; 11–347, *text*; [348–50] *blank*

PUBLISHED: 14 March 1924 (price $2.00)

COVER: Light blue cloth, dark blue letters and decorations

SIZE: 13.5×19.5 cm. (5¼×7⅝″)

NOTES: Herbert Jenkins reissued June 1924 (twelve titles on page 2 ending *Ukridge*); eleventh printing, ca. 1949, completing 77,400 copies; the Autograph Edition 1961, reprinted 1976.

Doran also reissued without the publisher's monogram on the copyright page. A. L. Burt reprinted 1925 ($.75).

Serial in *Saturday Evening Post*, 2 February 1923 – 17 March 1923, illustrated by May Preston Wilson; the ending was altered for the book. "I had a stream of letters cursing the end of *Leave It to Psmith*, and I shall have to rewrite it. But what a sweat it is altering a story that has grown cold!" (*Performing Flea*, p. 20.)

Dramatized with Ian Hay, 1930.

A32A Ukridge

UKRIDGE | BY | P. G. WODEHOUSE | HERBERT JENKINS LIMITED | 3 YORK STREET ST. JAMES'S | LONDON S.W.1 [ornament] MCMXXIV [double-rule frame]

COLLATION: [1] *half title*; [2] What This Story Is About, By the Same Author [*thirteen titles beginning* A Damsel in Distress *and ending with* Leave It to Psmith]; [3] *title page*; [4] *copyright page*: [publisher's device] Printed in Great Britain by Butler & Tanner Ltd., Frome and London; 5, *dedication*: Dedicated to Old Bill Townend; [6] *blank*; 7, Contents; [8] *blank*; 9–256, *text*

PUBLISHED: 3 June 1924 (price 7s6d); British Library reception date 3 June 1924

COVER: Green cloth, dark green letters and drawing

SIZE: 12.5×19 cm. (5×7½″)

CONTENTS: Ukridge's Dog College, pp. 9–31; Ukridge's Accident Syndicate, pp. 32–53; The Debut of Battling Billson, pp. 54–80; First Aid for Dora, pp. 81–103; The Return of Battling Billson, pp. 104–28; Ukridge Sees Her Through, pp. 129–51; No Wedding Bells for Him, pp. 152–80; The Long Arm of Looney Coote, pp. 181–208; The Exit of Battling Billson, pp. 209–32; Ukridge Rounds a Nasty Corner, pp. 233–56.

A32B First American edition

HE RATHER | ENJOYED IT | BY | P. G. WODEHOUSE | NEW [publisher's device] YORK | GEORGE H. DORAN COMPANY [double-rule frame]

COLLATION: [i–ii] *blank*; [1] *half title*; [2] By P. G. Wodehouse; [3] *title page*; [4] *copyright page*: Copyright, 1925, by George H. Doran Company [publisher's monogram] Copyright, 1923, by International Magazine Company, Inc. (Cosmopolitan) . . . –Q– . . . ; [5] *dedication*:

... to Old Bill Townend. My Friend from Boyhood's Days Who First Introduced Me to Stanley Featherstonehaugh Ukridge; [6] *blank*; [7] Contents; [8] *blank*; [9] *half title*; [10] *blank*; 11–316, *text*; [317–18] *blank*

PUBLISHED: 30 July 1925 (price $2.00)

COVER: Red cloth, black lettering

SIZE: 13 × 19.5 cm. (5¼ × 7⅝")

DUST WRAPPER: Illustrated by Herb Roth; $2.00; Jacket spine: Amusing Adventures in High Finance

CONTENTS: Ukridge's Dog College, pp. 11–37; Ukridge's Accident Syndicate, pp. 38–64; The Debut of Battling Billson, pp. 65–97; First Aid for Dora, pp. 98–126; The Return of Battling Billson, pp. 127–58; Ukridge Sees Her Through, pp. 159–87; No Wedding Bells for Him, pp. 188–223; The Long Arm of Looney Coote, pp. 224–57; The Exit of Battling Billson, pp. 258–86; Ukridge Rounds a Nasty Corner, pp. 287–316.

NOTES: Jenkins issued a second printing in 1924; the ninth printing, about 1939, completed 74,478 copies; the latest reprint is 1960.

A. L. Burt reprinted the American edition, 1927 ($.75).

The dedication refers to the idea for the plot of *Love among the Chickens* which Bill Townend had given him some twenty years earlier.

The short stories first appeared in *Cosmopolitan*, April 1923 – January 1924, and the *Strand*, May 1923 – February 1924.

A33A Bill the Conqueror

BILL | THE CONQUEROR | HIS INVASION OF ENGLAND | IN THE SPRINGTIME | BY | P. G. WODEHOUSE | METHUEN & CO. LTD. | 36 ESSEX STREET W.C. | LONDON

COLLATION: [i] *half title*; [ii] By the Same Author Uneasy Money, The Little Nugget, Something Fresh, The Man with Two Left Feet, The Man Upstairs; [iii] *title page*; [iv] *copyright page*: First published in 1924 Printed in Great Britain; [v] *dedication*: To My Father and Mother; [vi] *blank*; vii–viii, Contents; 1–296 *text* (*bottom of page 296, printer's note*: Printed in Great Britain by Butler & Tanner Ltd., Frome and London); [1]–8, A Selection from Messrs. Methuen's Publications [*undated advertising supplement inserted*]

PUBLISHED: 13 November 1924 (price 7s6d); British Library reception date 14 November 1924.

COVER: Red cloth, black letters

SIZE: 13 × 19.5 cm. (5 × 7¾")

DUST WRAPPER: Illustrated by Frank Marston; crown 8vo; 7s6d

A33B First American edition

BILL | THE CONQUEROR | *His Invasion of England in the* | *Springtime* | By | P. G. WODEHOUSE | NEW [publisher's device] YORK | GEORGE H. DORAN COMPANY [double-rule frame]

COLLATION: [1] *half title*; [2] By P. G. Wodehouse [*nine titles*]; [3] *title page*; [4] *copyright page*: Copyright, 1924, By P. G. Wodehouse [publisher's monogram] Bill the Conqueror –Q– . . . ; [5] *dedication*: To my Father and Mother; [6] *blank*; [7] Contents; [8] *blank*; [9] *half title*; [10] *blank*; 11–323, *text*; [324] *blank*

PUBLISHED: 20 February 1925 (price $2.00)

COVER: Yellow cloth, green lettering and decorations

SIZE: 13 × 19.5 cm. (5⅛ × 7⅝")

DUST WRAPPER SPINE: By the author of Leave It to Psmith; $2.00 net

NOTES: Methuen published at least seventeen times through 1950; the first and second editions in 1924, the third through seventh editions in 1925.

A. L. Burt, New York, reprinted the American edition in 1926, 323 pages ($.75).

Serialized in *Saturday Evening Post*, 24 May – 12 July 1924, illustrated by May Wilson Preston.

Part of the plot used for *Sitting Pretty*, 1924 Kern-Bolton-Wodehouse musical.

A34A Carry On, Jeeves!

CARRY ON, | JEEVES! | BY | P. G. WODEHOUSE | HERBERT JENKINS LIMITED | 3 YORK STREET · ST. JAMES'S | LONDON S.W.1 [two decorations] MCMXXV [double-rule frame]

COLLATION: [1] *half title*; [2] What This Book Is About, By the Same Author [*thirteen titles ending* Coming of Bill]; [3] *title page*; [4] *copyright page*: [publisher's device] Printed in Great Britain. Wyman & Sons Ltd., London, Reading and Fakenham; [5] *dedication*: To Bernard Le Strange; [6] *blank*; 7, Contents; [8] *blank*; 9–256, *text*

PUBLISHED: 9 October 1925 (price 3s6d); British Library reception date 9 October 1925

COVER: Apple-green pictorial cloth, black letters and illustration

SIZE: 13 × 19 cm. (5⅛ × 7½")

CONTENTS: Jeeves Takes Charge, pp. 9–34; *The Artistic Career of Corky, pp. 35–54; *Jeeves and the Unbidden Guest, pp. 55–77; *Jeeves and the Hard-Boiled Egg, pp. 78–99; *The Aunt and the Sluggard, pp. 100–129; The Rummy Affair of Old Biffy, pp. 130–57; Without the Option, pp. 158–85; *Fixing It for Freddie, pp. 186–207; Clustering Round Young Bingo, pp. 208–38; Bertie Changes His Mind, pp. 239–56. (*Asterisks indicate stories from *My Man Jeeves* [1919], extensively revised.)

A34B First American edition

Carry On, Jeeves! | By | P. G. WODEHOUSE | NEW YORK | GEORGE H. DORAN COMPANY [double-rule frame]

COLLATION: [i–ii] blank; [1] half title; [2] By P. G. Wodehouse [twelve titles]; [3] title page; [4] copyright page: Copyright, 1916, 1917, 1922, 1924, 1925 and 1927 By P. G. Wodehouse [publisher's monogram] Carry On, Jeeves! –Q– . . . ; [5] dedication: To Bernard Le Strange; [6] blank; [7] Contents; [8] blank; [9] half title; [10] blank; 11–316, text; [317–18] blank

PUBLISHED: 7 October 1927 (price $2.00)

COVER: Brown pictorial cloth, orange letters and drawings

SIZE: 13×19.25 cm. (5⅛×7⅛″)

DUST WRAPPER: M.F. $2.00; spine subtitle of dust wrapper: Jeeves the Incomparable

CONTENTS: Jeeves Takes Charge, pp. 11–42; The Artistic Career of Corky, pp. 43–66; Jeeves and the Unbidden Guest, pp. 67–94; Jeeves and the Hard-Boiled Egg, pp. 95–121; The Aunt and the Sluggard, pp. 122–58; The Rummy Affair of Old Biffy, pp. 159–93; Without the Option, pp. 194–228; Fixing It for Freddie, pp. 229–55; Clustering Round Young Bingo, pp. 256–93; Bertie Changes His Mind, pp. 294–316.

NOTES: The latest Jenkins reprint is 1976; the eleventh printing completed 90,830 copies, ca. 1939.

A. L. Burt reprinted 1912 ($.75).

Those stories not already used in *My Man Jeeves* (1919) were collected from various issues, 1922–1924, of the *Strand*; 1916, 1924–1925 issues of *Saturday Evening Post*; and the August 1922 issue of *Cosmopolitan*.

A35A Sam the Sudden

SAM THE SUDDEN | BY | P. G. WODEHOUSE | [publisher's device] | METHUEN & CO. LTD. | 36 ESSEX STREET W.C. | LONDON

COLLATION: [i] half title; [ii] By the Same Author [six titles ending Bill the Conqueror]; [iii] title page; [iv] copyright page: First published in 1925 . . . ; [v] dedication: To Edgar Wallace; [vi] blank; vii–viii, Contents; 1–248, text (bottom of page 248, printer's note: Printed in Great Britain by Butler & Tanner Ltd., Frome and London); [1]–8, A Selection from Messrs. Methuen's Catalogue of General Literature [advertising supplement inserted]

PUBLISHED: 15 October 1925 (price 7s6d); British Library reception date 15 October 1925

COVER: Red cloth, black lettering

SIZE: 12.75×19.5 cm. (5×7⅝″)

DUST WRAPPER: Illustrated by Frank Marston; 7/6

A35B First American edition

SAM IN | THE SUBURBS | BY | P. G. WODEHOUSE | NEW [publisher's device] YORK | GEORGE H. DORAN COMPANY [double-rule frame]

COLLATION: [i–ii] blank; [1] half title; [2] By P. G. Wodehouse [ten titles]; [3] title page; [4] copyright page: Copyright, 1925, by P. G. Wodehouse, [publisher's monogram] The Curtis Publishing Company, 1925 . . . –Q– . . . ; [5–6] Contents; [7] half title; [8] blank; 9–346, text; [347–48] blank

PUBLISHED: 6 November 1925 (price $2.00)

COVER: Pea green cloth, black lettering and picture (initialed W.T.A.)

SIZE: 12.5×19.25 cm. (5×7⅝″)

DUST WRAPPER: A commutation ticket with a real punch; $2.00

NOTES: Methuen reprinted through the thirteenth edition, 1950: twice in 1927, twice 1928, 1930, 1932, 1933, twice 1934, 1936, 1939, and 1950.

A. L. Burt, New York, reprinted the American title [1927], 346 pages ($.75).

Serial in *Saturday Evening Post*, 13 June – 18 July 1925, illustrated by F. R. Gruger, entitled "Sam in the Suburbs," for which Wodehouse was paid $25,000.

A36A The Heart of a Goof

THE HEART | OF A GOOF | BY | P. G. WODEHOUSE | HERBERT JENKINS LIMITED | 3 YORK STREET, ST. JAMES'S | LONDON S.W.1 [two decorations] MCMXXVI [double-rule frame]

COLLATION: [i] half title; [ii] What This Story Is About, By the Same Author [fourteen titles ending with The Coming of Bill]; [1] title page; [2] copyright page:

[publisher's monogram] Printed in Great Britain by Purnell and Sons Paulton, Somerset, England; [3] *dedication:* To my daughter Leonora . . . ; [4] *blank*; v–viii, Preface [*signed* P. G. Wodehouse, The Sixth Bunker, Addington]; [ix] Contents; [10] *blank*; 11–314, *text*; [315–18] *advertisements*

PUBLISHED: 15 April 1926 (price 7s6d); British Library reception date 15 April 1926

COVER: Green cloth, black letters and drawings

SIZE: 12.75×19.25 cm. (5×7½")

CONTENTS: The Heart of a Goof, pp. 11–46; High Stakes, pp. 47–80; Keeping in with Vosper, pp. 81–111; Chester Forgets Himself, pp. 112–49; The Magic Plus Fours, pp. 150–80; The Awakening of Rollo Rodmarsh, pp. 181–207; Rodney Fails to Qualify, pp. 208–43; Jane Gets off the Fairway, pp. 244–80; The Purification of Rodney Spelvin, pp. 281–314

A36B First American edition

DIVOTS | BY | P. G. WODEHOUSE | NEW [publisher's device] YORK | GEORGE H. DORAN COMPANY [double-rule frame]

COLLATION: [i–ii] *blank*; [1] *half title*; [2] By P. G. Wodehouse [*eleven titles*]; [3] *title page*; [4] *copyright page:* Copyright, 1923, 1924, 1925, 1926 and 1927, By P. G. Wodehouse [publisher's device] Divots –B– . . . ; [5] *dedication:* To my daughter, Leonora, . . . ; [6] *blank*; vii–x, Preface; [11] Contents; [12] *blank*; [13] *half title*; [14] *blank*; 15–316, *text*; [317–18] *blank*

PUBLISHED: 4 March 1927 (price $2.50)

COVER: Orange cloth, letters and drawing in black

SIZE: 14.5×21 cm. (5¾×8¼")

DUST WRAPPER: Decorated endpapers repeated on book jacket; jacket spine: On the Links at Squishy Valley; $2.50

CONTENTS: The Heart of a Goof, pp. 15–50; High Stakes, pp. 51–84; Keeping in with Vosper, pp. 85–115; Chester Forgets Himself, pp. 116–52; The Magic Plus Fours, pp. 153–82; The Awakening of Rollo Podmarsh, pp. 183–209; Rodney Fails to Qualify, pp. 210–45; Jane Gets off the Fairway, pp. 246–83; The Purification of Rodney Spelvin, pp. 283–316.

NOTES: Herbert Jenkins reissued August 1927, cheap edition; the eleventh printing, about 1945, completed 70,400 copies; the fourth printing, 1927, completed 41,400 copies; the Autograph Edition, 1956, reprinted 1978.

A. L. Burt, New York, reprinted the American edition [1929], 316 pages ($.75).

The short stories first appeared in the *Strand*, December 1922 – March 1926; *Red Book*, 1923; and *Saturday Evening Post*, 1924.

A37A The Small Bachelor

THE | SMALL BACHELOR | BY | P. G. WODEHOUSE | [publisher's device] | METHUEN & CO. LTD. | 36 ESSEX STREET W.C. | LONDON

COLLATION: [i] *half title*; [ii] By the Same Author [*seven titles ending* Sam the Sudden]; [iii] *title page*; [iv] *copyright page:* First published in 1927 Printed in Great Britain; 1–251, *text*; [252] *printer's note:* Printed in Great Britain by Butler & Tanner Ltd., Frome and London; [1]–8, Methuen's General Literature [*advertising supplement inserted*]

PUBLISHED: 28 April 1927 (price 7s6d); British Library reception date 27 April 1927

COVER: Blue cloth, lettered in black

SIZE: 13.5×19.5 cm. (5⅛×7⅝")

A37B First American edition

THE | SMALL BACHELOR | By | P. G. Wodehouse | NEW YORK | GEORGE H. DORAN COMPANY

COLLATION: [1] *half title*; [2] By P. G. Wodehouse [*twelve titles*]; [3] *title page*; [4] *copyright page:* Copyright, 1926, 1927, by P. G. Wodehouse [publisher's monogram] The Small Bachelor –Q– Printed in the United States of America; [5] *half title*; [6] *blank*; [7]–317, *text*; [318–20] *blank*

PUBLISHED: 17 June 1927 (price $2.00)

COVER: Yellow cloth, brown letters and decorations

SIZE: 13×19.5 cm. (5¼×7½")

DUST WRAPPER: Cover illustration signed Hartmann; on spine: The Small Bachelor / Wodehouse / George Finch Chases / Romance / $2.00 net

NOTES: Methuen published the first edition in a variant binding: tan cloth, black lettering and decoration, 12×18.25 cm. (4¾×7¼"); on the copyright page is "First Published in 1927." The publisher issued thirteen printings through 1950.

In New York, A. L. Burt reprinted [1928], 317 pages ($.75).

Based on play *Oh Lady! Lady!*, a Kern-Bolton-Wodehouse musical, 1918.

Serial in *Liberty* 18 September – 30 October 1926, illustrated by James Montgomery Flagg.

A38A Meet Mr. Mulliner

MEET | MR. MULLINER | BY | P. G. WODEHOUSE | HERBERT JENKINS LIMITED | 3 YORK STREET ST. JAMES'S | LONDON S.W.1 [three decorations] [double-rule frame]

COLLATION: [1] *half title*; [2] What This Story Is About, By the Same Author [*fifteen titles*]; [3] *title page*; [4] *copyright page:* [publisher's device] First printing . . 1927 Printed in Great Britain by William Clowes and Sons, Limited, London and Beccles.; [5] *dedication:* To the Earl of Oxford and Asquith; 6, Contents; 7–312, *text*; [313–20] *advertisements*

PUBLISHED: 27 September 1927 (price 7s6d); British Library reception date 27 September 1927

COVER: Green cloth, black lettering and designs

SIZE: 12.5×19.25 cm. (5×7½")

CONTENTS: The Truth about George, pp. 7–38; A Slice of Life, pp. 39–67; Mulliner's Buck-U-Uppo, pp. 68–101; The Bishop's Move, pp. 102–37; Came the Dawn, pp. 138–69; The Story of William, pp. 170–200; Portrait of a Disciplinarian, pp. 201–33; The Romance of a Bulb-Squeezer, pp. 234–65; Honeysuckle Cottage, pp. 266–312.

A38B First American edition

MEET | MR. MULLINER | By | P. G. WODEHOUSE | [publisher's device] | *Garden City, New York* | DOUBLEDAY, DORAN & COMPANY, INC. | 1928

COLLATION: [i–ii] *blank*; [iii] *half title*; [iv] By P. G. Wodehouse [*fourteen titles*]; [v] *title page*; [vi] *copyright page:* Copyright, 1928, by P. G. Wodehouse. Copyright, 1925, by the Curtis Publishing Company. Copyright, 1926, 1927, by Liberty Weekly, . . . Printed . . . at the . . . Country Life Press . . . First edition; [vi] *dedication:* To the Earl of Oxford and Asquith; [vii] *blank*; [viii] Contents; [ix] *blank*; 1–308, *text*; [309–10] *blank*

PUBLISHED: 2 March 1928 (price $2.00)

COVER: Orange cloth, red lettering

SIZE: 13×19.5 cm. (5½×7⅝")

CONTENTS: The Truth about George, pp. 1–33; A Slice of Life, pp. 34–62; Mulliner's Buck-U-Uppo, pp. 63–96; The Bishop's Move, pp. 97–132; Came the Dawn, pp. 133–64; The Story of William, pp. 165–95; Portrait of a Disciplinarian, pp. 196–228; The Romance of a Bulb-Squeezer, pp. 229–60; Honeysuckle Cottage, pp. 261–308.

NOTES: Herbert Jenkins first reissued January 1929, cheap edition; the eighth printing, about 1949, completed 68,021 copies; the latest reprint is 1956 in the Autograph Edition.

A. L. Burt reprinted the American edition 1929 ($.75).

Most stories first appeared in the *Strand*, February 1925 – October 1927, and *Liberty*, July 1926 – December 1927.

A39A Money for Nothing

MONEY FOR | NOTHING | BY | P. G. WODEHOUSE | HERBERT JENKINS LIMITED | 3 YORK STREET, ST. JAMES'S | LONDON, S.W.1 [double-rule frame]

COLLATION: [1] *half title*; [2] What This Story Is About, By the Same Author [*sixteen titles*]; [3] *title page*; [4] *copyright page:* [publisher's device] First printing 1928 Printed in Great Britain by Purnell and Sons Paulton Somerset) and London; [5] *dedication:* To Ian Hay Beith; [6] *blank*; [7] Contents; [8] *blank*; [9] *half title*; [10] *blank*; 11–312, *text*; [313–20] *advertisements*

PUBLISHED: 27 July 1928 (price 7s6d); British Library reception date 27 July 1928

COVER: Orange cloth, black letters and decorations

SIZE: 13×19 cm. (5×7")

A39B First American edition

MONEY | FOR NOTHING | BY | P. G. WODEHOUSE | [publisher's device] | GARDEN CITY, NEW YORK | DOUBLEDAY, DORAN & COMPANY, INC. | 1928

COLLATION: [i–ii] *blank*; [iii] *half title*; [iv] Books by P. G. Wodehouse; [v] *title page*; [vi] *copyright page:* Copyright, 1928 . . . First edition; [vii] *half title*; [viii] *blank*; 1–333, *text*; [334–36] *blank*

PUBLISHED: 28 September 1928 (price $2.00)

COVER: Light blue cloth, blue lettering, orange decorations

SIZE: 13×19.5 cm. (5⅛×7⅝")

NOTES: Herbert Jenkins issued a second printing 1928; the latest reprint, 1976; the eleventh printing, ca. 1949, completed 80,138 copies.

The American edition was reissued by A. L. Burt, New York, 1929 ($.75).

"I laid the scene of Money for Nothing at Hunstanton Hall." (*Performing Flea*, p. 46.)

The story was a serial in *Liberty* 7 July – 25 August 1928, illustrated by Wallace Morgan.

A40A Mr. Mulliner Speaking

MR. MULLINER | SPEAKING | BY | P. G. WODEHOUSE | HERBERT JENKINS LIMITED | 3 YORK STREET, ST. JAMES'S | LONDON, S.W.1 [three ornaments] [double-rule frame]

COLLATION: [1] *half title*; [2] What This Story Is About, By the Same Author [*eighteen titles*]; [3] *title page*; [4] *copyright page:* [publisher's device] First printing 1929. Printed in Great Britain by Purnell and Sons, Paulton Somerset and London; [5] Contents; [6] *blank*; [7] *half title*; [8] *blank*; 9–320, *text*

PUBLISHED: 30 April 1929 (price 7s6d); British Library reception date 30 April 1929

COVER: Orange cloth, black lettering and decoration

SIZE: 12.5×19 cm. (5×7½")

CONTENTS: The Reverent Wooing of Archibald, pp. 9–40; The Man Who Gave Up Smoking, pp. 41–73; The Story of Cedric, pp. 74–106; The Ordeal of Osbert Mulliner, pp. 107–40; Unpleasantness at Bludleigh Court, pp. 141–73; Those in Peril on the Tee, pp. 174–207; Something Squishy, pp. 208–44; The Awful Gladness of the Mater, pp. 245–87; The Passing of Ambrose, pp. 288–320.

A40B First American edition

MR. MULLINER | SPEAKING | BY | P. G. WODEHOUSE | GARDEN CITY, N.Y. | DOUBLEDAY, DORAN AND | COMPANY, INCORPORATED | 1930

COLLATION: [i] *half title*; [ii] Books by P. G. Wodehouse [*eighteen titles*]; [iii] *blank*; [iv] *drawing*; [v] *title page*; [vi] *copyright page:* [publisher's device] ... Printed ... at The Country Life Press ... First Edition; [vii] Contents; [viii] *blank*; [ix] *half title*; [x] *blank*; 1–334, *text*

PUBLISHED: 21 February 1930 (price $2.00)

COVER: Light blue cloth, darker blue lettering and drawing

SIZE: 13.5×19.75 cm. (5¼×7¾")

CONTENTS: The Reverent Wooing of Archibald, pp. 1–34; The Man Who Gave Up Smoking, pp. 35–70; The Story of Cedric, pp. 71–105; The Ordeal of Osbert Mulliner, pp. 106–41; Unpleasantness at Bludleigh Court, pp. 142–76; Those in Peril on the Tee, pp. 177–212; Something Squishy, pp. 213–51; The Awful Gladness of the Mater, pp. 252–98; The Passing of Ambrose, pp. 299–334.

NOTES: Herbert Jenkins reprinted in a cheaper edition, July 1930, completing 35,000 copies; the latest reprint is 1979.

A. L. Burt, New York, reprinted the American edition, 1929 ($.75).

The stories first appeared in various issues of the *Strand*, January 1925 – May 1929; in *Liberty*, May 1927 – May 1929; and in *Cosmopolitan*, August – September 1928.

A41A Fish Preferred

FISH PREFERRED | A NOVEL | BY | P. G. WODEHOUSE | [publisher's device] | 1929 | Doubleday, Doran & Company, Inc. | *Garden City, New York*

COLLATION: [i–ii] *blank*; [iii] *half title*; [iv] Books by P. G. Wodehouse; [v] *title page*; [vi] *copyright page:* copyright, 1929, ... First edition; [vii] *half title*; [viii] *blank*; 1–326, *text*; [327–28] *blank*

PUBLISHED: 1 July 1929 (price $2.00)

COVER: Brown cloth, yellow letters and decorations

SIZE: 13×19.25 cm. (5¼×7⅝")

DUST WRAPPER: Illustrations by Gaul; $2.00

A41B First English edition

SUMMER | LIGHTNING | BY | P. G. WODEHOUSE | HERBERT JENKINS LIMITED | 3 YORK STREET, ST. JAMES'S | LONDON S.W.1 [four ornaments] [double-rule frame]

COLLATION: [i] *half title*; [ii] What This Story Is About; [iii] *title page*; [iv] *copyright page:* [publisher's device] First printing 1929 Printed in Great Britain by Purnell and Sons, Paulton (Somerset) and London; [v] *dedication:* To Denis Mackail ... ; [vi] *blank*; vii–viii, Preface; [ix] Contents; [x] *blank*; [xi] *half title*; [xii] *blank*; 13–318, *text*; [319–20] *advertisements*

PUBLISHED: 19 July 1929 (price 7s6d); British Library reception date 27 June 1929

COVER: Orange cloth, black lettering and decorations

SIZE: 13.25×19.25 cm. (5¼×7⅝")

NOTES: An edition entitled *Fish Preferred* was issued by Herbert Jenkins in 1929, identical in binding, pagination, and size to the Doubleday edition. The only change is the imprint on the title page.

Herbert Jenkins reprinted through 1969; the tenth printing, about 1945, made 76,175 copies.

The American edition was reprinted by A. L. Burt, New York [1930], 326 pages ($.75).

From the Preface: "A certain critic—for such men, I regret to say, do exist—made the nasty remark about my last novel that it contained 'all the old Wodehouse characters under different names.' . . . With my superior intelligence, I have outgeneralled the man this time by putting in all the old Wodehouse characters under the same names. . . . This story is a sort of Old Home Week of my—if I may coin a phrase—puppets. Hugo Carmody and Ronnie Fish appeared in MONEY FOR NOTHING. Pilbeam was in BILL THE CONQUEROR. And the rest of them, Lord Emsworth, the Efficient Baxter, Butler Beach and the others, have all done their bit before in SOMETHING FRESH and LEAVE IT TO PSMITH. Even Empress of Blandings, that pre-eminent pig, is coming up for the second time, having made her debut in a short story called 'Pig-hoo-oo-ey!'

"The fact is, I cannot tear myself away from Blandings Castle. The place exercises a sort of spell over me. I am always popping down to Shropshire and looking in there to hear all the latest news, and there always seems to be something to interest me. . . .

". . . I thought of Summer Lightning. I recognized it immediately as the ideal title for a novel. My exuberance has been a little diminished since by the discovery that I am not the only one who thinks highly of it. Already I have been informed that two novels with the same title have been published in England, and my agent in America cables to say that three have recently been placed on the market in the United States. As my story has appeared in serial form under its present label, it is too late to alter it now. I can only express the modest hope that this story will be considered worthy of inclusion in the list of the Hundred Best Books Called Summer Lightning."

Serial in *Collier's*, 6 April 1929 – 22 June 1929, and in *Pall Mall*, March – May 1929, under the title "Summer Lightning."

Movie, 1933, starring Ralph Lynn and Winifred Shotter, entitled *Summer Lightning*.

A42A Very Good, Jeeves

Very Good, Jeeves | BY P. G. WODEHOUSE | AUTHOR OF "FISH PREFERRED," ETC. | [publisher's device] | GARDEN CITY, NEW YORK | DOUBLEDAY, DORAN & COMPANY, INC. | 1930

COLLATION: [i–ii] *blank*; [iii] *half title*; [iv] Books by P. G. Wodehouse; [v] *title page*; [vi] *copyright page:* Printed at the Country Life Press Garden City, N.Y., U.S.A. [publisher's device] Copyright, 1926, 1927, 1929, 1930 . . . First Edition; [vii] Contents; [viii] *blank*; [ix] *half title*; [x] *blank*; [1]–340, *text*; [341–44] *blank*

PUBLISHED: 20 June 1930 (price $1.00)

COVER: Orange cloth, black letters

SIZE: 13×19.5 cm. (5¼×7⅝")

CONTENTS: Jeeves and the Impending Doom, pp. *3–32*; The Inferiority Complex of Old Sippy, pp. *35–60*; Jeeves and the Yuletide Spirit, pp. *63–86*; Jeeves and the Song of Songs, pp. *89–116*; Jeeves and the Dog McIntosh, pp. *119–43*; Jeeves and the Spot of Art, pp. *147–77*; Jeeves and the Kid Clementina, pp. *181–209*; Jeeves and the Love That Purifies, pp. *213–41*; Jeeves and the Old School Chum, pp. *245–76*; The Indian Summer of an Uncle, pp. *279–306*; Tuppy Changes His Mind, pp. *309–40*.

A42B First English edition

VERY GOOD, | JEEVES! | BY | P. G. WODEHOUSE | HERBERT JENKINS LIMITED | 3 YORK STREET, ST. JAMES'S | LONDON, S.W.1 [three decorations] [double-rule frame]

COLLATION: [1] *half title*; [2] What This Book Is About; [3] *title page*; [4] *copyright page:* [publisher's device] First printing 1930 Made and Printed in Great Britain by Purnell and Sons, Paulton (Somerset) and London; [5] *dedication:* To E. Phillips Oppenheim; [6] *blank*; vii–ix, Preface [*signed* P.G.W.]; [10] *blank*; xi, Contents; [12] *blank*; [13] *half title*; [14] *blank*; 15–312, *text*; [313–20] *advertisements*

PUBLISHED: 4 July 1930 (price 7s6d); British Library reception date 14 July 1930

COVER: Orange cloth, black letters and decorations

SIZE: 13×19 cm. (5¼×7½")

CONTENTS: Jeeves and the Impending Doom, pp. *15–42*; The Inferiority Complex of Old Sippy, pp. *43–65*; Jeeves and the Yule-tide Spirit, pp. *66–91*; Jeeves and the Song of Songs, pp. *92–117*; Episode of the Dog McIntosh, pp. *118–41*; The Spot of Art, pp. *142–70*; Jeeves and the Kid Clementina, pp. *171–97*; The Love That Purifies, pp. *198–225*; Jeeves and the Old School Chum, pp. *226–55*; Indian Summer of an Uncle, pp. *256–83*; The Ordeal of Young Tuppy, pp. *283–312*.

NOTES: A. L. Burt, New York, reprinted 1931, 340 pages ($.75). The English edition was reprinted by Herbert Jenkins through 1958; the third printing, 1932, made 45,103 copies; the sixth printing, about 1935, made 65,103 copies.

The preface in the English edition, not included in the American edition, was reprinted in *Week-End Wode-*

house (1939) and *Selected Stories by P. G. Wodehouse* (1958).

The short stories first appeared in the *Strand*, April 1926, December 1926, December 1927, September 1929 – April 1930; *Cosmopolitan*, September 1929 – April 1930; and *Liberty*, 17 April 1926, 8 January 1927, 24 December 1927.

A43A Big Money

Big Money [in orange] | P. G. WODEHOUSE | [publisher's device in orange] | 1931 | DOUBLEDAY, DORAN & COMPANY, INC. | Garden City, New York

COLLATION: [i] *half title*; [ii] Books by P. G. Wodehouse [twenty titles]; [iii] *title page*; [iv] *copyright page:* Printed at the Country Life Press, Garden City, N.Y., U.S.A. copyright, 1930, 1931 . . . First edition; [v] *half title*; [vi] *blank*; [1]–316, *text*

PUBLISHED: 30 January 1931 (price $2.00)

COVER: Orange cloth, orange letters on green background

SIZE: 13.5×19.75 cm. (5¼×7¾″)

DUST WRAPPER: Drawings by Beckhoff (also endpapers); $2.00

A43B First English edition

BIG MONEY | BY | P. G. WODEHOUSE | HERBERT JENKINS LIMITED | 3 YORK STREET ST. JAMES'S | LONDON, S.W.1 [three ornaments] [double-rule frame]

COLLATION: [1] *half title*; [2] What This Story Is About; [3] *title page*; [4] *copyright page:* [publisher's device] First printing 1931 Printed in Great Britain by Wyman & Sons, Ltd., London, Fakenham and Reading; [5] *half title*; [6] *blank*; 7–314, *text*; [315–20] *advertisements*

PUBLISHED: 20 March 1931 (price 7s6d); British Library reception date 4 February 1931

COVER: Orange cloth, black letters

SIZE: 12.5×19 cm. (5×7½″)

DUST WRAPPER: Drawing by Batchelor, K.B. Studio

NOTES: Both publishers reissued the first edition but without the first edition or first printing statement.

Serialized in *Collier's*, 20 September 1930–6 December 1930, illustrated by Harry Beckhoff, and in the *Strand*, October 1930–April 1931, illustrated by Charles Crosbie.

A44A If I Were You

P. G. WODEHOUSE | IF | I WERE | YOU | DOUBLEDAY, DORAN & COMPANY, INC. | GARDEN CITY, NEW YORK | 1931

COLLATION: [i] *half title*; [ii] Books by P. G. Wodehouse; [iii] *title page*; [iv] *copyright page:* Printed at The Country Life Press . . . Copyright, 1931 by Pelham Grenville Wodehouse . . . First edition; [v] *dedication:* To Guy Bolton; [vi] *blank*; [1]–305, *text*; [306] *blank*

PUBLISHED: 3 September 1931 (price $2.00)

COVER: Orange cloth, red-brown letters

SIZE: 13.50×19.75 cm. (5¼×7¾″)

DUST WRAPPER: Drawing by Henrietta Starrett; $2.00

A44B First English edition

IF I WERE YOU | BY | P. G. WODEHOUSE | HERBERT JENKINS LIMITED | 3 YORK STREET ST. JAMES'S | LONDON, S.W.1 [three ornaments] [double-rule frame]

COLLATION: [1–2] *blank*; [3] *half title*; [4] What This Story Is About; [5] *title page*; [6] *copyright page:* [publisher's device] First printing 1931 Printed in Great Britain by Wyman & Sons, Ltd., London, Fakenham and Reading; [7] *half title*; [8] *blank*; [9]–280, *text*; [281–88] *advertisements*

PUBLISHED: 25 September 1931 (price 3s6d); British Library reception date 25 September 1931

COVER: Orange cloth, black lettering and decorations

SIZE: 13×19 cm. (5×7½″)

DUST WRAPPER: Illustration by W. Heath Robinson; green label books 3/6

NOTES: Herbert Jenkins reissued at least nine times, June 1933 through 1976. A. L. Burt, New York, reprinted the American edition, 1932 ($.75).

According to Richard Usborne, the book was purchased by M.G.M. in 1930 for $25,000 but has yet to be produced (*Wodehouse at Work*, p. 217).

Dramatized with Guy Bolton as *Who's Who* which opened at the Duke of York Theatre, London, 20 September 1934.

Serial in *American Magazine*, April – July 1931, illustrated by Frederick Chapman.

A45A Louder and Funnier

Louder | and Funnier | by | P. G. Wodehouse | London | Faber & Faber | 24 Russell Square

COLLATION: [1] *half title*; [2] *blank*; [3] *title page*; [4] *copyright page:* First published in MCMXXXII by Faber & Faber ... Printed ... by Butler & Tanner ... ; [5] *dedication*: To George Blake ... ; [6] *blank*; 7–12, About this Book; 13–14, Contents; 15–286, *text*; [287–88] *blank*

PUBLISHED: 10 March 1932 (price 7s6d); British Library reception date 7 March 1932

COVER: Yellow cloth, gold letters

SIZE: 13×19.25 cm. (5×7½″)

DUST WRAPPER: By Rex Whistler

CONTENTS: The Hollywood Scandal, pp. 15–30; Literature and the Arts (1. To the Editor – Sir ... , pp. 31–38; 2. My Gentle Readers, pp. 39–50; 3. Thrillers, pp. 51–76); Round about the Theatre (1. Fair Play for Audiences, pp. 77–93; 2. Looking Back at the Halls, pp. 95–105; 3. An Outline of Shakespeare, pp. 107–25); Sports and Pastimes (1. The Decay of Falconry, pp. 127–35; 2. A Day with Swattesmore, pp. 137–43; 3. Prospects for Wambledon, pp. 145–63); Fashionable Weddings and Smart Divorces, pp. 165–76; Happy Christmas and Merry New Year, pp. 177–91; Thoughts on the Income Tax, pp. 193–207; Butlers and the Buttled, pp. 209–23; A Word about Amusement Parks, pp. 225–32; The Small Gambler (1. Roulette, pp. 233–51; 2. Chemin de Fer, pp. 253–74); Photographs and Photographers, pp. 275–86.

NOTES: First edition also bound in yellow cloth but with bright blue-green letters on spine. Reissued 1932 in blue-green cloth, gold letters (12×18 cm. [4¾×7¼″]).

Most of the essays in this collection first appeared in *Vanity Fair*, where Wodehouse was called the drama critic. "Vanity Fair is a swanky magazine 'devoted to Society and the Arts,' and I used to write about half of it each month under a number of names—P. G. Wodehouse, Pelham Grenville, J. Plum, C. P. West, P. Brooke-Haven and so on." (*Performing Flea*, p. 13.) Wodehouse's comment on the book: "The best thing about Louder and Funnier is the jacket by Rex Whistler." (*Performing Flea*, p. 66.)

The entire dedication reads: "To George Blake a splendid fellow and very sound on Pekes*" [At bottom of page:] "*But he should guard against the tendency to claim that his Peke fights Alsatians. Mine is the only one that does this."

A46A Doctor Sally

DOCTOR SALLY | BY | P. G. WODEHOUSE | [publisher's device] | METHUEN & CO. LTD. | 36 ESSEX STREET W.C. | LONDON

COLLATION: [i] *half title*; [ii] By the Same Author [eight titles]; [iii] *title page*; [iv] *copyright page:* First published 1932 ... ; [1]–155, *text*; [156] *printer's note:* Printed by Jarrold and Sons Ltd. Norwich; [1]–8, Methuen's General Literature [advertising supplement inserted]

PUBLISHED: 7 April 1932 (price 3s6d); British Library reception date 7 April 1932

COVER: Blue cloth, black letters

SIZE: 13×19.5 cm. (5¼×7¾″)

NOTES: Methuen issued a second edition, 1932, reissued twice more in 1933, and in 1937.

Taken from the play *Good Morning, Bill*, based on the Hungarian play by Ladislaus Fodor.

Published in the United States as "The Medicine Girl" in the collection *Crime Wave at Blandings*.

Serialized in *Collier's* as "The Medicine Girl" 4 July – 1 August 1931, illustrated by Wallace Morgan.

A47A Hot Water

HOT WATER | BY | P. G. WODEHOUSE | HERBERT JENKINS LIMITED | 3 YORK STREET ST. JAMES'S | LONDON, S.W.1 [three decorations] [double-rule frame]

COLLATION: [1] *half title*; [2] What This Story Is About; [3] *title page*; [4] *copyright page:* [publisher's device] First printing 1932 Printed in Great Britain by Wyman & Sons, Ltd., London, Fakenham and Reading; [5] *dedication:* To Maureen O'Sullivan ... ; [6] *blank*; [7] *half title*; [8] *blank*; [9]–312, *text*; [313–20] *advertisements*

PUBLISHED: 17 August 1932 (price 7s6d); British Library reception date 17 August 1932

COVER: Orange cloth, black letters and designs

SIZE: 12.5×19 cm. (5×7½″)

DUST WRAPPER: Illustrated by Abbey and K.B. Studio; 7/6

A47B First American edition

P. G. WODEHOUSE | HOT WATER | [drawing from page 99] | DOUBLEDAY, DORAN & COMPANY, INC. [line in italics] | *Garden City, New York* | MCMXXXII

COLLATION: [i] *synopsis*; [ii] *blank*; [iii] *half title*; [iv] Books by P. G. Wodehouse [twenty-two titles]; [v] *title page*; [vi] *copyright page:* Printed at The Country Life Press, Garden City, ... with illustrations by Rea Irvin,

Copyright, 1932 . . . First edition; [vii] *dedication:* To Maureen O'Sullivan . . . ; [viii] *blank*; [ix] Illustrations; [x] *drawing*; [xi] *half title*; [xii] *blank*; [1]–307, *text*; [308] *blank*

PUBLISHED: 17 August 1932 (price $2.00)

COVER: Black cloth, red letters and drawing (same as on title page)

SIZE: 13.5×19.75 cm. (5¼×7¾")

DUST WRAPPER: By Rea Irvin

NOTE: Six illustrations by Rea Irvin.

NOTES: Herbert Jenkins has reprinted this title many times—the latest in 1978, 223 p.; the sixth printing completed 59,007 copies [1945?].

In the United States reprinted by A. L. Burt [1933] ($.75); and by P. F. Collier and Son Corporation.

Serialized in *Collier's*, 21 May – 6 August 1932, illustrated by Floyd M. Davis.

With Guy Bolton dramatized as *The Inside Stand*.

A48A Mulliner Nights

MULLINER NIGHTS | BY | P. G. WODEHOUSE | HERBERT JENKINS LIMITED | 3 YORK STREET ST. JAMES'S | LONDON, S.W.1 [three ornaments] [double-rule frame]

COLLATION: [1] *half title*; [2] What This Story Is About; [3] *title page*; [4] *copyright page:* [publisher's device] First printing 1933 Printed in Great Britain by Wyman & Sons Ltd., London, Fakenham and Reading; [5] Contents; [6] *blank*; [7] *half title*; [8] *blank*; [9]–312, *text*; [313–20] *advertisements*

PUBLISHED: 17 January 1933 (price 7s6d); British Library reception date 17 January 1933

COVER: Orange cloth, black lettering and designs

SIZE: 12.5×19 cm. (5×7½")

CONTENTS: The Smile That Wins, pp. [9]–40; The Story of Webster, pp. [41]–74; Cats Will Be Cats, pp. [75]–111; The Knightly Quest of Mervyn, pp. [112]–46; The Voice from the Past, pp. [147]–84; Open House, pp. [185]–217; Best Seller, pp. [218]–46; Strychnine in the Soup, pp. [247]–79; Gala Night, pp. [280]–312.

A48B First American edition

P. G. WODEHOUSE | MULLINER NIGHTS | [publisher's device] | DOUBLEDAY, DORAN & COMPANY, INC. [in italics] | *Garden City, New York* | MCMXXXIII

COLLATION: [i] *half title with drawing of man's face;* [ii] Books by P. G. Wodehouse; [iii] *title page;* [iv] *copyright page:* Printed at The Country Life Press . . . copyright, 1930, 1931, 1932, 1933 . . . First edition; [v] Contents; [vi] *blank*; [vii] *half title;* [viii] *blank*; [1]–312, *text*

PUBLISHED: 15 February 1933 (price $2.00)

COVER: Orange cloth, black and orange letters and drawing

SIZE: 13.5×19.75 cm. (5¼×7¾")

DUST WRAPPER: Illustrations by James Montgomery Flagg; $2.00

CONTENTS: The Smile That Wins, pp. 1–33; The Story of Webster, pp. 34–68; Cats Will Be Cats, pp. 69–105; The Knightly Quest of Mervyn, pp. 106–41; The Voice from the Past, pp. 142–80; Open House, pp. 181–214; Best Seller, pp. 215–44; Strychnine in the Soup, pp. 245–78; Gala Night, pp. 279–312.

NOTES: Herbert Jenkins has reprinted October 1934, June 1949, 1966 in the Autograph Edition, and 1980.

Doubleday reissued without the first edition statement on the copyright page. A. L. Burt reprinted 1934 ($.75).

Originally published in the *Strand*, June 1930 – June 1932. In the United States, first published in various issues of *American Magazine*, October 1931 – April 1932, and *Cosmopolitan*, May 1930 – April 1931. According to Richard Usborne, *American Magazine* paid Wodehouse $6,000 for the Mulliner series (*Wodehouse at Work*, p. 138).

A49A The Great Sermon Handicap

THE GREAT | SERMON HANDICAP | BY P. G. WODEHOUSE | HODDER AND STOUGHTON | LIMITED LONDON

COLLATION: [1] *half title*; [2] *blank*; [3] *half title*; [4] *copyright page:* Made and printed in Great Britain by Wyman and Sons, Ltd., Fakenham and Reading; 5–[64] *text*

PUBLISHED: March 1933 (price 9s); British Library reception date 3 April 1933

BINDING: Red paper (imitation leather), gold lettering and decorations

SIZE: 8×12 cm. (3×4¾")

DUST WRAPPER: Little Books of Laughter

NOTES: Reprinted London, St. Hugh's Press, 1949, 60 pages (British Library reception date 18 October 1949).

Originally collected in *The Inimitable Jeeves* (American title, *Jeeves*), published 1923.

A50A Heavy Weather

P. G. WODEHOUSE | HEAVY | WEATHER | [publisher's device] | 1933 | BOSTON | Little, Brown, and Company

COLLATION: [i] *half title*; [ii] *blank*; [iii] *title page*; [iv] *copyright page:* Copyright, 1933 All rights reserved Published July, 1933 . . . ; [1] *half title*; [2] *blank*; [3]–314, *text*; [315–16] *blank*

PUBLISHED: 28 July 1933 (price $2.00)

COVER: Black cloth, red lettering and decorations

SIZE: 13×19.5 cm. (5⅛×7⅝″)

DUST WRAPPER

A50B First English edition

HEAVY WEATHER | BY | P. G. WODEHOUSE | HERBERT JENKINS LIMITED | 3 YORK STREET ST. JAMES'S | LONDON S.W.1 [five decorations] [double-rule frame]

COLLATION: [1] *half title*; [2] What This Story Is About; [3] *title page*; [4] *copyright page:* [publisher's device] First printing 1933 Printed in Great Britain by Wyman & Sons Ltd., London, Reading and Fakenham; [5] *half title*; [6] *blank*; 7–311, *text*; [312] *blank*; [313–20] *advertisements*

PUBLISHED: 10 August 1933 (price 7s6d); British Library reception date 28 July 1933

COVER: Blue cloth, orange letters and decorations

SIZE: 12.75×19 cm. (5×7½″)

DUST WRAPPER: 7/6 green label; designed by K.B. Studio

NOTES: A. L. Burt, New York, reprinted September 1933, 314 pages ($.75); and Triangle Books, New York, reissued May 1938, 314 pages. About 1937, Blue Ribbon Books, New York, acquired A. L. Burt and published under the imprint Triangle Books.

Herbert Jenkins reprinted many times: cheap edition, April 1935; fifth printing [1939?], making 45,070 copies; ninth impression [1945?], making 73,070 copies; Autograph Edition, 1960; latest printing, 1978.

Sequel to *Summer Lightning*, 1929. (*Performing Flea*, p. 69.)

Serial in *Saturday Evening Post*, 27 May – 15 July 1933, illustrated by May Wilson Preston.

A51A Thank You, Jeeves

THANK YOU, | JEEVES | BY | P. G. WODEHOUSE | HERBERT JENKINS LIMITED | 3 YORK STREET · ST. JAMES'S | LONDON S.W.1 [four decorations] [double-rule frame]

COLLATION: [1] *half title*; [2] What This Story Is About; [3] *title page*; [4] *copyright page:* [publisher's device] First printing 1934 Printed in Great Britain by Wyman & Sons Ltd., London, Reading and Fakenham.; 5, Contents; [6] *blank*; [7]–312, *text*; [313–20] *advertisements*

PUBLISHED: 16 March 1934 (price 7s6d); British Library reception date 17 March 1934

COVER: Gray cloth, red letters and designs

SIZE: 13×19 cm. (5×7½″)

DUST WRAPPER: Illustrations by Abbey; 7/6

A51B First American edition

P. G. WODEHOUSE | THANK | YOU, | JEEVES! | [publisher's device] | LITTLE, BROWN, AND COMPANY | BOSTON · 1934

COLLATION: [1] *half title*; [ii] Books by P. G. Wodehouse; [iii] *title page*; [iv] *copyright page:* Copyright, 1933, 1934 . . . Published April, 1934 . . . ; [1] *half title*; [2] *blank*; [3]–307, *text*; [308] *blank*

PUBLISHED: 23 April 1934 (price $2.00)

COVER: Lavender cloth, black letters and illustration

SIZE: 13×19.5 cm. (5¼×7⅝″)

NOTES: Herbert Jenkins reprints: sixth printing [ca. 1949?], completing 50,273 copies; Autograph Edition, 1956; latest reprint, 1975.

Triangle Books, New York, reprinted several times: October 1938, February 1939, December 1939, April 1940, January 1941.

Serialized in the *Strand*, August 1933 – January 1934, illustrated by Gilbert Wilkinson and in *Cosmopolitan*, January – June 1934, illustrated by James Montgomery Flagg.

First novel dealing with Jeeves and Bertie Wooster; prior to this the books were collections of episodes.

Paramount produced as a film in 1936, starring Arthur Treacher, David Niven, and Virginia Fields. Wodehouse later said about the movie: "They didn't use a word of my story, substituting another written by some studio hack." (Letter to Guy Bolton, 15 August 1973.)

A52A Right Ho, Jeeves

RIGHT HO, | JEEVES | BY | P. G. WODEHOUSE | HERBERT JENKINS LIMITED | 3 YORK STREET · ST. JAMES'S | LONDON S.W.1 [two ornaments] MCMXXXIV [double-rule frame]

COLLATION: [1–2] *blank*; [3] *half title*; [4] What This Story Is About; [5] *title page*; [6] *copyright page:* [publisher's device] Printed . . . by Wyman & Sons . . . ; [7] *dedication:* To Raymond Needham K.C. . . . ; [8] *blank*; 9–312, *text*; [313–20] *advertisements*

PUBLISHED: 5 October 1934 (price 7s6d); British Library reception date 5 October 1934

COVER: Tan cloth, red letters and decorations

SIZE: 13×19 cm. (5×7½")

A52B First American edition

P. G. WODEHOUSE | BRINKLEY | MANOR | *A Novel About* | JEEVES | [publisher's device] | LITTLE, BROWN, AND COMPANY | BOSTON · 1934

COLLATION: [i] *half title*; [ii] Books by P. G. Wodehouse; [iii] *title page*; [iv] *copyright page:* Brinkley Manor appeared in *The Saturday Evening Post* under the title Right-Ho, Jeeves. Copyright 1933, 1934 . . . Published October 1934 . . . ; [1] *half title*; [2] *blank*; [3]–321, *text*; [322–24] *blank*

PUBLISHED: 15 October 1934 (price $2.00)

COVER: Orange-red cloth, black lettering and drawing

SIZE: 13×19.5 cm. (5×7⅝")

DUST WRAPPER: Cover drawing by James Montgomery Flagg; $2.00

NOTES: Herbert Jenkins reprints: Colonial Library, 1934; cheap edition, May 1936; Autograph Edition, 1959, reprinted 1978.

Little, Brown reprinted December 1934 and October 1937. The fourth printing, November 1938, was by Triangle Books who reprinted three more times through December 1940.

Serialized by *Saturday Evening Post*, 2 December 1933 – 27 January 1934, illustrated by Henry Raleigh, under the title "Right-Ho, Jeeves," for which Wodehouse received $40,000. In England the *Grand Magazine* (published by Newnes) serialized it April – September 1934.

Wodehouse said: "I was conscious all the time that the plot was not too strong so I developed every possible chance for bright dialogue." (Letter to Paul Reynolds, 25 January 1934.)

A53A Blandings Castle and Elsewhere

BLANDINGS | CASTLE | AND ELSEWHERE | BY | P. G. WODEHOUSE | HERBERT JENKINS LIMITED | 3 YORK STREET ST. JAMES'S | LONDON S.W.1 [design of five leaves] [double-rule frame]

COLLATION: [1] *half title*; [2] What This Story Is About; [3] *title page*; [4] *copyright page:* [publisher's device] First printing 1935 Printed in Great Britain by Wyman & Sons Ltd., London, Reading and Fakenham; 5, Contents; [6] *blank*; 7–8, Preface; [9] *half title*; [10] *blank*; 11–311, *text*; [312] *blank*; [313–20] *advertisements*

PUBLISHED: 12 April 1935 (price 7s6d); British Library reception date 12 April 1935

COVER: Turquoise cloth, black lettering

SIZE: 13×19 cm. (5×7½")

DUST WRAPPER: Drawing by Abbey; 7/6 green label

CONTENTS: Blandings Castle (The Custody of the Pumpkin, pp. 11–36; Lord Emsworth Acts for the Best, pp. 37–60; Pig – Hoo-o-o-o-ey!, pp. 61–87; Company for Gertrude, pp. 88–112; The Go-Getter, pp. 113–38; Lord Emsworth and the Girl Friend, pp. 139–63); Elsewhere – I, A Bobbie Wickham Story (Mr. Potter Takes a Rest Cure, pp. 167–93); Elsewhere – II, The Mulliners of Hollywood (Monkey Business, pp. 197–220; The Nodder, pp. 221–42; The Juice of an Orange, pp. 243–65; The Rise of Minna Nordstrom, pp. 266–87; The Castaways, pp. 288–311).

A53B First American edition

P. G. WODEHOUSE | BLANDINGS | CASTLE | [publisher's device] | Doubleday, Doran & Company, Inc. | *Garden City, New York* | 1935

COLLATION: [i] *half title*; [ii] Books by P. G. Wodehouse [*twenty-five titles*]; [iii] *title*; [iv] *copyright page:* Printed at the Country Life Press, Garden City, N.Y., U.S.A. Copyright, 1924, 1926, 1927, 1928, 1931, 1932, 1933, 1935 . . . First edition; v–vi, Preface; vii, Contents; [viii] *blank*; [1] *half title*; [2] *blank*; 3–311, *text*; [312] *blank*

PUBLISHED: 20 September 1935 (price $2.00)

COVER: Green cloth, dark green designs and letters

SIZE: 13.5×19.75 cm. (5⅜×7¾")

DUST WRAPPER: Roese; $2.00

CONTENTS: Blandings Castle (I, The Custody of the Pumpkin, pp. 3–29; II, Lord Emsworth Acts for the Best, pp. 30–54; III, Pig-Hoo-o-o-o-ey! pp. 55–82; IV, Company for Gertrude, pp. 83–108; V, The Go-Getter, pp. 109–34; VI, Lord Emsworth and the Girl Friend, pp. 135–60); Elsewhere (1. A Bobbie Wickham Story, VII, Mr. Potter Takes a Rest Cure, pp. 163–90, 2. The Mulliners of Hollywood, VIII, Monkey Business, pp. 193–217; IX, The Nodder, pp. 218–40; X, The Juice of an Orange, pp. 241–63; XI, The Rise of Minna Nordstrom, pp. 264–86; XII, The Castaways, pp. 287–311).

NOTES: Herbert Jenkins reissued the first edition in 1935 in blue cloth with black lettering and again October 1936; the fifth printing, ca. 1939, completed 45,244 copies; the Autograph Edition appeared in 1957.

Doubleday reissued the first edition in orange cloth with the first edition notice on the copyright page. A. L. Burt, New York, reprinted 1936, 311 pages ($.75).

From the Preface: "In point of time, these stories [the Blandings Castle set] come after *Leave it to Psmith* and before *Summer Lightning*. . . . Bobbie Wickham . . . appeared in three of the stories in a book called *Mr. Mulliner Speaking*."

The stories first appeared in various issues of the *Strand*, December 1924 – June 1933; *Liberty*, June 1926 – October 1928; *American Magazine*, December 1932 – February 1933; and *Saturday Evening Post*, 29 November 1924.

A54A The Luck of the Bodkins

THE | LUCK OF THE BODKINS | BY | P. G. WODEHOUSE | HERBERT JENKINS LIMITED | 3 YORK STREET ST. JAMES'S | LONDON, S.W.1 [three decorations] [double-rule frame]

COLLATION: [1–2] *blank*; [3] *half title*; [4] What This Story Is About; [5] *title page*; [6] *copyright page:* [publisher's device] First printing 1935 Printed in Great Britain by Wyman & Sons, Ltd., London, Fakenham and Reading.; [7] *half title*; [8] *blank*; [9]–311, *text*; [312] *blank*; [313–20] *advertisements*

PUBLISHED: 11 October 1935 (price 7s6d); British Library reception date 11 October 1935

COVER: Red cloth, black letters and decorations

SIZE: 12.5×19 cm. (5×7½″)

DUST WRAPPER: Illustration by Abbey; 7/6 green label

A54B First American edition

P. G. WODEHOUSE | THE LUCK | OF THE | BODKINS | [publisher's device] | 1936 | BOSTON | Little, Brown, and Company

COLLATION: [i] *half title*; [ii] Books by P. G. Wodehouse; [iii] *title page*; [iv] *copyright page:* Copyright, 1935, 1936, by P. G. Wodehouse . . . Published January, 1936 . . . ; [1] *half title*; [2] *blank*; [3]–298, *text*; [299–300] *blank*

PUBLISHED: 3 January 1936 (price $2.00)

COVER: Pale green cloth, black letters and designs

SIZE: 13×19.5 cm. (5⅛×7⅝″)

DUST WRAPPER: $2.00

NOTES: Herbert Jenkins reprinted the title in 1935 (blue cloth with gold lettering), in 1937, about 1939, in 1956 in the Autograph Edition, and most recently in 1975.

Little, Brown reissued May and October 1936. Triangle Books, New York, then reprinted April 1938, March 1940, and January 1941.

The story was reworked for the American edition.

A55A Young Men in Spats

YOUNG MEN IN | SPATS | BY | P. G. WODEHOUSE | HERBERT JENKINS LIMITED | 3 YORK STREET ST. JAMES'S | LONDON, S.W.1 [three decorations] [double-rule frame]

COLLATION: [1] *half title*; [2] What This Story Is About; [3] *title page*; [4] *copyright page:* [publisher's device] First printing 1936 Printed in Great Britain by Wyman & Sons, Ltd., London, Fakenham and Reading.; [5] Contents; [6] *blank*; [7] *half title*; [8] *blank*; [9]–312, *text*; [313–20] *advertisements*

PUBLISHED: 3 April 1936 (price 7s6d); British Library reception date 4 April 1936

COVER: Blue-green cloth, black lettering and decorations

SIZE: 12.5×18.75 cm. (5×7½″)

DUST WRAPPER: Jacket design from drawing by Gilbert Wilkinson; 7/6 green label; subtitle on spine: The Drones Club Book of the Month

CONTENTS: Fate, pp. [9]–37; *Tried in the Furnace, pp. [38]–66; *Trouble Down at Tudsleigh, pp. [67]–96; The Amazing Hat Mystery, pp. [97]–124; Good-bye to All Cats, pp. [125]–51; The Luck of the Stiffhams, pp. [152]–75; Noblesse Oblige, pp. [176]–202; Uncle Fred Flits By, pp. [203]–31; Archibald and the Masses, pp. [232]–60; The Code of the Mulliners, pp. [261]–86; The Fiery Wooing of Mordred, pp. [287]–312. (*Asterisks indicate stories not in the American edition.)

A55B First American edition

P. G. WODEHOUSE | YOUNG MEN | IN | SPATS | [publisher's device] | Doubleday, Doran & Company, Inc. | *Garden City 1936 New York*

COLLATION: [i] *half title*; [ii] Books by P. G. Wodehouse; [iii] *title page*; [iv] *copyright page:* Printed at the Country Life Press . . . copyright, 1931, 1933, 1934, 1935, 1936 . . . First Edition; [v] Contents; [vi] *blank*; [1]–297, *text*; [298] *blank*

PUBLISHED: 24 July 1936 (price $2.00)

COVER: Green cloth, darker green lettering and outline of drawing

SIZE: 13.5×19.75 cm. (5¼×7¾")

DUST WRAPPER: By Roese; $2.00

NOTE: Nine short stories of the London edition, plus three new stories.

CONTENTS: Fate, pp. [1]–26; The Amazing Hat Mystery, pp. 27–51; Good-bye to All Cats, pp. 52–75; The Luck of the Stiffhams, pp. 76–97; Noblesse Oblige, pp. 98–121; Uncle Fred Flits By, pp. 122–47; Archibald and the Masses, pp. 148–73; The Code of the Mulliners, pp. 174–96; The Fiery Wooing of Mordred, pp. 197–219; *There's Always Golf! pp. 220–44; *The Letter of the Law, pp. 245–71; *Farewell to Legs, pp. 272–97. (*Asterisks indicate stories not in the English edition.)

NOTES: Jenkins reissued in orange cloth with black letters in 1936 and 1937 and in the Autograph Edition, 1957.

The stories were first published in various issues of the *Strand*, May 1931, March 1934 – April 1936; *Cosmopolitan*, August 1933 – August 1935; *Red Book*, July 1935; and *This Week*, 14 July 1935.

A56A Laughing Gas

LAUGHING GAS | BY | P. G. WODEHOUSE | HERBERT JENKINS LIMITED | 3 YORK STREET ST. JAMES'S | LONDON, S.W.1 [three decorations] [double-rule frame]

COLLATION: [1] *half title*; [2] What This Story Is About; [3] *title page*; [4] *copyright page:* [publisher's device] First printing 1936 Printed in Great Britain by Wyman & Sons, Limited, London, Fakenham and Reading; [5] *half title*; [6] *blank*; [7]–311, *text*; [312] *blank*; [313–20] *advertisements*

PUBLISHED: 25 September 1936 (price 7s6d); British Library reception date 26 September 1936

COVER: Bright pink-red cloth, black letters and decorations

SIZE: 13×19 cm. (5×7½")

DUST WRAPPER: Illustrated by Abbey; 7/6

A56B First American edition

P. G. WODEHOUSE | *Laughing Gas* | [publisher's device] | Doubleday, Doran & Company, Inc. | *Garden City* 1936 *New York*

COLLATION: [i] *half title*; [ii] Books by P. G. Wodehouse; [iii] *title page*; [iv] *copyright page:* Printed at The Country Life Press, Garden City, N.Y., U.S.A. Copyright, 1935, 1936 by Pelham Grenville Wodehouse All Rights Reserved First Edition; [v] *half title*; [vi] *blank*; [1]–303, *text*; [304–6] *blank*

PUBLISHED: 19 November 1936 (price $2.00)

COVER: Orange cloth, black letters and drawing

SIZE: 14×19.75 cm. (5½×7¾")

DUST WRAPPER: Illustration by Roese; $2.00

NOTES: The subsequent printings by both publishers are without the first printing or first edition statements.

A57A Lord Emsworth and Others

LORD EMSWORTH | AND OTHERS | P. G. WODEHOUSE | HERBERT JENKINS LIMITED | 3 YORK STREET ST. JAMES'S | LONDON, S.W.1 [three decorations] [double-rule frame]

COLLATION: [1] *half title*; [2] What This Story Is About; [3] *title page*; [4] *copyright page:* [publisher's device] First printing 1937 Printed in Great Britain by Wyman & Sons, Ltd., London, Fakenham and Reading.; [5] Contents; [6] *blank*; [7] *half title*; [8] *blank*; [9]–312, *text*; [313–20] *advertisements*

PUBLISHED: 19 March 1937 (price 7s6d); British Library reception date 19 March 1937

COVER: Bright red cloth, black letters

SIZE: 12.5×19 cm. (5×7½")

DUST WRAPPER: Illustration by Abbey; 7/6 green label

CONTENTS: The Crime Wave at Blandings, pp. [9]–79; Buried Treasure, pp. [80]–107; The Letter of the Law, pp. [108]–36; Farewell to Legs, pp. [137]–64; There's Always Golf, pp. [165]–91; The Masked Troubadour, pp. [192]–224; Ukridge and the Home From Home, pp. [225]–55; The Come-Back of Battling Billson, pp. [256]–84; A Level Business Head, pp. [285]–312.

NOTES: Herbert Jenkins also issued the first printing in gray boards with red letters. Subsequent printings, so marked on the copyright page, are in orange cloth with black letters.

The three short stories added to the American edition of *Young Men in Spats* are included in this collection. All the short stories first appeared in the *Strand*, May 1926 – December 1936; *Saturday Evening Post*, 10–17 October 1936; *This Week*, 14 July 1935; and *Cosmopolitan*, February 1931, June 1935.

A58A Crime Wave at Blandings

P. G. WODEHOUSE | THE | CRIME WAVE | AT | BLANDINGS | [publisher's device] | Doubleday, Doran & Company, Inc. | *Garden City* 1937 *New York*

COLLATION: [i] *half title*; [ii] Books by P. G. Wodehouse; [iii] *title page*; [iv] *copyright page:* Printed at the Country Life Press, Garden City, N.Y., U.S.A. Copyright, 1931, 1936, 1937 . . . First Edition; [v] Contents; [vi] *blank*; [1]–330, *text*

PUBLISHED: 25 June 1937 (price $2.00)

COVER: Green cloth, darker green lettering and pictures

SIZE: 13.5 × 19.5 cm. (5½ × 7¾")

DUST WRAPPER: Drawing by Roese

CONTENTS: The Crime Wave at Blandings, pp. 1–68; The Medicine Girl, pp. 69–188; Buried Treasure, pp. 189–214; The Masked Troubadour, pp. 215–45; Romance at Droitgate Spa, pp. 246–74; All's Well with Bingo, pp. 275–303; Tried in the Furnace, pp. 304–30.

NOTES: "The Medicine Girl" appeared in 1932 separately published as *Doctor Sally*; three stories are from *Lord Emsworth and Others*. The title story was published in *Saturday Evening Post*, 10–17 October 1936.

A59A Summer Moonshine

P. G. WODEHOUSE | Summer Moonshine | [publisher's device] | Doubleday, Doran and Company, Inc. | GARDEN CITY *1937* NEW YORK

COLLATION: [i–ii] *blank*; [iii] *synopsis*; [iv] *blank*; [v] *half title*; [vi] Books by P. G. Wodehouse; [vii] *title page*; [viii] *copyright page:* Printed at The Country Life Press . . . copyright 1937 . . . First Edition; [ix] *half title*; [x] *blank*; [1]–322, *text*; [323–26] *blank*

PUBLISHED: 8 October 1937 (price $2.00)

COVER: Yellow-orange cloth, green lettering and drawings

SIZE: 13.5 × 20 cm. (5½ × 7¾")

DUST WRAPPER: Drawing by Roese; $2.00

A59B First English edition

SUMMER | MOONSHINE | BY | P. G. WODEHOUSE | HERBERT JENKINS LIMITED | 3 DUKE OF YORK STREET | ST. JAMES'S LONDON, S.W.1 [double-rule frame]

COLLATION: [1] *half title*; [2] What This Story Is About; [3] *title page*; [4] *copyright page:* [publisher's device] First printing 1938 Printed in Great Britain by Wyman & Sons Ltd., London, Fakenham and Reading.; [5] *half title*; [6] *blank*; [7]–312, *text*; [313–20] *advertisements*

PUBLISHED: 11 February 1938 (price 7s6d); British Library reception date 11 February 1938

COVER: Red cloth, black lettering

SIZE: 12.75 × 18.75 cm. (5 × 7½")

DUST WRAPPER: Drawing by Fenwick; 7/6 green label

NOTES: Doubleday reissued in 1938 in orange cloth with black lettering and without the first edition statement.

Herbert Jenkins reprinted March 1939 (3s6d), March 1940, June 1949, and in 1956 in the Autograph Edition.

For the serial in *Saturday Evening Post*, 24 July – 11 September 1937, illustrated by Wallace Morgan, Wodehouse was paid $40,000.

A60A The Code of the Woosters

P. G. WODEHOUSE | [drawing] | THE CODE | OF THE WOOSTERS | DOUBLEDAY, DORAN & CO., INC. NEW YORK 1938

COLLATION: [i] *half title*; [ii] Books by P. G. Wodehouse; [iii] *title page*; [iv] *copyright page:* Printed at The Country Life Press, Garden City, N.Y., U.S.A. CL Copyright, 1938 . . . First Edition; [v] *half title*; [vi] *blank*; [1]–298, *text*

PUBLISHED: 7 October 1938 (price $2.00)

COVER: Yellow cloth, yellow and blue decorations, letters and drawing; same drawing as on title page

SIZE: 14 × 19.75 cm. (5½ × 7¾")

DUST WRAPPER: Drawing by Roese; $2.00

A60B First English edition

THE CODE OF THE | WOOSTERS | BY | P. G. WODEHOUSE | HERBERT JENKINS LIMITED | 3 DUKE OF YORK STREET | ST. JAMES'S LONDON, S.W.1 [double-rule frame]

COLLATION: [1] *half title*; [2] What This Story Is About; [3] *title page*; [4] *copyright page:* [publisher's device] First printing 1938 Printed in Great Britain by Wyman & Sons, Ltd., London, Fakenham and Reading.; [5] *half title*; [6] *blank*; [7]–312, *text*; [313–20] *advertisements*

PUBLISHED: 7 October 1938 (price 7s6d); British Library reception date 7 October 1938

COVER: Green cloth, black letters and design

SIZE: 12.5×19 cm. (5×7½″)

DUST WRAPPER: Drawing by Fenwick; (number on license plate of car: PGW 38); green label books 7/6

NOTES: Jenkins reissued in orange cloth with black letters, 1939 and 1940, and reprinted again in June 1949, and in 1962 in the Autograph Edition.

Serial in *Saturday Evening Post*, 16 July – 3 September 1938, illustrated by Wallace Morgan.

Sequel to *Right Ho, Jeeves*.

A61A Uncle Fred in the Springtime

P. G. WODEHOUSE | Uncle Fred | in the | Springtime | 1939 | DOUBLEDAY, DORAN & CO., INC. | New York

COLLATION: [i–ii] *blank*; [iii] *half title*; [iv] Books by P. G. Wodehouse; [v] *title page*; [vi] *copyright page*: Printed at The Country Life Press ... CL Copyright, 1939 ... First Edition; [vii] *half title*; [viii] *blank*; [1]–292, *text*; [293–96] *blank*

PUBLISHED: 18 August 1939 (price $2.00)

COVER: Green cloth, brown letters and decoration

SIZE: 14.5×20.5 cm. (5¾×8″)

DUST WRAPPER: Drawing by Peggy Bacon; $2.00

A61B First English edition

UNCLE FRED IN THE | SPRINGTIME | by | P. G. WODEHOUSE | HERBERT JENKINS LIMITED | 3 DUKE OF YORK STREET, ST. JAMES'S | LONDON S.W.1

COLLATION: [1] *half title*; [2] What This Story Is About; [3] *title page*; [4] *copyright page*: [publisher's device] First printing 1939 Printed in Great Britain by Wyman & Sons Ltd., London, Fakenham and Reading.; [5] *half title*; [6] *blank*; [7]–311, *text*; [312] *blank*; [313–15] List of the Works of P. G. Wodehouse; [316] *blank*

PUBLISHED: 25 August 1939 (price 7s6d); British Library reception date 25 August 1939

COVER: Dark red cloth, gold lettering on spine

SIZE: 12.5×19 cm. (5×7⅜″)

DUST WRAPPER: By Fenwick; 7/6 green label

NOTES: Jenkins reissued in orange cloth with black letters, October 1940, and in the Autograph Edition, 1962 which was reprinted 1978.

The novel first appeared in *Saturday Evening Post*, 22 April – 27 May 1939, illustrated by James Williamson.

Uncle Fred is Frederick Altamount Cornwallis, fifth Earl of Ickenham, "a sort of elderly Psmith" (*Performing Flea*, p. 85), who first appears in "Uncle Fred Flits By," collected in *Young Men in Spats* (1936).

A62A Eggs, Beans and Crumpets

EGGS, BEANS AND | CRUMPETS | by | P. G. WODEHOUSE | HERBERT JENKINS LIMITED | 3 DUKE OF YORK STREET, ST. JAMES'S | LONDON S.W.1

COLLATION: [1] *half title*; [2] What This Story Is About; [3] *title page*; [4] *copyright page*: [publisher's device] First Printing 1940 Printed in Great Britain by Wyman & Sons Ltd., London, Fakenham and Reading.; [5] Contents; [6] *blank*; [7]–284, *text*; [285] Books by P. G. Wodehouse; [286–88] *advertisements for Wodehouse books*

PUBLISHED: 26 April 1940 (price 7s6d); British Library reception date 26 April 1940

COVER: Orange cloth with black lettering

SIZE: 12.5×18.75 cm. (5×7½″)

DUST WRAPPER: Fenwick; 7/6 green label

CONTENTS: *All's Well with Bingo, pp. [9]–39; Bingo and the Peke Crisis, pp. [43]–72; The Editor Regrets, pp. [75]–99; Sonny Boy, pp. [103]–28; Anselm Gets His Chance, pp. [131]–59; *Romance at Droitgate Spa, pp. [163]–91; A Bit of Luck for Mabel, pp. [195]–223; Buttercup Day, pp. [227]–55; Ukridge and the Old Stepper, pp. [259]–84. (*Asterisks indicate stories from the collection *Crime Wave at Blandings* [New York, 1937].)

A62B First American edition

P. G. WODEHOUSE | Eggs, Beans and Crumpets | [publisher's device] | 1940 | Doubleday, Doran & Company, Inc. | NEW YORK

COLLATION: [i] *half title*; [ii] Books by P. G. Wodehouse; [iii] *title page*; [iv] *copyright page*: Printed at the Country Life Press, Garden City, N.Y., U.S.A. CL Copyright, 1925, 1926, 1928, 1931, 1935, 1937, 1939, 1940 by Pelham Grenville Wodehouse. ... First Edition; [v] Contents; [vi] *blank*; [vii] *half title*; [viii] *blank*; [1]–312, *text*

PUBLISHED: 10 May 1940 (price $2.00)

COVER: Green cloth, darker green letters and illustration

SIZE: 14.5×20.5 cm. (5⅝×8¼″)

DUST WRAPPER: Drawing by Hal McIntosh; $2.00 (illustrated)

CONTENTS: Ukridge and the Old Stepper, pp. 1–23; A Bit of Luck for Mabel, pp. 24–48; *The Level Business Head, pp. 49–72; Buttercup Day, pp. 73–98; *Ukridge and the Home from Home, pp. 99–124; *The Come-Back of Battling Billson, pp. 125–48; Sonny Boy, pp. 149–71; The Editor Regrets, pp. 172–93; Bingo and the Peke Crisis, pp. 194–219; Trouble Down at Tudsleigh, pp. 220–43; Bramley Is So Bracing, pp. 244–64; Anselm Gets His Chance, pp. 265–90; Scratch Man, pp. 291–312. (*Asterisks indicate stories from the collection *Lord Emsworth and Others* [London, 1937] not included in the English edition of *Eggs, Beans and Crumpets*.)

NOTES: Herbert Jenkins reissued June 1949 (5s), 1951, 1963 in the Autograph Edition, reprinted 1976.

Stories published in *Saturday Evening Post* (1937–39) and *Strand* (1937–39).

A63A Quick Service

QUICK SERVICE | *by* | P. G. WODEHOUSE | HERBERT JENKINS LIMITED | 3 DUKE OF YORK STREET, ST. JAMES'S | LONDON, S.W.1

COLLATION: [1] *half title*; [2] What This Story Is About; [3] *title page*; [4] *copyright page*: [publisher's device] First printing 1940 Printed in Great Britain by Wyman & Sons, Ltd., London, Fakenham and Reading; [5] *half title*; [6] *blank*; [7]–252, *text*; [253] Books by P. G. Wodehouse; [254–56] *advertisements*

PUBLISHED: 4 October 1940 (price 7s6d); British Library reception date 4 October 1940

COVER: Dark red cloth, gold lettering and decoration

SIZE: 13 × 18.75 cm. (5 × 7⅜″)

DUST WRAPPER: Illustration by Fenwick; 7/6

A63B First American edition

P. G. WODEHOUSE | *Quick Service* | [publisher's device] New York 1940 | Doubleday, Doran & Co., Inc.

COLLATION: [i–ii] *blank*; [iii] *half title*; [iv] Books by P. G. Wodehouse; [v] *title page*; [vi] *copyright page*: Printed at the Country Life Press, Garden City, N.Y., U.S.A. CL Copyright, 1940 . . . First Edition; [vii] *half title*; [viii] *blank*; [1]–310, *text*; [311–12] *blank*

PUBLISHED: 27 December 1940 (price $2.00)

COVER: Beige cloth, black letters and illustrations

SIZE: 14.5 × 20.5 cm. (5¾ × 8⅛″)

DUST WRAPPER: Illustration by Donald McKay

NOTES: Jenkins reissued three times in orange cloth with black letters through September 1948; the Autograph Edition was issued 1960 and reprinted 1978.

Serial in *Saturday Evening Post*, 4 May – 22 June, 1940, illustrated by Gilbert Bundy.

A64A Money in the Bank

P. G. WODEHOUSE | Money In The Bank | [publisher's device] | Doubleday, Doran & Company | GARDEN CITY, NEW YORK | 1942

COLLATION: [i–ii] *blank*; [iii] *half title*; [iv] Books by P. G. Wodehouse; [v] *title page*; [vi] *copyright page*: Printed at the Country Life Press, Garden City, N.Y., U.S.A. CL Copyright, 1941, 1942 . . . First Edition; [vii] *half title*; [viii] *blank*; [1]–300, *text*; [301–304] *blank*

PUBLISHED: 9 January 1942 (price $2.00)

COVER: Dark red cloth, black letters and drawing

SIZE: 14.5 × 20.75 cm. (5¾ × 8⅛″)

DUST WRAPPER: Illustrations by Donald McKay; $2.00

A64B First English edition

MONEY IN THE BANK | BY | P. G. WODEHOUSE | HERBERT JENKINS LIMITED | 3 DUKE OF YORK STREET, ST. JAMES'S, S.W.1

COLLATION: [1] *half title*; [2] What This Story Is About; [3] *title page*; [4] *copyright page*: [publisher's device] First printing . . . ; [5]–253, *text* (*bottom of page 253, printer's note*: Printed in Great Britain by Wyman & Sons, Ltd., London, Fakenham and Reading.); [254] *blank*; [255] Books by P. G. Wodehouse; [256] *advertisement*

PUBLISHED: 27 May 1946 (price 8s6d); British Library reception date 27 May 1946

COVER: Orange cloth, black lettering

SIZE: 13 × 19 cm. (5 × 7½″)

DUST WRAPPER: Drawing by Frank Ford; 8/6

NOTES: Albert Bonniers, Stockholm, 1942, reprinted the title from American plates and bound the edition in brown boards with a cloth spine and corners and with the series note "Clipper Books."

The English edition was reprinted in Holland (about 1946) by Drukkerij Holland N.V. and appeared in gray cloth with orange-brown lettering, printed on cheap paper.

From *Performing Flea* (p. 113): ". . . the only novel I should imagine, that has ever been written in an internment camp. I did it at the rate of about a page a day in a room with over fifty men playing cards and ping-pong and talking and singing. . . ."

Serial in *Saturday Evening Post*, 7 November – 27 December 1941, illustrated by Rudolph Pott.

A65A Joy in the Morning

P. G. WODEHOUSE | *JOY* | *in the morning* | *Illustrations by Paul Galdone* | [publisher's device] | DOUBLEDAY & COMPANY, INC. | GARDEN CITY, NEW YORK 1946

COLLATION: [i] *synopsis*; [ii] Books by P. G. Wodehouse; [iii] *title page*; [iv] *copyright page:* Copyright, 1946 by Pelham Grenville Wodehouse . . . Printed . . . at The Country Life Press, Garden City, New York. First Edition; [v] *half title*; [vi] *blank*; [1]–281, *text*; [282] *blank*

PUBLISHED: 22 August 1946 (price $2.00)

COVER: Gray cloth with green letters and faces on spine

SIZE: 13.5 × 19.75 cm. (5⅜ × 7⅞")

DUST WRAPPER: Illustrations by Galdone

NOTE: Illustrations throughout text by Paul Galdone.

A65B First English edition

JOY IN THE MORNING | *By* | P. G. WODEHOUSE | HERBERT JENKINS LIMITED | 3 DUKE OF YORK STREET, ST. JAMES'S | LONDON, S.W.1

COLLATION: [1] *half title*; [2] What This Story Is About; [3] *title page*; [4] *copyright page:* [publisher's device] First printing . . . ; [5]–256, *text* (*bottom of page 256, printer's note:* Printed in Great Britain by Wyman & Sons, Ltd., London, Fakenham and Reading.)

PUBLISHED: 2 June 1947 (price 8s6d); British Library reception date 2 June 1947

COVER: Bright orange cloth, black letters

SIZE: 13 × 19 cm. (5 × 7½")

DUST WRAPPER: Illustrations by Frank Ford; 8/6 green label

NOTES: The Continental Book Company, Stockholm, reprinted as a paperback, 1947, in their series Zephyr Books 156.

Herbert Jenkins reissued twice between 1947 and 1949 marked "Second printing": bright red cloth, gold letters, and plum cloth with gold letters.

Doubleday reissued in rust colored cloth with green letters, and lacking first edition statement.

A66A Full Moon

P. G. WODEHOUSE | *Full Moon* | *Illustrated by Paul Galdone* | [publisher's device] | DOUBLEDAY AND COMPANY, INC. | GARDEN CITY, NEW YORK 1947

COLLATION: [i–ii] *blank*; [iii] *half title*; [iv] Books by P. G. Wodehouse; [v] *title page*; [vi] *copyright page:* Copyright, 1947, . . . Printed . . . at The Country Life Press, Garden City, N.Y. First Edition; [vii] *half title*; [viii] *blank*; [1]–276, *text*; [277–80] *blank*

PUBLISHED: 22 May 1947 (price $2.00)

COVER: Bright blue cloth, black letters and drawing on spine

SIZE: 13 × 19.75 cm. (5⅛ × 7¾")

DUST WRAPPER: Illustration by Paul Galdone; $2.00

NOTE: Illustrations throughout by Paul Galdone.

A66B First English edition

FULL MOON | *By* | P. G. WODEHOUSE | HERBERT JENKINS LIMITED | 3 DUKE OF YORK STREET, ST. JAMES'S | LONDON S.W.1

COLLATION: [1] *half title*; [2] What This Story Is About; [3] *title page*; [4] *copyright page:* [publisher's device] First printing; [5] *half title*; [6] *disclaimer*; [7]–252, *text* (*bottom of page 252, printer's note:* Printed in Great Britain by Wyman & Sons, Ltd., London, Fakenham and Reading.)

PUBLISHED: 17 October 1947 (price 8s6d); British Library reception date 17 October 1947

COVER: Orange cloth, black letters

SIZE: 12.75 × 19 cm. (5 × 7½")

DUST WRAPPER: Frank Ford; 8/6

NOTES: Condensed for *Liberty*, November 1947.

A67A Spring Fever

Spring Fever | P. G. WODEHOUSE | [illustration by Paul Galdone] | *Illustrated by Paul Galdone* | DOUBLEDAY & COMPANY, INC. | GARDEN CITY, NEW YORK, 1948

COLLATION: [1] *half title*; [2] Books by P. G. Wodehouse; [3] *title page*; [4] *copyright page:* Copyright, 1948, by Pelham Grenville Wodehouse Printed . . . at The Country Life Press, Garden City, N.Y. First Edition; [5] *half title*; [6] *blank*; 7–223, *text*; [224] *blank*

PUBLISHED: 20 May 1948 (price $2.44)

COVER: Brown cloth, white lettering and flowers on spine

SIZE: 13.5×20 cm. (5⅜×7¾″)

DUST WRAPPER: Illustrated by Galdone; photograph on back of jacket by Ray Platnick; $2.44

A67B First English edition (simultaneously published)
SPRING FEVER | *By* | P. G. WODEHOUSE | HERBERT JENKINS LIMITED | 3 DUKE OF YORK STREET, ST. JAMES'S | LONDON, S.W.1

COLLATION: [1] *half title*; [2] The Story–; [3] *title page*; [4] *copyright page*: [publisher's device] First Printing; [5] Contents; [6] *disclaimer*; [7]–256, *text* (*bottom of page 256, printer's note*: Printed in Great Britain by Wyman & Sons, Ltd., London, Fakenham and Reading)

PUBLISHED: 20 May 1948 (price 8s6d); British Library reception date 21 May 1948

COVER: Orange cloth, black letters

SIZE: 12.75×19 cm. (5⅛×7½″)

DUST WRAPPER: Jacket illustration by Frank Ford

NOTES: According to Richard Usborne (*Wodehouse at Work to the End*, Penguin Books, page 155) Wodehouse turned *Spring Fever* into a play for Edward Everett Horton with an American setting and characters. Horton, because of other commitments, was unable to use the play so Wodehouse turned it into a new novel, *The Old Reliable* (1951).

A68A Uncle Dynamite
UNCLE DYNAMITE | *By* | P. G. WODEHOUSE | HERBERT JENKINS LIMITED | 3 DUKE OF YORK STREET, ST. JAMES'S | LONDON, S.W.1

COLLATION: [1] *half title*; [2] *synopsis*; [3] *title page*; [4] *copyright page*: [publisher's device] First Printing; [5] *half title*; [6] *disclaimer*; [7]–249, *text* (*bottom of page 249, printer's note*: Printed in Great Britain by Wyman & Sons, Ltd., London, Fakenham and Reading); [250] *blank*; [251] Books by P. G. Wodehouse; [252] *advertisements*

PUBLISHED: 22 October 1948 (price 8s6d); British Library reception date 22 October 1948

COVER: Orange-red cloth, black letters

SIZE: 13×19 cm. (5×7½″)

DUST WRAPPER: Drawing by Frank Ford

A68B First American edition
P. G. Wodehouse | *UNCLE* | *DYNAMITE* | DIDIER · NEW YORK | [double-spread illustration by Hal McIntosh]

COLLATION: [i] *half title*; [ii] *drawing*; [iii] *title page*; [iv] *copyright page*: Copyright, 1948, by P. G. Wodehouse . . . ; [v–vii] Who's Who in Uncle Dynamite; [viii] *blank*; [1] *drawing*; [2] *blank*; 3–312, *text*

PUBLISHED: 29 November 1948 (price $2.95)

COVER: Red cloth, silver letters

SIZE: 14×20.75 cm. (5½×8¼″)

DUST WRAPPER: Illustration by Hal McIntosh; $2.95

NOTE: Illustrations by Hal McIntosh throughout text.

NOTES: Both publishers reissued this title: Jenkins in orange-yellow cloth (5s); Didier with "Second printing" on the copyright page.
From *Performing Flea*, page 118: ". . . read Chapter Nine. . . . The whole of that chapter was written in the Inspecteurs' room at the Palais de Justice [Paris], with the lads crowding round to see how the stuff was going."
Condensed in *Liberty*, April 1949.

A69A The Mating Season
THE MATING SEASON | *By* | P. G. WODEHOUSE | HERBERT JENKINS LIMITED | 3 DUKE OF YORK STREET, ST. JAMES'S | LONDON, S.W.1

COLLATION: [1] *half title*; [2] The Story—; [3] *title page*; [4] *copyright page*: [publisher's device] First Printing Printed in Great Britain by Wyman & Sons, Ltd., London, Fakenham and Reading.; [5] Contents; [6] *disclaimer*; [7]–246, *text*; [247] *advertisements*; [248] Books by P. G. Wodehouse

PUBLISHED: 9 September 1949 (price 8s6d); British Library reception date 7 September 1949

COVER: Orange-red cloth, black letters

SIZE: 13×19 cm. (5×7½″)

DUST WRAPPER: Drawing by Frank Ford; 8/6

A69B First American edition
P. G. WODEHOUSE | *THE* | MATING SEASON | DIDIER · NEW YORK [line in italics] [drawing on title page and facing page of two young men in a fountain with a policeman in the distance]

COLLATION: [i–ii] *blank*; [iii] *half title*; [iv–v] *blank*; [vi] *frontispiece* [part of double-spread illustration]; [vii]

title page; [viii] *copyright page:* Copyright, 1949 . . . Jacket design and illustrations by Hal McIntosh . . . ; [ix] *half title*; [x] *blank*; [xi–xiii] Who's Who in The Mating Season; [xiv] *blank*; 1–287, *text*; [288–90] *blank*

PUBLISHED: 28 November 1949 (price $2.95)

COVER: Brick-red cloth, silver lettering

SIZE: 14.25×21 cm. (5⅝×8¼″)

DUST WRAPPER: Drawing by Hal McIntosh

NOTE: Ten illustrations in text by Hal McIntosh.

NOTES: The later edition [1951?] published by Jenkins is in orange-yellow cloth.

A70A Nothing Serious

NOTHING SERIOUS | *By* | P. G. WODEHOUSE | HERBERT JENKINS LIMITED | 3 DUKE OF YORK STREET, ST JAMES'S | LONDON, S.W.1

COLLATION: [1] *half title*; [2] This Book; [3] *title page*; [4] *copyright page:* [publisher's device] First Printing Printed in Great Britain by Wyman & Sons, Ltd, London, Fakenham and Reading; [5] Contents; [6] *blank*; [7] *half title*; [8] *disclaimer*; [9]–254, *text*; [255] Books by P. G. Wodehouse; [256] *blank*

PUBLISHED: 21 July 1950 (price 8s6d); British Library reception date 20 July 1950

COVER: Yellow-orange cloth, black letters

SIZE: 13×19 cm. (5⅛×7½″)

DUST WRAPPER: Drawing by Frank Ford on blue background; 8/6

CONTENTS: The Shadow Passes, pp. [9]–38; Bramley Is So Bracing, pp. [39]–60; Up from the Depths, pp. [61]–77; Feet of Clay, pp. [78]–110; Excelsior, pp. [111]–35; Rodney Has a Relapse, pp. [136]–61; Tangled Hearts, pp. [162]–87; Birth of a Salesman, pp. [188]–205; How's That, Umpire? pp. [206]–24; Success Story, pp. [225]–54

A70B First American edition

P. G. WODEHOUSE | Nothing | Serious [title in script] | GARDEN CITY, NEW YORK | Doubleday & Company, Inc. [name in script] | 1951

COLLATION: [1] *half title*; [2] Books by P. G. Wodehouse; [3] *title page*; [4] *copyright page: disclaimer* Copyright, 1939, 1947, 1948, 1949, 1950, 1951 . . . Printed . . . at The Country Life Press, Garden City, N.Y. First Edition; [5] Contents; [6] *blank*; [7] *half title*; [8] *blank*; [9]–222, *text*; [223–24] *blank*

PUBLISHED: 24 May 1951 (price $2.50)

COVER: Red cloth, black lettering on spine

SIZE: 13.5×19.5 cm. (5½×7¾″)

DUST WRAPPER: Same drawing by Frank Ford as on English dust wrapper but on white background; photograph of Wodehouse on back cover by Ray Platnick; $2.50

CONTENTS: The Shadow Passes, pp. [9]–34; Bramley Is So Bracing, pp. [35]–53; Up from the Depths, pp. [54]–68; Feet of Clay, pp. [69]–97; Excelsior, pp. [98]–119; Rodney Has a Relapse, pp. [120]–42; Tangled Hearts, pp. [143]–64; Birth of a Salesman, pp. [165]–79; How's That, Umpire? pp. [180]–96; Success Story, pp. [197]–222

NOTES: The Herbert Jenkins edition was also issued in bright orange cloth (1953?, 5s).

The story "Bramley Is So Bracing" was first collected in the American edition of *Eggs, Beans and Crumpets* (1940). This was the last Wodehouse story ever published by the *Strand* (December 1940).

A71A The Old Reliable

THE OLD RELIABLE | *By* | P. G. WODEHOUSE | LONDON: HERBERT JENKINS

COLLATION: [1] *half title*; [2] This Story; [3] *title page*; [4] *copyright page:* [publisher's device] First published by Herbert Jenkins Ltd. 3 Duke of York Street London, S.W.1 1951 Printed in Great Britain by Wyman & Sons, Ltd., London, Fakenham and Reading; [5] Contents; [6] *blank*; [7] *half title*; [8] *disclaimer*; [9]–233, *text*; [234] *blank*; [235] Books by P. G. Wodehouse; [236] *advertisements*

PUBLISHED: 18 April 1951 (price 9s6d); British Library reception date 13 April 1951

COVER: Orange cloth, black lettering

SIZE: 12.75×19 cm. (5⅛×7½″)

DUST WRAPPER: Drawing by Frank Ford; 9/6

A71B First American edition

The | *Old Reliable* | P. G. WODEHOUSE | *Doubleday & Company, Inc., Garden City* | *New York*, 1951

COLLATION: [i–ii] *blank*; [1] *half title*; [2] Books by P. G. Wodehouse; [3] *title page*; [4] *copyright page:* . . . Copyright, 1950, 1951, by Pelham Grenville Wodehouse . . . Printed in the United States at The Country Life Press, Garden City, N.Y., First Edition; [5] *half title*; [6] *blank*; 7–217, *text*; [218–22] *blank*

PUBLISHED: 11 October 1951 (price $2.75)

COVER: Tan cloth, red lettering on spine

SIZE: 13×19.25 cm. (5¼×7½″)

DUST WRAPPER: Drawing by Hurst; photograph on back cover; $2.75

NOTES: Herbert Jenkins reissued in rose cloth, black letters, identified as "Second impression" on the copyright page.

From dust wrapper: "This novel has appeared in serial form in *Collier's* magazine under the title, 'Phipps to the Rescue'" [published 24 June – 22 July 1950, illustrated by Harry Beckhoff].

"... that play of mine, the one I made into my novel, *The Old Reliable*. I wrote about six versions of it, but couldn't get it right, and finally handed it over to Guy [Bolton], who wrote almost a completely new play, which was wonderful.... Joe E. Brown wants to star in it...." (*Performing Flea*, p. 170, section dated 20 June 1952.)

A72A Barmy in Wonderland

BARMY | IN WONDERLAND | *By* | P. G. WODEHOUSE | LONDON: HERBERT JENKINS

COLLATION: [1] *half title*; [2] *synopsis*; [3] *title page*; [4] *copyright page*: First Published ... 1952 ... Printed in Great Britain by Wyman & Sons, Ltd., London, Fakenham and Reading; [5] *half title*; [6] *disclaimer*; 7–[222] *text*; [223] Books by P. G. Wodehouse; [224] *advertisements*

PUBLISHED: 21 April 1952 (price 9s6d); British Library reception date 4 April 1952

COVER: Red cloth, black letters

SIZE: 12.75×19 cm. (5×7½″)

A72B First American edition

Angel Cake | P. G. WODEHOUSE | DOUBLEDAY & COMPANY, INC. | *Garden City, N.Y., 1952*

COLLATION: [1] *half title*; [2] Books by P. G. Wodehouse; [3] *title page*; [4] *copyright page*: [*disclaimer*] Library of Congress Catalog Card Number: 52–5767 Copyright, 1952, by Pelham Grenville Wodehouse ... Printed ... at The Country Life Press, Garden City, N.Y. First Edition; [5] *dedication*: To the onlie begetter of these insuing sonnets Mr. G.S.K. [*i.e.*, George S. Kaufman]; [6] *blank*; [7] *half title*; [8] *blank*; 9–222, *text*; [223–24] *blank*

PUBLISHED: 8 May 1952 (price $2.75)

COVER: Brown cloth with blue-green lettering on spine

SIZE: 14×21 cm. (5½×8¼″)

DUST WRAPPER: Designed by Earl Oliver Hurst; photograph on back cover by Ray Platnick; $2.75

NOTE: Novelization of George S. Kaufman's play *The Butler and Egg Man*.

A73A Pigs Have Wings

Pigs Have Wings | BY P. G. WODEHOUSE | *Doubleday & Company, Inc. Garden City, New York, 1952* [title page a double page]

COLLATION: [i–ii] *blank*; [1] *half title*; [2] *blank*; [3] By P. G. Wodehouse; [4–5] *title page*; [6] *copyright page: disclaimer* Library of Congress Catalog Card Number: 52–10997 Copyright, 1952, by Pelham Grenville Wodehouse ... Copyright, 1952, by The Crowell-Collier Publishing Company Printed ... at The Country Life Press, Garden City, N.Y. First Edition; [7] *half title*; [8] *blank*; [9]–[219] *text*; [220–22] *blank*

PUBLISHED: 16 October 1952 (price $2.75)

COVER: Gray cloth, white lettering on spine

SIZE: 13.5×20.5 cm. (5⅜×8⅛″)

A73B First English edition

PIGS HAVE WINGS | *By* | P. G. WODEHOUSE | LONDON: HERBERT JENKINS

COLLATION: [1] *half title*; [2] The Story—; [3] *title page*; [4] *copyright page*: First Published ... 1952 ... Printed in Great Britain by Wyman & Sons, Ltd., London, Fakenham and Reading; [5] *half title*; [6] *disclaimer*; 7–[220] *text*; [221] Books by P. G. Wodehouse; [222] *advertisement*; [223–24] *blank*

PUBLISHED: 31 October 1952 (price 9s6d); British Library reception date 29 October 1952

COVER: Red cloth, black lettering

SIZE: 12.5×18.75 cm. (5×7½″)

DUST WRAPPER: Sax; 9/6 net

NOTES: Serial in *Collier's* 16 August – 20 September 1952, illustrated by Robert Fawcett.

A74A Ring for Jeeves

RING FOR JEEVES | *By* | P. G. WODEHOUSE | LONDON: HERBERT JENKINS

COLLATION: [1] *synopsis*; [2] *blank*; [3] *title page*; [4]

copyright page: First Published . . . 1953 . . . Printed in Great Britain by Wyman & Sons, Ltd., London, Fakenham and Reading; [5] *half title*; [6] *disclaimer*; 7–[222] *text*; [223] Books by P. G. Wodehouse; [224] *blank*

PUBLISHED: 22 April 1953 (price 9s6d); British Library reception date 22 April 1953

COVER: Red cloth, black letters

SIZE: 12.5×19 cm. (5×7½″)

DUST WRAPPER: Illustrations by Sax; 9/6

A74B First American edition

P. G. WODEHOUSE | The Return | of | Jeeves | [publisher's device] | SIMON AND SCHUSTER | NEW YORK · 1954

COLLATION: [i] *publisher's device*; [ii] *blank*; [iii] *title page*; [iv] *copyright page:* All rights reserved . . . copyright, 1953, 1954, by P. G. Wodehouse . . . First Printing Library of Congress Catalog Card Number: 54–5469 Manufactured in the United States of America by American Book–Stratford Press, Inc., New York, N.Y.; 1–219, *text*; [220] A Note about the Author

PUBLISHED: 15 April 1954 (price $3.50)

COVER: Tan cloth spine, charcoal gray boards, orange-brown lettering

SIZE: 14×20.75 cm. (5½×8¼″)

DUST WRAPPER: Designed by Dick Dodge; $3.50

NOTES: First Wodehouse novel published by Simon and Schuster, who published all the rest of Wodehouse's books in the United States.

The American edition is much revised from the English edition; it appeared in *Ladies' Home Journal*, April 1954, a "complete-in-one-issue novel."

Novelized version of P. G. Wodehouse's and Guy Bolton's play *Come On, Jeeves*. "This . . . is Guy Bolton's eighty-ninth play. It is the twentieth he and I have written together. . . . After I and Guy had written the play, I turned it into a novel. . . ." (Preface to the acting edition.) Bertie Wooster is mentioned in the play but does not appear.

A75A Bring on the Girls!

BRING ON | THE GIRLS! | The Improbable Story of Our Life in | Musical Comedy, with Pictures to Prove It | by | P. G. WODEHOUSE | and | GUY BOLTON | SIMON AND SCHUSTER [publisher's device] NEW YORK, 1953 [single-rule frame]

COLLATION: [i–ii] *blank*; [iii] *publisher's device*; [iv] *blank*; [v] *title page*; [vi] *copyright page:* All rights reserved . . . Copyright, 1953, by P. G. Wodehouse and Guy Bolton . . . First Printing . . . Library of Congress Catalogue Card Number: 53–10807 Dewey Decimal Classification Number: 792 Manufactured in the United States of America by H. Wolff Book Mfg. Co., New York, N.Y.; [vii–viii] *half title*; [ix–xxiv] *thirty-two photographs*; [1]–278, *text*; [279–80] About the Authors

PUBLISHED: 5 October 1953 (price $3.95)

COVER: Black boards, green cloth spine, red and darker green lettering and decoration on spine

SIZE: 14.5×21.75 cm. (5⅝×8⅝″)

DUST WRAPPER: Jacket design by Paul Bacon; $3.95

NOTE: Sixteen pages of photographs.

A75B First English edition

BRING ON THE | GIRLS | *The Improbable Story of Our Life in | Musical Comedy, with Pictures to Prove it | By* | P. G. WODEHOUSE | *and* | GUY BOLTON | LONDON: HERBERT JENKINS

COLLATION: [1] *half title*; [2] *blank*; [3] *title page*; [4] *copyright page:* First published . . . 1954 . . . Made and Printed in Great Britain by Wyman & Sons, Limited, London, Fakenham and Reading; [5] Contents; [6] *blank*; [7] Illustrations; [8] *blank*; [9] *half title*; [10] *blank*; [11]–248, *text*

PUBLISHED: 21 May 1954 (price 16s); British Library reception date 5 May 1954

COVER: Rose cloth, gold lettering on spine

SIZE: 14.5×22 cm. (5¾×8¾″)

DUST WRAPPER: 16/; photograph of chorus line on front cover

NOTE: The sixteen inserted pages of photographs differ from those in the American edition.

NOTES: "It is now just forty years since we started working on Broadway, during which time we wrote twenty-three shows together and met every freak that squeaked and gibbered along the Great White Way, so it ought to make an interesting book. It may turn out something which we can publish only in America, but I don't think so, as there will be a lot of London stuff in it, so many of our shows having been produced in England." (*Performing Flea*, p. 171.)

The English edition is much rewritten to emphasize London productions.

A76A Performing Flea

PERFORMING FLEA | *A Self-Portrait in Letters* | *By* | P. G. WODEHOUSE | *With an Introduction and Additional Notes by* | W. TOWNEND | LONDON: HERBERT JENKINS

COLLATION: [1] *half title*; [2] Books by P. G. Wodehouse; *frontispiece: photograph of Wodehouse with his signature across lower right corner*; [3] *title page*; [4] *copyright page:* First Published by Herbert Jenkins Ltd. . . . 1953 . . . Made and Printed in Great Britain by Wyman & Sons, Limited, London, Fakenham and Reading; [5] Contents; [6] *blank*; [7] *half title*; [8] *blank*; [9]–12, Introduction by W. Townend; [13]–218, *text*; [219]–24, Index

PUBLISHED: 9 October 1953 (price 12s6d); British Library reception date 2 October 1953

COVER: Blue cloth, gold lettering on spine and autograph on front cover (lower right corner)

SIZE: 14 × 22 cm. (5⅝ × 8¾″)

DUST WRAPPER: Photograph of Wodehouse on front cover

A76B First American edition

AUTHOR! | AUTHOR! | *P. G. Wodehouse* | *New York 1962* | SIMON AND SCHUSTER [in frame of S's]

COLLATION: [1] *publisher's device*; [2] Books by P. G. Wodehouse; [3] *title page*; [4] *copyright page:* . . . Copyright © 1953, 1962 . . . First Printing Library of Congress Catalog Card Number: 62–12415 Manufactured . . . by H. Wolff Book Mfg. Co., Inc., New York; [5] *dedication:* To Peter Schwed but for whom . . . ; [6] *blank*; 7–10, Introduction by W. Townend; [11]–191, *text*; [192] *blank*

PUBLISHED: 20 June 1962 (price $4.50)

COVER: Yellow boards, yellow cloth spine, red lettering and decorations

SIZE: 15.5 × 23.5 cm. (6⅛ × 9¼″)

DUST WRAPPER: Design by Janet Halverson; author's photograph courtesy Ira Rosenberg, *New York Herald Tribune*; $4.50

NOTES: Jenkins "Reprinted January 1954," so noted on the copyright page.

Author! Author! is extensively revised from the London edition.

A77A Jeeves and the Feudal Spirit

JEEVES AND THE | FEUDAL SPIRIT | *By* | P. G. WODEHOUSE | LONDON: HERBERT JENKINS

COLLATION: [1] *synopsis*; [2] *blank*; [3] *title page*; [4] *copyright page:* First Published . . . 1954 . . . Printed in Great Britain by Wyman & Sons, Ltd., London, Fakenham and Reading; [5] *half title*; [6] *disclaimer*; [7]–222, *text*; [223] Books by P. G. Wodehouse; [224] *advertisements*

PUBLISHED: 15 October 1954 (price 9s6d); British Library reception date 15 October 1954

COVER: Red cloth, black letters

SIZE: 12.25 × 19 cm. (4⅞ × 7½″)

DUST WRAPPER: 9/6

A77B First American edition

Bertie Wooster | Sees It Through | *by* | P. G. Wodehouse | [publisher's device] | Simon and Schuster | *New York* | 1955

COLLATION: [i] *publisher's device*; [ii] Books by P. G. Wodehouse; [iii] *title page*; [iv] *copyright page:* . . . © 1954, 1955 . . . First printing Library of Congress catalog card number: 55–5948 Manufactured . . . by American Book–Stratford Press, Inc., N.Y.; [v–viii] *dedication:* . . . to Peter Schwed . . . (signed P. G. Wodehouse, Colney Hatch, 1954); 1–246, *text*; [247] About the Author; [248] *blank*

PUBLISHED: 23 February 1955 (price $3.50)

COVER: Gray-blue boards, gray-blue cloth spine; gold and brown lettering and decorations

SIZE: 14 × 21 cm. (5½ × 8¼″)

DUST WRAPPER: Designed by Dick Dodge; $3.50

NOTES: Herbert Jenkins reissued June 1957 (6s), in the Autograph Edition 1962 and again 1966 (12s6d).

A78A French Leave

FRENCH LEAVE | *By* | P. G. WODEHOUSE | [publisher's device] | HERBERT JENKINS | LONDON

COLLATION: [1] *synopsis*; [2] *blank*; [3] *title page*; [4] *copyright page:* First Published . . . 1955 . . . Printed in Great Britain by Wyman & Sons, Ltd., London, Fakenham and Reading; [5] *half title*; [6] *disclaimer*; [7]–206, *text*; [207] The Books by P. G. Wodehouse; [208] *blank*

PUBLISHED: 20 January 1956 (price 10s6d); British Library reception date 9 January 1956

COVER: Red cloth, black letters

SIZE: 12.5×19 cm. (4⅞×7½″)

DUST WRAPPER: Illustrations by Sax; 10/6

A78B First American edition

French Leave | *by* | P. G. WODEHOUSE | [*publisher's device*] | SIMON AND SCHUSTER · NEW YORK · 1959

COLLATION: [i] *publisher's device*; [ii] *blank*; [iii] Books by P. G. Wodehouse; [iv] *blank*; [v] *title page*; [vi] *copyright page*: . . . © 1956, 1959 by P. G. Wodehouse . . . First Printing Library of Congress Catalog Card Number: 59-13139 Manufactured . . . by American Book–Stratford Press, Inc., New York; [1] *half title*; [2] *blank*; 3–213, *text*; [214] *blank*; [215] About the Author; [216–18] *blank*

PUBLISHED: 28 September 1959 (price $3.50)

COVER: Blue cloth, dark blue letters with dark blue and green drawings and decorations

SIZE: 14×20.75 cm. (5½×8¼″)

DUST WRAPPER: Design by Robert Shore; photograph on back cover by William Cole

NOTES: "Some time ago Guy Bolton wrote a play [*Three Blind Mice*]. It was a success in London as a straight play, and I believe was done as a musical over here. It was also made into not one but three motion pictures, all successful. (One of them was called Moon over Miami. I can't remember the other two.) Anyway I liked the story and made a novel of it, changing it a good deal, of course, in the process. . . . It was serialized in the Toronto Star and in John Bull in England [9–30 November 1955] and published as a book by Herbert Jenkins Ld. . . . it sold 40,000 in England and was a book club choice. . . ." (Letter to Bennett Cerf, 27 August 1957.)

A79A America, I Like You

P. G. WODEHOUSE | America, | I like you | ILLUSTRATIONS BY MARC SIMONT | 1956 | SIMON AND SCHUSTER, NEW YORK

COLLATION: [i–ii] *blank*; [iii] *publisher's device*; [iv] Books by P. G. Wodehouse; [v] *title page*; [vi] *copyright page*: . . . © 1956 . . . First Printing Library of Congress Catalog Card Number: 56–7486 Manufactured . . . American Book–Stratford Press, New York; [vii] Contents; [viii] *blank*; [1] *half title*; [2] *blank*; 3–212, *text*; [213–16] *blank*

PUBLISHED: 3 May 1956 (price $3.50)

COVER: Blue boards, white cloth spine; red, blue, gray letters and decorations

SIZE: 14.5×21.25 cm. (5¾×8⅜″)

DUST WRAPPER: Design by Peter Hollander; line drawings by Marc Simont; $3.50

CONTENTS: Thanks for the Memory, Such As It Is, pp. 3–25; An Old Sweetheart Who Has Put on Weight, pp. 26–41; Archie Had Magnetism, pp. 42–51; Hi, Bartlett!, pp. 52–65; Put Me among the Earls, pp. 66–80; The Meteorite Racket, pp. 81–90; To the Critics, These Pearls, pp. 91–110; My Iron Resolve to Take Ish, pp. 111–28; The Slave of a Bad Habit, pp. 129–38; Life among the Armadillos, pp. 139–47; Thin Blessings in Disguise, pp. 148–57; Gaughan the Deliverer, pp. 158–67; The Girl in the Pink Bathing Suit, pp. 168–78; Francis Bacon and the Play Doctor, pp. 179–200; Say It with Rattlesnakes, pp. 201–12.

A79B First English edition

OVER SEVENTY | *An Autobiography With Digressions* | *By* | P. G. WODEHOUSE | [*publisher's device*] | HERBERT JENKINS | LONDON

COLLATION: [1] *half title*; [2] Books by P. G. Wodehouse; [3] *title page*; [4] *copyright page:* First published by Herbert Jenkins . . . 1957 . . . Made and printed in Great Britain by Wyman & Sons, Ltd. London, Fakenham and Reading; [5] Contents; [6] *blank*; [7] *half title*; [8] *blank*; [9]–13, Foreword; [14] *blank*; [15]–190, *text*; [191] *blurbs from reviews of* Performing Flea; [192] *advertisement for Autograph Edition*

PUBLISHED: 11 October 1957 (price 16s); British Library reception date 3 October 1957

COVER: Red cloth, gold lettering

SIZE: 14×22 cm. (5⅝×8⅝″)

DUST WRAPPER: 16/

CONTENTS: Introducing J. P. Winkler, pp. [15]–27; Getting Started, pp. [28]–37; Bring on the Earls, pp. [38]–51; Good-by to Butlers, pp. [52]–58; Critics and the Criticized, pp. [59]–69; Raw Eggs, Cuckoos and Patrons, pp. [70]–81; Some Thoughts on Humorists, pp. [82]–88; Lives of the Hunted, pp. [89]–96; Bridge, Snails and Meteorites, pp. [97]–102; Crime, Does It Pay?, pp. [103]–9; Armadillos, Hurricanes and What Not, pp. [110]–19; Healthward, Ho!, pp. [120]–30; Shaking a Head at New York, pp. [131]–38; Things Aren't the Same, pp. [139]–42; How I Became a Poet, pp. [143]–51; Television, pp. [152]–59; The Girl in the Pink Bathing Suit, pp. [160]–66; The Theatre, pp. [167]–77; Christmas and Divorce, pp. [178]–84; My Methods, Such As They Are, pp. [185]–90.

A80A Something Fishy

SOMETHING FISHY | *By* | P. G. Wodehouse | [publisher's device] | HERBERT JENKINS | LONDON

COLLATION: [1] *synopsis*; [2] *blank*; [3] *title page*; [4] *copyright page:* First published . . . 1957 Made and Printed in Great Britain by Wyman & Sons, Ltd., London, Fakenham and Reading; [5] *half title*; [6] *disclaimer*; [7]–199, *text*; [200] *blank*

PUBLISHED: 18 January 1957 (price 10s6d); British Library reception date 7 January 1957

COVER: Red cloth, black lettering

SIZE: 12.5×19 cm. (4¾×7½″)

DUST WRAPPER: Drawing by Sax; 10/6

A80B First American edition

The Butler | Did It | by | P. G. WODEHOUSE | [publisher's device] | Simon and Schuster | *New York* · *1957*

COLLATION: [i] *publisher's device*; [ii] Books by P. G. Wodehouse; [iii] *title page*; [iv] *copyright page:* . . . © 1956, 1957 by P. G. Wodehouse . . . First Printing Library of Congress Catalog Card Number: 57–5676 Manufactured . . . American Book–Stratford Press . . . ; [v] *half title*; [vi] *blank*; 1–214, *text*; [215–18] *blank*

PUBLISHED: 28 January 1957 (price $3.50)

COVER: Black boards, pea-green cloth spine, silver letters

SIZE: 14×21.25 cm. (5½×8⅜″)

DUST WRAPPER: Jacket design by Dick Dodge; $3.50

NOTES: Simon and Schuster issued a second printing, so noted on the copyright page. Barrie and Jenkins reprinted in 1978.

Copyright page, American edition: "A short version of this book, in substantially different form, appeared in *Collier's* under the title 'Something Fishy'" [31 August, 14 September 1956, illustrated by Ronald Searle].

A81A Cocktail Time

COCKTAIL TIME | *By* | P. G. WODEHOUSE | [publisher's device] | HERBERT JENKINS | LONDON

COLLATION: [1] *synopsis*; [2] Books by P. G. Wodehouse; [3] *title page*; [4] *copyright page:* First Published . . . 1958 © P.G. Wodehouse, 1958 . . . Printed in Great Britain by John Gardner (Printers) Ltd., Liverpool 20; [5] *half title*; [6] *disclaimer*; 7–222, *text*; [223–24] *advertisements for the* Autograph Edition

PUBLISHED: 20 June 1958 (price 12s6d); British Library reception date 10 June 1958

COVER: Bright red cloth, black lettering

SIZE: 12.5×19 cm. (5×7½″)

DUST WRAPPER: Illustration by Hall; 12/6

A81B First American edition

Cocktail Time | *by* | P. G. WODEHOUSE | [publisher's device] | *Simon and Schuster · New York · 1958*

COLLATION: [i] *publisher's device*; [ii] Books by P. G. Wodehouse; [iii] *title page*; [iv] *copyright page:* . . . First Printing Library of Congress Catalog Card Number: 58–10351 Manufactured . . . American Book–Stratford Press . . . ; 1–219, *text*; [220] About the Author

PUBLISHED: 24 July 1958 (price $3.50)

COVER: Pink cloth spine, black boards, green and black lettering on spine

SIZE: 14×21 cm. (5½×8¼″)

DUST WRAPPER: Design by Robert Shore; $3.50

NOTES: Jenkins reissued 1958(?) in blue cloth with gold letters. Simon and Schuster issued a second printing, so marked on the copyright page.

Condensed version, *Ladies' Home Journal*, April 1958, as "complete-in-one-issue condensed novel."

A82A A Few Quick Ones

A Few Quick Ones | *by* | P. G. WODEHOUSE | [publisher's device] | SIMON AND SCHUSTER · NEW YORK · 1959

COLLATION: [i] *publisher's device*; [ii] Books by P. G. Wodehouse; [iii] *half title*; [iv] *blank*; [v] *title page*; [vi] *copyright page:* . . . © 1948, 1958, 1959 by P. G. Wodehouse © 1947 by Hearst Magazine, Inc. © 1953 by Crowell-Collier Publishing Co. © 1954 by The McCall Corporation © 1958 by HMH Publishing Company, Inc. © 1958 by United Newspaper Magazine Corp. . . . First Printing Library of Congress Catalog Card Number: 59–9497, . . . Kingsport Press, Inc., Kingsport, Tenn.; [vii] Contents; [viii] *blank*; 1–213, *text*; [214] *blank*; [215] About the Author; [216] *blank*

PUBLISHED: 13 April 1959 (price $3.50)

COVER: Gray boards, white cloth spine; bright pink signature in lower right-hand corner of front cover; black and bright pink lettering on spine with yellow and bright pink stripes

SIZE: 14×21 cm. (5⅜×8½″)

DUST WRAPPER: Design by Paul Bacon; $3.50

CONTENTS: Big Business, pp. 1–20; Scratch Man, pp. 21–42; The Right Approach, pp. 43–61; The Word in Season, pp. 62–82; The Fat of the Land, pp. 83–104; Leave It to Algy, pp. 105–22; Joy Bells for Walter, pp. 123–38; Unpleasantness at Kozy Kot, pp. 139–59; Freddie, Oofy and the Beef Trust, pp. 160–90; Jeeves Makes an Omelet, pp. 191–213.

A82B First English edition

A FEW QUICK ONES | *By* | P. G. WODEHOUSE | [publisher's device] | HERBERT JENKINS | LONDON

COLLATION: [1] *synopsis*; [2] The Books by P. G. Wodehouse; [3] *title page*; [4] *copyright page:* First Published ... 1959 ... Printed in Great Britain by John Gardner (Printers) Ltd., Liverpool, 20; [5] Contents; [6] *disclaimer*; 7–207, *text*; [208] *blank*

PUBLISHED: 26 June 1959 (price 12s6d); British Library reception date 25 June 1959

COVER: Red cloth, black lettering on spine

SIZE: 12.5×19 cm. (5×7½")

DUST WRAPPER: 12/6

CONTENTS: The Fat of the Land, pp. 7–27; Scratch Man, pp. 28–48; The Right Approach, pp. 49–67; Jeeves Makes an Omelet, pp. 68–89; The Word in Season, pp. 90–109; Big Business, pp. 110–28; Leave It to Algy, pp. 129–45; Joy Bells for Walter, pp. 146–61; A Tithe for Charity, pp. 162–78; Oofy, Freddie and the Beef Trust, pp. 179–207.

NOTES: Herbert Jenkins reissued the first edition, 1959(?), in black boards, gold letters, and a plain yellow dust wrapper.

"A Tithe for Charity" is not in American edition. A few of the stories had been published earlier in magazines: "A Tithe for Charity" and "The Right Approach" in *Playboy*, April 1955 and January 1959 respectively; "Big Business" appeared both in *Collier's*, 13 December 1959, and in *Lilliput*, March/April 1953; "The Fat of the Land" in *This Week*, 2 November 1958; and "Leave It to Algy" in *John Bull Magazine*, 16 May 1959.

A83A How Right You Are, Jeeves

HOW RIGHT YOU ARE, | JEEVES | *by* | P. G. WODEHOUSE | [publisher's device] | SIMON AND SCHUSTER · NEW YORK · 1960

COLLATION: [i] *publisher's device*; [ii] *blank*; [iii] Books by P. G. Wodehouse; [iv] *blank*; [v] *title page*; [vi] *copyright page:* Copyright © 1960 ... First Printing Library of Congress Catalog Card Number: 60-6106 Manufactured ... by George McKibbin and Son, Inc.; [vi] *half title*; [vii] *blank*; 1–183, *text*; [184] *blank*

PUBLISHED: 4 April 1960 (price $3.50)

COVER: Orange and white decorated boards, white cloth spine, black letters on spine with orange decorations

SIZE: 14×21 cm. (5½×8¼")

DUST WRAPPER: Jacket design by Robert Shore; $3.50

A83B First English edition

JEEVES | IN THE OFFING | *By* | P. G. WODEHOUSE | LONDON: HERBERT JENKINS

COLLATION: [1] *synopsis*; [2] Books by P. G. Wodehouse; [3] *title page*; [4] *copyright page:* First published by Herbert Jenkins Ltd. ... 1960 ... Printed in Great Britain by Charles Birchall & Sons Ltd. Liverpool and London; [5] *half title*; [6] *disclaimer*; 7–205, *text*; [206–8] *blank*

PUBLISHED: 12 August 1960 (price 13s6d); British Library reception date 22 August 1960

COVER: Red cloth, gold lettering on spine

SIZE: 12×19 cm. (4¾×7½)

DUST WRAPPER: 13/6

NOTES: According to David Jasen the first printing had a half title for *A Few Quick Ones*, which was corrected in the second printing (*A Bibliography and Reader's Guide*, p. 231). This error, however, was repeated in the 1979 Barrie and Jenkins reprint.

Jenkins reissued in tan boards with black letters, price 7/6.

The story first appeared in *Playboy*, February 1960, illustrated by Seymour Fleishman, and was in *John Bull Magazine*, 29 August – 19 September 1959.

A84A Ice in the Bedroom

THE | ICE | IN | THE | BEDROOM | *P. G. WODEHOUSE* | SIMON AND SCHUSTER | New York · 1961

COLLATION: [i] *publisher's device*; [ii] *blank*; [iii] *title page*; [iv] *copyright page:* ... First Printing Library of Congress Catalog Card Number: 61-5849. Manufactured ... by American Book–Stratford Press, N.Y.; [v] *half title*; [vi] *blank*; 1–246, *text*; [247] About the Author; [248–50] *blank*

PUBLISHED: 2 February 1961 (price $3.75)

COVER: Black boards, black cloth spine; white, yellow, red lettering

SIZE: 14×20.75 cm. (5½×8¼″)

DUST WRAPPER: Jacket design by Paul Bacon

A84B First English edition

P. G. Wodehouse | ICE IN | THE BEDROOM | LONDON: HERBERT JENKINS

COLLATION: [1] *synopsis*; [2] *note:* Please turn to page 224 for a list of books by P. G. Wodehouse; [3] *title page*; [4] *copyright page:* First published . . . 1961 . . . Made and Printed in Great Britain by William Clowes and Sons, Limited, London and Beccles; [5] *half title*; [6] *blank*; [7]–223, *text*; [224] Books by P. G. Wodehouse

PUBLISHED: 15 October 1961 (price 13s6d); British Library reception date 13 October 1961

COVER: Bright red boards with gold lettering on spine

SIZE: 12.5×19 cm. (4⅞×7½″)

DUST WRAPPER

NOTES: Herbert Jenkins also issued the first edition in red boards with black lettering.

A85A Service With a Smile

Service | with a | Smile | P. G. WODEHOUSE | [publisher's device] | SIMON AND SCHUSTER · NEW YORK | *1961*

COLLATION: [i] *publisher's device*; [ii] *blank*; [iii] Books by P. G. Wodehouse; [iv] *blank*; [1] *title page*; [2] *copyright page:* . . . © 1961 . . . First Printing Library of Congress Catalog Card Number: 61–12864 Manufactured . . . by H. Wolff, Inc., New York, N.Y.; [3] *half title*; [4] *blank*; 5–218, *text*; [219] About the Author; [220] *blank*

PUBLISHED: 15 October 1961 (price $3.75)

COVER: Blue-purple cloth, black boards, white letters

SIZE: 14.5×21.25 cm. (5¾×8⅜″)

DUST WRAPPER: Jacket design by Paul Bacon; $3.75

A85B First English edition

P. G. Wodehouse | SERVICE | WITH A SMILE | LONDON: HERBERT JENKINS

COLLATION: [1] *synopsis*; [2] Books by P. G. Wodehouse; [3] *title page*; [4] *copyright page:* First published . . . 1962 © P. G. Wodehouse 1961 . . . Made and Printed in Great Britain by William Clowes and Sons, Limited, London and Beccles; [5] *half title*; [6] *disclaimer*; 7–192, *text*

PUBLISHED: 17 August 1962 (price 13s6d); British Library reception date 30 July 1962

COVER: Red boards lettered in gold

SIZE: 12.5×19 cm. (4⅞×7½″)

DUST WRAPPER

NOTES: Simon and Schuster issued a second printing, which is so marked on the copyright page. Herbert Jenkins also issued the first edition in blue boards with gold lettering.

A86A Stiff Upper Lip, Jeeves

Stiff Upper Lip, | Jeeves | *by* | *P. G. Wodehouse* | [publisher's device] | SIMON AND SCHUSTER · NEW YORK · 1963

COLLATION: [1] *publisher's device*; [2] *blank*; [3] Books by P. G. Wodehouse; [4] *blank*; [5] *title page*; [6] *copyright page:* . . . © 1962 . . . First Printing A condensed version of this novel was serialized in Playboy Magazine. Library of Congress Catalog Card Number: 63–7423 Manufactured . . . by The Book Press, Inc., Brattleboro, Vermont; [7] *dedication:* To David Jasen; [8] *blank*; 9–221, *text*; 222–24 *blank*

PUBLISHED: 22 March 1963 (price $3.95)

COVER: Gray boards, gray buckram spine, bright blue author's name and title on spine, bright yellow publisher's name on spine

SIZE: 14×21 cm. (5½×8¼″)

DUST WRAPPER: Jacket design by Paul Bacon; photograph on back cover by Ira Rosenberg; $3.95

A86B First English edition

P. G. Wodehouse | STIFF UPPER LIP, | JEEVES | LONDON: HERBERT JENKINS

COLLATION: [1] *half title*; [2] *blank*; [3] *title page*; [4] *copyright page:* First published . . . 1963 © P. G. Wodehouse 1963 . . . Printed in Great Britain by John Gardner (Printers) Ltd., Liverpool, 20; [5] Contents; [6] *blank*; [7] *half title*; [8] *blank*; 9–189, *text*; [190–92] *blank*

PUBLISHED: 16 August 1963 (price 13s6d); British Library reception date 19 August 1963

COVER: Red boards, gold letters

SIZE: 12.5×19 cm. (4⅞×7½″)

DUST WRAPPER: 13/6

NOTES: Jenkins reissued in blue boards, in light gray boards, and in beige boards, all with black lettering, and all having the same dust wrapper as the first edition.

The story appeared in *Playboy*, March 1963, illustrated by Charmatz.

A87A Biffen's Millions

Biffen's Millions | *by* | *P. G. WODEHOUSE* | [publisher's device] SIMON AND SCHUSTER, NEW YORK, 1964

COLLATION: [1] *publisher's device*; [2] *blank*; [3] *title page*; [4] *copyright page:* . . . © 1964 . . . First Printing Library of Congress Catalog Card Number: 64–17499 Manufactured . . . by American Book–Stratford Press, Inc., New York; [5] Books by P. G. Wodehouse; [6] *blank*; 7–222, *text*; [223–24] *blank*

PUBLISHED: 14 July 1964 (price $4.50)

COVER: Bright yellow boards, orange cloth spine, with black lettering and drawing

SIZE: 14×21 cm. (5½×8¼")

DUST WRAPPER: Jacket design by John Alcorn; $4.50

A87B First English edition

FROZEN ASSETS | P. G. Wodehouse | LONDON: HERBERT JENKINS

COLLATION: [1] *synopsis*; [2] Books by P. G. Wodehouse; [3] *title page*; [4] *copyright page:* First published by Herbert Jenkins, Ltd. . . . 1964 © P. G. Wodehouse 1964 . . . Made and Printed in Great Britain by John Gardner (Printers) Ltd., Hawthorne Road, Liverpool.; [5] Contents; [6] *blank*; [7] *half title*; [8] *blank*; 9–219, *text*; [220] *blank*; [221–223] *advertisements for the Autograph Edition*; [224] *blank*

PUBLISHED: 14 August 1964 (Price 15s); British Library reception date 14 August 1964

COVER: Pink-red boards, gold lettering

SIZE: 13.25×20.25 cm. (5¼×8")

DUST WRAPPER: Illustration by Payne; 15/– net

NOTES: The Herbert Jenkins edition adds a concluding sentence.

The spine of the American edition gives the author's name as P. J. Wodehouse.

The story first appeared in *Playboy*, February and March 1964, illustrated by Charmatz, entitled "Biffen's Millions."

A88A The Brinkmanship of Galahad Threepwood

THE | BRINKMANSHIP | OF GALAHAD | THREEPWOOD | A BLANDINGS CASTLE NOVEL BY | P. G. | WODEHOUSE | SIMON AND SCHUSTER · NEW YORK

COLLATION: [1] *publisher's device*; [2] *blank*; [3] Books by P. G. Wodehouse; [4] *blank*; [5] *title page*; [6] *copyright page:* . . . © 1964 . . . First Printing Library of Congress Catalog Card Number: 65–10386 Manufactured . . . by American Book–Stratford Press, Inc. Designed by Eve Metz; [7] *dedication*: To Scott Meredith, prince of literary agents and best of friends; [8] *blank*; [9] *half title*; [10] *blank*; 11–223, *text*; [224] *blank*

PUBLISHED: 31 December 1964 (price $4.50)

COVER: Mustard boards, yellow cloth spine, blue and gold lettering and decorations

SIZE: 14×20.75 cm. (5½×8⅜")

A88B First English edition

P. G. Wodehouse | GALAHAD AT | BLANDINGS | LONDON: HERBERT JENKINS

COLLATION: [1] *synopsis*; [2] Books by P. G. Wodehouse; [3] *title page*; [4] *copyright page:* First published by Herbert Jenkins Ltd., 3 Duke of York Street, London, S.W.1. 1965 © P. G. Wodehouse 1965 . . . Printed in Great Britain by Bristol Typesetting Co. Ltd. . . . Bristol 2; [5] *half title*; [6] *blank*; 7–224, *text*

PUBLISHED: 26 August 1965 (price 16s); British Library reception date 9 August 1965

COVER: Red boards, gold lettering on spine

SIZE: 13×20.5 cm. (5×8")

DUST WRAPPER: Jacket by Payne; 16/– net

NOTES: Jenkins issued a "Second impression," so marked on the copyright page, in the identical binding as the first.

A89A Plum Pie

P. G. WODEHOUSE | *Plum Pie* | HERBERT JENKINS | London

COLLATION: [1] *synopsis*; [2] Books by P. G. Wodehouse; [3] *title page*; [4] *copyright page:* © 1966 by P. G. Wodehouse First published 1966 . . . Printed in Great Britain by Northumberland Press Limited Gateshead; 5, Contents; [6] *blank*; [7] *half title*; [8] *blank*; 9–285, *text*; [286–88] *blank*

PUBLISHED: 22 September 1966 (price 25s); British Library reception date 1 September 1966

COVER: Purple cloth, silver lettering on spine

SIZE: 13.25×20.25 cm. (5¼×8″)

DUST WRAPPER: 25s net

CONTENTS: Jeeves and the Greasy Bird, pp. 9–54; Sleepy Time, pp. 58–73; Sticky Wicket at Blandings, pp. 77–93; Ukridge Starts a Bank Account, pp. 97–114; Bingo Bans the Bomb, pp. 119–36; Stylish Stouts, pp. 140–58; George and Alfred, pp. 163–78; A Good Cigar Is a Smoke, pp. 183–202; Life with Freddie, pp. 207–74; Time like an Ever-Rolling Stream, pp. 275–77; Printer's Error, pp. 278–80; A Note on Humour, pp. 281–85; Our Man in America, pp. 55–57, 74–76, 94–96, 115–18, 137–39, 159–62, 179–82, 203–6.

A89B First American edition

P. G. Wodehouse | [decoration] | PLUM | PIE | [decoration] | SIMON AND SCHUSTER | NEW YORK

COLLATION: [i–ii] blank; [1] publisher's device; [2] blank; [3] Books by P. G. Wodehouse; [4] blank; [5] title page; [6] copyright page: . . . © 1966, 1967 . . . First Printing Library of Congress Catalog Card Number: 67-10900 Designed by Edith Fowler Manufactured . . . by H. Wolff, New York acknowledgments; [7] Contents; [8] blank; 9–252, text; [253–54] blank

PUBLISHED: 1 December 1967 (price $4.95)

COVER: Plum cloth, blue-gray boards, silver letters and decorations

SIZE: 14×21 cm. (5½×8¼″)

DUST WRAPPER: Jacket design by Lawrence Ratzkin; $4.95

CONTENTS: Jeeves and the Greasy Bird, pp. 9–55; Sleepy Time, pp. 56–72; Sticky Wicket at Blandings, pp. 73–89; Ukridge Starts a Bank Account, pp. 90–107; Bingo Bans the Bomb, pp. 108–25; Stylish Stouts, pp. 126–44; George and Alfred, pp. 145–60; A Good Cigar Is a Smoke, pp. 161–81; Life with Freddie, pp. 182–252.

NOTES: Simon and Schuster issued a second printing, so marked on the copyright page. Herbert Jenkins also reissued several times, the latest being 1978.

The short stories originally appeared in various issues of *Playboy*, January 1965 – December 1967. The last three selections of the English edition and the "Our Man in America" pieces were originally articles in *Punch*, 1954–63, and were not included in the American edition.

A90A The Purloined Paperweight

THE PURLOINED | PAPERWEIGHT | BY P. G. | WODEHOUSE | SIMON AND SCHUSTER · NEW YORK [all in italics]

COLLATION: [i] publisher's device; [ii] blank; [1] Books by P. G. Wodehouse; [2] blank; [3] title page; [4] copyright page: © 1967 . . . First Printing Library of Congress Catalog Card Number: 67-16724 Designed by Eve Metz Manufactured . . . by American Book–Stratford Press, N.Y.; [5] dedication: To Peter Schwed, best of publishers; [6] blank; [7] half title; [8] blank; 9–188, text; [189–90] blank

PUBLISHED: 12 May 1967 (price $4.50)

COVER: Gray boards, yellow cloth spine, decoration and lettering in blue

SIZE: 14×21 cm. (5½×8¼″)

DUST WRAPPER: Seymour Chwast; $4.50

A90B First English edition

P. G. WODEHOUSE | Company for Henry | HERBERT JENKINS | LONDON

COLLATION: [1] synopsis; [2] Books by P. G. Wodehouse; [3] title page; [4] copyright page: © 1967 . . . First published 1967 . . . Printed in Great Britain by Northumberland Press Limited Gateshead; [5] half title; [6] blank; 7–[222] text; [223–24] blank

PUBLISHED: 26 October 1967 (price 21s); British Library reception date 20 September 1967

COVER: Rust-colored cloth, white lettering on spine

SIZE: 13×20.25 cm. (5⅛×8″)

DUST WRAPPER: Jacket design: Osbert Lancaster; 21s

A91A Do Butlers Burgle Banks?

P. G. WODEHOUSE | Do | Butlers | Burgle | Banks? | Simon and Schuster New York

COLLATION: [1] publisher's device; [2] Books by P. G. Wodehouse; [3] title page; [4] copyright page: . . . © 1968 . . . First Printing Library of Congress Catalog Card Number: 68-22974 Designed by Edith Fowler . . . ; [5] half title; [6] blank; 7–191, text; [192] blank

PUBLISHED: 5 August 1968 (price $4.50)

COVER: Mustard boards, gray-blue cloth spine, gold lettering on spine

SIZE: 14×20.75 cm. (5½×8⅛″)

DUST WRAPPER: Design by John Alcorn; photograph by Ira Rosenberg; $4.50

A91B First English edition

P. G. WODEHOUSE | Do Butlers Burgle | Banks? | HERBERT JENKINS | LONDON

COLLATION: [1] *synopsis*; [2] Books by P. G. Wodehouse; [3] *title page*; [4] *copyright page:* © 1968 . . . First published 1968 . . . Printed in Great Britain by Northumberland Press Limited Gateshead; [5] *half title*; [6] *blank*; 7–[189] *text*; [190–92] *blank*

PUBLISHED: 19 September 1968 (price 21s); British Library reception date 15 August 1968

COVER: Green buckram, silver lettering on spine

SIZE: 13×20.25 cm. (5⅛×8″)

DUST WRAPPER: Design by Osbert Lancaster; 21s

NOTES: Herbert Jenkins published 10,000 copies of the first printing and 3500 copies of the second printing.

A92A A Pelican at Blandings

P. G. WODEHOUSE | A Pelican at Blandings | HERBERT JENKINS | LONDON

COLLATION: [1] *half title*; [2] Books by P. G. Wodehouse; [3] *title page*; [4] *copyright page:* © 1969 . . . First published 1969 . . . SBN 257 65096 2 Printed in Great Britain by Northumberland Press Limited Gateshead; 5–222, *text*; [223–24] *blank*

PUBLISHED: 25 September 1969 (price 25s); British Library reception date 28 August 1969

COVER: Black cloth, silver lettering on spine

SIZE: 13×20.5 cm. (5¼×8⅛″)

DUST WRAPPER: Jacket design by Osbert Lancaster; photograph on back cover by Tom Blau, Camera Press; 25s

A92B First American edition

No Nudes Is | Good Nudes | by P. G. WODEHOUSE | [publisher's device] | *Simon and Schuster* | NEW YORK

COLLATION: [1] *publisher's device*; [2] Books by P. G. Wodehouse; [3] *title page*; [4] *copyright page:* . . . copyright © 1970 . . . First printing SBN 671-20464-5 Library of Congress Catalog Card Number: 73-101887 Designed by Irving Perkins Manufactured . . . by The Book Press, Brattleboro, Vt.; [5] *half title*; [6] *blank*; 7–220, *text*, [221–22] *blank*

PUBLISHED: 11 February 1970 (price $4.95)

COVER: Orange-pink cloth spine, orange boards, black letters

SIZE: 14×21 cm. (5½×8¼″)

DUST WRAPPER: Jacket design by Barry Zaid; $4.95

A93A The Girl in Blue

P. G. WODEHOUSE | The Girl In Blue | [publisher's device] | BARRIE & JENKINS | LONDON

COLLATION: [1] *half title*; [2] Books by P. G. Wodehouse; [3] *title page*; [4] *copyright page:* © 1970 First published 1970 . . . SBN 214 65276 9 Printed in Great Britain by Northumberland Press Limited Gateshead; 5–[192] *text*

PUBLISHED: 29 October 1970 (price 26s); British Library reception date 14 October 1970

COVER: Blue cloth, gold lettering on spine

SIZE: 13×20.25 cm. (5×8″)

DUST WRAPPER: Illustration by Osbert Lancaster; back of wrapper: a recent photograph of the author in his Long Island home; 26 /

A93B First American edition

The Girl in Blue | *by* | P. G. WODEHOUSE | SIMON AND SCHUSTER | NEW YORK [decorative frame]

COLLATION: [1] *publisher's device*; [2] *blank*; [3] Books by P. G. Wodehouse; [4] *blank*; [5] *title page*; [6] *copyright page:* . . . © 1971 . . . First printing SBN 671-20802-0 Library of Congress Catalog Card Number: 76-133098 Designed by Edith Fowler . . . ; 7–190, *text*; [191–92] *blank*

PUBLISHED: 22 February 1971 (price $5.95)

COVER: Bright blue cloth, silver lettering and decoration

SIZE: 14.5×21.25 cm. (5⅝×8⅜″)

DUST WRAPPER: Same as English edition; design by Osbert Lancaster, photograph of Wodehouse on back of jacket by Tom Blau, Camera Press; $5.95

NOTES: Simon and Schuster issued a second and third printing, which are so marked on the copyright page. Barrie and Jenkins reprinted in 1979.

A94A Much Obliged, Jeeves

P. G. WODEHOUSE | Much Obliged, Jeeves | [publisher's device] | BARRIE & JENKINS | LONDON

COLLATION: [1] *half title*; [2] Books in Print by P. G. Wodehouse; [3] *title page*; [4] *copyright page:* . . . First published 1971 . . . ISBN 0 214 65360 9 Printed in Great Britain by Northumberland Press Limited Gateshead; 5–[192] *text*

PUBLISHED: 15 October 1971 (price £1.60); British Library reception date 10 September 1971

COVER: Blue cloth, gold letters on spine

SIZE: 13×20.5 cm. (5×8″)

DUST WRAPPER: Jacket by Osbert Lancaster; £1.60; photograph of P. G. Wodehouse at home (in color)

A94B First American edition

P. G. WODEHOUSE | Jeeves and the | Tie That Binds | SIMON AND SCHUSTER | NEW YORK [decorative frame]

COLLATION: [1] *publisher's device*; [2] Books by P. G. Wodehouse; [3] *title page*; [4] *copyright page*: . . . copyright © 1971 . . . First printing SBN 671–21038–6 Library of Congress Catalog Card Number: 75–159142 Designed by Edith Fowler Manufactured . . . by H. Wolff Book Mfg. Co., Inc., New York; [5] *half title*; [6] *blank*; 7–189, *text*; [190–92] *blank*

PUBLISHED: 15 October 1971 (price $5.00)

COVER: Yellow cloth, black letters

SIZE: 14.5×21.5 cm. (5¾×8½″)

DUST WRAPPER: Jacket design by Osbert Lancaster; photograph by Tom Blau; $5

NOTES: Barrie and Jenkins reprinted in 1969. G. K. Hall, Boston, 1971, reprinted the American edition in a "Large Print Edition."

A95A Pearls, Girls and Monty Bodkin

P. G. WODEHOUSE | Pearls, Girls and | Monty Bodkin | [publisher's device] | BARRIE & JENKINS | LONDON

COLLATION: [1] *half title*; [2] Books by P. G. Wodehouse; [3] *title page*; [4] *copyright page*: . . . © 1972 . . . First published 1972 . . . ISBN 0 214 66814 2 Printed in Great Britain Northumberland Press Limited Gateshead; [5] *dedication*: To Sheran with love; [6] *blank*; 7–[192] *text*

PUBLISHED: 12 October 1972 (price £2.20); British Library reception date 2 October 1972

COVER: Green cloth, gold lettering on spine

SIZE: 12×20.5 cm. (5⅛×8″)

DUST WRAPPER: Illustration by Osbert Lancaster; photograph by Bernard Gotfryd on back cover; £2.20

A95B First American edition

THE | PLOT | THAT | THICKENED | P. G. WODEHOUSE | SIMON AND SCHUSTER · NEW YORK

COLLATION: [i] *publisher's device*; [ii–1] Books by P. G. Wodehouse; [2] *blank*; [3] *title page*; [4] *copyright page*: Copyright © 1973 . . . SBN 671–21572–8 Library of Congress Catalog Card Number: 73–8028 Designed by Edith Fowler . . . ; [5] *half title*; [6] *blank*; 7–221, *text*; [222] *blank*

PUBLISHED: 6 August 1973 (price $6.95)

COVER: Brown cloth, gold letters and decorations

SIZE: 14×21 cm. (5⅝×8¼″)

DUST WRAPPER: Design by Paul Bacon; photograph on back cover by Jill Krementz; $6.95

NOTES: The American Edition was reissued in a "Large Print Edition" by G. K. Hall, 1974.

A96A Bachelors Anonymous

P. G. WODEHOUSE | Bachelors Anonymous | [publisher's device] | BARRIE & JENKINS | LONDON

COLLATION: [1] *half title*; [2] Books by P. G. Wodehouse; [3] *title page*; [4] *copyright page*: First published in 1973 . . . ISBN 0 214 66889 4 . . . Printed in Great Britain by Northumberland Press Limited Gateshead; [5–6] *blank*; 7–[191], *text*; [192] *blank*

PUBLISHED: 15 October 1973 (price £1.95); British Library reception date 2 October 1973

COVER: Green cloth, gold lettering on spine

SIZE: 13×20.5 cm. (5⅛×8⅛″)

DUST WRAPPER: Illustration by Osbert Lancaster; photograph of P. G. Wodehouse in his Long Island home by Tom Blau, courtesy Camera Press; £1.95

A96B First American edition

Bachelors | *Anonymous* | P. G. Wodehouse | SIMON AND SCHUSTER · NEW YORK [decorated with cupids around title]

COLLATION: [i–ii] *blank*; [1] *publisher's device*; [2–3] Books by P. G. Wodehouse; [4] *blank*; [5] *title page*; [6] *copyright page*: copyright © 1974 . . . Designed by Edith Fowler . . . Library of Congress Cataloging in Publication Data . . . 74–5030 ISBN 0–671–21741–0; [7] *dedication*: To Peter Schwed, as always; [8] *blank*; 9–186, *text*; [187–90] *blank*

PUBLISHED: 28 August 1974 (price $6.95)

COVER: Blue cloth, silver letters and decorations

SIZE: 14×21 cm. (5½×8¼″)

DUST WRAPPER: Same as English edition; $6.95

NOTES: G. K. Hall, 1974, reissued the American edition in a "Large Print Edition."

A97A Aunts Aren't Gentlemen

P. G. WODEHOUSE | Aunts Aren't Gentlemen | *A Jeeves and Bertie Story* | [publisher's device] | BARRIE & JENKINS | LONDON

COLLATION: [1] *half title*; [2] Books by P. G. Wodehouse; [3] *title page*; [4] *copyright page:* First published in 1974 ... ISBN 0 214 20047 7 ... © P. G. Wodehouse 1974 ... Printed in Great Britain by Clarke, Doble & Brendon Ltd, Plymouth; 5–176, *text*

PUBLISHED: October 1974 (price £2.25); British Library reception date 3 September 1974

COVER: Blue cloth, gold letters and decorations

SIZE: 13×20.5 cm. (5¼×8⅛″)

DUST WRAPPER: Illustration by Osbert Lancaster; photograph of Wodehouse on back cover; £2.25

A97B First American edition

P. G. WODEHOUSE | *THE CAT-NAPPERS* | *A Jeeves and Bertie Story* | [drawing] | SIMON AND SCHUSTER · NEW YORK

COLLATION: [1] *publisher's device*; [2–3] Books by P. G. Wodehouse; [4] *blank*; [5] *title page*; [6] *copyright page:* Copyright © 1974 ... Designed by Edith Fowler ... Library of Congress Cataloging in Publication Data: ... 74-23181 ISBN 0-671-21972-3; [7] *half title (with drawing)*; [8] *blank*; 9–190, *text*; [191–92] *blank*

PUBLISHED: 14 April 1975 (price $6.95)

COVER: Brown boards, black drawing on front cover, gold lettering on spine

SIZE: 14×21 cm. (5½×8¼″)

DUST WRAPPER: Designs by Norman Green; photograph on back cover by Jill Krementz; $6.95

NOTE: Notice on inside of back flap of dust wrapper of Wodehouse's death.

A98A Sunset at Blandings

SUNSET AT | BLANDINGS | P. G. WODEHOUSE | With Notes and Appendices | *by* | RICHARD USBORNE | Illustrations by Ionicus | 1977 | CHATTO & WINDUS | LONDON

COLLATION: [1] *half title*; [2] *blank*; [3] *title page*; [4] *copyright page:* Published by Chatto & Windus Ltd ... Clarke, Irwin & Co. Ltd. Toronto ... British Library Cataloging in Publication Data ... ISBN 0-7011-2237-4 Text © The Estate of P. G. Wodehouse, 1977. Appendices, notes, and illustrations © Chatto & Windus Ltd., 1977. Printed in Great Britain by Ebenezer Baylis & Son Limited The Trinity Press, Worcester, and London; [5] Contents; [6] *blank*; [7] Illustrations; [8] *blank*; [9] *half title*; [10] *blank*; 11–213, *text*; [214–16] *blank*

PUBLISHED: 17 November 1977 (price £3.95); British Library reception date 24 October 1977

COVER: Bright blue boards, gold letters

SIZE: 13.25×20.5 cm. (8×5½″)

DUST WRAPPER: Illustrations by Ionicus; £3.95

ENDPAPERS: Map of Blandings Castle by Ionicus

NOTE: Peter Schwed indicated the English edition appeared 25 August 1977; the 17 November date was supplied by Richard Usborne.

CONTENTS: Chapters 1–16, pp. 7–103; Appendices by Richard Usborne: Work in Progress, pp. 104–68; The Castle and Its Surroundings, pp. 169–86; The Trains between Paddington and Market Blandings, pp. 187–99; Notes to the Text, pp. 200–13.

A98B First American edition

Sunset at Blandings | P. G. WODEHOUSE | [drawing of castle] | WITH NOTES AND APPENDICES BY | RICHARD USBORNE | ILLUSTRATIONS BY IONICUS | SIMON AND SCHUSTER · NEW YORK

COLLATION: [i] *blank*; [ii–iii] map of Blandings Castle and environs; [iv] *blank*; [v] *publisher's device*; [vi–1] Other Books by P. G. Wodehouse; [2] *blank*; [3] *title page*; [4] *copyright page:* Text copyright © 1977 ... ISBN 0-671-24293-8 ... 78-2188; [5] Contents; [6] *blank*; [7] Illustrations; [8] *blank*; [9] *half title*; [10] *blank*; 11–216, *text*; [217–218] *blank*

PUBLISHED: 19 September 1978 (price $8.95)

COVER: Brown and black cloth, white lettering and drawing

SIZE: 14.5×21.5 cm. (5¾×8½″)

DUST WRAPPER: Book jacket same as English edition; $8.95

CONTENTS: Sunset at Blandings, pp. 11–103; Work in Progress, pp. 104–68; The Castle and Its Surroundings, pp. 169–86; The Trains between Paddington and Market Blandings, pp. 187–99; Notes to the Text, pp. 200–13; Note to the American Reader, pp. 215–16; [217–18] *blank*

NOTES: Wodehouse had completed sixteen of twenty-two chapters for this novel when he died. Richard Usborne edited the incomplete manuscript and added all the notes Wodehouse had made for the last six chapters to show how Wodehouse crafted his novels.

Ionicus, the illustrator, provided the covers for most all of the Penguin Books editions of Wodehouse's work.

Quest

QUEST | By [in script] | P. G. WODEHOUSE | This story first appeared in the Strand Magazine in 1931. It later | appeared in the book Mulliner Nights, but with the beginning and end | materially changed. It is here, with the permission of the author, | reprinted in its original form, because I think it to be his masterpiece, | a plot to stir the envy of Sophocles, and a continual brilliance of | phrase to sparkle for ever on the forefinger of Time. | Alan Salisbury | Kingweston | Somerset | 1975

COLLATION: [1] *title page*; [2] *blank*; 3–14, *text*; [15–16] *blank*

PUBLISHED: Privately; British Library reception date 30 April 1975

COVER: Blue paper wrappers which have no lettering

SIZE: 16.67×24.67 cm. (6½×9⅝″)

NOTE: Illustrated by Treyer Evans; originally published in the *Strand*, LXXXII, July 1931, pages 2–14.

Omnibus Volumes

CHRONOLOGICAL LIST

1931	*Jeeves Omnibus*	1967	*A Carnival of Modern Humor*
1932	*Nothing But Wodehouse*	1973	*The Golf Omnibus*
1934	*P. G. Wodehouse (Methuen's Library of Humour)*	1974	*The World of Psmith*
1934	*A Century of Humour*	1975	*The World of Ukridge*
1935	*Mulliner Omnibus*	1976	*The World of Blandings*
1939	*The Week-End Wodehouse*	1976	*Jeeves, Jeeves, Jeeves*
1940	*Wodehouse on Golf*	1976	*The Uncollected Wodehouse*
1949	*The Best of Wodehouse*	1977	*Vintage Wodehouse*
1951	*The Best of Modern Humor*	1979	*The Swoop and Other Stories*
1952	*The Week-End Book of Humor*	1980	*The Eighteen-Carat Kid*
1958	*Selected Stories*	1980	*Wodehouse on Wodehouse*
1960	*The Most of P. G. Wodehouse*		

B1A Jeeves Omnibus

JEEVES | OMNIBUS | BY | P. G. WODEHOUSE | HERBERT JENKINS LIMITED | 3 YORK STREET ST. JAMES'S | LONDON S.W.1 [three ornaments] [double-rule frame]

COLLATION: [i] *half title*; [ii] *blank; frontispiece: photograph of Wodehouse*; [iii] *title page*; [iv] *copyright page:* First printing 1931 Made and Printed in Great Britain by Ebenezer Baylis and Son, Limited, The Trinity Press, Worcester, and London; v–viii, Introduction (*by* Wodehouse); ix–x, Contents; [xi] *half title*; [xii] *blank*; 13–847, *text*; [848] *blank*

PUBLISHED: 30 October 1931 (price 7s6d); British Library reception date 30 October 1931

COVER: Green cloth, black lettering and decoration

SIZE: 13.25×19.5 cm. (5⅛×7¾″)

CONTENTS: Jeeves Takes Charge, pp. 13–42; Jeeves in the Springtime, pp. 43–63; Scoring off Jeeves, pp. 64–81; Sir Roderick Comes to Lunch, pp. 82–100; Aunt Agatha Takes the Count, pp. 101–20; The Artistic Career of Corky, pp. 121–43; Jeeves and the Chump Cyril, pp. 144–69; Jeeves and the Unbidden Guest, pp. 170–96; Jeeves and the Hard-Boiled Egg, pp. 197–222; The Aunt and the Sluggard, pp. 223–57; Comrade Bingo, pp. 258–81; The Great Sermon Handicap, pp. 282–305; The Purity of the Turf, pp. 306–29; The Metropolitan Touch, pp. 330–57; The Delayed Exit of Claude and Eustace, pp. 358–83; Bingo and the Little Woman, pp. 384–409; The Rummy Affair of Old Biffy, pp. 410–42; Without the Option, pp. 443–75; Fixing It for Freddie, pp. 476–501; Clustering Round Young Bingo, pp. 502–37; Jeeves and the Impending Doom, pp. 538–66; The Inferiority Complex of Old Sippy, pp. 567–90; Jeeves and the Yule-Tide Spirit, pp. 591–617; Jeeves and the Song of Songs, pp. 618–45; Episode of the Dog McIntosh, pp. 646–70; The Spot of Art, pp. 671–700; Jeeves and the Kid Clementina, pp. 701–28; The Love That Purifies, pp. 729–57; Jeeves and the Old School Chum, pp. 758–88; Indian Summer of an Uncle, pp. 789–816; The Ordeal of Young Tuppy, pp. 817–47.

NOTES: Stories from *The Inimitable Jeeves* (1923); *Carry On, Jeeves!* (1925); *Very Good, Jeeves* (1930). Reissued by Herbert Jenkins in 1967 entitled *The World of Jeeves* (British Library reception date 13 July 1967) with the addition of three short stories: "Bertie Changes His Mind," "Jeeves Makes an Omelet," and "Jeeves and the Greasy Bird."

In the United States, this later edition was issued by Manor Books, New York, 1974.

B2A Nothing But Wodehouse

P. G. WODEHOUSE | Nothing But Wodehouse | EDITED BY OGDEN NASH | [publisher's device] | Doubleday, Doran & Company, Inc. | Garden City 1932 New York

COLLATION: [i] *half title*; [ii] Books by P. G. Wodehouse; [iii] *title page*; [iv] *copyright page*: . . . Printed . . . at The Country Life Press . . . First Edition; v–vi, Foreword (*signed by* Ogden Nash); vii–ix, Contents; [x] *blank*; [xi] Introduction: The work of P. G. Wodehouse needs no introduction. O.N.; [xii] *blank*; [various pagings (1051 p.)] *text*; [*last three unnumbered pages*] *blank*

PUBLISHED: 20 July 1932 (price $2.39)

COVER: Orange cloth, orange on black letters, black drawings on spine

SIZE: 13.75×21 cm. (5½×8¼")

CONTENTS: *Section One* (from *Jeeves*): Jeeves Exerts the Old Cerebellum, No Wedding Bells for Bingo; Introducing Claude and Eustace, Sir Roderick Comes to Lunch; The Great Sermon Handicap; The Purity of the Turf; (from *Very Good, Jeeves*): Jeeves and the Yuletide Spirit; Jeeves and the Song of Songs; Jeeves and the Love That Purifies; Jeeves and the Old School Chum; The Indian Summer of an Uncle; *Section Two* (from *He Rather Enjoyed It*): Ukridge's Dog College; Ukridge's Accident Syndicate; First Aid for Dora; Ukridge Sees Her Through; No Wedding Bells for Him; Ukridge Rounds a Nasty Corner; *Section Three* (from *Meet Mr. Mulliner*): The Truth about George; The Ordeal of Osbert Mulliner; Unpleasantness at Bludleigh Court; Something Squishy; *Section Four* (complete novel – *Leave It to Psmith*)

NOTES: Text is made from plates of the original edition throughout—page numbers and all—so they have no continuity.

The collection was reprinted in 1933 and 1936 by Garden City Publishing Company, Garden City, New York, with the same various paging. (The name of this publisher appears on the title page.) Doubleday issued in 1946 with the text reset throughout and numbering 696 pages; Section III, Mulliner Stories, was changed to include three extra Mulliner stories: "A Slice of Life," "Mulliner's Buck-U-Uppo," and "The Reverent Wooing of Archibald."

B3A P. G. Wodehouse (Methuen's Library of Humour)

Methuen's | Library of Humour | Edited by E. V. Knox | P. G. | WODEHOUSE | [drawing of comic mask] | Methuen & Co. Ltd. | 36 Essex Street, W.C.2 | LONDON [single-rule frame]

COLLATION: [i] *half title*; [ii] *series title* Each volume F'cap 8vo, 2s. 6d. net; [iii] *title page*; [iv] *copyright page*: First published in 1934 . . . ; v, Note; vi, Contents; 1–153, *text*; [154] *printer's note*: Printed by Jarrold and Sons Ltd. Norwich

PUBLISHED: February 1934 (price 2s6d); British Library reception date 22 February 1934

COVER: Orange-brown cloth, gold lettering (drawing of fool with comic mask stamped on front cover)

SIZE: 11×17.25 cm. (4¼×6½")

DUST WRAPPER: Drawing by Hendy; 2/6

CONTENTS: A Sea of Troubles, pp. 1–20 (from *The Man with Two Left Feet*); Painful Affair at a Coffee-

Stall, pp. 21–30 (from *Sam the Sudden*); Extricating Young Gussie, pp. 31–63 (from *The Man with Two Left Feet*); The Salvation of George Mackintosh, pp. 64–90; (from *The Clicking of Cuthbert*); Horace Changes His Mind, pp. 91–111 (from *Bill the Conqueror*); Love and Poetry, pp. 112–24 (from *The Small Bachelor*); Deep Waters, pp. 125–53 (from *The Man Upstairs*).

B4A A Century of Humour

A CENTURY OF | HUMOUR | *Edited by* | P. G. WODEHOUSE | *London:* | HUTCHINSON & CO. (PUBLISHERS) LTD.

COLLATION: [1] *half title*; [2] *blank*; [3] *title page*; [4] *copyright page:* Made and printed in Great Britain by The Hutchinson Printing Trust Ltd., London; [5–6] Acknowledgements; 7–9, Preface (*signed by* P. G. Wodehouse); [10] *blank*; xi–xiv, Contents; [15]–1024, *text*

PUBLISHED: September 1934 (price 3s6d); British Library reception date 23 November 1938

SIZE: 14×22 cm. (5½×8⅝″)

COVER: Yellow cloth, black letters and drawing

DUST WRAPPER: 3/6

CONTENTS: The Exit of Battling Billson, pp. 707–25 (only Wodehouse story).

NOTES: Hutchinson reissued December 1934 in two more expensive bindings: half-leather (7s6d) and imitation leather (5s6d).

Selections also from Ian Hay and Bill Townend.

B5A Mulliner Omnibus

MULLINER | OMNIBUS | BY | P. G. WODEHOUSE | HERBERT JENKINS LIMITED | 3 YORK STREET, ST. JAMES'S | LONDON, S.W.1 [three ornaments] [double-rule frame]

COLLATION: [1] *half title*; [2] *blank*; *portrait frontispiece*; [3] *title page*; [4] *copyright page:* [publisher's device] First printing 1935 ... Printed in Great Britain by Purnell and Sons Ltd. Paulton (Somerset) and London; v–vi, Contents; [7] *half title*; [8] *blank*; 9–864, *text*

PUBLISHED: 25 October 1935 (price 7s6d); British Library reception date 26 October 1935

COVER: Apple-green cloth, dark green letters and decorations

SIZE: 13.5×19.5 cm. (5¼×7⅝″)

DUST WRAPPER: Illustrated by Abbey; 7/6

CONTENTS: The Truth about George, pp. 9–31; A Slice of Life, pp. 32–52; Mulliner's Buck-U-Uppo, pp. 53–76; The Bishop's Move, pp. 77–102; Came the Dawn, pp. 103–25; The Story of William, pp. 126–47; Portrait of a Disciplinarian, pp. 148–71; The Romance of a Bulb-Squeezer, pp. 172–94; Honeysuckle Cottage, pp. 195–228; The Reverent Wooing of Archibald, pp. 229–54; The Man Who Gave Up Smoking, pp. 255–81; The Story of Cedric, pp. 282–317; The Ordeal of Osbert Mulliner, pp. 318–34; Unpleasantness at Bludleigh Court, pp. 335–61; Those in Peril on the Tee, pp. 362–88; Something Squishy, pp. 389–418; The Awful Gladness of the Mater, pp. 419–54; The Passing of Ambrose, pp. 455–81; The Smile That Wins, pp. 482–508; The Story of Webster, pp. 509–37; Cats Will Be Cats, pp. 538–68; The Knightly Quest of Mervyn, pp. 569–96; The Voice from the Past, pp. 597–628; Open House, pp. 629–56; Best Seller, pp. 657–81; Strychnine in the Soup, pp. 682–708; Gala Night, pp. 709–36; Monkey Business, pp. 737–63; The Nodder, pp. 764–87; The Juice of an Orange, pp. 788–812; The Rise of Minna Nordstrom, pp. 813–37; The Castaways, pp. 838–64.

NOTES: Stories from *Mr. Mulliner Speaking* (1929), *Meet Mr. Mulliner* (1927), *Mulliner Nights* (1933), *Blandings Castle* (1935). Reissued with ten additional stories in 1972 by Barrie and Jenkins, retitled *The World of Mr. Mulliner* (British Library reception date 16 June 1972). In New York the 1972 edition was issued by Taplinger Publishing Company, 1975, and Avon Books, April 1979.

B6A The Week-End Wodehouse

P. G. WODEHOUSE | *The Week-End* | *Wodehouse* | [double-page drawing by Roese of characters] | DOUBLEDAY, DORAN & CO., INC. NEW YORK 1939

COLLATION: [i] *half title*; [ii] *drawing continued on* [iii] *title page*; [iv] *copyright page:* Printed at the Country Life Press ... CL ... First Edition; [v] *publisher's note:* ... the publishers have not re-folioed the sheets; [vi] *blank*; [vii–viii] Contents; *text*

PUBLISHED: 20 January 1939 (price $2.50)

COVER: Brown cloth, blind-stamped on front cover, gold drawing and letters

SIZE: 14×20.5 cm. (5⅝×8″)

CONTENTS: *Part I – Mulliner Stories:* Archibald and the Masses; Monkey Business; The Rise of Minna Nordstrom; The Voice from the Past; The Smile That Wins;

Cats Will Be Cats; Best Seller; Strychnine in the Soup; *Part II – Jeeves Stories:* The Metropolitan Touch; Jeeves Takes Charge; Jeeves and the Hard-Boiled Egg; Clustering Round Young Bingo; Bertie Changes His Mind; Jeeves and the Impending Doom; Jeeves and the Spot of Art; *Part III – Drones and Others:* All's Well with Bingo; The Masked Troubadour; Tried in the Furnace; "Pig-Hoo-o-o-o-ey!"; The Go-Getter; *Part IV – A Complete Novel:* Fish Preferred

B6B First English edition

WEEK-END WODEHOUSE | Introduction by Hilaire Belloc | Decorations by Kerr | [drawing] | HERBERT JENKINS LIMITED | 3 DUKE OF YORK STREET, ST. JAMES'S | LONDON, S.W.1

COLLATION: [1] *half title*; [2] *blank*; [3] *title page*; [iv] *copyright page:* Made and printed in Great Britain by Purnell and Sons, Ltd., Paulton (Somerset) and London; v–x, Introduction by Hilaire Belloc; xi–xiii, Contents; [14] *blank*; xv–xvi, Classified Contents; 17–508, *text*; [509] *drawing*; [510] *blank*; [511] The Books by P. G. Wodehouse; [512] *blank*

PUBLISHED: 12 May 1939 (price 7s6d); British Library reception date 12 May 1939

COVER: Blue-green cloth, lettered in gold on cover and on green leather spine

SIZE: 12.5×19 cm. (5×7½")

DUST WRAPPER: 7/6

CONTENTS: Uncle Fred Flits By, pp. 17–42; Galahad on Tea, pp. 43–44; My Gentle Readers, pp. 45–52; The Salvation of George Mackintosh, pp. 53–73; The Artistry of Archibald, p. 74; Old Bill Townend, pp. 75–79; Gussie Presents the Prizes, pp. 81–115; Good News from Denmark, p. 116; Inside Information, p. 117; The Feudal Spirit, p. 118; Golfing Tigers and Literary Lions, pp. 120–23; The Soupiness of Madeline, p. 124; Lord Emsworth and the Girl Friend, pp. 125–50; One Moment!, pp. 151–52; The First Time I Went to New York, pp. 153–62; The Fiery Wooing of Mordred, pp.163–84; Le Vodeouse, pp. 185–87; Mr. Bennett and the Bulldog, Smith, pp. 189–90; Good-bye to All Cats, pp. 191–213; The Penurious Aristocracy, p. 214; I Explode the Haggis, pp. 215–19; Diet and the Omnibus, pp. 221–24; Ukridge's Accident Syndicate, pp. 225–48; High Stakes, pp.249–76; Archibald Goes Slumming, p. 277; Two Ways of . . . , p. 278; . . . Saying the Same Thing, p. 279; Conversation Piece, p. 280; Pig-Hoo-o-oo-ey!, pp. 281–308; Americans: "A" and "B," p. 309; To W. Townend, pp. 310–11; Back to Whiskers, pp. 312–16; Buried Treasure, pp. 317–42; The Defeat of a Critic, pp. 343–44; The Clicking of Cuthbert, pp. 345–64; The Saga Habit, pp. 367–68; Gallant Rescue by Well-Dressed Young Man, pp. 369–72; No Wedding Bells for Him, pp. 373–404; Good Gnus, pp. 405–6; The Pinheadedness of Archibald, p. 407; The Sinister Cudster, p. 408; In Which a Mother Pleads for Her Son, pp. 409–26; Chester Forgets Himself, pp. 427–57; A Damsel in Distress, pp. 459–68; Fore!, pp. 469–70; Hollywood Interlude, pp. 471–80; Sinister Behaviour of a Yacht-Owner, pp. 483–508.

NOTES: The American edition was reissued by Garden City Publishing Company in 1940, the pages still not refolioed. In London the Reader's Union reprinted in 1940, 508 pages. Jenkins issued a revised edition, November 1951, 432 pages (12s6d).

Except for the title and date of publication the American and English collections have little in common. The American edition is a reprinting of stories taken from the earlier collections *Young Men in Spats, Blandings Castle and Elsewhere, Mulliner Nights, The Inimitable Jeeves, Carry On, Jeeves!, Very Good, Jeeves,* and *Crime Wave at Blandings,* concluding with the novel *Fish Preferred* (1929) serialized as "Summer Lightning." The English edition reprints some of the short stories but also includes chapters from some of the novels, e.g., "Gussie Presents the Prizes" from *Right Ho, Jeeves.*

B7A Wodehouse on Golf

Wodehouse | on Golf | P. G. WODEHOUSE | [drawing] | Doubleday, Doran & Company, Inc. | NEW YORK 1940 [double-rule frame]

COLLATION: [1] *half title*; [2] Books by P. G. Wodehouse; [3] *title page*; [4] *copyright page:* Printed at The Country Life Press . . . CL . . . First Edition; [5] Contents; [6] *blank*; [7]–844, *text*; [845–48] *blank*

PUBLISHED: 23 August 1940 (price $2.50)

COVER: Green cloth, darker green letters and drawing

SIZE: 14.5×20.5 cm. (5¾×8⅛")

CONTENTS: Divots, pp. [7]–316; Golf without Tears, pp. [317]–640; The Medicine Girl, pp. [641]–762; There's Always Golf!, pp. [763]–89; The Letter of the Law, pp. [791]–819; Archibald's Benefit, pp. [821]–44.

NOTES: The anthology reprints the entire *Golf without Tears* (1924) (published in England as *The Clicking of Cuthbert,* 1922); the entire *Divots* (1927) (published in England as *The Heart of a Goof,* 1926); "The Medicine Girl" from *Crime Wave at Blandings* (1937) but which earlier was published in England as *Doctor Sally* (1932); and three stories from *Young Men in Spats* (1936).

B8A The Best of Wodehouse

THE | BEST | OF | WODEHOUSE | SELECTED AND WITH | AN INTRODUCTION BY | SCOTT MEREDITH | [publisher's device] | POCKET BOOKS, INC. | Rockefeller Center, New York

COLLATION: [i] *quote from introduction*; [ii] *blank*; [iii] *title page*; [iv] *copyright page:* The printing history of the Best of Wodehouse: Pocket Book edition published October, 1949, first printing September, 1949. This is an original Pocket Book published simultaneously in New York by Pocket Books, Inc. and in Montreal, Canada by Pocket Books of Canada, Ltd . . . published by arrangement with Doubleday & Company, Inc., Herbert Jenkins, Ltd., Tauchnitz, and Scott Meredith Literary Agency. Copyright, 1949, by Pocket Books; [v–vi] Contents; vii–xii, Introduction (*by* Scott Meredith); [xiii] *half title*; [xiv] *blank*; 1–266, *text*; [267–274] *advertisements*

PUBLISHED: 12 September 1949 (price $.25)

COVER: Pictorial cover by Paul Gallico on yellow background boards (paperback); series note on front cover and spine: Pocket Book 628

SIZE: 10.5 × 16.25 cm. (4⅛ × 6⅜″)

CONTENTS: Introduction, by Scott Meredith, pp. vii–xii; Introducing Jeeves, p. 1: Jeeves and the Yuletide Spirit, pp. 2–21; Introducing Freddie Widgeon, p. 22: Trouble Down at Tudsleigh, pp. 23–45; Introducing Mr. Wodehouse, p. 46: Good-bye to Butlers, pp. 47–54; Introducing Mr. Mulliner, p. 55: Strychnine in the Soup, 56–78; Introducing Stanley Featherstonehaugh Ukridge, p. 79: The Level Business Head, p. 80–102; Introducing Lord Emsworth, p. 103: The Crime Wave at Blandings, pp. 104–62; Introducing Bingo Little, p. 163: Sonny Boy, pp. 164–85; Introducing the Oldest Member, p. 186: The Letter of the Law, pp. 187–210; Introducing the Drones Club, p. 211: Tried in the Furnace, pp. 212–35; Introducing a New Story, p. 236: Freddie, Oofy and the Beef Trust, pp. 237–66.

NOTES: One story each from *Very Good, Jeeves*; *Louder and Funnier*; *Mulliner Nights*; *Young Men in Spats*; three stories from *Eggs, Beans and Crumpets* (American edition); and two from *Crime Wave at Blandings*. The last story, "Freddie, Oofy and the Beef Trust," was subsequently reprinted in *A Few Quick Ones* (1959).

"I have sold a few short stories and a couple of my books are being done in the Pocket Book edition, where they practically guarantee you a sale of two million per. . . ." (Letter to Guy Bolton, 7 September 1947.)

B9A The Best of Modern Humor

THE BEST OF | MODERN HUMOR | Edited by | P. G. WODEHOUSE and SCOTT MEREDITH | General introduction by Mr. Wodehouse | Introductions to selections by Mr. Meredith | [publisher's device] | *Medill McBride Company, Inc., New York*

COLLATION: [i–ii] *blank*; [iii] *title page*; [iv–vi] *copyright page:* Copyright, 1951, by P. G. Wodehouse and Scott Meredith . . . *copyright acknowledgments* . . . ; [vii] [*Dedications to each other*]; [viii] *blank*; [ix] Acknowledgments; [x–xiv] Introduction by P. G. Wodehouse; [xv] Contents; 1–264, *text*; [265] *blank*

PUBLISHED: 1951 (price $2.75)

SIZE: Approximately 5 × 8″

CONTENTS: Introduction pp. x–xiv; Sonny Boy, pp. 241–64 (the only Wodehouse story).

NOTES: All of the copies of the original volume that I have seen have been rebound and therefore the size given here is approximate and I am unable to supply a description of the original cover.

The title reissued under the Metcalf imprint is brown buckram with red letters on the spine. Medill McBride became Metcalf Associates and reissued this title under the new imprint in 1952.

"Sonny Boy" is from *Eggs, Beans, and Crumpets* (1940) and is often reprinted.

B10A The Week-End Book of Humor

The | WEEK-END BOOK | *of* HUMOR | Selected by | P. G. WODEHOUSE | and SCOTT MEREDITH | *General Introduction by Mr. Wodehouse* | *Introductions to Selections by Mr. Meredith* | [publisher's device] | IVES WASHBURN, INC. NEW YORK

COLLATION: [i] *half title*; [ii] *blank*; [iii] *title page*; [iv] *copyright page:* Copyright, 1952 . . . Manufactured in the United States of America Vail-Ballou Press, Inc., New York; [v]–vii, Acknowledgments; [viii] *blank*; [ix]–xi, Contents; [xii] *blank*; [1] *half title*; [2] *blank*; [3]–6, Introduction, by P. G. Wodehouse; [7]–251, *text*; [252–60] *blank*

PUBLISHED: 8 November 1952 (price $3.00)

COVER: Black buckram, silver lettering on spine

SIZE: 14 × 20.67 cm. (5½ × 8¼″)

CONTENTS: Introduction, pp. 3–6; Trouble Down at Tudsleigh, pp. 228–51 (the only Wodehouse story).

B10B First English edition

The | WEEK-END BOOK | *of* HUMOUR | *Selected by* | P. G. WODEHOUSE | (*and*) | SCOTT MEREDITH | LONDON: HERBERT JENKINS

COLLATION: [1] *half title*; [2] *blank*; [3] *title page*; [4] *copyright page:* First published in Great Britain . . . 1954 . . . Printed in Great Britain by Wyman & Sons Ltd., London, Reading and Fakenham; v–[6] Contents; vii, List of Humourous Drawings; [8] *blank*; [9] *half title*; [10] *blank*; xi–xiv, Introduction, by P. G. Wodehouse; 15–220, *text*; 221–23, Acknowledgments; [224] *blank*

PUBLISHED: 19 February 1954 (price 12s6d); British Library reception date 17 February 1954

COVER: Plum buckram, gold letters on spine

SIZE: 13×19.75 cm. (5⅛×7⅞″)

CONTENTS: Introduction by P. G. Wodehouse, pp. 11–14; Trouble Down at Tudsleigh, pp. 201–20 (the only Wodehouse story).

NOTES: The story "Trouble Down at Tudsleigh" is from *Eggs, Beans, and Crumpets* (1940).

In 1965, Grosset and Dunlap reprinted the Washburn edition, *P. G. Wodehouse Selects the Best of Humor* with cartoons by Syd Hoff.

The American edition was also reprinted by Books for Libraries, Freeport, N.Y., 1971.

World Distributors, London, reissued the Jenkins edition, 1960.

B11A Selected Stories

Selected Stories | by | *P. G. Wodehouse* | Introduction by John W. Aldridge | [publisher's device] | THE MODERN LIBRARY

COLLATION: [i] *series page*; [ii] *blank*; [iii] *title page*; [iv] *copyright page:* copyright, 1958, by Random House . . . Library of Congress Catalog Card Number: 58-11472 Random House is the Publisher of The Modern Library . . . Manufactured . . . by H. Wolff; v–viii, Foreword by P. G. Wodehouse; [ix] Contents; [x] *blank*; xi–xxv, Introduction: P. G. Wodehouse: the Lessons of the Young Master, by John W. Aldridge; [xxvi] *blank*; [1]–382, *text*; [383–90] *advertisements*

PUBLISHED: 25 August 1958 (price $1.95)

COVER: Red cloth, gold letters on black and gold drawing

SIZE: 12.25×18.5 cm. (4⅞×7¼″)

DUST WRAPPER: $1.95; Modern Library Books no. 126

CONTENTS: Jeeves Takes Charge, pp. 3–29; The Artistic Career of Corky, pp. 30–49; Jeeves and the Unbidden Guest, pp. 50–73; The Aunt and the Sluggard, pp. 74–104; The Rummy Affair of Old Biffy, pp. 105–33; Clustering Round Young Bingo, pp. 134–64; Bertie Changes His Mind, pp. 165–83; Jeeves and the Impending Doom, pp. 184–209; Jeeves and the Yuletide Spirit, pp. 210–33; Jeeves and the Song of Songs, pp. 234–57; Episode of the Dog McIntosh, pp. 258–79; Jeeves and the Kid Clementina, pp. 280–303; The Love That Purifies, pp. 304–28; Jeeves and the Old School Chum, pp. 329–55; The Ordeal of Young Tuppy, pp. 356–82.

NOTES: The first seven stories are from *Carry On, Jeeves!* (1925) and the rest are from *Very Good, Jeeves* (1930). The introduction is reprinted from *New World Writing*, no. 13 (New York: New American Library, 1958).

Letters between Wodehouse and Bennett Cerf concerning this collection are in the Rare Book and Manuscript Division of the Columbia University Libraries.

B12A The Most of P. G. Wodehouse

The | *Most* | *of* | *P. G. Wodehouse* | [publisher's device] | SIMON AND SCHUSTER · NEW YORK · 1960

COLLATION: [i] *publisher's device*; [ii] *blank*; [iii] *title page*; [iv] *copyright page:* . . . First printing Library of Congress Catalog Card Number: 60–12584 Manufactured . . . by American Book–Stratford Press, New York, N.Y.; [v]–vi, Contents; [1]–666, *text*

PUBLISHED: 15 October 1960 (price $6.50)

COVER: Blue-green boards, darker blue-green picture on cover of butler holding tray with Wodehouse books on it; white cloth spine with red and blue-green lettering and decoration

SIZE: 14.5×21.5 cm. (5¾×8½″)

DUST WRAPPER: Jacket design by Paul Bacon; $6.50

CONTENTS: *The Drones Club:* Fate, pp. 3–19; Tried in the Furnace, pp. 20–36; The Amazing Hat Mystery, pp. 37–52; Noblesse Oblige, pp. 53–68; Goodbye to All Cats, pp. 69–83; All's Well with Bingo, pp. 84–101; Uncle Fred Flits By, pp. 102–18; *Mr. Mulliner:* The Truth about George, pp. 121–34; A Slice of Life, pp. 135–47; Mulliner's Buck-U-Uppo, pp. 148–62; The Reverent Wooing of Archibald, pp. 163–78; The Ordeal of Osbert Mulliner, pp. 179–95; Monkey Business, pp. 196–211; The Smile That Wins, pp. 212–28; Strychnine in the Soup, pp. 229–45; *Stanley Featherstonehaugh Ukridge:* Ukridge's Dog College, pp. 249–64; Ukridge's Accident Syndicate, pp. 265–80; A Bit of Luck for Mabel, pp. 281–97; Buttercup Day, pp. 298–315; Ukridge and the Old Stepper, pp. 316–31; *Lord Emsworth:* "Pig-hoo-o-o-o-ey!," pp. 335–52; *The Golf Stories:* The Coming of Gowf, pp. 355–69; The Awakening of Rollo Podmarsh, pp. 370–84; The Clicking of Cuthbert, pp. 385–97; High Stakes, pp. 398–416; The Heel of Achilles, pp. 417–29; *Jeeves:* The Purity of the Turf, pp. 433–47; The Great Sermon Handicap, pp. 448–63; The Metropolitan Touch, pp. 464–80; Jeeves and the Song of Songs, pp. 481–98; Jeeves and the Impending Doom, pp. 499–517; *Quick Service* (the complete novel), pp. 521–666.

NOTES: The Drones Club stories are from *Young Men in Spats* (1936) and *Eggs, Beans and Crumpets* (1940); Mr. Mulliner stories are from *Meet Mr. Mulliner* (1927), *Mr. Mulliner Speaking* (1929), *Blandings Castle* (1935), and *Mulliner Nights* (1933); Stanley Featherstonehaugh Ukridge stories are from *Ukridge* (1924) and *Eggs, Beans and Crumpets* (1940); Lord Emsworth story is from *Blandings Castle* (1935); The Golf Stories are from *The Clicking of Cuthbert* (1932; American title: *Golf without Tears*) and *The Heart of a Goof* (1926; American title: *Divots*); Jeeves stories are from *The Inimitable Jeeves* (1923; American title: *Jeeves*) and *Very Good, Jeeves* (1930); Quick Service originally published 1940.

Simon and Schuster published this collection to celebrate Wodehouse's seventy-ninth birthday; they reissued as a paperback in 1969 and again in 1973.

B13A A Carnival of Modern Humor

A CARNIVAL OF | MODERN HUMOR | EDITED BY | P. G. WODEHOUSE | AND | SCOTT MEREDITH | [publisher's device] DELACORTE PRESS | NEW YORK

COLLATION: [i] *half title;* [ii] *blank;* [iii] *title page;* [iv] *copyright page:* copyright © 1967 . . . Library of Congress Catalog Card Number: 67-11020 . . . First printing; [v–vi] Acknowledgments; [vii] *blank;* [viii] *dedication:* To Don Fine; [ix] *blank;* [x–xii] Contents; [xiii] *blank;* [xiv] *half title;* [xv] *blank;* 1–240, *text*

PUBLISHED: 12 June 1967 (price $4.95)

COVER: Yellow cloth, red and black lettering on spine

SIZE: 14×22 cm. (5½×8½)

DUST WRAPPER: $4.95

CONTENTS: Introduction (by P. G. Wodehouse), pp. 1–5; Sonny Boy, pp. 222–40 (only Wodehouse story).

B13B First English edition

A CARNIVAL OF | MODERN | HUMOUR | EDITED BY | P. G. WODEHOUSE | AND | SCOTT MEREDITH | HERBERT JENKINS | LONDON

COLLATION: [i] *synopsis;* [ii] *blank;* [iii] *title page;* [iv] *copyright page:* Copyright © 1967 . . . First published in Great Britain by Herbert Jenkins Ltd . . . 1968 SBN 257.66696.6 Printed in Great Britain by Lowe and Brydone (Printers) Ltd., London; [v] *dedication:* To Don Fine; [vi] *blank;* [vii–ix] Contents; [x] *blank;* [xi] *half title;* [xii] *blank;* 1–[240] *text;* [241–43] Acknowledgments; [244] *blank*

PUBLISHED: September 1968 (price 25s); British Library reception date 6 September 1968

COVER: Orange buckram, black lettering

SIZE: 13.5×20.5 cm. (5¼×8″)

DUST WRAPPER: Jacket by D. Larkin

CONTENTS: Introduction (by P. G. Wodehouse), pp. 1–5; Sonny Boy (only Wodehouse story) pp. 222–40.

NOTE: "Sonny Boy" is from *Eggs, Beans and Crumpets* (1940).

B14A The Golf Omnibus

P. G. WODEHOUSE | The | Golf | Omnibus | [publisher's device] | BARRIE & JENKINS | LONDON

COLLATION: [1] *half title;* [2] Books by P. G. Wodehouse; [3] *title page;* [4] *copyright page:* © P. G. Wodehouse 1973 First published in this edition 1973 . . . ISBN 214 66850 9 . . . Printed in Great Britain by Redwood Press Limited, Trowbridge, Wiltshire; [5–6] Contents; [7–8] Preface (*by* Wodehouse); [9] *dedication:* . . . to the Immortal Memory of John Henrie and Pat Rogie . . . ; [10] *blank;* [11] *half title;* [12] *blank;* [13]–467, *text;* [468] *blank*

PUBLISHED: 12 April 1973 (price £3); British Library reception date 20 March 1973

COVER: Blue-green cloth, white lettering

SIZE: 15×22 cm. (6×8¾″)

DUST WRAPPER: Jacket design by David Pether; photograph of the Wodehouses by Bernard Gotfryd

CONTENTS: Archibald's Benefit, pp. [13]–24; The Clicking of Cuthbert, pp. [25]–35; A Woman Is Only a Woman, pp. [37]–50; A Mixed Threesome, pp. [51]–63; Sundered Hearts, pp. [65]–77; The Salvation of George Mackintosh, pp. [79]–90; Ordeal by Golf, pp. [91]–104; The Long Hole, pp. [105]–17; The Heel of Achilles, pp. [119]–29; The Rough Stuff, pp. [131]–44; The Coming of Gowf, pp. [145]–57; The Heart of a Goof, pp. [159]–175; High Stakes, pp. [177]–92; Keeping in with Vosper, pp. [193]–208; Chester Forgets Himself, pp. [209]–25; The Magic Plus Fours, pp. [227]–40; The Awakening of Rollo Podmarsh, pp. [241]–53;

Rodney Fails to Qualify, pp. [255]–71; Jane Gets off the Fairway, pp. [273]–89; The Purification of Rodney Spelvin, pp. [291]–306; Those in Peril on the Tee, pp. [307]–21; The Letter of the Law, pp. [323]–37; Farewell to Legs, pp. [339]–52; There's Always Golf, pp. [353]–66; Up from the Depths, pp. [367]–76; Feet of Clay, pp. [377]–95; Excelsior, pp. [397]–410; Rodney Has a Relapse, pp. [411]–25; Tangled Hearts, pp. [427]–41; Scratch Man, pp. [443]–56; Sleepy Time, pp. [457]–67.

B14B First American edition

The | Golf | Omnibus | P. G. WODEHOUSE | [publisher's device] | SIMON AND SCHUSTER · NEW YORK

COLLATION: [1] *publisher's device*; [2] Books by P. G. Wodehouse; [3] *title page*; [4] *copyright page:* Copyright © 1973 . . . SBN 671-21618-X Library of Congress Catalog Card Number: 73-6528 Printed in Great Britain by Redwood Press Limited, Trowbridge, Wiltshire . . . ; [5–6] Contents; [7–8] Preface by Wodehouse; [9] *dedication:* to the immortal memory of John Henrie and Pat Rogie . . . ; [10] *blank*; [11] *half title*; [12] *blank*; [13]–467, *text*; [468] *blank*

PUBLISHED: 12 April 1973 (price $7.95)

COVER: Green boards, gold lettering on spine

SIZE: 15×22.33 cm. (5⅞×8¾″)

DUST WRAPPER: Jacket designed by Michael Harvey; photograph of Wodehouses and dogs on back cover; $7.95

NOTES: Simon and Schuster brought out the Barrie and Jenkins edition with no changes except to title page and spine and with a correction in Preface: "Nicolaus" to "Nicklaus."

Barrie and Jenkins reprinted in 1975 and 1977.

Reprinting of *The Clicking of Cuthbert* stories (1922), all stories from *The Heart of a Goof* (1926), five stories from *Nothing Serious* (1950), three stories from *Young Men in Spats* (1936), and one each from *The Man Upstairs* (1914), *Meet Mr. Mulliner* (1929), *Eggs, Beans and Crumpets* (1940), and *Plum Pie* (1966).

B15A The World of Psmith

P. G. WODEHOUSE | The | World of | Psmith | [publisher's device] | BARRIE & JENKINS | LONDON

COLLATION: [i] *half title*; [ii] Books by P. G. Wodehouse; [iii] *title page*; [iv] *copyright page:* The story *Mike and Psmith* has also appeared under the title *Enter Psmith* . . . First published in this edition 1974 . . . ISBN 0 214 200000 0 . . . Printed in Great Britain by Northumberland Press Limited Gateshead; [v]–vi, Preface (*by* Wodehouse); [vii]–x, Contents; [1]–597, *text*; [598] *blank*

PUBLISHED: April 1974 (price £3.50); British Library reception date 28 March 1974

COVER: Green boards, white lettering on spine

SIZE: 15.25×22.25 cm. (6×8¾″)

DUST WRAPPER: Jacket design by Michael Harvey; £3.50; photograph on back of jacket of Wodehouse taken in October 1973 by Marina Schinz

CONTENTS: Mike and Psmith, pp. [1]–137; Psmith in the City, pp. [139]–262; Psmith, Journalist, pp. [263]–398; Leave It to Psmith, pp. [399]–597.

B16A The World of Ukridge

P. G. WODEHOUSE | The World | of Ukridge | BARRIE & JENKINS | COMMUNICA-EUROPA

COLLATION: [1] *half title*; [2] Books by P. G. Wodehouse; [3] *title page*; [4] *copyright page:* © The Estate of P. G. Wodehouse 1975. First published in this edition in 1975 by Barrie & Jenkins . . . ISBN 0 214 20137 6 . . . Printed in Great Britain by Redwood Burn Limited Trowbridge & Esher; [5] Contents; [6] *blank*; [7] *half title*; [8] *blank*; [9–12] *pages omitted because of misnumbering*; [13]–286, *text*; [287–88] *blank*

PUBLISHED: October 1975 (price £4.95); British Library reception date 8 October 1975

COVER: Red cloth, silver lettering on spine

SIZE: 15×22 cm. (6×8¾″)

DUST WRAPPER: Jacket design by Michael Harvey; photograph on back cover by John Marmaras; £4.95

CONTENTS: Ukridge's Dog College, pp. 13–26; Ukridge's Accident Syndicate, pp. 27–39; The Debut of Battling Billson, pp. 40–56; First Aid for Dora, pp. 57–71; The Return of Battling Billson, pp. 72–86; Ukridge Sees Her Through, pp. 87–100; No Wedding Bells for Him, pp. 101–18; The Long Arm of Looney Coote, pp. 119–35; The Exit of Battling Billson, pp. 136–49; Ukridge Rounds a Nasty Corner, pp. 150–64; Success Story, pp. 165–80; Ukridge Starts a Bank Account, pp. 181–91; A Bit of Luck for Mabel, pp. 192–205; Buttercup Day, pp. 206–20; Ukridge and the Old Stepper, pp. 221–33; A Tithe for Charity, pp. 234–43; Ukridge and the Home from Home, pp. 244–58; The Come-Back of Battling Billson, pp. 259–72; The Level Business Head, pp. 273–86.

NOTES: Reprinting of all of *Ukridge* (1924), six stories

from English edition of *Eggs, Beans and Crumpets* (1940), and one each from *Nothing Serious* (1950), *A Few Quick Ones* (1959), *Plum Pie* (1966).

B17A The World of Blandings

P. G. WODEHOUSE | The World | of Blandings | BARRIE & JENKINS | COMMUNICA-EUROPA

COLLATION: [i] *half title*; [ii] Books by P. G. Wodehouse; [iii] *title page*; [iv] *copyright page:* This edition © The Estate of P. G. Wodehouse 1976. First published 1976... ISBN 214 20250 X ... Printed in Great Britain by Redwood Burn Limited Trowbridge & Esher; [v] Contents; [vi] *blank*; [vii] *half title*; [viii] *blank*; [1]–357, text; [358–360] *blank*

PUBLISHED: March 1976 (price £4.95); British Library reception date 18 March 1976

COVER: Black boards, gold letters

SIZE: 15×22 cm. (8¾×5⅞")

DUST WRAPPER: Design by Michael Harvey; photograph by John Marmaras, courtesy Camera Press; £4.95

CONTENTS: Something Fresh, pp. 1–139; The Custody of the Pumpkin, pp. 140–54; Lord Emsworth Acts for the Best, pp. 155–67; Pig-Hoo-o-o-o-ey!, pp. 168–82; Summer Lightning, pp. 183–357.

NOTES: From the copyright page: "*Something Fresh* first published in book form 1915 *Summer Lightning* first published in book form 1929 *The Custody of the Pumpkin, Lord Emsworth Acts for the Best,* and *Pig-Hoo-o-o-o-ey* first published in book form in *Blandings Castle* 1935."

B18A Jeeves, Jeeves, Jeeves

Jeeves, | *Jeeves,* | *Jeeves* | *Three Novels* | *By P. G.* | *Wodehouse* | [publisher's device] AVON | PUBLISHERS OF BARD, CAMELOT AND DISCUS BOOKS

COLLATION: [i] *half title*; [ii] *blank*; [iii] *title page*; [iv] *copyright page:* ... Avon Books, A division of The Hearst Corporation ... New York ... ISBN: 0-380-00627-8 ... First Avon printing, March, 1976 ...; [v] Contents; [vi] *blank*; [vii] *story title*: How Right You Are, Jeeves; [viii] *blank*; 1–585, text; [586–92] *blank*

PUBLISHED: March 1976 (price $4.95)

COVER: Silver boards, black and red lettering, drawing by J. Zucker

SIZE: 13.33×20.33 cm. (5¼×8")

CONTENTS: How Right You Are, Jeeves, pp. 1–183; Stiff Upper Lip, Jeeves, pp. 187–399; Jeeves and the Tie That Binds, pp. 403–585.

NOTES: Avon reprinted at least five times, most recently in 1978.

B19A The Uncollected Wodehouse

The Uncollected | WODEHOUSE | EDITED AND INTRODUCED BY | DAVID A. JASEN | FOREWORD BY | MALCOLM MUGGERIDGE | A CONTINUUM BOOK | THE SEABURY PRESS · NEW YORK

COLLATION: [i] *half title*; [ii] *blank*; [iii] *title page*; [iv] *copyright page:* 1976 The Seabury Press ... Foreword copyright © 1976 by Malcolm Muggeridge. Introduction and new material copyright © 1976 by David A. Jasen ... ISBN 0-8164-9286-7; [v] *dedication*; [vi] *blank*; [vii]–viii, Contents; [ix]–xii, Foreword; [xiii] *half title*; [xiv] *blank*; 1, Introduction; [2] *blank*; 3–212, text; [213–14] *blank*

PUBLISHED: 18 October 1976 (price $8.95)

COVER: Blue boards, silver lettering on spine

SIZE: 14×21.5 cm. (5½×8½")

DUST WRAPPER: Jacket design by Donya Melanson Associates; $8.95; photograph inside back flap of Wodehouse and Jasen, 1963, in front of Remsenburg home

CONTENTS: *Part One: 1900–1909*, p. 5: Some Aspects of Game-Captaincy, pp. 6–7; An Unfinished Collection, pp. 7–8; Damon and Pythias, a Romance, pp. 9–11; The Haunted Tram, pp. 11–12; The New Advertising, pp. 12–13; *1914–1919*, p. 14: The Secret Pleasures of Reginald, pp. 15–16; My Battle with Drink, pp. 17–19; In Defense of Astigmatism, pp. 19–22; Photographers and Me, pp. 22–23; A Plea for Indoor Golf, pp. 24–25; The Alarming Spread of Poetry, pp. 25–27; My Life as a Dramatic Critic, pp. 28–29; The Agonies of Writing a Musical Comedy, Which Shows Why Librettists Pick at the Coverlet, pp. 30–33; On the Writing of Lyrics, pp. 33–36; The Past Theatrical Season and the Six Best Performances by Unstarred Actors, pp. 36–38; *Part Two:* Uncollected Short Stories, pp. 39: When Papa Swore in Hindustani, pp. 40–45; A Corner in Lines, pp. 45–58; The Autograph Hunters, pp. 58–64; Tom, Dick and Harry, pp. 64–73; The Good Angel, pp. 73–87; The Man Upstairs, pp. 87–102; Misunderstood, pp. 102–9; Pillingshot, Detective, pp. 109–20; When Doctors Disagree, pp. 120–35; The Best Sauce, pp. 135–149; Pots o' Money, pp. 149–63; Ruth in Exile, pp. 164–78; Death at the Excelsior, pp. 178–200; The Test Case, pp. 200–12.

NOTES: G. K. Hall, Boston, issued this title in a "Large Print Edition," 1977.

B20A Vintage Wodehouse

Vintage Wodehouse | edited by | RICHARD USBORNE | BARRIE & JENKINS | COMMUNICA-EUROPA

COLLATION: [1] half title; [2] Books by P. G. Wodehouse; [3] title page; [4] copyright page: First published in 1977 . . . ISBN 0 214 20350 6 . . . Copyright © 1977 The Estate of P. G. Wodehouse Arrangement and Notes Copyright © 1977 Richard Usborne Printed in Great Britain by The Anchor Press Ltd and bound by Wm Brendon & Son Ltd both of Tiptree, Essex; [5] Contents; [6] blank; [7] Foreword by Richard Usborne; [8] blank; [9]–287, text; [288] blank

PUBLISHED: November 1978 (price £5.95); British Library reception date 20 October 1978

COVER: Blue cloth, gold letters on spine

SIZE: 15×22.25 cm. (5⅞×8¾")

DUST WRAPPER: £5.95

CONTENTS: Boxing Final, pp. 9–14; Mike Meets Psmith, pp. 15–16; The Clicking of Cuthbert, pp. 17–27; Boyhood Memories, pp. 28–29; Dark Deeds at Blandings Castle, pp. 30–36; Dedications, pp. 37–39; Ukridge's Accident Syndicate, pp. 40–52; Grand Hotel, p. 53; Jeeves and the Yule-Tide Spirit, pp. 54–67; Franglais, p. 68; Anselm Gets His Chance, pp. 69–83; Militant Poet, p. 84; Gussie Presents the Prizes, pp. 85–105; Debut of Young Barrister, pp. 106–7; Rodney Has a Relapse, pp. 108–22; The Dreadful Duke, p.123; Uncle Fred Flits By, pp. 124–37; Lottie Blossom of Hollywood, pp. 138–39; Some Thoughts on Humorists, pp. 140–44; Lord Emsworth and the Girl Friend, pp. 145–58; Bertie's Saviour, p. 159; Honeysuckle Cottage, pp. 160–77; The Case against Sir Gregory, p. 178; The Machinations of Stiffy Byng, pp. 179–91; Uncle and Nephew, p. 192; The Amazing Hat Mystery, pp. 193–206; Myra Meets an Old Friend, p. 207; Pig-Hoo-o-o-o-ey!, pp. 208–23; A Top Hat Goes Flying, pp. 224–25; Tried in the Furnace, pp. 226–40; Gally and Sue, pp. 241–42; Two Good Dinners at Blandings Castle, pp. 243–45; Valley Fields the Blest, pp. 246–47; Romance at Droitgate Spa, pp. 248–62; Introducing Percy Pilbeam, pp. 263–66; Bramley Is So Bracing, pp. 267–79; Young Villain, pp. 280–81; The Plot So Far, p. 282; The Talks to America on the German Radio, pp. 283–87.

NOTE: Penguin Books reprinted 1979, 405 pages, with cover illustration by Ionicus.

B21A The Swoop and Other Stories

THE SWOOP! | and Other Stories by | P. G. WODEHOUSE | Edited and Introduced by | DAVID A. JASEN | [three decorations] | with an Appreciation by | MALCOLM MUGGERIDGE | A Continuum Book · The Seabury Press · New York

COLLATION: [i] half title; [ii] blank; [iii] title page; [iv] copyright page: 1979 . . . Designed by Victoria Gomez . . . 78–26758 ISBN 0-8164-9350-2; v, Contents; [vi] dedication; vii–xiv, Appreciation (by Malcolm Muggeridge); xv–xvii, Introduction by David A. Jasen; [xviii] blank; [1]–205, text; [206] blank

PUBLISHED: May 14, 1979 (price $9.95)

COVER: Light blue boards, gold lettering on spine

SIZE: 14×21.5 cm. (5½×8½")

DUST WRAPPER: Photograph of young Wodehouse on inside back flap; $9.95

CONTENTS: The Swoop, pp. [1]–65; Bradshaw's Little Story, pp. 67–74; A Shocking Affair, pp. 75–86; The Politeness of Princes, pp. 87–95; Shields' and the Cricket Cup, pp. 96–105; An International Affair, pp. 106–17; The Guardian, pp. 118–33; Something to Worry About, pp. 134–52; The Tuppenny Millionaire, pp. 153–69; Deep Waters, pp. 170–90; The Goal-Keeper and the Plutocrat, pp. 191–205.

B22A The Eighteen-Carat Kid

The | Eighteen-carat Kid | and Other Stories by | P. G. Wodehouse | Edited and Introduced by | DAVID A. JASEN | [three decorations] | CONTINUUM / New York

COLLATION: [i] half title; [ii] blank; [iii] title page; [iv] copyright page: 1980 . . . Introduction copyright © 1980 by David A. Jasen. . . . Designed by Victoria Gomez . . . ISBN 0-8264-0012-4; [v] Contents; [vi] blank; [vii], dedication; [viii] blank; ix–xii, Introduction by David A. Jasen; [1]–[164], text

PUBLISHED: August 1980 (price $10.95)

COVER: Blue buckram with gold lettering

SIZE: 14×21.5 cm. (5½×8½")

DUST WRAPPER: $10.95

CONTENTS: Introduction, pp. ix–xii; The Eighteen-carat Kid, pp. [1]–90; The Wire-Pullers, pp. [91]–103; The Prize Poem, pp. [105]–15; William Tell Told Again, pp. [117]–[63]; Epilogue, p. [164].

B23A Wodehouse on Wodehouse

P. G. Wodehouse | WODEHOUSE | ON WODEHOUSE | Bring On the Girls | (*with Guy Bolton*) | Performing Flea | Over Seventy | HUTCHINSON | London Melbourne Sydney Auckland Johannesburg

COLLATION: [1] *half title*; [2] Books by P. G. Wodehouse; [3] *title page*; [4] *copyright page:* . . . This edition first published 1980 Printed in Great Britain by The Anchor Press Ltd and bound by Wm Brendon & Son Ltd, both of Tiptree, Essex . . . ISBN 0 09 143210 3; [5] Contents; [6] Publisher's Note; [7]–645, *text*; [646] *blank*; [647]–55, Index; [656] *blank*

PUBLISHED: 10 November 1980 (price £9.95); British Library reception date 30 October 1980

COVER: Brown boards, gold lettering and decorations

SIZE: 14×22.5 cm. (5½×8¾")

DUST WRAPPER: Jacket design by John Gorham; cartoon of Wodehouse by David Low on front cover; £9.95

CONTENTS: Bring on the Girls, pp. 7–235; Performing Flea, pp. 237–464; Over Seventy, pp. 465–645.

NOTE: Reprint of *Bring on the Girls* (1954) with minor revisions by Guy Bolton, *Performing Flea* (1953), and *Over Seventy* (1957).

Published Plays (Including Adaptations)

CHRONOLOGICAL LIST

1926	*Hearts and Diamonds*	1934	*Candle-Light*
1927	*The Play's the Thing*	1936	*Anything Goes*
1928	*Good Morning, Bill*	1937	*The Three Musketeers*
1930	*A Damsel in Distress*	1952	*Don't Listen, Ladies*
1930	*Baa, Baa, Black Sheep*	1956	*Come on, Jeeves*
1932	*Leave It to Psmith*	1968	*Oh, Clarence*

C1 Hearts and Diamonds

HEARTS AND DIAMONDS | A NEW LIGHT OPERA | Adapted from | THE ORLOV | by | Ernst Marischka and | Bruno Granichstaedten | English Adaption by | P. G. WODEHOUSE | & LAURIE WYLIE | English Lyrics by | Graham John. | Music by | BRUNO GRANICHSTAEDTEN | and Max Darewski | KEITH PROWSE & Co. Ltd. | LONDON, W.1.

COLLATION: [1] [publisher's initials]; [2] *blank*; [3] *title page*; [4] *copyright page:* copyright 1925 by Edition Bristol, Musik- und Buhnenverlag A.G., Wien, Berlin. English version: – copyright 1926 by Keith Prowse & Co., Ltd., London, W.1; [5] Strand Theatre London. 1st June 1926.; [6] *blank*; [7] Characters; [8] *blank*; [9]–77, *text*; [78] *advertisement for Keith Prowse theatre tickets*; [79] *advertisement for music. Printer's note:* Lowe & Brydone Printers Ltd. N.W.10.; [80] *blank*

PUBLISHED: British Library reception date 15 June 1926

COVER: Blue paper, white lettering and decorations

SIZE: 7×10.75 cm. (2¾×4½″)

NOTE: A few copies were sold at the Strand Theatre, but the show was a failure and practically the entire edition was destroyed by the publishers. The only known copy is in the British Library.

C2 The Play's the Thing

[decoration] | *FERENC MOLNAR* | THE PLAY'S | THE THING [title in dark blue] | [decoration] | *Adapted from the Hungarian* | *By* P. G. WODEHOUSE | [decoration] | BRENTANO'S | *Publishers New York*

COLLATION: [i–ii] *blank*; [iii] *half title*; [iv] *blank*; [v] *title page*; [vi] *copyright page*: Copyright, 1927, by Charles Frohman, Inc., copyright statement; [vii] *original cast of characters*; [viii] *blank*; [1] *half title*; [2] The Characters; 3–139, *text*; [140] *blank*

PUBLISHED: 7 February 1927 (price $2.00)

COVER: Reddish brown cloth, dark blue and green decoration and lettering

SIZE: 13.25×19.5 cm. (5¼×7¾″)

DUST WRAPPER: $2.00

NOTES: The play was first presented Thursday, 21 October 1926, at Irving M. Lesser's Great Neck Playhouse, Great Neck, Long Island by Gilbert Miller, managing director, the Charles Frohman Company and featuring Holbrook Blinn. . . . "The play was presented for the first time in New York City under the same auspices at Henry Miller's Theatre on Wednesday, November the third, 1926 . . ." (p. vii). The play was again produced on Broadway at the Booth Theatre, opening 28 April 1948.

Samuel French published an acting edition in 1948 ($.85).

C3 Good Morning Bill

GOOD MORNING | BILL | A THREE-ACT COMEDY | (Based on the Hungarian of Ladislaus Fodor) [in small capitals] | By | P. G. Wodehouse | [publisher's device] | METHUEN & CO. LTD. | 36 ESSEX STREET W.C. | LONDON

COLLATION: [1] *half title*; [2] By the Same Author [*eight titles beginning* Uneasy Money, *ending* The Small Bachelor]; [3] *title page*; [4] *copyright page:* First published in 1928 Printed in Great Britain; [5] Characters; [6] Scenes; [7]–160, *text* (*bottom of page 160, printer's note:* Printed in Great Britain by Wyman & Sons, Ltd., London, Fakenham and Reading.); [1]–8, Methuen's General Literature (*advertising supplement inserted*)

PUBLISHED: 28 March 1928 (price 3s6d); British Library reception date 28 March 1928

COVER: Light blue cloth, lettered in black

SIZE: 13×19.5 cm. (5×7¾″)

DUST WRAPPER: Illustration by D. C. Eyles; 3/6

NOTE: Later printings, 1938, do not have advertising supplement but do have tipped-in notices from Messrs. Samuel French, Ltd., regarding amateur fees.

Produced at Duke of York's Theatre, Monday, 28 November 1927. Later became short novel, *Doctor Sally* (1932). Copyright in United States 18 May 1928.

C4 Damsel in Distress

A DAMSEL IN DISTRESS | A Comedy of Youth, Love and | Adventure in Three Acts | By | IAN HAY | AND | P. G. WODEHOUSE | Copyright, 1930, By Samuel French, Ltd. [all in small capitals] | *All rights reserved*

LONDON   NEW YORK
SAMUEL FRENCH, LTD.   SAMUEL FRENCH, INC.
PUBLISHERS   PUBLISHERS
26 SOUTHAMPTON STREET   25 WEST 45TH STREET
STRAND, W.C.2

COLLATION: [1] *title page*; [2] *copyright page: copyright notice regarding amateur performances.* Made and printed in Great Britain by Butler & Tanner Ltd., Frome and London; [3] *original cast*; [4] Scenes; *photograph of the set in Act I, Scene I*; 5–86, *text*; 87–88, Furniture and Property Plot; 89, Lighting Plot; [90] *blank*; [91] Plays by Ian Hay (*nine titles*); [92] The Plays of A. A. Milne

PUBLISHED: April 1930 (price 2s6d); British Library reception date 4 April 1930; © 13 April 1930 (price $.75)

COVER: Pale blue wrappers, black lettering

SIZE: 14×21.5 cm. (5½×8½″)

NOTES: First produced at the New Theatre, London, 12 August 1928.

Front cover: "French's Acting Edition no. 1281 . . . Two shillings and sixpence net."

The first issue should have the same advertisements on back cover as *Baa, Baa, Black Sheep*, beginning *Farmer's Wife*, and must have "Ian Hay and" together on the same line on front cover. Later editions have advertisements on back cover beginning *The Ghost Train* or *Full House*.

Four photographs of sets inserted: opposite pages 5, 14, 40, 67.

C5 Baa, Baa, Black Sheep

BAA, BAA, BLACK | SHEEP | A Farcical Comedy in Three Acts | BY | IAN HAY and | P. G. WODEHOUSE | Copyright, 1930, By Samuel French, Ltd. [all in small capitals] | *All rights reserved*

LONDON	NEW YORK
SAMUEL FRENCH, LTD.	SAMUEL FRENCH, LTD.
PUBLISHERS	PUBLISHERS
26 SOUTHAMPTON STREET	25 WEST 45TH STREET
STRAND, W.C.2	

COLLATION: [1] *title page*; [2] *copyright page: copyright notice regarding amateur performances.* Made and printed in Great Britain by Butler & Tanner Ltd., Frome and London; [3] Characters; [4] Scenes; *photograph for Scene I*; [5]–76, *text*; 77, *design of stage setting*; 78–79, Furniture and Properties; 80, Lighting Plot

PUBLISHED: August 1930 (price 2s6d); British Library reception date 23 May 1930; © 21 May 1930 (price $.75)

COVER Blue-gray paper wrappers, black letters

SIZE: 14×21.75 cm. (5½×8⅝″)

NOTES: Produced at the New Theatre, St. Martin's Lane, London, W.C., on 22 April 1929 by Ian Hay [pseud. of John Hay Beith].

On cover: "French's Acting Edition, no. 2022. Two shillings and sixpence net."

First edition is identified by advertisements on back wrapper, which must commence with *The Farmer's Wife* and end *Meet the Wife*. On front wrapper the words "Ian Hay and" must be on the same line. Later editions have advertisements on back cover which begin *The Ghost Train* or *Autumn Crocus*.

C6 Leave It to Psmith

LEAVE IT TO PSMITH | A Comedy of Youth, Love, and | Misadventure, in Three Acts | BY | IAN HAY and | P. G. WODEHOUSE | Copyright, 1932, by Samuel French, Ltd. [all in small capitals] | *All rights reserved*

LONDON	NEW YORK
SAMUEL FRENCH, LTD.	SAMUEL FRENCH, INC.
PUBLISHERS	PUBLISHERS
26 SOUTHAMPTON STREET	25 WEST 45TH STREET
STRAND, W.C.2	

COLLATION: [1] *title page*; [2] *copyright page: copyright notice regarding amateur performances.* Made and printed in Great Britain by Butler & Tanner Ltd., Frome and London; [3] *original cast of characters*; [4] Scenes; 5–80, *text*; 81–86, Furniture and Property Plot; [87] Lighting Plot; [88] The Plays of Ian Hay (*eleven titles*)

PUBLISHED: © 29 August 1932 (price $.75); September 1932 (price 2s6d); British Library reception date 29 August 1932

COVER: Light blue wrappers, black lettering

SIZE: 14×21.5 cm. (5½×8½″)

NOTES: First produced Shaftesbury Theatre, London, W.C., on 29 September 1930.

Front cover: "French's Acting Edition no. 1262. Two shillings and sixpence net."

Advertisements on back cover must begin with *Third Time Lucky* and end with *Important People*. The words "Ian Hay and" must appear on same line on front cover.

C7 Candle-Light

CANDLE-LIGHT | *A COMEDY IN THREE ACTS* | BY | SIEGFRIED GEYER | *Adapted by* | P. G. WODEHOUSE | Copyright, 1927 (under title, "Kleine Komoedie"), By | Georg Marton, Verlag | Copyright, 1929, by Gilbert Miller | Copyright, 1934, by Samuel French | All Rights Reserved | [ten-line copyright statement] | SAMUEL FRENCH, Inc. | 25 West 45th Street, New York, N.Y. | 811 West 7th Street, Los Angeles, Calif. | SAMUEL FRENCH, Ltd., London | SAMUEL FRENCH (Canada), Ltd., Toronto

COLLATION: [1] *title page*; [2] *copyright page: notice regarding amateur performances*; [3] Story of the Play; [4] *blank*; [5] copy of program of the first performance . . . produced at The Empire Theatre, New York; [6] *blank*; [7] Description of Characters; [8] *blank*; *photograph of Act I set*; 9–89, *text*; 90–94, Property Plot; 95, Electric Plot; 96, Cue Sheet; 97, Music Plot; 98–100, Publicity Through Your Local Papers; [101] *sketch of stage setting*; [102–4] *advertisements beginning* Berkeley Square *and ending* The Farmer's Wife

PUBLISHED: 8 June 1934 (price $2.00); British Library reception date 27 June 1934

COVER: Light brown paper wrappers, medium brown letters and decorations; on front cover: "French's Standard Library Edition," New York address

SIZE: 12.5×19 cm. (5×7½″)

NOTES: Photographs opposite pages 9, 52, 70; later printings have no photographs.

The copy in the British Library is the American edition.

C8 Anything Goes

ANYTHING GOES | A MUSICAL COMEDY | BY | GUY BOLTON | AND | P. G. WODEHOUSE | MUSIC AND LYRICS BY | COLE PORTER | copyright, 1936, by harms, incorporated, new york | copyright, 1936, by samuel french, limited | samuel french, ltd. | 26, Southampton Street, Strand, London, w.c.2 | 59, Cross Street, Manchester | samuel french, inc. | 25 West 45th Street, New York, U.S.A. | 811 West 7th Street, Los Angeles, Cal. | samuel french (canada), ltd. | 480 University Avenue, Toronto

COLLATION: [1] *title page*; [2] *copyright page: notice regarding royalties*. Made and printed in Great Britain by Butler & Tanner Ltd., Frome and London; iii, *Characters*; iv, *Synopsis of Scenes*; v, *Musical Numbers*; [6] *blank*; 7–61, *text*; [62] *blank*; 63, *Costume Plot*; 64, *Property Plot*; 65–67, *Switchboard Lighting Plot*; [68] *blank*

PUBLISHED: 14 August 1936 ($2.00); (price 2s6d); British Library reception date 18 August 1936

COVER: White cardboard covers, black letters

SIZE: 18.5×24.67 cm. (7⅜×9¾")

NOTES: Produced at the Palace Theatre, London, Friday, 14 June 1935.

French's Acting Edition 804.

C9 The Three Musketeers

The | Three Musketeers | *A Romantic Musical Play* | *Book by* | Wm. ANTHONY McGUIRE | *Lyrics by* | P. G. WODEHOUSE and | CLIFFORD GREY | *Music by* | RUDOLF FRIML | [decoration] | price 3 /- net |

| CHAPPELL & CO. LTD. | HARMS INC. |
| 50 New Bond St., London, W.1 and Sydney | 62 West 45th Street, New York |

Copyright mcmxxxvii by harms inc. | *All rights reserved* | 438 Printed in England

COLLATION: [1] *title page*; [2] *blank*; [3] *Cast of Characters. Synopsis of Scenes*; [4] *blank*; [5]–95, *text* (bottom of page 95, *printer's note*: Printed by Lowe & Brydone Printers Limited, London, N.W.10); [96] *advertisements*: Chappell & Co.'s Light Opera Successes (*thirteen titles beginning* The Rebel Maid *and ending* Lilac Time)

PUBLISHED (price 3s); British Library reception date 22 March 1937

COVER: Gray wrappers, black lettering

SIZE: 14×21.5 cm. (5½×8½")

DUST WRAPPER: Advertisement for *Lilac Time* on the back; advertisement for *Wildflower* inside back wrapper

NOTES: Variant edition had advertisement on page 96 for *The New Moon* by Sigmund Romberg.

Copyright in the United States by Harms, 19 March 1937.

C10 Don't Listen, Ladies

DON'T LISTEN, LADIES | A Comedy in Three Acts | by | STEPHEN POWYS and GUY BOLTON | From the French of | SACHA GUITRY | [decoration] | samuel french limited | london

COLLATION: [i] *title page*; [ii] *copyright page:* . . . Copyright, 1948, by Guy Bolton and P. G. Wodehouse [copyright notice] Made and Printed in Great Britain by Latimer, Trend and Co., Ltd, Plymouth Made in England; [iii] *cast of first performance Synopsis of Scenes*; [iv] *copyright notice regarding amateur performances*; *photograph of Scene I* (*inserted*); [1]–70, *text*; [71]–73, *Furniture and Property List*; [74–76] *blank*

PUBLISHED: July 1952 (price 5s); British Library reception date 16 July 1952

COVER: Tan boards, dark brown letters, brown and gold drawings and decorations

SIZE: 14×21.5 cm. (5½×8½")

NOTES: Opened at St. James's Theatre, London, September 2, 1948.

On cover: French's Acting Edition no. 330.

Stephen Powys had been used as a pseudonym before for *Wise To-Morrow* (1937) written by either Guy Bolton (see letter to Wodehouse, 23 February 1937) or by Guy's wife, Virginia (see Guy Bolton statement in the *New York Times*, 26 October 1939). This time, however, Wodehouse was Stephen Powys.

C11 Come On, Jeeves

ACTING EDITION | COME ON, JEEVES | *A Farcical Comedy in Three Acts* | by | P. G. WODEHOUSE | and | GUY BOLTON | [publisher's device] | london | evans brothers limited | general editor: lionel hale [triple-rule frame]

COLLATION: *photograph*; [1] *title page*; [2] *copyright page:* First published 1956. *Copyright notice regarding amateur performances*; [3–4] Author's Note (*by P. G. Wodehouse*); [5] Characters. Scenes; [6] *sketch set for Act I*; [7]–78, *text*; [79–80] Property Plot

PUBLISHED: (price 5s); British Library reception date 15 January 1960

COVER: Blue-gray wrappers, green decorations, black lettering

SIZE: 14×21.5 cm. (5½×8½")

NOTES: Front cover: "price 5s. net Evans Plays."

From the Author's Note: "Unless I have got my figures wrong, this—I allude to COME ON JEEVES—is Guy Bolton's eighty-ninth play. It is the twentieth he and I have written together. . . . A footnote. All students of the best in English literature are familiar with the novel *Ring for Jeeves*, and many must have supposed that *Come on, Jeeves* is a dramatization of that book. This is not so. After I and Guy had written the play, I turned it into a novel, and if anyone has not read it, there is a genuine treat in store for him."

C12 Oh, Clarence

GUILD LIBRARY | OH, CLARENCE! | A COMEDY | by | JOHN CHAPMAN | Adapted from 'Blandings Castle' | and other Lord Emsworth stories by P. G. Wodehouse | ENGLISH THEATRE GUILD LTD. | Ascot House, 52 Dean Street, London W.1.

COLLATION: [1] *title page*; [2] *copyright page: performance rights* © copyright John Chapman 1969 Printed in England by Stephen Austin and Sons, Hertford, Herts.; [3] Presented by Peter Saunders at the Opera House, Manchester on July 29th, 1968, and subsequently at the Lyric Theatre, London, W.1., on August 28th, 1968, with the following cast . . . ; [4] *blank*; [5] *list of scenes*; [6] *photograph of set in Act I*; 7–141, *text*; 142–43, *property plot*; 144, *sketch of stage*

PUBLISHED (price 7s); British Library reception date 11 December 1969

COVER: Red boards, black lettering

SIZE: 15×21 cm. (5⅞×8¼")

NOTE: Photographs also on pages 10 and 68. Errata sheet included.

NOTE: There are two titles which are lacking descriptions in this bibliography:

Uncle Fred Flits By, dramatized by Perry Clark (pseud. Christopher Sergel). Chicago: Dramatic Publishing Co., 1949 (copyright 10 February 1949).

Too Much Springtime, dramatized by Marjorie Duhan Adler. Chicago: Dramatic Publishing Company, 1955 (copyright 5 March 1955). Dramatization of *The Mating Season*.

Tauchnitz Editions

THE FIRM OF Bernard Tauchnitz published the Tauchnitz Edition, a paperback "Collection of British and American Authors," in Leipzig from 1841 until the Second World War and in Stuttgart for a few years after the war.

During these years British and American publishers had few sales for their expensive hardcover books outside of the English-speaking world. As a result, they authorized Tauchnitz to publish their titles in English in inexpensive paperback editions provided these were not sold in primary English-language markets. "Not to be introduced into the British Empire and U.S.A." was printed on the front cover of all Tauchnitz books.

From 1924 to 1954 Tauchnitz published forty-one different Wodehouse titles.

Published in Leipzig:

no. 4651 *Ukridge*, 1924
4669 *Bill the Conqueror*, 1925
4710 *Carry On, Jeeves!*, 1925
4714 *Sam the Sudden*, 1926
4740 *Love among the Chickens*, 1926
4741 *The Heart of a Goof*, 1926
4776 *Psmith, Journalist*, 1927
4777 *Leave It to Psmith*, 1927
4847 *The Small Bachelor*, 1928
4848 *A Damsel in Distress*, 1928
4852 *The Adventures of Sally*, 1928
4874 *Meet Mr. Mulliner*, 1929
4882 *Indiscretions of Archie*, 1929
4885 *Piccadilly Jim*, 1929
4963 *Mr. Mulliner Speaking*, 1931
4983 *Very Good, Jeeves*, 1931
4995 *Summer Lightning*, 1931
5035 *Big Money*, 1932
5061 *Louder and Funnier*, 1932
5068 *If I Were You*, 1932
5105 *Jill the Reckless*, 1933

5106 *Hot Water*, 1933
5112 *The Girl on the Boat*, 1933
5113 *The Clicking of Cuthbert*, 1933
5115 *Something Fresh*, 1933
5146 *The Little Nugget*, 1934
5170 *Thank You, Jeeves*, 1934
5184 *The Inimitable Jeeves*, 1935
5195 *The Man with Two Left Feet*, 1935
5206 *Money for Nothing*, 1935
5218 *Mulliner Nights*, 1935
5231 *The Coming of Bill*, 1936
5249 *Blandings Castle*, 1936
5271 *Young Men in Spats*, 1937
5280 *Laughing Gas*, 1937
5316 *Lord Emsworth and Others*, 1938
5347 *Summer Moonshine*, 1939
5357 *The Code of the Woosters*, 1939

Published in Stuttgart:
n.s. 16 *Money in the Bank*, 1949
n.s. 107 *The Mating Season*, 1952
n.s. 137 *Ring for Jeeves*, 1954

Autograph Editions

ONLY the copies of the Autograph Editions published between 1956 and 1963 were deposited in the British Library; the dates for November 1963 through March 1965 come from the *English Catalogue*. They were all published in uniform covers, bright blue or green cloth, and size 12.5×19.5 cm. (5×7½″). Many have Wodehouse's name written diagonally across the lower right-hand corner of the front cover. All should have P. G. Wodehouse's signature across the top of the title page.

BRITISH LIBRARY DATE	TITLE	ENGLISH CATALOGUE DATE AND PRICE
9 October 1956	*Thank You, Jeeves*	25 May 1956; 7s6d
	The Clicking of Cuthbert	
	Hot Water	
	Lord Emsworth and Others	
	The Girl on the Boat	
	The Inimitable Jeeves	
	Summer Moonshine	
	A Damsel in Distress	
28 November 1956	*The Heart of a Goof*	30 November 1956; 7s6d
	The Luck of the Bodkins	
	Meet Mr. Mulliner	
4 September 1957	*Young Men in Spats*	13 September 1957; 7s6d
	Right Ho, Jeeves	
	Blandings Castle	
18 April 1958	*If I Were You*	25 April 1958; 7s6d
	Jill the Reckless	
5 November 1958	*Barmy in Wonderland*	7 November 1958; 7s6d
	Very Good, Jeeves	
26 May 1959	*Laughing Gas*	29 May 1959; 7s6d
	Money for Nothing	
17 February 1960	*Quick Service*	February 1960; 8s6d
	Ukridge	
25 November 1960	*Carry On, Jeeves!*	25 November 1960; 8s6d
	Heavy Weather	
14 June 1961	*Leave It to Psmith*	16 June 1961; 8s6d
	Mr. Mulliner Speaking	
15 March 1962	*Code of the Woosters*	March 1962; 10s6d
	Jeeves and the Feudal Spirit	
21 November 1962	*A Gentleman of Leisure*	21 November 1962; 10s6d
	Uncle Fred in the Springtime	
21 June 1963	*Louder and Funnier*	29 November 1963; 10s6d
	Ring for Jeeves	
	Love among the Chickens	
18 October 1963	*Eggs, Beans and Crumpets*	10s6d
1964	*Summer Lightning*	9 October 1964; 10s6d
	Nothing Serious	
1965	*Big Money*	12 March 1965; 10s6d
	Indiscretions of Archie	
1966	*Piccadilly Jim*	10s6d
	The Coming of Bill	
	Mulliner Nights	

Anthologies with Wodehouse Contributions

A A. *The Laughter Omnibus Taken from Punch*, by A A [pseud. Anthony Armstrong Willis]. London: Faber and Faber, 1937. 667 pages. "The Sluggard."

Alden, Cecil. *The Cecil Alden Book*. London: Eyre and Spottiswoode, 1932. 193 pages. "Gone Wrong," pp. 84–90.

Armstrong, Anthony. *Laughter Parade*, compiled by A A [pseud. Anthony Armstrong Willis]. London: Faber & Faber, 1940. 512 pages. "The Great Sermon Handicap," pp. 227–50.

Asquith, Cynthia Mary Evelyn. *The Funny Bone*. New York: Scribner's, 1928. 303 pages. Also published under the title *New Tales of Humor by Leading Authors* (London: Jarrolds, 1928). "Keeping It from Harold," pp. 7–20.

Asquith, Cynthia Mary Evelyn. *The Treasure Ship: A Book of Prose and Verse*, ed. Lady Cynthia Asquith. London: Partridge; New York: Charles Scribner's Sons, 1926. 198 pages. "Pillingshot, Detective," pp. 118–31.

Barsley, Michael. *Life and Laughter, More Wit and Humour*. London: Phoenix House, 1962. 270 pages. "Pigs Have Wings" [the last chapter], pp. 18–34.

Benson, Theodora. *The First Time I . . .* , ed. and illus. the Hon. Theodora Benson. London: Chapman & Hall, 1935. 306 pages. "The First Time I Went to New York," pp. 265–79.

Bishop, Morris. *A Treasury of British Humor*. New York: Coward-McCann, 1942. 820 pages. "Tried in the Furnace," pp. 542–60.

Blair, Thomas M. H. *Fifty Modern Stories*. New York: Row, Peterson, 1960. 723 pages. "Jeeves and the Song of Songs," pp. 516–32.

Bradby, Christopher, and Anne Ridler. *Best Stories of Church and Clergy*. London: Faber and Faber, 1966. 224 pages. "The Great Sermon Handicap," pp. 205–23.

Briggs, Thomas Henry. *New Frontiers*, ed. Thomas H. Briggs, Lucille Prim Jackson, Emma Miller Bolenius, and Max J. Herzberg. New York: Houghton, 1940. 680 pages. "Pig-hoo-o-o-ey!"

Brown, Leonard Stanley. *Modern Short Stories*, enlarged ed. New York: Harcourt, 1937. 676 pages. "Uncle Fred Flits By."

Buckeridge, Anthony. *In and Out of School*, stories chosen by Anthony Buckeridge. London: Faber & Faber, 1958. 250 pages. "Mainly about Shoes."

Buckeridge, Anthony. *Stories for Boys*. London: Faber and Faber, 1957. 272 pages. "The Mixer," pp. 24–40.

Bullett, Gerald William. *Jackdaw's Nest: A Fivefold Anthology*. London: Macmillan, 1939. 1007 pages. "Amazing Hat Mystery," pp. 788–812.

Cerf, Bennett Alfred, and Henry Curran Moriarty. *Bedside Book of Famous British Stories*, intro. Bliss Perry. New York: Random House, 1940. 1233 pages. "Jeeves and the Song of Songs," pp. 826–42.

Cole, William. *The Fireside Book of Humorous Poetry*. New York: Simon and Schuster, 1959. 522 pages. "Printer's Error," pp. 334–36; "Song about Whiskers," pp. 355–58; "Time Like an Ever-Rolling Stream," pp. 364–66.

Cole, William. *Man's Funniest Friend: The [drawing of a dog] in Stories, Reminiscences, Poems and Cartoons*. Cleveland, New York: The World Publishing Company, 1967. 237 pages. "The Go-Getter," pp. 87–109.

Costain, Thomas B. *Read with Me*. New York: Doubleday, 1965. 623 pages. "The Clicking of Cuthbert," pp. 599–613.

Einstein, Charles. *The Fireside Book of Baseball*. New York: Simon and Schuster, 1956. 394 pages. "The Pitcher and the Plutocrat," pp. 370–75.

Erwitt, Elliott. *Son of Bitch*, with 100 Photographs; Unleashed by P. G. Wodehouse. London: Thames & Hudson, 1975. 127 pages. "About My Friends," pp. 9–14.

The Favourite Wonder Book. London: Odhams Pr., 1938. 768 pages. "William Tell Told Again," pp. 81–119.

Georgian Stories, 1924. London: Chapman and Hall, 1924. 296 pages. "Purity of the Turf," pp. 277–96.

Gray, Charles Wright. *Real Dogs: An Anthology of Short Stories*, New York: Holt, 1926. 352 pages. Reprinted Garden City: Sun Dial Pr., 1937. "Very Shy Gentleman."

Great Dog Stories. New York: Ballantine Books, 1955. 162 pages. "Very Shy Gentleman."

Hoke, Newton Wilson. *Double Entendre*. New York: Pocket Books, 1957. 202 pages. "The Model and the Sofa," by P. G. Wodehouse and Guy Bolton, pp. 17–22.

Holtzman, Jerome. *Fielder's Choice*. New York: Harcourt, Brace, Jovanovich, 1979. 395 pages. "The Pitcher and the Plutocrat," pp. 321–33.

Ingles, Rewey Belle. *Adventures in English Literature*, standard 3d ed. New York: Harcourt, Brace and

Company, 1945. 724 pages. "Uncle Fred Flits By," pp. 583–93.

Kahn, Joan. *Open at Your Own Risk*. Boston: Houghton Mifflin, 1975. 506 pages. "Sensational Occurence at a Poetry Reading," pp. 474–99.

Lardner, Rex. *Rex Lardner Selects the Best of Sports Fiction*. New York: Grosset & Dunlap, 1966. 249 pages. "The Clicking of Cuthbert," pp. 195–214.

The Legion Book, ed. Captain H. Cotton Minchin. London: Cassell and Company, 1929, 290 pages. Published in the United States by Doubleday, Doran, 1929. "Disentangling Old Percy," pp. 111–27.

Lines, Kathleen. *The Faber Book of Stories*. London: Faber & Faber, 1960. 334 pages. "Bill the Bloodhound."

Linfield, Eric G., and Egon Larsen. *Laughter in a Damp Cellar*. London: Herbert Jenkins, 1963. 397 pages. "Bertie and Jeeves," pp. 201–8; "Do Thrillers Need Heroines?" pp. 208–11.

Literary Treasures of 1929. Chicago: Hearst's International Cosmopolitan Magazine for private distribution only, 1929. 309 pages. "Jeeves and the Song of Songs," pp. 182–211.

London Omnibus, intro. Carl Van Doren. Garden City, N.Y.: Doubleday, 1932. Various pagings. "Jeeves and the Impending Doom," 32 pages.

McCloskey, Frank H. *A Pageant of Prose*. New York: Harper, 1935. 895 pages. "Mulliner's Buck-U-Uppo," pp. 495–507.

Maugham, William Somerset. *Tellers of Tales: 100 Short Stories from the United States, England, France, Russia and Germany*. Garden City, N.Y.: Doubleday, 1939. 1526 pages. "Uncle Fred Flits By," pp. 920–35.

Meany, Tom. *Collier's Greatest Sports Stories*. New York: A. S. Barnes, 1955. 299 pages. "The Pitcher and the Plutocrat."

Meredith, Scott. *The Fireside Treasury of Modern Humor*. New York: Simon and Schuster, 1963. 986 pages. "Jeeves and the Yuletide Spirit," pp. 949–63.

Miller, Richard. *Just Cats: Stories Grave and Gay of the Hearthside Tyrant*. Garden City, N.Y.: Doubleday, 1934. 293 pages. "Bishop's Cat," pp. 106–31.

Montgomery, John. *The World's Best Cat Stories*. New York: McGraw-Hill, 1970. 217 pages. "The Story of Webster."

My Funniest Story: An Anthology of Stories Chosen by Their Own Authors. London: Faber and Faber, 1932. 498 pages. "Honeysuckle Cottage," pp. 9–41.

Nash, Ogden. *I Couldn't Help Laughing*, stories selected and introduced by Odgen Nash. Philadelphia: J. B. Lippincott, 1957. 231 pages. "Uncle Fred Flits By," pp. 205–31.

Overton, Grant Martin. *Cream of the Jug: An Anthology of Humorous Stories*. New York: Harper, 1927. 336 pages. "Custody of the Pumpkin," pp. 30–63.

Overton, Grant Martin. *World's 100 Best Short Stories in 10 volumes*. New York: Funk and Wagnalls, 1927. 10 volumes. "Custody of the Pumpkin," vol. 10, pp. 43–68.

Panorama of Modern Literature, Contributed by 31 Great Modern Writers, intro. Christopher Morley. Garden City, N.Y.: Doubleday, 1934. 555 pages. "The Smile That Wins," pp. 315–35.

Parrish, J. M., and John R. Crossland. *The Great Book of Humour*. London: Odhams Pr., 1935. 768 pages. "The Ordeal of Young Tuppy," pp. 748–68.

Pence, Raymond Woodbury. *Short Stories of Today*. New York: Macmillan, 1934. 512 pages. "Unpleasantness at Bludleigh Court," pp. 469–89.

Playboy. *The Playboy Book of Humor and Satire*, selected by the editors of *Playboy*. Chicago: Playboy Pr., 1967. 407 pages. "Fox-Hunting—Who Needs It?" pp. 351–59.

Punch. *A Big Bowl of Punch: A Heady Potpourri of Cartoons, Prose and Verse from England's Humorous Weekly*, selected for Americans by William Cole. New York: Simon and Schuster, 1964. 336 pages. "Our Man in America," pp. 59–60, 63–64, 71–72, 77–78, 83–85; "Get Set," pp. 179–80; Richard Usborne, "The French for P. G. Wodehouse," pp. 99–102.

Punch. *Later Poems from Punch, 1887–1908*, intro. Arthur Waugh. London: Harrap, 1909. 235 pages. "Damon and Pythias," pp. 119–22.

Punch. *The Pick of Punch, 1956–1959: An Annual Selection*, ed. Nicolas Bentley. New York: E. P. Dutton; London: Andre Deutsch, 1956–59. 4 annuals. "America Day by Day," 1956, pp. 43–44; "Introduction," 1957, pp. 9–10; "America Day by Day," 1957, pp. 28–29; "America Day by Day," 1958, pp. 92–93; "Get Set," 1959, pp. 11–12; "America Day by Day," 1959, pp. 128–31.

Reppert, Emma L. *Modern Short Stories*. New York: McGraw, 1939. 564 pages. "Farewell to Legs," pp. 416–38.

Rhys, Ernest. *28 Humorous Stories, Old and New, by 20 and 8 Authors*. New York: Appleton, 1926. 341 pages. "Last of Battling Billson."

Schwed, Peter, and Herbert Warren Wind. *Great Stories from the World of Sport*. New York: Simon and Schuster, 1958. 3 volumes. "Heart of a Goof," vol. 1, pp. 203–22; "Clicking of Cuthbert," vol. 2, pp. 162–75.

Scoggin, Margaret Clara. *Chucklebait: Funny Stories for Everyone*. New York: Knopf, 1945. 383 pages. "Rummy Affairs of Old Biffy."

Smith, H. Greenhough. *"What I Think": A Symposium on Books and Other Things by Famous Writers of To-Day*, ed. H. Greenhough Smith (editor of the *Strand* magazine). London: George Newnes, 1936? 184 pages. "How I Write My Books," pp. 42–45.

Speare, Morris Edmund. *World's Great Short Stories: Masterpieces of American, English and Continental Literature*. Cleveland, New York: World Publishing, 1942. 334 pages. "Custody of the Pumpkin," pp. 68–85.

Stanley, Dave. *A Treasury of Golf Humor*, ed. Dave Stanley [pseud. David Dachs], illus. Cobbledick. New York: Lantern Pr., 1949. 383 pages. "Jane Gets off the Fairway," pp. 328–55. "The Heart of a Goof," pp. 356–83.

Stix, Thomas Louis. *"Say It Ain't So, Joe."* New York: Boni and Gaer, 1947. 342 pages. "High Stakes."

Thomson, H. Douglas, and C. Clark Ramsey. *The Holiday Book*. London: Odhams Pr., 1934. 1024 pages. "Jeeves in the Springtime," pp. 257–71.

The Times, London. *The First Cuckoo: A Selection of the Most Witty, Amusing and Memorable Letters to The Times, 1900–1975*, chosen and intro. Kenneth Gregory. London: Times Books and George Allen and Unwin, 1976. 350 pages. "The Wooster Chin," p. 160.

Twenty-Five Cricket Stories. London: George Newnes, 1909. 208 pages. "Tom, Dick—and Harry," pp. 7–15; "The Wire-Pullers," pp. 40–49; "The Lost Bowlers," pp. 78–87; "How Pillingshot Scored," pp. 118–24.

Untermeyer, Louis. *Treasury of Great Humor, Including Wit, Whimsy, and Satire from the Remote Past to the Present*, presented with a running commentary, by Louis Untermeyer. New York: McGraw-Hill Book Company, 1972. 683 pages. "Strychnine in the Soup," pp. 571–89.

Untermeyer, Louis. *A Treasury of Laughter Consisting of Humorous Stories, Poems, Essays, Tall Tales, Jokes, Boners, Epigrams, Memorable Quips, and Devastating Crushers*. New York: Simon and Schuster, 1946. 712 pages. "Uncle Fred Flits By," pp. 683–99.

Wait, Peter. *Stories by Modern Masters*. London: Methuen, 1936. 151 pages. "The Mixer—I and II," pp. 1–39.

Waranoff, Peter, and Norman Adler. *English Literature: Four Representative Types*. New York: Globe Book, 1965. 915 pages. "America, I Like You," pp. 754–910.

Wind, Herbert Warren. *The Complete Golfer*, intro. Robert T. Jones, Jr. New York: Simon and Schuster, 1954. 314 pages. "The Clicking of Cuthbert," pp. 3–10.

Yoder, Robert M. *The Saturday Evening Post Carnival of Humor*. Englewood Cliffs, N.J.: Prentice-Hall, 1958. 362 pages. "The Aunt and the Sluggard," pp. 61–75.

Zistel, Era. *Treasury of Cat Stories*. New York: Greenberg, 1944. 287 pages. "Cats Will Be Cats," pp. 130–43.

Introductions and Prefaces

Bolton, Guy. *Gracious Living, Limited*. London: Herbert Jenkins, 1966. 208 pages. "Introducing Guy Bolton," pp. 5–7.

Cuppy, Will. *How to Tell Your Friends from the Apes*. London: Methuen, 1934. 120 pages. Introduction, pp. ix–xii.

Doyle, Arthur Conan. *The Sign of the Four*. New York: Ballantine Books, 1975. 130 pages. Introduction, pp. vii–xi.

Graves, Charles. *And the Greeks*. London: Geoffrey Bles, 1930; New York: Robert M. McBride, 1931. 224 pages. Introduction, pp. 13–16.

Graves, Charles. *Leather Armchairs*. London: Cassell, 1963; New York: Coward McCann, 1964. 194 pages. Foreword, p. v (p. xiii in New York edition).

Jenkins, Herbert. *Bindle Omnibus*. London: Herbert Jenkins, 1932. 960 pages. "H.J.," pp. v–vii.

McAleer, John. *Rex Stout: A Biography*. Boston: Little, Brown, 1977. 621 pages. Foreword, pp. xv–xvi.

Mackail, Denis. *Romance to the Rescue*. Boston: Houghton, Mifflin, 1921. 329 pages. Telegram on dust wrapper.

MacKinlay, Leila. *Musical Productions*. London: Herbert Jenkins, 1955. 96 pages. Preface, pp. 7–8.

Punch. *The Pick of Punch: An Annual Selection*, ed. Nicolas Bentley. London: Andre Deutsch; New York: Dutton, 1957. 176 pages. Introduction, pp. 9–10.

Townend, William. *The Ship in the Swamp and Other Stories*. London: Herbert Jenkins, 1928. 320 pages. Introduction, pp. 9–13.

Translations

THIS LIST of translations is only a beginning, intended to demonstrate Wodehouse's great popularity outside England and the United States. Wodehouse has been translated into most of the twenty-odd European languages, which range across the Continent from Portuguese and Spanish to Finnish, Polish, and Hungarian, and, of course, Esperanto. Publishers in the Scandinavian countries, Holland, Germany, and Italy are still offering long lists of Wodehouse translations. Most of the titles listed here have been gleaned from bibliographies and library catalogs; many have not been examined; thus there are inconsistent and incomplete entries.

The Heincman collection includes representative copies of translations from most countries. The Boston Public Library and the University of South Carolina Library have collections of Italian translations.

The translations cited here are arranged by earliest date of publication under the name of the language. Within each entry the information is presented as on a catalog card: the translated title of a Wodehouse book followed by the English-language title in parentheses, the translator's name, place, publisher, date, and number of pages, series name if there is one. Subsequent printings and editions of the work are then listed immediately after the earliest translation. Blank spaces within an entry indicate a lack of information.

It is to be hoped that this initial effort at a checklist of translations will encourage bibliographers in other countries to correct and complete this list, and to emulate Uno Asplund[1] who compiled a bibliography of Swedish translations.

1. Uno Asplund, *Möt mir Wodehouse* (Göteborg: Bergendahls, 1971).

Czech Translations

1934 *Archibaldovy nerozvaznosti* (*Indiscretions of Archie*). A. Fleischer. Prague: J. Otto, 1934. 224 pp.

1934 *Děvče v nasnázích* (*A Damsel in Distress*). Louisa Szalatnayová. Prague: Novina, 1934. 285 pp.

1934 *Ukvapený Sam* (*Sam the Sudden*). W. F. Waller. Prague: Sfinz, Bohumil Janda, 1934. 272 pp. Knižnice Nové céle, 616.

1935 *Bill dobyvatel* (*Bill the Conqueror*). W. F. Waller. Prague: Sfinz, Bohumil Janda, 1935. 313 pp.

1935 *Zánek blissac* (*Hot Water*). O. Laurinová. Prague: Alois Srdce, 1935. 291 pp.

1974 *Maly pán na zemění* (*The Small Bachelor*). J. Z. Novák. [Prague:] Odeon, [1974]. [278] pp.

1977 *Letní bouřka* (*Summer Lightning*). Ladislav Smutek. Prague: Československý spesovatel, [1977]. [227] pp.

1977 *Vlna zlocinnosti na zámku Blandings* (*Lord Emsworth and Others*). J. Z. Novák. [Prague:] Odeon, [1977]. [335] pp. Světová četba, sv. 484.

Danish Translations

1927 *Miss Billie ombord* (*The Girl on the Boat*). Anna Høyer. Copenhagen: Jespersen i Pio, 1927. 198 pp. Aut. oversättelse for Danmark og Norge.

1928 *Mands overmand* (*Bill the Conqueror*). Anna Høyer. Copenhagen: Jespersen i Pio, 1928. 240 pp. Aut. oversättelse for Danmark og Norge.

1929 *Lad Psmith klare den—!* (*Leave It to Psmith*). Ulla Eiler-Nielson. Copenhagen: Jespersen i Pio, 1929. 238 pp. Aut. oversättelse for Danmark og Norge.

1930 *Sallys Eventyr* (*The Adventures of Sally*). Ulla Valentiner-Branth. Copenhagen: Jespersen i Pio, 1930. 204 pp. Aut. oversättelse for Danmark og Norge.

1931 *Godt klaret, Jeeves* (*Very Good, Jeeves*). Sigvard Lund. Copenhagen: Jespersen i Pio, 1931. 180 pp. Aut. oversättelse for Danmark og Norge.

1931 *Jeeves, den uforlignelige* (*The Inimitable Jeeves*). Ulla Valentiner-Branth. Copenhagen: Jespersen i Pio, 1931. 190 pp. Aut. oversättelse for Danmark og Norge.
    2 oppl. 1951. 180 pp.
    3 oppl. 1963. 191 pp. Pios Billigbøger. Copenhagen: Lindhardt og Ringhof, 1976. 180 pp. ISBN 87-7560-198-2.

1932 *Haeng i Jeeves* (*Carry On, Jeeves!*). Ulla Valentiner-Branth. Copenhagen: Jespersen i Pio, 1932. 182 pp.
    2 oppl. 1951. 174 pp.
    Copenhagen: Lindhardt og Ringhof, 1976. 173 pp. ISBN 87-7560-199-0.

1932 *Sommerpjank* (*Summer Lightning*). Ulla Valentiner-Branth. Copenhagen: Jespersen i Pio, 1932. 190 pp.
    ny udg. Copenhagen: Skrifola, [1963]. 200 pp.

1933 *I klemme* (*Hot Water*). Ulla Valentiner-Branth. Copenhagen: Jespersen i Pio, 1933. 182 pp.

1934 *Tak Jeeves* (*Thank You, Jeeves*). Ulla Valentiner-Branth. Copenhagen: Jespersen i Pio, 1934. 190 pp.

1935 *Bravo Jeeves* (*Right Ho, Jeeves*). Ulla Valentiner-Branth. Copenhagen: Jespersen i Pio, 1935. 186 pp.

1936 *Psmith i banken* (*Psmith in the City*). Ulla Valentiner-Branth. Copenhagen: Jespersen i Pio, 1936. 192 pp.

1937 *Psmith som journalist* (*Psmith, Journalist*). Ulla Valentiner-Branth. Copenhagen: Jespersen i Pio, 1937. 176 pp.

1938 *Mulliner* (*Mulliner Omnibus*). Ulla Valentiner-Branth. Copenhagen: Jespersen i Pio, 1938. 158 pp.

1939 *Paa'en igen, Jeeves* (*The Code of the Woosters*). Ulla Valentiner-Branth. Copenhagen: Jespersen i Pio, 1939. 180 pp.

1942 *En Wodehouse Cocktail*, rysptet of *The Wodehouse-Fellowship* (anthology). Ulla Valentiner-Branth and Arne Ungermann. Copenhagen: Jespersen i Pio, 1942. 218 pp. Contents: Uncle Fred in Springtime, Heavy Weather, The Luck of the Bodkins, Money in the Bank, Something Fresh.

1942 *Et tosset Foraar* (*Uncle Fred in the Springtime*). Ulla Valentiner-Branth. Copenhagen: Jespersen i Pio, 1942. 238 pp.
    ny udg. Copenhagen: Skrifola, [1963]. 247 pp.

1943 *Ude at Svømme* (*Luck of the Bodkins*). Arne Ungermann. Copenhagen: Jespersen i Pio, 1943. 272 pp.

1944 *Ta' med til Blandings* (*Something Fresh*). Ulla Valentiner-Branth. Copenhagen: Jespersen i Pio, 1944. 218 pp.

1945 *Kejserinden af Blandings* (*Heavy Weather*). U. Valentiner-Branth. Copenhagen: Jespersen i Pio, 1945. 232 pp.

1946 *Penge i banken* (*Money in the Bank*). Ulla Valentiner-Branth. Copenhagen: Jespersen i Pio, 1946. 224 pp.

1947 *Jeeves griber ind* (*Joy in the Morning*). Ulla Valentiner-Branth. Copenhagen: Jespersen i Pio, 1947. 240 pp.

1948 *Hurtig ekspedition* (*Quick Service*). Svend Kragh-Jacobsen. Copenhagen: Jespersen i Pio, 1948. 178 pp.

1950 *Onkel Dynamit* (*Uncle Dynamite*). Ulla Valentiner-Branth. Copenhagen: Jespersen i Pio, 1950. 222 pp.

1952 *Bill den ukuelige* (*The Old Reliable*). Ulla Valentiner-Branth. Copenhagen: Jespersen i Pio, [1952]. 180 pp.

1956 *Ring på Jeeves* (*Ring for Jeeves*). Ulla Valentiner-Branth. Copenhagen: Jespersen i Pio, 1956. 189 pp.

1960 *Jeeves muntrer sig* (*Jeeves and the Feudal Spirit*). Ulla Valentiner-Branth. Copenhagen: Jespersen i Pio, 1960. 184 pp.

1960 *P. G. Wodehouse's bedste muntre historier: Udvalgt af Tage la Cour* ( ). Kurt Kreutzfeld. Copenhagen: Carit Andersen, 1960. 319 pp. Omnibusbøgerne.

1962 *P. G. Wodehouse fortaeller: Udvalgt af Tage la Cour* ( ). Karen Meldsted, Poul Ib Liebe, and

Kurt Kreutzfeld. Copenhagen: Carit Andersen, [1962]. 320 pp. Omnibusbøgerne.

1964 *Jeeves traekker i trådene* (*Jeeves in the Offing*). Ulla Valentiner-Branth. Copenhagen: Jespersen i Pio, 1964. 153 pp.

1967 *Hold hovedat koldt, Jeeves* (*Stiff Upper Lip, Jeeves*). Otto Jacobsen. Copenhagen: Grafisk, 1967. 222 pp.

1967 *Diamanter i dynerne* (*Ice in the Bedroom*). Otto Jacobsen. Copenhagen: Grafisk, 1967. 222 pp.

1968 *Over hals og hoved* (*French Leave*). Otto Jacobsen. Copenhagen: Grafisk, 1968. 220 pp.

1968 *En lusket affaere* (*Something Fishy*). Otto Jacobsen. Copenhagen: Grafisk, 1968. 223 pp.

1968 *Altid til tjeneste* (*Service with a Smile*). Otto Jacobsen. Copenhagen: Grafisk, 1968. 224 pp.

1968 *Den ordner Galahad* (*Galahad at Blandings*). Otto Jacobsen. Copenhagen: Grafisk, 1968. 220 pp.

1975 *Tanter er ikke gentlemen* (*Aunts Aren't Gentlemen*). Vilhelm Topsøe. Copenhagen: Lindhardt og Ringhof, 1975. 152 pp. SBN 7560-176-1.

Dutch Translations

1927 *Het meisje in de taxi* (*A Damsel in Distress*). R.L.d'W. Harlaam: Uitg-zaak J. W. Boissevain, 1927. 217 pp.

1927 *Sam en zijn schat* (*Sam the Sudden*). Amsterdam: Drukkerij Jacob van Campen, 1927. 396 pp. Feuilleton-bibliotheek, 53.

Sam en de schat (*Sam the Sudden*). John van Dijken. Utrecht: Het Spectrum, 1972. 243 pp. Prisma-boeken, 1554. ISBN 90-274-0681-2.

1928 *Psmith knapt het op* (*Leave It to Psmith*). R. H. G. Nahuys. Utrecht: A. W. Bruna & Zoon's, 1928. 264 pp.

Psmith knapt het op (*Leave It to Psmith*). R. H. G. Nahuys & W. Wielek-Berg. Utrecht, Antwerp: Het Spectrum, 1956. 224 pp.

   3 druk. 1960. 208 pp. Prisma-boeken, 210.

   4 druk. 1976. 208 pp. Prisma-boeken, 1745.

1928 *Psmith aspirant bankier* (*Psmith in the City*). R. H. G. Nahuys. Utrecht: A. W. Bruna & Zoon's, 1928. 256 pp.

1928 *Psmith journalist* (*Psmith, Journalist*). R. H. G. Nahuys. Utrecht: A. W. Bruna & Zoon's, 1928. 238 pp.

1928 *Een vroolijke romance* (*Something Fresh*). R. H. G. Nahuys. Utrecht: A. W. Bruna & Zoon's, 1928. 255 pp.

Nieuwe bezems (*Something Fresh*). William N. Vandersluys. Utrecht: [Het Spectrum, 1963]. 192 pp. Prisma-boeken, 835.

1928 *Amor in het kippenhok* (*Love among the Chickens*). A. Vuerhard-Berkhout. Utrecht: A. W. Bruna & Zoon's, 1928. 248 pp.

   Antwerp: Helicon, [1949]. 175 pp.

   3 druk. Antwerp, Utrecht: Het Spectrum, 1957. 190 pp.

1933 *In de soep* (*Hot Water*). M. J. Landré-Tollenaar. Amsterdam: Drukkerij Jacob van Campen, 1933. 338 pp. Feuilleton-bibliotheek, 85.

   1948. 243 pp. Eekhoornreeks, 2.

   3 druk. Utrecht, Antwerp: Het Spectrum, [1956]. 228 pp. Prisma-boeken, 200.

1934 *Ukridge* (*Ukridge*). A. M. Buis. Amsterdam: Albert de Lange, 1934. 211 pp.

De dolende Schurk (*Ukridge*). A. J. Richel & John van Dijken. Antwerp: [Het Spectrum, 1965]. 219 pp. Prisma-boeken, 1124.

1935 *Knap jij 't maar op, Jeeves* (*Carry On, Jeeves!*). F. van Velsen. Tilburg: Het Nederlandsche boekhuis, 1935. 281 pp.

Jeeves fikst 't (*Carry On, Jeeves!*). A. J. Richel. Utrecht: Het Spectrum, [1970]. 208 pp. Prisma-boeken, 1462.

   2 druk. [1974]. 208 pp. Prisma-boeken, 1462. ISBN 90-272-0474-7.

1937 *Jimmy verliefd* (*Piccadilly Jim*). Jean H. P. Jacobs. Tilburg: Het Nederlandsche boekhuis, 1937. 352 pp.

Piccadilly Jim (*Piccadilly Jim*). C. A. Spiekerman-Machielse. Antwerp, Utrecht: Het Spectrum, [1961]. 220 pp. Prisma-boeken, 621.

1941 *De verlegen vrijgezel* (*The Small Bachelor*). Harlaam: De Spaarnestad, 1941. 315 pp. Kennemer serie, 35.

Antwerp: Het Spectrum, 1965, 1966. 240 pp.

1947 *Goeiemorgen, Bill* (*Good Morning, Bill*). J. Poort. Antwerp: Jos. Janssens, [1947]. 96 pp.

1950 *Uit de pekel* (*The Code of the Woosters*). Frank Deckers. Antwerp: Standaard Boekhandel, [1950]. 286 pp.

Het blazoen van de Woosters (*The Code of the Woosters*). Frank Deckers. Antwerp, Utrecht: Het Spectrum, [1954], 1955. 240 pp. Prisma-boeken, 121.

    3 druk. [1960]. 192 pp. Prisma-boeken, 121.

    4 druk. 1976. 232 pp. Prisma-boeken, 1722.

1950 *Veulens in galop* (*Young Men in Spats*). Norbert Helgard. Antwerp: Standaard-Boekhandel, [1950]. 239 pp.

1950 *Vooruit maar, Jeeves!* (*The Inimitable Jeeves*). G. Jo Steenbergen. Antwerp: Standaard-Boekhandel, 1950. 255 pp.

De onnavolgbare Jeeves (*The Inimitable Jeeves*). G. Jo Steenbergen. Antwerp, Utrecht: Het Spectrum, 1955. 224 pp.

    3 druk. 1960. 192 pp. Prisma-boeken, 126.

1951 *Familie—festival* (*Mr. Mulliner Speaking*). Antwerp: De Standaard-Boekhandel, [1951]. 272 pp.

1951 *Wat een familie* (*Meet Mr. Mulliner*). G. van Tichelen & Frank Deckers. Antwerp: Standaard-Boekhandel, [1951]. 239 pp.

Getapte verhalen (*Meet Mr. Mulliner*). Anne C. C. Toornvliet-Los. Antwerp, Utrecht: [Het Spectrum, 1968]. 157 pp. Prisma-boeken, 1309.

1953 *Phips is de man!* (*The Old Reliable*). G. Jo Steenbergen. Amsterdam: Standaard-Boekhandel, [1953]. 234 pp.

De krakende butler (*The Old Reliable*). Anne C. C. Toornvliet-Los. Antwerp, Utrecht: Het Spectrum, [1972]. 190 pp. Prisma-boeken, 1515. ISBN 90-274-0642-1.

1956 *De ontvoerde zeug* (*Summer Lightning*). W. Wielek-Berg [pseud. Willy Kwiksilber-Berg]. Antwerp: Het Spectrum, 1956. 229 pp. Utrecht: Het Spectrum, 1956. 232 pp.

    2 druk. Utrecht, Antwerp: Het Spectrum, 1960. 224 pp. Prisma-boeken, 219.

1956 *Rumoer op Blandings Castle* (*Heavy Weather*). W. Wielek-Berg. Utrecht, Antwerp: Het Spectrum, 1956. 232 pp.

    2 druk. [1960]. 221 pp. Prisma-boeken, 230.

    [1976]. 221 pp. Prisma-boeken, 1746.

1957 *De das met de blauwe hoefijzers* (*Ring for Jeeves*). W. Wielek-Berg. Utrecht, Antwerp: Het Spectrum, 1957. 197 pp.

    2 druk. 1960. 191 pp. Prisma-boeken, 257.

1957 *De hammenkonig* (*Quick Service*). W. Wielek-Berg. Utrecht, Antwerp: Het Spectrum, [1957]. 184 pp. Prisma-boeken, 244.

1957 *Er zit een luchtje aan* (*Something Fishy*). Lydia Belinfante. Antwerp, Utrecht: Het Spectrum, [1957]. 187 pp. Prisma-boeken, 305.

1958 *Gussie en katvis* (*The Mating Season*). W. Wielek-Berg. Antwerp, Utrecht: Het Spectrum, [1958]. 199 pp. Prisma-boeken, 338.

    2 druk. 1976. 199 pp. Prisma-boeken, 1721. ISBN 90-274-0848-3.

    3 druk. [1976]. 199 pp. Prisma-boeken, 1721.

1958 *Lachgas* (*Laughing Gas*). Lydia Belinfante. Antwerp, Utrecht: Het Spectrum, [1958]. 220 pp. Prisma-boeken, 323.

1958 *Lentekoorts* (*Spring Fever*). J. C. de Graaff. Antwerp, Utrecht: Het Spectrum, [1958]. 204 pp. Prisma-boeken, 382.

1958 *Wodehouse over Wodehouse: Een autobiografi met uitweidingen* (*Over Seventy*). B. H. Lohf. Antwerp: Het Spectrum, 1958; Utrecht: Het Spectrum, 1961. 187 pp. Prisma-boeken, 395.

1959 *Gevleugelde varkens* (*Pigs Have Wings*). R. Dekuyper. Antwerp, Utrecht: Het Spectrum, [1959]. 200 pp. Prisma-boeken, 480.

    2 druk. 1976. 200 pp. Prisma-boeken, 1748. ISBN 90-274-0875-0.

1959 *Borreluurtje* (*Cocktail Time*). Henriëtte van der Kop. Utrecht, Antwerp: [Het Spectrum, 1959]. 184 pp. Prisma-boeken, 441.

1959 *Bravo Jeeves.* (*Right Ho, Jeeves*). B. H. Lohf. Antwerp, Utrecht: Het Spectrum, [1959]. 197 pp. Prisma-boeken, 411.

1959 *Mickey Mous en het parelsnoer* (*Luck of the Bodkins*). Lydia Belinfante. Antwerp, Utrecht: [Het Spectrum, 1959]. 230 pp. Prisma-boeken, 408.

1959 *Volle maan* (*Full Moon*). Lydia Belinfante. Antwerp: Het Spectrum, [1959]. 187 pp. Prisma-boeken, 430.

    2 druk. Antwerp, Utrecht: Het Spectrum, 1962. 187 pp.

    3 druk. [1976]. 187 pp. Prisma-boeken, 1747.

1960 *De avonturen van Sally* (*The Adventures of Sally*). Fie Zegerius. Utrecht, Antwerp: Het Spectrum, [1960]. 192 pp. Prisma-boeken, 565.

1960 *Dokter Sally* (*Doctor Sally*). Henriëtte van der

Kop. Utrecht, Antwerp: Het Spectrum, [1960]. 157 pp. Prisma-boeken, 541.

    2 druk. 1961. 157 pp.

    3 druk. 1962. 157 pp. Prisma-boeken, 541.

1960 *Geld zat!* (*Big Money*). Leonore ter Laan. Antwerp, Utrecht: Het Spectrum, 1960. 208 pp. Prisma-boeken, 525.

1960 *Maneschijn in de zomernacht* (*Summer Moonshine*). H. Vernes & P. A. A. Vernes van der Weide. Antwerp, Utrecht: Het Spectrum, [1960]. 223 pp. Prisma-boeken, 584.

1960 *Met Jeeves door dik en dun* (*Jeeves and the Feudal Spirit*). A. J. Richel. Utrecht, Antwerp: [Het Spectrum, 1960]. 192 pp. Prisma-boeken, 568.

1961 *Bedankt, Jeeves!* (*Thank You, Jeeves*). J. M. H. van Heycop ten Ham-Frowein. Utrecht, Antwerp: Het Spectrum, [1961]. 187 pp. Prisma-boeken, 597.

    2 druk. 1976. 187 pp. Prisma-boeken, 1720. ISBN 90–274–0847–5.

    3 druk. 1976. 186 pp. Prisma-boeken, 1720.

1961 *Oompje Dynamiet* (*Uncle Dynamite*). Fredericka Adriana Valken. Antwerp: [Het Spectrum, 1961]. 217 pp. Prisma-boeken, 636.

1962 *Jeeves met valkantri* (*Jeeves in the Offing*). Charlie Burgers. Utrecht, Antwerp: [Het Spectrum, 1962]. 157 pp. Prisma-boeken, 700.

    3 druk. [1976]. 157 pp. Prisma-boeken, 1724.

1963 *Zeepneus & Co.* (*Ice in the Bedroom*). L. Montagne-Andres. Utrecht: [Het Spectrum, 1963]. 184 pp. Prisma-boeken, 876.

1963 *Aan Venus ontvloden* (*Joy in the Morning*). A. J. Richel. Utrecht, Antwerp: Het Spectrum, [1963]. 192 pp. Prisma-boeken, 921.

    2 druk. [1976]. 192 pp. Prisma-boeken, 1723. ISBN 90–274–0850–5.

1964 *Herberg "De rustende hengelaar"* (*Mulliner Nights*). M. E. Dreef. Utrecht, Antwerp: [Het Spectrum, 1964]. 187 pp. Prisma-boeken, 992.

1964 *Een heer op vrij ersvoeten* (*A Gentleman of Leisure*). A. J. Richel. Utrecht, Antwerp: [Het Spectrum, 1964]. 188 pp. Prisma-boeken, 1011.

1964 *De dienstevillige dienaar* (*Service with a Smile*). Joh. H. Van Dijken. Utrecht, Antwerp: [Het Spectrum, 1964]. 187 pp. Prisma-boeken, 1040.

    2 druk. [1976]. 186 pp. Prisma-boeken, 1749. ISBN 90–274–0876–9.

    3 druk. [1976]. 186 pp. Prisma-boeken, 1749.

1965 *De linke golfspeler* (*The Heart of a Goof*). A. J. Richel. Utrecht: [Het Spectrum, 1965]. 191 pp. Prisma-boeken, 1134.

1965 *Malle mensen* (*Uneasy Money*). J. M. H. van Heycop ten Ham-Frowein. Utrecht: [Het Spectrum, 1965]. 191 pp.

1966 *De lokkende Miljoenen* (*Frozen Assets*). Anne C. C. Toornvliet-Los. Utrecht: [Het Spectrum, 1966]. 191 pp. Prisma-boeken, 1206.

    2 druk. Antwerp, Utrecht: Het Spectrum, 1969. 191 pp. Prisma-boeken, 1206.

1967 *Jeeves blijft in de plool* (*Stiff Upper Lip, Jeeves*). A. J. Richel. Antwerp, Utrecht: [Het Spectrum, 1967]. 160 pp. Prisma-boeken, 1237.

1967 *Liefdesperikelen op Blandings Castle* (*Galahad at Blandings*). J. van der Wart-Kousemaker. Utrecht, Antwerp: [Het Spectrum, 1967]. 192 pp. Prisma-boeken, 1264.

    2 druk. [1969]. 192 pp. Prisma-boeken, 1264.

1968 *Plumpudding* (*Plum Pudding*). Jan Wart Kousemaker. Utrecht: [Het Spectrum, 1968]; Antwerp: Het Spectrum, 1970. 223 pp. Prisma-boeken, 1343.

1969 *Henry's grote liefde* (*Company for Henry*). C. M. Botje-Zoetmulder. Antwerp, Utrecht: [Het Spectrum, 1969]. 187 pp. Prisma-boeken, 1368.

    2 druk. [1969]. 191 pp. Prisma-boeken, 1206.

1970 *De verliefde Butler* (*Do Butlers Burgle Banks?*). A. J. Richel. Utrecht, Antwerp: Het Spectrum, [1970]. 157 pp. Prisma-boeken, 1450.

    2 druk. [1974]. 157 pp. Prisma-boeken, 1450. ISBN 90–274–0458–5.

1971 *Bloot op Blandingscastle* (*A Pelican at Blandings*). A. J. Richel. Antwerp, Utrecht: Het Spectrum, [1971]. 191 pp. Prisma-boeken, 1474.

    2 druk. [1974]. 191 pp. Prisma-boeken, 1474. ISBN 90–274–0498–4.

1971 *Det is het einde, Jeeves* (*Much Obliged, Jeeves*). A. J. Richel. Antwerp, Utrecht: Het Spectrum, [1971]. 174 pp. Prisma-boeken, 1503.

    2 druk. [1974]. 174 pp. Prisma-boeken, 1503. ISBN 90–274–0630–8.

1971 *Oom Fred versiert het* (*Uncle Fred in the Spring-*

time). Anne C. Toornvliet-Los. Antwerp: Het Spectrum, [1971]. 218 pp. Prisma-boeken, 1487. ISBN 90-274-0614-6.

1972 *Het meisje in het blauw* (*The Girl on the Boat*). A. J. Richel. Antwerp, Utrecht: Het Spectrum, [1972]. 175 pp. Prisma-boeken, 1528. ISBN 90-274-0655-3.

1972 *Goudklompje* (*The Little Nugget*). A. C. C. Toornvliet-Los. Antwerp, Utrecht: Het Spectrum, [1972]. 174 pp. Prisma-boeken, 1541.
    [1972]. 202 pp. Het Nederlandse pocketboek.

1972 *Jeeves omnibus* (anthology). G. Jo Steenbergen, B. H. Lohf, A. J. Richel. Utrecht, Antwerp; Het Spectrum, 1972. 565 pp. Contents: De omnavolgbare Jeeves [The Inimitable Jeeves], Bravo Jeeves [Right Ho, Jeeves], Met Jeeves door dik en dun [Jeeves and the Feudal Spirit].

1973 *Diefje met verlos* (*Pearls, Girls and Monty Bodkin*). Anne C. C. Toornvliet-Los. Utrecht: Het Spectrum, [1973]. 153 pp. Prisma-boeken, 1599. ISBN 90-274-0726-6.

1973 *Geld op de banken* (*Money in the Bank*). John van Dijken. Antwerp, Utrecht: Het Spectrum, [1973]. 204 pp. Prisma-boeken, 1562. ISBN 90-274-0689-8.

1974 *Vrijgezellen* (*Bachelors Anonymous*). Anne C. C. Toornvliet-Los. Utrecht: Het Spectrum, [1974]. 144 pp. Prisma-boeken, 1645. ISBN 90-274-0772X.

1975 *Archie ontdekt Amerika* (*Indiscretions of Archie*). John H. van Dijken. Utrecht: Het Spectrum, [1975]. 203 pp. Prisma-boeken, 1697. ISBN 90-274-0824-6.

1975 *Tantes zijn gun beren* (*Aunts Aren't Gentlemen*). J. J. P. Boezeman. Utrecht, Antwerp: Het Spectrum, [1975]. 142 pp. Prisma-boeken, 1706.

1976 *Uitstekend, Jeeves* (*Very Good, Jeeves*). A. C. C. Toornvliet-Los. Utrecht, Antwerp: Het Spectrum, 1976. 204 pp. Prisma-boeken, 1754; Het Nederlandse pocketboek. ISBN 90-274-0081-5.

1979 *Zonsondergang op Blandings* (*Sunset at Blandings*). Anne C. C. Toornvliet-Los. Utrecht, Antwerp: Het Spectrum, 1979. 107 pp. Prisma-boeken, 1881. ISBN 90-274-1011-9.

Esperanto Translations

1938 *La princo kaj Betty* (*The Prince and Betty*). C. Badesh. Heronsgate, Rickmansworth (Herts.): The Esperanto Publ. Co., Ltd., [1938]. 185 pp. La "Epoko" Libro-Klubo, III.

Finnish Translations

1923 *Vaikeasti valloitettu* (*A Gentleman of Leisure*). Väinö Nyman. Hämeenlinna: Arvi A. Karisto oy, 1923. 187 pp. Matkaromaane ja, 3.
    2 pain. 1936. 248 pp. Kariston, 10.

1924 *Rauhatonta rahaa!* (*Uneasy Money*). Väinö Meltti. Hämeenlinna: Arvi A. Karisto oy, 1924. 274 pp.

1925 *Jotakin uutta* (*Something Fresh*). Aino Tuomikoski. Hämeenlinna: Arvi A. Karisto, 1925. 263 pp.

1925 *Neitonen ah dingossa* (*A Damsel in Distress*). J. V. Korjula. Hämeenlinna: Arvi A. Karisto, 1925. 258 pp. Vihreäleimaisia kirjoja, 7.
    Ojassa ja allikossa (*A Damsel in Distress*). S. S. Taula [Taube]. Jyväskylä: KJG, 1951. 249 pp.

1926 *Prinssi ja Betty* (*The Prince and Betty*). Salme Setälä (Cornér). Helsinki: Otava, 1926. 152 pp. Kirsikkasarja, 9.
    2 pain. 1952. 197 pp.

1927 *Onnen portaat* (*The Adventures of Sally*). Alpo Kupiainen. Hämeenlinna, Helsinki: A. Karisto, 1927. 352 pp. Uusia romaaneja, 7.

1928 *Antaa Psmithin hoitaa* (*Leave It to Psmith*). Aino Tuomikoski. Hämeenlinna: A. Karisto, 1928. 379 pp. Uusia romaaneja, 16.

1929 *Sukkela Sam* (*Sam the Sudden*). Eino Palola. Helsinki: Otava, 1929. 277 pp. Kirsikkasarja, 35.
    2 pain. 1949. 323 pp. Kirjan ystävien kerho, 1949:7.

1931 *Kesäinen rajuilma* (*Summer Lightning*). Eino Auer. Jyväskylä: K. J. Gummerus, 1931. 296 pp.
    2 pain. 1942. 252 pp.
    3 pain. 1943. 251 pp.

1934 *Huimapää Jill* (*Jill the Reckless*). Tellervo Laurila. Helsinki: Otava, 1934. 375 pp. Kymmenen uutta, 2.

1936 *Ville Valloittaja* (*Bill the Conqueror*). O. A. Joutsen. Porvoo: Werner Söderström, 1936. 295 pp. Kymmenen markan romaaneja, 90.
    2 pain. Porvoo, Helsinki: Werner Söderström, [1960]. 295 pp. Riksin sarja, 96.

1937 *Onnenpotku* (*The Luck of the Bodkins*). Helsinki: Otava, 1937. 327 pp.

1938 *Rahaa kuin roskaa* (*Big Money*). Tauno Nuotio. Porvoo: Werner Söderström, 1938. 253 pp.
    2 pain. 1960. 253 pp. Riksin sarja, 98.

1939 *Piccadillyn Jim* (*Piccadilly Jim*). Tuulikki Routamo. Helsinki: Otava, 1939. 277 pp.
    2 pain. 1962. 238 pp. Otavan taskuromanit, 31.

1939 *Kesäinen kuutamo.* (*Summer Moonshine*). Olavi Linnus. Porvoo, Helsinki: Werner Söderström, [1939]. 247 pp.
    2 pain. 1960. 247 pp. Riksin sarja, 97.

1939 *Puelmallinen Viikonloppu* (*The Code of the Woosters*). Tauno Nuotio. Porvoo: Werner Söderström, 1939. 242 pp.
    2 pain. 1960. 242 pp. Riksin sarja, 99.

1940 *Jäähyvaiset kissoille* ( ). Helsinki: Otava, 1940. 33 pp. 5 markan sarja, 10.

1948 *Kuutamokuhertelu* (*Full Moon*). Taimi Tanskanen. Hämeenlinna: Nide, 1948. 283 pp.

1948 *Rakkauden hullus* (*Joy in the Morning*). Risto Kalliomaa. Helsinki, Hämeenlinna: Nide, 1948. 360 pp.

1948 *Verraton Jeeves* (*The Inimitable Jeeves*). Annikka Jäntti. Helsinki: Kustannusoy Karhu, 1948. 271 pp.

1949 *Kuka teki kenelle mitä?* (*If I Were You*). Olli Nuorto. Jyväskylä: KJG, 1949. 244 pp.

1950 *Antaa Jeevesin hoitaa* (*Carry On, Jeeves!*). Katri Jylhä. Helsinki: Pellervoo, 1950. 295 pp.

1950 *Fred-setä järjestää* (*Uncle Dynamite*). S. S. Taula [Taube]. Jyväskylä: KJG, 1950. 256 pp.

1950 *Kevätkuumetta* ( ). S. S. Taula [Taube]. Jyväskylä: KJG, 1950. 236 pp.

1952 *Kunnon vanha Bill* (*The Old Reliable*). S. S. Taula [Taube]. Jyväskylä: KJG, 1952. 191 pp.

1953 *Aina vain paranee* (*Barmy in Woderland*). S. S. Taula [Taube]. Jyväskylä: KJG, 1953. 208 pp.

1954 *Mutkan kautta väärään: Herra Mullinerin iltapakinoita* (*Mulliner Nights*). S. S. Taula [Taube]. Jyväskylä: KJG, 1954. 214 pp.

1955 *Possut pilosilla* (*Pigs Have Wings*). S. S. Taula [Taube]. Jyväskylä: KJG, 1955. 232 pp.

1956 *Jalomielinen Jeeves* (*Jeeves and the Feudal Spirit*). Risto Kalliomaa. Hämeenlinna: Nide, Rauma, 1956. 183 pp.

1957 *Ranskalaista rakkautta* (*French Leave*). Mario Talaskivi. Hämeenlinna: Nide, 1957. 160 pp.

1971 *Outo lintu linnassa* (*A Pelican at Blandings*). Raija Mattila. Porvoo, Helsinki: Werner Söderström, [1971]. [230] pp.

1973 *Suurenmoista, Jeeves* (*Much Obliged, Jeeves*). Raija Mattila. Porvoo: Werner Söderström, 1973. [201] pp.

French Translations

1929 *Le petit trésor* (*The Little Nugget*). Suzanne Flour. Paris: Gallimard, 1929. 253 pp. Les Livres du jour.

1932 *Une affaire étourdissante* (*Love among the Chickens*). Suzanne Flour. Paris: Les Editions des Portiques, [1932]. 255 pp.

1932 *La Petite garçonnière* (*The Small Bachelor*). Marion Gilbert et Madeleine Duvivier. Paris: A. Michel, 1932. 253 pp. Les "Albin Michel" à 6 fr., 18.

1933 *Gendre et martyr* (*The Indiscretions of Archie*). Marion Gilbert et Madeleine Duvivier. Paris: Éditions cosmopolites, [1933]. 250 pp. Collection du lecteur, n.s., 103.

1934 *Les Caprices de Miss Bennett* (*The Girl on the Boat*). Marguerite d'Avenel. [Paris:] Hachette, 1934. 244 pp. Les Meilleurs romans étrangers.

1934 *Monsieur est servi* (*Carry On, Jeeves!*). E. Rinon. Paris: Éditions de la Nouvelle revue critique, 1934. 224 pp. Collection "Tours d'horizon," 8. Reissued in 1948.

1935 *Un riche filon* (*Big Money*). Marguerite d'Avenel. [Paris]: Hachette, 1935. 254 pp. Les Meilleurs romans étrangers.

1936 *Monsieur Mulliner* (*Meet Mr. Mulliner*). Jean Calvel. Paris: Hachette, 1936. 187 pp. Les Meilleurs romans étrangers.

1937 *J'ai trois amoureux* (*The Adventures of Sally*). Marion Gilbert et Madeleine Duvivier. Paris: Hachette, 1937. 240 pp. Les Meilleurs romans étrangers.

1938 *Jim, l'excentrique* (*Piccadilly Jim*). Maurice Rémon. [Paris]: Hachette, 1938. 256 pp. Les Meilleurs romans étrangers.

1944 *Sous pression* (*Hot Water*). Denyse et Benoît de

Fonscolombe. Paris: F. Sorlot, 1944. 255 pp. Les Maîtres étrangers, 65.

1946 *Merci, Jeeves* (*Thank You, Jeeves*). Benoît de Fonscolombe. Paris: Le Portulan, 1946. 381 pp. Les Grands écrivains de langue anglaise, Angleterre, 2.

1947 *Eclair de chaleur* (*Summer Lightning*). Denyse et Benoît de Fonscolombe. Paris: Vent du large, 1947. 352 pp.

1947 *Jeeves, au secours* (*Joy in the Morning*). Denyse et Benoît de Fonscolombe. Paris: Vent du large 1947. 374 pp. Les Grands écrivains de langue anglaise, 6.

1948 *Valeurs en coffre* (*Money in the Bank*). Charles Thiollier. Paris: Vent du large, 1948. 381 pp. Les Grands écrivains de langue anglaise, Angleterre, 9.

Paris: [Amiot-Dumont] Vent du large, [1948]. 377 pp. (paper).

1950 *Baronnets et bars bonnêtes* (*Young Men in Spats*). P. A. Gruénais. Paris: Éditions Jean Froissart, 1950. 285 pp.

1950 *Bravo, oncle Fred!* (*Uncle Fred in the Springtime*). Charles Thiollier. Paris: Amiot-Dumont, 1950. 299 pp. Périples, Bibliothèque étrangère, 1.

Lausanne: La Thune du Quay, 1957. 237 pp.

1950 *Une pluie de dollars* (*Uneasy Money*). Marion Gilbert et Madeleine Duvivier. Paris: Amiot-Dumont, 1950. 261 pp. Périples, Bibliothèque étrangère, 2.

Verviers: Marabout, 1958. 187 pp.

Verviers: Gérard, 1959. 187 pp. Collection Marabout, 242.

1951 *Ça va, Jeeves?* (*Right Ho, Jeeves*). Josette Raoul-Duval. Paris: Amiot-Dumont, 1951. 293 pp.

Verviers: Gérard, 1956. 223 pp.

Verviers: Gérard, [1957]. 223 pp. Collection Marabout, 186.

1951 *Oncle Dynamite* (*Uncle Dynamite*). Josette Raoul-Duval. Paris: Amiot-Dumont, 1951. 299 pp. Périples, Bibliothèque étrangère, 3.

1952 *Hollywood follies* (*The Old Reliable*). Michel Chrestien. Paris: Amiot-Dumont, 1952. 251 pp.

1952 *Le Plus beau cochon du monde* (*Pigs Have Wings*). Charles Mauban et Robert Carme. Paris: Amiot-Dumont, 1953. 272 pp.

1953 *Tous cambrioleurs* (*Leave It to Psmith*). Josette Raoul-Duval. Paris: Amiot-Dumont, 1953. 286 pp. Périples, Bibliothèque étrangère, 4.

Verviers: Gérard, 1958. 221 pp. Collection Marabout, 229.

Lausanne: La Thune du Quay, 1960. 243 pp.

1954 *S.O.S. Jeeves* (*The Code of the Woosters*). Josette Raoul-Duval. Paris; Amiot-Dumont, 1954. 254 pp. Les Meilleurs traductions, 6.

Verviers: Gérard, [1958]. 224 pp. Collection Marabout, 225.

German Translations

1927 *Abenteuer eines Bumpgenies* ( ). Heinrich Fraenkel. Stuttgart: J. Engelhorns, 1927. 142 pp. Engelhorns Romanbibliothek, 1004.

Munich: Domino Verlag Brinek, 1964. 132 pp.

1927 *Nimrods Tochter* (*Sam the Sudden*). Franz Fein. Berlin: Th. Knaur Nachf., [1927]. 312 pp. Romane die Welt.

1928 *Ein Glücklicher* (*Bill the Conqueror*). Franz Fein. Berlin: Th. Knaur Nachf., [1928?]. [320] pp. Romane die Welt.

1928 *Da lachen die Hühner* (*Love among the Chickens*). Alice Weisskopf. Leipzig: Reclam, [1928]. 221 pp. Reclams Universalbibliothek, 6878/6880.

1928 *Ein hilfsbereiter Freund* (*My Man Jeeves*). Heinrich Fraenkel. Stuttgart: Engelhorns, 1928. 141 pp. Engelhorns Romanbibliothek, 1019.

Jeeves macht alles (*My Man Jeeves*). Heinrich Fraenkel. Stuttgart: Engelhorns, 1929. 139 pp. Engelhorns Romanbibliothek, 1026.

1929 *Der schüchterne Junggeselle* (*The Small Bachelor*). Franz Fein. Berlin: Ullstein, [1929]. 255 pp. Die gelben Ullsteinbücher, 56.

1931 *Er kann nicht nein sagen* ( ). Alice Weisskopf. Leipzig: Goldmann, [1931]. 263 pp. Die heiteren Goldmann-Bücher.

Fritz Pütsch. Leipzig: Goldmann, 1939. 214 pp.

1932 *Die Fürstin von Blandings* (*Summer Lightning*). Ravi Ravendro. Berlin: Delta-Verlag, [1932]. 240 pp.

Berlin: Aufwärts-Verlag, [1937]. 95 pp. Dreissig-pfennig-Roman, 48.

1932 *Vertauschte Rollen* (*If I Were You*). Lola Lorm.

Munich: Goldmann, [1932]. 275 pp. Die heiteren Goldmann-Bücher.

    Munich: Goldmann, 1966. 183 pp.

    2 Aufl. 1970.

    3 Aufl. [August 1978]. [188] pp. Goldmann-Bücher, 1715. ISBN 3–442–01715–7 (pa.).

1933 *Jeeves rettet der Situation* (*Carry On, Jeeves!*). Leipzig: Goldmann, [1933]. 279 pp. Die neuen blauen Goldmann-Bücher.

1933 *Jill geht durch dick und dünn* (*Jill the Reckless*). Hans Barbeck. Lorch: K. Rohm, 1933. 251 pp.

1933 *Pass auf Berry* (*Big Money*). Marianne Kempner. Leipzig: Goldmann, [1933]. 279 pp. Die neuen blauen Goldmann-Bücher.

    Munich: Goldmann, 1967. 164 pp.

    Munich: Wilhelm Goldmann, [1973?]. [187] pp. (pa.). ISBN 3–442–01672–X.

1934 *Besten Dank, Jeeves* (*Thank You, Jeeves*). Ernst Simon. Berlin, Basel, Leipzig, Wein: Zinnen-Verlag, 1934. 285 pp.

1935 *Ein X für ein U* (*Heavy Weather*). Ernst Simon. Basel, Leipzig, Wein: Zinnen-Verlag, 1935. 287 pp.

    Berlin: Aufwärts-Verlag, [1938]. 96 pp. Dreissig-pfennig-Roman, 96.

1935 *Piccadilly Jim* (*Piccadilly Jim*). Hans Barbeck. Berlin: P. J. Oestergaard, [1935]. 256 pp.

1937 *Billie welchen meinst Du?* (*The Girl on the Boat*). Mittel-Ostrau: Kittel, [1937]. 314 pp.

1937 *Wenn der Vater mit der Sohne* ( ). Hans Barbeck. Berlin: Aufwärts-Verlag, [1937]. 96 pp. Dreissigpfennig-Roman, 52.

1955 *Psmith macht alles* (*Leave It to Psmith*). Kathe Illch. Frankfurt: Das goldene Vlies, 1955. 184 pp.

    Eine Lord in Nöten (*Leave It to Psmith*). Gretl Friedmann. Munich: Wilhelm Heyne, 1977.

    3 Aufl. 1979. 254 pp. Heyne-Buch, 5339.

1959 *Hier ist etwas faul* (*Something Fishy*). George S. Martin. Frankfurt: Ullstein Taschenbücher Verlag, 1959. 173 pp.

1964 *Die liebe Not mit jungen Damen* (*Damsel in Distress*). Kristin Weber und Hans Roesch. Tübingen: Rainer Wunderlich, 1964. 271 pp.

    Frankfurt am Main: Fischer, 1971. 202 pp. Fischer-Bücherei, 1196.

1964 *Lustige Geschichten* (anthology). Günther Eichel. [Zurich:] Diogenes Verlag, [1964]. [399] pp.

1966 *Maskerade in St. Rocque* (*Hot Water*). Hartmut Georgi. Tübingen: Rainer Wunderlich, 1966. 271 pp.

    Frankfurt: Fischer, 1968. 186 pp. Fischer-Bücherei, 893.

1967 *Die Feuerprobe und sieben andere Geschichten aus dem Drohnen-Club* (*Young Men in Spats*). Karl-Ulrich von Hutten. Tübingen: Rainer Wunderlich, 1967. 241 pp.

    Munich: Wilhelm Goldmann, [1968]. 185 pp. Goldmanns Gelbe Taschenbücher, 2339. ISBN 3–442–02339–4.

1971 *Terry lebt versheuenderisch* (*French Leave*). Monika Eckert. Munich: Wilhelm Goldmann, [1971]. 192 pp. (pa.). ISBN 3–442–03349–7.

1972 *Stets zu Diensten: die heitere Geschichte der Lord Ickenham* (*Service with a Smile*). Monika Eckert. Munich: Wilhelm Goldmann, 1972.

    [1979]. [184] pp. (pa.). ISBN 3–442–03860–X.

1974 *Frühlingsgefühle* (*Spring Fever*). Gretl Friedmann. Munich: Wilhelm Heyne, [1974]. [143] pp. Heyne-Buch, 5125.

    4 Aufl. 1979 (pa.). ISBN 3–453–00464–7.

1975 *Geld spielt (k)eine Rolle* (*Do Butlers Burgle Banks?*). Walter Paul. Munich: Wilhelm Heyne Verlag, 1975. [144] pp. Heyne-Buch 5208.

    3 Aufl. 1977. 144 pp. (pa.). ISBN 3–453–00568–6.

1975 *Kleiner Schwindel in grossen Schloss* (*Company for Henry*). Gretl Friedmann. Munich: Wilhelm Heyne Verlag, [1975]. [144] pp.

    3 Aufl. 1977. 144 pp. (pa.). ISBN 3–453–00516–3.

1976 *Das Hält Man doch im Kopf nicht aus* (*Ice in the Bedroom*). Gretl Friedmann. Munich: Wilhelm Heyne, 1976. [190] pp. Heyne-Buch, 5285.

    3 Aufl. 1978. ISBN 3–453–00652–6.

    4 Aufl. 1979.

1976 *Lieber Reich und Glücklich* (*Pearls, Girls and Monty Bodkin*). Iris und Rolf Hellmut Foerster. Munich: Wilhelm Heyne Verlag, [1976]. 174 pp. Heyne-Buch, 5249.

    4 Aufl. 1979. 174 pp. (pa.). ISBN 3–453–00611–9.

1976 *Herr auf Schloss Blandings* (*Blandings Castle and Elsewhere*). Annemarie Arnold-Kubina. [Munich:] Wilhelm Goldmann, 1976. [123] pp.
    2 Aufl. 1978. 123 pp. (pa.). ISBN 3-442-03418-3.

1977 *Ohne Butler geht es nicht* (*Much Obliged, Jeeves*). Monika Eckert. [Munich:] Wilhelm Goldmann, 1977. [190] pp. ISBN 3-442-03500-7.
    2 Aufl. 1979.

1977 *Ein Goldjunge, heiterer Roman* (*The Little Nugget*). Petra Vogt. Beyreuth: Hestia Verlag, 1977. 311 pp.
    Munich: Wilhelm Heyne Verlag, [1979]. [207] pp. (pa.). ISBN 3-453-00959-2.

1978 *Grosse Liebe, kleine Diebe* (*Money for Nothing*). Ilse Pauli. Munich: Wilhelm Heyne, [1978]. 240 pp. Heyne-Buch, 5398.
    2 Aufl. 1978. 240 pp. (pa.).
    3 Aufl. 1978. 240 pp. (pa.). ISBN 3-453-00791-3.

1978 *Reichtum schützt vor Liebe nicht* (*Galahad at Blandings*). Iris und Hellmut Foerster. Munich: Wilhelm Heyne Verlag, [1978]. [176] pp. Heyne-Buch, 5441.
    2 Aufl. 1978. 176 pp. (pa.). ISBN 3-453-00836-7.
    3 Aufl. 1979.

1978 *Keine Ferien für Jeeves* (*Jeeves in the Offing*). Annemarie Arnold-Kubina. [Munich:] Wilhelm Goldmann, [1978]. [185] pp. (pa.). ISBN 3-442-03658-5.

1979 *Seine Lordschaft und das Schwein* (*Heavy Weather*). Iris und Rolf Hellmut Foerster. [Munich]: Wilhelm Heyne Verlag, 1979. [256] pp. Heyne-Buch, 5592. ISBN 3-453-01004-3.

1979 *Das Mädchen in Blau* (*The Girl in Blue*). Annemarie Arnold-Kubina. [Munich:] Wilhelm Goldmann, [1979]. [185] pp. (pa.). ISBN 3-442-03718-2.

1979 *Erben Sie Wohl, Mylord!* (*Uneasy Money*). Ulrike von Sobbe. [Beyreuth:] Hestia, [1979]. [300] pp. ISBN 3-7770-0183-X.

1979 *Jeeves übernimmt das Ruder, Jeeves Takes Charge* (English and German on facing pages). Harald Raykowski. [Munich:] Deutscher Taschenbüch Verlag, [1979]. 125 pp.

1980 *Barmy in Wunderland* (*Barmy in Wonderland*). Iris und Rolf Hellmut Foerster. Munich: Wilhelm Heyne, [1980]. (pa.) Heyne-Buch, 5664. ISBN 3-453-01109-0.

Hungarian Translations

1928 *Betty és a hereeg* (*The Prince and Betty*). Budapest: Legrády Testvérek kiadása, [1928]. 256 pp. Pesti hirlap könyvek, 45.

1928 *Nimrod leanya* (*Sam the Sudden*). Maria Dobosi-Pécsi. Budapest: A. Pesti Hirlap kiadása, 1928. 256 pp. Pesti hirlap könyvek, 3.
    Eszményi Samuel (*Sam the Sudden*). György Várady. Budapest: Széchenyi, 1940. 344 pp.
    Hübele Samuel (*Sam the Sudden*). László Munkaja. Budapest: Kozmoz Könyvek, 1975. [327] pp.

1928 *Psmith, mint ujságiró* (*Psmith, Journalist*). Balogh Barna. Budapest: Pantheon-R. T. Kiadasa, 1928. 258 pp.

1941 *Köszönöm Tóbiás!* ( ). György Várady. Budapest: Széchenyi, 1941. 271 pp.

1941 *Majd a Tóbiás* ( ). György Várady. Budapest: Széchenyi, 1941. 302 pp.

1948 *Kedelyes kastely* (*Full Moon*). Magda Gabor. Budapest: Corvina, 1948.

1957 *Forduljon Psmithhez* (*Leave It to Psmith*). Erzsebet Guthi. Budapest: Magvelö, 1957. 2 v.
    Budapest: Europa, 1972. 297 pp.

1957 *Renegeteg penz* (*Big Money*). Jegyz Antal. [Budapest: Tancsics kiado, 1957.] 351 pp.

Icelandic Translation

1973 *Látum Psmith leysa vandann* (*Leave It to Psmith*). Sunna Stéfansdotter. Hafnarfjörður: Rauðskinna, 1973. 245 pp.

Indian Translations

1969 *Nevai Oo hnint saikju* (*Uncle Fred in the Springtime*). Bo Aye Maung. Rangoon: Aye Nyunt Swe Pub. House, 1969. 346 pp.

Italian Translations

1928 *Avanti Jeeves* (*Carry On, Jeeves!*). Silvio Spaventa Filippi. Milan: Monanni, 1928. 334 pp.

Milan: Bietti, 1933, 1934, 1936. 335 pp. Nuovissima collezione letteraria, 10.

Milan: Bietti, [1973]. 273 pp.

1929 *L'amore fra i polli* (*Love among the Chickens*). Silvio Spaventa Filippi. Milan: Monanni, 1929. 311 pp. Nuovissima collezione letteraria, 27.

Milan: Bietti, 1932. 312 pp. Nuovissima collezione letteraria, 27.

Milan: Bietti, 1935. 284 pp. Biblioteca reclame, 115.

[Milan:] Bietti, [1964]. 284 pp. Il Picchio, 13.

L'amore fra i polli (*Love among the Chickens*). Dienne Carter. Milan: Aurora, 1938. 252 pp.

L'amore fra i polli (*Love among the Chickens*). O. Previtali. Milan: Rizzoli, 1961. 197 pp. Biblioteca universale Rizzoli, 1693/1694.

1930 *L'inimitable Jeeves* (*The Inimitable Jeeves*). Aldo Traverso. Milan: Monanni, 1930. 318 pp. Nuovissima collezione letteraria, 41.

Milan: Bietti, 1933, 1937. 316 pp. Nuovissima collezione letteraria, 41.

Milan: Bietti, [1966]. 316 pp. Il Picchio, 19.

1931 *Indiscrezione di Archibaldo* (*Indiscretions of Archie*). Alfredo Pitta. Milan: Bietti, 1931. 297 pp. Biblioteca internazionale, 131.

Milan: Bietti, 1934. 299 pp. Nuovissima collezione letteraria, 56.

Milan: Bietti, 1966. 297 pp. Il Picchio, 12.

Indiscrezione di Archibaldo (*Indiscretions of Archie*). Francesco Palumbo. Milan: Monanni, 1931. 317 pp. Nuovissima collezione letteraria, 56.

Archibaldo conquista l'America (*Indiscretions of Archie*). Alfredo Pitta. Milan: Bietti, 1931. 297 pp. Biblioteca internazionale, 131.

Florence: Novissima editrice, 1931. 264 pp. Umorista, 2.

1931 *Jill, ragazza bizzarra* (*Jill the Reckless*). Alfredo Pitta. Milan: Bietti, [1931]. 293 pp.

Milan: Bietti, 1933. 293 pp. Biblioteca internazionale, 129.

Milan: Bietti, 1936. 293 pp. Nuovissima collezione letteraria, 67.

Jill, ragazza bizzarra (*Jill the Reckless*). C. Ferri. Milan: Bietti, [1966]. 293 pp. Il Picchio, 24.

Giulia la bizzarra (*Jill the Reckless*). M. B. Raffanelli. Milan: Monanni, [1932]. 511 pp.

1931 *Jim di Piccadilly* (*Piccadilly Jim*). Ida Lori. Milan: Bietti, 1931. 299 pp. Biblioteca internazionale, 130.

Milan: Bietti, 1938. 299 pp. Nuovissima collezione letteraria, 53.

[Milan:] Bietti, [1966]. 299 pp. Il Picchio, 25.

Jim di Piccadilly (*Piccadilly Jim*). Mario Malatesta. Milan: Monanni, 1932. 341 pp. Nuovissima collezione letteraria, 53.

Jim di Piccadilly (*Piccadilly Jim*). Milan: Aurora, 1937. 331 pp.

1931 *Mister Mulliner* (*Meet Mr. Mulliner*). Alberto Tedeschi. Milan: Monanni, [1931], 1932. 237 pp. Nuovissima collezione letteraria, 51.

Milan: Bietti, 1933. 237 pp. Nuovissima collezione letteraria, 51.

[Milan:] Bietti, [1966]. 237 pp. Il Picchio, 26.

1931 *Parla Mister Mulliner* (*Mr. Mulliner Speaking*). Alberto Tedeschi. Milan: Monanni, 1931. 269 pp. Nuovissima collezione letteraria, 52.

Milan: Bietti, 1933, 1936. 269 pp. Nuovissima collezione letteraria, 52.

[Milan:] Bietti, [1966]. 269 pp. Il Picchio, 27.

1931 *Una signorina in imbarazzo* (*A Damsel in Distress*). A. Mozzato. Milan: Bietti, 1931. 225 pp. Biblioteca internazionale, 132.

[Milan:] Bietti, [1966]. [255] pp. Il Picchio, 37.

Una donzella in imbarazzo (*A Damsel in Distress*). Francesco Palumbo. Milan: Monanni, 1932. 331 pp. Nuovissima collezione letteraria, 55.

Un capriccio e poi (*A Damsel in Distress*). Alfredo Bianchini. Milan: SACSE, 1935. 254 pp.

Un matrimonio complicato (*A Damsel in Distress*). A. Bianchini. Milan: SACSE, 1935. 254 pp.

1931 *Un gentiluomo in ozio* (*A Gentleman of Leisure*). M. B. Raffanelli. Milan: Bietti, 1931. 257 pp. Biblioteca internazionale, 128.

Milan: Bietti, 1935. 259 pp. Nuovissima collezione letteraria, 61.

[Milan:] Bietti, [1966]. 257 pp. Il Picchio, 38.

Un gentiluomo in ozio (*A Gentleman of Leisure*). Milan: Monanni, 1932. 363 pp.

Jimmy all'opra (*A Gentleman of Leisure*). Milan: SACSE, 1935. 255 pp.

1932 *Battaglie sportive* (*The Gold Bat*). Lina Baraldi.

Milan: Bietti, 1932. 243 pp. Biblioteca internazionale, 139.

1932 *Il capo della Kay* (*The Head of Kay's*). Francesco Palumbo. Milan: Bietti, 1932. 259 pp. Biblioteca internazionale, 142.

Il capo della Kay (*The Head of Kay's*). F. Leon Shipley. Milan: Monanni, 1933. 226 pp. Nuovissima collezionne letteraria, 72.

1932 *Denaro incomodo* (*Uneasy Money*). Francesco Palumbo. Milan: Bietti, 1932. 243 pp. Biblioteca internazionale, 134.

[Milan:] Bietti, [1966]. 243 pp. Il Picchio, 6.

Denaro incomodo (*Uneasy Money*). Milan: SACSE, 1935. 255 pp.

Denaro difficile (*Uneasy Money*). M. Carlisimo. Milan: Monanni, 1932. 278 pp. Nuovissima collezione letteraria, 58.

1932 *I conquistatore di coppe* ( ). Mario Benzi. Milan: Bietti, 1932. 231 pp. Biblioteca internazionale, 149.

1932 *Mike, storia di un collegio* (*Mike*). Mario Benzi. Milan: Bietti, 1932. 292 pp. Biblioteca internazionale, 140.

Milan: Bietti, 1933. 292 pp. Nuovissima collezione letteraria, 75.

1932 *Una penna di coda* ( ). Mario Benzi. Milan: Bietti, 1932. 251 pp.

1932 *Pepita d'oro* (*The Little Nugget*). Mario Malatesta. Milan: Monanni, [1932]. 306 pp. Nuovissima collezione letteraria, 54.

La piccola pepita (*The Little Nugget*). Alfredo Pitta. Milan: Bietti, 1932. 255 pp. Biblioteca internazionale, 148.

[Milan:] Bietti, [1966]. 255 pp. Il Picchio, 15.

1932 *Il principe e Betty* (*The Prince and Betty*). Maria Martone. Milan: Monanni, 1932. 205 pp. Nuovissima collezione letteraria, 60.

Il principe e Betty (*The Prince and Betty*). Francesco Palumbo. Milan: Bietti, 1932. 240 pp. Biblioteca internazionale, 138.

Milan: Bietti, 1966. 240 pp. Il Picchio, 30.

1932 *Psmith in banca* (*Psmith in the City*). Alfredo Pitta. Milan: Bietti, 1932. 251 pp. Biblioteca internazionale, 141.

Milan: Bietti, 1934, 1936. 251 pp. Nuovissima collezione letteraria, 74.

[Milan:] Bietti, [1966]. [251] pp. Il Picchio, 31.

1932 *Psmith giornalista* (*Psmith, Journalist*). Alfredo Pitta. Milan: Bietti, 1932. 274 pp. Biblioteca internazionale, 144.

Milan: Bietti, 1933. 275 pp. Nuovissima collezione letteraria, 73.

[Milan:] Bietti, [1966]. [275] pp. Il Picchio, 30.

Psmith giornalista (*Psmith, Journalist*). Gian Dauli. Milan: Lucchi, 1940. 286 pp.

1932 *Qualcosa di nuovo* (*Something New*). L. Bernardini. Milan: Monanni, 1932. 314 pp. Nuovissima collezione letteraria, 66.

[Milan:] Bietti, [1966]. [256] pp. Il Picchio, 32.

Qualcosa di nuovo (*Something New*). L. Fratta. Milan: Bietti, 1932. 255 pp. Biblioteca internazionale, 137.

1932 *Quattrini a palate* (*Big Money*). Mario Benzi. Milan: Monanni, 1932. 354 pp. Nuovissima collezione letteraria, 59.

Milan: Bietti [1964], [1966]. 318 pp.

Il filone d'oro (*Big Money*). Gian Dauli. Milan: Lucchi, 1940. 255 pp.

1932 *Racconti di Sant'Agostino* (*Tales of St. Austin's*). Ida Lori. Milan: Bietti, 1932. 260 pp. Biblioteca internazionale, 143.

1932 *L'uomo con due piedi sinistri* (*The Man with Two Left Feet*). G. V. Pisano. Milan: Bietti, 1932, 1938. 252 pp. Biblioteca internazionale, 138.

Milan: Bietti, 1936. 252 pp. Nuovissima collezione letteraria, 76.

[Milan:] Bietti, [1966]. 252 pp. Il Picchio, 23.

1932 *L'uomo del piano di sopra.* (*The Man Upstairs*). Francesco Palumbo. Milan: Bietti, 1932. 243 pp.

Milan: Bietti, 1935. 243 pp. Nuovissima collezione letteraria, 68.

[Milan:] Bietti, [1966]. 243 pp. Il Picchio, 22.

L'uomo dell piano di sopra (*The Man Upstairs*). Maria Martone. Milan: Monanni, 1933. 311 pp.

1932 *La venuta di Bill* (*The Coming of Bill*). Alfredo Pitta. Milan: Monanni, 1932. 376 pp. Nuovissima collezione letteraria, 57.

La venuta di Bill (*The Coming of Bill*). Teresita Casale Rossi. Milan: Bietti, 1932. 312 pp. Biblioteca internazionale, 133.

[Milan:] Bietti, [1966]. 312 pp. Il Picchio, 18.

La venuta di Bill (The Coming of Bill). Rome: An Romana, 1932. 312 pp.

1932 *Lo zio del prefetto (A Prefect's Uncle)*. Naples: Casella, 1932. 232 pp.

1933 *Acqua bollente (Hot Water)*. M. B. Rafanelli. Milan: Bietti, 1933, 1937. 310 pp. Nuovissima collezione letteraria, 82.

[Milan:] Bietti, [1964], [1966]. 310 pp. Il Picchio, 1.

1933 *Acqua pesante (Heavy Weather)*. Zoe Lampronti. Milan: Bietti, [1933]. 285 pp.

1933 *Benissimo Jeeves! (Very Good, Jeeves)*. Alberto Tedeschi. Milan: Bietti, 1933, 1936, 1938. 331 pp. Nuovissima collezione letteraria, 45.

Benissimo Jeeves! (Very Good, Jeeves). Claudio Redi. Milan: Bietti, [1974], [1977]. 277 pp.

1933 *Il colpo di Cuthbert (The Clicking of Cuthbert)*. Mario Malatesta. Milan: Bietti, 1933. 273 pp. Nuovissima collezione letteraria, 9.

Milan: Bietti, [1973]. 260 pp.

1933 *Il Cuore di un coniglio (The Heart of a Goof)*. Mario Malatesta. Milan: Bietti, 1933. 292 pp. Nuovissima collezione letteraria, 12.

Milan: Bietti, [1973]. [253] pp.

1933 *Doctor Sally (Doctor Sally)*. Roberto Roberti. Milan: Monanni, 1933. 276 pp. Nuovissima collezione letteraria, 71.

Milan: Bietti, 1934. 288 pp. Nuovissima collezione letteraria, 77.

[Milan:] Bietti, [1966]. 288 pp. Il Picchio, 8.

1933 *Lampi d'estate (Summer Moonshine)*. M. B. Raffanelli. Milan: Monanni, 1933. 429 pp. Nuovissima collezione letteraria, 69.

[Milan:] Bietti, [1964], [1966]. 351 pp. Il Picchio, 14.

1933 *Lasciate fare a Psmith (Leave It to Psmith)*. Mario Gilli. Milan: Monanni, 1933. 391 pp.

Milan: Bietti, 1933, 1936. 391 pp. Nuovissima collezione letteraria, 70.

[Milan:] Bietti, [1966]. 304 pp. Il Picchio, 16.

1933 *Se io fossi voi (If I Were You)*. A. Zanini. Milan: Bietti, 1933, 1936. 286 pp. Nuovissima collezione letteraria, 14.

Milan: Bietti, 1965, [1966]. 286 pp. Il Picchio, 35.

1933 *Le serate di Mulliner (Mulliner Nights)*. Alberto Tedeschi. Milan: Bietti, 1933. 287 pp. Nuovissima collezione letteraria, 83.

[Milan:] Bietti, [1966]. 287 pp. Il Picchio, 21.

1933 *Ukridge (Ukridge)*. Mario Malatesta. Milan: Bietti, 1933, 1936. Nuovissima collezione letteraria, 5.

Ukridge (Ukridge). Maria Martone. Milan: Bietti, [1962]. 333 pp. Il Picchio, 39.

1934 *Grazie, Jeeves (Thank You, Jeeves)*. Giulia Brugiotti. Milan: Bietti, 1934, 1935, 1937. 315 pp. Nuovissima collezione letteraria, 86.

[Milan:] Bietti, [1966]. 315 pp. Il Picchio, 10.

1934 *Più forte e più allegro (Louder and Funnier)*. Zoe Lampronti. Milan: Bietti, [1934]. 237 pp. Nuovissima collezione letteraria, 84.

[Milan:] Bietti, [1966]. 237 pp. Il Picchio, 29.

1934 *Sam il dinamico (Sam the Sudden)*. M. B. Raffanelli. Milan: Bietti, 1934, 1935, 1936. 284 pp. Nuovissima collezione letteraria, 81.

[Milan:] Bietti, [1966]. 284 pp. Il Picchio, 34.

1935 *Alla buon'ora Jeeves (Right Ho, Jeeves)*. Cina Sacchi-Perego. Milan: Bietti, 1935, 1938. 270 pp. Nuovissima collezione letteraria, 100.

Milan: Bietti, 1976, 1977. 290 pp.

1936 *Bill il conquistatore (Bill the Conqueror)*. M. B. Raffanelli. Milan: Bietti, 1936. 342 pp. Nuovissima collezione letteraria, 50.

[Milan:] Bietti, [1966]. 342 pp. Il Picchio, 5.

1936 *La fortuna dei Bodkin (The Luck of the Bodkins)*. Zoe Lampronti. Milan: Bietti, 1936. 302 pp. Nuovissima collezione letteraria, 102.

[Milan:] Bietti, [1973]. 322 pp.

1936 *Giovannoti con le ghette (Young Men in Spats)*. Zoe Lampronti. Milan: Bietti, 1936, 1937. 287 pp. Nuovissima collezione letteraria, 103.

[Milan:] Bietti, [1966]. [287] pp. Il Picchio, 9.

1936 *La ragazza del transatlantico (The Girl on the Boat)*. Alfredo Pitta. Milan: Bietti, 1936. 304 pp. Nuovissima collezione letteraria, 62.

[Milan:] Bietti, [1966]. 304 pp. Il Picchio, 16.

1938 *Gas esilarante (Laughing Gas)*. Alberto Tedeschi. Milan, Verona: Mondadori, 1938. 109 pp. I romanza della palma, 106.

2d. ed. 1938. 273 pp. I capolavori della palma, 6.

1955. 182 pp. Biblioteca economica Mondadori, 30.

1938 *Il piccolo scapolo* (*The Small Bachelor*). A. Zanini. Milan: Bietti, 1938. 359 pp. Nuovissima collezione letteraria, 65.

    [1966]. 359 pp. Il Picchio, 28.

1939 *Poi, tutto s'accomoda* (*Summer Moonshine*). Alberto Tedeschi. Milan, Verona: A. Mondadori, 1939. 120 pp. I romanzi della palma, 118.

    1955. 191 pp.

1939 *Il gentiluomo spensierato* ( ). Gian Dauli. Milan: Lucchi, 1939. 252 pp.

1939 *Una magnifica avventura* ( ). Gian Dauli. Milan: Lucchi, 1939. 252 pp.

1939 *Jeeves non si smentisce* (*The Code of the Woosters*). Alberto Tedeschi. Milan, Verona: A. Mondadori, 1939. 108 pp. I romanzi della palma, 124.

    1956. 192 pp. Biblioteca economica Mondadori, 52.

    1962. 223 pp. I libri del pavone, 296.

    1976. 229 pp. Gli Oscar, 440.

1949 *Quattrini in banca* (*Money in the Bank*). Sirio Agnati. Milan: Elmo, 1949. 289 pp.

    [Verona:] Mondadori, 1974. [188] pp. Gli Oscar, 534.

    Milan, Verona: Mondadori, 1958. 180 p. Il girasole. Biblioteca economica Mondadori, 96.

    Milan, Verona: Mondadori, 1964. 180 pp. I libri del pavone, 403.

    1974. [188] pp. Oscar del ridere, 534.

1949 *La gioia de col mattino* (*Joy in the Morning*). Giorgio Monicelli; pref. George Orwell. Milan: F. Elmo, 1949. 388 pp. L'Olimpo.

    1961. 319 pp. Moderna libreria straniera, 2.

1949 *Le zio dinamite* (*Uncle Dynamite*). Adriana Motti. Milan: F. Elmo, 1949. 363 pp. Moderna libreria straniera Elmo.

    [1962?]. 303 pp. Moderna libreria straniera, 15.

1950 *Genero al verde* (*Galahad at Blandings*). Sario Agnati. [Milan:] Federico Elmo, [1950?]. [216] pp.

1950 *Sotto le fresche frasche* (*The Mating Season*). Adriana Motti. Milan: Elmo, 1950. 310 pp.

1951 *Servizio espresso* (*Quick Service*). Adriana Motti. Milan: F. Elmo, [1951]. 265 pp. Elmo, della moderna libreria straniera.

    [1962?]. [234] pp. Moderna libreria straniera, 13.

1953 *Diario segreto* (*The Old Reliable*). Adriana Motti. Milan: Elmo, 1953. 223 pp. Moderna libreria straniera.

1953 *Grullo nel paese delle Meraviglie*. (*Barmy in Wonderland*). Adriana Motti. Milan: Elmo, 1953. 287 pp. Moderna libreria straniera, 3.

1954 *Luna piena* (*Full Moon*). Vittoria Comucci. Milan, Verona: A. Mondadori, 1954. 192 pp. Biblioteca economica Mondadori, 5.

1954 *Chiamate Jeeves* (*Ring for Jeeves*). Adriana Motti. Milan: F. Elmo, 1954. 287 pp. Elmo, della moderna libreria straniera.

1958 *Qualcosa di losco* (*Something Fishy*). Adriana Motti. Milan: F. Elmo, 1958. 252 pp.

1961 *Mister I. ci sa fare* (*Cocktail Time*). Adriana Motti. Milan: F. Elmo, 1961. [291] pp. Moderna libreria straniera, 1.

1962 *Ghiaccio in una stanza da letto* (*Ice in the Bedroom*). S. Agnati. Milan: F. Elmo, [1962?]. [258] pp. Moderna libreria straniera, 17.

1962 *Jeeves taglia la corda* (*Jeeves in the Offing*). Adriana Motti. Milan: F. Elmo, [1962?]. 204 pp. Moderna libreria straniera, 10.

1962 *I porci hanno le ali* (*Pigs Have Wings*). Adriana Motti. Milan: F. Elmo, [1962?]. 269 pp. Moderna libreria straniera, 11.

1962 *Non c'è da preoccuparsi* (*Nothing Serious*). Sario Agnati. [Milan:] Federico Elmo, [1962?]. [246] pp. Moderna libreria straniera.

1962 *Il club dei nati stanchi* (*Eggs, Beans and Crumpets*). Sario Agnati. [Milan:] Federico Elmo, [1962?]. [246] pp. Moderna libreria straniera.

1962 *Lei è unico, Jeeves* (*Stiff Upper Lip, Jeeves*). Sario Agnati. [Milan:] Federico Elmo, [1962?]. [225] pp. Moderna libreria straniera.

1962 *I signori, sono serviti* (*Service with a Smile*). Adriana Motti. [Milan:] Federico Elmo, [1962?]. [215] pp. Moderna libreria straniera.

1964 *Zio Fred in primavera* (*Uncle Fred in the Springtime*). A. Tedeschi. [Milan:] A. Mondadori, 1964. 262 pp. I libri del pavone, 387.

    Milan: A. Mondadori, 1972. [274] pp.

    1977. 274 pp. Gli Oscar, 425.

1965 *L'eredità sotto chiave* (*Frozen Assets*). Sario Agnati. [Milan:] Federico Elmo, [1965]. [238] pp. Moderna libreria straniera.

1966 *Il castello di Blandings (Blandings Castle)*. Luigi Brioschi. [Milan:] Bietti, [1966]. 166 pp. Il Picchio, 51.

1966 *L'avventura di Sally (The Adventures of Sally)*. [Milan:] Bietti, [1966]. 348 pp. Il Picchio, 20.

1966 *E, chi s'è visto s'è visto (French Leave)*. Adriana Motti. [Milan:] Federico Elmo, [1966]. [215] pp. Moderna libreria straniera.

1970 *Il pellicano di Blandings (A Pelican at Blandings)*. Caterina Longanesi. Milan: Mondadori, [1970]. 216 pp. Gli Oscar, 290.

[Jan. 1976]. [217] pp. Gli Oscar, 290.

1972 *Molto obbligato, Jeeves (Much Obliged, Jeeves)*. Elena Spagnol. Milan: Arnoldo Mondadori, [1972]. [197] pp.

[1976]. [197] pp. Gli Oscar, 403.

1973 *Un eroe da romanza (Lord Emsworth and Others)*. Giulia Brigiotti. [Milan:] Bietti, [1973]. 181 pp. Contents: Un eroe da romanza, Il menestrello mascherato, L'albergo del "dolce soggiorno," L'allenamento di Battler Billson, Il benoccolo degli affari.

1973 *Lord Emsworth i altri racconti (Lord Emsworth and Others)*. Giulia Brigiotti. [Milan:] Bietti, [1973]. 186 pp. Contents: Aria di delitto a Blandings, Tesori sepolti, Amore e golf, Sorti di un bellimbusto.

1973 *La ragazza in blu (The Girl in Blue)*. Elena Spagnol. [Milan:] Arnoldo Mondadori, [1973]. [196] pp. Gli Oscar del ridere, 449.

1974 *I gioielli di Monty Bodkin (Pearls, Girls and Monty Bodkin)*. Elena Spagnol. [Verona:] Arnoldo Mondadori, [1974]. 221 pp. (paper). Gli Oscar del ridere, 509.

1975 *Anonima scapoli (Bachelors Anonymous)*. Elena Spagnol. [Milan:] Arnoldo Mondadori, [1975]. [163] pp. Gli Oscar, 614.

1976 *Le zie non sono gentiluomini (Aunts Aren't Gentlemen)*. Elena Spagnol. [Milan:] Arnoldo Mondadori, [1976]. [158] pp. Gli Oscar, 690.

1977 *In compagnia di Henry (Company for Henry)*. Adriana Motti. [Milan:] Arnoldo Mondadori, [1977]. [189] pp. Gli Oscar, 739.

1977 *I maggiordomi rapinano le banche? (Do Butlers Burgle Banks?)*. Adriana Motti. [Milan:] Arnoldo Mondadori, [1977]. [171] pp. Gli Oscar, 785.

Japanese Translation

1969 *Mulliner-shi go-shôkai (Meet Mr. Mulliner)*. Inoue Kazuo. Tokyo: Chikuma shobû, 1969. 383 pp.

Norwegian Translations

1928 *Frøken Jill ved teatret (Jill the Reckless)*. Anna Sparre Nelson. Oslo: H. Aschehoug, 1928. 154 pp.

1934 *Høk over høk (Hot Water)*. Bjørn Bunkholdt. Oslo: H. Aschehoug, 1934. 263 pp.

Oslo: Aschehoug, 1973. [228] pp. ISBN 82-03-05299-1.

1934 *"Utmerket, Jeeves!" (Very Good, Jeeves)*. Axel Kielland. Oslo: H. Aschehoug, 1934. 243 pp.

2 oppl. 1951. 247 pp.

3 oppl. 1971. 211 pp.

1935 *Keiserinnen av Blandings (Summer Lightning)*. Sverre Halse. Oslo: H. Aschehoug, 1935. 275 pp.

2 oppl. 1972. [224] pp. ISBN 82-03-04826-9.

1935 *La Psmith greie det! (Leave It to Psmith)*. Axel Kielland. Oslo: H. Aschehoug, 1935. 290 pp.

2 oppl. 1951. 290 pp.

3 oppl. 1971. [247] pp.

1935 *Takk skal Da ha, Jeeves! (Thank You, Jeeves)*. Sverre Halse. Oslo: H. Aschehoug, 1935. 237 pp.

2 oppl. 1973. [196] pp. ISBN 82-03-05300-9.

1938 *En jomfru i nød (A Damsel in Distress)*. Hans Geelmuyden. Oslo: H. Aschehoug, 1938. 256 pp.

1939 *Piccadilly Jim (Piccadilly Jim)*. Hans Geelmuyden. Oslo: H. Aschehoug, 1939. 260 pp.

2 oppl. 1951. 259 pp.

1940 *Jeeves og diktatoren (The Code of the Woosters)*. Birger Rygh-Hallan. Oslo: H. Aschehoug, 1940. 228 pp.

2 oppl. 1977. 202 pp. ISBN 82-03-08703-5.

1940 *Psmith som journalist (Psmith, Journalist)*. Jacob Brinchman. Oslo: H. Aschehoug, 1940. 172 pp.

1941 *Onkel Fred i värstemning (Uncle Fred in the Springtime)*. Hans Geelmuyden. Oslo: H. Aschehoug, 1941. 241 pp.

2 oppl. 1976. 234 pp. ISBN 82-03-08304-8.

1941 *Jeeves den uforlignelige (The Inimitable Jeeves)*. Jacob Brinchman. Oslo: H. Aschehoug, 1941. 230 pp.

1941 *Psmith i banken (Psmith in the City)*. Birger Rygh-Hallan. Oslo: H. Aschehoug, 1941. 166 pp.

1948 *Penger i skjul* (*Money in the Bank*). Carl Keilhau. Oslo: H. Aschehoug, 1948. 248 pp.

    2 oppl. 1976. 246 pp. ISBN 82-03-08305-6.

1949 *Lett tjente penger* (*Money for Nothing*). Steen Forvald Øhrn. Oslo: H. Aschehoug, 1949. 269 pp.

    2 oppl. 1977. 256 pp. ISBN 82-03-08704-3.

1949 *Unge Mordreds ildfulle kjærlighet og-and re-foretillinger* ( ). Axel Kielland. Oslo: H. Aschehoug, 1949. 157 pp.

1950 *Månelyst på Blandings* (*Full Moon*). Steen Forvald Øhrn. Oslo: H. Aschehoug, 1950. 258 pp.

    2 oppl. 1977. 217 pp. ISBN 82-03-08705-1.

1951 *Bryllupsløyer* (*The Small Bachelor*). Axel Seeberg. Oslo: H. Aschehoug, 1951. 252 pp.

    2 oppl. 1975. [214] pp. ISBN 82-03-06461-2.

1951 *Penger som gress* (*Big Money*). Axel Seeberg. Oslo: H. Aschehoug, 1951. 272 pp.

1952 *Den tjenende ånd* (*Quick Service*). Axel Seeberg. Oslo: H. Aschehoug, 1952. 196 pp.

    2 oppl. 1977. 175 pp. ISBN 82-03-08702-7.

1952 *Kjenner De Mr. Mulliner?* (*Meet Mr. Mulliner*). Axel Seeberg. Oslo: H. Aschehoug, 1952. 215 pp.

    2 oppl. 1974. [176] pp. ISBN 82-03-06013-7.

1953 *Alle tiders fulltreffer* (*Barmy in Wonderland*). Axel Seeberg. Oslo: H. Aschehoug, 1953. 212 pp.

1954 *Ring på Jeeves* (*Ring for Jeeves*). Axel Seeberg. Oslo: H. Aschehoug, 1954. 259 pp.

    2 oppl. 1975. [183] pp. ISBN 82-03-06462-0.

1956 *Jeg stoler på Jeeves* (*Jeeves and the Feudal Spirit*). Axel Seeberg. Oslo: H. Aschehoug, 1956. 234 pp.

    2 oppl. 1974. 184 pp. ISBN 82-03-06012-9.

1957 *Franskbrød og arme riddere* (*French Leave*). Axel Seeberg. Oslo: H. Aschehoug, 1957. 221 pp.

    2 oppl. 1978. 176 pp. ISBN 82-03-09365-5.

1958 *Ungkarslotteriet* (*Something Fishy*). Axel Seeberg. Oslo: H. Aschehoug, 1958. 204 pp.

    2 oppl. 1978. 160 pp. ISBN 82-03-09369-8.

1959 *Prøv noe annet* (*Something Fresh*). Axel Seeberg. Oslo: H. Aschehoug, 1959. 214 pp.

1960 *Onkel Dynamitt* (*Uncle Dynamite*). Axel Seeberg. Oslo: H. Aschehoug, 1960. 202 pp.

    2 oppl. 1978. 189 pp. ISBN 82-03-09366-3.

1961 *Handlingens mann* (*Sam the Sudden*). Axel Seeberg. Oslo: H. Aschehoug, 1961. 175 pp.

1962 *S.O.S. Jeeves* (*Jeeves in the Offing*). Greta Molander. Oslo: H. Aschehoug, 1962. 162 pp.

    2 oppl. 1978. 155 pp.

1963 *Gjemt, men ikke glemt* (*Ice in the Bedroom*). Greta Molander. Oslo: H. Aschehoug, 1963. 172 pp.

1964 *Svin på skogen* (*Service with a Smile*). Axel Seeberg. Oslo: H. Aschehoug, 1964. 167 pp.

1965 *Friskt mot, Jeeves!* (*Stiff Upper Lip, Jeeves*). Axel Seeberg. Oslo: H. Aschehoug, 1965. 171 pp.

1973 *Perler, piker og Monty Bodkin* (*Pearls, Girls and Monty Bodkin*). Axel Seeberg. Oslo: H. Aschehoug, 1973. 146 pp. ISBN 82-03-05824-8.

1974 *Anonyme peppersvenner* (*Bachelors Anonymous*). Axel Seeberg. Oslo: H. Aschehoug, 1974. [122] pp. ISBN 82-03-06193-1.

1975 *Tanter er ikke gentlemen* (*Aunts Aren't Gentlemen*). Axel S. Seeberg. Oslo: H. Aschehoug, 1975. [132] pp. ISBN 82-03-06463-9.

Tanter er ikke gentlemen (*Aunts Aren't Gentlemen*). Vilhelm Topsøe. [Aalborg:] Lindhardt og Ringhof, 1975. [152] pp.

1979 *Salig i sin tro* (*Heavy Weather*). Axel Seeberg. Oslo: H. Aschehoug, 1979. 221 pp. ISBN 82-03-09960-2.

1979 *Superdupert, Jeeves* (*Much Obliged, Jeeves*). Axel Seeberg. Oslo: H. Aschehoug, 1979. 142 pp. ISBN 82-03-09959-9.

Polish Translations

1933 *Grube pieniądze* (*Big Money*). J. P. Zajączkowski. Warsaw: Rój, 1933. 319 pp.

1934 *Ptaszek z Piccadilly* (*Piccadilly Jim*). Warsaw: Swiat, [1934?]. 316 pp.

1936 *Goscie spod ciemmej geviazdy* (*Hot Water*). Herminja Bukowska. Warsaw: Rój, 1936. 282 pp.

1936 *Na Kawalerce* (*The Small Bachelor*). J. P. Zajączkowski. Warsaw: Rój, 1936. 287 pp.

1936 *Ucésniona dziewica* (*A Damsel in Distress*). J. P. Zajączkowski. Warsaw: Rój, 1936. 290 pp.

1937 *Panna Dr. Sally* (*Doctor Sally*). H. Bukowska. Warsaw: Rój, 1937. 207 pp.

1977 *Wielce zobowiązany, Jeeves* (*Much Obliged, Jeeves*). Juliusz Kydrynski. Warsaw: Książka i Wiedza, 1977. [254] pp.

Portuguese Translations (Portugal and Brazil)

1936 *Por sua dama* (*A Damsel in Distress*). J. E. Paula Rosa. Lisbon: Edicões Europa, 1936. 355 pp.

1938 *Isso é consigo* ( ). Eduardo Paula Rosa. Lisbon: Oficinas Gráficas de Edicões Europa, 1938. 376 pp.

1949 *Homeva de visão* ( ). Estevão Reis. Lisbon: Soc. Nacional de Tipografia, 1949. 271 pp.

1958 *Dinheiro molesto* (*Uneasy Money*[?]). João Ervedosa. Lisbon: Aster, [1958?]. 228 pp.

1960 *O código dos Woosters* (*The Code of the Woosters*). Ernesto de Carvalho. Lisbon: Aster, [1960?]. 240 pp.

1961 *O tio Fred à Solta* (*Uncle Fred in the Springtime*). Luis de Andrade Pina. Lisbon: Aster, [1961?]. 278 pp.

Tio Fred na primavera (*Uncle Fred in the Springtime*). Luzia Machada da Costa. Rio de Janeiro, Saõ Paulo: Record, [1973?]. 251 pp.

1971 *Muito grato, Jeeves* (*Much Obliged, Jeeves*). Luzia Machada da Costa. Rio de Janeiro, Saõ Paulo: Record, [1971?]. 180 pp.

1973 *Jeeves ao largo* (*Jeeves in the Offing*). Luzia Caminha Machada da Costa. Rio de Janeiro, Saõ Paulo: Record, [1973]. 184 pp.

1973 *Um castello sem Fantasmas* (*Blandings Castle*). Luzia Caminha Machado da Costa. Rio de Janeiro: Record, 1973. 230 pp.

1973 *O incomparável Jeeves* (*The Inimitable Jeeves*). Luzia Caminha Machado da Costa. Rio de Janeiro: Record, 1973. 230 pp.

Spanish Translations

1935 *Le genialidades de Sam* (*Sam the Sudden*). G. López Hipkiss. Barcelona: Hymsa, 1935. 64 pp.
Sam el Brusco (*Sam the Sudden*). Emilia Bertel. Barcelona: José Janés, Ediciones Lauro, 1946. 247 pp. El Club de la Alegría.
   Madrid: Aguilar, 1952. 424 pp. Colección Cristol, 362.
   Madrid: Aguilar, 1961. 362 pp.

1942 *Luna de verano* (*Summer Moonshine*). Juan G. de Luaces. Barcelona: Augustín Núñez, 1942. 270 pp. Colección Al Monigote de Papel.
   2 ed. Barcelona: Aléu y Domingo, 1944. 270 pp. Al Monigote de Papel.

1943 *El tío Fred de primavera* (*Uncle Fred in the Springtime*). B. Palazón. Barcelona: Ediciones Anfora, Imp. de Augustín Núñez, 1943. 272 pp. Colección Anfora.

1944 *El castillo de Blandings* (*Blandings Castle*). Manuel Bosch Barrett. Madrid: Ediciones Anfora, 1944. 286 pp. Colección Anfora.

1944 *Dejádselo a Psmith* (*Leave It to Psmith*). Claudio Matons Rossi. Barcelona: Imp. Ponsa, 1944. 314 pp. Al Monigote de Papel.
   Barcelona: José Janés, 1952. 265 pp.

1944 *Dinero molesto* (*Uneasy Money*). José A. de Larrinaga y Gorostiza. Barcelona: Imp. La Académica, 1944. 253 pp. Al Monigote de Papel.
   Barcelona: José Janés, 1952. 203 pp.
   Barcelona: G.P., 1959. 192 pp. Libros de Humor "El Gorrión," 49.

1944 *Un dineral* ( ). Simón Santainés. Barcelona: José Janés, 1944. 282 pp. Al Monigote de Papel.

1944 *Un par de solteros* (*The Small Bachelor*). Emilia Bertel. Barcelona: Imp. Rubí, 1944. 284 pp. Al Monigote de Papel.

1944 *El gas de la risa* (*Laughing Gas*). Gregorio H. Alonso de Grimaldi. Madrid: Ediciones Anfora, Imp. Aléu y Domingo, 1944. 266 pp. Colección Anfora.
   2 ed. Barcelona: José Janés, 1955. 243 pp.

1944 *Guapo, rico y distinguido* ( ). Luis Ignacio Bertrán. Barcelona: La Pléyade, Imp. La Académica, 1944. 298 pp. Novelistas ingleses, 8.
   2 ed. Barcelona: José Janés, 1956. 257 pp.

1944 *Jim de Piccadilly* (*Piccadilly Jim*). Emilia Bertel. Barcelona: José Janés, Ediciones Lauro, 1944. 306 pp. La Hostería del Buen Humor.
   3 ed. Barcelona: José Janés, 1955. 246 pp.

1944 *Pobre, vago y optimista* ( ). Juan G. de Luaces. Barcelona: Imp. Rubí, 1944. 262 pp. Al Monigote de Papel.
   4 ed. Barcelona: José Janés, 1956. 209 pp.

1944 *Psmith, periodista* (*Psmith, Journalist*). Fernando Trías Beristain. Barcelona: La Académica, 1944. 269 pp. Al Monigote de Papel.
   Barcelona: José Janés, 1952. 193 pp.

Barcelona: G.P., 1959. 192 pp. Libros de Humor "El Gorrión," 54.

1944 *Señorita en desgracia* (*A Damsel in Distress*). Fernando Trías Beristain. Barcelona: José Janés, Ediciones Lauro, 1944. 301 pp. La Hostería del Buen Humor.

    4 ed. Barcelona: José Janés, 1956. 245 pp. *Señorita en desgracia* (*A Damsel in Distress*). Fernando Trías Beristain. [Madrid: Aguilar, 1952.] 460 pp.

    2 ed. Madrid: Aguilar, [1959]. 450 pp. Colección Cristol, 345.

1945 *Amor y gallinas* (*Love among the Chickens*). Carlos Botet. Barcelona: José Janés, Ediciones Lauro, 1945. 364 pp. La Hostería del Buen Humor.

    3 ed. Barcelona: José Janés, 1955. 176 pp. *Amor y gallinas* (*Love among the Chickens*). Carlos Botet. Madrid: Dédalo, 1961. 68 pp.

1945 *¡Adelante, Jeeves!* (*Carry On, Jeeves!*). Luis Jordá. Barcelona: Ediciones Lauro, 1945. 254 pp.

    Barcelona: José Janés, 1952. 218 pp.

1945 *El código de los Woosters* (*The Code of the Woosters*). Manuel Bosch Barrett. Barcelona: Ediciones Lauro, 1945. 268 pp.

    Barcelona: José Janés, 1952. 230 pp.

1945 *De acuerdo, Jeeves* (*Right Ho, Jeeves*). Emilia Bertel. Barcelona: Ediciones Lauro, 1945. 223 pp. Colección Leda.

    Barcelona: José Janés, 1952. 233 pp.

1945 *Dinero para nada* (*Money for Nothing*). Manuel Bosch Barrett. Barcelona: José Janés, Ediciones Lauro, 1945. 339 pp. La Hostería del Buen Humor.

    2 ed. Barcelona: José Janés, 1956. 245 pp.

1945 *¡Gracias Jeeves!* (*Thank You, Jeeves*). Juan G. de Luaces. Barcelona: José Janés, Ediciones Lauro, 1945. 243 pp. Colección Leda.

    Barcelona: José Janés, 1952. 201 pp.

    Barcelona: G.P., [1959]. 192 pp. Libros de Humor "El Gorrión," 61.

    Barcelona: Círculo de Lectores, 1971. 214 pp.

1945 *Guillermo el Conquistador y su invasión de Inglaterra en primavera* (*Bill the Conqueror*). Luis Jordá. Barcelona: Imp. Aléu y Domingo, 1945. 320 pp. Al Monigote de Papel.

    2 ed. Barcelona: Al Monigote de Papel, [1947]. 304 pp.

    Barcelona: José Janés, 1951. 314 pp.

1945 *El hombre con dos pies izquierdos* (*The Man with Two Left Feet*). Fernando Trías Berstain. Barcelona: José Janés, 1945. 236 pp. Al Monigote de Papel.

1945 *¡Muy bien, Jeeves!* (*Very Good, Jeeves*). Juan G. de Luaces. Barcelona: Ediciones Lauro, 1945. 230 pp. Colección Leda.

    Barcelona: José Janés, 1952. 209 pp.

    Barcelona: G.P., [1960]. 190 pp. Libros de Humor "El Gorrión," 76.

    Barcelona: Círculo de Lectores, 1967. 234 pp.

1945 *La suerte de los Bodkin* (*The Luck of the Bodkins*). E. Toda Valcárcel. Barcelona: José Janés, Ediciones Lauro, 1945. 322 pp. La Hostería del Buen Humor.

    [Madrid: Aguilar, 1953.] 440 pp. Colección Cristol, 377.

    2 ed. Madrid: Aguilar, [1962]. 450 pp.

1946 *Archie, el indiscreto* (*The Indiscretions of Archie*). Juan G. de Luaces. Barcelona: José Janés, 1946. 274 pp. Al Monigote de Papel.

    3 ed. Barcelona: José Janés, 1956. 222 pp.

1946 *El inimitable Jeeves* (*The Inimitable Jeeves*). Emilia Bertel. Barcelona: José Janés, 1946. 206 pp. Colección Leda.

    Barcelona: José Janés, 1952. 205 pp.

    Barcelona: G.P., [1960]. 160 pp. Libros de Humor "El Gorrión," 67.

1946 *Jovencitos con botines* (*Young Men in Spats*). Luis Jordá. Barcelona: José Janés, 1946. 251 pp. Al Monigote de Papel.

    Barcelona: José Janés, 1952. 209 pp.

    Barcelona: G.P., 1959. 160 pp. Libros de Humor "El Gorrión," 51.

1946 *Les presento a Mr. Mulliner* (*Meet Mr. Mulliner*). Emilia Bertel. Barcelona: José Janés, Ediciones Lauro, 1946. 179 pp.

    2 ed. Barcelona: José Janés, 1956. 158 pp.

    Barcelona: José Janés, 1961. 192 pp.

1946 *Mal tiempo* (*Heavy Weather*). Pedro Reverter. Barcelona: José Janés, 1946. 259 pp. Al Monigote de Papel.

1946 *Mr. Mulliner tiene la palabra* (*Mr. Mulliner*

Speaking). Emilia Bertel. Barcelona: José Janés, Ediciones Lauro, 1946. 189 pp. El Club de la Alegría.

    2 ed. Barcelona: José Janés, 1956. 189 pp.

    Barcelona: G.P., 1961. 192 pp.

1946 *Las noches de Mulliner* (*Mulliner Nights*). Manuel Márquez. Barcelona: José Janés, Ediciones Lauro, 1946. 193 pp. El Club de la Alegría.

    2 ed. Barcelona: José Janés, 1955. 188 pp.

    Barcelona: G.P., 1961. 160 pp.

1946 *Un caballero extravagante* (*A Gentleman of Leisure*). A. Martinez del Rincón. Barcelona: Ediciones Lauro, 1946. 257 pp. La Hostería del Buen Humor.

    2 ed. Barcelona: José Janés, 1956. 223 pp.

1947 *El advenimiento de Bill* (*The Coming of Bill*). Manuel Bosch Barrett. Barcelona: José Janés, 1947. 217 pp. Al Monigote de Papel.

    Barcelona: José Janés, 1952. 261 pp.

1947 *Algo fresco* (*Something Fresh*). Manuel Bosch Barrett. Barcelona: José Janés, 1947. 239 pp. Al Monigote de Papel.

    Barcelona: G.P., [1960]. 192 pp. Libros de Humor "El Gorrión," 73.

    Buenos Aires: Plaza y Janés, [1960]. 192 pp.

1947 *Una alhaja de niño* (*The Little Nugget*). R. Coll Robert. Barcelona: José Janés, 1947. 217 pp. Al Monigote de Papel.

1947 *Las aventuras de Sally* (*The Adventures of Sally*). R. Coll Robert. Barcelona: José Janés, 1947. 246 pp. Al Monigote de Papel.

    Barcelona: José Janés, 1952. 248 pp.

1947 *Dieciocho agujeros* (*The Heart of a Goof*). Luis Jordá. Barcelona: José Janés, 1947. 175 pp. Al Monigote de Papel.

    Barcelona: José Janés, 1952. 205 pp.

1947 *Dinero en el Banco* (*Money in the Bank*). Manuel Bosch Barrett. Barcelona: José Janés, 1947. 198 pp. Al Monigote de Papel.

    Barcelona: José Janés, 1952.

1947 *El hombre del piso de arriba* (*The Man Upstairs*). Claudio Matons Rossi. Barcelona: José Janés, 1947. 217 pp. Al Monigote de Papel.

    2 ed. Barcelona: José Janés, 1955. 237 pp.

1947 *Jeeves, tú eres mi hombre* (anthology). Luis Jordá, Juan G. de Luaces, Emilia Bertel. Barcelona: José Janés, 1947. 256 pp. Manantial que no cesa, 15.

1947 *Servicio rápido* (*Quick Service*). Gregorio H. Alonso de Grimaldi. Barcelona: José Janés, 1947. 193 pp. Al Monigote de Papel.

    Barcelona: José Janés, 1952. 191 pp.

1948 *Luna llena* (*Full Moon*). Manuel Bosch Barrett. Barcelona: José Janés, 1948. 239 pp. Al Monigote de Papel.

    Barcelona: José Janés, 1952. 211 pp.

1948 *El príncipe y Betty* (*The Prince and Betty*). Ornella Bertel. Barcelona: José Janés, 1948. 152 pp. El Club de la Alegría, 15.

1949 *Ola de crímenes en el castillo de Blandings* (*Crime Wave at Blandings*). Manuel Bosch. Barcelona: José Janés, 1949. 235 pp. Al Monigote de Papel.

    2 ed. Barcelona: José Janés, 1956. 212 pp.

1950 *La chica de a bordo* (*The Girl on the Boat*). Fernando J. Platero. Barcelona: José Janés, 1950. 279 pp. Al Monigote de Papel.

    2 ed. Barcelona: José Janés, 1955. 236 pp.

1950 *Júbilo matinal* (*Joy in the Morning*). Manuel Bosch. Barcelona: José Janés, 1950. 267 pp. Los Escritores de Ahora.

    Barcelona: José Janés, 1952. 228 pp.

1950 *Si yo fuera usted* (*If I Were You*). Manuel Bosch. Barcelona: José Janés, 1950. 241 pp. Al Monigote de Papel.

    2 ed. Barcelona: José Janés, 1956. 180 pp.

    Barcelona: G.P., 1958. 159 pp.

1953 *En las redes de Broadway* (*Angel Cake*). Luís Conde Vélez. Barcelona: Bruguera, 1953. 222 pp. Autores famosos, 78; serie azul, 5.

1957 *Fiebre primaveral* (*Spring Fever*). Rosa S. de Naveira. Barcelona: José Janés, 1957. 223 pp. Al Monigote de Papel.

1960 *Cara de tonto, cara de palo* (*Eggs, Beans and Crumpets*). Rosa S. de Naveira. Barcelona: G.P., [1960]. 192 pp. Libros de Humor "El Gorrión," 78.

1960 *Obras* (anthology). Buenos Aires: Plaza y Janés; [Madrid: Castilla], 1960. 1348 pp.

    2 ed. Buenos Aires: Plaza y Janés; Barcelona: [Saturno], 1963. Contents: ¡Muy bien, Jeeves!; ¡Adelante, Jeeves!; ¡Gracias, Jeeves!; El código de los Woosters; De acuerdo, Jeeves; El inimitable Jeeves.

1961 *Jeeves está de vacaciones* (*Jeeves in the Offing*). Consuela González de Ortega. Buenos Aires: Plaza y Janés, [1961]. 196 pp.
    Barcelona: G.P., 1968. 208 pp. Colección "Alcotán," 142.

1963 *Joyas en el dormitorio* (*Ice in the Bedroom*). M. a del Carmen Pascual. Buenos Aires: Plaza y Janés, [1963]. 200 pp.

1966 *Buenas obras y sonrisas* (*Service with a Smile*). Rosa S. de Naveiro. Barcelona: Plaza y Janés, 1966. 311 pp.

Swedish Translations

1920 *Piccadilly Jim* (*Piccadilly Jim*). H. Flygare. Stockholm: Fahlcrantz, 1920. 274 pp.
    Stockholm: B. Wahlström, 1937. 256 pp. Blå biblioteket.
    1941. 256 pp.

1921 *En flicka i trångmål* (*A Damsel in Distress*). Ulla Rudebeck. Stockholm: Hökerberg, 1921. 245 pp.
Flicka i fara (*A Damsel in Distress*). Birgitta Hammar. Stockholm: Bonnier, [1979]. [211] pp. ISBN 91-0-043918-5.

1921 *Rörliga pengar* (*Uneasy Money*). Stockholm: Fahlcrantz, 1921. 213 pp.
Rörliga pengar (*Uneasy Money*). Emil Langlet. Stockholm: B. Wahlström, 1938. 254 pp.; 1941. 254 pp.

1922 *Psmith som journalist* (*Psmith, Journalist*). Stockholm: Bonnier, 1922. 261 pp.
    ny utg. Stockholm: Ahlén & Åkerlund (Bonnier), 1939. 198 pp.

1922 *Vannen Archies missöden* (*The Indiscretions of Archie*). Harald Johnsson. Stockholm: Bonnier, 1922. 264 pp.

1923 *Dick Underhills fästmö* (*Jill the Reckless*). Harald Johnsson. Stockholm: Hökerberg, 1923. 296 pp.

1925 *Den okända son han älskade* (*A Gentleman of Leisure*). Stockholm: Hökerberg, 1925. 232 pp.

1929 *Börsspel och kärlek* ( ). Signe von Vegesack. Stockholm: Bonnier, 1929. 293 pp.

1931 *Lord Emsworth misstag* (*Something Fresh*). Elsa Jonason. Stockholm: Hökerberg, 1931. 299 pp.
Det våras på Blandings (*Something Fresh*). Birgitta Hammar. Stockholm: Bonnier, [1978]. [212] pp. ISBN 91-0-043548-1.

1931 *Den oförliknelige Jeeves* (*The Inimitable Jeeves*). Kerstin Wimnell. Stockholm: Skoglunds, 1931. 269 pp.
Den oefterharmlige Jeeves (*The Inimitable Jeeves*). Birgitta Hammar. Stockholm: Bonnier, 1957. 405 pp.
    Stockholm: Aldus/Bonnier, 1960. 204 pp. En Delfinbök, D25.

1933 *Billie och hennes friare* (*The Girl on the Boat*). Kerstin Wimnell. Stockholm: Fritzes, 1933. 266 pp.
    Stockholm: Saxon & Lindström, [1936?]. 255 pp.
    Stockholm: Saxon & Lindström, 1939. 262 pp.
    4 uppl. Stockholm: Ardor, 1942. 220 pp.

1934 *Hett om öronen* (*Hot Water*). Stig Facht. Stockholm: Fritzes, 1934. 303 pp. ny uppl. 1936. 303 pp.
    ny utg. Stockholm: Lindqvist, 1941. 239 pp.
    ny utg. Stockholm: Fritzes, [1951?]. 270 pp.

1934 *Psmith ordnar saken* (*Leave It to Psmith*). Vilgot Hammarling. Stockholm: Bonnier, 1934. 295 pp.
    2-3 uppl. 1934; 4-5 uppl. 1935; 6 uppl. 1936; 7 uppl. 1938. 295 pp.
    ny utg. 1945. 373 pp.
    ny uppl. 1959. 271 pp.
    [1978]. [272] pp. I Delfinserien. ISBN 91-0-043771-9.

1935 *Blixt och dunder* (*Summer Lightning*). Vilgot Hammarling. Stockholm: Bonnier, 1935. 295 pp.; 2-3 uppl., 1935. 295 pp.; 4 uppl., 1936. 295 pp.; 5 uppl., 1940. 295 pp.
    ny uppl. Stockholm, Aldus/Bonnier, 1959. 267 pp.
    [1978]. [263] pp. ISBN 91-0-043778-6.

1935 *Pengar till skänks* (*Money for Nothing*). Stig Facht. Stockholm: Fritzes, 1935. 334 pp.
    2 uppl. 1935. 334 pp.; 3 uppl. 1936. 334 pp.
    [ny utg.] Stockholm: Lindqvist, 1942. 272 pp.
    [ny utg.] 1946. 224 pp. Folksbiblioteket, 36.
    [Stockholm:] Aldus, [1975]. [247] pp. ISBN 91-0-040522-1.

1935 *Sam hos tidningskungen* (*Sam the Sudden*). Stig Facht. Stockholm: Fritzes, 1935. 332 pp.
    2-3 uppl. 1935. 332 pp.

ny utg. Stockholm: Lindqvist, 1942. 267 pp.

[Stockholm:] Aldus, [1975]. [242] pp. ISBN 91-0-040526-6.

1935 *En blyg ung man* (*The Small Bachelor*). Martin Loya. Stockholm: Fritzes, 1935. 306 pp.

2 uppl. 1935. 306 pp.

ny uppl. Stockholm: Lindqvist, 1943. 223 pp.

1936 *Fina papper* (*Big Money*). Stig Facht. Stockholm: Fritzes, 1936. 320 pp. 2 uppl. 1936. 320 pp.

3 uppl. Stockholm: Lindqvist, 1941. 222 pp.

4 uppl. 1943. 222 pp.

1936 *Karlek i hönsgården* (*Love among the Chickens*). Stockholm: Saxon & Lindström, 1936. 237 pp.

1936 *Åska i luften* (*Heavy Weather*). Vilgot Hammarling. Stockholm: Bonnier, 1936. 281 pp.

2–5 uppl. 1936; [6 uppl.] 1940. 281 pp.

[ny uppl.] 1959. 261 pp.; ny uppl. 1961. 221 pp.

1936 *Tack, Jeeves* (*Thank You, Jeeves*). Vilgot Hammarling. Stockholm: Bonnier, 1936. 251 pp.

2 uppl. 1936. 251 pp.

ny utg. [1952]. [208] pp. Trumf-serien.

[ny uppl.] 1959. 240 pp.; 1961. 240 pp.

1937 *Bill erövraren* (*Bill the Conqueror*). Vilgot Hammarling. Stockholm: Bonnier, 1937. 319 pp.

Stockholm: Aldus/Bonnier, [1965]. [239] pp. 1968. 239 pp. En Delfinbök, D184.

[1978]. 238 pp. ISBN 91-0-043773-5.

1937 *I knipa* (*The Pothunters*). Emil Langlet. Stockholm: Wahlströms, 1937. 156 p. Wahlströms ungdomböcker, 253.

1937 *Lagets kapten* (*A Prefect's Uncle*). Emil Langlet. Stockholm: Wahlströms, 1937. 157 p. Wahlströms ungdomböcker, 254. 2 uppl. 1943. 157 p.

1937 *Jeeves klarer skivan* (*Carry On, Jeeves!*). Vilgot Hammarling. Stockholm: Bonnier, 1937. 252 pp.

2–3 uppl. 1937. 252 pp.; 4 uppl. 1938. 252 pp.

ny utg. Stockholm: Bonnier/Aldus, 1966. 229 pp.

[1978]. [230] pp. ISBN 91-0-043769-7.

1938 *Sommarpippi* (*Summer Moonshine*). Martin Loya. Stockholm: Bonnier, 1938. 304 pp.

[ny utg.] 1946. 382 pp.

1939 *Som det anstår en Wooster* (*The Code of the Woosters*). Birgitta Hammar. Stockholm: Bonnier, 1939. 266 pp.

2–7 uppl. 1939. 266 pp.; 8 uppl. 1940. 266 pp.

[ny utg.] 1955. 299 pp.

ny utg. 2 uppl. [1964]. 208 pp. Delfinserien, D109.

1939 *Den vita fjädern* (*The White Feather*). Axel Essén. Stockholm: Saxon & Lindström, 1939. 240 pp.

1940 *Farbror Fred i vårhumör* (*Uncle Fred in the Springtime*). Birgitta Hammar. Stockholm: Bonnier, 1940. 251 pp. 2–7 uppl. 1940. 251 pp.; [ny utg.] 1952. 208 pp.

[ny uppl.] 1959. 242 pp.

1941 *Nära ögat* (*The Luck of the Bodkins*). Birgitta Hammar. Stockholm: Bonnier, 1941. 331 pp.

2–5 uppl. 1941. 331 pp.

Stockholm: Aldus, [1975]. 279 pp. ISBN 91-0-040520-5.

1941 *Luft i luckan* (*Mike*). Gösta Högelin. Stockholm: Wahlströms, 1941. 138 pp. Wahlströms ungdomsböcker, 329.

1942 *Odågorna* (*The Head of Kay's*). Gösta Högelin. Stockholm: Wahlströms, 1942. 138 pp. Wahlströms ungdomsböcker, 343.

1942 *Pengar på banken* (*Money in the Bank*). Birgitta Hammar. Stockholm: Bonnier, 1942. 352 pp.

2–5 uppl. 1942. 352 pp.; [ny uppl.] 1959. 259 pp.

1942 *Ferm expedition* (*Quick Service*). Birgitta Hammar. Stockholm: Bonnier, 1942. 211 pp.

2–4 uppl. 1942. 211 pp.

Stockholm: Aldus, 1975. [245] pp. ISBN 91-0-040516-7.

1943 *All right, Jeeves!* (*Right Ho, Jeeves*). Birgitta Hammar. Stockholm: Bonnier, 1943. 337 pp.

2–7 uppl. 1943. 337 pp.

[Stockholm:] Aldus, [1975]. [224] pp. ISBN 91-0-040508-6.

1944 *Guldklimpen* (*The Little Nugget*). Birgitta Hammar. Stockholm: Bonnier, 1944. 314 pp.

2–7 uppl. 1944. 314 pp.; [ny uppl.] 1959. 245 pp.

1945 *Får jag föreställa Mr. Mulliner?* (*Meet Mr. Mulliner*). Birgitta Hammar. Stockholm: Bonnier, 1945. 245 pp.

[Stockholm:] Aldus, [1975]. [245] pp. ISBN 91-0-040516-7.

1946 *Mr. Mulliner har ordet* (*Mr. Mulliner Speaking*).

Birgitta Hammar. Stockholm: Bonnier, 1946. 279 pp.

    2–9 uppl. 1946. 279 pp.

    [ny uppl.] 1959. 227 pp.

    Stockholm: Aldus/Bonnier, 1971. [197] pp.

1947 *Bravo, Jeeves!* (*Joy in the Morning*). Birgitta Hammar. Stockholm: Bonnier, 1947. 295 pp.

    2–10 uppl. 1947. 295 pp.

1948 *Fullmåne* (*Full Moon*). Birgitta Hammar. Stockholm: Bonnier, 1948. 279 pp.

    2–10 uppl. 1948. 279 pp.

    [ny uppl.] 1959. 250 pp.

    [1967]. 218 pp. Delfinserien, D266.

1949 *Vårkänslor* (*Spring Fever*). Birgitta Hammar. Stockholm: Bonnier, 1949. 277 pp.

    2–10 uppl. 1949. 277 pp.

    Stockholm: Aldus, [1975]. 213 pp. ISBN 91-0-040527-2.

1950 *Alla tiders Wodehouse*, (anthology), redigerad och inledd av Georg Svensson. Birgitta Hammar. Stockholm: Albert Bonniers Forlag, [1950]. 533 pp.

1950 *Farbror Dynamit* (*Uncle Dynamite*). Birgitta Hammar. Stockholm: Bonnier, 1950. 312 pp.

    Stockholm: Aldus, [1975]. [250] pp. ISBN 91-0-040512-4.

1951 *Kaka söker maka* (*The Mating Season*). Birgitta Hammar. Stockholm: Bonnier, [1951]. 288 pp.

1952 *Kvällar med Mr. Mulliner* (*Mulliner Nights*). Birgitta Hammar. Stockholm: Bonnier, 1952. 238 pp.

1953 *Svinhugg går igen* (*Pigs Have Wings*). Birgitta Hammar. Stockholm: Bonnier, 1953. 269 pp.

    Stockholm: Aldus/Bonnier, 1961. 211 pp. I Delfinserien.

    2 uppl. 1964. 269 pp.; 3 uppl. 1967. [212] pp.

1954 *Ring på Jeeves!* (*Ring for Jeeves*). Birgitta Hammar. Stockholm: Bonnier, 1954. 245 pp.

    3 uppl. Stockholm: Aldus/Bonnier, 1968. 182 pp.

1955 *Jeeves och feodalandan* (*Jeeves and the Feudal Spirit*). Birgitta Hammar. Stockholm: Bonnier, 1955. 247 pp.

    Stockholm: Aldus, 1975. [247] pp. ISBN 91-0-040518-3.

1956 *Fransysk visit* (*French Leave*). Birgitta Hammar. Stockholm: Bonnier, [1956]. [239] pp.

1957 *Den oumbärlige Jeeves* (anthology), red. och inledd av Georg Svensson. Birgitta Hammar. Stockholm: Bonnier, 1957. 405 pp.

1957 *Rävspel* (*Something Fishy*). Birgitta Hammar. Stockholm: Bonnier, [1957]. [205] pp.

1958 *Skrattgas* (*Laughing Gas*). Birgitta Hammar. Stockholm: Bonnier, [1958]. [292] pp.

1959 *Cocktaildags* (*Cocktail Time*). Birgitta Hammar. Stockholm: Bonnier, 1959. 226 pp.

    ny utg. Stockholm: Aldus/Bonnier, [1969]. [209] pp. Delfinserien, 324.

1960 *Sängfösare* (*A Few Quick Ones*). Birgitta Hammar. Stockholm: Bonnier, 1960. 225 pp.

1961 *När Jeeves är borta* (*Jeeves in the Offing*). Birgitta Hammar. Stockholm: Bonnier, [1961]. [211] pp.

1962 *Sköna juveler* (*Ice in the Bedroom*). Birgitta Hammar. Stockholm: Bonnier, [1962]. [249] pp.

1963 *Alltid till Er tjänst* (*Service with a Smile*). Birgitta Hammar and Mons Mossner. Stockholm: Bonnier, 1963. 224 pp.

1964 *Upp med hakan, Jeeves* (*Stiff Upper Lip, Jeeves*). Birgitta Hammar. [Stockholm:] Bonnier, [1964]. [227] pp.

1966 *Galahad på Blandings* (*Galahad at Blandings*). Birgitta Hammar. Stockholm: Bonnier, 1966. [216] pp.

1967 *Ett upp för Cuthbert* (*The Clicking of Cuthbert*). Birgitta Hammar. Stockholm: Bonnier, 1967. 213 pp. Stockholm: Aldus, [1975]. [214] pp. ISBN 91-0-040510-8.

1968 *Sammelsurium* (*Company for Henry*). Birgitta Hammar. Stockholm: Bonnier, 1968. [202] pp.

1969 *Brukar betjänter begå bankrån?* (*Do Butlers Burgle Banks?*). Birgitta Hammar. Stockholm: Bonnier, [1969]. [193] pp.

1970 *En pelikan på Blandings* (*A Pelican at Blandings*). Birgitta Hammar. Stockholm: Bonnier, [1970]. [200] pp.

1971 *Flickan i blått* (*The Girl in Blue*). Birgitta Hammar. Stockholm: Bonnier, 1971. 199 pp.

1972 *Underbart, Jeeves* (*Much Obliged, Jeeves*). Birgitta Hammar. Stockholm: Bonnier, [1972]. [202] pp. ISBN 91-0-020091-3.

1973 *Smycken, tycken och Monty Bodkin* (*Pearls, Girls and Monty Bodkin*). Birgitta Hammar. Stock-

	holm: Bonnier, [1973]. [215] pp. ISBN 91-0-038272-8.
1974	*Inbitna Ungkarlar* (*Bachelors Anonymous*). Birgitta Hammar. Stockholm: Bonnier, [1974]. [201] pp. ISBN 91-0-038973-0.
1975	*Fastrar är inga gentlemän* (*Aunts Aren't Gentlemen*). Birgitta Hammar. Stockholm: Bonnier, [1975]. [196] pp. ISBN 91-0-040040-8.
1976	*Oss golfare emellan* (*The Heart of a Goof*). Birgitta Hammar. Stockholm: Bonnier, [1976]. [231] pp. ISBN 91-0-040896-4.
1977	*Lita på Bill* (*The Old Reliable*). Birgitta Hammar. Stockholm: Bonnier, [1977]. [193] pp. ISBN 91-0-041724-6.

Turkish Translations

1956	*Macun hokkasi* ( ). Celâl Dağlar. Istanbul: Yeni Matbaa, 1956. 191 pp.
1958	*Dolar yağmuru* (*Big Money*). Celâl Dağlar. Istanbul: Yeni Matbaa, 1958. 91 pp.

Ukrainian Translation

1928	*Psmit-zhurnalist* (*Psmith, Journalist*). I. Iu. Kulik. Kharkov: Derzhavne Vydavnytstvo, 1928. 214 pp.

The Dramatic Wodehouse: Stage and Screen

P. G. WODEHOUSE and Guy Bolton wrote of their experiences in the theatre in *Bring on the Girls*.[1] Because different stories are included, both the London and the American editions should be read, but both should be taken with a pinch of salt for the authors were interested first in telling good stories. Wodehouse also refers to some of his experiences in the theatre and in Hollywood in *Performing Flea*.[2]

Besides the Heineman collection, much information on both the American and English theatre and cinema is available in the Theatre Division of the Museum of the Performing Arts Library which is part of the Research Libraries of the New York Public Library.

David Jasen has compiled an account of Wodehouse and the stage in *The Theatre of P. G. Wodehouse*,[3] reproducing programs, photographs, and reviews, and giving cast lists of many of the plays.

Three other more general reference sources should be mentioned which are available in most large libraries: *Who's Who in the Theatre*,[4] published in London since 1912. This directory, frequently issued in new editions, gives brief biographies and, more importantly, number of performances, opening dates, and cast lists for the London stage and, in later editions, for Broadway. For the United States, *The Biographical Encyclopedia and Who's Who of the American Theatre*[5] succeeded by *Notable Names in the American Theatre*[6] do much the same thing; although the period of coverage for playbills is brief, 1959–64, the listing of New York production opening dates and number of performances is extensive through 1975.

Stanley Green's *Encyclopedia of the Musical Theatre*[7] is a handy dictionary for information on songs, performers, productions (including revivals), composers, etc., of the major musicals on the New York and London stages. Here, for example, one finds a

---

1. P. G. Wodehouse and Guy Bolton, *Bring on the Girls* (New York: Simon and Schuster, 1953; London: Herbert Jenkins, 1954).
2. P. G. Wodehouse, *Performing Flea* (London: Herbert Jenkins, 1953).
3. David A. Jasen, *The Theatre of P. G. Wodehouse* (London: B. T. Batsford, 1979).
4. *Who's Who in the Theatre*, eds. 1–16, ed. John Parker and currently by Ian Hamilton (London: Pitman, 1912–77).
5. *The Biographical Encyclopedia and Who's Who of the American Theatre*, ed. Walter Rigdon (New York: James H. Heineman, 1966).
6. *Notable Names in the American Theatre*, ed. Raymond D. McGill (Clifton, N.J.: John T. White and Co., 1976).
7. Stanley Green, *Encyclopedia of the Musical Theatre* (New York: DaCapo, 1976).

summary of the peregrinations of the Wodehouse-Kern song "Bill."

Similar works for the cinema exist; two very good dictionaries are compiled by Leslie Halliwell: *The Filmgoer's Companion* and *Halliwell's Film Guide*.[8] Together they offer definitions, brief biographies of actors, producers, directors, and film writers, and brief synopses of major films.

Finally, a word should be said about the pseudonym Stephen Powys. Wodehouse used the name only once, for the play *Don't Listen, Ladies* (1948). Stephen Powys made his debut as the author of *Wise Tomorrow* which opened in London 17 February 1937. Guy Bolton in a letter to Wodehouse (23 February 1937) stated, ". . . I've written a comedy that opened last week at the Lyric. . . . I wrote the play under a pseudonym and so far I have been able to preserve it from everyone." And yet in an interview published in the *New York Times*, 26 October 1939, Guy Bolton credited his wife, Virginia, with writing the play and being Stephen Powys.

Thus we come to *Three Blind Mice* by Stephen Powys which Wodehouse turned into *French Leave*. Wodehouse wrote Bennett Cerf (27 August 1957) that Guy Bolton had written this play. This play had quite a few incarnations: first as a movie, *Three Blind Mice*, 1938, produced by Twentieth Century Fox; *Three after Three*, performed by a touring company in the United States, 1939; *Walk with Music*, a Broadway play opening 4 June 1940 for fifty-five performances, with music by Hoagy Carmichael and lyrics by Johnny Mercer; and finally *Moon over Miami*, 1941, produced by Twentieth Century Fox.

---

8. Leslie Halliwell, *The Filmgoer's Companion*, 6th ed. (New York: Hill and Wang, 1977).
Leslie Halliwell, *Halliwell's Film Guide*, 2d ed. (New York: Charles Scribner's, 1979).

WODEHOUSE AND THE STAGE

1904   *Sergeant Brue*; book by Owen Hall; music by Liza Lehmann; lyrics by J. Hickory Wood
London, Strand Theatre, opened 10 December 1904, 280 performances; producer, Frank Curzon; musical director, Frederick Rosse
New York, Knickerbocker Theater, opened 24 April 1905, 152 performances; producer, Charles B. Dillingham; musical director, Watty Hydes
Wodehouse lyric: Put Me in My Little Cell (music by Frederick Rosse)

1906   *The Beauty of Bath*; book by Seymour Hicks and Cosmo Hamilton; music by Herbert E. Haines; lyrics by Charles H. Taylor
London, Aldwych Theatre, opened 19 March 1906, 287 performances; producer, Seymour Hicks; stage director, Edward Royce
Wodehouse lyric: Mister Chamberlain (music by Jerome Kern)

1907   *The Gay Gordons*; book by Seymour Hicks, music by Guy Jones, lyrics by Arthur Wimperis
London, Aldwych Theatre, opened 11 September 1907, 229 performances; producer, Seymour Hicks; dances and choral effects by Edward Royce; stars, Ellaline Terriss, Seymour Hicks
Wodehouse lyrics: Now That My Ship's Come Home; You, You, You

1907   *The Bandit's Daughter*; book by P. G. Wodehouse and Herbert Westbrook; music by Ella King Hall
Camden Town, England, Bedford Music Hall, 11 November 1907

1911   *A Gentleman of Leisure*; book by John Stapleton and P. G. Wodehouse
New York, The Playhouse, opened 24 August 1911, 76 performances; producer, William A. Brady; director, Edward Elsner; stars, Douglas Fairbanks, Ruth Shepley

1913   *A Thief for a Night*; book by John Stapleton and P.G. Wodehouse
Chicago, McVicker's Theatre, opened 30 March 1913; stars, John Barrymore, Alice Brady

1913   *Brother Alfred*; book by Herbert Westbrook and P. G. Wodehouse (based on the short story "Rallying Round Old George")
London, Savoy Theatre, opened 8 April 1913, 14 performances; producer, Lawrence Grossmith; stars, Lawrence Grossmith, Faith Celli, Arthur Chesney

1914   *Nuts and Wine*; book by C. G. Bovill and P. G. Wodehouse; music by Frank E. Tours and Melville Gideon; lyrics by Bovill, Wodehouse, and Guy Jones

London, Empire Theatre, opened 4 January 1914, 7 performances; producer, Oscar Barrett, Jr.; director, Julian Alfred

1916 *Pom Pom*; book and lyrics by Anne Caldwell and P. G. Wodehouse; music by Hugo Felix

New York, Cohan Theatre, opened 28 February 1916, 114 performances

1916 *Miss Springtime*; book by Guy Bolton; music by Emmerich Kalman and Jerome Kern; lyrics by P. G. Wodehouse and Herbert Reynolds

New York, New Amsterdam Theatre, opened 25 September 1916, 224 performances; producer, Klaw and Erlanger; director, Herbert Gresham; stars, Georgia O'Ramey, Charles Meakins

Wodehouse lyrics: Throw Me a Rose; My Castle in the Air; All Full of Talk; Saturday Night; Once upon a Time

1917 *Have a Heart*; book and lyrics by Guy Bolton and P. G. Wodehouse; music by Jerome Kern

New York, Liberty Theatre, opened 11 January 1917, 78 performances; producer, Henry W. Savage; director, Edward Royce; stars, Billy B. Van, Marjorie Gateson

Wodehouse lyrics: You Said Something; And I Am All Alone; I'm So Busy; The Road That Lies Before; Have a Heart; They All Look Alike; Daisy; Honeymoon Inn; Napoleon; Polly Believed in Preparedness; Samarkand; I'm Here Little Girls, I'm Here

1917 *Oh, Boy!*; book and lyrics by Guy Bolton and P. G. Wodehouse; music by Jerome Kern

New York, Princess Theater, opened 20 February 1917, 463 performances; producer, William Elliott and F. Ray Comstock; director, Edward Royce and Robert Milton

Oh, Joy!; retitled for the London production

London, Kingsway Theatre, opened 27 January 1919, 167 performances; producer, George Grossmith and Edward Laurillard; director, Austen Hurgon; debut of Beatrice Lillie

Wodehouse lyrics: Nesting Time in Flatbush; An Old-Fashioned Wife; Till the Clouds Roll By; Words Are Not Needed; A Pal Like You; You Never Knew About Me; A Package of Seeds; Every Day; Rolled into One; Be a Little Sunbeam

1917 *Leave It to Jane*; book by Guy Bolton based on *The College Widow* by George Ade; music by Jerome Kern; lyrics by P. G. Wodehouse

New York, Longacre Theatre, opened 28 August 1917, 167 performances; producer, William Elliott, F. Ray Comstock, Morris Gest; staged by Edward Royce; stars, Oscar Shaw, Georgia O'Ramey, Edith Hallor

New York, Sheridan Square Playhouse, opened 25 May 1959, 928 performances; presented by Joseph Beruh and Peter Kent; director, Lawrence Carra; stars, Kathleen Murray, Dorothy Greener, Angelo Mango

Wodehouse lyrics: The Sun Shines Brighter; The Siren's Song; The Crickets Are Calling; What I'm Longing to Say; Cleopatterer; A Peach of a Life; It's a Great Big Land; Poor Prune; I'm Going to Find a Girl Someday; Leave It to Jane; Sir Galahad; There It Is Again; Why?; Just You Watch My Step; Wait Till Tomorrow

1917 *Kitty Darlin'*; book and lyrics by Guy Bolton and P. G. Wodehouse; based on David Belasco's *Sweet Kitty Bellairs*; music by Rudolf Friml

Buffalo, Teck Theatre, opened 10 September 1917; producer, William Elliott, F. Ray Comstock, Morris Gest; director, Edward Royce; stars, Alice Nielsen, John Phillips (*Kitty Darlin'* opened in New York, 7 November 1927, with book and lyrics by Otto Harbach)

Wodehouse lyrics: When She Gives Him a Shamrock Bloom; Dear Old Dublin; The Land Where Dreams Come True; Noah

1917 *The Riviera Girl*; book and lyrics by Guy Bolton and P. G. Wodehouse; music by Emmerich Kalman and Jerome Kern

New York, New Amsterdam Theatre, opened 24 September 1917, 78 performances; producer, Klaw and Erlanger; director, Herbert Gresham; stars, Wilda Bennett, Carl Gantvoort, Sam Hardy

Wodehouse lyrics: A Little Bungalow in Quoque; Just a Voice to Call Me Dear; Will You Forget; Life's a Tale; Half a Married Man; There'll Never Be Another Girl Like Daisy; Gypsy, Bring Your Fiddle (The Lilt of a Gypsy Strain); Man, Man, Man

1917 *Miss 1917*; book and lyrics by P. G. Wodehouse and Guy Bolton; music by Jerome Kern

New York, Century Theatre, opened 5 November 1917, 48 performances; producers, Charles Dillingham and Florenz Ziegfeld; staged by Ned Wayburn; stars, Vivienne Segal, Lew Fields, Cecil Lean, Marian Davies, Irene Castle

Wodehouse lyrics: We're Crooks; Peaches; The Picture I Want to See; Tell Me All Your Troubles, Cutie; Land Where the Good Songs Go; I'm the Old Man in the Moon

1918 *Oh, Lady! Lady!*; book and lyrics by Guy Bolton and P. G. Wodehouse; music by Jerome Kern

New York, Princess Theatre, opened 1 February 1918, 219 performances; producer, F. Ray Comstock and William Elliott; staged by Robert

Milton and Edward Royce; stars, Vivienne Segal, Carl Randall

Wodehouse lyrics: Oh, Lady! Lady!; You Found Me and I Found You; When the Ships Come Home; Waiting Round the Corner; Not Yet; Greenwich Village; Wheatless Days; Some Little Girl; Our Little Nest; Moon Song; Before I Met You; It's a Hard, Hard World for a Man; Dear Old Prison Days; A Picture I Want to See; The Sun Starts to Shine Today; Do Look at Him

1918 *See You Later*; book and lyrics by Guy Bolton and P. G. Wodehouse; music by Jean Schwartz and William F. Peters

Baltimore, Academy of Music, opened 15 April 1918; producer, A. H. Woods; director, Robert Milton

Wodehouse lyrics: Isn't It Wonderful?; Young Man; The Train That Leaves for Town; I'm Going to Settle Down; In Our Little Paradise; Anytime Is Dancing Time!; Honeymoon Island; Desert Island; See You Later, Girls; I Never Knew; It Doesn't Matter; Love's a Very Funny Thing; Nerves; Lovers' Quarrels; Mother Paris; You Whispered It; Young Man

1918 *The Girl behind the Gun*; book and lyrics by Guy Bolton and P. G. Wodehouse, based on *Madame et son filleul* by Maurice Hennequin and Pierre Veber; music by Ivan Caryll

New York, New Amsterdam Theatre, opened 16 September 1918, 160 performances; producer, Klaw and Erlanger; director, Edgar MacGregor; stars, Ada Meade, Wilda Bennett, Donald Brian, John E. Hazzard

Kissing Time; retitled for the London production, with additional lyrics by Clifford Grey

London, Winter Garden Theatre, opened 20 May 1919, 430 performances; producer, George Grossmith and Edward Laurillard; director, Willy Redstone; stars, Stanley Holloway, George Grossmith, Yvonne Arnaud, Isobel Jeans

Wodehouse lyrics: Back to the Dear Old Trenches; The Girl behind the Man behind the Gun; A Happy Family; I Like It, I Like It; Oh, How Warm It Is Today; Some Day Waiting Will End; There's a Light in Your Eyes; There's Life in the Old Dog Yet; Women Haven't Any Mercy on a Man; I've Just Come Back from Paris

1918 *The Canary*; book by Harry B. Smith; music by Ivan Caryll, Irving Berlin, Harry Tierney; lyrics by Anne Caldwell and P. G. Wodehouse; based on book by George Barr and Louis Verneuill

New York, Globe Theatre, opened 4 November 1918, 152 performances; producer, Charles Dillingham; directors, Fred G. Lathem and Edward Royce; stars, Julia Sanderson and Joseph Cawthorne

Wodehouse lyrics: The Hunting Honeymoon; Julie and Her Johnnies; That's What Men Are For; Thousands of Years Ago; I Have Just One Heart for Just One Boy; Only in Dreams

1918 *Oh, My Dear!*; book and lyrics by Guy Bolton and P. G. Wodehouse; music by Louis A. Hirsch

New York, Princess Theatre, opened 26 November 1918, 189 performances; producers, F. Ray Comstock and William Elliott; directors, Robert Milton and Edward Royce; stars, Roy Atwell, Ivy Sawyer, Joseph Santley, Julliette Day

Wodehouse lyrics: City of Dreams; I Wonder Whether I've Loved You All My Life; You Never Know; I Shall Be All Right Now; Come Where Nature Calls; It Sorta Makes a Fellow Stop and Think; Childhood Days; I'd Ask No More; If They Ever Parted You from Me; Isn't It Wonderful?

1919 *The Rose of China*; a romantic musical comedy by Guy Bolton; music by Armand Vecsey; lyrics by P. G. Wodehouse

New York, Lyric Theatre, opened 25 November 1919, 47 performaces; producer, F. Ray Comstock and Morris Gest; staged by Robert Milton; stars, Oscar Shaw, Jane Richardson

Wodehouse lyrics: Yesterday; Bunny Dear; In Our Bungalow; Tao Loved His Li; Yale; College Spirit; Down on the Banks of the Subway

1920 *Sally*; book and lyrics by Guy Bolton and Clifford Grey, based on Bolton and Wodehouse's unproduced musical *The Little Thing*; music by Jerome Kern; ballet music by Victor Herbert

New York, New Amsterdam Theatre, opened 21 December 1920, 570 performances; producer, Florenz Ziegfeld; director, Edward Royce; stars, Marilynn Miller, Leon Errol

London, Winter Garden Theatre, opened 10 September 1921, 387 performances; producer, George Grossmith and J. A. E. Malone; director, Charles A. Maynard; stars, George Grossmith, Dorothy Dickson, Leslie Henson

The Wild Rose; revision of *Sally* by Frank Eyton and Richard Hearne

London, Prince's Theatre, opened 6 August 1942, 205 performances; producer, Firth Shephard; director, Robert Nesbitt; stars, Richard Herne, Jessie Mathews, Linda Gray

Sally; New York, Martin Beck Theatre, opened 10 May 1948, 36 performances; presented by Hunt Stromberg, Jr. and William Berney; staged by Billy Gilbert; stars, Bambi Lynn, Willie Howard, Jack Goode

Wodehouse lyrics: The Church 'Round the Corner; You Can't Keep a Good Girl Down

1921 *The Golden Moth*; book by Fred Thompson and P. G. Wodehouse; music by Ivor Novello; lyrics of five songs by Adrian Ross

London, Royal Adelphi Theatre, opened 5 October 1921, 281 performances; producer, Austen Hurgon and Thomas F. Dawe; musical director, Ernest Longstable; stars, W. H. Berry, Nancy Lovat, Thorpe Bates, Cecily Debenham, Robert Michaelis

Wodehouse lyrics: My Girl; Fairy Prince; Give Me a Thought Now and Then; Romance Is Calling; Dear Eyes That Shine; If Ever I Lost You

1922 *The Cabaret Girl*; book and lyrics by George Grossmith and P. G. Wodehouse; music by Jerome Kern; lyrics by Grossmith, Wodehouse, and Anne Caldwell

London, Winter Garden Theatre, opened 19 September 1922, 361 performances; producer, George Grossmith; musical director, John Ansell; stars, George Grossmith, Dorothy Dickson

Wodehouse lyrics: Chopin ad lib; Mr. Gravins—Mr. Gripps; Journey's End; Looking All Over for You; First Rose of Summer; Oriental Dreams; London, Dear Old London; These Days Are Gone Forever; Dancing Time

1923 *The Beauty Prize*; book and lyrics by George Grossmith and P. G. Wodehouse; music by Jerome Kern

London, Winter Garden Theatre, opened 5 September 1923, 213 performances; producer, George Grossmith; director, Charles A. Maynard; stars, Leslie Henson, Dorothy Dickson, George Grossmith, Heather Thatcher

Wodehouse lyrics: You Can't Make Love by Wireless; Non-Stop Dancing; Moon Love; Honeymoon Isle; Meet Me down on Main Street

1924 *Sitting Pretty*; book by Guy Bolton and P. G. Wodehouse; music by Jerome Kern; lyrics by P. G. Wodehouse

New York, Fulton Theatre, opened 8 April 1924, 95 performances; producer, F. Ray Comstock and Morris Gest; director, Fred G. Latham and Julian Alfred; stars, Queenie Smith, Gertrude Bryan, Rudolph Cameron

Wodehouse lyrics: A Year from Today; The Enchanted Train; All You Need Is a Girl; Mr. and Mrs. Rorer; Shadow of the Moon; Bongo on the Congo; Tulip Time in Sing Sing; Shuflin' Sam; Worries; Sitting Pretty; On a Desert Island with You

1925 *City Chap*; book by James Montgomery based on *The Fortune Hunter* by Winchell Smith; music by Jerome Kern, lyrics by Anne Caldwell

New York, Liberty Theatre, opened 26 October 1925, 72 performances; stars, Richard (Skeet) Gallagher, Irene Dunn, John Rutherford

Wodehouse lyric: Journey's End

1926 *Hearts and Diamonds*; English adaptation by P. G. Wodehouse and Laurie Wylie from *The Orlov* by Ernst Marischka and Bruno Granichstadten; music by Bruno Granichstadten; additional numbers by Max Darewski; lyrics by Graham John

London, Strand Theatre, opened 1 June 1926, 46 performances; producer, Arthur Bourchier; director, Theodore Komisarjevsky; stars, Charles Stone, Lupino Lane, Eric Roland, Wilfrid Caithness, George Metaxa

1926 *The Play's the Thing*; from *Spiel im Schloss* by Ferenc Molnar, adapted by P. G. Wodehouse

New York, Henry Miller's Theatre, opened 3 November 1926, 313 performances; producer and director, Gilbert Miller; stars, Holbrook Blinn, Catherine Dale Owen

New York, Empire Theatre, opened 9 April 1928, 24 performances; director, Gilbert Miller; star, Holbrook Blinn

London, St. James's Theatre, opened 4 December 1928; producer, Gerald du Maurier; director, Gilbert Miller; stars, Gerald du Maurier, Ursula Jeans

New York, Booth Theatre, opened 28 April 1948, 244 performances; producer, Gilbert Miller, James Russo, and Michael Ellis; director, Gilbert Miller; stars, Louis Calhern, Faye Emerson

New York, Roundabout Theater, opened 9 January 1973, 64 performances; director, Gene Feist; stars, Hugh Franklin, Elizabeth Owens

New York, Bijou Theater (moved from the Roundabout), opened 7 May 1973, 23 performances and 14 previews

Brooklyn, Brooklyn Adademy of Music, opened 22 February 1978, ran through 19 March 1978; director, Frank Dunlop; stars, René Auberjonois, Carole Shelley

1926 *Oh, Kay!*; book by Guy Bolton and P. G. Wodehouse; music by George Gershwin; lyrics by Ira Gershwin

New York, Imperial Theatre, opened 8 November 1926, 256 performances; producers, Alex A. Aarons and Vinton Freedley; director, John Harwood; choreography, Sammy Lee; stars, Victor Moore, Oscar Shaw, Gertrude Lawrence, Betty Compton, Fairbank twins

London, His Majesty's Theatre, opened 21 September 1927, 214 performances; presented by Musical Plays Ltd. with Aarons and Freedley; director, William Ritter; choreography, Elsie Neal; stars, Gertrude Lawrence, Harold French

London, Century Theatre, opened 2 January 1928, 16 performances

New York, East 74th Street Theatre, opened 16 April 1960, 89 performances; producer, Leighton K. Brill, Frederick Lewis, Jr., and Bertram Yarborough; director, Bertram Yarborough; stars, Marti Stevens, David Daniels, Bernie West, Murray Matheson

1927 *The Nightingale*; book by Guy Bolton, based on the life of Jenny Lind; music by Armand Vecsey; lyrics by P. G. Wodehouse

New York, Jolson's Theatre, opened 3 January 1927, 96 performances; producer, Shubert Brothers; director, Lewis Morton; stars, Ralph Erroll, Eleanor Painter, Stanley Lupino, Thomas A. Wise

Wodehouse lyrics: Homeland of Mine; May Moon; Two Little Ships; Breakfast in Bed; Another One Gone Wrong; Love like Yours Is Rare Indeed; Rabbit Song

1927 *Her Cardboard Lover*; book by Valerie Wyngate and P. G. Wodehouse adapted from the comedy *Dans sa candeur naïve*, by Jacques Deval

New York, Empire Theatre, opened 21 March 1927, 152 performances; producer, Gilbert Miller and A. H. Woods; director, Gilbert Miller; stars, Leslie Howard, Jeanne Eagles

London, Lyric Theatre, opened 21 August 1928, 173 performances; producer, Leslie Howard; stars, Tallulah Bankhead, Leslie Howard

1927 *Good Morning, Bill!*; adapted from the Hungarian of Ladislaus Fodor by P. G. Wodehouse

London, Duke of York's Theatre, opened 28 November 1927, 146 performances; producer, Athole Stewart; director, Sam Lysons; stars, Lawrence Grossmith, Vera Lennox

London, Daly's Theatre, opened 20 March 1934, 78 performances; producer, Peter Haddon; director, Reginald Bach; stars, Lawrence Grossmith, Peter Haddon, Winifred Shotter

1927 *Show Boat*; book by Oscar Hammerstein II, based on Edna Ferber's novel; music by Jerome Kern; lyrics by Oscar Hammerstein II

New York, Ziegfeld Theatre, opened 27 December 1927, 572 performances; producer, Florenz Ziegfeld; directed by Hammerstein and Zeke Colvan; choreography, Sammy Lee; orchestrations, Robert Russell Bennett; stars, Norma Terris, Howard Marsh, Charles Winninger, Helen Morgan, Jules Bledsoe

London, Drury Lane Theatre, opened 3 May 1928, 572 performances; producer, Alfred Butt; director, Felix Edwardes; stars, Edith Day, Howett Worster, Cedric Hardwicke, Marie Burke, Paul Robeson, Alberta Hunter

New York, Ziegfeld Theatre, opened 5 January 1946, 418 performances; presented by Kern and Hammerstein; directed by Hassard Short and Hammerstein; stars, Jan Clayton, Ralph Dumke, Carol Bruce, Kenneth Spencer

London, Adelphi Theatre, opened 29 July 1971, 910 performances; presented by Harold Fielding; directed and choreographed by Wendy Toye; stars, André Jobin, Cleo Laine, Thomas Carey, Lorna Dallas

Wodehouse lyric: Bill

1928 *Rosalie*; book by Guy Bolton and William Anthony McGuire; music by George Gershwin and Sigmund Romberg; lyrics by Ira Gershwin and P. G. Wodehouse

New York, New Amsterdam Theatre, opened 10 January 1928, 335 performances; producer, Florenz Ziegfeld; staged by Flo Ziegfeld, Seymour Felix, William A. McGuire; stars, Frank Morgan, Marilyn Miller, Gladys Glad, Bobbe Arnst

St. Louis, Municipal Opera, 1960; stars, Dorothy Collins, Bobby Van, Arthur Treacher

Wodehouse lyrics: Hussars March; West Point Bugle; Why Must We Always Be Dreaming?

Wodehouse and Gershwin lyrics: Say So; Oh, Gee! Oh, Joy!; New York Serenade

1928 *The Three Musketeers*; book by William Anthony McGuire; music by Rudolf Friml; lyrics by Clifford Grey and P. G. Wodehouse

New York, Lyric Theatre, opened 13 March 1928, 319 performances; producer, Florenz Ziegfeld; staged by William Anthony McGuire; stars, Vivienne Segal, Harriet Hoctor, Dennis King, Lester Allen

London, Theatre Royal, Drury Lane, opened 28 March 1930, 240 performances; producer, Felix Edwardes; director, Alfred Butt; stars, Dennis King, Adrienne Brune

New York, Equity Library Theatre, opened 8 May 1975, 22 performances; directed and choreographed by Charles Abbott; stars, Jason McAuliffe, Tricia Ellis, David Pursley, Ray Cox, Jane Altman

Wodehouse lyrics: March of the Musketeers; Your Eyes

1928 *A Damsel in Distress*; play by Ian Hay and P. G. Wodehouse

London, New Theatre, opened 13 August 1928, 234 performances; produced by Nicholas Hannen; stars, Basil Foster, Jane Baxter, Reginald Gardiner

1929 *Baa, Baa, Black Sheep*; by Ian Hay and P. G. Wodehouse

London, New Theatre, opened 22 April 1929, 115 performances; produced by Ian Hay; stars, Reginald Gardiner, Jane Baxter

1929 *Candle-Light*; adapted by P. G. Wodehouse from Siegfried Geyer's *Kleine Komoedie*

New York, Empire Theatre, opened 30 September 1929, 128 performances; producer and director, Gilbert Miller; stars, Gertrude Lawrence, Reginald Owen, Leslie Howard

1930 *Leave It to Psmith*; by Ian Hay and P. G. Wodehouse

London, Shaftesbury Theatre, opened 29 September 1930, 156 performances; producer, Frank Cellier; stars, Jane Baxter, Basil Foster

1934 *Who's Who*; by P. G. Wodehouse and Guy Bolton (based on Wodehouse's novel *If I Were You*)

London, Duke of York's Theatre, opened 20 September 1934, 19 performances; producer, Lawrence Grossmith; stars, Lawrence Grossmith, Violet Vanbrugh

Who's Who, Baby; adapted by Guy Bolton; music and lyrics by Johnny Brandon

New York, The Players Theater, opened 2 February 1968, 16 performances (Guy Bolton asked to have his and Wodehouse's names removed from the program)

1934 *Anything Goes*; book by Guy Bolton and P. G. Wodehouse; lyrics and music by Cole Porter; revised by Howard Lindsay and Russel Crouse

New York, Alvin Theatre, opened 21 November 1934, 415 performances; presented by Vinton Freedley; staged by Howard Lindsay; stars, William Gaxton, Ethel Merman, Victor Moore, Bettina Hall

London, Palace Theatre, opened 14 June 1935, 261 performances; presented by Charles B. Cochran; director, Frank Collins; stars, Sydney Howard, Jeanne Aubert, Jack Whiting

New York, Orpheum Theatre, opened 15 May 1962, 239 performances; presented by Jane Friedlander, Michael Parver, and Gene Andrewski; director, Lawrence Kasha; stars, Eileen Rodgers, Hal Linden

1935 *The Inside Stand*; by P. G. Wodehouse based on the novel *Hot Water*

London, Saville Theatre, opened 21 November 1935, 50 performances; producer, Jack Waller; director, Geoffrey Norman; stars, Ralph Lynn, Olive Blakeney

1948 *Don't Listen Ladies*; by Stephen Powys (pseudonym of P. G. Wodehouse) and Guy Bolton from the French of Sacha Guitry

London, St. James's Theatre, opened 2 September 1948, 219 performances; producers, Alec L. Rea, E. P. Clift; director, William Armstrong; stars, Constance Cummings, Pamela Bevan, Denholm Elliott, Francis Lister

New York, Booth Theatre, opened 28 December 1948, 15 performances

1968 *Oh, Clarence*; a comedy in two acts (seven scenes) by John Chapman, based on stories by P. G. Wodehouse

London, Lyric Theatre, opened 28 August 1968; presented by Peter Saunders; staged by Charles Hickman; stars, Nauton Wayne, James Hayter, Jon Pertwee

1975 *Jeeves*; book by Alan Ayckbourn, music by Andrew Lloyd Webber

London, Her Majesty's Theatre, opened 22 April 1975; presented by Robert Stegwood; directed by Eric Thompson; stars, David Hemmings, Michael Aldridge

1980 *Jeeves Takes Charge*; by P. G. Wodehouse, adapted and devised by Edward Duke

London, The Studio, Lyric Theatre, Hammersmith; presented by Theobald Dickson Productions; star, Edward Duke

London, Fortune Theatre, opened 30 September 1980; presented by Bernard Theobald; star, Edward Duke

WODEHOUSE AND THE MOVIES

1915 *Gentleman of Leisure*; © 2 March 1915; silent; John Stapleton, P. G. Wodehouse, and Cecil B. DeMille, scriptwriters

Jesse L. Lasky Feature Play Co., Inc.; star, Wallace Eddinger.

1917 *Uneasy Money*; © 8 December 1917; 75 minutes; silent

Essanay Film Mfg.; released through George Kleine System; director, Lawrence C. Windom; adaptation, Raymond E. Dakin

1919 *Oh Boy!*; © 19 June 1919; 6 reels; silent
   Pathé Exchange; adapted, directed, and produced by Albert Capellani

1919 *Piccadilly Jim*; © 4 December 1919; 5 reels; silent
   Selznick Pictures Corporation

1920 *The Prince and Betty*; © 2 January 1920; silent
   Pathé Exchange; presented by Jesse D. Hampton; director, Robert Thornby; stars, William Desmond, Mary Thurman

1920 *Damsel in Distress*; © 18 March 1920; silent
   Pathé Exchange; Albert Capellani Productions; stars, June Caprice, Creighton Hale

1920 *Oh Lady! Lady!*; © 2 November 1920; 5 reels; silent
   Realart Picture Corporation; director, Maurice Campbell; scenario, Ethel Kennedy from Bolton and Wodehouse play; stars, Bebe Daniels, Walter Hiers

1920 *Their Mutual Child*; © 13 December 1920; 6 reels; silent
   American Film Company; director, George L. Cox; scenario, Daniel F. Whitcomb from the story by P. G. Wodehouse

1921 *Stick Around*; © 6 December 1921; silent
   Pathé Exchange

1923 *A Gentleman of Leisure*; © 17 July 1923, released 15 July 1923; 6 reels; silent
   Famous Players—Lasky, distributed by Paramount Pictures; director, Joseph Henabery; adaptation, Anthony Coldeway, Jack Cunningham; star, Jack Holt

1924 *The Clicking of Cuthbert* (series); December 1924; silent
   Stoll Pictures; director, Andrew P. Wilson; 1. *The Clicking of Cuthbert*, 1960 feet; 2. *Chester Forgets Himself*, 2160 feet; 3. *The Long Hole*, 2450 feet (reissued as *The Moving Hazard*); 4. *Ordeal by Golf*, 2100 feet; 5. *Rodney Fails to Qualify*, 2100 feet; 6. *The Magic Plus Fours*, 1930 feet

1925 *Sally*; © 12 March 1925, released 29 March 1925; 9 reels; silent
   First National Pictures; director, Alfred E. Green; scenario, June Mathis based on Ziegfeld's musical comedy by Bolton and Kern with lyrics by Wodehouse; stars, Colleen Moore, Leon Errol, Lloyd Hughes

1926 *Der goldene Schmetterling*; 1926; 11 reels
   Sacha-Film (Austria); director, Michael Curtiz; scenario, Adolf Lantz and Jane Bess from *The Golden Moth* by Fred Thompson and Wodehouse; stars, Nils Asther, Lilli Damita

1927 *The Small Bachelor*; © 12 July 1927, released 6 November 1927; 7 reels; silent
   Universal Pictures-Jewel; director, William A. Seiter; story, Edward J. Montague from the serial in *Liberty* magazine 18 September – 25 December 1926

1928 *Oh Kay!*; © 17 August 1928, released 26 August 1928; 6 reels (copyrighted as 7 reels); silent
   First National Pictures; presented by John McCormick; director, Mervyn LeRoy; scenario, Carey Wilson; adaptation, Elsie Janis; from the musical comedy by Bolton, Wodehouse, and Kern; stars, Colleen Moore, Lawrence Gray

1929 *Her Cardboard Lover*; April 1929
   British Phototone; director, Clayton Hutton; scenario, Jacques Deval, Valerie Wyngate, P. G. Wodehouse; star, Tallulah Bankhead

1929 *Show Boat*; © 27 April 1929, released 28 July 1929; 12 reels
   Universal Pictures; presented by Carl Laemmle; director, Harry Pollard; scenario, Charles Kenyon; stars, Laura La Plante, Joseph Schildkraut, Alma Reubens, Stepin Fetchit
   Wodehouse lyric: Bill

1930 *Sally*; © 11 February 1930, New York premiere 23 December 1929, released 12 January 1930; 12 reels; 1 hour 43 minutes
   First National Pictures; director, John Francis Dillon; screen version, Waldemar Young; stars, Joe E. Brown, Marilyn Miller, Lawrence Gray

1930 *Those Three French Girls*; © 23 October 1930; 8 reels
   Cosmopolitan distributed by Metro Goldwyn Mayer; director, Henry Beaumont; adaptation and continuity by Sylvia Thalberg and Frank Butler from an original story by Dale Van Every, Arthur Freed, Richard Schayer; dialogue by P. G. Wodehouse; stars, George Grossmith, Fifi Dorsay

1931 *The Man in Possession*; © 1 July 1931; 9 reels
   Metro Goldwyn Mayer; producer, Sam Wood; screen adaptation by Sarah Y. Mason from the play by H. M. Harwood; additional scenes by P. G. Wodehouse; stars, Robert Montgomery, Charlotte Greenwood

1932 *Brother Alfred*; April 1932; 77 minutes
   British International Pictures; director, Harry Edwards; screenplay, P. G. Wodehouse and Herbert Westbrook; adaptation by Henry Edwards and Claude Gurney; stars, Gene Gerrard, Molly Lamont

1933 *Summer Lightning*; May 1933; 78 minutes; reissued 1937
   British and Dominions Film Corporation; pro-

ducer, Herbert Wilcox; director, Maclean Rogers; stars, Ralph Lynn, Winifred Shotter

1933 *Leave It to Me*; April 1933; 76 minutes
British International Pictures; director, Monty Banks; screenplay by Gene Gerard, Frank Miller, Cecil Lewis based on *Leave It to Psmith* by P. G. Wodehouse and Ian Hay; stars, Gene Gerrard, Molly Lamont

1934 *Have a Heart*; © 4 September 1934; 8 reels
Metro Goldwyn Mayer; producer, John W. Considine, Jr.; director, David Butler; story by B. G. DeSylva and David Butler from the play by Bolton, Wodehouse, and Kern; stars, Jean Parker, James Dunn, Una Merkel, Stuart Erwin

1935 *Dizzy Dames*; © 20 May 1935; 9 reels
Liberty Pictures; producer, M. H. Hoffman; director, William Nigh; story by George Waggner suggested by the Wodehouse story "The Watchdog"; stars, Marjorie Rambeau, Lawrence Gray

1936 *Piccadilly Jim*; © 10 August 1936; 10 reels
Metro Goldwyn Mayer; a Robert Z. Leonard production; producer, Harry Rapf; director, Robert Z. Leonard; screenplay, Charles Brackett and Edwin Knopf; stars, Robert Montgomery, Madge Evans, Frank Morgan, Eric Blore, Billie Burke, Robert Benchley

1936 *Anything Goes*; © 30 January 1936; 10 reels
Paramount Pictures; presented by Adolph Zukor; producer, Benjamin Glazer; director, Lewis Milestone; music and lyrics by Cole Porter; stars, Bing Crosby, Ethel Merman, Charles Ruggles

1936 *Show Boat*; © 13 May 1936; 12 reels
Universal Productions; producer, Carl Laemmle, Jr.; director, James Whale; screenplay and lyrics by Oscar Hammerstein II; music by Jerome Kern; stars, Irene Dunne, Allan Jones, Charles Winninger, Helen Morgan, Paul Robeson
Wodehouse lyric: Bill

1936 *Thank You, Jeeves*; © 2 October 1936; 6 reels
Twentieth Century Fox; executive producer, Sol M. Wurtzel; director, Arthur Greville Collins; screenplay, Joseph Hoffman and Stephen Gross based on the novel by P. G. Wodehouse; stars, Arthur Treacher, David Niven, Virginia Fields

1937 *A Damsel in Distress*; © 19 November 1937; 11 reels
RKO-Radio Pictures; producer, Pandro S. Berman; director, George Stevens; screenplay, P. G. Wodehouse, Ernest Pagano, S. K. Lauren; music, George Gershwin; lyrics, Ira Gershwin; stars, Fred Astaire, Joan Fontaine, Gracie Allen, George Burns, Ray Noble, Reginald Gardner

1937 *Rosalie*; © 20 December 1937; 13 reels
Metro Goldwyn Mayer; director, W. S. Van Dyke III; words and music by Cole Porter; screenplay and production by William Anthony McGuire; stars, Nelson Eddy, Eleanor Powell

1937 *Step Lively, Jeeves*; © 9 April 1937; 6160 feet
Twentieth Century Fox; director, Eugene Forde; original story, Frances Hylan based on the character Jeeves; screenplay, Frank Fenton and Lynn Root; stars, Arthur Treacher, Patricia Ellis, Robert Kent

1946 *Till the Clouds Roll By*; based on the life of Jerome Kern; © 4 December 1946; 120 minutes
Metro Goldwyn Mayer; producer, Arthur Freed; director, Richard Whorf; story by Guy Bolton; screenplay, Myles Connolly, Jean Holloway; star, Robert Walker
Wodehouse lyrics: The Land Where the Good Songs Go; Till the Clouds Roll By; Cleopatterer; Leave It to Jane; Go Little Boat

1951 *Showboat*; © 11 June 1951; 107 minutes
Metro Goldwyn Mayer; producer, Arthur Freed; director, George Sidney; screenplay, John Lee Mahin; stars, Kathryn Grayson, Howard Keel, Ava Gardner, Marge and Gower Champion, Joe E. Brown, William Warfield
Wodehouse lyric: Bill

1956 *Anything Goes*; © 21 March 1956; 106 minutes
Paramount Pictures; producer, Robert Emmett Dolan; director, Robert Lewis; new songs by James Van Heusen and Sammy Cahn; stars, Bing Crosby, Zizi Jeanmaire, Mitzi Gaynor, Donald O'Connor

1957 *The Helen Morgan Story*; © 5 October 1957; 118 minutes
Warner Brothers Pictures; director, Michael Curtiz; written by Oscar Saul, Dean Rusner, Stephen Longstreet, Nelson Gidding; stars, Ann Blyth, Paul Newman
Wodehouse lyric: Bill (sung by Gogi Grant)

1961 *The Girl on the Boat*; January 1961; 91 minutes
Knightsbridge/United Artists; producer, John Bryan; director, Henry Kaplan; scenario, Reuben Ship; stars, Richard Briers, Norman Wisdom

Works about P. G. Wodehouse

THE SECONDARY bibliography includes major studies and biographies of Wodehouse. Book reviews are not listed, which precludes the citation of such interesting ones as Evelyn Waugh's reply to a review of *French Leave*, "Dr. Wodehouse and Mr. Wain";[1] however, the reader can identify reviews through the standard tools. Nor are directory-type volumes included because the information given is not unique. Newspaper articles are not listed unless of great interest, e.g., the reprint of Evelyn Waugh's BBC speech in *The Sunday Times Magazine* of 16 July 1961.

There are few foreign language studies cited here. Along with translations, this is an area that needs much work. One aid is Professor Evelyne Ginestet's dissertation "Le Monde de P. G. Wodehouse"[2] which gives a number of French-language citations.

1. Evelyn Waugh, "Dr. Wodehouse and Mr. Wain," *The Spectator* 196, no. 6661 (24 Feb. 1956): 243–44.

2. Evelyne Ginestet, "Le Monde de P. G. Wodehouse (1881–1975)," 4 vols. (Litt.D. diss., Sorbonne, Paris, 1980).

BIBLIOGRAPHIES

Asplund, Uno, *Möt mir Wodehouse: 90 år – 93 Böcker; en bibliografi av Uno Asplund*. Göteborg, Bergendahls Boktryckeri, 1970. 53 pages. Chronological listing of all Swedish translations through 1971; does not give translators' names.

Jasen, David A. *A Bibliography and Reader's Guide to the First Editions of P. G. Wodehouse.* [Hamden, Conn.]: Archon Books, 1970. x, 290 pages. Bibliography of first editions published through 1969 with a brief description of characters appearing in each novel. Includes list of some magazine stories, songs in musicals, movies.

Whitt, J. F. *The Strand Magazine, 1891–1950: A Selective Checklist Listing All Material Relating to Arthur Conan Doyle, All Stories by P. G. Wodehouse, and a Selection of Other Contributions, Mainly by Writers of Detective, Mystery, or Fantasy Fiction*. London: J. F. Whitt, 1979. 48 pages. Chronological listing of Wodehouse articles; includes names of illustrators.

FULL-LENGTH STUDIES

Arquié, Marie-José. "Jeeves, héros comique de P. G. Wodehouse." Diss., Université de Rouen, 1975. 235 pages.

Carlson, Richard Stocks. "An Analysis of P. G. Wodehouse's Team of Bertie Wooster and Jeeves." Ph.D. dissertation, Michigan State University, 1973. 192 pages. Abstract in *Dissertations Abstracts International*, vol. 34 (1973), pp. 1233A.

Connolly, Joseph. *P. G. Wodehouse: An Illustrated Biography with Complete Bibliography and Collector's Guide*. London: Orbis Publishing, [1979]. 160 pages. The bibliography concentrates on the English editions and includes descriptions of the dust wrappers.

Edwards, Owen Dudley. *P. G. Wodehouse: A Critical and Historical Essay*. London: Martin Brian and O'Keefe, [1977]. 232 pages.

French, R. B. D. *P. G. Wodehouse*. Writers and Critics. Edinburgh, London: Oliver and Boyd, [1966]. 120 pages. Also issued in New York by Barnes and Noble, [1967].

Gauthier, Evelyne. "Étude structurale du récit chez Wodehouse." Diss., Université François Rabelais, Tours, 1975. 235 pages.

Ginestet, Evelyne. "Le Monde de P. G. Wodehouse (1881–1975)." Litt.D. diss., Sorbonne, Paris, 1980. 4 volumes.

Hall, Robert A., Jr. *The Comic Style of P. G. Wodehouse*. Hamden, Conn.: Archon Books, 1974. 147 pages.

Homage to Wodehouse, ed. Thelma Cazalet-Keir. London: Barrie and Jenkins, [1973]. 146 pages. Contents: Lord David Cecil, Preface; Richard Usborne, "Dear Mr. Wodehouse"; Claud Cockburn, "Wodehouse All The Way"; Henry Longhurst, "That Varied Neverending Pageant that Men Call Golf"; Sir John Betjeman, "Seaside Golf"; Basil Boothroyd, "The Laughs"; Richard Ingrams, "Much Obliged, Mr. Wodehouse"; Malcolm Muggeridge, "Wodehouse in Distress"; Guy Bolton, "Working with Wodehouse"; The Hon. William Douglas Home, "P. G. Wodehouse in the Theatre"; Sir Compton Mackenzie, "As a Contemporary"; Auberon Waugh, "Father of The English Idea."

Jaggard, Geoffrey. *Blandings the Blest and The Blue Blood: A Companion to the Blandings Castle Saga of P. G. Wodehouse, LL.D. with a Complete Wodehouse Peerage, Baronetage, & Knighthood, Embodying a Bulk of Butlers: Caledonia, Stern and Wild: Royalty, Vintage and Modern: Who's Who in the Nobility and Gentry: Taverns in the Town: A Genealogical Tree of the Threepwood Family of Shropshire: Together with All That High-Mettled and Exalted Brouhaha, Tan-Tantara, Tzing-Boom!* London: Macdonald, [1968]. 227 pages.

Jaggard, Geoffrey. *Wooster' World: A Companion to the Wooster-Jeeves Cycle of P. G. Wodehouse, LL.D., containing a Modicum of Honey from the Drones and Reviewing a Surging Sea of Aunts: Brief Instances: Collectors' Corner: A Pleasing Diversity of Dumbchummery: Racing Intelligence: The Stately Homes of England Together with All That Stimulating Brouhaha the Laughing Love God Has Hiccoughs with Some Consideration of What the Well-Dressed Young Man Is Not Wearing and a Useful Now We Know Department.* London: Macdonald, [1967]. 203 pages. Also issued as Coronet paperback.

Jasen, David A. *P. G. Wodehouse: A Portrait of a Master.* New rev. ed. New York: Continuum, 1981. 298 pages. Also issued in paperback by Continuum. First edition: New York: Mason and Lipscomb, [1974]; London: Garnstone Pr., [1975]. 294 pages.

Jasen, David A. *The Theatre of P. G. Wodehouse.* London: B. T. Batsford Ltd., [1979]. 120 pages.

Sharma, M. N.. *Wodehouse the Fictionalist.* Meerut, India: Munakski Prakashan, 1980. 224 pages.

Usborne, Richard. *Dr. Sir Pelham Wodehouse—Old Boy: The Text of an Address Given by Richard Usborne at the Opening of the P. G. Wodehouse Corner in the Library of Dulwich College, October 15, 1977.* London: James H. Heineman, 1978. 34 pages.

Usborne, Richard. *Wodehouse at Work to the End,* rev. ed. London: Barrie and Jenkins, [1976]. 255 pages. Also issued by Penguin Books, 1978. First edition: *Wodehouse at Work: A Study of the Books and Characters of P. G. Wodehouse across Nearly Sixty Years.* London: Herbert Jenkins, 1961. 224 pages.

Voorhees, Richard J. *P. G. Wodehouse.* New York: Twayne Publishers, [1966]. 205 pages.

Wind, Herbert Warren. *The World of P. G. Wodehouse.* New York, Washington: Praeger Publishers, [1972]. 104 pages. Most of the contents originally appeared under the title "Chap with a Good Story to Tell," in *The New Yorker,* 15 May 1971.

CHAPTERS DEVOTED TO WODEHOUSE

Clarke, Gerald. "P. G. Wodehouse." In *Writers at Work: The Paris Review Interviews.* 5th series, pp. 1–19. New York: Viking, 1981. 387 pages. Also issued by Penguin Books, 1981.

Flannery, Harry W. *Assignment to Berlin.* London: Michael Joseph, 1942. pp. 117–18, 244–51.

Hall, Robert A., Jr. "Primicias estilísticas de P. G. Wodehouse." In *Linguistic and Literary Studies in Honor of Archibald A. Hill,* ed. Mohammad Ali Jazayery, vol. 4, pp. 55–61. The Hague: Mouton, 1978. 4 volumes.

Hamilton, Cosmo. "P. G. Wodehouse: A Mere Humourous Person." In *People Worth Talking About,* 95–99. London: Hutchinson, 1934. 283 pages.

Kingsmill, Hugh. "P. G. Wodehouse." In *The Progress of a Biographer,* pp. 139–42. London: Methuen, 1949. 194 pages. (Originally published in *New English Review* 1945–48.)

Lancaster, Osbert. "Great Houses of Fiction Revisited: Blandings Castle." In *Scene Changes,* pp. 35–37. London: John Murray, [1978]. 101 pages.

Medcalf, Stephen. "The Innocence of P. G. Wodehouse." In *The Modern English Novel: The Reader, the Writer, and the Work,* ed. Gabriel Josipovici, pp. 186–205. New York: Barnes and Noble, 1976. 281 pages.

Mikes, George. "P. G. Wodehouse." In *Eight Humorists.* pp. 153–75. London: Allan Wingate, 1954. 175 pages.

Muggeridge, Malcolm. *Tread Softly for You Tread on My Jokes.* London: Collins, 1966. 287 pages. "The Wodehouse Affair," pp. 83–93. Also issued in paperback by Collins, Fontana, 1968.

New Statesman and Nation. "P. G. Wodehouse...." In *Twelve Biographies . . . ,* pp. 9–10. London: New Statesman and Nation, 23 December 1933. "These biographies are appearing with the series of caricatures by Low, each biography with its subject, in the issues of The New Statesman and Nation between October 21st, 1933 and January 6th, 1934" (note).

Nicholls, Beverley. "P. G. Wodehouse or a Few 'Plums.'"

In *Are They the Same at Home?* pp. 248–52. London: Jonathan Cape, 1927. 256 pages.

Sheed, Wilfrid. "P. G. Wodehouse: Leave It to Psmith." In *The Good Word and Other Words*, pp. 215–22. New York: Dutton, 1978; London: Sidgwick and Jackson, 1979. 300 pages. Originally published as the introduction to the paperback reprint (New York: Vintage Books, 1975).

Swinnerton, Frank. "Some Later Novelists: David Garnett, P. G. Wodehouse, J. B. Priestley, A. P. Herbert." In *The Georgian Literary Scene*, pp. 479–500. London: Hutchinson, 1935; rev. ed., 1938. 548 pages. See especially pp. 485–89.

Thompson, Anthony Hugh. *Censorship in Public Libraries in the United Kingdom during the Twentieth Century.* [Epping, Essex:] Bowker, 1975. 236 pages. Chapter 3: "The P. G. Wodehouse Affair," pp. 34–55.

PERIODICAL ARTICLES

Aldridge, John W. "P. G. Wodehouse: The Lesson of a Young Master." *New World Writing* no. 13 (1958). Reprinted as the introduction to *Selected Stories by P. G. Wodehouse* (New York: Random House, 1958) and in Aldridge, *Time to Murder and Create: The Contemporary Novel in Crisis* (New York: David McKay, 1966).

Appia, Henry. "O Rare P. G. Wodehouse." *Études anglaises* 26 (1973): 22–34.

Belloc, Hilaire. "Homage to Wodehouse." *John O' London's Weekly* 43 (30 Aug. 1940): 1–2.

Benson, Donald R. "Exclusive Interview with P. G. Wodehouse." *Writer's Digest* 51 (Oct. 1971): 22–24, 43.

Bowen, Barbara C. "Rabelais and P. G. Wodehouse: Two Comic Works." *Espirit créateur* 16 (1976): 63–77.

Bradshaw, Leslie Havergal. "Impressions of P. G. Wodehouse." *Captain* 22 (Mar. 1910): 500–501.

Cannadine, David. "Another 'Last Victorian': P. G. Wodehouse and His World." *South Atlantic Quarterly* 77 (Autumn 1978): 470–91.

Clarke, Gerald. "Checking in with P. G. Wodehouse: Notes in Passing on a Life *Still* in Progress." *Esquire* 81 (May 1974): 98–99, 202, 204, 208, 210–11.

Green, Benny. "The Truth behind the Fiction." *Spectator* 234, no. 7653 (1 Mar. 1975): 234–35.

Green, Martin. "Carry on, Wodehouse." *New York Times Magazine* (19 Nov. 1978): pp. 64–65, 69, 71, 78.

Hall, Robert A., Jr. "Incongruity and Stylistic Rhythm in P. G. Wodehouse." *Annali* (Istituto Orientale Universitario, Naples, Sezione Germanica) 9 (1969): 135–44.

Hall, Robert A., Jr. "P. G. Wodehouse and the English Language." *Annali* (Istituto Orientale Universitario, Naples, Sezione Germanica) 6 (1964): 103–21.

Hall, Robert A., Jr. "The Transferred Epithet in P. G. Wodehouse." *Linguistic Inquiry* 4 (1973): 92–94.

Hayward, John. "P. G. Wodehouse and the Edwardians." *Spectator* 155, no. 5602 (8 Nov. 1935): p. 771.

Hayward, John. "P. G. Wodehouse." *Saturday Book, 1941–1942* 1 (1941): 372–89.

Jasen, David A. "Bolton, Wodehouse and Kern." *Cakes & Ale* 9 (25 Apr. 1977): 7, 17.

Magee, David. "On Collecting P. G. Wodehouse." *Quarterly News-Letter* (Book Club of California) 29 (Spring 1964): 29–35.

Muggeridge, Malcolm. "The Wodehouse Affair." *New Statesman* 62, no. 1586 (4 August 1961): 150, 152. Reprinted in *Tread Softly for You Tread on My Jokes*.

Muir, Augustus. "The Popularity of P. G. Wodehouse." *Strand* 73 (Feb. 1927): 128–36.

Olney, Clarke. "Wodehouse and the Poets." *Georgia Review* 16 (1962): 392–99.

Orwell, George. "In Defence of P. G. Wodehouse." *The Windmill* no. 2 (1945): 10–19. Reprinted in *Critical Essays* (London: Secker and Warburg, 1946, pp. 179–95) and in *Collected Essays* (London: Secker and Warburg, [1961], pp. 248–64).

Robinson, Robert. "Of Aunts and Drones: P. G. Wodehouse Talks to Robert Robinson." *Listener* 92 (17 Oct. 1974): 496.

"Seaside Home of Famous Humorist: Villa at Le Touquet." *Arts and Decoration* 50 (Aug. 1939): 16–18.

Stephenson, William. "The Wodehouse World of Hollywood." *Literature/Film Quarterly* 6 (1978): 190–203.

Stevenson, Lionel. "The Antecedents of P. G. Wodehouse." *Arizona Quarterly* 5 (1959): 226–34.

Svensson, Georg. "Nationalmonumentet Wodehouse." *Böckernas Värld* (1971): 16–21.

"Talk of the Town." *New Yorker* 47 (30 Oct. 1971): 40–41.

Usborne, Richard. "My Blandings Castle." *Blackwell's Magazine* 312 (Nov. 1972): 385–401.

Usborne, Richard. "P. G. Wodehouse's Family of Friends." *Blackwell's Magazine* 316 (July 1974): 47–58.

Voorhees, Richard J. "The Jolly Old World of P. G. Wodehouse." *South Atlantic Quarterly* 61 (Spring 1962): 213–22.

Wallace, Malcolm T. "The Wodehouse World I: Classical Echoes." *Cithara* 12 (1973): 41–57.

Watkins, Alan. "The Young Wodehouse." *New Statesman* 74 (1 Dec. 1972): 834.

Waugh, Evelyn. "An Act of Homage and Reparation." *The Sunday Times Magazine Section*, 16 July 1961, pp. 21, 23. "The text of this article is from last night's broadcast by Mr. Waugh in the Home Service."

Wind, Herbert Warren. "Profile: Chap with a Good Story to Tell." *New Yorker* 47 (15 May 1971): 43ff. Most of the material republished in *The World of P. G. Wodehouse.*

Wodehouse, Leonora. "P. G. Wodehouse at Home." *Strand* 77 (Jan. 1929): 20–25.

Wodehouse, Leonora. "What His Daughter Thinks of P. G. Wodehouse." *American Magazine* (Oct. 1931): 77, 78, 122.

Wodehouse, P. G. "Berlin Broadcasts." *Encounter* 3, nos. 4–5 (Oct.–Nov. 1954): 17–24, 39–47.

REFERENCES TO WODEHOUSE IN MEMOIRS AND BIOGRAPHIES

There are many reminiscences and biographies of people with whom Wodehouse worked in the theatre. Most of these have at most a page or two relating specifically to Wodehouse. Following is a list of a few to indicate the possibilities of gleaning an incident concerning Wodehouse or of reaching an understanding of the musical comedy world.

Bordman, Gerald. *Jerome Kern: His Life and Music.* New York, Oxford: Oxford University Press, 1980. 438 pages.

Freedland, Michael. *Jerome Kern: A Biography.* London: Robson Books, 1978. 182 pages.

Gershwin, Ira. *Lyrics on Several Occasions.* New York: Alfred Knopf, 1959. 362 pages.

Grossmith, George, Jr. *GG.* London: Hutchinson, 1933. 288 pages.

Hicks, Seymour. *Hail Fellow Well Met.* London, New York: Staples Pr., 1949. 206 pages.

Nolan, Frederick. *The Sound of Their Music: The Story of Rodgers and Hammerstein.* New York: Walker and Company, 1978. 272 pages.

Skinner, Cornelia Otis. *Life with Lindsay and Crouse.* Boston: Houghton Mifflin, 1976. 242 pages.

Terriss, Ellaline. *Just a Little Bit of String.* London: Hutchinson, 1955. 296 pages.

RELATED MATERIALS

Blundell, N. H. *Old Alleynian Rugby Football Club, 1898–1948.* London: Dulwich College [1949?]. 182 pages.

Chesterton, G. K. "Mystery of Mr. Jeeves." *G. K.'s Weekly* 10 (18 Jan. 1930): 295.

Leake, W. R. M. *Gilkes and Dulwich, 1885–1914: A Study of a Great Headmaster.* [Dulwich College:] Alleyn Club, 1933. 278 pages.

Magee, David. *Infinite Riches: The Adventures of a Rare Book Dealer*, introduction by Lawrence Clark Powell. New York: Paul Eriksson, 1973. 274 pages.

Newth, J. D. *Adam and Charles Black, 1807–1957: Some Chapters in the History of a Publishing House.* London: Black, 1957. 115 pages.

Ormiston, Thomas Lane. *Dulwich College Register 1619–1926*, compiled for the Alleyn Club. [London: Dulwich College, 1927.] 717 pages.

IMITATIONS AND PARODIES

Boothroyd, Basil. "Jeeves for Hire." *Punch* 263 (8 Mar. 1972): 314.

Disney, T. "De Poor Dumb Animal with Apologies to Mr. P. G. Wodehouse." *Captain* 22 (Feb. 1910): 445.

Fuller, Timothy. "Story of Jack and Jill as It Might Be Told by W. Faulkner, P. G. Wodehouse and A. Woollcott." *Saturday Review* 15 (19 Dec. 1936): 10–11.

Kingsmill, Hugh. "Parodies I: Clubs Are Trumps by P. G. W-d-h—se (A Sequel to 'The Purity of the Turf')." *English Review* 53 (Oct. 1931): 574–85.

Kington, Miles. "Black Jeeves." *Punch* 268 (7 May 1975): 812.

Parkinson, C. Northcote. *Jeeves: A Gentleman's Personal Gentleman*. London: Macdonald and Jane's Publishers, 1979. 191 pages.

"Psmith, Special Reporter." *Captain* 20 (Jan. 1909): 362.

Roberts, S. C. *Distinguished Visitors*. Cambridge: Printed at the University Press, Cambridge, for Private Distribution, Christmas 1937. 22 pages. Contents: "Bertie Wooster in Cambridge"; "Mr. Mulliner in the Combination Room."

Sheffield, Charles. "The Marriage of True Minds." *Fantasy & Science Fiction* 32 (Nov. 1980): 130–46.

HAEC OLIM MEMINISSE JUVABIT
This book has been composed, printed by letterpress,
and bound by The Stinehour Press, with illustrations
printed by The Meriden Gravure Company.
The design is by Stephen Harvard.
The text is set in Monotype Bell, a modern recutting
of the design originally engraved by Richard Austin
and issued in 1788 by John Bell through his
British Letter Foundry.

DATE DUE

Demco, Inc. 38-293

Book Shelves
PR6045.O53 Z83
P.G. Wodehouse, a centenary
celebration, 1881-1981

PR
6045
.O53
Z83

A TAPESTRY OF
WODEHOUSE
CHARACTERS,
SITUATIONS &
PREDICAMENTS

DEPICTED BY
PETER VAN STRAATEN

[KEY ON PAGE IX]